REGIONAL POLITICS
and
WORLD ORDER

REGIONAL POLITICS
and
WORLD ORDER

Edited by

RICHARD A. FALK
PRINCETON UNIVERSITY

SAUL H. MENDLOVITZ
RUTGERS UNIVERSITY

W. H. FREEMAN AND COMPANY
San Francisco

Library of Congress Cataloging in Publication Data

Falk, Richard A.   comp.
    Regional politics and world order.

    Includes bibliographical references.
    CONTENTS: Masters, R. A multi-bloc model of the
international system.—Young, O. R. Political
discontinuities in the international system.—Miller,
L. H. The prospects for order through regional
security.—Nye, J. S. Regional institutions. [etc.]
JX1979.F34   341.24   73–7787
ISBN 0–7167–0783–7
ISBN 0–7167–0798–5 (pbk.)

Printed in the United States of America

1 2 3 4 5 6 7 8 9

Contents

Preface

This book on regionalism is a continuation of the educational enterprise that we began in 1966 with the publication of the four-volume collection of materials, *The Strategy of World Order*. In the present book, we attempt to make a sustained inquiry into the character and prospects of regionalism as a movement in world affairs.

It is evident that in dealing with regionalism we are dealing with a multifaceted reality, the study of which has produced a variety of methodological, ideological, and geographical orientations. In this volume we hope to introduce the student to this rich variety of treatment but seek to maintain intellectual cohesion by giving particular attention in the Discussion and Questions sections to matters bearing on world order. It is this focus on regionalism as a world-order issue that differentiates this book from others in the same general field.

We worked on this book for several years and benefited from all sorts of help and encouragement. We acknowledge here only the most notable contributions.

As with prior collaborative work, we have undertaken this project on behalf of the World Law Fund, now renamed the Institute for World Order. As always, Harry Hollins has encouraged, helped, prodded, and inspired us.

The Carnegie Corporation made a generous grant that enabled this project to go forward, and we are pleased to express our thanks.

At various stages we have been greatly helped in many ways by a series of bright and efficient research assistants. It is a pleasure to thank Claudia Cords, Frances Headley, and Andrea Praeger for taking from our labors and adding to our joys.

June Traube has helped this undertaking by her usual outstanding performance of secretarial duties.

And, finally, in the spirit of love and dedication, we both want to mention our children, who, after all, have the greatest stake in the future of world order: Chris, Noah and Dimitri Falk; Jessica, Michael, Jamie, John, and Martha Mendlovitz. In the same spirit, Richard Falk wants to thank his wife, Florence, who, among other virtuous doings, managed to live graciously with regionalism during one long summer period that had previously been designated "vacation."

February 1973

Richard A. Falk
Saul H. Mendlovitz

REGIONAL POLITICS
and
WORLD ORDER

General Introduction

In this volume we try to provide a basis for full-scale appraisal of the relevance of regional developments to the future of world order. Our subject is so extensive and diverse that we cannot deal with particular regional movements in any depth or examine very fully the role of regional efforts in the areas of security, economic development or human rights. What we do attempt, is to raise general questions about the positive, negative, and neutral implications of regional movements for the present and future quality of world order.

Our orientation is avowedly normative. We wish to use the process of study and inquiry to sharpen our perception of social problems on the world scene and to investigate plausible lines of solution as creatively and critically as possible. We believe that knowledge developed in this way encourages thoughtful and appropriate action.

In the course of working with scholars from various parts of the world in the World Order Models Project,[1] we have come to consider five social problems as predominant in our historical era:

1. War
2. Poverty
3. Racial oppression and colonialism
4. Environmental decay
5. Alienation

Each of these problems can be expressed as a world-order value:[2]

1. The minimization of violence
2. The maximization of social and economic welfare
3. The maximization of social and political justice
4. The maximization of ecological balance
5. The maximization of participation in authority processes

Our inquiry is directed toward the discovery of effective tactics and effective strategies for

[1]For a description of the project in its early stages, see Ian Baldwin, Jr., "Thinking about a New World Order for the Decade of the 1990's," *War/Peace Report* (January 1970), pp. 3-7.

[2]Mendlovitz has developed a definition of world order that we shall present in the final section of this General Introduction.

promoting and balancing these four interrelated values. Although we are convinced that part of the answer is some increase in central guidance capacities at the global level, we adopt no dogmatic position as to what kind of structural development would be most appropriate. Furthermore we share the concern of many people throughout the world that special dangers and costs arise from the increasing influence of government on people's lives. Innovations in such fields as computer technology and satellite broadcasting create frightening potentialities for the manipulation, suppression, and alienation of the majority of the human race. On the other hand, certain forms of political centralization could help to reduce the extent of governmental influence by lessening the significance of political boundaries. Furthermore, technological innovations could be used to increase citizen participation in government by providing means for rapid and widespread communication of popular sentiments.

We believe that the rise of concern about environmental quality, especially in the industrial countries, has a significant bearing on the future shape of world society. The mounting pressures on the ecosystems of the world require some kind of management on a global scale. Otherwise, the continuing process of industrialization and the increasing extraction of natural resources, including activity on and below the oceans, are sure to cause further environmental decay and to increase the risk of an ecological collapse of catastrophic proportions. These dangerous trends are so abundantly documented by now that it seems inevitable that the future shape of international society will be largely determined by the interplay between the war system and environmental pressure. Such an interplay is made more ominous by the steady growth of world population, adding to the pressures of every sort that are already taxing the capacities of overburdened governments. These pressures are also accentuated by the rising demand for scarce resources. By the year 2000 these will be almost double the number of people on earth at present, a frightening prospect when one appreciates that at the present time about one-third of the world's population is hungry and an additional one-third malnourished.[3] It is against this background that we undertake our investigation of regional phenomena.

We ask the following questions about regional developments.

1. Under what conditions does regionalism promote, and under what conditions does it retard, the solution of the four global social problems that we have stated? How do various regional movements bear on the prospects of realizing the five world-order values?

2. Which regional movements and which features of a particular regional movement are positive and which are negative with regard to the five world-order values? Such an inquiry seeks an appraisal of specific regional developments of both functional (security, economic, general purposes) and geographical (European, African, Latin American) character.

3. What is the relationship between the levels of political organization in international society? Does the rise of regional actors cause primarily sovereignty-cutting, sovereignty-insulating, or sovereignty-shifting? Or, more aptly, under what conditions does the growth of regionalism have an impact upon the scope and character of "sovereignty" at the national level?

4. What kinds of regional development promote and what kinds retard the potentiality for the rise of an adequate system of central guidance in world affairs? We make a distinction between *first order integration* (institutional cohesion within a region) and *second-order integration* (*external* linkages among regional actors and their degree of capacity for global integration.)

5. Is it necessary to take a position for or against regionalism in light of an overriding commitment to the creation of a more just and moderate system of world order?

In organizing the materials on regionalism contained in this book our principal aim is to explore the extent to which regionalist conceptions of world order promote the five goal values we feel are imperative to foster. Perhaps we should note at the outset, however, that the nature of the regionalist literature has made this task somewhat difficult and awkward to accomplish. It seems fair to say that the literature on

---

[3]These issues are more completely discussed in Paul R. Ehrlich and Anne H. Ehrlich, *Population, Resources, Environment: Issues in Human Ecology,* Second edition, W. H. Freeman and Company, San Francisco, 1972, and in R. A. Falk, *This Endangered Planet,* Random House, New York, 1971.

regionalism has concerned itself almost exclusively with measuring the extent to which *integration* is taking place, and only implicitly, if at all, with how best to promote security, welfare, social justice, and environmental quality either within the region or what the implications of regionalism are for the resolution of these issues at the global level. In general, social scientists who have attempted to measure world and regional political unity have been explicitly concerned with stability and have sought to answer the question: is it possible to keep the system going? (See especially the Roger Masters article in Part I). Recently two writers have acknowledged the somewhat one-sided emphasis of past writings in the field. In "Domestic and International Consequences of Regional Integration," reprinted in Part II, Stuart A. Scheingold says: "What has been missing from all this work is some attention to the difference it makes whether or not such regional entities are created. As a result, after more than a decade of research, we have only a very limited understanding of the costs and benefits of integration" (p. 133). Near the beginning of his article, "The Study of Regional Integration: Reflections on the Joy and Anguish of Pretheorizing," also reprinted in Part II, Ernst B. Haas says, "In the following pages I shall attempt an evaluation of fifteen years of research on regional integration. I should like to confess at the outset that while inferences about learning, adaptation, and the evolution of shared tasks among nations have provided the foci for research, the normative uses to which the findings could be put have not received the attention they deserve" (p. 104). It is to be hoped that this recognition foreshadows a new emphasis of study for regional processes and institutions. Since the main body of literature does not deal with the value issues we seek to examine, it is necessary then for us to come to terms with the material and to relate it to our conerns. This we attempt to do by means of (1) essays that introduce the readings and (2) comments and questions that follow the readings.

Within the large body of literature on regionalism that has been accumulating since World War II, there is considerable emphasis upon the study and promotion of regional integration for Western Europe.[4] Recent studies have evaluated this most impressive (provided we exclude great empires) of all regionalist experiments.[5] Other recent scholarly work has been designed both to extend the European experience to the study of other geographical areas and to adapt that experience to a variety of distinct regional settings throughout the world. As a result, a more disciplined and globalist literature of comparative regionalism is beginning to emerge.[6]

The idea of regional development has been closely tied to the idea of an association of states linked, above all, by a condition of geographical proximity. Such proximity often coincides with shared features of history, climate, and culture. In addition to the regional boundaries of natural geography, boundaries of a region may be drawn either by considerations of *ideology* (Western and Eastern Europe) or by reference to *ethnic* factors (the Arab world). In our inquiry we shall adhere to the traditional emphasis on geographical proximity, although we also shall consider associations among states that are geographically separated (for example, the British Commonwealth, and the Communist International System) as well as global agencies of specialized function (such as the International Labor Organization). The decline of the British Commonwealth, as well as the Sino-Soviet split, has—when compared to the continuing growth of European regionalism, despite all stops and diversions—stimulated a renewed belief in the critical importance of geography in building political units larger than the nation-state.

A debate continues, however, whether such a regional building process can ever cross thresholds of national sovereignty—and even if it does, whether the emerging unit will be any more responsive to the five world-order values either in its internal development or in its external relations. As yet, there is no relevant experience, hence no real evidence; we must depend upon speculation. David Mitrany argues, for instance,

---

[4]Ernst B. Haas, *The Uniting of Europe*, Stanford University Press, Stanford, 1958, rev. ed., 1968.

[5]For assessments of the European experience, see Leon N. Lindberg and Stuart A. Scheingold, *Europe's Would be Polity*, Prentice-Hall, Englewood Cliffs, N.J., 1970; Carl J. Friedrich, *Europe: An Emergent Nation?*, Harper and Row, New York, 1970.

[6]See especially Louis J. Cantori and Stephen L. Spiegel, *The International Politics of Regions*, Prentice-Hall, Englewood Cliffs, N.J., 1970.

that a regional political unit will be so preoc-cupied with the task of maintaining the deli-cate balance of internal pressures that it will be virtually closed to the global system and will tend to be incapable of initiating or participating in second-order integation movements. Will regional actors develop a doctrine of regional sovereignty both to resist penetration by extra-regional actors and to aggregate capabilities for dealing with economic and political rivalries going on outside the region? The OAU has certainly regarded its role as partly to create a shield that blocks the reassertion of colonial in-fluence by way of military intervention in intra-regional affairs. Perhaps the OAS could pursue a comparable goal if it were reconstituted to ex-clude the United States.

We are also concerned with structures and organizations that evolve out of the regional impetus to coordinate and integrate separate national policies. We contend that the ideology and institutions associated with the state system are incapable of coping with the problems of the nuclear age, or with the emerging concerns of the ecological age. Traditions of rivalry are accentuated by the concentration of power and authority in national governments. Such statist emphasis is being broken down by a variety of developments:

1. The growth of nonstate actors in the eco-nomic sphere, especially multinational cor-porations;
2. The use of global functional agencies to cope with many technological developments that occur on a global scale;
3. The rise of transnational sentiments and movements in the professions and among ethnic, ideological, and age reference groups (for example, blacks, the third world, the young) and the decline in advanced coun-tries of national patriotism;
4. The rise of subnational militancy that seeks to disperse authority of national govern-ments;
5. The rise of regional movements and the growth of regional loyalties.

It is within this larger setting of organizational developments that the regional movement must be placed for evaluation.

Because of our concern with the politics of world order, we examine the politics of regions that have not yet evolved a distinct movement for integration or agreed upon the creation of impor-tant regional entities. Such an unintegrated polit-ical system is found in the Middle East—Israel, the Arab countries, and the liberation movements are the main actors—and there is a complex in-ternal dynamic, as well as a complicated set of external linkages both with the global system and with other political systems. Studies of Middle Eastern affairs usually emphasize intraregional conflict and are contrary to the tendency of much "regionalist" literature to emphasize the achieve-ments and prospects of regional cooperation.

Finally, we assess the effects of regional tendencies upon the present role and future prospects of the United Nations. In this regard, we shall present two kinds of inquiry.

The first kind of inquiry pertains to the useful-ness of the regional concept within the opera-tions of the United Nations, especially with respect to regional economic commissions and the extension of such regionalist organization to matters in the spheres of security, human rights, and the environment. Regionalism within the UN framework often brings together rival po-litical groups that would refuse to form a project based on intergovernmental decision. The rela-tive success of the European Economic Com-mission in promoting cooperative relations be-tween East and West Europe has led Johan Galtung to propose a comparable organizational apparatus within the UN for security issues.[7]

The second kind of inquiry pertains to a consideration of the relationship between the UN and the regional actors organized outside its control. The regional actor can be either a useful intermediary or an obstructive alternative to UN action. Minerva Etzioni has studied this relationship between regionalism and the UN in the Western Hemisphere and has taken due note of the extent to which the OAS has been used, especially by the United States, to interfere with, rather than to facilitate, compliance with the UN Charter.[8]

---

[7]This proposal is briefly considered in Part IV.
[8]See Minerva Etzioni, *The Majority of One: Towards a Theory of Regional Compatability*, Sage, Beverly Hills, California, 1970.

Table 1
Matrix for the Study of World Order

Actor	Year	Minimization of Violence			Maximization of Welfare	Maximization of Justice	Maximization of Ecological Balance	Maximization of Participation
		Arms Policy	Peace Keeping	Conflict Resolu-tion	_Impact on Key Processes and Their Elements (Can be ranked on a 5-point achievement scale; 1-low, 5-high.)_			
World (e.g., the UN)	1970 1980 1990 2000							
International	1970 1980 1990 2000							
Regional	1970 1980 1990 2000							
Transnational	1970 1980 1990 2000							
National	1970 1980 1990 2000							
Infranational	1970 1980 1990 2000							
Individual	1970 1980 1990 2000							

DEFINITION OF WORLD ORDER

In conclusion, we offer readers the following definition of world order together with a crude matrix (Table 1) that fits the main categories of study to be found in this volume into an over-all framework of inquiry.

World order is used here to designate that study of international relations and world affairs that focuses primarily on the questions: how can the likelihood of international violence be reduced significantly? And how can tolerable conditions of worldwide economic welfare, social justice, and ecological stability be created? (In more connotative but less precise terminology the questions would read: how can a warless and more just world be achieved and maintained? And how can the quality of human life be improved?)

So understood, *world order* encompasses a range of entities—world institutions, international organizations, regional arrangements, transnational movements, nation-states, infranational groups, and individuals—as they relate to the following world political and community processes: peace-keeping, third-party resolution of disputes, and other modes of pacific settlement of disputes; disarmament and arms control; economic development and welfare; the technological and scientific revolutions; the attainment of ecological stability; and the protection of human and social rights.

Methodologically, this inquiry will evaluate *relevant utopias* and culminate in statements of investigators' *preferred worlds*.

A *"relevant utopia"* is a projection of a reasonably concrete behavioral model or image of a system of world political and social processes capable of dealing with the set of global problems at some tolerable level of human satisfaction.

In addition, relevant utopias must describe in as rigorous a manner as possible, the trends and prognoses with respect to these problems over a one-to-three-decade period. (Within this context "relevance" means that both the model and the *transition* must be sufficiently described in behavioral terms so that the intelligent reader as well as the formulator has a reasonable basis for making a statement about the probabilities of the emergence of such a model. It does *not* mean that the model has been proven to be politically feasible.)

"Transition" is the process by which the present system is likely to and/or will be transformed into the relevant utopia. In dealing with transition, special emphasis is given to the possibility of system change without recourse to large-scale violence.

A *"preferred world"* is the culmination of the preceding investigations; it comprises a blueprint of a recommended structure *and* a list of recommended guidelines and steps for achieving that structure, described in reasonably concrete behavioral terms. It is from testing alternative world-order models and transition processes, structures and strategies (that is, from a set of relevant utopias), that the investigator is able to select or invent his preferred world.

Throughout the following inquiry, formalized authoritative structures and processes of world legal order are given special emphasis, especially as they relate to all the various political, economic, and social processes and structures that either favor or militate against the achievement and maintenance of a warless, more just, and ecologically stable world.

Finally, a continuous effort must be made to define "world interest" operationally, in terms of the central world-order problems under discussion.

REGIONS AND WORLD ORDER: BLOCS, SUBSYSTEMS, AND ORGANIZATIONS

It is desirable to avoid two tendencies, both of which are sometimes evident in the literature on regional studies:

1. the tendency to distinguish too sharply between regionalist movements and other collective techniques for organizing the economic and political activities of a region (to avoid this, our book includes blocs, subsystems, and even collective security pacts within its conception of regionalism);
2. the tendency to distinguish too rigidly between the process of integration and the structure of the activities that have been integrated (to avoid this, our inquiry tries to prevent the confusion of dynamic and static modes of inquiry, but acknowledges the validity of each mode).

Part I and Part II take into account some of the principal multinational, nonglobal approaches to the study of international society. The emphasis on partial structures in the over-all setting of the world political system in Part I should be distinguished from the emphasis of Part II on the regional integration process taken as a distinct object for study.

As we emphasize in the General Introduction, we explore the subject matter of regionalism from a normative perspective of world order. Such a perspective implies a concern with assessing the various effects of regionalist tendencies upon the present and future quality of world order. This approach is in some sense managerial in character, investigating the phenomenon of regionalism to assess whether it is having a positive effect on the over-all quest for a better system of world order as identified primarily in relation to the five goals: war-prevention, international welfare, the promotion of human rights, the maintenance of environmental quality, widespread participation in government.

The managerial outlook depends upon a good deal of conceptual clarity. Part I is an introduction to the main modes of thought embraced within a broad interpretation of what constitutes regionalism. We offer leading examples of four analytical orientations toward the subject matter; each main selection is followed by a Discussion and Questions section that presents the reader with various related considerations.

The first selection is an essay by Roger Masters that puts forward a "multibloc model" of international society. Such a model is in one sense a response to those who analyzed international society as "bipolar," consisting mainly of two rival blocs under Soviet and American leadership. The decay of the Cold War, the disintegration of both blocs, the spread of nuclear weapons, and the challenge of the less modern, poorer states have been among the factors that have led students of international society to grow dissatisfied with the bipolar image that dominated thought in the years after World War II up through the late 1950's. Masters' article is one of the first formulations of a multibloc alternative to bipolarity. The analysis is built upon the theory of oligopolistic competition in a market dominated by a few large firms. It retains its attractiveness for present analysis because it clearly depicts the elements of a multibloc model world as it proposes, although quite tentatively, this multibloc world as a desirable world-order alternative to be achieved by conscious, directed action during the next fifty to a hundred years. Masters, along with many Western thinkers, seems to exhaust the content of world order by a concern with the inhibition of large-scale, catastrophic violence through a new formulation of the conditions for equilibrium in international society. He gives little attention in his article to the North-South category of welfare issues or to the promotion of human rights or even to drastic disarmament.

The second selection, "Political Discontinuities in the International System," by Oran R. Young, is a later piece that carries on in a somewhat altered idiom the line of thinking initiated by Masters. Young's inquiry here is "analytical" rather than "normative." Unlike Masters, he is not offering readers an image of a better system of world order. Rather he is hoping to improve tools of analysis to enable a better understanding of what is happening in international society. His overriding interest is to gain insight into the present functioning of the international political system as a whole. Young depicts several international "subsystems," thereby adding a new element to conventional analysis of international relations, and makes several novel and significant points. First of all, he emphasizes the extent to which these "subsystems" (patterns of substantial interaction in relation to a spatial core of sovereign states) are different from one another. The conception and operation of subsystems will be treated more fully in Part V. Second, he calls attention to the various kinds of interactions between global patterns of politics and regional subsystems, suggesting that these interactions between the whole and the various parts are determined both by the common attributes of the global systems and by the distinctive attributes of each subsystem. And third, he points to the lateral linkages between these subsystems as an element of present international society, made more pronounced by the fact that advancing technology diminishes the importance of the distance between subsystems and of the size of the global system. In this connection it should be noted that by looking at the emerging interconnectedness between the European and the Asian subsystems of today—a relationship generally overlooked by American political scientists—Young suggests a fruitful line of inquiry in terms of understanding and controlling global processes in relation to the five world-order goals posited in our General Introduction.

Using a somewhat more traditional rhetoric and mode of analysis, Lynn Miller in the third selection categorizes the regional actors concerned with the maintenance of international peace and security. Such an inquiry raises questions of theory and practice about the relationships between regionalism and globalism in contemporary international society. To begin with, there is apparent an occasion for making comparisons between the United Nations Charter and the comparable constitutional instruments of regional authorization. Such a comparison suggests the broader relevance of legal standards and procedures to the development of larger political units in world affairs. Miller's analysis of diplomatic practice also directly raises the difficult question: have regional actors in different sets of circumstances implemented or frustrated the ideals of world order as embodied in the Charter? The growth of regionalism in the security area responded to certain trends in international politics, most especially to the narrow limits of

Soviet-American cooperation. If these limits sharply diminish or disappear in the years ahead, then new global trends (to some extent already emerging) will soon reshape the function and role of regional security actors. Miller also brings into focus the problems of imperialism that exist whenever a regional framework accommodates one state that is predominant in relation to the rest of the membership. The relations between the United States and Latin American regionalism or between the Soviet Union and Eastern European regionalism are obvious arenas within which to conduct this inquiry into the extent to which regionalism is an *instrument for* or a *brake upon* great-power domination.

The last selection in this chapter, by Joseph S. Nye, is entitled "Regional Institutions." To some extent this article is a theoretical overview of approaches to the study of integration at the regional level and anticipates the concerns of Part II. Nye proposes an interesting scheme for the classification of regional actors (a problem that is dealt with more extensively in Part III). He uses quantitative data to interpret the regional phenomenon and to expose and correct certain oversimplifications that are common in the literature. In suggesting that regionalism as an emergent movement has a range of alternative futures centering around either effective international organization or the possibility of functional arrangements less territorially based, Nye provides us with a sophisticated appraisal of regional developments, their ebb and flow, patterns of success and failure, and the limits of what existing data make it possible to conclude about the future of regionalism. Nye's explicit concern with the future is typical of a growing tendency among students of international society to focus inquiry on the future.

A study of these three selections should help clarify the main distinctions between blocs, subsystems, alliances, and regional organizations. Additional political forms relevant to a comprehensive appreciation of regionalism include empires, commonwealths, specialized international agencies, and caucuses. These related forms of organization on an international level will be discussed from time to time throughout the text of this volume.

1

A Multi-bloc Model of the International System

ROGER D. MASTERS

This essay will attempt to define an abstract model of the international system (or, more precisely, a model of the *structure* of that system), as a supplement to the types presented by Morton A. Kaplan.[1] Before attempting such a construction, it is well to show the utility of the "multi-bloc system" as an alternative to his six models. Kaplan's "balance-of-power" and "unit veto" systems are essentially defined in terms of nation-states as "actors";[2] and his "universal" and "hierarchical" systems have essentially but one "actor," though in the former the nation-state subsists as an administrative and local political unit.[3] The two "bipolar" models ("loose" and "tight") have, by definition, two major bloc "actors," with uncommitted nation-states on the margin and an "international actor" such as the U.N. playing a limited role in the former model.[4] It is true that his "unit veto" system may have blocs instead of nation-states for "actors," but by this very token the *difference* between a system with a multiplicity of states and one with a multiplicity of blocs is not suggested by Kaplan's typology.[5]

---

[1] *System and Process in International Politics* (New York, 1957), ch. 2. For a more general presentation, see also his "Balance of Power, Bipolarity, and Other Models of International Systems," *American Political Science Review*, Vol. 51 (September, 1957), pp. 684–95.

[2] *System and Process*, pp. 22, 50.

[3] *Ibid.*, pp. 45–49.

[4] *Ibid.*, pp. 36–44.

[5] *Ibid.*, p. 78. A note on the use of the word "bloc" is in order. This term will be used to describe a group of nation-states to the extent that they act as a unit in international relations. Although at the outset it will be *assumed* that each bloc acts as a unit, the word "bloc" itself implies neither particular institutional structures nor any measure of unity of action. Indeed, one might consider alliances as the generic term for relationships between states; in this case a "bloc" would be regarded as a species of alliance—i.e., an alliance having a "functional organization" as an ongoing institution. For the purposes of theoretical exposition, however, the reverse usage will be adopted here. A "bloc" will be considered as a genus or general category,

From *American Political Science Review*, vol. 55, no. 4, Dec. 1961, pp. 780-798. Reprinted by permission of the author and publisher.

I. INTRODUCTION

The possibility of an international system composed of a multiplicity of blocs has been considered by a number of writers in the past few years. Even before the end of the Second World War, Walter Lippmann wrote:

> The question is whether some sixty to seventy states, each acting separately, can form a universal organization for the maintenance of peace. I contend that they cannot, and that single sovereign states must combine in their neighborhoods, and that the neighborhoods must combine into larger communities and constellations, which then participate in a universal society.[6]

More recently, Stanley Hoffmann has argued that, to the unpleasant alternatives of nuclear war or continued rigid bipolarity

> there remains a third possibility . . . the progressive transformation of the non-communist world, not into a series of States . . . but into a series of supranational communities, at first regional, and continuously enlarging themselves. Such communities, built according to a confederal model, . . . would be formed parallel to the international organization, whose survival will be necessary for the settlement of disputes between States outside partial communities or [between] members of different communities, as long as the international arena remains based essentially on States.[7]

Ernst B. Haas, in describing the useful function of the UN in permitting the uncommitted nations to "balance" the Eastern and Western blocs, has concluded:

> International organization, understood in these terms, would not produce the millennium of law, progress, and order expected by ardent advocates of international cooperation. But it might ensure the international breathing spell necessary to develop a multi-polar and multi-functional pattern of policy expectations, and thereby further the habits of peaceful adjustment of basic tensions.[8]

Clearly, if only from these references, it has been considered *possible* that the international system could develop into a multiplicity of blocs.

In addition, it has recently been suggested that the development of supra-national organisms, at least in the West, is *desirable* and should be encouraged. For example, it has been said that the United States should consider a partial surrender of its sovereignty to NATO. But little careful thought has been directed to the characteristics of a world order in which the nation-state is no longer the "sovereign" unit (or "actor") which makes foreign policy decisions. Before one can make a well informed *political* choice concerning the desirability of federated or regional institutions, it seems essential to speculate on the consequences, for world politics, of the replacement of nations by regional blocs. Any long-range foreign policy goals must consider the possible choice between a world composed of sovereign states and a world in which alliances or blocs act as units. Although the model to be proposed does *not* imply a preference for any given policy, the ultimate need to determine long-run policy aims provided the impetus for the present essay, which will try to specify the characteristics of a multi-bloc world order.

John Herz, having seen this possibility, has argued that a system of multipolarity would take the form of the "unit veto" system as defined by Kaplan. Since this assertion, if correct, would render superfluous the specification of the unique characteristics of a multiple bloc system, perhaps it is justifiable to quote him at some length:

---

describing all types of relationships between a group of nation-states. This usage is advantageous because, although the term "alliance" usually connotes a relationship in which *states* are the constituent units, it is possible to conceive of alliances between *blocs* as well as between states. Hence, considering the entire international system as the frame of reference, an alliance is but one way in which several "actors" (nation-states or blocs) may coordinate their political, military, and economic actions. From a general theoretical perspective, the varying degrees of coordination between nation-states can best be expressed in terms of a continuum; for a typology expressing the range of possibilities in this continuum, see below, Table 1.

[6]*U.S. War Aims* (Boston, 1944), p. 187. *Cf.* Edward Hallett Carr, *Nationalism and After* (New York, 1945), pp. 53–54, 60–62.

[7]*Organisations Internationales et Pouvoirs Politiques des États*, Cahiers de la Foundation Nationale des Sciences Politiques, No. 52 (Paris: Librairie Armand Colin, 1954), pp. 416–17. (My translation.)

---

[8]"Regionalism, Functionalism, and Universal International Organization," *World Politics*, VIII (January, 1956), 263.

For bipolarity . . . may already be passing, and, with the rise of countries like China, Western Germany, and possibly Japan and India, its disintegration into a new multipower system may be in the offing. . . . If, or when, in addition to the present two atomic powers or power blocs, an indefinite number of other countries possess atomic capabilities, any new multipower system thus arising will have aspects vastly different from what those who talk in terms of a "return" to a five-power or six-power system are envisaging. It would be radically new in the sense that it would add to the present two nuclear blocs an indefinite number of units which, whether "big," "medium," or "small" in traditional terms, would all exist on a basis of fundamental "equality" as possessors of the new weapon. "Multipolarity" (on the pattern of the term "bipolarity"), or "polycentrism," might be terms better fitting a situation, or system, in which each unit constitutes a center or pole of absolute power. This is something utterly different from the classical constellation of "multinational" or "multipower" system with its graduated power of comparable "powers."[9]

At this point, Herz adds in a footnote: "If I understand him correctly, this is the system Mr. Kaplan has in mind when he calls one of his 'models' the 'unit-veto system'." As the lengthy citation implies, the term "multipolarity" is applied to an international system in which each "actor," regardless of size, possesses an invulnerable nuclear capability such that it may destroy any other actor (even if being destroyed itself in the process). This problem is inherent in the diffusion of nuclear weapons among a large number of nation-states, creating an approximation of Hobbes' "war of all against all."

But is it necessary to assume that a "multipolarity" of states with nuclear striking forces will be identical with a multiplicity of blocs, each composed of a number of states? Such an argument could be based on the assertion that the hydrogen bomb is an "absolute weapon" to such an extent that it equalizes a single state and a bloc of states with respect to their defensive security (or "impermeability," to use Herz' term):

In principle, such countries [*i.e.*, with nuclear capabilities] acquire equal power status. True, as I have indicated before, possession of nuclear weapons as such does not necessarily equal power to destroy or retaliate, especially when nuclear units included in defense blocs with some amount of coordinated policy are involved. But when any number of uncommitted and uncoordinated units have this power, the situation may be different. . . . The world would not only be at the mercy of each power as such but would also be dependent on whoever—that is, which person, group, regime within each unit—was controlling the military establishment. . . .[10]

In other words, Herz concludes that the "equalization" caused by nuclear diffusion would have its "unit veto" effects when a *large number* of states or blocs attain the capability to destroy any rival. Despite his use of the term multipolarity in this context, Herz leaves open the possiblity that "defense blocs with some amount of coordinated policy" may *not* stand in a "unit veto" relationship with one another.[11]

If the "unit veto" system implies a large number of actors, therefore, it is not at all certain that Kaplan's model describes the behavior of a small number of blocs (say less than ten), even assuming each is armed with nuclear weapons. In economic theory, for example, small-numbers markets (oligopolies) have been found to differ fundamentally from systems with large numbers of actors. This suggests that it might be desirable to construct a "multi-bloc" model while ignoring the effects of nuclear weapons; their introduction can be made later as a more "realistic" assumption. This follows the method used by Herz, since his brilliant analysis of the post-World War II international system rests on a distinction between the effects of bipolarity (a structure of power) and

---

[9]John H. Herz, *International Relations in the Atomic Age* (New York: Columbia University Press, 1959), pp. 34–35.

[10]*Ibid.*, p. 182.

[11]Kaplan himself has implied that a multiplicity of blocs might arise if the use of nuclear weapons were prohibited by joint agreement. (*System and Process*, p. 52). This suggests that, for Kaplan, the "unit veto" model describes a *state* of an international system rather than a determinant structure. But certain structures are more likely to produce self-limiting agreements than others, as will be argued below. Kaplan's "unit veto" model, by stressing the implications of nuclear capabilities, ignores the power context within which such military weapons are placed.

nuclear weapons (a crucial implement of military power).[12]

There is one additional reason why a model of the type proposed may be useful. Although the current discussions of the "cold war" generally assume the existence of a "bipolar" situation, there are in fact a multiplicity of regional alliances of varying degrees of intergration. In the West, to be sure, this multiplicity has been well described as a "wheel," with the United States at the hub and its many allies distributed around the circumference.[13] Nonetheless the theoretical implications of the rise of many multilateral organizations deserve study apart from this apparently overriding bipolar orientation; American participation in any one bloc (*e.g.*, NATO) need not determine the behavior of another bloc (*e.g.*, OAS), particularly with respect to intra-regional problems. Although the model which follows is not intended as a descriptive one, therefore, it may not be without significance for an understanding of the numerous regional organizations currently in existence.

II. GENERAL CHARACTERISTICS OF THE MULTI-BLOC SYSTEM

In order that the construction of the "multi-bloc model" may serve as a theoretical extension of Kaplan's typology, it is helpful to define the system with reference to his work. Once the characteristics of this model have been established on the basis of Kaplan's propositions, it will be feasible to introduce elements unique to a system composed of a plurality of bloc actors. This procedure has a further advantage, because it enables one to begin with the assumption that a small number of blocs would behave like a small number of nation-states, at least while ignoring the effect of nuclear weapons. To determine the specific elements of a multi-bloc (or "balance of bloc") system, therefore, we can conveniently start with an analysis of the changes resulting from the substitution of bloc actors for the states in Kaplan's "balance of power" model. This sub-

stitution will suffice for the establishment of the general characteristics of the model proposed.

In brief, then, the "pure" multi-bloc system is merely Kaplan's "balance of power" model with five or more regional blocs as actors. For the sake of illustration, the blocs might be the Western Hemisphere, Western Europe, the Soviet Union and East Europe, an Asian region dominated by China, and an African region. Other actors are possible (*e.g.*, an Indo-Australian or Middle Eastern bloc, not to mention states not committed to a bloc), and of course other patterns are conceivable. Each region must be sufficiently integrated to act as a unit in its relations with external powers or actors.[14] If two crucial variables—the extent of integration and the effect of nuclear weapons—are temporarily ignored, the system will approximate a rivalry of power between regional blocs comparable to that which existed, say, in Italy in the Fifteenth Century between the Italian city-states[15] or in Europe in the Nineteenth Century between the European nation-states.[16] That is to say, the actors would use the means of internal growth and consolidation, alliances, claims of prestige, and war to compete for the achievement of conflicting but limited goals. These characteristics of the multi-bloc model can be described with reference to Kaplan's rules for the "balance of power" system.

Rule 1. "Act to increase capabilities, but negotiate rather than fight."[17] It might be objected that the emergence of regional blocs or "super-States" as international actors would render negotiation impossible. According to this view, because each member of the international system would be so large, a "titanic conflict" would in-

---

[12]*International Politics*, chs. 7, 8. See esp. p. 111.

[13]Arnold Wolfers, "Stresses and Strains in 'Going It with Others'," in Arnold Wolfers, ed., *Alliance Policy in the Cold War* (Baltimore: Johns Hopkins Press, 1959), p. 7.

[14]The definition of "integration," the extent to which it may vary, and the effects of different degrees of integration must all be of crucial importance for the operation of the system. Although it is convenient, in order to establish the general configuration of the multi-bloc model, to assume that all blocs are equally integrated, this assumption will be examined, in Section V.

[15]*Cf.* Garrett Mattingly, *Renaissance Diplomacy* (London: Jonathan Cape, 1955), Pt. II.

[16]The bibliography on the "balance of power" system is, of course, quite large. For a survey of the operations of the system after 1848, see A. J. P. Taylor, *The Struggle for the Mastery of Europe* (Oxford, 1954).

[17]Kaplan, *System and Process*, p. 23.

evitably result.[18] There are, however, several important theoretical reasons why this inability to negotiate need not follow. First, a study of the process of the "integration" of states into larger political communities has developed the hypothesis that such integration is normally followed by inward or "selfish" orientation rather than by outward "aggression."[19] Secondly, the decision-makers of a regional bloc, being responsible to a large, multi-national "constituency," would be forced to take into consideration a multiplicity of considerations and cross-pressures; as the famous argument of the *Federalist*, No. 10, suggests, such broader units tend to be *less* dangerous than narrow and homogeneous societies.[20] A similar consideration is suggested by Kaplan's proposition that the more numerous the roles occupied by decision-makers, the more information they will consider and hence the more flexible their policies will be.[21] If it be assumed that blocs would tend to require complex institutional structures with some "federal" basis, this hypothesis suggests that those responsible for a bloc's foreign policy would tend to be somewhat "flexible."

It is not being suggested here that a multi-bloc system would necessarily be peaceful. Although Hoffmann apparently makes this assumption, it is certainly gratuitous if not utopian.[22] But if a plurality of blocs need not be peaceful, there is equally no reason to believe that bloc actors would be *necessarily* incapable of preferring negotiation to war. Even if one introduces the possession of nuclear capabilities (which will not be attempted formally until Section IV), there is no need to assume that the behavior of a bloc-actor would be more "aggressive" than that of a nation-state. Certainly the experience of NATO with respect to nuclear warheads shows that in a regional organization including conflicting interests, "immobilism" and indecision are as likely as an expansionist hostility. And this is so in a relatively rigid bipolar system, in which NATO is opposed by a homogeneous bloc, *i.e.*, the Warsaw Pact nations. To say the least, therefore, a multi-bloc system seems compatible with Kaplan's first rule; war in such a system would not arise from sources fundamentally different from those in a "balance of power" model.

Rule 2. "Fight rather than pass up opportunities to increase capabilities."[23] No structure of the international system precludes conflict. The conception of a "stable" system does not mean that no violence occurs or that no change takes place, but that violence and change remain within "tolerable" limits such that the identity or underlying structure of the system is not overthrown.[24] While it has been argued above that a total war of annihilation is not implicit in the structure of a multi-bloc system (as distinguished from the weapons likely in that system), it has also been suggested that blocs are not intrinsically "peaceful" either. Indeed, it seems impossible to determine, in the abstract, the relative likelihood of conflict in the multi-bloc system, since the outbreak of violence depends on the goals (*i.e.*, the kinds of "capabilities" to be increased) and the power situation of the actors.

One can suggest, however, the kinds of "opportunities" for fighting which might exist in the multi-bloc model, since these are partially determined by the structure of the system. Four possi-

---

[18]Lippmann's reply to this argument with reference to World War II is not irrelevant: "It will be feared that great constellations like the Atlantic Community, the Russian Orbit, the Chinese Community will become engaged in a titanic conflict. The members of these communities are now engaged in a titanic conflict, and in order to survive they have had to organize impromptu and tardily, the strategical combinations which, in my view, they ought to maintain and perfect. It cannot be said that this titanic conflict was caused by regional combinations. It can be said that it was not prevented and has very nearly been lost because they did not exist." *U.S. War Aims*, p. 191.

[19]Karl W. Deutsch et al., *Political Community and the North Atlantic Area* (Princeton: Princeton University Press, 1957), p. 25.

[20]"The smaller the society, the fewer probably will be the distinct parties and interests composing it; the fewer the distinct parties and interests, the more frequently will a majority be found of the same party; and the smaller the number of individuals composing a majority, and the smaller the compass within which they are placed, the more easily will they concert and execute their plans of oppression." *The Federalist*, Edward Mead Earle, ed. (New York: Modern Library, n.d.), pp. 60–61. While Madison here refers to internal oppression, the same argument could be made with reference to foreign policy.

[21]Kaplan, *System and Process*, pp. 104–105.

[22]*Cf. Organisations Internationales*, pp. 417–18. Hoffman even implies that the unique virtue of regional associations is that they *couldn't* engage in "power politics," at least if properly regulated.

[23]Kaplan, *Systems and Process*, p. 23.

[24]*Ibid.*, pp. 6–7. See below, Section III.

bilities can be distinguished: (1) Occupation of territory outside the blocs, either "marginal" to a bloc or "uncommitted" to any bloc (the device employed by European nation-states, especially with respect to colonies);[25] (2) division of a rival bloc, rendering it impotent (the classic "divide and rule"); (3) control over a rival bloc, resulting either in direct amalgamation or indirect subversion and dominance (comparable to the means of Soviet control over Eastern Europe); or (4) forcible establishment of world government. The last of these "opportunities" clearly involves changing the very structure of the international system, creating something approximating Kaplan's "hierarchical" or "universal" model. While this indicates the obvious fact that a multi-bloc system, if established, could not be expected to be permanent, it is not especially interesting as an indication of the workings of the multi-bloc system itself. To be sure, in any "realistic" sense, it would be necessary to assume that a bloc or blocs (*e.g.*, the Soviet bloc) would attempt to establish their hegemony, but this is explicity dealt with by Kaplan's rules four and five.

Of the remaining three kinds of "opportunities" to increase a bloc's "capabilities" by fighting, two depend upon the internal vulnerability of rival blocs: division, and subversion or conquest of a bloc are unlikely whenever intra-bloc integration provides the regional organization with sufficient means to maintain control over its "constituency." Since a high degree of integration is being assumed, these objectives would be relatively unpromising in the "pure" model.[26] The remaining type of "opportunity" (fighting to occupy marginal territories) is, it will be noted, a "limited" one. That is, the likely cause of overt hostilities in the "pure" multi-bloc model is compatible with the third rule formulated by Kaplan.

Rule 3. "Stop fighting rather than eliminate an essential national actor."[27] The relevance of this rule does not depend on the possession of a nuclear capability, as is evident from Hitler's overt violation of it. As the example shows, there is no assurance that a bloc (any more than a state in classical international relations) would tolerate a competitive relationship with other power equals. It is necessary, however, to distinguish between the ideological goals of an actor and the power limitations placed upon him by the structure of the international system as he perceives it. For example, the Soviet Union is now committed to the "victory of socialism" throughout the world, but this has not prevented the emergence of a doctrine of "peaceful coexistence" which explicity claims to accept the present bipolar system, especially with respect to Germany. While hegemonic goals are possible, therefore, the existence of a number of rivals, capable of forming a coalition, can force any given "actor" (nation or bloc) to limit his objectives, at least with regard to the destruction of any other major member of the system.[28] However, this circumspection, created by the interdependence of a small number of significant international "actors," need not apply to those entities which are of lesser size and importance.

As a corollary to this rule, it therefore follows that one could "eliminate any non-essential actor when convenient." As was implied by the definition of the "opportunities" in a multi-bloc system, the uncommitted states between blocs are the most likely objectives of "aggression." It might even be assumed that no such intermediate states would ultimately remain outside of the major blocs, thus producing what Kaplan has called (with reference to bipolarity) a "tight" rather than a "loose" system.[29] While such a procedure might be violent, it need not cause "total" war, since the continued existence of any bloc would not be at stake. The implications of this corollary suggest the possible "realism" of a multi-bloc model, since it describes one possible means of absorbing the

---

[25]The possibility of the opening of space to conquest, while not absurd, is ignored for these purposes (if only because its consequences seem hard to predict, although the parallel with the exploration and control of the non-European world after the Sixteenth Century obviously suggests itself).

[26]This restriction will, as has been suggested, be removed in Section V.

[27]Kaplan, *System and Process*, p. 23.

---

[28]It may not be irrelevant in this respect that the Soviet Union rejected suggestions, after World War II, that its Eastern European satellites join the U.S.S.R. as integral member-republics. If the maintenance of the form of nation-states, even with reference to minor ones, was compatible with Soviet ideology and political domination, self-restraint with major rivals might also be expected.

[29]*Ibid.*, p. 43.

many nation-states of Asia and Africa into the structure of the international system.[30] Since Kaplan's other models do not provide a completely satisfactory framework for integrating the "uncommitted nations,"[31] this may be claimed as an "advantage" for the multi-bloc model.

Rule 4. "Act to oppose any coalition or single actor which tends to assume a position of predominance with respect to the rest of the system."[32] If the assumptions made to this point are accepted, it is unlikely that the substitution of bloc actors for nation-states would change the operation of this rule. The most ready objection would be, of course, the ideology of the Soviet bloc and the danger that should other Communist blocs emerge (*e.g.*, a Chinese-centered region in Asia), they would combine in a drive for hegemony due to their common ideology. Such ideological solidarity was not, historically speaking, absent from the "balance of power" system.[33] As is shown by the policies of France in the Thirty Years' War, beliefs need not prevent "unholy" alliances for the purpose of checking a hegemonic power.[34] Indeed, if one contrasts the "containment" policy under which one state (the United States) has an ultimate commitment to preserve the *status quo* everywhere in the world, a system with a multiplic-

ity of regional units might well be *more* capable of checking threats to predominance than a bipolar system, whose rigidities make even a slight change of position a dangerous sign of "predominance."[35]

Rule 5. "Act to constrain actors who subscribe to supra-national [here supra-regional] organizing principles."[36] It is conceivable that a multi-bloc system could exist without an "international actor" such as the UN, and it is even likely that the regional institutions would be as jealous of their "sovereignty" as are nation-states today. Indeed, Lippmann argued that this is one of the great advantages of regional organizations, since they preclude the conversion of "local" issues into global conflicts.[37] Because the weakening of national loyalties might well imply the substitution of regional allegiances—and not the automatic emergence of "universalism"—world government would be likely to serve the hegemonic interests of one bloc even if it emerged out of the multi-bloc system. Unless statesmen suddenly decide to accept the preponderance of a single power or bloc, therefore "supra-regional" sovereignty over the internal affairs of blocs would probably be opposed.[38]

---

[30]*Cf.* Robert C. Good, "The U.S. and the Colonial Debate," in Wolfers, *Alliance Policy*, esp. pp. 269–70.

[31]In Kaplan's models, these nonaligned states might be: (*a*) "neutral" balances within an international actor ("loose bipolar system"), (*b*) powerlessly integrated into two opposed blocs ("tight bipolar"), (*c*) relatively equal members of a world government ("universal system") or largely dissolved into a world government ("hierarchical system"), or, finally, (*d*) all either provided with an invulnerable nuclear capability or destroyed ("unit veto system"). The first of these roughly corresponds with the present situation, and does not indicate how the rising power of these areas will affect the "balancing" procedure; the second and third are relatively unlikely. The last ("unit veto") would be not only highly unstable, but, in any prudent sense, "undesirable".

[32]Kaplan, *System and Process*, p. 23.

[33]The religious wars of the Sixteenth and Seventeenth Centuries are a frequently cited illustration of this; the "liberal"–"monarchist" split after the Congress of Vienna is a more recent example.

[34]An even more extreme proof may be found in the tacit opposition of the Papacy to Hapsburg expansion (most especially when directed toward Italy) and the somewhat less than messianic zeal of the Pope's opposition to the Protestant princes on some occasions.

[35]Herz, *International Relations*, pp. 153–56. *Cf.* Walter Lippmann's definition of a "solvent" foreign policy, *U.S. Foreign Policy* (Boston, 1943), pp. 9–10.

[36]Kaplan, *System and Process*, p. 23.

[37]*U.S. War Aims*, pp. 189–90.

[38]It would seem that this is the weakest point in Herz' analysis, for he appears to leap from the era of allegiance to nation-states (now "obsolete" because of nuclear weapons) to "universalism" (*International Relations*, ch. 12). In point of fact, men's loyalties have been shifted from narrow to broader communities, but rarely has the scope of the community involved such a revolutionary change. To commit himself to world government, the average American citizen would be forced to "identify" himself with Laos, South Africa, and Yemen as well as South Carolina. Herz is forced to argue that the threat of nuclear annihilation must induce this change, but popular apathy would seem to belie the actuality of this process. Of course, a nuclear war or an attack from Mars might do the trick. . . . In the meantime, worldwide organization, if it assumes direct powers over *all* regions and states, is likely to do so under the "guidance" of a hegemonic power center. *Cf.*: "A world organization may be a necessary convenience as well as a valuable symbol. But the intermediate unit is more likely to be the operative factor in the transition from nationalism to internationalism." Carr, *Nationalism and After*, pp. 46–47.

Although according to Kaplan's propositions the multi-bloc system would not include a "universal actor," an international organization like the UN will be included in the model for the sake of "realism." As a symbol of the interdependence of regional blocs, the UN or a parallel agency would primarily serve mediating functions—*i.e.*, providing a locus for diplomatic contacts and implement agreed solutions under an "impartial" aegis.[39] In other words, the international organization would be likely to continue its current functions, rather than to develop punitive sanctions as a "pure" collective security system. Within a framework of a system of a limited number of blocs—especially if their power is relatively equal—it is possible that something like the Concert of Europe mechanisms might develop in the context of the UN, as indeed was apparently intended in the Security Council. Trends in this direction might lead to an approximation of what George Liska has defined as a "multiple equilibrium," in which regional and universal organizations complement one another.[40]

Should an international organization play at least the minimum role of providing "diplomatic sanction" (or acting as the "policeman" for agreements between powers), its effectiveness as a "balancer" would be somewhat different from its role today. In a loose bipolar system with relatively equal power constellations, the "balancing" function is extraordinarily delicate and cannot replace a rough parity between blocs.[41] It is at least arguable, in contrast, that in a multi-bloc system the UN would have a more independent function as

a mediator or formulator of the predominant views. In the classical "balance of power" system, it was necessary for one state to act as the "balancer." Usually England, the so-called "swing" power, played this role, so that when the English followed isolationist policies, the flexibility of the entire system was threatened. An organization (and especially a civil service) identified with the international "community" would be forced to perform its "balancing" functions or lose its *raison d'être*; since experience shows the tendency of organizations to maintain themselves, the UN might stabilize the multi-bloc system by insuring that changes in power constellations were met with an effective "balancing" response.

Rule 6. "Permit defeated or constrained national actors to reenter the system as acceptable role partners or act to bring some previously unessential actor within the essential actor classification.[42] Treat all essential actors as acceptable role partners."[43] The condition in the last sentence is perhaps the most essential factor when comparing current regional agreements with the blocs in the model being proposed. In order to ensure the "perfect" or "pure" model, the requirement of absolute flexibility of alignment implies that no state can participate in more than a single bloc. Such regional integrity and separateness is radically different from the present structure of overlapping bloc ties or networks of alliances.[44] This aspect of the model can be clarified by the contemporary example of the United States as a member of both NATO and the OAS. Regardless of the future integration of either of these two regions, it would be difficult for them to be aligned against one another; the overlapping membership

---

[39]This is not the place to enter into an extensive discussion of the current role of the UN or its possibilities. See Inis L. Claude, Jr., *Swords Into Plowshares* (New York, 1959) for a balanced judgment. *Cf.* Ernst B. Haas, "Regional Integration and National Policy," *International Conciliation*, No. 513 (May, 1957), esp. pp. 438–42.

[40]See his *International Equilibrium* (Cambridge: Harvard University Press, 1957), esp. chs. 5, 6, 7. Because of the general unwillingness of statesmen to surrender power to an external organization beyond their control, it has seemed wiser to take Kaplan's "balance of power" model rather than Liska's "multiple equilibrium" as a theoretical starting point. Nonetheless the effects of the possession of nuclear weapons by a small number of actors may well create a congruence of the two seemingly diverse schemes. See below, Section IV.

[41]*Cf.* Haas, "Regionalism, Functionalism, and Universal International Organization."

[42]This part of the rule is implied in Rule 3. However, since the changes in the identity of actors are not instantaneous, this rule also implies that the number of members of the system may change. This part of the rule will not be analyzed in any detail, save for passing references to the influence of numbers in Section III.

[43]Kaplan, *System and Process*, p. 23.

[44]*Cf.* Haas, "Regional Integration and National Policy," pp. 381–83, 433–37; William Lee Miller, "The American Methods and the Alliance System," in *Alliance Policy*, pp. 33–34; and William Welch, "Soviet Commitments to Collective Action," *ibid.*, pp. 280–81. This remark ignores, obviously, the varying integration in different blocs; moreover, current regional agreements are integrated at a low level, whereas the "pure" model assumes uniformly and highly integrated units.

of the United States introduces a "rigidity" which is perhaps comparable to the dynastic rigidities of classical diplomacy.[45] As the example shows, such a rigidity would not make a "balancing" system impossible, especially since dynastically allied states often diverged when "reason of state" seemed to override family ties. Nonetheless, overlapping membership in more than one bloc would seriously reduce the flexibility of alignments, and in so doing would make the operation of all the other rules more difficult. In particular, the rigidity of alliances would make more likely the expansion of any conflict into a total war with total aims.[46]

To specify completely the effects of overlapping membership, however, it is necessary to go somewhat further. The extent of rigidity introduced by the simultaneous membership of one state in two blocs is determined by the relative power of the central decision-making units of the two blocs with respect to the power of the state with overlapping membership. For example, if both NATO and OAS had an institutional body with the authority and power to override the United States (as one federated member-state among equals), clearly the rigidity would be of limited importance in a crucial case. But where both regions are absolutely dependent upon the power of a common member, the model as defined above could not operate. As an aside, it might be noted that the opposition of many "new nations" to regionalism has been based precisely on the fear that such overlapping membership would enable the ex-colonial powers to dictate to

regions of which they are not geographically contiguous members.[47] Yet conceivably the relations between the former colonies and their erstwhile mother countries may be sublimated into a tacit preference for alliances between the "new" blocs and the bloc containing the European powers. Such an alignment would imply a rigidity, but one less stringent than the rigidity caused by overlapping membership.[48]

The foregoing discussion indicates some of the difficulties involved in "realizing" a model of the present type. The value of such models lies, however, not in their immediate descriptive virtues, but in their ability to indicate an underlying structure and thereby to suggest alternative modes of organizing the international system. As with Weber's "pure types" of authority, such a method is dangerous, for it is always tempting to take the abstraction as a "norm" which should be a guide for policy and a standard of judgment. And while such a norm may not be undesirable, it should be a conscious choice.

In what has been said to this point, a multi-bloc system following Kaplan's rules for a "balance of power" model has been proposed, with the addition of a "universal actor" as a presumably unavoidable part of the structure. To do so, it has been necessary to make three assumptions: first, that Kaplan's rules all apply; second, that nuclear weapons are irrelevant; and third, that each bloc is a perfectly integrated whole, acting as a unit. The following sections will remove these assumptions one at a time.

III. THE STABILITY OF THE SYSTEM

To this point, the multi-bloc model has been described with reference to Kaplan's six rules for the "balance of power" system. It is important to ascertain whether the stability of the multi-bloc model would be undermined should these rules

---

[45]"Rigidity" here does not mean that two blocs with a common member state could not conceivably be aligned against each other, but only that the presence of the common member makes them less likely to choose allies according to the needs of the moment. E.g., the dynastic union of the states of Austria and Spain under the Hapsburg family (and later of France and Spain under the Bourbons) limited the ability of the "branches of the family" to oppose one another. It might be added that if a single nation-state is a member of two blocs, these two blocs might be encouraged to oppose one another should each bloc seek sole control over the common member; in this case the "rigidity" introduced by overlapping membership is an increase in the probability of opposition, rather than an increase in the probability of alliance.

[46]E.g., it is often argued that the rigidity of the Austro-German alliance brought about World War I as a "total" rather than a "limited" war, because it forced conflict with any European state to become conflict with all. Cf. Kaplan, *System and Process*, p. 29.

[47]Hence an Indian author has opposed a regional organization in the Indian Ocean having "punitive" collective security powers, largely on the ground that English participation in the bloc would enable Great Britain to maintain a kind of quasi-colonial control. K. M. Pannikar, "Regionalism and World Security," in Pannikar *et al., Regionalism and Security* (New Delhi: Indian Council of World Affairs, 1948), pp. 3–6.

[48]This type of rigidity might be comparable to the English preference for the Austrian alliance prior to the "Diplomatic Revolution" of 1756.

not apply completely. "Stability" here means only that a system, in reacting to internal and external changes, remains within certain arbitrary bounds which define the system; rigid maintenance of the *status quo* is not implied. In other words, a stable system is capable of adapting itself to altered conditions so that it can survive.[49] The limits within which a system can "find" an "appropriate" response to its surroundings are of course variable, and the unique element in the "balance of power" system was its extraordinary flexibility, and hence the wide range of arrangements which were possible within it. One can therefore distinguish highly flexible or adaptive systems from more rigid ones.[50] Moreover, it should be noted that the flexibility of a system does not, *a priori*, determine its stability as measured by the capacity to persist through time; stability is a function of both the flexibility of response and the type of stimulus, and a system with a great multitude of possible reactions, if it can be upset by a minor change, may be unstable.

Kaplan has argued that the inconsistency between his rules 1 and 2 is a necessary element of the model, since without the contradiction between the desire to negotiate and the desire to fight there would be less flexibility.[51] While it is true that a highly flexible system is able to adapt itself to quite varied circumstances, however, there are limits to the rapidity with which any social system can change. Hence Kaplan's "pure" model of infinitely changeable alliances within a system of five or more powers is, like the economic theory of perfect competition, rarely achieved in its complete form.[52]

---

[49] Kaplan, *System and Process*, p. 6.

[50] In the terminology of system-theory, a highly flexible system is "ultra-stable" since, in responding to stimuli, it can "search" for the *level* or general type of response. In contrast, a system which can only adapt to its environment on a given level or "field" of behavior is technically called "stable." See W. Ross Ashby, *Design for a Brain* (New York, 1952), p. 99; Kaplan, *System and Process*, pp. 6–8. An ultra-stable system can be illustrated by a system of five powers in which a large number of alliances is possible; within any set of alliances, the system would be capable of adapting to changes and maintaining itself. In contrast, a bipolar system may be "stable" (since it can maintain itself in the face of internal and external changes), but no different arrangement of power is possible without altering the very structure of the system.

[51] *Ibid.*, p. 52.

[52] Kaplan recognized that the "balance of power" model could be stable only if the rate of change of

Apart from this consideration of "realism," should rules 1 and 2 not be followed because an actor did not desire to increase his capabilities or fight, although the system would be less adaptable in its response to disturbances, such disturbances themselves might be less likely. On the other hand, actors violating rule 1 because they refuse to negotiate would radically increase the instability of the system, in the sense of the likelihood of violent change through war. Generally speaking, however, these two rules are the most "natural" ones since they conform to the calculating self-interest of competitors. Therefore, although it is possible that the traditional pattern of diplomacy would be transformed in a multi-bloc system into a kind of declaratory propaganda exchange, the competitive elements of the "balance of power" system are not likely to be absent—and if absent, the model might well be further stabilized.

The one exception to this, the bloc with hegemonic ambitions, violates even more clearly rules 3 and 4. Certainly ideological ties between blocs would be possible (if not likely), and these would gravely weaken the operation of rule 4. However, as long as those blocs having a preponderance of power opposed any bloc with hegemonic tendencies, the stability of the system would not be destroyed. Still leaving nuclear weapons aside, this would depend on the number of blocs in the model. Kaplan's definition holds for a system with five or more actors, but historically there have been international systems or sub-systems with four or three actors as well. Clearly, in the five-bloc instance, violation of rules 3 and 4 by more than two blocs would tend to destroy the system; similarly a hegemonic pair in the three-bloc system could be expected to reduce the number of independent actors and alter the system. But whereas systems with an odd number of members require a majority of "rule-abiding" blocs, an even number of blocs may be stable (although rigid) when there is a standoff. This is so in the current bipolar antagonism of East vs. West, and might hold for a two-to-two division of four blocs (*e.g.*, Western Europe and the Western Hemisphere vs. Communist Chinese-dominated Asia and the USSR). Thus it appears that the more numerous the blocs, the more

---

alliances is within limits (*ibid.*, p. 35), but his rules themselves contain no provision for this "realistic" limitation.

stable the system will be, since the number of "aggressive" actors required to destroy the system increases.

This holds under the condition that all blocs are relatively equal, and with the proviso that systems with odd numbers of actors will be relatively flexible whereas those with an even number of member-blocs will tend toward rigidity.

In Kaplan's "pure" model, a high degree of flexibility is required not only by the provision for five or more actors, but by rules 4 and 6, which demand opposition to *any* threatening state and willingness to ally with *any* state. While violation of these rules would doubtless reduce the range of possible responses, however, it is not clear how far the resulting rigidity would necessarily lead to violent instability. It has often been pointed out that rigidity of alliance policy often contributed to war in the classical state system, but overly rapid adjustments, too delicately attuned to some presumed "balance," were more important as the source of conflict.[53] Rigidity of alliances *will* cause the system to be unstable if a bloc is forced to go to war against its own self-interest merely to protect a disintegrating ally, as is likely to occur when the two allied blocs are both isolated and unable to find other possible alliance partners. But this type of rigidity, which may be said to have destroyed the Nineteenth Century European system by "causing" World War I, is an extreme case—and its importance may be reduced by the impact of nuclear weapons, since these make the danger of such a war more immediately apparent to the stronger of the two isolated actors. In contrast, the highly "flexible" system derives its stability not from its ability to avoid conflict, but due to a configuration of power which tends to limit the violence and objectives of any war. Nevertheless, when the classical state system was "flexible," peace and even the stability of the system were far from assured; on the contrary, the attempt to "balance" every change in every rival's power position often led to extended wars which were limited only by the resources available to monarchs, and not by a voluntary restriction of the scope of violence. The current tendency to "idealize" the classic "balance of power" era, while understandable as a reaction against the utopian desire to banish power from

international politics, should not be accepted uncritically as a theoretical proposition. Hence it is not at all clear that the "pure" multi-bloc model, which would be highly flexible according to Kaplan's rules, would necessarily be the most stable system with a plurality of blocs.

At this point it is desirable to introduce theoretical properties developed in economics with reference to systems of a small number of interdependent, rival actors. In oligopolistic markets (*i.e.*, those with few firms), each decision-maker is aware of the effects of his policies on the actions of each of his competitors and *vice versa*. Economic theorists have called this situation "mutual interdependence recognized."[54] That is, each firm is aware that an apparently advantageous action will lead to a response by the others nullifying the original act. The clearest example is price-cutting; firm A may be tempted to cut its price in order to increase sales, but if it does so, firms B, C, etc. are likely to "retaliate," and may even reduce their prices below A's. What ensues is significantly called a "price *war*." Prices charged by all firms fall, so that no one firm gains the additional sales anticipated when it was first decided to undersell the rivals. The only result is that *all* firms suffer, especially if each continues to sell roughly the same quantity of merchandise, but at far lower prices than before.[55]

Under these circumstances, price wars are in fact relatively rare, as the repeated prosecution of oligopolistic industries for violating the Sherman Anti-Trust Act shows. Rather, a tendency develops toward what has been called "quasi-agreement" or "tacit collusion." Each actor, aware that any change on his part will bring about immediate responses by others, refrains from making overt price cuts unless he is quite certain that the others will "follow" him exactly. Thus prices of all firms tend to be the same (or nearly so), with prices changing at the same time and by the same amount. In connection with this pattern, one firm has often become traditionally accepted as the "leader" responsible for initiating all changes. In

---

[53]*Cf.* Kaplan's image of the precarious nature of the "balancing" process, *ibid.*, p. 32.

[54]See especially William Fellner, *Competition Among the Few* (New York, 1949), pp. 15–16, 24–50, 120–136 and *passim*.

[55]Elasticity of demand can be ignored, at least for those "price wars" in which the selling price is reduced below total average cost. Since such severe price wars are not incomparable with large scale modern warfare in their effects, the parallel seems justified.

this way no one firm can maximize its profits, but all firms are able to practice what Fellner has called "limited joint profit maximization."

The relevance of this type of behavior to international relations is obvious. The interdependence of actors in the international system has normally been recognized, since any change can normally be attributed to a single actor and normally affects others. And while states have not, in the past, been reluctant to enter into the international analogue to "price wars," this has largely been due to the considerable opportunities for gain present in the emerging European state system, which were not overshadowed by the consequences of losing a war. By the Nineteenth Century, this situation began to change radically (save with respect to non-European territories, which continued to be the object of conflicts), and the emergence of the Concert of Europe after 1815 could even be attributed to a recognition of this fact. Indeed, the European state system after the Congress of Vienna provides a striking example of an international "quasi-agreement," since competition between states (or alliances of states) for direct or indirect control over territories on the margins of Europe was tacitly limited. Nevertheless, as long as power was relative and hence alliance a prime means of increasing one's capabilities, the behavior of states only partially approximated that of oligopolistic firms. With the appearance of nuclear weapons which equalize all actors and which render violent competition (*i.e.*, "war") mutually disadvantageous—the possibility of "quasi-agreement" becomes of great importance. Hence it is advisable to remove the assumption that only conventional military means are available to members of a multi-bloc system.

IV. NUCLEAR WEAPONS

Under contemporary technological conditions, Arthur Lee Burns has distinguished three types of nuclear capability: "The independent, the triggering, and the minimum atomic variety."[56] An independent or complete deterrent requires that a nuclear power be able to retaliate effectively after suffering a surprise ("first strike") attack. At present such a deterrent seems to require submarine launched, mobile, or hard-site ICBMs, which provide an invulnerable "second strike" capability

large enough to make the costs of a nuclear exchange prohibitive to all rivals. In contrast, the possessor of a "triggering" deterrent, while not having an invulnerable second-strike capacity, is assured that a nuclear exchange with any rival actor having an independent capability would render that rival vulnerable to a third (or *n*th) independent nuclear power.[57] That is, even though a delivery system (*e.g.*, long-range manned bombers) is vulnerable to surprise attack, it may deter more powerful rivals with invulnerable striking forces, provided that the invulnerability and number of weapons comprising the rival's independent deterrent are not unlimited. If, however, two or more independent nuclear powers have virtually infinite quantities of weapons, the triggering effect would not ensue; all powers lacking an independent deterrent would then be reduced, *vis-à-vis* the greatest powers, to the third or lowest class of nuclear capabilities.

This lowest or "minimum atomic" category is capable of anything less than unambiguously deterring all rivals from engaging in a total nuclear exchange. By means of its ability to destroy several cities, such an actor (even without allies) might nonetheless still deter an attack from a neighbor having an independent deterrent.[58] Moreover, the possession of a few isolated atomic

---

[56] "Power Politics and the Growing Nuclear Club," *Policy Memorandum Number 20* (Princeton University, Center of International Studies, 1959), p. 18 and *passim*. The following analysis will assume the unlikelihood of technological changes which make an invulnerable second-strike capability impossible; such an innovation would probably lead to hegemony for its possessor, total war, or both.

[57] Burns distinguishes between "passive triggering" (in which the expenditure of missiles by an attacking independent power would remove the invulnerability of the attacker's second-strike capability *vis-à-vis* a third, independent nuclear power) and "active triggering" (in which the triggering power, by using its weapons in a first strike on an independent nuclear power, renders the victim vulnerable to a succeeding first strike by another nuclear power). *Ibid.*, pp. 12–13. It should be noted that while the two types of triggering are different, especially under the technological assumptions which Burns makes, they could well reinforce one another.

[58] This would follow when the more powerful nuclear actor wished to avoid both the initiation of nuclear attack (necessary to neutralize the small, vulnerable stockpile of its neighbor) and the loss of one or two cities (which would result from any non-nuclear attack). See the example of Sweden deterring Russia, *ibid.*, p. 17, and George W. Rathjens, Jr., "NATO Strategy:

weapons falling short of even this capability might deter conventional attacks from non-nuclear or similarly armed powers. Considerable variation in the nuclear weapons systems within this "weakest" class might well be crucial when such actors are rivals among themselves, granted that each "minimum" deterrent power would be vulnerable to attack by all actors with an independent deterrent. Let us now apply these categories of military potential to the multi-bloc model as it has been developed to this point.

To begin, it will be assumed that all blocs have symmetrical military establishments, including both an independent deterrent and the means (as well as the strategy) for conventional or limited warfare. This approximates a rather "pure" instance of the "nth country problem" where n is equal to about five.[59] Burns, who analyzed the calculus of deterrence for systems with two, three, and four actors, concluded that the "strain" of five or more nuclear powers on the balance of terror is increased, and that triggering effects would be "quite unreliable as deterrents."[60] His conclusion is to the point: "These very uncertainties, however, *might* constrain all parties to be conservative, eschew blackmail, and subscribe to international projects for reducing the possibility of surprise attack."[61]

In order to be stable, such a reaction to uncertainty would have to take the form of either express treaties or "quasi-agreements." This possibility suggests that the strategies of nuclear powers may not be based solely upon a rational calculation of deterrence. In other words, one must distinguish between an analysis of deterrence (which depends on calculating the likely action of each individual actor in response to specified acts of each rival) and an analysis of systems of small numbers of competitors, studied as a system. One is therefore tempted to turn to the characteristics developed by oligopoly theory in economics in order to determine the likelihood of

the emergence of a tacit (or overt) agreement to limit the use, or at least the initial use, of nuclear weapons.[62]

The danger of nuclear annihilation has often been traced to the disproportion between the possible goals of policy and the destructive power of nuclear weapons. Yet this danger is similar to that of a price war for an oligopolistic firm. To be sure, bankruptcy is not the immediate result of a price cut, whereas nuclear annihilation is commonly believed to be the likely result of "push-button" missile warfare;[63] but the ultimate effects are roughly the same.[64] Once the decision-makers of blocs are aware of the implications of nuclear warfare, a tacit agreement not to initiate an all-out nuclear strike would have a rather high probability of effectiveness, especially if violations are unambiguous. This possibility is attested to by the length of the recent "tacit agreement" prohibiting nuclear testing, and the fact that when it was terminated some advance notice was publicly given—abroad at least, where it was indispensable, if not at home in the USSR. Although the awareness of mutual interdependence, necessary for such an agreement, would probably be weakest in the early years of each actor's possession of a nuclear capability,[65] it is possible that "experimenting" with the results of a nuclear exchange need not require the explosion of bombs.[66]

The main problem facing an "anti-nuclear quasi-agreement" is the requirement that violations be ambiguous. In a system with few actors, unlike a large-numbers system such as the "unit-veto" model, it is less likely that an actor could use nuclear weapons anonymously. Radar missile

Total War," in Klaus Knorr, ed., *NATO and American Security* (Princeton: Princeton University Press, 1959), ch. 4, pp. 88–89.

[59]Note that although the "unit veto" model assumes that each of a large number of countries has an independent deterrent, nuclear symmetry is far less likely to be realized on the level of nation-states, where economic and technical prerequisites are often limited by sheer size, than on the level of regional blocs.

[60]*Op. cit.*, p. 16.

[61]*Ibid.* (original italics).

[62]*Cf.* Fellner, *op. cit.*, pp. 120 ff.

[63]It is, however, uncertain that nuclear war would be as rapid as is generally assumed in the West. The Russians apparently plan for a more protracted battle. See Raymond L. Garthoff, *Soviet Strategy in the Nuclear Age* (New York, 1958), pp. 87–89.

[64]The experience of those who tried to compete with John D. Rockefeller's Standard Oil Company attests to this similarity. *Cf.* Ida Tarbell, *The History of the Standard Oil Company* (New York, 1904), II, *passim.*

[65]Compare the behavior of the United States, England, and the USSR on attaining a nuclear capability with their strategic attitudes (as well as that of France) at the present time.

[66]It is, however, true that the emergence of a "tacit agreement" requires the kind of "learning" and "testing" which is associated with the "stochastic" model in game theory. See Kaplan, *System and Process*, pp. 225 ff, 247.

tracking is presumably sufficiently sophisticated to distinguish the *continent* from which missiles are launched. Although missiles launched from submarines (or space platforms) might enable an unidentified power to launch a nuclear strike, each region in a system of five or six blocs would probably be aware of those enemies who might initiate a nuclear attack. Moreover, the effect of this order of numbers could well reinforce the quasi-agreement in another sense. Although Herz has noted that, in a bi-polar world, a pledge not to begin a nuclear war has advantages,[67] a self-denying agreement would be more stable with more than two parties to the accord. This follows simply because, in a face-to-face encounter, relative power is easier to compute; the state (or bloc) losing a bi-polar conventional war or armaments race may unleash nuclear war rather than suffer ultimate defeat. By contrast, when there are about five rivals, it is more difficult to ascertain whether a further decline in power will be disastrous. Since alliance, neutrality, or protection by a stronger power remain alternatives, even defeat in war—provided it is limited—may be more acceptable than nuclear suicide.

Even if it were possible to establish a stable agreement preventing the initiation of all-out nuclear war, of course, it does not follow that all nuclear weapons would necessarily be "out-lawed." In the first place, it can be assumed that no actor would surrender his nuclear weapons, since it is impossible to conceive of a system of arms control which would insure that all rivals could not possibly cheat.[68] Secondly, there are two possible uses for nuclear weapons which need not be prevented

by the existence of an agreement not to initiate all-out, "strategic" strikes against the civilian population of rivals: "tactical" or limited nuclear war,[69] and "limited retaliation" by the selective use of "strategic" weapons.[70] In both these instances, the "catalytic" eruption of a general nuclear war would be a distinct possibility, and the greater the probability of that eruption, as judged by all actors, the more likely that any agreement against the initial use of nuclear weapons would be extended to include these less-than-total initiatives.

"Tactical" nuclear warfare and "limited retaliation" are not necessarily identical in this respect. Since the latter requires a willingness to "play the game," a selective attack by a few long-range missiles will elicit "massive retaliation" unless the distinction between all-out and limited strategic nuclear war is considered politically and militarily legitimate. At present, for example, popular abhorrence of the idea of nuclear devastation might well make this strategy politically impracticable, even should its military effects be deemed favorable.[71] As long as this remains the case, any quasi-agreement prohibiting the initial use of nuclear weapons would probably include limited nuclear retaliation. Because cleaner, low-yield warheads have been developed, on the other hand, it is somewhat more likely that "tactical" weapons could be used without violating a self-limiting nuclear agreement. Although this is still questionable, it would seem that the most effective check on the use of battlefield nuclear weapons would be (paradoxically) a dispersed deployment of combat troops in anticipation of tactical nuclear warfare.[72] Otherwise a bloc losing a conventional war would probably consider the gains from using such weapons to be greater than the risks of unleashing an all-out nuclear exchange.

Despite the doubts of some students concerning the feasibility of a distinction between limited nuclear attacks (be they "tactical" or "strategic") and total nuclear war, the initiation of the latter

---

[67]*International Politics*, pp. 285–86.

[68]Current discussions of disarmament, with their emphasis on controls, usually fail to recognize that the *possession* of nuclear weapons, as distinct from their manufacture, is now probably beyond any feasible system of international inspection. Agreements to disarm should be restricted to those armaments whose presence can be detected with a relatively high probability—*i.e.*, especially conventional forces. Extending agreements, especially in writing, beyond this point merely invites the least scrupulous power to violate the agreement, since a cheater has some grounds for believing his rivals will not cheat. It is one of the great advantages of quasi-agreements in general that the certainty of being the only cheater is denied the unscrupulous; hence when a quasi-agreement covers an action which can be detected by suspicious rivals (*e.g.*, weapons testing or all-out nuclear assault), violations are relatively unlikely, though by no means impossible.

[69]See Henry A. Kissinger, *Nuclear Weapons and Foreign Policy* (New York, 1957), ch. 6.

[70]See Morton A. Kaplan, "The Strategy of Limited Retaliation," *Policy Memorandum Number 19* (Princeton University, Center of International Studies, 1959).

[71]*Cf.* Kaplan's discussion of limited retaliation in the context of NATO policy: "Problems of Coalition and Deterrence," in Knorr, *NATO and American Security*, ch. 6, pp. 142–48.

[72]*Cf.* Kissinger, *Nuclear Weapons*, pp. 178–82.

(and possibly the former as well) might be prohibited by an overt or quasi-agreement in a multi-bloc system. Such an agreement might well serve, however, to make limited warfare, especially with conventional weapons, less dangerous and therefore more attractive. Indeed, when only political factors were under consideration, it was suggested that in a well-integrated multi-bloc system, limited aims would be likely to have priority for all actors. The presence of nuclear weapons held equally by all blocs would further increase the likelihood of limited conventional warfare by changing considerably the character of alliances.

In a world of roughly equal blocs, each with independent nuclear capabilities, every actor would presumably have approached a level of "absolute" power which renders alliances unattractive unless they serve to check a specific opponent; the commitment to defend an ally against *his* rivals entails dangers which are not likely to be overbalanced by the advantages of the alliance. It is far more to be expected that the "friendly" blocs would agree to oppose specific rivals in specific areas; rigid commitments for mutual protection (*e.g.*, "collective security" pacts) would be hardly credible and hence of little use. Because the small-numbers situation of a multi-bloc system would be conducive to ideological rivalry, often as a substitute for open warfare, subversion or revolution within rival blocs may well become a major aim of an aggressive actor. But inter-bloc alliances formed to counter an actor (or actors) with subversive or hegemonic ambitions could hardly be expected to preclude overt military conflict: since it is unlikely that any single bloc would be completely isolated, replacement of the currently fashionable "collective security" treaties by limited purpose alliances might *encourage* blocs to conduct restricted warfare. As long as allies could be expected to prevent annihilation of a bloc, a limited aggressor would have "insurance" against total defeat.

It is now necessary to remove the assumption of an equality of military capabilities, and with it, the implied equality of economic and technical potential. It is scarcely probable that any set of five or more regional actors would be as nearly identical as the foregoing analysis has assumed. Given that some actors in a multi-bloc system have large, invulnerable missile forces and that others have lesser capabilities, what would be the deterrent effect? The factor of the size of regional blocs would be crucial; invulnerability would be easier to achieve at any level of technology, but a tremendous nuclear strike would be required in order to achieve the objectives of a total strategic attack. Because the damage resulting even from an extensive strategic attack might no longer seem decisive to a unit of continental size, it might follow that complete nuclear independence would be rare if not impossible.

Again due to the sheer size of regional blocs, it would be necessary to expend a considerable number of missiles in a first or counter-force strike in order to be relatively certain of success against any rival except a victim having a handful of weapons in vulnerable and known locations. This means that "passive triggering" would be more likely than "active triggering," although neither would be possible against a bloc with a very large supply of invulnerable missiles. Because of these factors, it would seem most probable that regions with lesser nuclear forces would be in the position of states having a "minimum atomic capability" which could, under certain conditions, act as a "passive trigger." These considerations suggest that in a multi-bloc system, actors with nuclear capabilities would most probably be divided into the powerful (*i.e.*, those with large supplies of long-range, invulnerable missiles) and the weak (*i.e.*, those whose delivery systems were limited in numbers, accuracy, or invulnerability). More accurate predictions seem impossible because of the uncertainties arising from the size of the units.

It appears, therefore, that it is virtually impossible to specify in detail the deterrent abilities of blocs possessing different types of nuclear weapons. Fortunately, however, it may not be necessary to go into great detail. While the calculus of deterrence is crucially dependent on the forces-in-being of each actor, the analysis of a system in which "mutual interdependence" is recognized does not. In oligopolistic markets, the analogy to unequal nuclear potential is the phenomenon of "price leadership" arising out of size or cost differentials. In a market with limited numbers, one or two of the largest firms may become accepted, by tacit convention, as the only actors who may legitimately initiate changes of price; smaller actors may compete freely in matters of product quality or (to some extent) conditions of sale, but they are normally aware that they operate under the "umbrella" of those larger firms who set the prevailing price level of the industry. A multi-bloc model might well operate in a similar way. The blocs with the largest nuclear arsenals, provided that more than one of this class exists, would have the most to lose by the initiation of all-out nuclear warfare; barring an alliance between the powerful blocs to oppress the weaker ones, each "great power" would have to be the prime target of similarly armed rivals in the event of extensive nuclear exchanges. Hence, as long as at least two "giants" can maintain a rough parity in the qualitative arms race, they might expect to be followed by lesser nuclear powers in establishing an overt or tacit agreement limiting the initiation of nuclear war.[73] Such an agreement might be stable simply because the calculations of deterrence by each actor would be so uncertain that it would be impossible to initiate the use of nuclear weapons without an intolerably high probability that such weapons would be used in return by one or another actor.

Assuming that the agreement would have roughly the same characteristics as outlined under the assumption of nuclear parity, the only additional qualification might arise out of alliances. A treaty which preempted the friendship of most or all major nuclear powers might, by reducing the likelihood of nuclear attack, also reduce the uncertainty of the deterrent calculus to the point at which a nuclear strike might seem profitable. But alliances are only likely to give such assurance to the partners when there is considerable asymmetry between the nuclear potentials of the participating blocs; otherwise the weaker of the allies would gain little, and the stronger might lose a great deal, from a pact which was believed to restrict the freedom of action of the partners. Even with large power differentials, if the more powerful ally possesses an invulnerable deterrent he gains relatively little advantage from the alliance, since the commitment to a weaker ally always carries the risk of involvement with other great nuclear powers. Indeed, this consideration might induce rival great powers to make tacit or explicit agreements creating non-nuclear zones in the area of a weaker bloc, in return for which the weaker

bloc might forego or limit its own development of nuclear weapons.

It is more likely, however, that a "nuclear giant" would make a kind of sharing alliance with a more "backward" bloc; in return for an alliance excluding the influence of rivals, the more powerful bloc would undertake to provide its weaker ally with whatever nuclear weapons the latter would need for self-defense.[74] Such "nuclear sharing" would be necessary in order to convince the weaker ally of the will of the stronger to defend it in case of attack (or rather, to replace the incredibility of such an intention). Only if there existed a generally trusted and enforced agreement prohibiting the initiation of nuclear warfare might an "under-developed" bloc be willing to ally with a "protecting" nuclear power without receiving nuclear weapons of its own. As the current behavior of the uncommitted nations indicates, however, such alliances might still be unlikely unless stimulated by a direct and clear threat of hegemony by one power, which would then either attract or repel the weaker blocs. As long as those blocs with large, invulnerable nuclear capabilities are relatively equal, it is to be expected that weaker blocs would attempt to play the more powerful rivals off against each other, using the rivalry as a source of economic and military (and most especially nuclear) aid. And even if the more advanced nuclear powers should attempt to prevent the diffusion of nuclear weapons and delivery systems, the very process of economic development may sooner or later provide the opportunities for the autonomous development of at least "minimal" nuclear capabilities.

This suggests that rival "nuclear giants" might well prefer some form of "controlled diffusion," in which adherence to an explicit agreement not to initiate the use of these weapons was the condition for their delivery. While such a condition would require the preexistence of a more general overt or quasi-agreement to the same effect (without which conditional diffusion could hardly be effective), within such a general agreement different "giants" might well be understood to be entitled to supply different "underdeveloped" blocs, after the manner of territorial divisions of oligopolistic markets. In this way the emergence

---

[73]In contrast, "leadership" should not be expected to prevent other blocs or powers acquiring nuclear weapons, because on this issue each actor may feel that without nuclear weapons he is not really a participant in the system. See Burns, "Power Politics," pp. 6–9.

[74]This type of "controlled diffusion" is discussed by Arthur Lee Burns, "NATO and Nuclear Sharing," in Knorr, *NATO and American Security*, ch. 7.

of dangerous nuclear powers might be avoided by insuring that no power has an atomic capability which is too *weak*. The bloc receiving nuclear weapons need not be tempted to use them, provided that its nuclear capability is so great that its decision-makers must be conscious of their participation in a "mutually interdependent" system, in which self-restraint is necessary. Although this reasoning emphasizes the tenous stability of any international system with a plurality of nuclear powers, it also indicates the great difference between a large-numbers system and a small-numbers system. And it is largely on the grounds of this distinction that a multi-bloc model might approximate the only international system in which the diffusion of nuclear weapons does not have catastrophic results.

V. INTEGRATION OF BLOCS

Although it has been assumed up to this point that each bloc acts as a common unit, extensive theoretical problems are raised by the notion of "integration." Of the many variables which would determine the integration of regional political communities, and thereby provide the foundation for the political behavior of the multi-bloc system, only one—the structural organization of the bloc—can be analyzed here. Other crucial factors, especially the goals of regional communities and their size or "scope of control," could not be ignored in an exhaustive treatment. Typologies of the structures possible in an integrated supranational political community have been proposed, but they provide little general assistance.[75] It is likely that the best approach is to postulate a continuum, extending from the least to the most extensively organized structure.[76] At one end

of the spectrum would be a "null bloc" (*i.e.*, a group of nation-states with no alliance or other common policy relating them), at the other end a unitary "bloc-state" operating directly on individual subjects.[77] It should be added that the range set forth in Table 1 is a theoretical abstraction; it is not assumed that a structure at any point on the continuum can or will "grow" to the next stage. Relating this typology to Kaplan's terminology, the extent of "system dominance"[78] (*i.e.*, structural centralization) varies from none ("null bloc") to complete (unitary "bloc-state"); each type may be more or less "directive"[79] (*i.e.*, autocratic or politically centralized) according to the proportion of bloc decisions at all levels which are made by the group formally (or actually) responsible for "bloc-wide" decision-making.

Ex hypothesi, the more structurally centralized ("system dominant") as well as the more autocratic ("directive") the organizational structure of a bloc, the greater the potential energy with which the bloc could act. Obviously, however, the common institutions could direct their policies either "inward" to intra-bloc problems or "outward."[80] It may be suggested that priority is more likely to be given to inter-bloc problems if the bloc is either very autocratic ("highly directive") or structurally decentralized ("sub-system dominant"). The former type of bloc, because of its control over resources, can readily respond to external threats or opportunities, but is equally capable of turning to internal problems should they be more pressing. A structurally decentralized ("sub-system dominant") bloc—*i.e.*, an alliance between nation-states—is likely to hold

---

[75]*E.g.*, Kaplan has suggested a distinction between "hierarchical," "mixed-hierarchical," and "non-hierarchical" blocs (*System and Process*, pp. 74-83); Deutsch *et al.* have proposed a simpler dichotomy between "amalgamated" and "pluralistic" "security communities." (*Political Community*, pp. 6-7). In neither case, however, do the authors propose any general relationships between the types of integration and the kind of behavior which is likely.

[76]*Cf.* David Easton, "Political Anthropology," in Bernard J. Siegal, ed., *Biennial Review of Anthropology, 1959* (Stanford: Stanford University Press, 1959), pp. 239-41. It should be noted that the theoretical problems concerning the political structures of

so-called "primitive societies" are closely parallel to those concerning the international system. Incidentally, this parallel shows the weakness of Kaplan's definition of the "political system" (*System and Process*, pp. 12-14)—or rather, of his interpretation that the international system has a null political sub-system. Here Kaplan equates the political *system* with political *structures*, thereby risking an error made in some early studies of what have been called "stateless societies." *Cf.* the debate on this point in the literature of anthropology (largely cited in Easton's article, just noted).

[77]Easton's continuum, applied to primitive societies, is based on three interrelated variables: the differentiation among political roles (*i.e.*, their number), and the specialization of roles by kind or by level. These variables are implicit in Table 1.

[78]Kaplan's *System and Process*, p. 16.

[79]*Ibid.*, p. 18.

[80]*Cf. ibid.*, pp. 56-58.

Table 1
Types of Bloc Structures

Type	Characteristics
Null bloc	Unrelated states
Tacit alliance	No formal commitments, but awareness of common interest
Friendship alliance	Purely verbal commitment of good intentions[a]
Formal alliance commitment:	At least tacit material commitment:
One state dominant	Stronger committed to protect weaker[b]
Between equals	Tacit division of labor[c]
- -	- -
Decentralized functional bloc organizations:	Dependence on accord of "sovereign" members (*i.e.*, veto or "concurrent majority")
One state dominant	Stronger has disproportionate influence[d]
Between equals	General parity[e]
* *	* *
Centralized functional bloc organizations	Independent authority of specialized organization[f]
Federal bloc-state	All bloc-wide political decisions in competence of central structures, but action is through member states[g]
Unitary bloc-state	Bloc-wide institutions act directly on individuals[g]

[a]The classic form of international treaty in the Sixteenth through Nineteenth Centuries, implying no structure or organization whatsoever.

[b]E.g., American bilateral assistance treaties with S. Korea or Nationalist China.

[c]E.g., the Concert of Europe. Common institutions are "contingent," being created for particular problems, e.g., the conference system.

[d]In Kaplan's terms, the "mixed-hierarchical bloc" when highly "directed" by a key member state (e.g., the Warsaw Pact); the "non-hierarchical bloc" if "non-directive" (e.g., NATO). Cf. Kaplan, System and Process, p. 80. Note that NATO may tend toward the following type, especially where the key member state does not use its leadership.

[e]E.g., the Western European Union (WEU) and, often, NATO.

[f]E.g., the European Coal and Steel Community.

[g]Included in the "hierarchical" bloc in Kaplan's terminology (ibid., pp. 74–75); the structural difference is similar to that between the "hierarchical" and "universal" international systems, only on the bloc level.

- - -: Approximate point of the emergence of permanent, institutionalized structures.

* * *: Approximate point of the emergence of "amalgamated" communities (cf. Deutsch et al., Political Community, pp. 5–6).

together only in opposition to some external "enemy," and therefore generally lacks the capacity to deal effectively with internal problems.

Should these hypotheses be correct, a multi-bloc system would be most stable if all of its members were both structurally centralized ("system dominant"), at least to the extent of being "amalgamated," and "democratic" ("non-directive"). In this case, each bloc would be most likely to devote its energies to intra-bloc development, while at the same time being capable of taking effective action in response to external challenges. But since increased structural centralization creates opportunities for increasing power within a bloc, the development of authoritative common institutions is more determinant of behavior than "democracy" (or "autocracy") within the institutions.[81]

To be effective, a self-denying nuclear "quasi-agreement" would require that each bloc have at least an authoritative functional organization controlling the military establishment, independent of veto by any member-state in the bloc. Otherwise those bloc-members with access to nuclear weapons could use them independently in a crisis, and the system would risk degeneration

[81]E.g., note the foreign policy of the French revolutionaries of 1848, which did not differ from the policy of the July Monarchy in its effect, despite verbal differences. Taylor, Struggle for the Mastery of Europe, pp. 8–11, 15–16. This does not mean that "directive" blocs may not be more "aggressive" than "non-directive" ones, but it suggests that the difference lies in the goals motivating decision-makers (and not in structure per se). Cf. the Second Empire and the Second Republic on the one hand, and present day Spain with Imperialist England on the other.

into a "unit veto" relationship. Moreover, weaker or "sub-system dominant" structures (*i.e.*, alliances), since they permit—and encourage—overlapping memberships, would restrict the ability of a bloc to align itself with other blocs, in violation of Kaplan's rule 6. To the extent that nuclear capabilities reduce the need for inter-bloc alignments, this effect may not be too serious. But because few nations are powerful enough to make a considerable military and economic contribution to more than one regional grouping, a more important result of "interlocking" membership might be to reduce the capacity of those blocs which contain members with multiple allegiances.[82]

Finally, the more vulnerable and disorganized a bloc is internally, the greater the "opportunity" it presents to a rival bloc (or blocs) for attack. Just as the disintegration of once great Empires (Turkey and Austro-Hungary) underlay the two greatest European wars in the century after the Congress of Vienna,[83] similar violence would be the likely result of a decaying bloc. From these considerations, a significant structural integration of *all* blocs would seem necessary for the stability of the multi-bloc system. Any large differentials of integration will tend to invite more integrated blocs to attack (or subvert) less integrated ones, and such direct attacks would be the most likely cause of total or nuclear war. In particular, a bloc in which foreign policies were merely "concerted" would be, in all probability, insufficiently integrated to become a stable member of a multi-bloc system; experience with such "consultation" in the West has shown the overwhelmingly negative nature of agreements, which tend toward policies of *immobilisme*. Nonetheless the degree of structural integration need not approach that of a "super-state"—and indeed, such a development may be "undesirable" on other grounds. But the emergence of functional organizations with "veto-proof" control over all weapons—or at least nuclear ones—is neither completely utopian nor, *a priori*, undesirable *qua* policy.[84] Such

a development would presumably make possible a "tacit agreement" to refrain from initiating the use of nuclear weapons, and might well enforce a higher degree of policy coordination than now exists in most regional groupings. Perhaps with the growing threat of nuclear diffusion, such a development will appear as a welcome alternative to a "unit veto" relationship between a large number of "nuclearized" nation-states.

VI. CONCLUSION

It may be useful to summarize the characteristics of the multi-bloc model as it has been developed above. In the "pure" model, based solely on *political* considerations, five or more integrated regional blocs participate in a "balance of power" system not unlike the traditional historical system of European nation-states. This implies a considerable flexibility in alignments, a willingness to limit all warfare (especially in order not to destroy a major bloc), and a tendency to absorb all uncommitted states into one or another bloc. The complete flexibility of alliances is not, however, a necessary feature of the system as long as the rigidities preventing realignment are not so strong that a commitment to weak or disintegrating allies overrides a bloc's own interest in self-preservation. It is even possible for the multi-bloc system to operate with less than five actors, though the maintenance of the necessary adaptability is somewhat more difficult. The introduction of an invulnerable nuclear capability considerably alters the influence of numbers by

---

[82]*E.g.*, the United States would of course be capable of devoting more resources to its NATO commitments if it did not have commitments to SEATO, etc.

[83]The other major war of the century (the American civil war) might well have produced an international cataclysm but for the logistic and technological isolation of the American continent at the time and the relative strength of the contending parties.

[84]In fact, one can visualize the international political system as already having a structure similar to what has been described, in the context of African tribes, as a "segmentary state." Aiden W. Southall, *Alur Society* (Cambridge: W. Heffer and Sons, n.d. 1956?), esp. ch. 9. *Cf.* John Middleton and David Tait, eds., *Tribes Without Rulers* (London: Routledge and Kegan Paul, 1958), esp. Introduction; and M. G. Smith, "On Segmentary Lineage Systems," *Journal of the Royal Anthropological Institute*, Vol. 86 (July–December, 1956), pp. 39–80. In this respect, the emergence of bloc organs, functionally responsible for nuclear weapons, represents merely a further trend in contemporary developments—and a development which has already been suggested with respect to NATO. See Roger Hilsman, "On NATO Strategy," in *Alliance Policy*, ch. 6; Morton A. Kaplan, "Problems of Coalition and Deterrence," in Knorr, *NATO and American Security*, ch. 6, esp. pp. 139–42.

reducing the desirability of alliance as a means of achieving objectives. Unlike the "unit veto" model, in which a large number of actors have "absolute" military power, the multi-bloc system is likely to produce a "quasi-agreement" limiting the initiation of nuclear warfare. This depends, however, on the attainment of a minimal degree of functional integration within all blocs, so that common decision-makers control such weapons free from the veto of member-states.

In conclusion, it may be in order to relate the theoretical abstraction to substantive policy choices now facing this country. Much has been written about our alliances and especially NATO, but since there has been little analysis of the theoretical implications of regionalism, alternatives to the present bipolar network of alliances have rarely been offered. But if the multi-polar system appears to be potentially viable as a world order, it may be legitimate to orient policies toward that end. Of course, even if the model suggested above is considered as a realistic and desirable objective, it may be impossible for this country to influence trends in favor of its emergence. But granted the limits on America's ability to alter the structure of the international system single-handed, the choice of an objective in terms of a concept of "world order" (*i.e.*, as a structure of power rather than as a *state* of a structure, such as "peace" or "freedom") remains both prudent and desirable. It is prudent because our Communist rivals have such a goal and the willingness to exploit our indecision; it is desirable because *without* such a goal the United States loses whatever influence it *might* have among other nations.[85] Moreover, if power is the ability to influence, there is something absurdly contradictory in the tendency to assert the limits of America's capacity to alter future world developments (real though it be) while simultaneously accepting a "containment" policy which requires military "forces-in-being" which the United States seems to be unwilling (though capable) to provide.

If the multi-bloc system were adopted as a long-run (50 to 100 year) goal, the United States would face two supremely difficult choices: first, are we willing to surrender our "sovereignty" to a highly integrated "American" regional bloc;

and second, are we willing to withdraw our commitment from Europe and NATO, exchanging our troop withdrawal for the unification of Germany inside a European region? Such a European bloc would have to be in the possession of an independent nuclear capability, in order to avoid the trap of a "disengagement" in Europe which would open a power vacuum to Soviet exploitation. The advantage of this type of development is that our commitments could then be brought into a closer balance with our available forces. The disadvantage is that to reunify Germany in a European bloc (and, ideally, to attract the Soviet satellites into such a regional organization), the Soviets would have to be convinced that: (a) they had no chance to advance in Europe by other means, and that (b) the new region would be "neutral" in the East-West conflict. This in turn would be completely unacceptable to the West, unless the Sino-Soviet axis was split, so that the two Communist collossi could potentially be aligned against each other.[86] Since the conditions for mutual acceptability are unlikely, the most promising approach to the model suggested here may well be a Western European regional bloc and an American bloc, tied in a rather close alliance, as a counter-weight to the Sino-Soviet axis. Such a system of four major "actors" divided two-against-two might be described as "bi-axial,"[87] and could well be the prelude to a broader multi-bloc system as new regions attained world power status.[88] Of course, the model presented here may be weak in theory or utopian in policy, but it seems absolutely necessary that, at least in academic circles, the search be begun for long run alternatives to the dilemmas which our overextended commitment to mere containment threaten to cause in the next decades.

---

[85]*Cf.* the argument of Nitze, "Coalition Policy and the Concept of World Order."

[86]*Cf. ibid.*, p. 29.

[87]*Cf.* the general pattern of mid-Eighteenth Century diplomacy, in which the Anglo-Austrian alliance opposed France and Prussia prior to the "Diplomatic Revolution."

[88]Such a "bi-axial" system is rendered all the more likely (at least in the short run) by current weapons technology, in which the United States and the USSR seem likely to maintain a considerable superiority both in quantitative and qualitative terms. Nonetheless, the bi-axial alignment need not be taken as the only possible form of a multi-bloc system; the present model has been conceived in highly abstract, long run terms (*i.e.*, as a possibility for the next 100 years).

Discussion and Questions

1. The distinction Masters makes between blocs and alliances is a useful and sensible one. In footnote 5 he defines "bloc" as a "group of nation-states to the extent that they act as a unit in international relations." ➤ How does this definition of a "bloc" relate to the idea of an "alliance"? (See Henry A Kissinger, "Coalition Diplomacy in the Nuclear Age," *Foreign Affairs*, vol. XLII, no. 4 [July 1964], pp. 525–545; George Liska, *Nations in Alliance—The Limits of Interdependence* [Johns Hopkins Press, Baltimore, 1962].) ➤ Is an alliance bound together by more fluctuating interests than a bloc is? ➤ Are the members of an alliance freer to withdraw from the association than are members of a bloc?

2. ➤ Does "bloc" imply formal organization of any kind? Would a multibloc world system of the sort that Masters proposes have a different structure than the present international system? ➤ If formalized and given institutional expression, then would the resulting network of relationships constitute a move toward some species of world government? ➤ Has Masters provided us with any basis for answering these questions? It is important to note that we use the term "world order" differently than does Masters. "World order" to Masters means a stable system; "world order" to us means a system that is appraised in relation to the realization of our five world-order values or to some alternative set of values.

3. ➤ How likely is it that a multibloc world will emerge in the twentieth century? ➤ What factors would promote such a development in international society? In a later book Masters advocates a reorientation of American foreign policy designed to make a multibloc world more likely (Masters, *The Nation is Burdened: American Foreign Policy in a Changing World* [Knopf, New York, 1967]).

4. The whole notion of multipolarity has been given dramatic relevance by the views of the future held by President of the United States, Richard M. Nixon, and his foreign policy adviser, Henry Kissinger. The most formal statement of multipolarity as prediction and prescription was made by Mr. Nixon in an Address to Midwestern Newspaper Executives in Kansas City, Missouri, on July 6, 1971. In that speech he spoke of a "five-power world" (the U.S., the U.S.S.R., China, Japan, and Western Europe) in which ideological confrontation would be displaced by economic competition. Note that all the poles except Japan have nuclear weapons and that Western Europe is included as a participating unit, thereby breaking the statist monopoly over first-rank international diplomacy. ➤ Does India have as good or better basis for inclusion than Japan or China? ➤ By what criteria? ➤ Does this five-power world underestimate the North-South axis of struggle in world affairs? (For two responses to the "five-power world", see Edmund Stillman, "America after Vietnam," *Commentary*, October 1971, pp. 45–52; James Chace, "The Five-Power World of Richard Nixon," *N.Y. Times Magazine*, February 20, 1972, pp. 14–15, 42–47.)

5. ➤ What are the principal advantages and disadvantages of a multibloc system of world order? ➤ Does a multibloc world have more appeal for the rich countries or the poor countries, for the socialist countries or the capitalist countries, for the superpowers or the secondary and tertiary states, for Asia or Europe, and so on?

6. ➤ How does the multibloc model compare with the Clark-Sohn world in terms of *attainability? desirability?*

7. Masters bases his discussion of the conception of a multibloc model on Morton A. Kaplan's presentation of the balance-of-power system. (See Kaplan, *System and Process in International Politics* [Wiley, New York, 1957], pp. 22–36). ➤ Is this your conception of the classical operation of the balance of power? There is a discussion of the balance of power by Raymond Aron (*Peace and War* [Doubleday, New York, 1966],

pp. 128–36) that is quite critical of Kaplan's approach. ➤ To what extent has the emergence of nuclear weapons altered the classical operation of the balance of power?

8. ➤ Does the economist's model of oligopolistic competition shed much light on the operations of international society? There are two major reasons to raise the issue. First of all, political competition is actuated by more complex goals than is economic competition. Even if politics is associated with power and economics with wealth, there is a difference in the degree of tangibility that may be quite important. Fluctuations in profits can be measured and provide a focus and test for the operations of a business firm, whereas fluctuations in the power of a government are relative and often intangible. Second, in historical situations—for instance, Europe in the nineteenth century—the observed interaction among governments does not seem to resemble the observed interaction among competitors in the American automobile industry. With respect both to cooperation and conflict, the international milieu is more complex and is influenced much more by considerations of sentiment (and so-called irrational factors) than are the workings of any marketplace.

9. Many of the discussions of whether a multi-bloc model would be desirable, if attainable, assume conditions of *international stability*. Many politically astute observers appraise an international system by the extent to which it is, or appears to be, stable. "Stability" is an illusive concept. Here is one formulation offered by two leading political scientists:

> Stability may, of course, be considered from the vantage point of both the total system and the states comprising it. From the broader, or systemic, point of view, we shall define stability as the probability that the system retains all of its essential characteristics; that no single nation becomes dominant; that most of its members continue to survive; and that large-scale war does not occur. And from the more limited perspective of the individual nations, stability would refer to the probability of their continued political independence and territorial integrity without any significant probability of becoming engaged even in limited wars. (From Karl W. Deutsch and J. David Singer, "Multipolar Power Systems and International Stability," *World Politics*, vol. 16, no. 3 [April 1964], pp. 390–406, at pp. 390–91).

It should be noticed that stability as the criterion of assessment is *(a)* biased in favor of the maintenance of the *status quo* and *(b)* exclusively concerned with the avoidance of large-scale warfare.

The relationship between stability and polarity has been explored in an article by Michael Haas's ("International Subsystems: Stability and Polarity," *American Political Science Review*, vol. 64, no. 1 [March 1970], pp. 98–123). The article takes up seriously the question of whether a multipolar system is more stable than a bipolar system. Discussing the work of Rosecrance, Singer, Small, Deutsch, and Waltz, and taking account of empirical data, Haas's main finding is "a negative relation between system stability and number of power centers." (p. 121). His main conclusion is that multipolarity entails a higher incidence of violence and war; bipolarity entails fewer but longer wars. ➤ Is stability a goal shared by governments of diverse culture, ideology, foreign policy, or stage of economic development? ➤ Why? ➤ Why not?

Socialist states and third-world countries have supported "wars of national liberation" that are justified either by appeals to the logic of history or by concepts of social justice. ➤ Are such positions inconsistent with support for stability in international relations? ➤ Is the advocacy of revolution and counterrevolution destructive of our five world-order values under all conditions of international stability?

The following statement on the relevance of military technology to international stability should also be considered:

> The apparent contradiction between arms-control concepts and traditional balance-of-power theory arises, in part, from the different ordering of conditions believed to create stability, particularly with respect to the effects of military technology. Arms control focuses on the role of nuclear weapons, making deterrence the indispensible condition of international stability. It sees a unique correlation between the stability of deterrence at various levels of national armaments and the stability of the international system. International relations theory, on the other hand, does not generally give preeminence to nuclear technology in the calculus of stability. . . . The invention of intercontinental missiles and nuclear warheads has brought into question

traditional concepts about the nature of war, the uses of military force in pursuit of national policy, and the role of military power in the maintenance of international stability. In the balance-of-power system, war was a legitimate, if not a preferred, means of reestablishing stability in the system. Neither the number of wars nor the participation in them were crucial determinants of stability. Moreover, provided the existence of so-called essential actors was not threatened in defeat, minor states could be conquered, partitioned, or incorporated as a matter of political adjustment. An essential characteristic was that war was not to be fought for unlimited objectives by any of the great powers. [From Ciro Elliott Zoppo, "Nuclear Technology, Multipolarity, and International Stability," *World Politics*, vol. 18, no. 4 (July 1966), pp. 578–606, at pp. 580–89.]

➤ How critical has nuclear technology been to the avoidance of warfare in Asia and Africa? ➤ Would the spread of nuclear technology to these "subsystems" increase or decrease their respective stability?

➤ Is a multibloc image of the future compatible with drastic disarmament? There is some impression given by Masters that the classical ideas of "balance," "equilibrium," and "stability" are being adapted to the special features of the nuclear age—the mutual destructiveness of general war, the unrestrained objectives arising from ideological confrontation, and the geographical dispersion of concern as a result of worldwide participation in international life.

➤ Would the stability that minimizes violence help to maximize social and economic welfare, and political and social justice? ➤ Or does the preoccupation with stability introduce rigidity into the system in such a way as to inhibit the realization of these values?

Note that stability theorists generally presuppose a fixed structure for international society. Stability is concerned with unit identity and systemic coherence *within* the existing structure. Alternative systems are not contemplated, nor are values additional to those associated with power and survival much taken into account by the theorists of international stability.

10. Some analysts have felt that the multibloc model, erected as an alternative to the bipolar model (for a descriptive analysis and prescriptive endorsement of a bipolar international system,

see Kenneth Waltz, "The Stability of a Bipolar World," in Richard A. Falk and Saul H. Mendlovitz, Eds., *The Strategy of World Order*, vol. I [World Law Fund, New York, 1966], pp. 186–214.) was an oversimplification of international reality. Richard Rosecrance has depicted international society as multilayered. Bipolarity is descriptive for strategic nuclear deterrence; multipolarity is descriptive for a range of supplemental security relationships. Rosecrance outlines the principal features of an "intermediate international system, a system of bi-multipolarity," in his article, "Bipolarity, Multipolarity, and the Future" (*Journal of Conflict Resolution*, vol. 10, no. 3 [September 1966], pp. 314–27). The objective Rosecrance has in mind is "to avoid the extremes of conflict, or if conflict could not be averted to dissociate bipolar interests from outcomes in the area. . . . The two major states would act as regulators for conflict in the external areas; but multipolar states would act as mediators and buffers for conflicts between bipolar powers" (p. 322). ➤ Is it at all likely that an international system organized along these lines will emerge (or has emerged)? ➤ If it does emerge, can it be managed by rational calculations without a central structure of management?

Wolfram Hanrieder has produced a sophisticated example of the multipolar style of analysis. His effort is mainly directed at drawing analytical distinctions that will strengthen our awareness of the real character of the international system. He points out that on some international issues the two superpowers are predominant, and within this category, their relationship to one another can be based either on equality or on inequality. Hanrieder calls these patterns, respectively, "symmetrical" and "asymmetrical." In other issue-areas the superpowers are equal to each other, but share their predominance with an additional number of states, whereas in still others the superpowers are unequal but share predominance. The first set of issues is labeled "hetero-symmetrical," the second "hetero-asymmetrical." (See Wolfram F. Hanrieder, "The International System: Bipolar or Multibloc," *Journal of Conflict Resolution*, vol. 9, no. 3 [September 1965], pp. 299–308). A focus on issue-areas broadens inquiry beyond the central preoccupation with nuclear deterrence, but greatly complicates the framework of inquiry. Human rights, civil strife, and international economic disputes each require individual analysis and the results of each issue-area are distinct.

11. ➤ Is a "bloc" or "pole" (as in bipolar) a spatial concept? ➤ Are these concepts properly studied as an aspect of "regionalism?" ➤ Does a concert of action on a range of salient issues establish bloc identity? ➤ Can a single state ever be appropriately regarded as a "pole"? "Bipolarity" is often used to refer to the dominance of international affairs by two adversaries, the Soviet Union and the United States, because of their preeminent nuclear status. ➤ But is "bipolarity" also descriptive of a generalized technological preeminence, as evidenced, for instance, in space exploits?

12. ➤ Is a multibloc image of the future compatible with the growth of regional and global supranationalism?

2

Political Discontinuities in the International System

ORAN R. YOUNG

The international political system is currently undergoing changes that are both rapid and extensive. Especially since the early sixties, a number of trends have manifested themselves and become interrelated in such a way that, taken together, they are substantially altering the fundamental postwar patterns of international politics. These indications of change and flux have engendered a substantial debate concerning appropriate concepts for the analysis of the international system. Nevertheless, the resultant debate about the significance of these trends has evolved, for the most part, around the dichotomy between bipolar and multipolar models of the international system.[1] As a result, the debate has been cast in terms of a somewhat narrow conception of essentially structural problems. I submit, however, that the dichotomy between bipolar and multipolar models is clearly inadequate to deal with a number of the principal aspects and axes of change which are becoming increasingly important in international politics in the current period. Nor is the range of mixed types along a spectrum between the poles of bipolarity and multipolarity sufficent for a clear analysis of contemporary shifts.[2] While the notion of a vertically layered system combining elements of bipolarity and multipolarity at the same time, for example, is an interesting one, it too fails to capture much of the essence of the contemporary flux.[3] What are needed instead, therefore, are

---

[1] For a clear discussion of the bipolar model, see Kenneth Waltz, "The Stability of a Bipolar System," *Daedalus* (Summer 1964), 881–909. A somewhat parallel effort to develop the multipolar model is Karl W. Deutsch and J. David Singer, "Multipolar Power Systems and International Stability," *World Politics*, xvi (April 1964), 390–406.

[2] For various conceptions of the range of mixed types, see Arthur Lee Burns, "From Balance to Deterrence: A Theoretical Analysis," *World Politics*, ix (July 1957), 494–529; and Ciro Elliott Zoppo, "Nuclear Technology, Multipolarity, and International Stability," *World Politics*, xviii (July 1966), 579–606.

[3] This notion of a layered system has been developed by Richard Rosecrance in his aritcle "Bipolarity, Multipolarity, and the Future," *Journal of Conflict Resolution*, x (September 1966), 314–27.

From *World Politics*, vol. 20, no. 3 (copyright © 1968 by Princeton University Press), pp. 369–392. Reprinted by permission of Princeton University Press.

some new modes of conceptualizing the international political system. It is the thesis of this article that a constructive start in this direction can be made by emphasizing the growing interpenetration of the global or systemwide axes of international politics on the one hand and several newly emerging but widely divergent regional arenas or subsystems on the other hand.

THE DISCONTINUITIES MODEL

The alternative model I propose for the analysis of international politics in the present period is one that encompasses the concurrent influence of global and regional power processes in patterns that are strongly marked by elements of both congruence and discontinuity. In general, the concepts of congruence and discontinuity refer to the extent to which patterns of political interests and relationships of power are similar or dissimilar as between the global arena and various regional arenas and as between the different regional arenas themselves. There are, however, several more specific characteristics of this model of international politics that should be made explicit at the outset.

First, there are some actors and some substantive issues that are relevant throughout the whole international system, or at least throughout most of its subsystems. The superpowers, though their *effective* influence on many issues is declining, clearly fall into this category in the current international system. Similarly, substantive issues such as communism, nationalism, and economic development have systemwide as well as local aspects. Second, relevant actors, substantive interests, patterns of conflict, and specific power balances differ significantly from one subsystem to another. While global actors and issues are of some importance in each subsystem, the individual subsystems also contain a variety of unique features. Asian and African power balances, for example, are quite different from the more classical arrangements in Europe. And Asian communism is considerably more intertwined with the problems of active nationalism than is the case with communism in Europe. Third, the regional subsystems of the international system are therefore significantly discontinuous with one another in a number of respects. The degree of discontinuity between any two subsystems may of course vary, but for the moment it is the existence of discon-

tinuities in general that needs to be stressed. Fourth, in all cases the subsystems are by no means totally discontinuous with one another since each is in fact an amalgam of global and local features. The existence of systemwide actors and issues is not the only source of congruence between the various subsystems. Several other types of links between subsystems are of some importance. To begin with, with regard to issues of reputation there is a spread effect that is important in shaping regional manifestations of systemwide issues. For example, the alliance behavior of a superpower in one subsystem can affect the posture of that power's allies in other subsystems. In addition, there are various demonstration effects that exercise a considerable influence on the atmosphere of international politics across subsystems. In other words, there are perceptual links between the subsystems as well as more substantive links. These perceptual links tend to be substantially spread and strengthened through the existence of various universal organizations, such as the United Nations, that serve as channels of communication. The fifth characteristic of the model is that the specific mixture between global and regional elements is apt to differ in a variety of ways from one subsystem to another. In short, levels and patterns of discontinuity are likely to be relatively volatile both horizontally across space and vertically over time.

It is important to clarify the essential differences between the discontinuities model outlined above and the other important models that have appeared in the contemporary discussion of international politics.[4] Bipolar models emphasize the importance of a single, dominant axis of conflict and the tendency for regional actors and issues to be conceptualized in relationship to the underlying bipolar axis of the system. The discontinuities model, on the other hand, stresses the importance of both systemwide and regional factors and emphasizes the complex patterns of their interpenetration, leaving room for shifting weights with regard to the question of which type of factor is dominant. For its part, the multipolar model tends to stress the existence of a multiplicity of axes of conflict and the phenomenon of

---

[4] Perhaps the single most important statement of abstract models of the international system remains Morton A. Kaplan, *System and Process in International Politics* (New York 1957).

crosscutting relationships among these axes.[5] The discontinuities model differs in several respects from the multipolar perspective: it deals primarily with subsystems rather than with individual actors; it stresses the differences between system-wide and regional axes of conflict; and it focuses on the complex interpenetrations between universal and regional issues rather than on the much less "lumpy" notion of a number of individual actors dealing with each other on a variety of issues in ways that produce numerous intersecting lines of conflict. Next, the distinctions between the discontinuities model and the model based on the notion of a small number of relatively distinct regional blocs are easily discernible.[6] Above all, the discontinuities model emphasizes both the combination of global and regional factors within individual subsystems and the various interconnections between subsystems. Finally, there is a hypothetical model of the international system based on the notion of political fragmentation that would produce a situation somewhat similar to the old conception of atomistic liberalism within individual polities. In this case, the discontinuities model with its repeated stress on interactions and interpenetrations offers a conception of international politics that constitutes one form of direct opposition to the fragmentation model.[7]

One of the most interesting features of the discontinuities model of the international system is the extent to which it contains logical ambiguities that are very much analogous to some of the central problems of international politics in the current era. The sources of these ambiguities fall into several distinct categories. First, the tension between congruence and discontinuity among the various subsystems generates "limited adversary" relationships of a very peculiar nature, especially among the great powers.[8] In short, black-and-white distinctions are impossible in such a situation. The great powers, and especially the superpowers, are increasingly constrained to modify their conflicts in any given subsystem by the fact that they are apt to have important common interests in other subsystems which they do not want to jeopardize. At the same time, these powers are often hampered in the exploitation of common interests both within subsystems and on the global level by the fact that they find themselves engaged in sharp conflicts in other subsystems. There is little doubt, for example, that one important source of change in the postures of the United States and the Soviet Union in Europe is the development of incipient common interests between these powers in the Asian subsystem. Or to take another example, a major barrier to Soviet-American cooperation on the global issues of arms control arises from their conflicting interests in such concrete situations as Germany and Vietnam.

Second, there are important possibilities for manipulation across subsystems which tend to lend further ambiguities to the system, in addition to those emerging directly from the tension between congruence and discontinuity. These possibilities emerge, in essence, from the fact that, while the various subsystems are significantly discontinuous, there are nevertheless important interconnections between them. For this reason, it is sometimes possible to achieve advantages by utilizing political credit and reputation across subsystems. Victories won in a subsystem that is relatively easy to deal with may serve a country in pursuing its interests in other subsystems. Or again, it is sometimes possible to stir up trouble in one subsystem as a means of sowing confusion and of diverting attention from a country's prime area of interest.[9] There are also in a system of this kind some less tangible manipulatory possibilities arising out of perceptual problems. Especially in a dynamic and fast-changing world, it is sometimes possible to define and conceptualize emerging power balances in terms of perspectives and concepts developed originally for other

---

[5]In its intellectual origins, the multipolar model of the international system really stems from the conceptions of the American group theorists concerning domestic politics. For the original and in some ways clearest statement of these conceptions, see Arthur F. Bentley, *The Process of Government* (Chicago 1908).

[6]For conceptualizations of models along these lines, see Roger Masters, "A Multi-Bloc Model of the International System," *American Political Science Review*, LV (December 1961), 780–98; and Wolfram Hanrieder, "The International System: Bipolar or Multibloc," *Journal of Conflict Resolution*, IX (September 1965), 299–308.

[7]Another form of direct opposition to fragmentation would be the development of genuine political integration among the units of the international system.

---

[8]The concept of "limited adversary" relationships is introduced and developed in Marshall D. Shulman, *Beyond the Cold War* (New Haven 1966).

[9]This particular possibility has always been a major source of American concern with regard to East-West problems in the postwar period.

arenas. Though this effort sometimes leads to dangerous misconceptions and rigidities (more on these problems below), the process can work to the advantage of an actor that can succeed in shaping perceptions about realities and relevant norms in a specific area in ways that work to its own advantage.

Third, the logical ambiguities that can arise from a discontinuities model increase considerably when we begin to move from a world of two important subsystems to one that contains a number of important subsystems. Both the specific issues and the mixture between regional and global concerns will vary from one subsystem to the next. From the point of view of the powers with systemwide interests, the complexities are increased on a straight numerical basis since there are a greater number of combinations of issues and of discontinuities to be dealt with in a situation of multiple subsystems. Moreover, the shift to multiple subsystems raises the possibility of new types of international problems that are not unique to any individual subsystem but that are still not universal problems since they do not arise in all of the subsystems of the overall system. And finally, the number of possibilities for manipulation, mentioned above, rises rapidly as the system shifts from two subsystems to multiple subsystems.

Given the complexities and ambiguities of the system summarized in the discontinuities model, it is hardly surprising that it tends to generate various intellectual problems and confusions that plague the work of analysts and decision-makers alike. In particular, the mixed and interpenetrated nature of the situation seems to go against the grain of very deep-seated psychological needs for clarity and relative simplicity in efforts to conceptualize reality. Perhaps because of these needs, there are two characteristic classes of simplifying devices that tend to crop up repeatedly in efforts to deal with a world of significant discontinuities. Though these classes of devices are, in a sense, opposites, both involve substantial distortions of reality which are apt to generate very serious difficulties for sound analysis and decision-making.

The first class of simplifying devices falls under the heading of *segmentation* or *compartmentalization* and is based on a form of cognitive dissonance. The main thrust of these devices is an overemphasis on the uniqueness of individual, regional subsystems and a tendency to deny, at least

tacitly, the extent of interpenetration and congruence between them. More specifically, segmentation is the characteristic failing of analysts who operate on the basis of area specialization and of decision-makers and bureaucrats who work through the country or regional-office system. This orientation not infrequently leads to an inability to assess the impact of systemwide actors and issues on regional power processes. Even more serious, however, is the extent to which segmentation of this kind tends to result in a failure to take account of interconnections between subsystems in such areas as reputation, demonstration effects, and the problems of manipulation across subsystems.

The second class of simplifying devices falls under the heading of *fusion* or *universalization* and stems from the search for a few underlying dimensions or concepts in terms of which it is possible to conceptualize all of international politics. This device is perhaps even more common than segmentation, especially among the lay public, because it satisfies the felt need for some sense of "understanding" concerning the basic meaning or significance of the whole of international politics. At the same time, fusion is apt to be even more distorting than segmentation, both because it requires simplification on an even more grandiose scale and because it leads to a polarized conception of the whole world rather than, as with segmentation, to a differentially inadequate conceptualization of particular regional subsystems. Even the most cursory consideration of such polarized conceptions as democracy versus communism, capitalism versus socialism, or the world city versus the countryside is ample to demonstrate the extent of distortion that the device of fusion is likely to produce.

THE EMERGENCE OF DISCONTINUITIES IN THE INTERNATIONAL SYSTEM

The problems arising from multiple power balances and political discontinuities are necessarily relatively modern developments in international politics. The fundamental precondition of reasonable extensive contacts between regional subsystems has been met, for the most part, only in the modern era. Within these limitations, however, there are some interesting historical examples of significant discontinuities between several regional subsystems. And some concrete examples of the ways in which such problems have manifested themselves in the past may lend perspective to our subsequent discussion of political discontinuities in the contemporary international system.

In the period between the Franco-Prussian War and the First World War several interesting discontinuities began to unfold more or less simultaneously in the international arena. From the 1880's onward, England and France were engaged in a variety of conflicts concerning the division of territories in Africa, a situation that created important rigidities when the common interests of the two countries on the European continent began to grow stronger, around the turn of the century, in the wake of various changes in Germany's posture. During the same period, England and Russia were in almost constant opposition to each other in the Middle East and in the Far East despite the existence of common interests between them in Europe and despite the growing Franco-Russian friendship on European issues. In fact, before the Anglo-Russian arrangement of 1907 concerning Persia, these two powers represented the principal axis of contention in the Middle East. Then, even during the First World War, England maintained a treaty relationship with Japan despite the fact that Russia and Japan were clear opponents in the Far East. Moreover, all of these divergent axes of contention were further complicated by the participation of all the major European powers except Austria-Hungary and Italy in the process of extracting concessions from China. Throughout this period, the lines of conflict in the Chinese arena, in which Japan and the United States also participated, tended to shift along different lines and at a different pace than the evolving pattern of conflict in Europe itself.

It is also possible to find important examples of discontinuities in international politics during the interwar years, though for the most part the complexities of this period seem somewhat less striking than those that characterized the system immediately prior to the First World War. England and France, in this period, developed sharply disparate views concerning the organization of security in Eastern Europe and, especially, concerning the appropriate role for the Soviet Union in this connection. More generally, the extensive and relatively acrimonious disputes between England and France in the Middle Eastern arena during the twenties and the thirties clearly played

a role in producing the uncertainty and unhappiness that marked Anglo-French efforts to coordinate in response to the resurgence of Germany in Europe. Even into the late thirties, for example, there were no formal alliance commitments or coordination procedures between the two countries. The United States in the interwar period allowed itself to become increasingly involved in the Far East, even while it continued to maintain an insistently isolationist posture with regard to developments in the European arena. Finally, the Second World War itself produced a striking example of political discontinuity in the efforts of the Soviet Union to remain on nonbelligerent terms with Japan long after the opening of the war in the Pacific and the entry of the United States into the European contest had polarized the war on a global basis. The sharpness of this discontinuity is particularly striking in the light of both the clear-cut interdependence of the allied powers in the European arena and the willingness of Britain to join the United States, at least formally, in the war in the Pacific.

Throughout most of the modern history of international politics, however, other types of relationships have tended to be considerably more salient and influential than the patterns of discontinuity under discussion in this article. To a very real extent, in fact, patterns of this kind have emerged on an extensive, worldwide scale and assumed a position of recognized importance only in the present international system. Several significant sets of causal factors underlie this present relevance of a discontinuities model of international politics.

To begin with, the impact of systemwide or global actors and issues is now much more strongly felt than has ever been the case before. The aftermath of the Second World War has seen a sharp acceleration in the rates of development of communications, transportation, and military technologies. As a result, the extent of interdependence of the various components of the overall international system, which has now become a full-fledged world system, has risen dramatically in the contemporary period.[10] Moreover, the period

---

[10]Interdependence refers here to the extent to which actions in one part of the system affect the other parts of the system. It is therefore not a measure of common or overlapping interests. Interdependencies may be either positive or negative.

since World War II has witnessed the rise of two superpowers, in contrast to a larger number of great powers, as well as the emergence of several substantive issues that are relevant throughout the international system. Therefore, the contemporary system is not only more interdependent (in the general sense that what happens in any part of it is capable of exercising a very substantial influence on developments in any other part of it), but is also characterized by the existence of several discrete actors and issues of global significance which play very concrete and specific roles in the various regional subsystems.

These developments actually represent the acceleration of a fundamental trend that began in the second half of the nineteenth century. In themselves, however, they are not sufficient to produce an international system such as the one portrayed in the discontinuities model. In the period following World War II, for example, the dominance of the two superpowers became so clear-cut that some version of the bipolar model seemed to be the most accurate representation of reality. During these years, regional subsystems were nonexistent, effectively dominated by the superpowers, or sufficiently peripheral that the conditions of the discontinuities model other than its systemwide features were rarely met. In more recent years, however, a number of important developments in international politics have come together to reduce the salience of the bipolar axis in international politics and to generate a variety of unique features in the power processes of the various subsystems of the international system.

First, a considerable period of time has passed without a large-scale international war to polarize and simplify the patterns of international politics. Because of this, the setting for political discontinuities has been growing increasingly favorable. Second, there has been a gradual diffusion of effective power in the system, despite the superpowers' great superiority in the physical elements of power. Third, the system has witnessed the rise or resurgence of a small number of new power centers that are of major significance even though they are still far less influential than the superpowers. Powers such as France, Germany, China, Japan, and India belong in this category. Fourth, the number of independent states in the system has grown rapidly since 1945, especially in the new regional subsystems of Asia and Africa. Here, the demise of colonialism represented the end of a major simplifying factor of earlier periods of international politics. Fifth, these shifts in the numbers and types of actors in the system have been accompanied by a general rise in levels of political consciousness and by the spread of active nationalism among the "new states." At the present time, even with such an avowedly international movement as communism, it is often difficult to tell whether its specific manifestations in particular states are based more on internationalism or on nationalism. Sixth, as effective influence diffuses in the system and as new lines of conflict emerge, the superpowers themselves are becoming more aware of their own common interests, even while they continue to prosecute a variety of conflicting interests in the various regional subsystems. The upshot of all these developments is that the major simplifying assumptions of the bipolar world of the fifties either are no longer valid or are increasingly hedged about by a variety of complicating relationships on a subsidiary level. The regional subsystems, therefore, are now coming more and more into their own as a complement to the global nature of the overall international system.

ASIA AND EUROPE

Let me continue this analysis of contemporary international politics by shifting to some more concrete remarks about the positions of the European and Asian subsystems in the overall international system. Increasingly, the relationships between these two subsystems offer illustrations of a number of the principal aspects of the general discontinuities model outlined above. At the same time, the emerging interconnections between Europe and Asia in contemporary international politics, which have become the subject of a number of ambiguities and misunderstandings, can be at least partially unraveled by applying the perspectives of the discontinuities model.

During most of the first half of the twentieth century, the Asian subsystem was essentially subordinate to rather than coordinate with the European subsystem. The degree of European dominance rose and fell in various patterns in the course of this period. Moreover, the various European powers were frequently at odds with one another over particular Asian issues during these years. The fact remains, nevertheless, that a great deal of the tone of Asian politics prior to World War II was set by the participation of various outside, and primarily European, powers in the Asian subsystem. In this perspective, the Second World War constitutes a sharp and decisive break with the previous pattern of relations between Europe and Asia that had, in any case, already begun to deteriorate during the thirties as the influence of Japan expanded.[11] For several reasons, however, the opening of the war did not lead immediately to the development of an independent or fully autonomous pattern of international politics in the Asian subsystem. First, Japan became the dominant political force in Asia during the war years, thereby effectively replacing the European powers in functional terms rather than exerting a significant pressure for the creation of a self-sustaining political system within Asia. Second, the outbreak of the war resulted in a thorough polarization of the patterns of conflict in the overall international system. For the duration of the war, the regional subsystems were effectively merged into a global pattern of dichotomous conflict.

The War itself destroyed the preconditions of the previous pattern of European dominance in Asia, but it did not, in the process, produce the makings of a new and autonomous Asian subsystem. In fact, in the years immediately following the war the Asian subsystem was almost entirely lacking in international relations of an indigenous variety. The individual units of the subsystem were often more deeply involved in bilateral relations with various external powers than in relations with one another. There were several important causes of this absence of local international relations in Asia. On the one hand, the situation was related to the activities of the outside powers. France, Britain, and Holland, for example, attempted to reestablish their former positions of dominance in Indochina, Malaya, and Indonesia, a posture that led to *inter*regional patterns of interaction as well as to a number of sharp conflicts. At the same time, its dominant role in the war in the Pacific and in the final defeat of Japan made the United States a prominent Asian

power almost automatically. As a result, the aftermath of the war found the United States deeply involved in a number of Asian problems, a development that also tended to hinder the emergence of an autonomous Asian political system. On the other hand, this lack of genuine international relations within Asia after the war was also caused by a number of local, Asian factors. First, the most important Asian countries, including Japan and China, had been severely shattered by the war. The principal powers of the subsystem were therefore unable to function effectively as international actors. Second, a number of Asian countries were involved to a great degree with civil wars and a variety of other internal preoccupations during this period. China, Indonesia, Malaya, the Philippines, and various parts of Indochina all belong in this category. Third, many of the new states of Asia had not yet fully emerged from the ties of colonialism at this time. Much of the international effort of these states, therefore, was directed toward breaking the remaining bonds of colonial relationships, an interest that in fact complemented the concurrent attitudes of the European states in producing patterns of *inter*regional interactions. Among those states to which this set of problems was relevant were India, Pakistan, Indonesia, the Philippines, Korea, and the states of Indochina. In summary, then, the aftermath of the war witnessed a sharp break from the previous pattern of unequal relations between Asia and Europe, but it led, in the first instance, only to a peculiar ferment characterized by an absence of local international politics rather than to a new and independent format for international politics in Asia.

Starting from this rather chaotic base, the international politics of Asia have begun to change rapidly and extensively in recent years. The European powers ultimately lost their colonial conflicts. A number of new states appeared on the scene within the Asian subsystem. Though civil strife is still important in Asia, the most important civil war, in China, came to an end relatively early in the postwar period, thereby paving the way for the emergence of the People's Republic of China as an important force in Asian politics. At the same time, Japan reemerged very rapidly as a dynamic state and a key factor to be reckoned with in any current analysis of the Asian subsystem. In passing, even though these changes have also, to a very great degree, destroyed the physical

---

[11]It may be appropriate to take the Japanese invasion of Manchuria in 1931 as an important turning point. But the expansion of Japanese influence throughout the Asian subsystem continued on a fairly gradual basis until the actual beginning of the war.

bases of the tutelary position of the United States in Asia, American perceptions have often been quite slow in adapting to the consequences of this shift.

The unsettled quality of the Asian subsystem clearly remains in evidence today. But a number of fundamental issues have been either settled decisively or thrown into channels whose ultimate outcome is relatively clear. As a result, for the first time in the twentieth century a unique brand of Asian politics is beginning to take its place alongside the long-standing traditions of international politics within the European subsystem. In the contemporary world, of course, there is a great deal of interpenetration among all the regional subsystems in political relationships. And this interpenetration between the European and Asian subsystems is very evident. To an increasing degree, however, the postition of the Asian subsystem is becoming coordinate rather than subordinate.

The global features and components of this emerging Asian subsystem are not difficult to locate. Many specific issues in Asian politics still bear the imprint of the dominance of outside states in earlier years. The last vestiges of colonialism are only now disappearing. Many individual states in Asia are presently in the throes of various post-colonial shakedown processes. And the United States has not yet shown itself willing to draw back from its *de facto* emergence as a preeminent Asian power at the end of World War II. At the same time, Asian politics have been shaped in a number of ways by the global contours of the various ideological problems underlying the so-called cold war. Some form of communism has become a dominant, or at least powerful, force in a number of Asian countries.[12] The Asian states in general have become involved in the competition between the superpowers for the political favor of the world. And in Asia especially the ideologically tinged debate about which models of economic development are most appropriate has become virulent.[13] Finally, the global aspects

of the Asian subsystem are further emphasized by the fact that the two superpowers have extensive power interests in the area. These interests have manifested themselves both in the extension of alliance systems to Asia and in the efforts of the United States to construct an Asian defense perimeter that is periodically probed and tested by Communist or Communist-influenced forces.[14] The existence of these interests in Asia on the part of both superpowers underlines the interconnection between the Asian subsystem and the overall international system, but it also tends to open up new possibilities for maneuver on the part of various second-order powers in Asia.

The global aspects of the Asian subsystem are therefore quite evident. More interesting perhaps are the unique features of the subsystem which are becoming increasingly evident and influential as Asian politics move away from their formerly subordinate role vis-à-vis the European arena. These unique features are particularly evident when defined in terms of discontinuities between the Asian and European subsystems. First, the Asian subsystem contains a large number of new states that are often lacking in the internal viability that characterizes most of the older and more established states of Europe. As a result, Asian politics are characterized by boundary problems, internal civil strife and shakedown processes, and the dangers of competitive external intervention in upheavals. Second, though the dividing lines are not always clear with regard to individual states, the two subsystems operate, for the most part, at very different levels of economic development. While the European states are increasingly interested in the politics of affluence, the states of Asia, by and large, are still struggling to reach the stage of sustained economic growth. Third, the brands of communism that have become prominent in Asia are quite different from the mainstream of European communism. In general, as was suggested earlier, Asian communism is more deeply colored by nationalism and agrarianism in the current period, a fact that has produced great variations in the Communist movements even within the Asian subsystem. Fourth, while

[12]At the present time, some form of communism is dominant in China, North Korea, and North Vietnam. There are, in addition, Communist movements of some significance in a number of the other Asian states.

[13]The models debated range from the pure forms of a free market economy to the pure forms of socialism. At the present time, many of the developing countries are becoming increasingly interested in various mixed forms.

[14]The most obvious cases of testing include (1) the attack on South Korea in 1950, (2) the probes in the Taiwan Strait in 1954–1955 and in 1958, (3) Laos, at least until the Geneva agreement of 1962, and (4) Vietnam from 1959 until the present.

European politics in the postwar period have been marked by a relatively clear demarcation between the Soviet and Western blocs, the Asian subsystem has always been rather amorphous with regard to these problems of political delineation. To some extent, this quality is related to geopolitical complexities and to the peculiar features of nonalignment and neutralism in Asia. More fundamentally, perhaps, the quality is also related to the fact that the basic East-West dichotomy essentially originated in Europe and spread only subsequently to the peculiar environment of the Asian subsystem. Fifth, though the superpowers are of critical importance in both subsystems, there are major differences between the second-order powers in the two subsystems. This point relates to such European states as Britain, France, and Germany and to such Asian powers as China, Japan, and India. Among other things, the second-order powers of the two subsystems differ on such matters as the nature of their political alignments, the extent and importance of sources of local conflict among the second-order powers, and the degree of revisionism, directed toward the prevailing international system, manifested by these states.

While the European and Asian subsystems are related to one another in a number of important ways, therefore, they also exhibit a variety of very significant discontinuities. And it is essentially the mixed and complex quality of this relationship that accounts for a considerable amount of the confusion currently evident in efforts to understand the unfolding course of international politics. For this reason, let me now turn to an exploration of several sets of problems that emerge with some clarity from the application of the perspectives of the discontinuities model to the connections between the European and Asian subsystems in the current period.

First, despite the fact that the postwar patterns of international politics in Europe are now beginning to change, the Asian subsystem is characterized by a substantially greater fluidity or power relationships. In Europe we are now witnessing a gradual breaking down of the hard lines of conflict that emerged in the late forties and early fifties. Even with the appearance of a distinctive brand of international politics in Asia, on the other hand, no hard-and-fast lines of division and conflict have emerged. This fluidity in the Asian sub-

system is ultimately related both to the peculiarities of communism in Asia and to the ambiguities created by the lack of internal viability in many of the individual states of the subsystem. Moreover, this political fluidity has manifested itself in a number of specific areas that generate problems for conceptions of international politics that stem primarily from the bipolar-multipolar spectrum.

Though the superpowers have attempted, from time to time, to extend their interbloc conflicts into Asia, this effort has met with increasing obstacles in recent years. On the Western side, the SEATO alliance has never become fully operational as a major factor in Asian politics.[15] And even from a very early stage in its history the Sino-Soviet alliance was more nearly a relationship of ideology, fraught with important ambiguities, than of complementary power positions.[16] As a result, there are no really solid alliance systems in Asia at the present time, a fact that produces considerably greater opportunities for shifts and alterations in power relationships than is presently the case in Europe. In addition, this picture has been further complicated in recent years by the growth of various common interests of a straightforward political nature which cut across the nominal lines of ideological alignments. Among the major powers, the current growth of common interests between the Soviet Union and Japan and between Japan and China is particularly significant. And the emerging pattern of crosscutting lines of conflict in Asia is further emphasized by the development of a number of very complex local conflicts involving, in the first instance, such states as Indonesia, Malaysia, India, and Pakistan. The consequences of this pronounced fluidity in

---

[15]Even at the outset in 1954, the SEATO alliance was notable for its failure to include many of the significant Asian states. In the intervening years, the alliance has occasionally been an instrument of American foreign policy, but has seldom functioned in any other way.

[16]Even in 1950 there were several aspects of the relationships between the Soviet Union and China that were obvious sources of potential disagreement. At the time, however, the weakness of China served to camouflage these problems. As a direct function of the emergence of China as a power of significance at least in the Asian sub-system, the basic political difficulties in the Sino-Soviet relationship have become increasingly prominent. In this sense, the relationship is essentially reverting to the patterns that predominated in the early years of the twentieth century.

the Asian subsystem are to create a political environment in which the simplifying assumptions of the European subsystem are often irrelevant, as well as to produce an expanding range of political opportunities and dangers in international relationships.

Second, we are now entering a period in which the coordinate relationships among the various second-order powers of the European and Asian subsystems are becoming increasingly interesting and important. This new type of interconnection between the subsystems is related to the gradual diffusion of effective influence in the overall international system as well as to the general development of coordinate rather than subordinate relations between Europe and Asia. As the overall international system begins to shift in these directions, a number of the second-order powers in the European and Asian subsystems are gradually coming to occupy positions in international politics which are somewhat analogous in structural terms. Under these circumstances, these states are becoming more and more interested in developing relationships with each other across the lines of the subsystems, not so much because they have strong common interests of a positive nature but because the analogous nature of their situations gives them common problems and, in some cases, common opponents in the form of the superpowers.

Although these developments are still at an early stage, these new forms of relationships across the subsystems are already manifesting themselves in a number of concrete areas. The French decision to recognize the People's Republic of China in 1964, for example, was the harbinger of a number of new trends in relations between France (and to some extent Germany) and China. At the present time, there are several sets of ideas emerging in France and Germany about the political value of relations with China for purposes of increasing European leverage in dealings with both the United States and the Soviet Union.[17]

And the potential utility for China of developing ties with the major powers of Europe is evident. Moreover, these new interconnections between the subsystems are also emphasized by the increasing extent to which second-order powers in one subsystem are becoming independently active with regard to issues originating in the other. France, for example, has recently shown a growing interest in developing an independent and decidedly postcolonial position of influence with regard to the problems of Indochina. And the Japanese, as a result of their rapidly expanding economic power, have begun to participate extensively in several primarily Europe-based activities in the realm of international economics. This is true, for example, of both the programs of the GATT and the growing efforts among the major powers to coordinate the means of regulating international monetary conditions.

Third, related to the general diffusion of effective influence in the international system and emphasized by developments such as the growth of relationships among the second-order powers in the system is the emerging trend toward the operationalization of common interests between the two superpowers. As is the case with the second-order powers, the superpowers are coming to occupy increasingly similar structural positions in the overall international system. Perhaps the most interesting feature of this trend in the context of this discussion, however, is the fact that the superpowers are finding it generally easier in the current period to activate their common interests in the Asian subsystem than in the European subsystem.[18] There are several reasons why this is so. As we have seen, the Asian subsystem has never been as rigidly structured as the European subsystem in the postwar period. International politics are more fluid in Asia than in Europe, a condition that provides more opportunities for significant change and therefore requires greater attention on a day-to-day basis. The Asian subsystem contains China, which is currently the most threatening of the emergent powers from the point of view of the power positions of the superpowers in the overall system. And finally, the Asian subsystem currently appears to be more actively dangerous

---

[17]There are several alternative lines of thinking in this area at the present time. Some of these ideas have been discussed in a particularly interesting way by Richard Löwenthal. See his "China's Impact on the Evolution of the Alliances in Europe," in *Western and Eastern Europe: The Changing Relationship,* Institute for Strategic Studies, Adelphi Paper No. 33 (London, March 1967), 20–29.

---

[18]This point is especially interesting because of the fact that it is generally true despite the complexities and difficulties of the current struggle over Vietnam.

than the European subsystem because of the challenges it generates for the stability of the overall international system. Under these circumstances, the superpowers have recently begun to show a noticeable interest in coordinating their activities in the Asian subsystem both generally, in order to maintain at least a minimally stable balance of power in the subsystem, and more specifically, in order to deal with the desires and the geopolitically critical position of China.

These growing interests of the superpowers in coordinating their activities in Asia have manifested themselves in a number of concrete situations.[19] The Indian subcontinent, for example, has in recent years been the focus of several issues that have served as catalysts for at least tacit coordination between the superpowers. Notable cases in point include the Sino-Indian conflict of the fall of 1962,[20] the problems of creating favorable expectations about the future security of India in the wake of the Chinese nuclear test of October 1964,[21] and the various India-Pakistan clashes, which reached a high point in August and September 1965 and which shifted considerably in the wake of the Tashkent Declaration of January 1966.[22] In addition, the Soviet Union, as well as the United States, is currently beginning to show an interest in supporting the continued development of Japan, at least for the time being, to provide a balancing force that is likely to become increasingly important as a function of the emergence of China as an important actor in the Asian

[19]These concrete efforts at coordination in the Asian subsystem are particularly interesting in contrast to the continuing strength of rigidities impeding the realization of common interests between the superpowers in the European subsystem.

[20]The temporal juxtaposition of this situation with the Cuban missile crisis makes the efforts at tacit coordination between the superpowers with regard to the Sino-Indian conflict even more significant.

[21]It was during this period that guarantees, and especially a tacit coordination of guarantees by both superpowers, began to become prominent in discussions of Indian security problems.

[22]In this connection, the *de facto*, though publicly denied, coordination of the superpowers in the United Nations Security Council was a prominent feature of the efforts to stop the overt hostilities between India and Pakistan during September 1965. During January 1966, the Soviet Union took the lead in playing the role of intermediary at Tashkent, but the United States operated in a manner that indicated *de facto* approval and support of the Soviet initiative.

subsystem. Then, to take another example, the two superpowers have demonstrated considerable caution with regard to the disputes in the Maphilindo area in recent years and have tended to agree tacitly to avoid any possibility of being dragged into local disputes in this area. Thus, in 1962 the Soviet Union acquiesced in the American efforts to settle the West Irian issue, and in 1965 and 1966 the two superpowers were able to agree on an essentially "hands off" policy with regard to the internal upheavals in Indonesia. Finally, the current situation in Vietnam is extraordinarily peculiar in this perspective not only because the superpowers are in fact engaged on opposite sides of the principal conflict but also because this posture is at odds with some important common interests between the superpowers in the whole Indochina area. Underneath the current conflict and regardless of the future political status of South Vietnam, there is an important vein of common interests among the United States, the Soviet Union, and North Vietnam in the creation of viable political structures in Indochina capable of maintaining a stable balance in the area without succumbing to outside dominance.[23] And despite the current activities of the Soviet Union in aiding North Vietnam, it is undoubtedly a sense that the ongoing Vietnamese conflict is counterproductive of a stable balance in Indochina which lies behind both the half-hearted actions of the Soviet Union in this arena and the clear indications of Soviet unhappiness with the current course of events in Vietnam. For its part, the United States is not wholly oblivious to interests along these lines in Indochina. But the American perspectives on these issues at the present time are rather seriously confused by the influence of a set of doctrines which goes under the heading of containment and which raises a number of problems when applied to the politics of the Asian subsystem.

Fourth among the sets of problems under discussion, these American doctrines of containment,

[23]The fundamental problem for the Soviet Union and the United States in this area is that there is every reason to suppose that the development of new patterns of outside dominance in Indochina would effectively mean Chinese dominance. The geopolitical features of the area are such that it is much more plausible to foresee a situation in which a Chinese sphere of influence has reemerged than a situation characterized by the predominance of either superpower.

whose origins lie in the development of policies for Europe in the forties and fifties,[24] do not stand the strains of transfer to the Asian subsystem very well.[25] Although there has been in the contemporary period a considerable effort to accomplish this transfer, the effort has so far produced one fundamental ambiguity and a number of unanswered problems. The basic ambiguity stems from the fact that it has never become clear whether the focus of containment in the Asian context falls on the objective of containing China as an emerging great power or on the goal of restraining manifestations of communism in all forms throughout the Asian arena. This ambiguity is a crucial one because the two goals are not only not fully congruent in Asian politics, but also tend to require positions that are seriously incompatible on various specific issues. The fact is, as we have noted, that there are many brands of communism within Asia and that there are, in addition, important differences between most of the Asian brands of communism and the predominant European varieties. In containing China on the basis of power considerations, for example, the United States would have a strong positive interest in supporting the development of a strong and essentially nationalistic political system in the Democratic Republic of Vietnam, whereas this is clearly not the case if the objective is to restrain all forms of communism. Or again, Soviet-American common interests in Asia are increasingly evident from the perspective of the straight-forward political interests of both countries in maintaining a minimally stable balance of power in the Asian subsystem. The growth of these common interests seems far less impressive, though, when filtered through the vestiges of the Communist versus non-Communist pattern of conflict in the global East-West arena.

In addition to this fundamental ambiguity, moreover, containment also runs into several more specific problems when applied to the Asian subsystem. To begin with, the political fluidity of the Asian arena and the absence of any clear geographical demarcations between Communist and non-Communist areas make it almost impossible to develop meaningful blocs or systematic alignments based on the issue of communism in Asia. In addition, the frequent lack of political viability within individual states in the Asian subsystem makes it extraordinarily messy and costly to attempt to meet all manifestations of communism with forceful means. Whereas containment in Europe was largely a matter of constructing international coalitions and clarifying international boundaries, containment in Asia requires very extensive interventions in the internal politics of individual states. These interventions are generally ambiguously related to the basic goal of dealing with the sources of communism and are almost always politically costly in a variety of secondary effects.[26] It is primarily this lack of political viability in individual states, for example, that has led to a number of costly American interventions in Asian politics aimed at propping up dubious non-Communist regimes or at combating Communist-tinged insurgency movements. Finally, communism is only one of a number of important issues in Asian Politics, and it has never acquired the overriding salience that it achieved in the European subsystem during the fifties. For this reason, any set of doctrines that ascribe a dominant role to the issue of communism is apt to produce both serious distortions and political contradictions when applied to the politics of the Asian subsystem.

These ambiguities of the concept of containment are also important in explaining the present American tendency to ascribe to the United States an especially critical balancing role in the Asian subsystem. Here again the key problem is one of conceptual confusion. Insofar as the principal goal is to contain all manifestations of communism in Asia, it is probably true that no country other than the United States will be both able and willing to shoulder major burdens in the Asian subsystem in the foreseeable future. This goal, however, is a highly ambiguous one in any case, both because communism in general is not considered as important an issue by most Asians

---

[24]The classic formulation of this doctrine is the famous article by "X" (George Kennan), "The Sources of Soviet Conduct," *Foreign Affairs*, xxv (July 1947), 566–82.

[25]For some interesting additional points in this area see David Mozingo, "Containment in Asia Reconsidered," *World Politics*, xix (April 1967), 361–77.

[26]These secondary effects range from the costs of a continuing commitment to support a shaky or unpopular regime to detrimental consequences for the reputation of the intervening state in the other subsystems of the overall international system.

as it is by many Americans and because there are so many varieties of communism in the Asian arena that it is exceedingly difficult to generalize about Asian communism, let alone worldwide communism. Insofar as the fundamental goal is to manage power successfully in the Asian subsystem in the face of the emergence of China, it is simply inaccurate to argue that the United States is the only important bulwark of stability. On the contrary, an interesting feature of the current Asian arena is the extent to which the emergence of China is serving as a catalyst in clarifying the common or overlapping interests of a number of powers that have previously been separated by various ideological divergences.

Fifth, the development of a coordinate international subsystem in Asia has produced a number of new types of problems for the management of power in international politics, as well as some new ideas concerning specific regulatory mechanisms. Above all, it is difficult to conceive of any viable procedures for balancing the Asian subsystem in the absence of prominent participation on the part of both superpowers. This is so for a number of reasons including the political fluidity of the Asian arena, the lack of internal viability of many individual participants in the Asian subsystem, the sharpness of specific conflicts arising in this arena, and the extensiveness of the *ad hoc* political interests of both superpowers in the area. From the point of view of managing power, this involvement of the superpowers in Asian politics is currently producing several consequences of interest. On the one hand, it opens up various possibilities for Asian powers to manipulate the interests and the commitments of the superpowers for local purposes. Both Chinas, for example, have successfully played this game in the various confrontations in the Taiwan Strait.[27] And increasingly, both Vietnams in the current struggle in Indochina are acting to lock the two superpowers into the conflict even though it means an actual or potential reduction in their own freedom of action on a number of issues.[28] While this process is sometimes of considerable importance in determining the specific outcomes of local conflicts, it carries with it some important dangers to overall international stability by involving the superpowers in situations of conflict that they are frequently unable to control very precisely.[29] On the other hand, however, this enforced coexistence of the superpowers in the Asian subsystem is increasingly leading to the growth of tacit agreements between these powers in the interests of developing rules for the maintenance of at least minimal stability in the Asian arena. Among other things, this limited and *de facto* coordination between the superpowers seems at present to be generating a new willingness to allow long-delayed processes of political shakedown to occur in a number of Asian states without attempting to exploit them very seriously for cold-war purposes.[30] In this sense, the current political environment in Asia may be considerably more conducive to a process of decisively throwing off the last vestiges of colonialism, in a genuine rather than a formal sense, than was the environment of the late forties and fifties, when the virulence of the cold war operated to freeze matters artificially in such a way that the necessary shakedowns were often prevented from being played out.

Perhaps the most characteristic problems of managing power in the contemporary Asian subsystem are those that arise from situations involving simultaneous and competitive interventions on the part of several outside parties in civil upheavals within individual states. The problem of competitive intervention is peculiarly charac-

---

[27]During the 1958 crisis, activities along these lines were particularly evident in relationships between the People's Republic of China and the Soviet Union on the one hand and between the Nationalists and the United States on the other.

[28]For some interesting points concerning this problem in the Vietnam context, consult John T. McAlister, Jr., "The Possibilities for Diplomacy in Southeast Asia," *World Politics,* xix (January 1967), 258–305.

[29]The possibilities of catalytic actions on the part of the local powers are particularly important. These dangers of catalytic actions do not refer, in the first instance, to nuclear exchanges, but rather to the possibilities of touching off escalatory sequences that are difficult to control.

[30]Many of the Asian states emerged from colonialism with regimes that were highly successful in revolutionary activities but ill-suited to the requirements of creating viable political structures on a long-term basis. Adaptation problems of this kind are, in fact, relatively common in revolutionary situations. And they are an important cause of the continued political ferment that often follows the successful termination of a struggle for independence. In the Asian context, however, independence was gained by a number of states at a time when the bipolar conflict in the overall system placed artificial impediments in the way of this shakedown process. The current political ferment in several Asian states is actually a kind of delayed shakedown process that never occured in the late forties and early fifties.

teristic of Asia, as compared with Europe, in the current period, and it is peculiarly dangerous in the existing international system, given the possibilities of escalation to superpower confrontations and the quality of military technologies available at the strategic level. Though this problem has not yet generated any clear-cut regulatory responses, it has produced some interesting movements in the direction of regulation. As mentioned above, the superpowers are now proceeding with considerable caution, for the most part, in the Asian arena, and they are showing increasing signs of a willingness to coordinate at least tacitly on procedures that will allow for political shakedowns in individual countries without disrupting the stability of the whole subsystem. More specifically, there is at the present time a growing interest in various arrangements of a more formal nature, such as neutralization agreements,[31] designed to allow the various outside parties with an interest in specific situations of internal upheaval to coordinate in setting up for the area a regime designed to prevent competitive intervention while still allowing the various internal forces to prosecute their conflicts in a manner that is as free of artificial impediments as possible.[32] In the final analysis, however, the growth of thinking about the regulation of power along these lines in the Asian subsystem is not important so much for the merits of various specific formulations as for the fact that it constitutes evidence of the development of concepts in this area tailored especially for the Asian problems rather than borrowed from prior experiences in the European subsystem.

CONCLUSION

The discontinuities model discussed in this article has no particular status as a set of answers concerning international politics. On the contrary, it is offered more as a set of concepts designed to generate fruitful insights concerning the changing state of the contemporary international system. And in this sense, it seems to me that the discontinuities model opens up a number of interesting lines of thought and problems for analysis which tend to be overlooked by the bipolar and multipolar models underlying most current debate in this area. It leads, for example, to ideas about a variety of types of complex interpenetration among subsystems each of which is sufficiently *sui generis* that it is impossible to assume direct correspondences among them. In this connection, the trade-offs and possibilities for manipulation across subsystems are particularly interesting in the contemporary world. In addition, the discontinuities model offers some useful perspectives on the problems of the actors with systemwide interests. Such perspectives are particularly useful in understanding current developments in international politics. Inconsistencies in Soviet and American behavior, for example, are far easier to explain when it is understood that both of these countries have patterns of interests that diverge substantially and are not infrequently incompatible with one another as between the various subsystems of the overall international system. The contrasts between the European and Asian subsystems, for example, offer illustrations of these problems.

The introduction of concrete material on the European and Asian subsystems also emphasizes some interesting triangular relationships. Here we have two important subsystems that are increasingly coordinate in their influence patterns, even though there are a number of very significant discontinuities between them. At the same time, the global pattern of relations between the superpowers intersects, at a number of points, with the patterns within each of the subsystems as well as with the interconnections between the two subsystems. As a result, an overall pattern of interaction is formed that contains two distinct classes of discontinuities. In addition to the discontinuities between the two subsystems, there are also discontinuities between the conceptually analogous patterns of international politics within the subsystems on the one hand and the global format

---

[31]For an exploration of the concepts of neutralization see "Neutralization in Southeast Asia: Problems and Prospects," A Study Prepared at the Request of the Committee on Foreign Relations, United States Senate, 89th Cong., 2nd Sess. (Washington 1966). This study was prepared by Cyril E. Black, Richard A. Falk, Klaus Knorr, and Oran Young.

[32]Ideas of this kind have already been tried to a certain extent. Laos, for example, was formally neutralized by

---

international agreement under the terms of the Geneva Convention of 1962. And Cambodia is presently a self-neutralized state whose act of neutralization has been recieved favorably by most of the relevant outside states.

of international politics focusing on the direct relationships between the superpowers on the other hand. Under these circumstances, it is hardly surprising that a substantive issue influenced simultaneously by several of these divergent patterns of international politics is virtually bound to become extremely complex and ambiguous. For example, a considerable degree of the opaqueness of the problems of Germany and of Southeast Asia at the present time is a result of this phenomenon of several distinct patterns of international politics focusing simultaneously on a given complex of substantive issues.

Finally, it is important to emphasize that the· European and Asian problems discussed in this article are, in general terms, illustrative of a broader class of phenomena in contemporary international politics. In short, the relationships between various subsystems as well as between individual subsystems and the global patterns of international politics could be analyzed on a similar basis for such cases as Africa, Latin America, and the Middle East. While the particular substantive problems would vary from case to case, the general perspectives of the discontinuities model are equally relevant throughout the international system. Moreover, a shift from a focus on two subsystems to a consideration of a larger number of subsystems would raise additional questions that could be analyzed profitably. In general, a shift along these lines would open up possibilities for increasingly subtle analyses of the basic power processes of the contemporary international system.

Discussion and Questions

1. ➤ How does the idea of a "subsystem" relate to notions of a "bloc" or "pole"? ➤ What are the boundaries of a particular subsystem? ➤ Is "subsystem" a spatial concept similar to the idea of a "region"?

To some extent Oran Young applies within each subsystem the general notions of "balance" and "stability" that multibloc theorists have applied to their analysis of the global international system.

In Part V, several principal subsystems are examined in more detail.

2. Note Young's concern with avoiding what he calls "segmentation" or "compartmentalization," namely, the tendency to examine an area or region of international society as if it were an autonomous unit that could be detached from the global system for purposes of inquiry. Young insists that the configuration of global relations has a definite set of impacts upon each particular subsystem and that these impacts have not been adequately taken into account by traditional modes of regionalist or internationalist thinking.

Young is also concerned with avoiding the opposite tendency of thought, toward "fusion" or "universalization," whereby distinctions are blurred in a search for overarching explanatory principles. These principles tend to explain conflict by adversary images such as "democracy vs. communism, imperialism vs socialism, or the world city vs. the countryside" (p. 37). Such images are too abstract and draw attention away from the variations among subsystems. Global patterns affect each subsystem differently as a consequence of its distinctive features.

3. ➤ How does Oran Young's presentation of the international system assist our thinking about attainable and preferable systems of world order? ➤ Do we need to evolve subsystemic strategies of transition? ➤ Should the world-order possibil-

ities at the subsystemic level be meshed with those that exist at the global level? ➤ Is it incompatible with Young's mode of analysis to introduce world-order preferences?

4. Young's presentation encourages us also to analyze links between major areas of the world. One argument that is often made is that these linkages disclose the hierarchy of power in world society. Africa, Asia, and Latin America are linked by their economic and political dependence on Europe, the United States, and the Soviet Union, but they are largely unlinked with one another.

3

The Prospects for Order through Regional Security

LYNN H. MILLER

I. INTRODUCTION

Although regional organizations of all descriptions have received the attention of scholars during recent years, most of the best work in this area has been centered either upon problems of transnational integration and community-building or on the "functional" activities of regional associations.[1] Studies dealing specifically with the peace and security role of regional organizations—at

[1] These two foci are, of course, generally considered to be related. Ernst B. Haas has led in the study of the functional integration of regional groupings. See, for example, his "Regionalism, Functionalism, and Universal International Organization," *World Politics*, VIII, 2 (January 1956), 238-63; "International Integration: The European and the Universal Process," *International Organization*, XV, 3 (Summer 1961), 366-92; *Beyond the Nation-State* (Stanford 1964). See also Ben. T. Moore, *NATO and the Future of Europe* (New York 1958), 263 pp. Karl W. Deutsch has made a unique contribution in this area with his elaboration of the idea of the security-community. See Deutsch and others, *Political Community and the North Atlantic Area* (Princeton 1957).

Analyses of particular regional groupings and their activities are much too numerous for an exhaustive listing. Some of the better, recent studies in this category dealing primarily with political aspects might include the following: Inis L. Claude, "The OAS, the UN, and the United States," *International Conciliation*, No. 547 (March 1964); J. Lloyd Mecham, *The United States and Inter-American Security, 1889-1960* (Austin 1961); B. Y. Boutros-Ghali, "The Arab League: 1945-1955," *International Conciliation*, No. 498 (May 1954); Robert W. Macdonald, *The League of Arab States* (Princeton 1965); George Modelski, ed., *SEATO: Six Studies* (Melbourne 1962), 302; M. Margaret Ball, *NATO and the European Union Movement* (London 1959), 486; John C. Dreier, *The Organization of American States and the Hemisphere Crisis* (New York 1962), 147; Charles G. Fenwick, *The Organization of American States: The Inter-American Regional System* (Washington 1963), 601; Jerome Slater, "The United States, The Organization of American States, and the Dominican Republic, 1961-1963," *International Organization*, XVIII, 2 (Spring 1964), 268-91; Zbigniew K. Brzezinski, "The Organization of the Communist Camp," *World Politics*, XIII, 2 (January 1961), 175-209; B. Y. Boutros-Ghali, "The Addis Ababa Charter," *International Conciliation*, No. 546 (January 1964).

least in any generalized fashion—have been fewer.[2] Some commentators on this aspect of regionalism have tended to dichotomize regional and universal approaches to international security in the abstract—usually as a prelude to asserting that the former principle is incompatible with and inferior to the latter for the organization of peace. Often, however, they have not explored satisfactorily the question as to whether or not, or to what extent, the dichotomy actually exists in the practice of states since World War II.

On the other hand, proponents of effective regional organization as a pathway to order have been inclined to dismiss the multilateral treaty organizations of the postwar period as not "genuine" regional agencies of the type accounted for in Chapter VIII of the United Nations Charter. Both views may be essentially correct, but neither seems to take adequate account of the likely effects of regional security activity—through whatever agencies it has been expressed—that has been characteristic of much international conduct during the past twenty years. Empirical analysis that focuses upon this regional security activity, regardless of the instrumentalities used, should provide the base for sounder judgments as to its compatibility with the goals of universal order.

Any attempt to determine the prospects for international order through regional efforts to achieve security must consider two distinct, though clearly related, issues. One is basically a normative concern, i.e., whether or not the regional approach to security characteristic of much current international practice is compatible with the goals of universal order. The other, a problem for empirical analysis, concerns the trends currently operating that can suggest whether the amount and quality of current regional security activity will become either more or less significant in the future.

The approach to be undertaken here will begin by analyzing relevant tendencies discernible in the structure and conduct of international politics during approximately the past twenty years. The

year 1945 is taken as a rough bench mark since the phenomenon of regionalism discussed here is almost exclusively the product of the postwar world. This is not to say, of course, that regional security activity was unknown prior to the war; indeed, as the experience of an earlier period may be seen to have relevance to the behavior of the present or near future, it will be drawn upon. The fact remains, however, that the post-1945 period differs in many fundamental respects from previous eras of political history: bipolarity and bloc politics, the creation of new nation-states out of the ashes of colonial empires, the threat of atomic devastation—these and other factors are essentially new ones in the international system (certainly so in combination). More importantly, they are not factors which can be expected to vanish overnight. They undoubtedly will continue to affect international political structures and behavior for some time into the future. Thus, the first part of the analysis which follows will emphasize the recent historical developments that have helped to shape and alter the parameters of regional security activity. The primary focus of attention will be upon both the changing and the comparatively constant relationships among national actors and international institutions.

Secondly, attention will shift more specifically to the developments in patterns of political behavior and normative standards as they apply to regional security activity. This section, too, is empirical-analytical, but discussion will deal primarily with types and functions of recent regional security activity as seen within the environmental framework presented previously. Finally, extrapolation from those tendencies drawn from analysis of the operation of the international system and those working at present at the regional level in particular then should permit a sketch of the likely security role of regionalism in the future, and, thus, of its potential contribution or noncontribution to international order.

II. POSTWAR POLITICS AND THE ORGANIZATION OF INTERNATIONAL SECURITY

With the close of World War II and the development of plans for a new international organization to replace the defunct League of Nations, there was discussion within the governments of both the

---

[2]The terms "peace and security role" or simply "security role" will be used throughout this chapter to denote (1) the potential of a regional organization, through its peacekeeping machinery or diplomatic techniques, for controlling the forceful settlement of disputes among its own members, and (2) the potential of the organization to present a common military front against an outside actor or actors. Variations in this role are treated more fully in Part III of this discussion.

United States and the United Kingdom as to the principle of order which should be incorporated into the organization's Charter, regionalism or universalism. Although Winston Churchill and Sumner Welles were the two principal spokesmen for the regional security approach, the proposals which emerged from the Dumbarton Oaks conference clearly favored a universal security attempt, somewhat on the pattern of the collective security scheme of the League of Nations. Nonetheless, regional arrangements were granted a rather conditional endorsement on the grounds that they be consistent with the purposes and principles of the universal organization. The draft provided that enforcement action by regional agencies could be taken only with the authorization of the Security Council.

At the San Francisco conference, however, many of the Latin American delegates in particular objected to this clear subordination of regional organizational activity to the UN, presumably on the grounds that it would give an already powerful Security Council even more authority. Such additional authority, too, would be granted by apparently denying permission to small states in regional groupings the chief responsibility for their own security. As the result of these objections, the UN Charter which emerged from the conference contained two provisions that seemed to grant regional organizations somewhat more authority than had been envisaged at Dumbarton Oaks.[3] Yet, in doing so, the prescribed relationship between regional organizations and the United Nations was left somewhat more ambiguous than it had been in the earlier draft proposals. Even so, the implication of Chapter VIII as a whole was relatively clear in its suggestion that even though regional groupings might play a more positive role in the peace and security field than had been anticipated by the leaders of the great powers, still, such activity was meant to be subordinate, in the final analysis, to the directives of the Security Council. On paper, at least, the Charter was far more explicit than the Covenant had been in attempting "to relate the regional organizations to the world organization and to reconcile the principles of universalism and regionalism."[4]

What manner of security system had the framers of the Charter attempted to devise? In their determination to make the Security Council the effective authority of international security, the participants in the San Francisco conference had partially abandoned the "pure" collective security rationale of the League of Nations, but only partially so. As Claude has argued cogently, grant of the veto power to the Council's permanent members ensured that they would be able to prevent any enforcement action being taken against their will. "The veto rule is an explicit declaration that the framers of the Charter rejected the idea of making . . . the United Nations an instrument of collective security in cases involving aggressive action by great powers."[5] Nonetheless, implicit in the international police powers granted the Security Council was the assumption that genuine collective security action could and, no doubt, would be undertaken against any other members guilty of aggressive action. It was in this kind of action that regional arrangements might play an important security role—not as the focal points of great power opposition but as either (a) the agents of universal collective action under the supervision of the Security Council, or (b) the instruments of settlement at the stage of a conflict when the involvement of the entire world community is not required.

The transformation of international politics that followed hard on the heels of the San Francisco conference soon undermined most of the assumptions built into the UN Charter about the way in which peace should be organized in the postwar world. Although most of the changes wrought in the security functions of regional groups can be traced directly to the onset of the cold war, this was not the only factor responsible for altering the structure of world politics. Several

---

[3]First, Article 52 (2) provided that members of regional organizations "shall make every effort to achieve pacific settlement of local disputes through such regional arrangements . . . before referring them to the Security Council." Secondly, the first Article of Chapter VI, dealing with the pacific settlement of disputes, listed the resort to regional arrangements among the other techniques contained in the Dumbarton Oaks proposal which should be explored before resorting to the Security Council (Article 33/1).

[4]Gerhard Bebr, "Regional Organizations: A United Nations Problem," *American Journal of International Law*, XLIX, 2 (April 1955), 168.

[5]Inis L. Claude, Jr., "The United Nations and the Use of Force," *International Conciliation*, No. 532 (March 1961), 329.

rather diverse factors have been at work within the international system since San Francisco to alter the role of regionalism in the ordering process. Although any extraction of certain historical trends as of greater explanatory value than others is in some sense arbitrary, those to be considered here are regarded as of primary importance (a) because of the persisting quality of the political problems they have induced and (b) because of their clear impact upon the conduct of politics in regional groupings.

Bipolarity and International Organization

The chief, immediate consequence of bipolarity for regionalism was the creation of a new kind of regional association in the cold war period, one apparently not anticipated by the framers of the Charter. Beginning with the creation of the North Atlantic Treaty Organization in 1949, several multilateral security organizations came into existence which, while meant to act as "regional" instruments of mutual defense (primarily in the sense that their membership was limited), deliberately avoided describing themselves as "regional arrangements" under the terms of Chapter VIII of the Charter. Instead, their adherence to the principles of the charter was expressed through the provisions of Article 51. That article, included in Chapter VII rather than Chapter VIII of the Charter, guaranteed members "the inherent right of individual or collective self-defense." Adherence to Article 51 was designed to eliminate the control of the Security Council over the responses of regional agencies to armed attack.

This development could be read at first as specifically the Western response to the implacable hostility which now divided them from the Soviet camp. With the permanent membership of the Soviet Union in the Security Council, the West recognized the impossibility of directing regional security activity in their interests through the medium of that UN organ. Thus, Western leaders created three new multilateral pacts during the next several years which could operate outside the scope of Chapter VIII—NATO, SEATO, and the Baghdad Pact (later CENTO).[6] The United States also encouraged the adoption within the OAS, heretofore a regional organization of the type whose relationship to the UN was specified

in Chapter VIII, of a new defense pact for the Organization which likewise invoked Article 51 of the Charter for its authority.[7] But then, in 1950, the Arab League—whose operations like those of the OAS, previously had been accounted for by Chapter VIII of the Charter—also invoked Article 51 in drawing up its collective defense pact.[8] What orginally had been a Western ploy to avoid Soviet involvement in regional security activity in which the Western powers had a stake was adopted by the "original" regional organizations as well, thus altering their legal relationship to the United Nations.

However much the functions of the original regional organizations and the new multilateral security organizations might differ in practice, they could now be regarded as comparable instruments of security in their relationship to the United Nations. The slight ambiguity of the Charter

---

[6]The Baghdad Pact arrangement, which did not include the United States as a member, was the alternative pursued by the West after their suggestion of a Middle East Defense Pact, to be tied to NATO in some way, was summarily rejected by the Egyptians.

[7]Inter-American Treaty of Reciprocal Assistance:

"*Article 2:* As a consequence of the principle set forth in the preceding Article [condemning war], the High Contracting Parties undertake to submit every controversy which may arise between them to methods of peaceful settlement and to endeavor to settle any such controversy among themselves by means of the procedures in force in the Inter-American System before referring it to the General Assembly or the Security Council of the United Nations.

"*Article 3 (1):* The High Contracting Parties agree that an armed attack against an American State shall be considered as an attack against all the American States and, consequently, each one of the said Contracting Parties undertakes to assist in meeting the attack in the exercise of the inherent right of individual or collective self-defense recognized by Article 51 of the Charter of the United Nations."

[8]Macdonald argues, in his *Arab States* that Arab and Latin American delegates at UNCIO had supported the provisions of Article 51 on the assumption that they would be incorporated into Chapter VIII. Then he adds, "inexplicably, the result of the maneuver has been that the original regional organizations . . . and the newer collective-defense organizations . . . both invoked Article 51 and not Article 52 when they drafted their security treaties" (p. 222). Such a move may have been nearly "inexplicable" so far as the Arab League was concerned, but with regard to the Rio Treaty, U.S. membership in the Organization and U.S. leadership of the West in the cold war certainly encouraged the decision to remove the security activity of the OAS from the veto power of the Soviet Union.

regarding the place of the original regional groupings within the UN system was not, thereby,
resolved. On the contrary, that ambiguity was intensified, at least so far as the original regional
groupings were concerned. Now they had set
themselves up as agencies independent of Security
Council control in matters regarding threats to
their security from outside their membership,
while they apparently remained bound by the provisions of Chapter VIII in other activities. This
question of the legal relationship between the regional body and the universal one was to become
further entangled, as will be seen in the next section, when these regional security pacts came to
be applied to peace-threatening action by members of the group.

The development of bipolarity, in addition to
destroying all hope of great power concert, also
served to alter the assumptions present at San
Francisco as to the limited applicability of Coun-
cil-directed collective security measures. Here one
can discern at least three shifts in attitude toward
the utility of universal collective action to maintain the peace in the UN period. The first such
shift took place at the beginning of the cold war,
prior to the clash of arms in Korea in 1950. This
was the period of the formation of NATO, when
the Charter's peace-keeping and enforcement provisions were rather suddenly and widely regarded
as almost totally irrelevant to the political cleavages which had developed among the former Allied powers. The East-West split was seen as so
pervasive that it seemed unlikely that any aggressive action by a lesser power could be taken without cold war ramifications. Even the limited
collective security provisions of the Charter had
assumed that the great powers would have a common interest in preventing aggression by other
states; now however, the tendency was to try to
bring all other states into the spheres of interest
of the superpowers and, thus, to incorporate most
of the world into an area of vital concern to one
or the other of the polar powers. The practicality
of any sort of collective security action was questioned seriously.[9]

In the West, these assumptions as to the potentialities of collective security action were reversed
rather suddenly at the time of UN entry into the
Korean War. In that case, the fortuitous absence
of the Soviet delegate from the Security Council
permitted the Council to undertake a collective
enforcement action somewhat similar in character
(albeit directed against the satellite of a great
power) to that which may have been anticipated
at San Francisco. Even though a single member,
the United States, became the chief agent of the
military operation undertaken in the name of the
organization, it was significant that most other
members were willing to associate themselves with
the official position of the Council. It was recognized that the circumstance which had permitted
Security Council action in Korea would not likely
be repeated. The surge of enthusiasm for collective security which grew in the first weeks of the
UN action soon was expressed in the Uniting for
Peace resolution, which was passed in the General
Assembly in November 1950.[10] The resolution was
intended to restore, insofar as possible, at least an
approximate collective security system to the
UN—this, at any rate, was the gist of many of the
comments favoring passage recorded in the General Assembly at the time.[11] Specifically, of course,
it provided General Assembly action in the event
of Security Council deadlock over a peace-threatening situation. Authorizing the Assembly to designate the aggressor on the basis of a two-thirds
majority vote, the resolution then provided for
collective action—although necessarily on a voluntary basis—somewhat similar to that which the

---

[9]By "collective security," I of course mean the idea
of a universal or nearly universal commitment to thwart
aggression no matter what state undertakes it. See
Claude's excellent discussion of the theoretical suppo-
sitions of Wilsonian collective security in his *Power and
International Relations* (New York 1962). The issue is
confused by the fact that many commentators and
statesmen, particularly in the West, have insisted upon
dubbing the multilateral alliances of the postwar period
"collective security organization." Perhaps they have
done so in the deliberate attempt to cast a greater aura
of legitimacy upon the new arrangements by implying
that they were simply variations on the accepted principle for maintaining peace and security. As Claude has
noted, application of the term to these two very different
approaches to the problem of security has served the
unfortunate purpose of rendering extremely unclear the
original, and essential, principles it was meant to
describe.

[10]"Uniting for Peace" resolution. General Assembly
Resolution 377 (V).

[11]See GAOR: 5th Session, 299th–302nd Plenary Mtgs.,
November 1, 1950–November 3, 1950. See also the address of the President of the General Assembly, Nas-
rollah Entezam, at the 295th Mtg.

Charter had authorized the Council to direct. Growing as it did out of the Korean experience, it was clear that the Uniting for Peace resolution was meant to provide the machinery needed for universal collective action even against a great power involved in a situation of aggression.

This was a step beyond what had been agreed upon at San Francisco, and it soon became clear that the Western powers that sponsored the resolution did so on the assumption that it probably would only come into play to permit collective action against expansionist tendencies of the Communist states.[12] Although the United States, in particular, remained a strong champion of the resolution, it was opposed bitterly by the Soviet Union and her allies. Moreover, as the fighting in Korea dragged on, the enthusiasm for collective security action which had been expressed in the resolution in 1950 gave way to greater feelings of caution and the recurrent, if not strengthened, conviction on the part of many that the United Nations—and perhaps the General Assembly in particular—really was not a very appropriate instrument for enforcement action against the major cold war antagonists. The resolution's suggestion that member states designate military units to be available for future collective security action under the General Assembly was virtually ignored in the aftermath of Korea. Still, even though the Uniting for Peace resolution never became the instrument of organization-wide collective security hoped for by its most ardent supporters, it nonetheless was to remain the effective instrument for greater General Assembly involvement in UN enforcement action in the future. This second phase of predominant UN attitudes toward the utility of collective security, then, was characterized by a temporary commitment to expanding the scope of such action well beyond that thought feasible at San Francisco, followed by an increased reluctance to implement such a scheme very effectively.

A third shift in attitude and practice orginated, perhaps, in the UN action surrounding the creation of UNEF at the time of the Suez crisis in 1956. That case, and several since then, have illustrated a UN approach to peace and security matters that constitutes a rather novel adaptation of collective security theory to deal with one type of threat to the peace that is characterisic of the loose bipolar period. In the Suez affair—as later in the Congo and in Cyprus—UN intervention took the form of sending in an international military contingent, not to wage war on behalf of the international community against a designated "aggressor," but to try to stabilize a troubled political situation and ward off countervailing interventions by outside great powers. In 1960, Dag Hammarskjold described the rationale for UN action of this sort which would attempt to localize conflicts before they became entrenched within an inflamed cold war context, labeling such a role "preventive diplomacy."[13] As Claude has noted, preventive diplomacy "was conceived by Hammarskjold as an international version of the policy of containment, designed not to restrict the expansion of one bloc or the other, but to restrict the expansion of the zone permeated by bloc conflicts; it was put forward as a means for containment of the cold war."[14] The evident difficulties of the attempt to make this conception of the role of the UN fit the intricacies of the Congolese situation—especially in its later phases—must be granted. Nonetheless, there was a growing awareness by the 1960's that it was precisely this kind of UN action, whereby the organization became involved in a situation to prevent a dangerous confrontation, which was essential to international security.

Preventive diplomacy, in containing the cold war, thereby helps to stabilize and perhaps even encourage neutralism on the part of states not members of the polar blocs. Moreover, at the operational level, it must rely upon the political support of neutrals to be effective. As a partial theory of international security, it has both contributed to and been based upon the growing respectability of neutralism in the postwar period. Thus, it is not bipolarity in its early cold war manifestation—a period characterized in the West by the Dulles strictures against neutralism—that gave rise to the preventive diplomatic role for the United Nations; rather, that role has been made possible in

---

[12]See Claude's discussion of the Western rationale behind the Uniting for Peace Resolution in his "The United Nations and the Use of Force," *International Conciliation*, No. 532 (March 1961), 361.

[13]*Introduction to the Annual Report of the Secretary-General on the Work of the Organization, 16 June 1959-15 June 1960*, GAOR: Fifteenth Session, Supplement No. 1A (A/4390/Add. 1).

[14]Inis L. Claude, Jr., *Swords into Plowshares*, 3rd rev. edn. (New York 1964), 286.

the period of superpower stalemate and the growth in the number of national adherents to an uncommitted position in the cold war contest. Although by no means all of the conditions of bipolarity had been eliminated by the late 1960's, the structure of international politics was once more in the process of change.

I leave to the next section a consideration of the extent to which this shifting emphasis upon ways to stabilize the conditions of loose bipolarity has been paralleled in the security action of regional organizations. First, it is necessary to consider the impact of other factors at work in the postwar international system upon the security role of regionalism.

Nuclear Technology

Until the current period, most of the impact of nuclear technology upon international politics could be subsumed under that of bipolarity. Since the U.S. and Soviet arsenals of atomic and nuclear weapons were the only ones that were competitive from the point of view of their military or deterrent quality, these capabilities of the superpowers simply contributed to the bipolarity of the international political structure. More precisely, even in the period before Soviet nuclear strength came to match that of the United States, the effective monopoly over the use of atomic and nuclear weapons that each of the superpowers possessed within its own bloc had far-reaching consequences both within and outside their spheres of interest. (1) Within each bloc, this effective monopoly of the ultimate instruments of warfare produced a *de facto* dependence of their middle and small power allies upon the two atomic giants that called into question their very sovereignty as independent states. It is true that the effect of nuclear monopoly was considerably less compelling within the Soviet bloc than in the West because of Moscow's political control over the governments of the satellite states; indeed, some of the Eastern European states have somewhat increased their freedom to maneuver as Moscow's nuclear strength has grown. Nonetheless, they remain dependent upon the Soviet Union for large-scale military protection and vulnerable to Soviet military encroachment. In the Atlantic area, however, where no overt attempt has been made by the United

States to abridge the sovereignty of its allies, the nuclear weapons issue is more clearly the chief source of the radically altered political relationships among this group of states.

When the North Atlantic Treaty came into being, it constituted primarily a unilateral guarantee by the United States to oppose the destruction of the weakened nations of Western Europe by the powerful Soviet army. Because of their vastly inferior strength vis-à-vis the Soviet bloc even in this early period before the Soviet Union developed its own atomic capacity, it is questionable whether the Western European nations were faced with a rational alternative to an alliance with the United States. Since America was the only power capable of restraining the imperialistic tendencies of the Soviet Union, and because opposition to Soviet expansion was the only means perceived as leading to the avoidance of conquest by the Soviet army, an alliance with the United States became the goal of Western European governments. It was felt on both sides of the Atlantic that only by binding the United States to aid the Europeans in their defense through such an alliance could Europe safely count on U.S. support. Unable to foresee the long-range implications of deterrence for the alliance structure, however, the basic assumption of the NATO members was that they could cooperate on European military matters while maintaining, indeed, strengthening, their independent political systems.

In fact, however, almost from the beginning, NATO's deterrence goal demanded the creation of extensive organizational machinery. Whether or not these organizational structures that developed were the most important distinguishing feature of the new alliance, the fact that they were required as a matter of course if the business of the alliance were to be done served to indicate something of the alterations that had taken place in the security sphere of the changed international system.[15] As was recognized generally at the time

---

[15]NATO's purpose "is that of defending Western Europe's independence without any resort to war. NATO will fail in its fundamental purpose at the moment the nuclear war comes to Europe . . . ," Norman A. Graebner, "Alliances and Free World Security," *Current History*, xxxviii, 224 (April 1960), 216. But the credibility of the U.S. deterrent as applied to the NATO area depends upon the creation of devices making retaliation to an attack on any member state as

of NATO's creation, the new alliance differed radically from the general pattern of alliances of the pre-war period in the matter of its ideological unity. With the creation of NATO, the operation of the classic balance of power principle upon alliance formation and behavior seemed an impossibility for the foreseeable future. Two implacably hostile groups of states now confronted each other, each avowing its own peaceful intentions and the defensive qualities of its alliance, but both sides showing a considerable desire to see the enemy grouping eliminated.[16] In short, the complex *organizational* structure characteristic of NATO could be regarded as the consequence of the loose bipolar system that had emerged, combined with the deterrent requirements of the atomic age.

Yet neither in NATO nor in NATO's alliance counterparts in other areas of the world was the complex organizational structure ever transformed into an integrated unit.[17] Only one member state had the "sovereign" capability to undertake effective nuclear warfare; its allies have been forced to rely, for the most part, upon that power's professed intentions to defend the alliance, and have not acquired an institutionalized guarantee that such a decision will be made. The nuclear factor set in an organizational context has made it nearly impossible for alliance members to calculate with reasonable accuracy what could be expected from its partners in the event of an enemy attack. The issue was stated unequivocally by

Hans Morgenthau when he insisted that "the availability of nuclear weapons to the United States and the Soviet Union has administered a death blow to the Atlantic Alliance, as it has to all alliances. . . . In the prenuclear age a powerful nation could be expected to come to the aid of a weak ally provided its interests were sufficiently involved, risking at worst defeat in war, the loss of an army or of territory. But no nation can be relied upon to forfeit its own existence for the sake of another."[18] One logical response to this dilemma has been that characterized by de Gaulle's *force de frappe*, which attempts the restoration of national military "sovereignty" in an atomic age. An alternative response would be the genuine transformation of the NATO organization into a supranational military authority—an alternative which had not been effectively dealt with in NATO circles before General de Gaulle's growing challenge to the alliance in 1965 and 1966.

Although it is NATO which exemplifies, *par excellence*, the challenge wrought by nuclear deterrence upon regional alliance organizations at the present time, that challenge lurks in the background in the other regional groupings in which the United States is a member as well. Neither in SEATO nor the OAS have the members consistently perceived a real Soviet atomic threat to the territories concerned in anything like the degree to which NATO members were preoccupied throughout with this threat during the 1950's. Moreover, neither the Latin American states in the OAS nor the smaller Asian members of SEATO were in the position a decade ago, in con-

---

nearly automatic as possible. Since the raison d'être of NATO is to deter aggression against the members, rather than to "defend" the territory in traditional terms once hostilities have broken out, the advance planning on the part of the alliance members requires altogether more complex a multilateral arrangement than did "defensive" alliances in the pre-atomic period. Most simply put, in the absence of a need to fight together once nuclear war breaks out, there is a greater impetus to work together to provide an effective deterrent force.

[16]Of the numerous statements—both official and unofficial—indicating the hostility on both sides of the Iron Curtain at the time of the creation of NATO, reports in the Soviet and American press of the time probably were most vitriolic.

[17]Although there has long been talk in NATO of the "integrated command structure" of the alliance, this does not mean, of course, that ultimate authority over use of nuclear weapons has been "integrated." By "integrated unit," then, I mean a genuinely supranational military body.

[18]Hans J. Morgenthau, "The Crisis in the Western Alliance," *Commentary*, xxv, 3 (March 1963), 187. Clearly, this view of Morgenthau's as to the obsolescence of all alliances is not one that he has developed fully in his writings. Elsewhere, his observations on alliances reveal a bias in favor of alliance formation and alliance policy that conforms to a balance of power international system (cf. his "Alliances in Theory and Practice," Arnold Wolfer, ed., *Alliance Policy in the Cold War*), and he pays little attention to any systemic changes that may have taken place as the result of a nuclear technology. The implication of the *Commentary* article—which analyzes the rationale of the French *force de frappe*—is that the "proper" response to this problem today is the abandonment of alliance for the construction of national independent nuclear arsenals, rather than the military integration of the alliance to restore calculability to military policy without encouraging nuclear proliferation.

trast to some Western European states, to develop even limited atomic capabilities of their own. Nonetheless, when Soviet missiles were emplaced in Cuba in October 1962, Latin American acquiescence in the demands of the United States that they be removed was clear indication of the total dependence of these states upon U.S. policy where nuclear issues were involved.

Outside the spheres of interest of the two super- powers, two regional security organizations exist, none of whose members possess atomic weapons. In both the Arab League and the Organization of African Unity the tendency developed (and in fact was made explicit in the OAU's Charter[19]) to make the organization a vehicle for preventing the intrusion of the cold war into the area. Such a policy was both demanded and made possible by the fact that no member states had access to atomic or nuclear weapons. But this nonatomic status of all the members may also have contributed to the capacity of those members to oppose each other. Thus, it may have made more difficult the creation of an effective police power to seal off the area from outside interference. Nonetheless, this "containment" role for the Arab League and, a bit later, the OAU developed perceptibly in the late 1950's as the theory and practice of "preventive diplomacy" grew within the United Nations. The role just ascribed to the Arab League and the OAU is clearly a concomitant of preventive diplomacy from the regional perspective—a fact with important inplications for world order.

The Rise of New States

The growth of regionalism in the uncommitted areas of the world was, of course, made possible by the achievement of national independence in many regions long under the colonial domination of European powers. Two points need to be made in this connection. First, both the Arab League and the OAU could be described at least to some extent as vehicles for the solidification of national independence within the region as well as instruments of cooperation and regional order. Thus, al-

most since its inception, Arab League policy has been directed toward abetting the national independence movement of Arab regions still under the domination of foreign powers.[20] Similarly, the OAU Charter looks to the liberation of the remaining African colonies as one of the fundamental aims of the organization.[21] As the case of Kuwait within the Arab League indicated, this policy may be as much the result of rivalries among the membership (and their corresponding unwillingness to permit one power to annex a new territory at the expense of other members) as it is the product of an abstract dedication to the right of self-determination. Nonetheless, one result of the policy has been to emphasize the form of the grouping as the instrument of *national independence* rather than of *regional integration*.

Secondly, as the anticolonial movement has come to fruition throughout most of the world, the "neo-colonial" rationale of a continued Western hegemony in SEATO and CENTO has become increasingly less acceptable. Since nonalignment on cold war issues has become virtually the official doctrine of the new states, the continued alignment of a few Asian states with the Western powers in these two organizations now appears somewhat anachronistic; not simply to leaders of the third world, I would suggest, but even within Western circles.[22] Even at the time of the Iraqi-Turkish alignment in the Baghdad Pact, the move was so ill-received in the rest of the Arab world

---

[19]Article III of the Charter of the Organization of African Unity lists the "principles" of the Organization, the last of which reads "affirmation of a policy of non-alignment with regard to all blocs."

[20]Cf. Macdonald, *Arab States*, 94–96.

[21]The Charter's preamble includes affirmation of the conviction "that it is the inalienable right of all people to control their own destiny," adding that the signatories are "determined to safeguard and consolidate the hard-won independence as well as the sovereignty and territorial integrity of our States, and to resist neo-colonialism in all its forms." Under Article II, the "purposes" of the Charter include those of promoting "the unity and solidarity of the African and Malagasy States," and eradication of "all forms of colonialism from the continent of Africa." Finally, one of the Organization's "principles" is listed (Article III) as "absolute dedication to the total emancipation of the African territories which are still dependent."

[22]Any number of American commentators have taken this line in recent years. Typical is an article by C. L. Sulzberger in the *New York Times,* June 3, 1964, which criticizes the Dulles conception of SEATO as an extension of Western influence and protection into Southeast Asia: "SEATO was a classic example of closing the barn door on a missing horse. In this case the horse was the Anglo-French empire. SEATO was written on the

as to make Iraq something of a pariah within the membership until a *coup d'état* in that country brought Iraq's withdrawal from the Pact. Within SEATO it appears that only Thailand and the Philippines, of the Asian membership, remain generally willing to accept the anti-Communist orientation of the Pact.

Trans-National Integration Movements

Although this study attempts to focus on regional organization rather than regional integration, the two phenomena are inextricably linked in some respects at the empirical level. First, it seems clear that because integration movements have been relatively powerful throughout most of the postwar period, this process has served especially in Europe as a parallel legitimizing norm for the development of regional organization in the peace and security area. Although a maze of contradictory purposes and programs with unexplained and perhaps unintended ramifications has so far inhibited the development of an integrated community in the North Atlantic area, there can be little doubt but that the integrative aspirations of many leaders within this area have helped to make acceptable (in their own eyes as well as those of their followers) the growth and development of NATO. For them the North Atlantic alliance has been not simply a coalition of powers whose only function is a firm military posture in the bloc politics of the cold war but rather an instrument providing for the military and political integration of the member states. The current challenge of de Gaulle, as already indicated, has brought into sharp relief the contradictions inherent in lip service to community-building and policy that is organizationally oriented. Still, the fact that an inchoate integrative aspiration lay behind the work of the alliance has helped make it appear as a legitimate instrument of regional order to those disinclined to look with favor upon the creation of a limited-member alliance.

assumption of British and French armed strength that didn't exist. . . .

"During the pactomania phase of American policymaking, we allowed ourselves to be deceived by shadowy illusions. We believed such organizations as SEATO and CENTO were realities, but they weren't. . . ."

On the other hand, the ideal of integration sometimes has served to inhibit realistic assessments of the utility of the multilateral organization as an end in itself. This seems to be at least as true in the case of the Arab League as it is with NATO (and it is within these two regional security organizations that the integrative aspiration most often is verbalized). Although it is easy to show that in both cases the constitutional document provides for an international organization and not a supranational community, nevertheless, both organizations sometimes are criticized by integrationists for not having accomplished what apparently they were not intended to accomplish. This would be largely irrelevant to the questions under investigation here except that it may help to focus upon a real issue for regional international organization in the current period—an issue already touched upon in the discussion of the impact of nuclear weapons: Is the organizational level within a region a practicable stopping place in the quest for security once the decision has been made (presumably for practical security reasons) to move beyond the principle of national self-sufficiency for the protection of desired values? If the current experience of NATO is now indicating that the return to national self-sufficiency appears a more practical alternative in some cases, it also must point up the impossibility of such a move—at least for the short run—for states that do not possess the resources for a large military establishment even in conventional terms. Otherwise put, the question at issue is whether or not the organizational dynamic is sufficient to provide the security demanded by member states (and this may entail security from other members as well as from external actors, it should be remembered), or whether and to what extent regional organization must be regarded as necessarily a temporary, half-way house between national independence and supranational integration.

III. THE DYNAMICS OF REGIONAL ORGANIZATION

One of the premises of this study is that the multilateral alliances of the postwar period have been as deeply involved, in some respects, in regional security activity as the "original" regional organizations that were treated in Chapter VIII of the UN Charter. Now, however, it will be useful to distinguish the security roles of these two types of organizations somewhat more clearly than was done in the previous section. This is not a distinction which can be made fruitfully solely on the bases of the differences in authoritative structures of each type of grouping; yet, such an examination can indicate the general *security orientation* of the grouping. Then it will be necessary to consider differences in types of *security activities*, which may or may not coincide with the group's distinctive orientation.

Original Regional Organizations[23]

Here are included those organizations which have arisen as the expression of some sort of regional solidarity vis-à-vis the outside world, and which possess the machinery, at least in embryo, to maintain security within their own region. In the most fully developed of these groups, the OAS, the machinery involved permits both (1) the settlement of disputes among member states, and (2) the development of a common policy in the face of intervention from outside the region. For the other two groupings which fall into this regional type (the Organization of African Unity and the Arab League), the provisions for settlement of intra-member disputes are less fully developed than are those for the second provision above. Characteristic of this group, however, is the fact that they are not alliances in the traditional sense, but are "ostensibly more permanent groups whose professed first aim is to keep the peace within a given area."[24] Their raison d'être, then, springs from territorial unity, made coherent by at least a modicum of recognized ideological or ethnic common ground.

In groupings of this type, the desire to maintain security among the members seems to have been the chief impetus to the creation of the organization. Thus, both the legal structures and political practice are likely to emphasize the aspect of the state actor-in-organization. Moreover, the language of Chapter VIII of the UN Charter seems to assume that the proper security activities of regional associations would be confined to issues involving conflicts among the member states.[25] Still as indicated above, both the OAS and the Arab League took steps in the years after the San Francisco conference to strengthen the security role of the organization-as-actor.[26] At the diplomatic level, all three of these groupings have experienced some measure of effectiveness in the elaboration of organizational policy vis-à-vis external actors. Thus, the primary orientation of these organizations toward the resolution of intra-group conflicts has been counterbalanced somewhat in practice through the elaboration of a more important role for the organization-as-actor.

Regional Alliance Organizations

This type of regional grouping includes many of the alliances of the postwar world, such as NATO, the Warsaw Pact, SEATO, and CENTO. The treaty arrangements containing a common defense pledge that do not fall within this category are those which are bilateral and not multilateral. These lack the so-called permanent institutions of the multilateral arrangements, such as secretariats, councils, and the like, and generally make no provisions at all for a coordination of military policy prior to outright military involvement with a third power. As to the multilateral arrangements which can be classed as regional organizations, however,

---

[23]This is a shorthand phrase to denote the kind of regional organization in existence at the time the UN Charter was adopted and, thus, the type referred to in Chapter VIII of the Charter. The term is, of course, misleading if taken literally, since one extant organization of this type—the OAU—was not "original" in the sense that it existed when Chapter VIII was written. Rather, it is regarded as "original" because it is basically like the OAS and the Arab League in its conception.

[24]Peter Calvocoressi, *World Order and New States* (New York 1962), 59.

[25]Cf. Article 52 (2): "The Members . . . entering into such [regional] arrangements . . . shall make every effort to achieve pacific settlement of local disputes through such regional arrangements . . . before referring them to the Security Council."

It is true that the discussion in Article 53 (1) of measures which may be taken by a regional agency against former enemy states seems to reveal that the organization may deal as a single actor with external threats to its members. Nevertheless, the main thrust of the chapter's provisions is in the direction of internally directed security action.

[26]See notes 7 and 8 above.

their very strong emphasis has been upon united organization-wide policy—especially military policy—in the face of challenges from external actors. These are "outer-directed" associations which came into being expressly as the result of a felt threat from a common external enemy, and their concern with the intra-organizational relations of the members is largely subsumed within their concern for developing an effective security role for the organization-as-actor.

The external orientation of regional alliance organizations was, at the time of their creation, considerably more dominant than was the internal orientation of the original regional groupings. Nor has the emphasis shifted back toward the other security orientation as strongly in the alliance groupings as in the original organizations. Nonetheless, and particularly as disagreement has grown among the members of alliance groupings as to the nature and quality of the external threat to the region, the attention of the members inevitably has turned in greater measure to use of the organization to help resolve these issues which divide them. In both types of regional organizations some attempt has been made to ensure the inviolability of the area of jurisdiction in security issues.[27] In other words, the tendency in all regional security organizations has been to attempt to make the regional agency the primary, if not the only, authoritative structure for dealing with security issues in the area. Thus, both types of organizations have had to deal with internally divisive issues as well as with external challenges to regional security.

Hegemonial Action and "Good Neighborliness"

Turning next to a consideration of types of security activities engaged in by regional groupings, the crucially important distinctions in practice correspond roughly to the dual view of regional-

ism that has long been characteristic of the literature on the subject. On the one hand, most commentators who have looked with favor upon the regional approach to security have described a regionalism wherein motivation for common action arises out of mutual interest in the problems of the area and from a recognition of the value of good neighborliness. This is the sort of regionalism that might emerge as the logical extension of the provisions on the subject in the UN Charter, where the attempt is made to demonstrate the way in which the regional and universal organizations can work together harmoniously—each in its proper sphere. On the other hand, other commentators clearly have regarded the regional approach to security with disfavor, suggesting that such activity is in fact detrimental to international order. Clearly, however, what they have had in mind is the use of regionalism either as a means of asserting the hegemonic domination of a major power, or as a feeble attempt on the part of small-power neighbors to forestall or regulate such domination. According to the extreme form of this view, regionalism "is the establishment of the paramountcy of a Great Power in a defined geographical region."[28]

In fact, of course, both views of regional security activity are partially accurate perceptions of reality; all existing regional security organizations would seem to contain elements of both kinds of activities. Although it appears that the regional alliance organizations in particular were conceived as instruments for making explicit the hegemony of a great power in a specific geographical region, this aim has not been entirely absent in the formation of the original regional groupings. The dominant role of the United States within the OAS is perhaps the clearest example in groupings of this type, but in the Arab League, the Egyptian desire for leadership of the Arab states—and the continuing opposition of successive Iraqi governments to a dominant Egyptian role—also illustrates the he-

---

[27]However, the U.S. reservation to its adherence to the SEATO Pact—that would undertake to defend the territory of the Southeast Asian members and protocol states only in the event of *Communist* aggression—underscores the limitations, and perhaps the ambiguity, of the SEATO security role in the area. Since the function of the organization-as-actor has always been somewhat less clear than in the case of NATO, it is reasonable to sup-

pose, not only that the actors-in-organization role may have suffered in consequence, but also that there is less than total agreement among the members as to making SEATO the sole authoritative structure for dealing with security issues in the area.

[28]K. M. Panikkar, "Regionalism and World Security." in Panikkar and others *Regionalism and Security* (Bombay 1948), 1.

gemonic principle in a regional organization.[29] Moreover, in the Organization of African Unity, even though no single member has yet established itself as the dominant or decisive force in organizational affairs, it seems clear that several statesmen with ambitions of Pan-African unity under their leadership concluded that such aspirations could be pursued more effectively through the creation of an African organization.

At the risk of oversimplifying the complex varieties of relationships among states members of the various regional organizations, it can be said that the real dynamic in effective regional security activity is provided by the coexistence within each grouping of the opposing tendencies of "good neighborliness" on the one hand, and the hegemonic domination of the region by a powerful member on the other. This is not to say, of course, that these dual tendencies are contained in effective balance in all existing regional associations; rather it suggests that in each such grouping members must continually come to terms with both demands if the organization is to function effectively as an instrument of security and regional order. Generally it has been appreciated that regional stress on "good neighborliness," i.e., upon the actors-in-organization, is conducive to the settlement of international disputes on a basis of cooperation rather than coercion. Ideally, the equal rights of participating states are emphasized and just settlements are the product of a mutual willingness to accept those rights. It is less often acknowledged, however, that in practice such emphasis may lead, not to cooperation but to fragmentation, and not to just settlements so much as anarchy. Thus, the inclination toward hegemonic domination of a regional grouping, i.e., toward stress upon the organization-as-actor, may be a necessary antidote to fragmentation. Moreover, when external considerations are included, the tendency toward hegemony on a regional organization basis is at least useful in delimiting spheres of great power interest.

This analysis suggests that a "proper" balance must be maintained in each regional grouping between these dual tendencies (a) to dwell upon security issues among the members at the expense of effective concerted policy, and (b) to make the

regional institution an instrument of the hegemony of one powerful member. Where the emphasis becomes wholly one-sided, it seems to be impossible to maintain the organization as a viable agent of security even for the limited purposes proclaimed for it. For example, when CENTO and SEATO were created, their emphasis was almost exclusively upon the organization-as-actor. Western powers sought to solidify their spheres of influence, thereby making clear to their opponents that these areas of the Middle East and Southeast Asia constituted legitimate regions of Western hegemony. The refusal of neighboring states in these areas to join these alliances cast doubt upon the assertions of the Western powers from the beginning. Still, had it been possible (not that it was even seriously attempted) to make of these organizations instruments for the settlement of regional problems, these organizations might, over time, have solidified Western ties to these areas, thereby making credible the assertion of Western hegemony. Instead, in ignoring the possibilities of these groupings in the area of intra-regional security, the Western powers involved found their claims to hegemony regarded as increasingly tenuous: by the 1960's CENTO was nearly moribund and SEATO was almost without credibility as an effective anti-Communist alliance.

In NATO, a one-sided emphasis upon the organization's security role did not have such drastic short-range consequences because the claim of a community of interest binding these member states together was perceived both by participants and by many non-participants as a legitimate claim. With NATO at the very core of the Western bloc, the issue seemed less one of extending Western hegemony than of consolidating Western interests, and those interests, for the most part, were conceived as sufficiently strong as to make unnecessary concern with intra-group security. Even so, by the 1960's NATO's role as the instrument of organization-wide security was threatened seriously by fissures within the membership. Although it may be questioned that an *organizational* approach (as opposed to an integrational one) to intra-regional cooperation and conflict resolution could have resolved the issues of military independence which threaten to split the alliance, still, such an added emphasis

---

[29]Macdonald, *Arab States*, 74–82.

from the beginning might have laid the groundwork for greater political unity when the external threat to the area was seen to be diminishing. In the most serious war-threatening issue to divide the members of NATO—the Cypriote conflict, particularly as it was rekindled in 1963–1964—the attempt to make NATO the instrument of regional order was challenged successfully by Archbishop Makarios and Premier Khrushchev, and the issue was turned over to the United Nations.[30] It could be argued, of course, that even had NATO had a record of intra-regional security practice of this type, the option of UN treatment would have remained open. Indeed, it would have, but the experience of the OAS shows that where this type of security role is firmly established, the regional organization is likely to maintain its claim to jurisdiction.

On the other hand, the "original" regional groupings—with their clearer orientation toward the actors-in-organization—have managed to survive the strains of intra-regional conflict, and even to ameliorate it in some cases, while in the process they have developed a framework for common organizational policy. The experience of the Arab League is perhaps most illustrative here. Polarization of power between Egypt and Iraq has afflicted the League since its inception, preventing the effective cooperation of League members on mutual problems in many cases. Of the major recurring issues which confront the League, these two Arab states have been generally in agreement only in their opposition to rapprochement with Israel.[31] In spite of the inability of either state to establish its hegemony over the organization, however, the Arab states have joined increasingly in playing an identifiable role vis-à-vis external actors. The League has consistently supported the independence movements of the Arab territories in North Africa, has caucused and voted *en bloc* in the United Nations, and while under the leadership of Egypt's President Nasser,

the policy of Arab nonalignment with the cold war blocs has been accepted widely.[32] While lip service still is paid to the idea of Arab political unity, intra-Arab rivalry continues to prevent any real progress in this respect. More significantly, however, this rivalry has been channeled through the organizational framework successfully enough to ensure the solidification of Arab independence movements and the growth in strength of an Arab bloc, as opposed to an Arab state.

The OAS is the only "original" regional organization to have one of the superpowers as a member. Yet in spite of the overwhelmingly dominant role of the United States in the Americas (or rather, perhaps, because of it), the actors-in-organization aspect of the grouping remains strong and important. In fact, most of the history of regional organization in this hemisphere can be read as the continuing attempt of the Latin American states to secure U.S. adherence to standards of nonintervention and noninterference in political affairs south of the Rio Grande, and, conversely, of the continuing U.S. attempt to make the inter-American organization a vehicle for the assertion of North American hegemony. U.S. acceptance of the nonintervention doctrine by the 1930's undoubtedly encouraged Latin American statesmen to champion the cause of the organization at San Francisco; they were persuaded that it was now "their" organization, in large measure, and that it could be utilized to prevent the arbitrary intrusion both of the United States and of other great powers into Latin American affairs. In the context of the cold war, however, the United States set about the task of utilizing the reorganized regional organization to attempt to strengthen the U.S. hold on the Western hemisphere. If U.S. hegemony in the area could no longer be exercised effectively by means of "Big Stick" diplomacy, it could, nonetheless, be maintained by upholding OAS primacy in hemispheric security, where U.S. policy demands almost always could be made to prevail. Thus, within a few years after San Francisco, Latin and U.S. roles were nearly reversed, and the United States took the lead in insisting upon the right of OAS primary jurisdiction in all inter-American disputes.

---

[30]See the *New York Times*, January 27–February 9, 1964. Considered in terms of spheres of influence, the outcome of the jurisdictional issue in the Cyprus case marked an indication on the part of Britain and the United States that, in acquiescing in UN action there, they no longer would regard Cyprus as coming under the protective umbrella of NATO.

[31]Macdonald, *Arab States*, 84–85.

---

[32][Macdonald, *Arab States*,] 105–18.

Secondly, and concurrently, the United States urged the elaboration of a more clear-cut organization-as-actor role for the OAS—specifically, one which would transform the organization into an anti-Soviet coalition. For a time in the 1950's, the United States seemed to be succeeding in this attempt almost entirely to the neglect of hemispheric problems and Latin American interests. The Caracas Declaration of 1954 was conceived as the chief instrument for exorcising Communism from the hemisphere, and was prompted specifically by the fact that a left-leaning government had come to power in Guatemala.[33] In the end, however, the United States chose to take covert unilateral action to secure the ouster of the Arbenz regime, and as a result, was hard-pressed to secure the support of the Latin Americans and of its other allies in insisting upon the right of the OAS to deal with the Guatemalan issue.[34] In effect, the attempt by the United States to assert the autonomy of the regional grouping was read by many as a subterfuge for what appeared to entail the unilateral accomplishment of U.S. policy goals through the guise of a multilateral agency.

In the years since the Guatemalan crisis, the United States has worked somewhat more assiduously to encourage development of the principle of collective intervention in the Americas for purposes of promoting democratic goals, thereby attempting to escape the onus of a thinly disguised unilateralism. The relatively democratic Latin American governments generally have been most willing to elaborate such a doctrine, for they have recognized increasingly that it is dictatorial regimes which have had the most to gain from a rigid doctrine of nonintervention.[35] U.S. support and even leadership of the OAS intervention in the Dominican Republic in 1960 and 1961—a policy urged on the OAS by certain Latin statesmen following Generalissimo Trujillo's attempted assassination of Betancourt of Venezuela—provided the United States with an effective *quid pro quo* for Latin American support of the U.S. demand to isolate the Castro government in hemispheric affairs. These two operations mark what have been perhaps the most effective multilateral interventionary actions undertaken in the spirit of organization-wide cooperation.[36] When, in 1965, the United States government again reverted to unilateral action in sending the Marines into the Dominican Republic, it was faced once again with the considerable reluctance of most Latin American governments to endorse such a move. Again, U.S. officials were reminded

---

[33]John C. Dreier, *The Organization of American States and the Hemisphere Crisis* (New York 1962), 53. See also C. Neale Ronning's discussion of the Caracas Resolution in similar terms in his article, "Intervention, International Law, and the Inter-American System," *Journal of Inter-American Studies*, III, 2 (April 1961), 249–71. An ironic element of the Caracas Declaration was, however, as Dreier has pointed out, that by stipulating that the "domination or control" of the "political institutions" of an American state by the Communists was the prerequisite to OAS action, it actually may have made such action under its terms more difficult by requiring proof of Communist domination.

[34]SCOR: 9th Yr., 671st–686th Mtgs. In the Security Council debate over the jurisdiction issue, only two states—Colombia and Turkey—were willing to back the U.S. unequivocally in its contention that the Security Council need not endorse OAS consideration of the case before such action could be regarded as legal under the terms of the Charter. Of the other states which voted with the U.S. in opposing the adoption of the agenda, the Brazilian delegate implied that the Council might take action once it had heard a report from the Inter-American Peace Committee.

[35]Jerome Slater, "The United States, the Organization of American States and the Dominican Republic, 1961–1963," *International Organization*, XVIII, 2 (Spring 1964), 287, gives evidence of these differences in attitude among Latin American elites.

[36]Definitive action against the Castro regime was taken finally at the Eighth Meeting of Consultation of Ministers of Foreign Affairs of the OAS at Punta del Este, Uruguay, from January 22 to 31, 1962. As reported in *International Organization*, XVI, 3 (Summer 1962), 654–55:

> After many consultations, conferences, private meetings . . . and compromises, the foreign ministers adopted seven main resolutions. (1) The adherence of any member of the OAS to Marxism-Leninism was incompatible with the . . . American system . . ; the vote was 20 for, 1 against (Cuba), no abstentions. (2) On the grounds of the first point, the present Cuban regime was incompatible with the principles and objectives of the inter-American system; the vote was 20 for, 1 against (Cuba), no abstentions. (3) Such incompatibility excluded Cuba from participation in the inter-American system, and the OAS was instructed to adopt . . . the measures required to put this resolution into effect; the vote was 14 for, 1 against (Cuba), and 6 abstentions (Argentina, Bolivia, Brazil, Chile, Ecuador and Mexico). The exclusion of Cuba had to be referred to the OAS Council . . . before being put into effect. The six abstaining delegations . . . took their action on the

almost immediately of the deficiencies of uni- lateral intervention of this kind, and, as in the case of Guatemala, experienced difficulty in trans- lating that action into one that was ostensibly regional in scope.

In sum, the two contrasting concerns of re- gional security are visible most clearly within the OAS. There, experience has indicated that the two approaches are not, or need not be, mutually exclusive ones, that, in fact, their healthy coex- istence gives the regional organizational approach much of its dynamism. At the same time, the OAS experience reminds us that the hegemonic power in such a grouping must be able to perceive the long-range advantages of multilateral as opposed to unilateral security action, just as the smaller- power members must be willing to use the organ- ization for something more than simply the containment of the regional great power. If the shibboleth of nonintervention can render the or- ganization impotent to deal with many of the practical regional problems that arise in this age of interdependence, so can the periodic unilater- alism of Santo Domingo.

---

legal grounds that existing inter-American law did not provide the basis for such exclusion. . . . On February 14, 1962, Cuba's exclusion from inter-Amer- ican affairs was made formal when the OAS Council received the resolutions aimed against Cuba that had been approved at the foreign ministers' meeting. The Council's meeting fulfilled the instructions of the foreign ministers for action. . . . For all practical purposes, the Cuban regime of Premier Fidel Castro ceased to be a member of the principal organ of the OAS. The other bodies of the OAS were subse- quently to act separately to make formal the exclu- sion of Cuba.

In the case of OAS action in the Dominican Republic, the Sub-Committee of the Inter-American Peace Com- mittee justified OAS intervention on these grounds:

Taking into account the existing relationship be- tween the violation of human rights and the lack of effective exercise of representative democracy on the one hand, and the political tensions that affect the peace of the hemisphere on the other, the Sub-Com- mittee considers that there must be evidence of more progress than has thus far been attained before it can be concluded that the Dominican government has ceased to be a threat to the peace and security of the hemisphere. [Council of the OAS, *Second Report of the Sub-Committee of the Special Committee to Carry Out the Mandate Received by the Council Pursuant to Resolution I of the 6th Meeting of Con- sultation,* OAS Document CE/RC V–26, 1961.]

The United Nations and Regional Security

The elaboration of a preventive diplomacy ap- proach to security in the United Nations can be regarded, in part, as a response to the claims of regional organizations to primacy in certain kinds of security issues. One of the postulates of pre- ventive diplomacy is that the UN may take ef- fective security action in areas where the claims of interest by cold war antagonists are recognized to be in conflict. Put in terms of regionalism, this is to say that UN action is required where effective regional action is not possible. To illustrate, the Suez crisis of 1956 was characterized by the at- tempt of two Western powers to reassert their lost hegemony in an area then controlled by gov- ernments in the process of constructing a doctrine of nonalignment. The claim to Western hege- mony was challenged not only by the Arabs them- selves and the Soviet Union, but even—tacitly—by the United States, which refused to accept the legitimacy of Anglo-French claims to an interven- tionary right in the area. Almost concurrently, however, the Soviet intervention in Hungary re- minded the world—as had the U.S. intervention in Guatemala two years earlier—of the near impo- tence of the universal organization to counter the unilateral intrusion of a superpower in the affairs of one of its own bloc members. If effective re- straints were to be exercised over this kind of hegemonic action, they had to originate within the regional grouping whose members were most directly affected.

There was frustration with these limitations upon the United Nations' ability to secure orderly and just settlement of issues that took place within the orbit of a superpower. Nonetheless, the little authority that the UN did possess in such cases could be marshaled, if not to ensure just solutions, at least to discourage the hege- monic state from flouting in such blatant fashion the principle of sovereignty and noninterference. The UN role in the Guatemalan situation is particularly instructive here. As indicated pre- viously,[37] the fact that the U.S. insistence on re- gional settlement was made to prevail in this case did not disguise the fact that almost all other Se- curity Council members were unwilling to accept

---

[37]See note 34 above.

the U.S. interpretation of the outcome as providing the regional organization with a *carte blanche* to take exclusive jurisdiction in such cases in the future. According to one commentator on the Guatemalan incident, "the victory of the United States was Pyrrhic, as well as incomplete. The United States had its way in Guatemala, but instead of establishing a precedent that the United Nations would be inclined to follow, it stimulated a persistent wariness against allowing the recurrence of such episodes."[38] While the Guatemalan case did not provide an effective United Nations alternative to the intervention of a hegemonic power in the affairs of a member of its own bloc, it may, at least, have encouraged such powers to secure the cooperation of their regional associates in advance whenever possible. At least, the United States was considerably more aware of the need for the genuine support of the Latin Americans by the time the issue of Castroism came to the United Nations. Even so, the jurisdiction issue was resolved somewhat more equivocally than it had been in the Guatemalan case, and an increased number of Latin American governments had by this time recognized that the doctrine of the absolute primacy of the OAS in hemispheric security affairs served no useful purpose to themselves.[39] Latin American support for U.S. sponsored regional settlement was becoming a commodity which had to be bargained for.

Within the Communist orbit, the prospects were somewhat less encouraging that the United Nations could help persuade the Soviet Union to seek genuinely multilateral solutions to intrabloc conflicts. The questionable sovereignty of the East European states seemed to make unilateral Soviet interventions efficacious in a way that their counterparts by the United States in Latin America could not be. Yet, an important fact stands out in the post-Hungarian development of the Soviet bloc: the "satellite" status of the East European states—once an accurate description—must be questioned increasingly today, as the former "puppet" governments of Moscow display varying degrees of independence. The change is obvious even in the attempted reassertion of monolithic control from Moscow. When the Soviet Union invaded Czechoslovakia in the summer of 1968, a much greater effort was made than a dozen years earlier in Hungary to cloak the operation in multilateral legitimacy. Soviet troops entered the country with contingents from four Warsaw Pact allies, while the Soviet government strove to make credible the fiction that the invasion was carried out at the behest of Czechoslovak authorities. In spite of these efforts, it is by no means clear that Soviet officials have had reason to be satisfied with the outcome of their intervention. An interim assessment suggests that they have paid a high price both politically and economically. The reasons for the loosening of ties within the Soviet bloc are many and complex, and it is not suggested here that condemnations in the UN of Soviet behavior in Hungary and Czechoslovakia have figured very importantly among those reasons. Nonetheless, it is apparent that unilateral "solutions" by the Soviet Union to the security problems of Communist states become increasingly hard to sustain while the loosening of ties within the Soviet bloc continues.[40] It is doubtful that the Soviet Union yet needs to be as responsive to the wishes of her allies in most issues of security as the United States must be to hers; still, the challenge of Peking China to the dominant role of Moscow does require that the Soviet government make cooperation rather than coercion the basic principle of her relations with other Communist powers.

---

[38]Inis L. Claude, Jr., "The OAS, the UN, and the United States," *International Conciliation*, No. 547 (March 1964), 34. A full discussion of the case is included in Claude's article, 21–34.

[39]For the debates on the Cuban question in the Security Council, see SCOR: 15th Yr., 874th–876th Mtgs., 18–19 July, 1960; SCOR: 16th Yr., 921st–923rd Mtgs., 4–5 January, 1961. General Assembly consideration of the Cuban complaints is contained in GAOR: 15th Sess., 872nd, 909th, and 995th Plenary Mtgs., in the 131st Mtg. of the General Committee, and in the 1149th–1161st Mtgs. of the First Committee.

---

[40]Haas has noted of the Soviet bloc that:

Integration was *least* successful when the Communist Party of the Soviet Union possessed an organizational monopoly over the process. . . . The Stalin period witnessed a minimum of military cooperation, no joint economic planning, no exchange of information apart from the slavish imitation in Eastern Europe of Soviet examples, and no successful value-sharing among fellow-communists. Integration was a one-way process in which the aims of the European satellites were simply subordinated to those of the Soviet Union. . . . Now, there is little central direction, but, paradoxically, a good deal of practical integration.

It goes without saying that so long as great power rivalry exists, the United Nations will be seized upon as the principal forum of opposition to hegemonic interventionary action—whether undertaken unilaterally or under the guise of a regional organization. The Soviet Union has never championed the principle of universal collective action so vigorously as when opposing OAS jurisdiction in the Guatemalan and Cuban cases, nor has the United States paid greater lip service to the principles of the Charter than in the Hungarian and Czechoslovak interventions.

Since the idea of preventive diplomacy assumes that UN action is called for in those marginal areas between spheres of great power interest, where countervailing interventions by those powers could result in a serious threat to world peace, a logical corollary of the theory would be that nonhegemonic regionalism be strengthened in those areas, both to inhibit interventions from external actors and to bolster UN security action when it is required. The emergence of the Organization of African Unity is a hopeful development in this direction, even though it would be naive to assume that its existence will automatically strengthen orderly security procedures in Africa. Two conditions often may exist in practice which will serve to qualify the theoretical assumption that such an organization will harmonize with the preventive diplomatic approach. The first is the unlikelihood that such a grouping would be sufficiently united politically or strong militarily to prevent the determined intrusion of a superpower. Neither the Arab League nor the OAU has been successful in developing a genuine security for the use of the organization-as-actor. On the other hand, world order would not likely be better served if these groupings were to acquire atomic weapons with which they could threaten external states. So long as they remain weak militarily but cohesive in regional security activities, they should be able to help deter the incursions of external actors into their affairs.

This latter suggestion, however, points to the second, and probably more serious, practical qualification that needs to be noted. It is probably utopian to expect such nonhegemonic groupings consistently to bolster UN preventive diplomatic action within their regions. Where the interests of neighboring states are involved in a regional issue, the intervention of a United Nations force into the area may come to be regarded as an unwarranted intrusion by some of the regional states just as it may be welcomed by others because of national advantages they may hope to attain from it. Again, however, at the risk of oversimplifying the real problems which may develop in this respect, it may be that the "threat" of UN security action in an area nominally under the jurisdiction of a nonhegemonic regional organization may act to encourage the states of the area to develop effective techniques of settlement at the regional level, so that UN intrusion becomes less necessary, just as the cost to external great powers of their intervention becomes too high for the risks involved. So long as a "political vacuum" exists which the regional organization is unable to cope with, it must pay the price of UN involvement to achieve settlement.

It is no accident of history that during the past several years the most persistent and intractable international conflicts have taken place in Southeast Asia, for this is an area where neither regional nor universal techniques of settlement are politically appropriate. And they are not appropriate because of the current confusion and disagreement as to the proper place of the area within the international system. While the claim of Western hegemony in much of the area is increasingly difficult to justify on the basis of an objective appraisal of the political facts there, it is not a claim which has been relinquished by the United States government. Competing Western and Communist claims to influence in Southeast Asia—combined, perhaps, with the continuing refusal of India to associate herself with, much less lead, a regional security movement in the area—have prevented the development of a nonhegemonic regional organization on the Asian subcontinent to deal with the problems of local security. By the same token, the preventive diplomatic role of the United Nations has been inapplicable, since no way has been found to bring about effective UN intervention that would be acceptable to both the superpowers.[41]

---

[41] It is true that on January 31, 1966, U.S. Ambassador Arthur J. Goldberg addressed a letter to the president of the Security Council requesting an urgent meeting of the Council to consider the situation in Vietnam. Simultaneously a draft resolution was submitted by the United States to the Council calling for immediate discussions to arrange a peace conference, with participation by "the appropriate interested governments." Three days later, nine Security Council members voted to inscribe the resolution on the agenda, two opposed the

Regardless of the outcome of the current conflict in Vietnam, it would appear that any effective long-range approach to security in the area must proceed from a recognition of the interests of the states located in the region. Such an approach would necessarily include China, although to admit this much is not to suggest that the smaller states in the vicinity must inevitably fall under Chinese tutelage. An organizational approach conforming to the patterns of the "original" regional associations could be made to contribute to orderly conflict resolution in approximately the same way that similar organizations elsewhere in the world are able to make such a contribution. No doubt, justice would not be done in every dispute that might arise, any more than it is done when powers external to the region seek to control the destinies of the area. Yet, the Asian solution of Asian problems—tempered by the right of appeal to the universal forum to prevent the harshest of regional solutions from being attempted—would do much to eliminate the nearly constant threats to world peace that will remain so long as *external* great powers continue to compete for influence there. But this brings us to the question of the prospective future of regional security.

IV. FUTURE PROSPECTS FOR REGIONAL PATTERNS OF ORDER

The norms of regional security action that have been taking shape during the past twenty years are the product of an international system which was rather rigidly bipolar during the first years of this period, and which had evolved into a "tripolar" or "multipolar" system by the mid-1960's. Thus, the crucial question for the future is whether the system itself is not changing to the point that the patterns of regional behavior appropriate to the present may be utterly inappropriate to the conduct of international politics ten or twenty years from now. Therefore, it is essential to attempt to determine what will be the basic features of the international system during the next few decades.

Of course, no such projection can be genuinely descriptive of reality at any given point in time in the future; rather, it must constitute a partial model whose basic form is determined by extrapolation from what are seen to be the dominant and dynamic trends at work today. Therefore, its construction must assume a basic continuity in the conduct of international politics from the present into the near future. For example, if widespread nuclear devastation were to occur, the system quite likely would be so transformed as to render such a model of the future nearly irrelevant to reality. Certainly there is no desire in what follows to propound a deterministic view of the future of world politics; neither current nor past history forecloses the way in which the future will unfold, even though it surely helps to delimit it. The dangers of deterministic analysis and the fallacies of models might well render useless and even harmful the attempt at prognostication if the projected period of study were a very long one. But in assuming the more modest goal of projecting certain current trends into the immediate future, it is submitted that these problems —while they cannot be eliminated—can, at least, be controlled.

The International System of the Future

My general view of the near future is one of a loosely multipolar system in which international coalitions and alignments will be relatively durable although, perhaps, not until after a continuing period involving some readjustments and shifting allegiances. Thus, this model of the future is not that of the "balance of power" system as Kaplan has described it,[42] even though it envisages the coexistence of several actors— whether individual states or groups of states—of approximately comparable strength and influence. Due in part to the comparatively more rigid and durable alignments than were characteristic of the "balance of power" system, transnational

move and four abstained. Once inscribed, however, the resolution was left undebated and the United States rested content, apparently, with having got the issue onto the agenda.

[42]Cf. Morton A. Kaplan, "Balance of Power, Bipolarity and Other Models of International Systems," *American Political Science Review,* LI (1957), 684–93. For a full treatment of the normative patterns that were produced by the historic balance of power and loose bipolar international systems, see also Kaplan's work (with Nicholas deB. Katzenbach), *The Political Foundations of International Law* (New York 1961).

actors can be expected to play an important role. These would include both the universal international organization and lesser groupings of states, most of which would form partially integrated security-communities.[43]

The most obvious reason for viewing the international system of the near future as multipolar is the patent fact of the crumbling of bipolarity at the present time.[44] The Russo-Chinese split, which until quite recently may have appeared as a temporary aberration which could be healed with a change of personnel in the governing elites, now can be regarded as a long-term feature of the international landscape. Competition between these two Communist giants has intensified and the breach between them has widened steadily during the 1960's. Moreover, as the Chinese increase their economic and military strength and develop an atomic arsenal and delivery capability during the next few years, the incentives for their return to a bloc role subordinant to the Soviet Union can only decline in number and importance. Meanwhile, in the West, the incongruities of the idea of Atlantic partnership become more obvious with each passing month. Without attempting to predict in detail the shape of Western area politics in the years ahead, it can be safely ventured that the trend is not toward the monolithic unity of the area, but is rather in the direction of the bifurcation of the grouping so far as integrated units are concerned (which is not necessarily to say that wide-ranging cooperation and coordination of policy may not continue in important areas). This division conceivably could take one of several forms, e.g., between the "Anglo-Saxon" powers and those of continental Europe, as seems to be suggested by the Gaullist vision; between Europe, including Britain, and North America; or even on the basis of a Washington-Bonn, London-Paris dual axis. This analysis is not meant to foreclose the possibility of the eventual amalgamation of, say, the entire Atlantic area or the Soviet and Chinese states; rather, it concludes that for the short run, the dynamic tendencies are producing greater intra-bloc autonomy than has been characteristic of the recent past.

There are good reasons for concluding that this trend toward greater autonomy will not soon be carried to the point of genuine state equality, however. Perhaps the most important of these is the atomic weapons factor. Although the principal nuclear powers have agreed upon a nonproliferation treaty, it is still possible that a few other states will become atomic powers during the next few years. The costs, however, of developing atomic and nuclear arsenals appear to be so great that it is doubtful that many of these states could enter the ranks of the first-class nuclear powers without a considerable cooperative effort. "Competitive" atomic powers, then, may be expected to remain few, and if more actors are to achieve superpower status in the near future, very few individual states will be able to do so. A more feasible pattern may be the military integration of more than one existing political unit.[45] The atomic factor has introduced the requirement of

---

[43]The term is that of Karl W. Deutsch and others, *Political Community*: "The pluralistic security-community (a group of people which have become 'integrated') . . . retains the legal independence of separate governments." (p. 6)

[44]Richard N. Rosecrance has argued cogently that neither the bipolar nor multipolar model of the international system constitutes a "relevant utopia" for the near future (see his "Bipolarity, Multipolarity, and the Future," *The Journal of Conflict Resolution*, x (3), 314–27). Instead, he suggests that the attractive features of each be combined in a systemic model of "bi-multipolarity": (p. 320) "Bipolarity provides for well-nigh automatic equilibration of the international balance; in addition, while reinforcing conflict between the two poles, it at least has the merit of preventing conflict elsewhere in the system. Multipolarity reduces the significance of major-power conflict by spreading antagonism uniformly through the system. What we should wish for . . . is to combine the desirable facets of each without their attendant disabilities."

The bi-multipolar concept which Rosecrance then describes constitutes a more deliberately deductive attempt than I have made to construct a model of the system's hope-for future. Nonetheless, in general, what I project here in the way of future trends is compatible with the bi-multipolar model. I have eschewed use of the term, however, because I am not engaged here in rigorous model-building. Thus, it has seemed more useful in this empirical context to describe the future system as "loosely multipolar, in which international coalitions and alignments will be relatively durable."

[45]This at least seems a possibility in the case of Western Europe, where the amalgamation of British and French atomic forces combined with the conventional military capabilities of these and other continental states could conceivably produce a unified military capacity that would make these states militarily competitive with the United States and the Soviet Union and, in this sense, "independent" as a single actor in questions of ultimate security.

long-term and relatively close-knit alignment into coalition policy that was not present in the pre-atomic age. Nor does the trend away from bi-polarity eliminate that requirement. An atomic or nuclear deterrent that is both credible and competitive with the capabilities of existing superpowers cannot be constructed by the tem-porary coalescence in a short-term alliance of small national arsenals. Credibility of the deter-rent demands an integrated command structure with undivided authority to act in the name of the unit or units to be protected, while a com-petitive capability will entail, for most states, the joining of independent national forces under a single authority. The relatively long-term align-ments of the future must, like those of the bipolar period, place much greater emphasis upon their internal organization than did those alliances of the more distant past.

A second reason for insisting upon the multi-polarity of the near future, characterized by rather stable groupings of states, is the likely continuation of relatively great disparities among the major potential groupings of the world in the goals which they seek, the styles of their politics, and their levels of political and economic devel-opment. If the dominant issue of world politics is no longer perceived as a simple contest between Communism and non-Communism, other kinds of divisions have come into focus elsewhere, but these, too, are characteristically differences be-tween groups of states rather than between individual states. Whereas nationalism in the European context can only be regarded today and in the future as a reactionary movement, in many of the underdeveloped areas of the world the overwhelming need to construct na-tional political units where they have not existed before tends to make the ideology of nationalism a progressive and even a revolutionary doctrine. In these areas, nationalism is not likely to become a justification for the preservation at all costs of existing state boundaries so much as it will be-come the vehicle of the trans-state integration of a larger "nation," however defined. The marriage of national liberation movements to the doctrine of Pan-Africanism is particularly instructive here.[46]

---

[46]Cf., Immanuel Wallerstein, "Pan-Africanism as Pro-test," in Morton A. Kaplan, ed., *The Revolution in World Politics* (New York 1962), 137–51.

While much of the West must devote increas-ing energy to coping with the problems of afflu-ence and automation, much of the rest of the world will be involved in a life-and-death struggle for physical survival. While a part of the world—including, no doubt, some of the Communist states—will be engaged in the effort to democra-tize and liberalize the conduct of politics within their state systems, elsewhere authoritarian and totalitarian forms of government may be ex-pected to wax strong. None of this is likely to encourage the formation of a world polity or a universal community in any meaningful sense of the term. Many of these disparities simply were camouflaged by the working of bipolarity, at least in its early days, and only now are they coming to be recognized as having been there all along.

This discussion is not meant to discount the fact that inter-state conflicts in the traditional sense will continue to form much of the basic stuff of international politics. The point is, rather (a) that limited groupings of states—and often of states that are relatively close geographically—will find that the numerous problems which they face in common will encourage them to take coopera-tive measures for their resolution; and (b) that these are not issues which can be treated mean-ingfully through constantly shifting, ad-hoc coali-tions. Moreover, it is not implied here that the factors working toward greater regional solidarity are so overwhelming that the splendid isolation of regional blocs will be the result. While the diversity of political issues just alluded to should encourage the growth of regional efforts to pro-vide for the security of the area, in functional terms the problems of development and democra-tization require the continuing cooperation of states in the Northern and Southern hemispheres.

The Organization of Security in a Multipolar World

As was seen in Part III the gradual loosening of the bipolar structure during the past decade has been accompanied on the one hand by the declining utility of the multilateral alliance *per se*, and on the other by the increased importance of regional security activity that focuses on intra-group problems. With the evolution of a more clearly multipolar system, the factors which have encouraged this trend should continue to operate. Thus, we can expect to see fewer attempts to extend the protective hegemony of great powers over distant territories and a greater effort to consolidate the interests of local powers in the more limited areas of their greatest interest.

It should be added immediately, however, that such an evolution will scarcely be smooth or simple. The revolutionary, transnational ideology of Marxism undoubtedly will continue to guide the elites of the Communist world in their foreign policies, encouraging them to promote revolution in distant countries and to maintain strong political ties with like-minded political cadres around the globe. Similarly, even though Western leaders seem to have learned that their former colonial subjects do not become automatic allies with independence, the diverse ties which have remained between many of them after nationhood no doubt will persist into the immediate future. There will, then, continue to be conflicting claims to the protection of various elite groups in far-flung areas, even though it is true that an increasing amount of security activity will rest with the groups most immediately involved in the vicinity.

Still, with the decline of bipolarity and the increased importance of new states in the international system, why should not an expanded security role for the United Nations be developed? The new states are, after all, among the most ardent champions of a dynamic universal organization, and the fact of bipolarity long has been regarded as the chief obstacle in the path of genuine collective security. In fact, however, there is little reason to assume that the principle of great power concert on which the security provisions of the Charter were built will be any more applicable to the realities of politics in the near future than it has been in the past two decades. Even if it be assumed that a rapprochement between the United States and the Soviet Union will extend to the point that these two powers may see eye to eye on measures of peaceful settlement and enforcement to be undertaken by the United Nations, the admission of Communist China to a seat on the Security Council—an event which surely will take place within the near future—does not portend great harmony among the permanent members. The current demands of the Peking regime upon the world are, perhaps, somewhat akin in quality to those of the Soviet Union in the immediate postwar period. If so, we may expect Chinese behavior in the Security Council to resemble that of the Russians during much of the recent past.

Given this situation, it is likely that the principal security role left to the UN will be some variation on that currently described as preventive diplomacy. Expansion of this role, however, will be fraught with difficulties from two quarters: In the first place, it will be necessary to secure the acquiescence in UN action of several permanent members that will be more nearly equal in their *de facto* relationships than the current members have been heretofore. To do so need not depend upon the willingness of these states to accept the status quo in all cases so much as it will require from them realistic appraisals of the limitations of their own power in extended areas. Experience indicates that such appraisals may not come readily to states unaccustomed to their role as great powers. Secondly, if even this limited security role is to be maintained for the United Nations, concrete steps must be taken soon to ensure its acceptance on a regularized basis. There was healthy recognition in the Twentieth General Assembly that world order could be better served than by permitting preventive diplomacy to continue to grow "like Topsy," on an ad hoc and uneven basis without due regard for the most effective means of financing such activity. Even though steps were undertaken beginning in 1965–1966 to reexamine the existing peace-keeping machinery of the organization, no specific proposals have yet emerged for strengthening the UN role in this area.

These facts, taken together, should induce a certain pessimism as to the short-range possibilities for a more extensive UN security role than now exists. On the other hand, they help emphasize the need, if not the likelihood, that much of the attempt to secure a more orderly world should be directed to the regional level. From a normative point of view, it is essential that the regional approach to security be strengthened by the construction of viable regional organizations whose members are viewed objectively, i.e., by actors external to those organizations, as forming a unified and responsible grouping for purposes of treating some security issues. Yet, the qualifier "some" must be emphasized here, for an effective universal organization will be required that is capable of responding to the need for peacekeeping action where regional intervention would be unacceptable to the international community as a whole. If United Nations preventive diplomacy can be regarded as complementing rather than opposing the regional approach to security, then the regional approach must be made to conform to acceptable standards of international behavior.

Regionalism and Political Order

It should not be impossible to set down general guidelines which may help to ensure the evolution of regional security activity that conforms with the goals of human dignity. At the same time, any attempt to specify the precise forms of regional security organization that should be developed in all such groupings must be regarded as chimerical. What follows, then, is simply an attempt to make explicit the primary social and political requisites to the orderly development of a transnational, subsystemic organization.

Although it may be possible to regard political authority built wholly upon the use or threat of force as ensuring "order" within the social structure, that is a superficial kind of order which inevitably breeds chaos over the long run. Genuine order permits the ever-greater realization of goals based upon shared values that are sought by members of the group, and not rigidity of social and political structures. Authority that is firmly built upon "a consistent pattern of shared value realization" is itself productive of order, whereas tension and conflict can only result when authority is maintained by a resort to power that inhibits the goal-gratification of members of the group.[47] Considered in terms of regional politics, this proposition is, of course, the principal explanation of the fact that the unrestrained exercise of hegemony by a great power over lesser ones is so likely to have disorderly and destabilizing consequences. At the same time, it assumes the necessity of authoritative structures if coherent policy is to be produced. The requirement, then, is for an organization at the regional level that can act effectively without permitting it to become the

instrument of the monolithic imposition of a single state's demands upon the wider area.

By an exacting definition, the regional association remains as the *organization* of "sovereign" states, rather than a single polity and, as such, may be regarded as an intermediate level of political integration between the (theoretically) fully integrated state units and the largely unintegrated international system as a whole. The proposition of orderly development sketched in the preceding paragraph, however, assumes as the ultimate norm of social and political life the fully integrated unit, where authority rests upon a consistent pattern of shared value realization. Thus, it cannot be regarded as accurately descriptive of the aims of transnational, subsystemic organization. Since regional organizations constitute a half-way house of transnational association, their authoritative structures are the creation of the states which comprise them, and their purpose is to help realize some of the goals of states rather than the values of individuals. The characteristic tensions (described in Part III) between hegemonic and nonhegemonic tendencies constitute— in the language of the present analysis—tensions which arise from the requirements of authoritative action on the one hand, and preservation of the relevant values of all associated states on the other.

Insistence upon the requirement of regional organizations to deal with some of the important security problems of the future does not stem from an inclination to hypostatize political development at the regional level. The goal of world order must be predicated upon the realization of human values, and should refuse to give absolute allegiance to particular political forms and structures as the only ones conducive to order. By the same token, our concern must be to fit the political structures which are available to the realization of those goals. Fully recognizing the tentative quality of regional organization in a world where universal order is demanded, I would posit as a normative goal of regional organizational development in the future what might be called the pluralistic unity of the organization, based upon the national "independence" of the constituent members. Such a goal attempts to account realistically for the apparently contradictory phenomena of current international politics, i.e., (*a*) the continuation of the nation-state as the basic

---

[47]The quotation is from Kenneth S. Carlston, *Law and Organization in World Society* (Urban 1962), 85–86.

unit of world politics (even though it can no longer be the final arbiter or ultimate protagonist in all international conflictual situations) and (b) the technological and political developments which, in large measure, render the nation-state as traditionally constituted unable ultimately to protect its own national values. However contradictory the demand may seem to be, the governing principle of regional organizational development should account for both the continuing "sovereign" independence of the nation-state and for the breakdown (or transformation) of national "sovereignty."

In part, then, the goal of pluralistic unity for the regional organization is posited on the assumption that a fuller scale political amalgamation of constituent member states is not a realistic goal for the near future—at least not in many areas of the world. But it is also suggested that, in the absence of genuinely democratic integrative processes, such a goal is more acceptable for the short run because it would entail restraint upon the violation of national values through a centralized authoritative structure. The existence of a pluralistic structure can prevent the unilateral expansion of the values of a particular elite at the expense of other members of the group; at the same time, however, it can encourage the harmonization of interests through a sharing of the instruments of power by which values are realized. A nonhierarchical regional grouping, in which diverse interests are recognized in the decision-making process, is far likelier to impose restraints upon its own security activity than is a body that is hierarchically structured. The result may, of course, merely be ineffective action or no action at all, but recognition of such a possibility itself encourages agreement on a common policy where such a policy is possible, without sacrificing values held vital by important members of the organization.

The Challenge of the Future

It is, of course, one thing to suggest the guidelines which ought to govern the operations of regional security organizations so that they are not disruptive of basic human values and quite another to suppose that they will be adhered to in practice. Undoubtedly, it would be utopian to suppose

that the kind of pluralistic unity at the regional level set forth as a goal in the preceding discussion will be realized throughout the world in the near future. In some areas, and particularly where the locally dominant power combines expansionist goals with authoritarian methods, the pluralistic unity of the regional powers will be virtually impossible. For the short run, hegemonic domination in those regions probably must go nearly unchecked; lesser regional powers will scarcely have the capabilities to do so and external actors will find that any such attempt on their part would be too costly in terms of their own security and that of the international community generally. External actors will be well advised to contain expansionist tendencies, but not to attempt seriously coercive action within the area dominated by a locally hegemonic power. The realization of shared values through authoritative political structures must be postponed, in such instances, in the interests of general international security.

On balance, however, most of the lessons and developments of the recent past support the case for regional action that is conducive to order at both the regional and universal levels in the near future. First, the attempt to maintain alliances essentially like those of the past—wherein emphasis upon the common external threat has taken precedence over the attempt to harmonize mutual relations authoritatively—must be regarded as inadequate for purposes of preserving an effective coalition in a multipolar world. Since it will be in the interests of the great powers to maintain as effectively as possible the allegiance and the loyalties of other national actors within their blocs, these powers should be encouraged to take the lead in building pluralistic unity in their regional associations through strong emphasis upon the functions of the actors-in-organization.

Secondly, experience has shown that action undertaken in the name of a regional body which has only a tenuous organizational development tends to be both ineffective in the immediate sense that it fails to increase importantly the capabilities of the major national actor involved, and in the more general sense of encouraging settlement that is acceptable to other national and universal actors. If this factor should discourage the great and superpowers from the attempt to form military alliances with states where the impetus to organizational or integrative development is lacking, it may encourage them, nonetheless, to concentrate their efforts upon the building of authority within those more restricted areas where the requisites for such development are present.

Finally, growing recognition of the futility to the great powers of attempting to maintain organizational commitments in areas of the world beyond those of their immediate interests already has encouraged the establishment, at least in one area, of a nonaligned regional body, potentially capable of dealing with the actors-in-organization in an orderly fashion. If the current level of conflict in Southeast Asia can be reduced before other major actors are pulled into the vortex, a similar approach may come to be recognized as the most feasible means of attaining greater security in that area. All three of these historical factors can be viewed as encouraging the potential contribution of regionalism to security that is compatible with order. All three developments hold out the prospect—although certainly not the promise—that international security can be promoted in a context which permits the increasing realization of many fundamental human values.

Discussion and Questions

1. Lynn Miller's emphasis on regional-security arrangements is both more specific in content and more standard in treatment than is either Masters' or Young's. ➤ Which of these three modes of thinking is the most illuminating for the world-order effort? ➤ Can each contribute something useful to our over-all knowledge of international affairs?

2. ➤ Have regional-security organizations minimized violence at the expense of social and political justice and of social and economic welfare?

3. Miller's analysis leads to an inquiry into the relationship between regionalism and globalism as organizational efforts. ➤ Do regional organizations impede or promote efforts by the United Nations in the peace and security field? ➤ Does the answer depend partly upon which subsystem is the arena of concern? partly on the global setting of time and place? partly on a series of contextual variables relating to leadership, perception, and domestic political forces? For instance, regionalism might be a barrier to the operation of the United Nations in Latin America or the Middle East but a complement to its operation in Africa. ➤ What factors in each system seem to explain the relationship between the activities of a given regional organization and the United Nations?

Some developments on the regional level have resulted from the limitations of the United Nations. The UN has been often unable to take effective action to uphold international peace and security. The Security Council voting procedure requires that the five permanent members agree on any line of proposed substantive action; a regional organization may have an even stronger underlying consensus built into its constitutional structure. Regional organizations tend, however, to exclude antagonistic units within the physical confines of the region. One can hardly imagine Israel as a member of the Arab League or South Africa as a member of the Organization of African Unity. A particularly dramatic instance of this tendency of regional organizations to condition membership on an effective community of interests occured at Punta del Este in 1962 when Cuba was officially excluded from participation in the inter-American system on the proclaimed ground that the Cuban government had embraced the ideology of Marxism-Leninism, which was found to be "incompatible with the principles and objectives of the inter-American system." (See Final Act, Second Punta del Este Conference, January 1962, Eighth Meeting of Consultation of Foreign Ministers, Inter-American Treaty of Reciprocal Assistance.)

➤ How do regional organizations differ from traditional kinds of alliances? ➤ Is it important to differentiate an arrangement for collective self-defense under Chapter VII of the Charter from a regional organization formed under Chapter VIII? These issues are discussed further by Inis L. Claude in an article reprinted in Part IV. (See also Ernst B. Haas, "Regionalism, Functionalism, and Universal International Organization," *World Politics*, vol. 8, no. 2 [January 1956], pp. 238-63. An excellent case study of these issues in the setting of the OAS, but with some wider complications, is Minerva Etzioni's *The Majority of One* [Sage, Beverly Hills, 1969].)

4. ➤ Why do national governments seek to form and to participate in regional organizations? ➤ Do regionalizing tendencies have to do mainly with security, economic development, and ethnic solidarity? Regional arrangements are one way to enhance the capability of national governments to fulfill their functions and realize their goals in relation to a given national society. There is no incompatibility between regionalism and nationalism unless the regional organization has an integrationist mission. Integration by its very character, as we shall see in Part II, entails the transfer of functions from the national level to a regional actor, and it may eventually lead to the merging of separate sovereignties in some new supranational unit. Without an integrationist dimension, the main activity of regional organizations may be to promote national causes and to proclaim supranationalist sentiments without implementing them, as in Africa, where the OAU is devoted, above all, to the triumph of *national* self-determination for Angola, Rhodesia, Nambia, Mozambique, and South Africa, and to the proclamation of African brotherhood.

In connection with regionalism in Southeast Asia, Bernard K. Gordon poses two questions and proceeds to provide the following answers:

> . . . why has so little been achieved, and why, in the face of so little success, have so many continued to advocate regionalism?

The first question has two answers. Regionalism has not taken root in Southeast Asia, first, because of the many political conflicts among the nations there, and second, because there is so little agreement, even among its advocates, on what "cooperation" would mean in practice. That same imprecision also helps to answer the second question. In large part, regionalism continues to attract supporters because the concept, vaguely defined, seems to promise different benefits to different national leaders. To many, regionalism has meant a revival of cultural, and perhaps political, ties among Asian "brothers," long divided during the period of European colonialism. For many others regional cooperation has offered hope for a more efficient path to national economic development. To another group, regionalism has seemed to offer small nations a stronger guarantee of defense and security. ["Regionalism and Instability in Southeast Asia," *Orbis*, vol. 10, no. 2 (Summer 1966), pp. 438-57, at p. 438.]

Note that Gordon seems to ignore the relevance of global political patterns to the dilemmas of regionalism in Southeast Asia. In this respect, Oran Young's article (above) provides a good basis for responding to Gordon's analysis. See also Leonard Binder's article in Part V.

5. Regional organizations also, as Miller points out, may be concerned with questions of hegemony and containment. The dominant state (or the state that aspires to be dominant) may use the mantle of regionalism to disguise patterns of domination and to make conditions of dependency more acceptable to the subordinate system. Such a pattern is likely to appear during an era such as the present one, when explicit modes of domination—colonialism, imperialism—have lost their legitimacy. At the same time, and in quite contradictory fashion, a regional organization may be used by subordinate members to moderate or even avoid the exertion of dominance by the strongest member. Both processes go on simultaneously, although in different settings one or the other is more prominent. Again, subsystemic and issue-area differentiation is critical to useful analysis. Also, in certain regional settings the hegemonial issue is more muted than in others, being most salient in any regionalist framework that includes one or the other superpower as an active member.

Doudou Thiam, the Foreign Minister of Senegal, has written an interesting cautionary passage on the hegemonial issue, in the course of his exposition of pan-Africanism. The section is entitled "Pan-Africanism as a pretext for neo-imperialism":

> Our analysis would not be complete, however, without reference to another aspect of pan-Africanism involving personal or national ambitions. Many African politicians suffer from a new disease called leadership. Their support of pan-Africanism and their pronouncements on African unity barely disguise their secret ambition to be leading men, the controllers of a united Africa. This propensity has been denounced vigorously on occasions. Frequently, too, certain African countries which have become independent dream of enlarging their territory. There is a nostalgia for the great empires of the past, which finds expression in the names given to certain states (e.g., Ghana, Mali). This is *historical* fantasy-building. Neither is it a rare occurrence for one country to make territorial claims on a neighbour. Colonial rulers are accused of having parcelled out certain African territories which were ethnic or geographic units before colonization. The theory of *national frontiers* is invoked in support of this theory. The claims of Ghana on Togo, or Morocco on Mauritania and the recent dispute between Nigeria and the Cameroon Republic about the former British Cameroons are significant of this tendency.
>
> Our analysis shows that pan-Africanism has many different aspects. Sometimes it appears as a way of defending Africans against outside ideologies, and at other times as a weapon in the struggle against colonialism. These are the negative aspects of pan-Africanism—anti-communism and anti-colonialism. They show pan-Africanism as a means of protection and self-defense. But beyond these two aspects of the pan-African doctrine there is a further, positive, constructive aspect; this is the ideal of African unity.
>
> But all this analysis does not reflect the total complex reality. When all is said, pan-Africanism is still a concept with ill-defined boundaries, based upon both *realities* and *myths*. The realities include the facts of belonging to the same continent, of having similar economic and social conditions, of the solidarity engendered by the colonial status under which all the peoples of Africa have lived or still live. The myths are a deposit of ideas, impressions, beliefs, even legends, which sustain the pan-African ideal, and the belief of Africans in a common destiny.
>
> Besides combining reality and myth, pan-Africanism is also a mixture of warring ingredients. It is a super-nationalism which claims to include the whole of Africa or else the whole of a part of Africa. In this respect, in its extreme form, it is akin to a continentalism not unlike the Monroe Doctrine. But it is a super-nationalism which sometimes bears within itself the germs of imperialism. It is a *movement of unity*, but one which meets centrifugal forces and contains elements of discord and disruption. All these conflicting elements are at work simultaneously in varying degrees according to circumstances, the interests involved, the national temperaments and the demands of societies and groups.
>
> Nevertheless the dominant factor is African nationalism, the affirmation of the authenticity of the African world. This world is trying to find its own true direction, to clear a path for itself through the tough, dense jungle of international relations. But just because of the many conflicting elements of which pan-Africanism is made up the present course of the African nations shows many twists and turns, as we shall have many opportunities of observing. [From Doudou Thiam, *The Foreign Policy of African States*, New York: Praeger, 1965, pp. 19–21. Reprinted by permission of the publisher.]

Note that Thiam is concerned with the use of regionalist pretexts to encroach within an *intra-organizational* context. There is also the related problem of aggressive intentions against a unit situated within the region that has been excluded from membership in the relevant organization. The whole problem of regional coercion against an incompatible unit is one of the basic issues of world order: Israel, Cuba, South Africa, and Taiwan are each targets of a hostile regional animus. ➤ What are (or should be) the limits on the right of regional organizations to use force with (or without) authorization from the political organs of the United Nations? See Article 53 of the Charter, but consider the patterns of diplomatic practice, especially the authorizations of coercion by the Organization of American States against Cuba in 1962 and against the Dominican Republic in 1965. As well, consider the reliance by the Johnson Administration upon the SEATO treaty framework to justify use of military power in the Vietnam War.

6. Consider the various conceptions of "regionalism" developed by Masters, Young, and Miller. (a) It is possible, as Masters contends, to map the polar centers of power in international society or to map the clusterings of states around these polar centers of power. (b) It is also possible, as Young contends, to map the arenas of interaction that develop quasi-autonomous patterns of statecraft in international society. (c) And, finally, it is possible, as Miller contends, to map the organized groupings of sovereign states on the basis of existing regional organizations in the formal sense. It is our contention that each of these conceptions aids our understanding of the relationship between *parts* and *wholes* in international society. In this volume the focus is upon "parts" that are larger in *scope* than a single sovereign state and the interaction of such parts with the whole.

7. ➤ In a highly structured system of world order—wherein some type of world government prevailed—would it not still be possible, even essential, to respect the quasi-autonomy of subsystems and of regional organizations? Blocs might seem to be incompatible, almost by definition, with any drastically disarmed international environment. It is possible to conceive of a regionally implemented disarmament plan with regional police forces and military capabilities. The execution of such a model would be an illustration of a "multibloc utopia." ➤ Is it a relevant utopia? ➤ Why? ➤ Why not? ➤ Under what conditions relevant? ➤ How does it compare with the Clark-Sohn scheme for world order? ➤ Is it more or less attainable? ➤ What evidence is available to facilitate responses to such queries?

4

Regional Institutions

JOSEPH S. NYE

From *The Structure of the International Environment,* Vol. IV of Cyril E. Black and Richard A. Falk, *The Future of the International Legal Order* (Copyright © 1972 by Princeton University Press), written under the auspices of the Center of International Studies, Princeton University, pages 425 through 447. Reprinted by permission of Princeton University Press.

The number and proportion of international regional institutions has been increasing, as shown in Table 1, but it is not clear what conclusions we should draw from this fact. In the opinion of Jean Rey, "the political life of the world is becoming less at the level of national states and more at the level of continents."[1] Even Charles de Gaulle has said that, "it is in keeping with the conditions of our times to create entities more vast than each of the European states."[2] We shall argue, however, that there is not a clear trend toward regionalization of world politics in the sense that the most important sets of interdependence are based on geographical contiguity. At best the evidence is ambiguous, and there are alternative hypotheses for explaining the meaning of the growth of the number of regional institutions.

REGIONAL TRENDS

Has world politics become increasingly "regionalized"? The evidence is varied, and different types of behavior point in different directions. On the one hand, those who see a trend toward regionalism cite the fact that non-regional organizations like the Commonwealth, which once represented the paragon of effective international organization, have undergone a decline,[3] and Britain has sought to limit its military obligations "East of Suez" and prove its Europeanness.

Intra-Commonwealth trade in 1967 was roughly a quarter of the total trade of member countries, but the figure has declined steadily and even the report of the Commonwealth Secretariat refers to "the drive towards regional economic emphasis"

[1]Quoted in *European Community,* No. 103 (June 1967), 8.
[2]Press Conference, September 9, 1965.
[3]"The Commonwealth stands today as a foremost example of international cooperation." Daniel S. Cheever and H. Field Haviland, *Organizing for Peace* (Boston 1954). In addition, other nonregional selective efforts such as Francophone or Afro-Asian organizations have not prospered.

Table 1
New Regional and Quasi-Regional
Intergovernmental Organizations
Founded, 1815–1965

*Intergovernmental Organizations
Newly Founded*

	Total	Regional	Regional as Percent of Total
1815–1914	49	14	28%
1915–1944	73	27	37%
1945–1955	76	45	60%
1956–1965	56	41	73%
Founded	254	127	50%
Terminated	−65	−27	
Total	189	100	53%

Source: J. David Singer and Michael Wallace, "Intergovernmental Organization in the Global System, 1815–1964," *International Organization*, 24 (Spring 1970). This table was constructed by the author and David Handley (scoring regional and quasi-regional on the basis of geographical restriction in an organization's name or practice) from an early version of the list kindly made available by J. David Singer. The trends are corroborated by Kjell Skjelsbaek, "Development of the Systems of International Organizations," International Peace Research Association Paper, September 1969.

among its members.[4] At the same time, the countries of the European Community more than tripled their intraregional trade in the first decade. This striking success caused other countries to try to imitate it. Further evidence frequently cited is the fact that regional voting blocs have come to characterize the politics of the United Nations and the principle of regional representation within the U.N. is firmly established. Finally, not only has the number and proportion of new intergovernmental organizations increased but, what is probably a more accurate indicator of transactions, the same has been true for nongovernmental organizations. From 1957 to 1963 international nongovernmental organizations of the regional type increased some five times as rapidly as other nongovernmental organizations.[5]

This evidence, however, is far from conclusive.

[4]Commonwealth Secretariat, Second Report of the *Commonwealth Secretary-General* (London 1968), 3.
[5]Robert Angell, "The Growth of Transnational Participation," *The Journal of Social Issues*, XXIII (Jan. 1967), 125. See also *Peace on the March* (New York 1969), Chap. 9.

In some cases, for example the broadening of the "Atlantic" OECD to include Japan in 1964, or the establishment of the nonregional Group of Ten in the politically important international monetary system, the important trend does not seem to be regional. As for behavior in the U.N., many of the caucuses are "regional" only in a loose sense of the word,[6] and "regional" caucusing behavior in the U.N. arena is not a reliable indicator of political behavior outside the U.N. Turning to international trade, it is true that geography remains an important determinant[7] and there have been dramatic increases in trade among members of regional organizations, but there have also been dramatic increases between distance partners such as the United States and Japan[8] (see Table 2).

Steven Brams and Bruce Russett have made systematic efforts to map the pattern of transactions

Table 2
Trade Growth

	1958 $billion	1967 $billion	1958 = 100
US/Canada	3.3	13.9	420
US/Japan	1.7	5.7	340
Intra EEC	7.5	24.5	326
Intra EFTA	2.8	7.0	249
World Trade	108.0	214.1	194

Sources: United Nations, *Yearbook of International Trade Statistics* OECD, *Overall Trade by Countries.*

[6]For instance, UNCTAD groups are partly by region and partly by level of development. See J. S. Nye, "UNCTAD," in Robert Cox and Harold Jacobson, *The Anatomy of Influence: Decision Making in International Organization*, Yale, New Haven, 1972. In the words of Robert Keohane, "the most striking feature of the Regional Groups is their weakness." "Political Influence in the General Assembly," *International Conciliation*, No. 557 (March 1966).
[7]See Hans Linnemann, *An Econometric Study of International Trade Flows* (Amsterdam 1966).
[8]Indices of relative acceptance which correct for the effects of the size of trading partners show a more marked rise from 1954 and 1964 in trade from Japan to the U.S. than vice versa. On the other hand, there is a slight decline in the indices of relative acceptance between the U.S. and Canda. I am endebted to Karl Deutsch, Richard Chadwick, I. Richard Savage, and Dieter Senghaas for this data from their forthcoming *Regionalism, Trade and Political Community.*

in the international system. Looking at exchange of diplomatic personnel, trade, and shared membership in intergovernmental organizations in the early 1960's, Brams found that "geographical proximity seemed to be the dominant influence in the structuring of most of the sub-groups." However, bearing out our suspicions, he also found that neither diplomatic exchanges nor trade showed as clear a regional principle as was apparent in memberships in international organizations.[9]

Russett factor analyzed socioeconomic homogeneity, U.N. voting patterns; trade; shared memberships, and geographical proximity among states in the 1950's and 1960's. He notes that for the indicators he chose, "the lowest correlation for a given analysis is almost always between it and the pattern of geographical proximity," and that the average correlation among his factor analyses for the 1960's is slightly lower than for the 1950's.[10]

One of the problems of interpreting Russett's results is that his factor analysis is designed to find the fewest (and thus often the largest) clusters of states to account for the variance in the data.[11] The resulting factors are then given "regional" labels though in some cases the fit between the general meaning of the labels and the factors is very imperfect. However, if we take the three factors for which Russett has data over time and rather arbitrarily give regional labels only to those factors of which three-quarters (or alternatively two-thirds) of the states listed fall in an intuitively recognizable contiguous region, we find that Russett's data, like Bram's, seems to substantiate our suspicion that there may have been more regionalization in international organization than in other international behavior (see Table 3).

In a more recent factor analysis of Bram's data on the exchange of diplomatic personnel in the early 1960's, Russett and Lamb found that most groupings were regionally based, but three of their nine factors were nonregionally labeled "Large powers; China and friends; Common-

wealth and Outer Seven." Moreover, several of their "regional" factors included distant nonregional large powers.[12]

II. THE NATURE AND USES OF REGIONAL INSTITUTIONS

If there does not seem to be a strong trend toward or away from regional systems as the dominant sets of interdependence, how then do we explain the increase in the number and proportion of regional institutions? To answer the question, we must look more carefully at the nature and functions of regional organizations.

First, regions are relative. There are no absolute naturally-determined regions. Relevant geographical boundaries vary with different purposes, and these purposes differ from country to country and change over time.[13] Regional core areas can be determined and various boundaries delineated by analysis of mutual transactions and other interdependences, but which of a large number of potential regions become relevant for organization depends on political decision. Physical contiguity can be misleading, not only because technology, history, and culture can make "effective distance" differ from linear distance,[14] but also because images of what constitutes a region is affected by different political interests.

A political region "needs essentially a strong belief. Regionalism has some iconography as its foundation."[15] But even these beliefs or icons change, or are differently applied. For example, do "oceans divide men" or do "oceans unite men"? For Western Europeans at the time of NATO's foundation the Atlantic Ocean was the historic highway of Atlantic culture. Less is heard of this

[9]Steven Brams, "Transactions Flows in the International System," *American Political Science Review,* LX (Dec. 1966), 889.

[10]Bruce Russett, *International Regions and the International System* (Chicago 1968), 213.

[11]This tendency to find quasi- and macroregional clusters also means that a number of Russett's generalizations about regions are not relevant (and sometimes misleading) when applied to microregions.

[12]See also Bruce Russett and W. Curtis Lamb, "Global Patterns of Diplomatic Interchange," *Journal of Peace Research,* No. 1 (1969), 42.

[13]In Russett's words, "there is *no* region or aggregate of national units that can in the very strict sense of boundary congruence be identified as a subsystem of the international system" (fn. 10), 69.

[14]Karl Deutsch and Walter Isard, "A Note on a Generalized Concept of Effective Distance," *Behavioral Science* (January 1961), 308–10.

[15]Jean Gottmann, "Geography and International Relations," in W. A. Douglas Jackson, ed., *Politics and Geographic Relationships* (New York 1964), 28.

Table 3
"Regional Group" Factors as a Fraction of Total Number of Factors

		Early 1950's	Early 1960's	Change
3/4 of states in the factor are "regional"	U.N. Voting	3/4	1/7	Decline
	Trade	1/8	2/9	Small rise
	I.O. Membership	2/7	6/7	Large rise
2/3 of states in the factor are "regional"	U.N. Voting	3/4	4/7	Decline
	Trade	2/8	2/9	Slight decline
	I.O. Membership	4/7	6/7	Slight rise

in recent years. In the eyes of African anticolonialists, however, salt water was a clear dividing line. "France belongs to the continent of Europe; Algeria belongs to the continent of Africa"—though Algeria and France are both Mediterranean and close, while Algeria and Ghana (fellow members of the OAU) share neither of these characteristics. In short, geographical milieu may be interpreted in very different ways by decision-makers.[16]

Added to the confusion stemming from the relativity of regional images has been the value-laden character of the regional organization label. Diplomatic efforts to define regional arrangements or agencies under both the League and the United Nations were not successful because they were essentially political struggles over legitimacy. For example, at the San Francisco Conference on International Organization in 1945, Egyptian diplomats pressed for a definition of a regional organization that closely resembled the recently founded Arab League, while American delegates pressed for language on regional organization that would clearly benefit the Inter-American system without giving too much leeway to organizations like the Arab League. Similarly, the Soviet Union has consistently denied that NATO was a legitimate regional organization.[17]

Academic authors have also used the term "regional organization" in a variety of ways. Some use the term "regional" for all organizations which are not globally inclusive in their membership (including, for instance, the Commonwealth), no matter how geographically dispersed the members are. Others use the term to refer to geographically contiguous states, but differ on the degree of contiguity necessary. Still others apply "regional" to selective membership organizations which restrict membership on the basis of a geographical principle regardless of geographical contiguity.

Definitions are not right or wrong, but more and less useful. As Oran Young has argued, a conception of region that abandons geographical contiguity as a necessary condition means that "the term 'region' is apt to become so inclusive that it is useless."[18] Since we wish to distinguish the effects of geographical contiguity from selective membership, we will define a regional organization as one in which (1) membership is restricted in principle and in practice on a basis of geographical contiguity (i.e., there are no nonregional members); and (2) this contiguity involves a proximity and compactness.[19]

We will define as "quasi-regional" an organization (1) whose membership is restricted in part

[16]E. N. van Kleffens, "Regionalism and Political Pacts," 43; *American Journal of International Law,* 668 (1949). Kwame Nkrumah's views quoted in Ali Mazrui, *Towards a Pax Africana* (Chicago 1967), 43; Harold and Margaret Sprout, *The Ecological Perspective* (Princeton 1965).

[17]Ruth B. Russell, *A History of the United Nations Charter* (Washington 1958), Chap. 27; and Arthur H. Vandenburg, Jr., *The Private Papers of Senator Vandenburg* (Boston 1952), 190; G. I. Morozov, "Notion et Classification des Organisations Internationales," *Associations Internationales,* No. 6 (1967), 412.

[18]Oran Young, "Professor Russett: Industrious Tailor to a Naked Emperor," *World Politics,* xxi (April 1969), 488.

[19]The precise degree of contiguity one demands is a matter of choice. For example, 6000 miles between the most distant capitals (half the maximum distance between capitals of U.N. members) and no country more than 1500 miles from the others makes NATO "quasi-regional." To make NATO "regional" would require a threshold of 3000 miles.

on the basis of geographical contiguity or a geographical area of concern; but (2) which in practice includes nonregional members. We will treat all other restrictive membership organizations (as well as universal ones) as nonregional.

Where one draws the line between regional or quasi-regional organizations is, of course, an arbitrary decision. So also are the lines we use to distinguish different types of regional and quasi-regional organizations by their degree of contiguity. We shall call "macroregional" those organizations that encompass vast "regions"—where the maximum distance between members' capitals is one-fourth to one-half that of the "global" United Nations (i.e., 3100 to 6200 miles). We shall use the term "microregional" for those organizations where the maximum distance between members' capitals is less than one-eighth that of the United Nations (i.e., less than 1500 miles). Of course, one can object that these distances are arbitrary. But some such arbitrary decision is essential in constructing typologies, and this one leads to interesting patterns as we shall see in Table 4. Also one might object that "effective distance" measured in communications cost is more important than linear distance. Such an objection misses the point, however, since we are interested in analyzing the (perhaps mistaken) regionalist belief in a relationship between linear distance and effective international organization.

Finally, in constructing a typology we also categorize regional organizations by whether their primary declared or manifest function is military security (defense against an external military threat), primarily political (including diplomatic and cultural activities affecting a group's security, rank, or identity); or primarily economic (concerned with the creation, acquisition, or allocation of resources). Table 4 takes a table of "principle regional organizations in 1966" from a recent text and reconstructs it according to the geographical criteria that we have elaborated above.[20]

Table 4 provides evidence for our earlier statement that the role of contiguity in what is conceived of as a region for organizational purposes varies with the type of function involved. One of the things apparent from the table is that military security organizations tend to be of the low contiguity macroregional type and quasi-regional membership. Political organizations tend to be regional rather than quasi-regional—perhaps because of the important role of identity. Economic organizations involved in promoting high levels of trade integration or common services among their members tend to be microregional, with high geographical contiguity and identity seemingly playing an important role. This pattern would not hold, however, if regional and quasi-regional economic organizations involved in providing aid and finance (e.g., U.N. Regional Commissions and Regional Development Banks) were added to this table. Like military organizations, the relevant power for their functions seems frequently to be beyond the microregional scale.

To return to our question of why the number and proportion of regional organizations have increased though the evidence of increased importance of regional systems is ambiguous, perhaps the most useful perspective is to ask what incentives there are for elites and statesmen to use them. From this perspective, it would be a mistake to see the politics of regional organizations as purely the politics of cooperation. Regional organizations, like all international organizations, have derivative uses as well as declared ones. They may serve a number of diplomatic purposes, whether as a means of holding conferences without quibbling over schedules, gathering information, or exerting pressure on other states. In a world in which communications make other societies "penetrable," an aspect of power is the ability to communicate over the heads of governments (i.e., not by diplomacy alone) to create sympathy and a basis for legitimizing one's policies. The conference or parliamentary diplomacy aspects and sometimes the

---

[20]Jack C. Plano and Robert Riggs, *Forging World Order* (New York 1967), Table 4–1. The "principal" organizations selected by Plano and Riggs correspond with eighteen of the twenty-five regional organizations given by Donald Blaisdell, *International Organization* (1966); eighteen of twenty-five in Ruth Lawson, *International Regional Organizations* (New York 1962); eighteen of twenty-one nonmilitary regional organiza-

tions in J. S. Nye, *International Regionalism* (Boston 1968); and ten of ten military organizations in Philip Jacob and Alexine Atherton, *The Dynamics of International Organization* (Homewood, Ill. 1965). ANZUS, OECD and the Commonwealth are nonregional and not included in our table.

Table 4
Types of Regional Organization

MILEAGE BETWEEN MOST DISTANT CAPITALS	Principal Declared Function					
	I. *Military Security*		II. *Political*		III. *Economic*	
	Regional	Quasi-Regional	Regional	Quasi-Regional	Regional	Quasi-Regional
6,000 (and over)		SEATO 11,500 NATO 5,500	ASPAC 6,000 OAU 5,800 OAS 5,300			COLOMBO PLAN
5,000				OCAM 4,900	LAFTA 4,700	
4,000	WTO 3,900	CENTO 3,700	Arab League 3,100 Council of Europe 3,100		CMEA 3,900	
3,000						
2,000			Nordic Council 1,500		EFTA 1,900 UDEAC 1,100	
1,000	WEU 900		Entente 700 ODECA 500		Eur. Com. 800 E. Af. Com. 700 CACM 500 Benelux 200	

(Left axis: MILEAGE BETWEEN MOST DISTANT CAPITALS — Macro-Region ↑ — Micro-Region ↑)

administrative actions of regional organizations are among the many means available for communicating to foreign populations. In some cases, regional secretariats act as pressure groups in domestic political processes. These derivative uses may also include a symbolic role, for example, something comparable to statements of good will, nonaggression treaties, or an indication of a weak alignment. A seemingly useless organization today may provide a useful diplomatic instrument in the future.[21]

---

[21]There are also "private-regarding" derivative uses. International organizations may become cozy little clubs staffed by routineers; or be promoted by diplomats who see them as an opportunity for such personal goals as prestige, exile, or corruption.

These derivative uses often seem more important than the declared functions for the political regional organizations, particularly the macro-regional political ones such as the Arab League, OAU, OAS and Council of Europe. But military and economic regional organizations can also be put to the same diplomatic use. Control of Germany was a major derivative function of the ECSC. More recently de Gaulle tried to use the EEC as a means to press his economic partners toward a French conception of a European foreign policy. A 1969 struggle over the right of the WEU to discuss the Middle East was in reality a pretext for some of the EEC states to associate with Britain.

One can speculate that these derivative uses have made regional organizations particularly attractive to the statesmen because of the nature of power in the current international system. As Stanley Hoffmann has described the current system, the combination of the self-defeating costliness of nuclear weapons; the sanctification of the legitimacy of the nation-state (enshrined in the United Nations), and the costliness of ruling socially mobilized (rather than colonially inert) alien populations have reduced the role of force and enhanced the psychological components of power in world politics today. For the large powers, milieu goals (concern with the general environment of the international system) have become more important than possession goals (direct territorial, economic, or other concrete interests). Prestige and capacity to communicate effectively have taken on special importance. Loose arrangements among small weak states are no longer useless.[22]

The following examples show the way in which these characteristics of the current international system have enhanced the attractiveness of regional organization as a diplomatic tool. (1) As the less tangible psychological components of power have increased in importance, statesmen have sought the prestige of regional leadership as a symbol of power—witness the foreign policies of France, Ethiopia, and Egypt in the EEC, OAU,

and Arab League respectively. (2) Given the increased importance of domestic populations in world politics, coupled with the legitimacy of national sovereignty, regional organizations provide an opportunity to appeal over the heads of governments to groups in other states (despite the sovereignty clauses often written into the charters), as the successful and unsuccessful efforts of the Ivory Coast and Ghana to influence their neighbors through the Conseil de l'Entente and the OAU, respectively, demonstrate.[23] (3) With the diminished utility of military force, in many settings traditional military alliances have lost some of their attractiveness. Nonetheless, statesmen still feel the need to draw lines and introduce even a faint element of predictability into their search for security by creating political alliances under the guise of regional organization—witness ASPAC, RCD, and the Association of Southeast Asian Nations.[24] (4) With the predominance of milieu goals over possession goals, regional organizations can serve as useful tools for shaping conditions beyond one's national boundaries, whether it be creating more favorable conditions for aid for economic development (e.g., the regional development banks); or creating regional balances of power (a major motive for ASPAC). (5) Finally, with the increased importance of communications and signals, regional organizations have been useful as "no trespassing" signs, either between the Superpowers (the OAS or the Warsaw Pact) or from the weak to the Superpowers (OAU).

In addition to the incentives provided by the derivative diplomatic uses, political leaders may create and use regional organizations in response to personal or elite desires to express a collective identity in world politics. Particularly in less-developed areas where foreign policy is less bureaucratized, a leader may succumb to the heady wine of "instant brotherhood" sometimes felt at

[22]For these arguments see Stanley Hoffmann, *Gulliver's Troubles* (New York 1968), Part I; also Karl Deutsch, "The Future of World Politics," *Political Quarterly* (Jan. 1966); Robert Rothstein, *Alliances and Small Powers* (New York 1968).

[23]I. William Zartman, *International Relations in the New Africa* (Englewood Cliffs, N.J. 1966); also Claude Welch, *Dream of Unity* (Ithaca 1966); and Scott Thompson, *Ghana's Foreign Policy, 1957–1966* (Princeton 1969).

[24]"They may properly be seen as publicizing cherished ideas, as providing a forum, or rather forums, and as a means of launching pilot schemes which might possibly lead to future political unification. . . . ," Peter Lyon, *War and Peace in Southeast Asia* (New York 1969), 156.

summit conferences, or he may shrewdly calculate that he must make a token concession to regional identity to satisfy domestic elites who wish to assert their status or defend their culture in the world arena.

The results are sometimes paradoxical. For example, East African leaders met under U.N. ECA auspices in Lusaka in 1965 and agreed to the formation of an Eastern African Common Market at the same time that they were unable to work out the more immediate problems plaguing their existing common market. Central Americans have a long history of agreeing to protocols at regional meetings and then failing to ratify them after the leaders have returned home.[25] Similarly, a Latin American president could have chosen either to break the spell of brotherhood at the 1967 Summit Conference or agree to the formation of a Common Market by 1985—when he would almost certainly be out of power. At approximately the same time, the member states of LAFTA were unable to agree on the more modest (but immediate) goal of a contractually overdue second list of goods to be freely traded.

This is not to suggest that the fault lies solely with the leaders. The demands for a sense of identity and status as a larger group in world affairs may be sufficiently widespread among politically relevant groups to make the creation of regional organizations "good politics" from a leader's point of view. But public opinion is not monolithic. Nor as the literature on opinion polls has shown, is it always consistent, even in the same person. Most people have multiple loyalties and senses of identity, and they can switch from one to another according to the situation and their perception of the personal cost involved. For example, Ugandan trade unionists called for a Pan-African foreign policy at the same time that they demanded the exclusion of Kenyan workers.[26] A leader may feel impelled by domestic political needs to agree to the foundation of a regional organization, and later severely limit his commitment to it in response to foot-dragging by civil servants, representatives of low-income areas, or threatened industries (not to mention the possibility of a threat to his personal position).

In other words, we have suggested two alternative hypotheses (derivative diplomatic uses, ambivalent political identities) as possible ways to account for the increase in the number and proportion of regional institutions. If they are valid, the equilibrium condition for most regional organizations may be minimal existence that fills the identitive or diplomatic needs without incurring any additional costs. This appears to be particularly true of such manifest "political" organizations as ODECA or the Arab League, but it is probably also true of a number of manifest "economic" organizations such as the Association of Southeast Asian Nations, the Maghreb Council, RCD, or the proposed West African Customs Union. The type of organization which is based on these derivative or identitive functions alone could be said to represent "token integration" at the international level. The increase in the numbers of such regional institutions would not mean an increase in the effectiveness of regional institutions in the future international legal order.

III. THE FUTURE OF REGIONAL INSTITUTIONS

If the existing evidence about the importance of regional institutions is rather mixed, what can we say about future trends? Will the future remain as ambiguous as the present or will there be clear trends toward or away from a greater importance for regional institutions? Obviously we can merely speculate about the future of these institutions, and the longer the time we assume, the less likely to remain the same are the other things we hold constant.

Nonetheless we can inform our speculations by making explicit our projections of four important determinants: (1) the policies of the Superpowers; (2) technological changes that may affect economic and political decisions; (3) the systems transformation effects of existing regional organizations; and (4) large-scale changes in public opinion resulting from particular events, new issues, or generational change.

---

[25]A crucial protocol on standardization of industrial incentives was delayed for seven years. In early 1968, one-third of the protocols signed during the life of the CACM have not been ratified. See *Latin America* (April 11, 1969), 114.

[26]J. S. Nye, *Pan-Africanism and East African Integration* (Cambridge, Mass. 1965), 199.

Predicting the policies of the U.S. and the U.S.S.R. is beyond the scope of this enterprise. If we project current policies, we find that the United States has been a major promoter of regional organizations in the past quarter decade. United States attitudes toward regional organizations stemmed from a series of *ad hoc* responses: in the Western Hemisphere, from a long historical tradition; in Europe, from a desire to reconstruct a continent left fragmented by war and threatened by cold war; in Africa, representing a response both to economic logic and isolationist impulses; in Asia, relating to American efforts to create a non-Chinese pole of power. A policy toward regional organization *per se* has been raised as an issue in foreign policy debate only twice: once, in the period of planning for a new world organization during the latter part of World War II, and again in the late 1960's, as part of the Vietnam imbroglio.

For the Johnson administration, regionalism offered a means of promising that the costs incurred in Vietnam would not be repeated endlessly by a United States acting as a global policeman. In President Johnson's words, "Our purpose in promoting a world of regional partnerships is not without self interest. For as they grow in strength inside a strong United Nations, we can look forward to a decline in the burden that America has had to bear in this generation."[27] As the London *Economist* noted in 1968, the word regionalism "pops up regularly and has established itself in the Administration's vocabulary to connote a vague kind of principle by which distant continents may get themselves into better order."[28] Not only in declaratory policy, but in practice as well, the rising costs of Vietnam created constraints which increased the emphasis on regionalism in U.S. policy. One of the strands underlying the incorporation of regional criteria in U.S. aid programs for Africa was a Congressional "neo-isolationism" which was heightened by the Vietnam situation and came to be expressed in Congressional resolutions limiting the number of countries to which aid could be given. Similarly, the need to offer something dramatic

yet with minimal budgetary implications, at the meeting of Western Hemisphere presidents in 1967, was an important reason for upgrading U.S. support for Latin American regional organization.[29] And in Asia the connection was even more clear. As one administration spokesman told Congress in 1967, "a better Southeast Asia . . . less likely to produce a series of Vietnams can be furthered by regional integration. . . ."[30]

Critics point out that efforts to create regional balances of power—from which the United States as the stronger superpower could stand back and intervene only occasionally to right the scales, in an analogy to Britain's nineteenth century European policy—were at odds with the ideological doctrine of containing Communism sometimes expressed as a goal. So long as ideological containment had priority, the United States could only intervene on one side of the scales. In any case, after the 1968 election and change of administration, there was a marked decrease in the rhetoric of regionalism in U.S. foreign policy, and, more important, a diminished emphasis on support of regional organization in specific areas such as Europe and Africa.

At the same time that U.S. support for regional organizations was becoming less intense, the interest of the U.S.S.R. in regional organization began to increase. While the U.S.S.R. had consistently followed a policy of a *de facto* regional sphere of influence in Eastern Europe in the postwar period, it had shown far less interest in supporting, and in some cases even a hostility toward, regional organizations in other parts of the world.[31] At the end of the 1960's, however, the U.S.S.R. promoted the idea of an Asian regional collective security idea to include India, Pakistan, Afghanistan, Burma, Cambodia and Singapore as well as a regional trade plan that

---

[27]Lyndon Johnson, *Department of State Bulletin* (September 26, 1966), 453.

[28]*The Economist* (January 27, 1968), 31.

[29]See Robert Denham, "The Role of the U.S. as an External Actor in the Integration of Latin America," *Journal of Common Market Studies*, VII, 3 (March 1969). Also confirmed in interviews by this author.

[30]Rutherford Poats before the House Appropriations Committee, *Foreign Assistance and Related Agencies Appropriations for 1968* (April 26, 1967), 837. I am indebted to Robert Denham for the research that uncovered this and several other references in this chapter.

[31]Klaus Tornudd, *Soviet Attitudes Towards Non-Military Regional Cooperation* (Helsinki 1963).

might also include Turkey and Iran.[32] Initial Soviet efforts were met with coolness, and there is reason to believe that the U.S.S.R. would meet the same limitations in the promotion of regional organizations that confronted the U.S.[33] External actors are only one of a number of factors that support the growth of effective institutions. A rapid growth in the power of China, however, and a concerted Chinese foreign policy effort to create its own regional sphere and organizations might change the situation. Indeed, the unintended effects of superpower policies could have a more important impact on the growth of regional institutions than will their policies of deliberate promotion of such institutions. For example, policies that are perceived in Europe or Asia as a rapid expansion of Soviet power or a rapid withdrawal of American power might seriously alter public attitudes toward transferring power from existing states to regional institutions. We will return to this question below.

A second factor, technological changes that affect political and economic decisions, is likely to have indeterminate effects. On the one hand, skeptics about the future of regional organizations tend to base their argument on the probable direction of technological change. They argue that the revolution in transport, communications, and defense technology is rapidly foreshortening effective distances and calling into question the basis for regionalist schemes.[34] For example, the creation of jumbo air freighters, giant supertankers, and large-scale data-processing that facilitates capital movements and central control in multinational corporations, will make reduction of trade barriers and achievement of economies of scale less dependent on geographical contiguity. Paul Streeten argues that "modern economic facts make for inter-continental groupings be-

cause sea freights have fallen compared with land transport costs."[35] According to Samuel Lawrence, "From a transport viewpoint, it is now essentially immaterial whether the manganese brought to the United States originates in Africa or Brazil or whether the iron ores discharged in Rotterdam are brought from one of those regions or Australia."[36]

The growth of global corporations may be a more significant trend in international organization than the growth of regional organizations. In 1965, the 87 largest corporations (of which 60 were domiciled in the United States) had sales greater than the gross national product of the 57 smallest sovereign states. Increasingly such corporations are developing global strategies and absorbing the business done abroad into the mainstream of corporate strategy.[37] In the eyes of some, they are seen as private global decision systems, staffed by Saint-Simonian technocrats responding to criteria of economic rationality rather than regional or national identity in their choices as to the location of industry, employment, or earnings.[38]

In the defense field, nuclear and missile technology has already reduced the role of geographical distance in military security, and further changes of a similar type can be expected from satellite technology, and possibly also from developments in chemical and biological warfare. From a satellite in a synchronous orbit 22,300 miles above the earth, distances beneath are immaterial. It costs no more to send a signal between Alaska and Madagascar than between next door neighbors.[39] In the view of Thomas Schelling, a new type of global geography may be taking over,

---

[32]*New York Times*, September 20, 1969. The ironies were not missed by the Chinese who accused the Russians of having "picked from the garbage-heap of the notorious warmonger John Foster Dulles." *The Economist* (July 5, 1969), 26.

[33]J. S. Nye, "United States Policy Toward Regional Organization," *International Organization*, XXIII (Summer 1969), 724–25.

[34]Albert Wohlstetter, "Illusions of Distance," *Foreign Affairs* (Jan. 1968), 250. Also Institute for Strategic Studies, *The Implications of Military Technology in the 1970s* (London, Adelphia Paper 46, 1968).

[35]Paul Streeten, "A New Commonwealth," *New Society*, 353 (July 3, 1969).

[36]Samuel A. Lawrence, "Ocean Shipping in the World Economy," *World Affairs*, CXXXII (Sept. 1969), 123.

[37]George Modelski, "The Corporation in World Society," *Yearbook of World Affairs* (1968), 68; Raymond Vernon, "Economic Sovereignty at Bay," *Foreign Affairs*, XLVII (Oct. 1968), 115.

[38]See Sidney Rolfe, *The International Corporation* (Paris 1969); Howard Perlmutter, "Multi-national Corporations," *Columbia Journal of World Business* (Jan.–Feb. 1969); and Charles Kindleberger, *American Business Abroad* (New Haven 1969). For a skeptical view, see "Notes on the Multinational Corporation," *Monthly Review* (Oct.–Nov. 1969).

[39]*The Economist* (Feb. 22, 1969), 58.

in which earth spin and cloud cover may become as important in the world of satellites as Suez and Gibraltar were for a seapower. In Albert Wohlstetter's words, "the upshot of these considerations of technology in the 1970's, is that basic interests in safety will extend further out than they ever have before."[40]

It would be mistaken, however, to conclude from the projection of technological trends that there will not also be important regional systems —whether economic or military. For one thing, such a conclusion would be somewhat premature, at least for the early 1970's. Despite falling transport costs, geography will still have an impact on price. Despite missile and satellite technology, local and conventional defense techniques will remain relevant, particularly for less-developed countries. Moreover, some technological changes may have a positive effect on regional organization. Technological changes may reduce the autonomy of the nation-state, but if for historical or psychological reasons this leads to the redistribution of only *part* of these national powers at the regional level, the result would be a strengthening of regional organization. For example communications technology may make possible direct and inexpensive regional communications in areas like Latin America or Africa, where intraregional communications now often have to go through New York, London, or Paris. Large international corporations, to take another example, may prove to be important catalysts by regarding groups of countries as regions and acting accordingly.[41]

Technology and systems of transactions are not the only determinants of international politics. As Pierre Hassner points out, "political geography is made of history, anthropology, and psychology, as much as of physical geography." Oceans, skin color, and other crude images of regions constitute points of salience "which emerge out of history and leave their mark on psychology." Unlike the United States, China need not establish the credibility of her long-term presence in Asia.[42] Nor is it technology that made three Arab states

contribute two-thirds of Jordan's budget after the June war of 1967.[43] Moreover, popular images tend to lag considerably behind technology changes—witness the relative indifference in American public attitudes toward Japan, or the limitation of public commitment to geographically proximate areas.[44] As long ago as 1943 some commentators were predicting that the development of modern transport and communications would probably "destroy both the objective and subjective grounds for regionalism."[45]

If there were a one to one relationship between systems of interdependence, as measured by transactions or technological links and states' willingness to consent to international organization, we might have more confidence in projections about regional organization that are based solely on technology or transactions. In fact, the relationship is made more complex by the fact that elite perceptions of different types of interdependence is an essential link in the causal chain. For example, when there are various types of interdependence, why do states choose to form organizations on the basis of some rather than others?

If we think of "states" in terms of elites or groups of competing bureaucracies instead of as single rational units, we can see that different types of interdependence will affect the interests of (and be recognized by) different groups in different ways. An insecure political elite may be more concerned with interdependence in public opinion (and might create an organization in response to such opinion), while a technocratic elite might pay more attention to trade interdependence. For example, in Central America in 1951, the traditional political elite founded an organization reflecting diplomatic and domestic political interdependence, while a new generation of technocrats was allowed by default to found another (and ultimately more successful) organization—not on the basis of actual trade transactions (which were extremely low) but on the basis of *anticipated* transactions.

[40]Speech to Foreign Policy Association, New York (May 1968); Wohlstetter (fn. 34), 252.

[41]For evidence of this type of effect, see Raymond Vernon, "Multinational Enterprise and National Sovereignty," *Harvard Business Review*, XLV (March—April 1967), 156ff.

[42]Pierre Hassner, "The Nation-State in the Nuclear Age," *Survey* (April 1968), 12, 13.

[43]*International Herald Tribune*, February 19, 1969. By the end of 1969 Kuwait, Saudi Arabia, and Libya had contributed $321 million to Egypt and Jordan. *New York Times*, December 24, 1969.

[44]See *The Economist* (November 15, 1969), 44; Louis Harris poll in *Time* (May 2, 1969).

[45]Pittmann B. Potter, "Universalism Versus Regionalism in International Organization," *American Political Science Review*, XXXVIII (1943), 852.

A third factor that might determine the future is the effect of existing regional organizations on their related state systems. Given the impact of its demonstration effect on the rest of the world, this is particularly interesting in the case of Europe. In Haas' words, one model of international system transformation "credits the international organization with the capacity to produce feedbacks that result in changed perspectives on the part of national actors." The other model "puts the emphasis on autonomous changes within nations. Developments in the various domestic social, economic and political sectors are conceived as proceeding more rapidly and decisively than the learning of lessons fed back from the international system."[46] According to the regionalist doctrine, microregional economic organizations serve as particularly effective generators of the forces that can lead to the overcoming of national sovereignty and the transformation of the international system.

We would argue, however, on the basis of a model elaborated elsewhere, that integration processes slow down rather than accelerate over time, particularly in less-developed areas.[47] First, in most settings the process of politicization means that low-cost integration and technocratic style decision-making procedures are unlikely to last very long; certainly not until widespread popular support or a powerful coalition of intensely concerned interests have developed to the point where they determine the decisions of political leaders.

Second, the ability to reach difficult political agreement on "positive integration" measures to cope with the problems created by redistribution is likely to lag behind the forces created by more easily agreed-upon liberalization measures. Alternatively, in settings where market forces are weak and liberalization cannot be agreed upon, it seems likely that process forces will also be weak.

Third, the sense of reduced alternatives and the precipitation of larger crises will probably fail to have an integrative effect the closer the issues come to the security and identitive areas that are of greatest concern to popular political leaders. These are also the areas in which they are least likely to have the clear overriding common interests that make crises productive rather than destructive. Finally, the pressures both inside and outside the region for a common external policy are likely to develop more rapidly than popular or group support for a high degree of integration in these generally more controversial fields.

In brief, unless the structure of incentives offered by the international system is seriously altered, the prospects for microregional economic organizations leading in the short run of decades to federation, or to some sort of political union capable of an independent defense and foreign policy, do not seem very high. This does not mean, of course, that coordination of economic policies cannot help provide a basis for more coordination of foreign and defense policies so long as that is desired by the relevant political leaders. But this is a far cry from political union and a single external policy.

If common markets do not lead to federation, does this mean that they must slip back or fall apart? Is there no point of equilibrium in between? The belief that common markets must go forward or fall back is widely accepted. It has even been accepted by such skeptics as Stanley Hoffmann, who argues that "half-way attempts like surpranational functionalism must either snowball or roll back."[48]

Our basic hypothesis is that most political decision-makers will opt for the *status quo* at any level so long as the process forces or popular pressures are not so strong as to make this choice unbearable for them. If the process forces are too strong, political decision-makers may downgrade commitments to a point where they are tolerable, as happened in East Africa. But though equilibrium may not be tolerable at a given level, it does not follow that the only equilibrium point is in the cellar of disintegration. On the contrary, a certain amount of economic integration, particularly if it can be handled by the "hidden hand" of market forces and thus not involve costly political decisions, may go part way to meet the concerns of those who argue that existing states are too small to provide adequate welfare. Half-measures may take the edge off the urgency of the

---

[46]Ernst Haas, *Tangle of Hopes* (Englewood Cliffs, N.J. 1968), 29.

[47]J. S. Nye, *Peace in Parts: Integration and Conflict in Regional Organization* (Boston 1971), Chap. 3.

[48]"Obstinate or Obsolete? The Fate of the Nation State and the Case of Western Europe," in J. S. Nye, ed., *International Regionalism* (Boston 1968), 229.

situation, reduce the force of the demands of the "new feudalists" who wish to reduce the role of the sovereign states, and strengthen regional institutions at the subnational and supranational levels.

Moreover, as Krause and Lindberg have pointed out and the case of EFTA shows, this type of market integration need not greatly strengthen the regional institutions.[49] In short, it seems most likely that under the current structure of international incentives, most political decision-makers will find some point of equilibrium at which they would rather tolerate the inconvenience of the existing level of process forces than incur the greater political costs of full integration or disintegration.

Barring dramatic events or pressures from the international environment and barring forces released by generational change, a rapid transformation as the result of existing integration processes is unlikely. System transformation will occur, indeed has occurred, in the sense of altering the locus of decision-making between states and region in a number of issue areas. But the result is what we might call a functional-region, rather than a highly unified region.[50] Even under relatively favorable conditions, such as in Europe, it seems doubtful that the integration process forces will be strong enough to bring about major shifts in the locus of decision-making for most spheres of activity between member states and regional organizations in the next decade or so.

This leads us to the fourth factor we will consider—large-scale changes in public opinion resulting from factors exogenous to our model. Public-opinion studies show that mass opinion determines elite behavior only when it is strong and intense. Despite popular expressions favorable to regional organization, opinion in Europe and elsewhere has tended to provide only a permissive concensus rather than a clear direction.[51]

When probed for intensity, public opinion tends to become rather ambiguous. While 60 percent to 80 percent of Europeans favored a united Europe, only half that number favored a federation.[52] A majority of Frenchmen voted Gaullist and supported the political unification of Europe at the same time.[53] Nor was elite opinion consistently intense. For instance, a majority of French and German elites favored limited sovereignty in principle, but preferred to rely on national defense measures in practice.[54]

One potential source of a more intense public opinion is generational change. There is evidence to show that younger groups in regions like Europe are more favorable to unity than their elders.[55] In addition many activist youth groups respond to a technologically transmitted transnational culture that deliberately downplays national identity.[56] But their attitude that "Europe exists," without paying attention to institutional ways to replace existing national organizations, probably means that they will either be socialized by the existing pattern of interests and institutions that respond to the needs of the more national majority or will be relegated to ineffectiveness.

Another possible source of intensification of opinion could be the impact of particular cataclysmic events in one of the Superpowers, between the Superpowers, or in their policies toward given areas. The rise of a dictatorial regime, inadvertent wars, a renewed military threat, or sudden withdrawal of support might have such an effect.[57]

---

[49]Leon Lindberg, "Integration as a Source of Stress on the European Community System," in Nye (fn. 48). Lawrence Krause, *European Economic Integration and the United States* (Washington 1968), 24.

[50]This term implies that some functions, e.g., nuclear defense, may be handled in large part outside the region. See Alastair Buchan, *Europe's Future, Europe's Choices* (London 1969).

[51]See Leon Lindberg and Stuart Scheingold, *Europe's Would Be Polity* (Englewood Cliffs, N.J. 1970); also

William E. Fisher, "An Analysis of the Deutsch Sociocausal Paradigm of Political Integration, *International Organization* (Autumn 1969), 289.

[52]Jacques René Rabier, *L'Opinion Publique et L'Europe* (Brussels 1966), 23.

[53]See Alain Lancelot and Pierre Weill, "Les Français et l'Unification Politique de l'Europe, d'Après un Sondage de la SOFRES," *Revue Française de Science Politique*, xix (February 1969), 166, 147.

[54]See Robert Weissberg, "Nationalism, Integration and French and German Elites," *International Organization* (Autumn 1969), 341.

[55]See Ronald Inglehart, "An End to European Integration?" *American Political Science Review* 67 (March 1967); also Anitra Karsten, *Comment les Jeunes Allemands Voient Les Autres Peuples* (Brussels 1969).

[56]See the description in Anthony Sampson, *The New Europeans* (London 1968), Chap. 21.

[57]See the argument on withdrawal of American troops in Buchan (fn. 50).

A less dramatic source of change in public opinion might come from the gradual politicization of the environmental pollution problem. Pollution is not merely a regional problem; nor is it a problem that attracts the attention of elites in all regions. Nonetheless, there are signs of a growing awareness of the regional aspects of pollution in Europe. Pollution of the Rhine and North Sea has become something of an issue between the Netherlands and Germany. Newspapers have carried accounts of "black snow" falling in Norway as the result of pollutants dispersed into the air in the Ruhr.[58] The UN Economic Commission for Europe has begun to look at pollution in both Eastern and Western Europe. As yet, however, environmental pollution tends to be treated as a problem requiring technical cooperation rather than as a problem calling for a major regional political solution.

Barring such changes, the growing obsolescence of the nation-state is unlikely to induce a dramatic shift in public opinion. As Herz describes it, the rise of the nation-state followed the invention of gunpowder and the development of professional infantry, which destroyed the impenetrability of the medieval castle. Now with air warfare, nuclear weapons, economic blockades, and ideological warfare, the hard protective shell of the state has become "permeable." Or in Boulding's terms, there are no longer any snugly protected centers of national power, and all states are only "conditionally viable."[59] But this is already accepted in a verbal way by many European elites.[60]

The argument that the state is obsolete, in terms of welfare functions, emphasizes the enormous costs of research and development in such technologically modern industries as electronics, aircraft, space satellites, and nuclear energy, and cites the fact that the United States spends more on research and development in three weeks than Germany or France spends in a year.[61] For many developing countries, the argument is that their internal markets are too small to achieve economies of scale in any but a small range of industries.

But the obsolescence of the nation-state is nowhere near as complete as it is sometimes claimed to be. Take the failure to provide security. Nuclear deterrence has made viability conditional, but not as a fact of daily life in such a way as to weaken national loyalties. In terms of welfare, the argument is mainly against the *size* of some states, and tends to neglect the question of distribution. After all, one role of the state has been to preserve inequality of welfare vis-à-vis outsiders, and this has done and will continue to do all too well—witness the response of the wealthy states to poverty in the Third World.

One thing that many nation-states no longer successfully provide, however, is a sense of identity, of pride, of "counting for something in the world" for some of their elite groups. As we argued earlier, in Africa, Latin America, and Europe, the desire by some elites to achieve equality of status and to project an image of power in world affairs is an important motive for the creation of regional organizations. But we also argued that the strength of the organizations that can be built on this sense of regional identity has not so far been such as to challenge the nation-states.

Welfare and security often prove to be stronger incentives than the sense of identity that is expressed at the regional level.[62] Take, for example, European responses to the "challenge" of direct investment by large American corporations. Some Europeans urge a nonregional response of accepting close economic linkages with the North American (and to a lesser extent Japanese) economy, carving out areas of comparative advantage through specialization as the Swiss and Swedes have done. Others like J. J. Servan Schreiber argue that maximizing welfare is not enough, and that European identity and power are also important. Too close linkages with the global or Atlantic economy could hinder these objectives by making Europe overly dependent on imports of technological innovations. It is not enough for

[58]*New York Times,* January 11, 1970. See also "Europe Unfit to Live In," *Agenor,* No. 14 (Dec. 1969), 27–43.

[59]John Herz, "The Rise and Demise of the Territorial State," *World Politics,* IX (July 1957), 473–93. Kenneth Boulding, *Conflict and Defense* (New York 1962).

[60]See Morton Gorden and Daniel Lerner, "The Setting for European Arms Control: Political and Strategic Choices of European Elites," *Journal of Conflict Resolution,* IX (December 1965), 428.

[61]See Robert Gilpin, *France in the Age of the Scientific State* (Princeton 1968), Chap. 2.

[62]In 1969, among British reluctant to join the Common Market, a possible rise in cost of living outweighed all other fears by ten to one. *The Economist* (September 27, 1969), 1.

Europeans to live like Swiss or Swedes.[63] Rather they must build a strong regional unit capable of being an independent power in world politics. An individual European manufacturer, however, much as he might agree with Servan Schreiber in principle, would probably put welfare first if faced with the choice of merging with another weak European firm to counter the threat of an American intruder, or merging with the American firm to reap the profits of the imported technology and skills.[64]

The net effect of these four factors is, unhappily, indeterminate. Technology is shrinking the importance of distance. Other factors, however, work to enhance the importance of the iconographic aspects of geographical images.[65] Most believers in regionalism do not see "regions" as a technocratic planner might—as a set of variable and overlapping or, in some cases, concentric geographical units. On the contrary, regionalists see regions as groups of states with a similar concern about loss of status or defense against outside forces, who have chosen a geographical symbol around which to aggregate their power, at either high or low levels of integration.[66]

Given the growing imbalance among nations in the world, the disproportionate size of the United States and its capacity to penetrate other societies, the increasing role of multinational corporations, and the perceived threat to indigenous cultures from mass communications, there will continue to be strong incentives for elites to create and use regional organizations.

If the demand for identity should lead to widespread dissatisfaction with existing nation-states and the development of strong regional attitudes, the technological changes that are reducing—but not eliminating—the importance of proximity could lead statesmen to support more *effective* regional institutions. If identitive demands are not intense at the regional level, it seems more likely that technological changes will lead in the direction of functional type organizations. Such organizations might have a regional core such as the OECD or the Group of Ten have, but the common denominator would be less a geographic proximity or imagery than a mutual high level of development.[67] Such institutions at different levels may fulfill various needs—if not perfectly, at least sufficiently to reduce pressing problems to second-order ones of inefficiency. We reach these conclusions, however, with awareness that the unknowns are generally the most important terms in equations about the future.

[63]J. J. Servan Schreiber, *The American Challenge*, trans. R. Steel (New York 1968), 111.

[64]See Raymond Aron, quoted in Gilpin (fn. 61), 425.

[65]The novelty of elites' concern for world status should not be overestimated. *The Economist* (October 15, 1864) noted "the desire now manifesting itself in so many quarters of the world for aggregation, the wish to belong to a great and powerful community able to defend itself, and able also to exert a powerful influence on the progress of the world."

[66]See Gustavo Lagos, "The Political Role of Regional Economic Organizations in Latin America," *Journal of Common Market Studies*, vi (June 1968).

[67]See Edward L. Morse, "The Politics of Interdependence," *International Organization* (Autumn 1969).

Discussion and Questions

1. ➤ What is Nye's view of the nature and functions of regional organizations? ➤ How does it compare to the views of Masters, Young, and Miller?

2. ➤ How would you compare the relative importance of the growth of global corporations with the growth of regional institutions? ➤ Do you agree with Nye's discussion of this question? In our nonspatial use of the regional idea, global corporations would qualify as "regional" actors.

3. ➤ Do you agree with the indicators of regional growth relied upon by Nye? Note also the distinction between the growth of regional organizations and the persistence of preorganizational patterns of behavior.

4. ➤ Is Nye's discussion of the future of regionalism persuasive? ➤ Does he assume too much political continuity at the global level? ➤ Would it be more useful to rely upon several alternative images of the future of world society as the basis for forecasting the prospects for regionalism? Note that we can discuss the future either from the viewpoint of a passive observer or from the viewpoint of an engineer—a participant eager to discover the conditions that must be satisfied to attain a desired outcome.

PART **II**

INTEGRATION AT THE REGIONAL LEVEL: A THEORETICAL ORIENTATION

Part I presented several major modes of thinking about the relevance of regional units to a comprehensive conception of world order. Whether the conceptual focus was blocs, subsystems, or regional organizations, the overriding concern of the selections was with the ways in which these units fitted together and influenced the shape and operations of the international system. Such a concern is indicative of a trend away from the idea that international society consists simply of interactions among sovereign states (with perhaps some peripheral influence by the United Nations).

In Part II we consider various points of view about what regional units have been or might be formed. The Discussion and Questions sections raise issues that pertain to linkages between regional and global integration; issues that are studied in greater detail elsewhere in the volume. Here we are particularly concerned with theories of supranational integration that have evolved in the period since the end of World War II, and

we consider the extent to which supranational integration has actually evolved during this period. In this connection we are concerned with several approaches to supranational integration. First of all, there is an attempt to gain insight into integration by identifying those factors that appear to facilitate or block its initiation and continuation. Second, there is strong concern with determining in what respects experience with regional integration (first-level integration) is transferable to thought about the future of global integration (second-level integration). Third, there is an interest in assessing (*a*) under what circumstances and in what form integration is beneficial for a particular subsystem and (*b*) under what conditions regional integration makes positive contributions toward the creation of a just and peaceful world.

Through an understanding of regional integration, it becomes possible to specify some of the conditions that work for and against different kinds of global integration. As yet, however, social scientists have not looked closely at the interactions between regionalist and globalist strategies of system change. In fact, the issues that would permit such examination have not been defined.

There are, however, some general issues that should guide your reading of this chapter:

1. Does success and failure of movements for regional integration arise from the same or similar considerations that determine the progress of movements for global integration?

2. Do governments that commit themselves to regional activities tend to diminish or increase their constructive participation in global activities, such as those administered by the United Nations?

3. What sorts of circumstances and experiences determine whether regionalism is perceived and structured as an *alternative* to rather than as a *transition* toward a stronger set of central political institutions in international life?

4. Under what circumstances does a commitment to regional integration act to promote the growth of more universal symbols and institutions of political authority? Does regional political loyalty facilitate or block the formation of a global political consciousness?

5. Is it desirable, from the perspective of second-order integration, that various experiments with integration within the principal regions reach roughly convergent results and achieve institutional forms that are similar to one another?

To introduce these inquiries we present an excerpt from George Liska's book *International Equilibrium: A Theoretical Essay on the Politics and Organization of Security* (Harvard University Press, Cambridge, 1957), pp. 162–67. Note that throughout Liska's analysis the significance of the authoritative process and structures is a major concern. In evaluating this material it might be fruitful to compare his view of these matters with the position on world authority taken by Clark and Sohn in *World Peace through World Law* and by Lynn Miller's selections in Parts I and V.

Integration translates into functional and institutional terms the awareness of larger interdependence for security and welfare. It can be a matter of spontaneous growth, be deliberately instituted, or, most likely, be a compound of the two. Interdependence does not ensure integration, it merely constitutes a challenge.

International integration may be seen as a dynamic process involving emerging community ties, functional and treaty relationships, and organs that range along an ideal continuum from more or less sporadic connections between sovereign states under international law to federal and unitary supranational institutions governed by constitutional law. Conceptually, there is no dramatic break; it is therefore often difficult to determine where international organs cease and supranational ones begin. Nor does the denial of *de jure* supranational powers necessarily exclude the *de facto* supranational character of institutions formally ruled by international law and sovereignty. When the integrative process passes into the federalizing stage, however, political and juridical sovereignty is definitely pooled and some of it transferred to joint institutions. There emerge into coordinate status interrelated central and component state organs, reciprocally autonomous within their defined spheres; and the federative institutional structure corresponds to a similarly composite pattern of inclusive and exclusive community feelings, needs, and interests. Traditional dichotomies between international, federal, and confederal systems are dissolved.

Any form of integration presents thus two major aspects at any particular moment. It constitutes, first, a static quantity or density of integration within the continuum. Second, it is a phase in the dynamic integrative process, progressive or regressive in relation to its own revolutionary potential and to other more or less advanced forms.

It is impossible to square the idea of an integrative continuum and process with a static view of sovereignty. On the one hand, it is still the rule to regard sovereignty as an intrinsic, fixed, and equal quantity of rights and immunities accruing automatically to any state. Sovereignty stands then for "complete freedom of action regarding peace and war" and is a "symbol for concentrated power." It is tempting to reject completely such an idea. On the other hand, one may prefer the notion of differential sovereignty as a variable aggregate of legal rights and claims, and try to preserve the concept of sovereignty as a functionally divisible and juridically unifying normative principle of a consistent organization of power. This seems to be the more constructive procedure. Some kind of order is preferable to the legal anarchy of uncoordinated powers, which would logically result both from rejecting altogether the idea of sovereignty as an ordering principle and from subscribing to the absolutist pretensions made on its behalf.

Unlike Austin, Grotius believed that sovereignty retained its essential character despite limitations and disabilities imposed on its subject. And in fact, no state in reciprocally dependent relations with other states can preserve an absolute and unlimited sovereignty. Rather it employs its autonomy to render less onerous its adjustment to other states. This is inevitably truer of weaker states whose diminishing power implies increasing power deformation of their sovereignty no less than of other institutions. Unless the contact of a sovereign self-will with another self-will produces a collective will, the alternative will be curtailment for the weaker self. It is thus impossible to uphold absolute, equal, and indivisible sovereignty against the facts of power differentials and the pressures of interdependent needs. Instead, substantial or effective sovereignty appears as a dynamic function following, as it were, the shifting point at which intersect the two continua of greater or lesser national power and *de facto* international integration. To elaborate, effective sovereignty is, on the one hand, a variable on the scale of actual coordination of policies and resources among states, corresponding to a range of attitudes from extreme ethnocentrism to cooperative internationalism reflecting the recognition of interdependence; on the other hand, effective sovereignty is a variable depending on the power of a state and its role and responsibility in international relations and organization. This may mean actual dissovereignty for weaker states and actual or institutional extension of the effective sovereignty of greater Powers as contemplated, for instance, by the United Nations Charter.

Such a view may imply graduation of differential sovereignty among factually unequal states; it certainly implies the pooling of divisible sovereignty in a way which would distribute national and international or supranational functions and powers in conformity with the structure of individual and group needs, and the progressive transfer of such functions and powers from domestic to international and supranational jurisdiction. This brings together the juridical-normative view of sovereignty and a realistic interpretation of international society. The former points to functionally diversified organization of institutional powers as a prerequisite of national, federal, and international legal order. The latter points out the basis of such an order in actual facts about national power and international interdependence. In a power-normative situation, the two approaches join to provide a rationale for a growing scope of international organization and integration as an alternative to legal and political anarchy.

To the extent that it is deliberate, integration represents a manipulative approach to order, security, and welfare. It supplements, to say the least, the discredited automatism of the "laws" of political balance of power and economic equilibrium on the one hand, and of the normative laws of collective security on the other. It is supposed to stabilize (but not freeze) the operation of these laws among the integrated parties and, in the case of only regional integration, consolidate the joint position of the parties in the global equilibrium and security systems. This is, to be sure, only the barest skeleton of integration, which is overlaid by the softer tissue of community feelings in a finished organic whole. Yet, like the theory of sovereignty, the theory of integration, too, must place into unifying focus not only the element of community and institutions, but also of power and, in addition, military security and socio-economic well being. This is especially true of integration among unequal communities with a tradition of personal and group insecurity, which stimulates the naturally anti-integrative tendencies implicit in nationalism.

Nations may be pulled together, among other things, by an active sense of larger community, needs of interdependence, and the anticipation of advantages flowing from a more inclusive union. They may seek joint security against common external threat. But nations with an antagonistic past and fears for the future may be induced to closer integration, including federation, also by the desire to be secure against each other. Security has been traditionally sought by means of a successful war or alliance, producing a favorable balance of power. Collective security was designed to modify this pattern. Yet within a menaced fragment of the state system, like

Western Europe today, internal war may be out of the question and the area for diplomatic maneuver too narrow. Security by means of federal association with the feared neighbor may then appear as the alternative to his containment by war, alliance with the countervailing states, or disarmament. Still more obviously, federalism as a vehicle of expansion may be substituted for warlike conquest. And in the realm of economics, a cooperatively integrated economy is a fairly close alternative to competitive trade war. Mutual attraction and repulsion characteristic of so many neighbors is thus paralleled by an equally ambivalent relation between federation and war. Nations in an intense contact may have no option but to be joined. The question then is whether they are to be joined in recurrent struggle or in a federal embrace.

If federation, or any other type of integration, is to fulfill its security function and be protected against its hegemonic potential, it must provide effective safeguards for the weaker parties. This is essential. Preoccupation with security will not promote forms of integration which fail to implement their *raison d'être*. Insecurity in separate diversity will be preferred to a union which is merely a medium for the aggrandizement of the nuclear nation. Just as there is only a narrow dividing line between federation and war, so is there only a thin partition between the anti- and the pro-federalizing effect of apprehensions among many unequal communities. A paralyzing concern about the future is less easily submerged than past antagonisms, and tends to cling to the known if precarious *status quo*. Hence, military-security arrangements and trusted safeguards against political, economic, and other peaceful penetration may easily be the decisive factor in the equation. They must counterbalance the threat of intrafederal supremacy by stronger partners or an extrafederal regional Great Power.

All this points to a proposition in terms of our conceptual framework. A successful integrative and federalizing process requires that military-political and socio-economic equilibrium in the larger security and welfare area be promoted through institutions in equilibrium with respect to their structure, security commitment, and both functional and geographic scope, as a means to an expanding functional and moral community. A reliable equilibrium cannot always be established from elements within the prospective area. Then, an external balancer or equilibrator may be required to intervene as a *deus ex machina* in the crisis and break through the dilemma. His function is to guarantee the crucial period of consolidation and thus to tip the balance of negative security fears from their natural anti-integrative to a pro-integrative expression.

It is, therefore, futile to deny the ultimate unity of politics by postulating an antithesis between the balance of power and the federal principle of equal rights in a "coordinate state." Quite to the contrary, federation may be the necessary condition of maintaining safe equilibrium among democratically governed nations; and internal equilibrium is essential for reinsuring the coordinate autonomy and legal equality of member-states, especially in incipient federations. [Reprinted by permission of the publishers from George Liska, *International Equilibrium*, Cambridge, Mass.: Harvard University Press, Copyright, 1957, by the President and Fellows of Harvard College.]

In a widely read early study of "community-building" on the regional level, a group of scholars working under the direction of Karl Deutsch made a fundamental distinction between those political communities that were "security-communities" and those that were not. A security-community was characterized by the Deutsch group as "one in which there is real assurance that the members of that community will not fight each other physically, but will settle their disputes in some other way. If the entire world were integrated as a security-community, wars would be automatically eliminated" (Deutsch *et al.*, "Political Community and the North Atlantic Area," in *International Political Communities* [Doubleday-Anchor, New York, 1966], pp. 1, 2). But note that the authors do not postulate any supranational institution building, nor do they even imply a transfer of loyalties to some new larger political entity. In their analysis, the Deutsch group distinguishes between security-communities that are "amalgamated" and those that are "pluralistic":

By *Amalgamation* we mean the formal merger of two or more previously independent units into a single larger unit, with some type of common government after amalgamation. This common government may be unitary or federal. The United States today is an example of the amalgamated type. It became a single governmental unit by the formal merger of several independent units. It has one supreme decision-making center.

The *Pluralistic* security-community, on the other hand, retains the legal independence of separate governments. The combined territory of the United States and Canada is an example of the pluralistic type. Its two separate governmental units form a security-community without being merged." [P. 2]

Note that the term "integration" is defined to include both types of security-communities. Canada and the United States became "integrated" at the point in time when the perceived expectation of violent resolution of disputes no longer existed. More typical usage would confine the concept "integration" to a situation of amalgamation, but would not isolate the intracommunity security element from other transfers of sovereignty to a higher-than-state political unit. Integration in this latter sense is much more *a matter of degree, of structure, and of shifting substantive or functional roles.*

The prospects for building a security-community are improved if the integration process is initiated in relation to such sharply delimited and perceived common interests as creating a common market or a free-trade area. The success of these interest-oriented integration ventures may then produce—although such an effect is controversial and as yet unverified—a security "spillover" as an eventual consequence of beneficial experience with economic integration.

Integration projects of a voluntarist character are almost exclusively undertaken by states that do not have hostile relations with each other. Often an "external" adversary helps cement the integrationist sentiment. It is probably useful to consider integration by force of arms in relation to integration by voluntary action. Empires can be regarded as examples of successful varieties of coercive integration, depending on the definition. Etzioni considers an empire to be an example of a "premature" expansion of a political unit: "The premature nature of empires has been demonstrated by showing that they did not have the cybernetic capacity and power, the communication and transportation means, and the consensus-formation structures necessary to keep a large or extending polity integrated and guided" (Amitai Etzioni, *The Active Society* [Free Press, New York, 1968], p. 580). Etzioni employs a more elaborate multidimensional conception of "political community" and "integration" than is used by the Deutsch group.

Although today's methodology for studying integration phenomena is more sophisticated than it was at the time Etzioni wrote *Political Unification* (Holt, Rinehart, and Winston, New York, 1965), he was interested even then not only in finding out how integration could be measured but also in determining what kinds of values integration would further.

As a highly creative political sociologist, Etzioni is concerned with political unification, that is, with the pursuit of a wider political community than the nation-state, and not with the internal dynamics of economic and functional integration of interest to many specialists, in particular, economists. He has developed quite an elaborate mix of concepts, of which a basic one is *political community*. Community exists only when a political aggregate is self-sufficiently integrative, and any political community, in order to maintain itself, must have three kinds of integration: (1) control over force; (2) control over allocation of resources; (3) provision of chief focus of identification. Etzioni introduces the concept of *unions* to refer to international systems whose level of integration is lower than that of community, but higher than that of a typical international organization. He then develops a systematic three-stage model of the integration process. At each stage Etzioni isolates those variables that determine whether the integration (or unification) process is likely to get started, and if started, whether it is likely to move to the next stage, stagnate, or relapse to an earlier stage.

Etzioni argues that integration proceeds along rather definite paths rather than by trial and error. Do you agree with this argument? For an extension of Etzioni's thinking to problems of integration at the global level, see *The Active Society*, pp. 550–613. Is it possible that the notion of federation could underlie Etzioni's thinking to such a degree that it limits the utility of his approach as the basis for a general inquiry into supranational integration?

It is important to consider how Etzioni's conception of "political community" differs from that of the Deutsch group. Does what the Deutsch group calls a "security community" amount to a "union" in Etzioni's terminology? If of the pluralistic variety, might it not merely constitute an atmosphere of harmony such that no expectation of inter-unit violence exists? In this latter instance, there is no occasion for structural modifications of inter-unit relations. Is it imaginable that a pluralistic security community might emerge on a global level? Under what circumstances? Some proposals for world order move in such a direction. See, for instance, Walter Millis and James Real, *The Abolition of War* (Macmillan, New York, 1963).

The federalist conception of volitional integration contrasts with coercive forms of integration associated with empire-building. Max Beloff, in a provocative essay, argues that historical evidence strongly suggests that integration along federal lines has not been successful in those cases where the process sought to integrate previously independent units. Beloff's main point, supported by such examples as the United States, the Swiss federation of 1848, Canada, and Australia, is that federal solutions have only worked on the basis of some *shared* prefederal experience, especially the experience of a group of units enduring together some form of prior imperial domination. See Max Beloff, "Federalism as a Model for International Integration," *Yearbook of World Affairs 1959* (Praeger, New York, 1959), pp. 188–204. The ideas of Beloff and Etzioni could be combined to suggest a two-step integration process: Step one—a world empire disintegrating because of premature expansion after a period of dominion; Step two—a world federal state arising from the common political institutions and experience that were developed during the stage of empire. A period of world empire becomes the necessary preparatory precondition for successful federalism.

The type of empire is related to its role as a preparation for more genuine varieties of integration. It would be tempting to consider Soviet domination of Eastern Europe during the period immediately after World War II as an imperial preparation for the integration of socialist states. John Pinder demonstrates, however, that the model of autarkic operations appropriate for the Soviet Union in the decades after the Russian Revolution, a gigantic country that found itself ideologically isolated until after World War II, was improperly transferred to the postwar East European societies. These smaller units in Eastern Europe were parts of an over-all Communist system. The Eastern European states developed highly planned economies and their affirmation of the prerogatives of national sovereignty made them less able to work toward economic integration than were the more ideologically diverse states of Western Europe. One factor in this process was, of course, their continuing struggle to achieve higher degrees of national independence by liberating themselves from Soviet hegemony.

The Eastern European example also suggests the importance of the domestic economic system in determining the prospects for integration. Latin American countries, although many of them are also seeking to dissolve a hegemonial subservience to the United States, have actually been led toward integration as a strategy of containment. These national societies, with their market economy and with their ideology of regional identity, seem most inclined to and capable of gradual stage-by-stage integration.

There is also the degree to which integration undertaken for economic reasons—to expand markets, to lower trade barriers, to increase the bargaining power of a group of states—might lead to political integration. Is there a sequence of stages? Does the sequence depend upon subsystemic varibles? In Beloff's terms, might not a relatively nonpolitical, inorganic form of economic integration provide the basis of common experience and harmonized institutions that will prepare the way for federation at a later stage? What is the integration potential of a defense arrangement such as NATO or the Warsaw Pact? Does such a concert of action for common defense "disintegrate" when the external threat disappears or diminishes? For an argument about the positive integration potential of NATO, see Henry A. Kissinger, *The Troubled Partnership* (McGraw-Hill, New York, 1965).

If the principal objective of integration is, despite a series of preparatory phases of uncertain duration, to create eventually an amalgamated security-community that embraces more than one previously independent state, then it seems correct to pursue a sequential strategy of regionalism. The move toward political community is gradual, perhaps beset by periodic reversals of direction. The European experience is our best case in history, and it confirms the twisting road that leads to supranationality.

The same reasoning, by analogy, has obvious consequences for a strategy of integration at the global level. It may well be that it would be best to initiate the process of integration unobtrusively, stressing subject matter that does not threaten either existing patterns of political loyalty or the status of and scope of control exercised by the sovereign state. Only later, as shared experiences become a reality, might it become possible to erode or challenge the prerogatives of sovereignty. The pacing and phasing of such a strategy of integration at the global level has yet to be worked out in detail comparable to that which is available at the regional level. And we do not know, given the diversities and conflicts present in international society, whether the experience at the regional level is properly transferrable to the global level. Perhaps it is necessary to work out a quite separate strategy for global integration, taking full account of the distinctive features of the international setting.

There is, finally, another kind of globalist concern that should be considered, although the readings here do not deal directly with it: namely, whether a world of regionally (or subregionally) merged sovereignties would be beneficial from the perspective of our concerns (1) with world peace, (2) with social and economic welfare for the poorer countries, and (3) with human rights. Would the move beyond the nation-state end, or at least diminish significantly, the baneful influence of national sovereignty on human existence? Or would such a regionalization of world society merely transfer the baneful aspects of sovereignty to these larger communities? Does the answer to such questions depend, partly at least, upon the motivations and ideology of each *particular* integration process? Does it depend, especially, upon whether governments and their populations can be persuaded to support the regional idea for reasons other than the improvement of their competitive position in international society? For one pessimistic analysis of these prospects, arguing that balancing of internal pressures tends to make regional units "closed systems" with respect to global politics, see David Mitrany, "The Prospect of Integration: Federal or Functional," *Journal of Common Market Studies*, vol. 4, no. 2 (December 1965), pp. 119-149.

The three selections in this chapter all appeared in an issue of *International Organization* entitled "Regional Integration: Theory and Research", vol. 24, no. 4 (Autumn 1970). This particular set of papers clearly represents the outstanding attempt to date to evaluate theory building and research results in relation to regionalist subject matter and is recommended in its entirety.

Two of the three selections have been chosen for inclusion in this volume because they provide a useful overview and synthesis of theory and research. Furthermore, these pieces reinforce our own advocacy of a more explicitly normative orientation toward regionalism.

The first selection in Part II, by Ernst Haas, is entitled "The Study of Regional Integration: Reflections on the Joy and Anguish of Pretheorizing." Professor Haas considers empirical generalizations that regional integration studies have given us and the confusion in the field resulting from differences inherent in the three main "pretheories" of integration. He demonstrates the need for a reassessment of past work and a new direction for the future, complementing our contention that insufficient time has been devoted to the normative aspects of regional integration. A theory of regional integration is needed, Haas contends, that will delineate consistently and specifically the dependent variable—the eventually resulting condition aimed at—and will explain which combination of independent variables will produce particular terminal results. The existing pretheories of federalism, communications theory, and neofunctionalism have neither done this nor have they even been clear in delimiting the independent variables that will interact to produce the final result.

In the last few pages of the article Haas discusses the direction future work should take. Rapid progress is already being made to specify, operationalize, and establish clear links between independent variables. From the three pretheories, we can draw empirical generalizations sharpening our understanding of these independent variables. Beyond this, to link variables together, Haas posits several "evaluative concepts", which he describes as "intellectual constructs that command general acceptance for their utility without being fully validated and without having found a clear and final niche in some as yet to be formulated theory. . . . Appropriately scored concepts associated with the explanation of one of our postulated outcomes constitute an 'action path'" (p.

124). The next step for integrationists to take is to compare regional and national experiences systematically on the basis of such evaluative concepts. To aid in doing this, Haas suggests computer simulation, which has the additional benefit of requiring systematic links between variables— thereby approximating a theory. Simulation would enable us to see alternative shapes for future world order as well, since regional integration studies contribute analytical and empirical tools to study the links between the international system and the nation-state.

This article could be usefully reread after reaching the end of this book, since it summarizes existing theories. Thus it can serve both as an introduction and as a summary of principal perspectives and methodologies now employed in the study of regionalism. It would also be helpful to read Haas' article in conjunction with the Cantori and Spiegel article reprinted in Part V.

The second selection is "Domestic and International Consequences of Regional Integration," by Stuart A. Scheingold, who draws upon the European experience with integration to illustrate the limits of present research and to identify the sorts of problems that remain to be approached in the study of regional integration. The basic point Scheingold makes here has been mentioned in the General Introduction, and is consistent with what Ernst B. Haas says in the preceding article: the study of integration must give attention to the *consequences* of integration, as well as to the *process* of integration. Value-sensitive empirical research must be carried out in order to see whether integration makes any impact on the five values. Scheingold suggests that cost-benefit analysis, which so far has been on a national level primarily, could be widened in scope in a number of ways.

The third selection is "Theory and Practice of Regional Integration: The Case of Comecon" by Andrzej Korbonski. It is presented here primarily to indicate the kind of empirical materials that have been utilized by theoreticians in the field of regional integration. Although throughout this volume there are many references to regional experiments and groupings in the rest of the world, this article in particular provides us with an occasion to gain some understanding of regional developments in Eastern Europe. Korbonski's analysis enables a comparison to be made between the integration experience of socialist Eastern Europe and that of nonsocialist Western Europe. It also encourages a sophisticated comparison between the role of the Soviet Union as a hegemonial actor in relation to Eastern European "regionalism" with that of the United States as a hegemonial actor in relation to "regionalist" forms in Latin America, especially Central America. For an emphasis on interregional comparison, see Louis J. Cantori and Steven L. Spiegel, *The International Politics of Regions* (Prentice-Hall, Englewood Cliffs, N.J., 1970).

5

The Study of Regional Integration: Reflections on the Joy and Anguish of Pretheorizing

ERNST B. HAAS

I. WHY STUDY REGIONAL INTEGRATION?

Why have we been studying something we call "regional integration" for about fifteen years? We were stimulated by two otherwise unrelated trends: the flowering in the United States of systematic social science and the blooming in Europe of political efforts to build a united continent, to "integrate" Western Europe at least.[1] But the story of integration encompassed a mixed bag of heroes ranging from such regional "integrators" as Napoleon Bonaparte and Simón Bolívar to nation-building statesmen such as Otto von Bismarck and Camillo Cavour. Some saw even in Adolf Hitler and Hideki Tojo certain characteristics of the political actor who seeks to integrate nations into a regional unit. Are we then studying *any* kind of political unification?

Often one gets the impression that the study of regional integration is the same as the study of regional cooperation, of regional organizations, of regional systems and subsystems, or of regionalism. All these terms are widely used. They compound the general uncertainty of whether regional conquerors and nation builders are also actors on the stage of regional integration. To delimit the field, therefore, it must be stressed that the study of regional integration is unique and discrete from all previous systematic studies of political unification because it limits itself to *noncoercive* efforts. The study of federalism, national unification, nation and empire building is necessarily replete with attention to the use of force by the federalizer or the catalytic agent—external colonizing elite, military conqueror, or hegemony-seeking

From *International Organization*, vol. 24, no. 4, Autumn 1970, pp. 607–646. Copyright 1970, World Peace Foundation, Boston, Mass. Reprinted by special permission. This article was also published in L. N. Lindberg and S. Scheingold, Eds., *Regional Integration: Theory and Research* (Harvard University Press, 1970.)

[1] I consider the pioneering work in this field to be Karl W. Deutsch's *Political Community at the International Level: Problems of Definition and Measurement* (Garden City, N.Y.: Doubleday & Company., 1954). Deutsch raised all the major questions and introduced many of the concepts that still preoccupy and guide the research effort.

state. Our task is to explain integration among nations without recourse to these historical agents not because they have not been important but because they make the explanation too simple and too time-bound. The dominant desire of modern students of regional integration is to explain the tendency toward the voluntary creation of larger political units each of which self-consciously eschews the use of force in the relations between the participating units and groups.

The main reason for studying regional integration is thus normative: The units and actions studied provide a living laboratory for observing the peaceful creation of possible new types of human communities at a very high level of organization and of the processes which may lead to such conditions. The study of regional integration is concerned with tasks, transactions, perceptions, and learning, not with sovereignty, military capability, and balances of power. It refuses to dichotomize the behavior of actors between "high" political and "low" functional concerns; it is preoccupied with all concerns of actors insofar as they can be used for sketching processes of adaptation and learning free from coercion.

This central reason should not obscure other normative uses to which the study of regional integration can also be put; they are in fact suggested by the overarching concern just stated. We can discover whether regional peace-keeping machinery is more effective than United Nations procedures, an important lesson for future modes of conflict resolution. We can also discover when and where regional processes are merely a facade for the hegemony of one member state. We can get more information about which elite learns from whom in the interactions triggered by regional processes, discover what is learned, and trace the use to which the new insight is put. Again we can contrast this with similar events at the global level. We can discover whether regional common markets are really better for industrialization and effective welfare policies than is a global division of labor, whether they lead to redistribution and the equitable sharing of scarce resources—or to more competition for such spoils.

All this should be self evident. But it has been hidden by the concern of some students of integration for the canons of social science and its language. Nor is this to be regretted. Apart from and

beyond the normative importance of these studies the empirical theory of international relations is advanced by clearly delineating and establishing recurrent practices. Moreover, the study of regional integration makes it possible to use the comparative study of foreign policy, even of domestic policies, and connect it with the study of international processes. In short, the field of "linkage politics"—as a conceptual bridge between theories of the international system and theories of national behavior—can be given real life if the empty boxes of its matrices can be filled with the interactions studied in the process of regional integration.[2]

In the following pages I shall attempt an evaluation of fifteen years of research on regional integration. I should like to confess at the outset that while inferences about learning, adaptation, and the evolution of shared tasks among nations have provided the foci for research, the normative uses to which the findings could be put have not received the attention they deserve. Nor has the field been systematically pressed into the service of theory building in the area of comparative foreign policy studies. This must be our first evaluative finding. But the effort at evaluation forces us to pose some other questions as well. They constitute a grab bag of nagging doubts and uncertainties rather than a methodologically satisfying scheme of analysis. Moreover these questions do

---

[2]For an identification of highly or closely linked national polities with the notion of "integrated international system" see Michael K. O'Leary, "Linkages Between Domestic and International Politics in Underdeveloped Nations," in James Rosenau (ed.), *Linkage Politics: Essays on the Convergence of National and International Systems* (New York: The Free Press, 1969), pp. 324–346. See also the argument of W. F. Hanrieder to the effect that regional integration movements provide a key way of isolating linkages. Wolfram F. Hanrieder, "Compatibility and Consensus: A Proposal for the Conceptual Linkage of External and Internal Dimensions of Foreign Policy," *American Political Science Review*, December 1967 (Vol. 61, No. 4), pp. 972–973.

This approach is rejected by James N. Rosenau, "Compatibility, Consensus, and an Emerging Political Science of Adaptation," *American Political Science Review*, December 1967 (Vol. 61, No. 4), pp. 983–988. He argues that the questions addressed in integration frameworks of study cannot be combined with questions which hinge on adaptation. This is a more restrictive definition of adaptation and integration than is necessary or desirable.

not rest on a consensus as to what the field *should* yield, and therefore they are far from constituting a paradigm against which a variety of ongoing work can be judged. They are, in short, just questions which guided the effort of evaluation.[3]

(1) I shall inquire whether these studies have yielded a set of generalizations of empirically founded truths about integration. (2) Further, I wish to know whether these truths are equally "true" everywhere. This necessitates further questions as to whether these generalizations apply to all regional efforts or only to selected geographical locales, to all conditions of modernization or social organization or only to some. (3) I wish to know whether these generalizations are applicable at identical levels of meaning or abstraction; that is, do they talk about facts or about descriptive variables unequivocally identified with appropriate indicators, or can they be grouped into more abstract concepts endowed with greater explanatory or predictive sweep? (4) I wish to ascertain the degree of methodological and epistemological rigor which characterizes the work of establishing generalizations and abstractions. (5) Most importantly, I wish to know whether the theories with which we have been working actually possess any substantial power.

Power to do what? Theories can and should be evaluated in a variety of ways. We would wish to know (1) whether a theory adequately *describes* what happens. Does it contain variables sufficient to account for what appears to be going on in a given regional integration process or is it sufficient for comparing several such processes? Does it identify the sequence, or the stages, through which such processes appear to pass? (2) We also wish to know whether the theory adequately *explains* why the stages occur. This is a matter of being able to recount how the variables interact so as to produce a given outcome. (3) Finally, we wish to know how well a given theory *predicts* future outcomes, whether it tells us which conditions must prevail in order to enable us to say, "If a certain number of variables are present in sufficient strength, then integration in area X will occur." No cat is being let out of any intellectual bag if I reveal at this

stage that none of the theories used in integration studies fully meets any of these criteria.

A final preliminary step is essential. Semantic confusion about "integration" must be limited even if it cannot be eliminated. The study of regional integration is often confounded with overlapping and cognate activities which, however, usually address somewhat different problems. Unless care is taken to exclude these pursuits from the discussion, the search for evaluative clarity will prove fruitless. Specifically, it is necessary to distinguish between "regional integration" and such competing terms as regionalism, regional cooperation, regional organization, regional movements, regional systems, or regional subsystems of a global system.[4]

The study of regional integration is concerned with explaining how and why states cease to be wholly sovereign, how and why they voluntarily mingle, merge, and mix with their neighbors so as to lose the factual attributes of sovereignty while acquiring new techniques for resolving conflict between themselves. Regional cooperation, organization, systems, and subsystems may help describe steps on the way; but they should not be confused with the resulting condition.[5]

Even fifteen years of work have not quite sufficed to create a consensus on a clear delimitation. Amitai Etzioni treats "integration" as the terminal condition, not as the process of getting there. Philip Jacob and Henry Teune regard integration both as a process and as a terminal condition, a condition achieved when an unspecified threshold is passed by an unspecified mix of ten process variables (independent or intervening?). Karl Deutsch speaks of integration as a process leading to the creation of security communities; I consider

---

[3] I wish to acknowledge my great debt to Ivan Vallier in seeking to come to grips with these issues even though I fall short of attaining his ideal.

[4] For a representative agenda of topics and articles illustrating the rubrics regionalism, regional cooperation, regional organization, regional systems, etc., see Joseph S. Nye, Jr. (ed.), *International Regionalism: Readings* (Boston: Little, Brown and Co., 1968).

[5] This stab at a definition differs appreciably from the working definition of integration involving a shift in the loyalties of political actors with which I had worked previously. In abandoning the earlier definition I am expressing my agreement with the criticism Nye leveled at my own and at Deutsch's definitions. See Joseph S. Nye, "Comparative Regional Integration: Concept and Measurement," *International Organization*, Autumn 1968 (Vol. 22, no. 4), pp. 856–858.

it a process for the creation of political communities defined in institutional and attitudinal terms, a condition also described by Jacob and Teune. Federalists, finally, see the end of the integration process in the growth of a federal union among the constituent nations.[6]

Hence anything which contributes to a better understanding of integration, as provisionally defined above, provides valuable data or a relevant variable. But the study of regionalism or regional cooperation or regional organizations furnishes simply materials on important activities of actors or on their beliefs. The study of regional integration is concerned with the *outcomes* or *consequences* of such activities in terms of a "new deal" for the region in question even though these activities could of course be analyzed for other purposes as well.

The study of regional cooperation, for instance, may be considered as a part of the study of regional integration or as a separate interest. Regional cooperation is a vague term covering any interstate activity with less than universal participation designed to meet some commonly experienced need. Such activities often contain lessons and data for the study of regional integration. But judgments as to whether cooperation is "successful" must be based on criteria very different from those appropriate to the study of integration. The study of regional organizations sums up activities of interstate cooperative enterprises and links to these activities observations concerning institutional evolution. Integration studies derive much of their information from the activities of international organizations including nongovernmental groupings. Some integration theorists even prefer to use measures of organizational tasks and institutionalization as indicators of integration or disintegration. Still, the study of organizations seeks to pinpoint the "success" of such entities in terms which make the organizations the centers of concern rather than to focus on their impact on the members.[7] Integration studies must rely on the study of comparative politics and economics because the regional organizations through which integrative/disintegrative activity is carried on are properly considered intervening variables which help explain our real concern, the attainment of the possible later conditions in which the region may find itself.

Some writers refer to regional subsystems and regional systems. If they mean an especially intense network of international links within a defined geographical compass, they are talking about regional cooperation, transactions, or organizations though at a higher level of abstraction. A "regional system" is no more than a figure of speech summing up and describing such interactions. To be useful for dealing with the essentially dynamic concerns of the student of integration the portrait of the totality as a "system" must yield to the analysis of the separate strands of which the system is made up.[8] Regional "sub-

---

[6]These definitions are too well known to require extensive recapitulation. For discussions see Amitai Etzioni, *Political Unifications: A Comparative Study of Leaders and Forces* (New York: Holt, Rinehart and Winston, 1965), chapter 1; the process of "political unification" is described in chapter 2. Philip E. Jacob and James V. Toscano (ed.), *The Integration of Political Communities* (Philadelphia: Lippincott, 1964), chapter 1; chapters 2 and 3 of this volume contain an admirable summary by Karl Deutsch of the communications-transactions approach to integration. The federalist case is made in a sophisticated fashion by Dusan Sidjanski, *Dimensions européennes de la science politique: Questions méthodologiques et programme de recherches* (Paris: Librairie générale de droit et de jurisprudence, 1963).

[7]Phillippe C. Schmitter, "La dinámica de contradicciones y la conducción de crisis en la integración centroamericana," *Revista de la integración,* November 1969 (No. 5), pp. 140–147, offers the notion of self-encapsulation which highlights the problem of identifying organizational success with progressive integration.

[8]Discussion of the "Inter-American system," for instance, usually includes descriptions of all regional organizations, programs, and commitments of the member states of the Organization of American States (OAS) as well as of the relations between separate organizations. The "European system" is sometimes taken as a descriptive term for the totality of Western European organizations and programs without regard to any impact on the reciprocal integration of the member nations.

The level of political integration is the main characteristic that distinguishes political communities from other political systems. *System* is the more encompassing concept, indicating that changes in the action of one (or more) unit(s) affect actions in one (or more) other units, and that these latter changes in turn have repercussions on the unit or units in which or from which the change was initiated. . . . In short, units of systems are interdependent; members of communities are integrated. [Etzioni, p. 6.]

systems" involve descriptions of the particularly intense interactions in a given locale, e.g., the Middle East, explained largely in terms of the inputs of the "system" (i.e., the global network of international relations). Regional subsystems, then, are devices for explaining the interdependence between local ties and concerns and the larger world which constrain them.[9] This may be terribly important in helping to explain why regional integration efforts do or do not progress; but since the basic concern is not the explication of integration, the concepts and measures appropriate in one realm do not carry over into the other. Further, the phenomenon of "regionalism" is sometimes equated with the study of regional integration. Regionalism can be a political slogan; if so, it is ideological data that the student of integration must use. Regionalism can also be an analytical device suggesting what the world's "natural" regions are (or ought to be?).[10] As such it has so far not helped students of the processes of regional integration or disintegration because the actors who make integrative decisions do not always worry about the naturalness of their region.

With these preliminaries out of the way we can now turn to the actual work of evaluation. We shall, in turn, seek to establish the number and character of empirical generalizations which studies of regional integration have given us, locate these on a ladder of abstraction, and seek to group them under some kind of master variables. We shall discover that these variables are dependent on assumptions drawn from three well-known theories of regional integration, and we

must therefore summarize and evaluate the power of these theories. Having done so, we shall discover that the theories are lamentably unspecific and inconsistent as to the dependent variable to which they address themselves. Nor are they clear with respect to the key independent variables which, in combination, are to result in the eventual condition which is described by the dependent variable. The evaluation completed, we can then propose some ways of doing better in the future.

II. EMPIRICAL GENERALIZATIONS AND THEIR LIMITS

We are now in a position to summarize some things which the study of regional integration seems to have established. Enormous quantities of information have been uncovered about common markets, parliamentarians, regional interest groups, trade and mail flows, attitudes of masses, self-definitions of interest by elites, career patterns of civil servants, role perceptions, relations between various kinds of economic tasks, links between economic, political, and military tasks, and the influence of extrasystemic actors. Moreover, this is by no means randomly collected information. Few of the studies undertaken are so primitively empirical as to ignore hypotheses drawn from a variety of sources and models. One major achievement is the willingness to use comparative analysis as a test of the generality of the empirical findings instead of withdrawing into the safe shell of geographical uniqueness and complacently noting that "things are different in Pago Pago." Comparative analysis has been more than a drive for higher-level generalizations; it is also a device for finding and explaining intraphenomenal variation.[11] True, as of now our empirical generalizations are strongest when they simply sum up the

---

To confuse matters further the notion of "system" is sometimes assimilated into that of a "model," a recurrent and/or typical way in which integration is thought to go forward. This usage is reserved for the discussion of how variables are to be organized, not for the delimitation of the field.

[9]Leonard Binder, "The Middle East as a Subordinate International System," *World Politics*, April 1958 (Vol. 10, No. 3), pp. 408–429. Michel Brecher, "International Relations and Asian Studies: The Subordinate State System of Southern Asia," *World Politics*, January 1963 (Vol. 15, No. 2), pp. 213–235.

[10]This is shown in Bruce M. Russett, *International Regions and the International System: A Study in Political Ecology* (Chicago: Rand McNally & Co., 1967). See the comment on such treatments of regionalism in Oran R. Young, "Professor Russett: Industrious Tailor to a Naked Emperor," *World Politics*, April 1969 (Vol. 21, No. 3), pp. 486–511.

[11]The list of studies dealing with aspects of law, economics, military strategy, current diplomacy, and ideology is immense. For an excellent selection of recent studies see Nye, pp. 73–74, 145–146, 282–283, 428–429. For Europe in particular also see European community Institute for University Studies (Brussels), *University Studies on European Integrations*, 1969 (No. 5). For an exhaustive list of documents relating to economic cooperation in the third world see Miguel S. Wionczek (ed.), *Economic Cooperation in Latin America, Africa, and Asia* (Cambridge, Mass: M.I.T. Press, 1969). The

experiences of discrete regional groupings. But some findings of general relevance also emerge.

The generalizations which follow are untidy and often unclear with respect to the level of abstraction at which they are supposed to operate. Some appear to be of universal validity; others are conditional. Some sum up discrete facts; others seem to order groups of facts under some concept which is not encountered "in nature." All of these statements, in some sense, are verified hypotheses. But the phenomena summed up under these hypotheses exist at various levels of meaning. How does one cope with such a mixed bag if we lack an accepted hierarchy of key terms, concepts, and constructs?

I shall suggest one which I have found useful in coping with the imperfect pretheories that have guided the work of regional integration studies, imperfect precisely because each pretheory has its own internal hierarchy. The facts sought so diligently by all scholars constitute the first level in

following studies, in addition to the ones included in these bibliographies, are highly relevant to the conclusions here reported: Carl J. Friedrich (ed.), *Politische Dimensionen der europäischen Gemeinschaftsbildung* (Cologne: Westdeutscher Verlag, 1968); Gerda Zellentin (ed.), *Formen der Willensbildung in den europäischen Organisationen* (Frankfurt: Athenäum Verlag, 1965); Kai Ewerlöf Hammerich, *L'union des industries de la Communauté européenne dans le Marché commun* (Stockholm: Federation of Swedish Industries, 1969); Werner Feld, *The European common Market and the World* (Englewood Cliffs, N.J.: Prentice-Hall, 1967); Study Group of the Graduate Institute of International Studies (Geneva), *The European Free Trade Association and the Crisis of European Integration* (London: Michael Joseph, 1968); Henry G. Aubrey, *Atlantic Economic Cooperation* (New York: Frederick A. Praeger, 1967); Robert W. Gregg (ed.), *International Organization in the Western Hemisphere* (Syracuse, N.Y.: Syracuse University Press, 1968); Dusan Sidjanski, *Dimensiones institucionales de la integración latino americana* (Buenos Aires: Instituto para la Integración de América Latina, 1967); Armando Pruque, *Siete años de acción de la ALALC* (Buenos Aires: Instituto para la Integración de América Latina, 1968); Francisco Villagrán Kramer, *Integración económica centroamericana: Aspectos sociales y politicos* (Estudios Universitarios, Vol. 4) (Guatemala City: University of San Carlos, 1967); Roger D. Hansen, *Central America: Regional Integration and Economic Development* (National Planning Association Studies in Development Progress, No. 1) (Washington: National Planning Association, 1967); Donald Rothchild (ed.), *Politics of Integration: An East African Documentary* (EAPH Political Studies 4) (Nairobi: East African Publishing House, 1968).

the hierarchy. But which facts do they select? We treat as facts the items which we call our independent variables, i.e., events, conditions, attitudes, behaviors, considered to be of causative significance in explaining the condition or the outcome which preoccupies us. Items grouped and arranged in such a fashion as to lend themselves to explanation are facts categorized as variables. Groups of variables so related to each other as to explain successfully some outcome *but not justified in terms of some more comprehensive intellectual structure* we call empirical generalizations. The findings of regional integration studies, insofar as they are understood and accepted by all students, are thus no more than empirical generalizations. They are "true," i.e., they are verified hypotheses. But their distance from the primitive facts of behavior is unclear, and hence their theoretical status is doubtful because their relationship to still other variables and their relative weight in a group of potentially important variables is not specified. Nor is their position in a recurring sequence of trends or events spelled out.

Empirical Generalizations: Global

1. Members of regional groupings perceive themselves as being increasingly interdependent as the volume and rate of transactions between them rises as compared to third countries. This remains true despite debate as to the most appropriate statistical techniques and indices.

2. (a) Actors will evaluate interdependence as negative if they feel their regional partners profit more than they; negative evaluations can be predicted in common markets and free trade areas of less developed countries.

   (b) Actors will evaluate interdependence as positive if they feel they benefit equally with their partners in *some* issue area though not necessarily in all or in all simultaneously; such a pattern can be predicted in economic arrangements between industrialized countries.

3. The relative size of the member states in a regional grouping is not a good overall predictor of the success of integration. Inequality may spur integration in some economic and military task settings if the "core area" can provide special payoffs. Inequality is certain

to hinder integration, however, when such payoffs are not provided, e.g., the role of the Union of Soviet Socialist Republics in the Council for Mutual Economic Assistance (COMECON), of Argentina, Brazil, and Mexico in the Latin American Free Trade Association (LAFTA), or of the United States since 1963 in the North Atlantic Treaty Organization (NATO). Differentials in size may advance the integration of diplomatic groupings when one purpose is perceived as the control of the "core area" by the smaller partners, as in the Organization of American States (OAS).

4. The proliferation of organization channels in a region (both governmental and private) stimulates interdependence among the members as they increasingly resort to these channels for the resolution of conflicts. However, a positive evaluation of such interdependence on the part of the actors cannot be predicted, e.g., the reactions of the Federal Republic of Germany in the European Economic Community (EEC) and of Nicaragua in the Central American Common Market (CACM).

5. A critical mass composed of integrative activities in a number of issue areas likely to result in a culmination of de facto or de jure political union is difficult to identify and hazardous to predict. Many fields of potentially integrative activity, after successful accomplishments, result in "self-encapsulation" organizationally and attitudinally and therefore may not contribute to the evolution of new demands by actors. Other areas of perceived interdependence result in the creation of rival organizations whose activities may or may not contribute to overall integration, leading to the "spill-around" situation which defies political centralization. Self-encapsulation has been observed especially in activities relating to telecommunications, transportation, the protection of human rights, military strategy and procurement, and public health.[12]

6. Of all issues and policy areas the commitment to create a common market is the most conducive to rapid regional integration and the maximization of a spillover. Military alliances, even if equipped with far-ranging competences and standing organs, have triggered very little permanent integrative consequences.[13] Arrangements limited to the setting up of common technical and scientific services tend toward self-encapsulation.[14] Regional arrangements for the protection of human rights (confined to Western Europe and to the Western Hemisphere) have so far not contributed to the integration of values and attitudes and have generated few new institutions.[15] Organizations with an economic mandate short of creating a common market or a free trade area have great difficulty in influencing the policies of their members.

---

[12]This distinction was first clearly elaborated by Schmitter in the article cited in footnote 7. It may be observed also in Africa and in Eastern Europe. For a European example see Robert L. Pfaltzgraff and James L. Deghand, "European Technological Collaboration: The Experience of the European Launcher Development Organization (ELDO)," *Journal of Common Market Studies*, September 1968, (Vol. 7, No. I), pp. 22–34.

[13]The definitive study probing the ability of NATO to trigger integrative results outside the narrow military field is Francis A. Beer, *Integration and Disintegration in NATO: Processes of Alliance Cohesion and Prospects for Atlantic Community* (Columbus: Ohio State University Press, 1969). Modelski makes the same point about SEATO and Slater about the OAS (see Nye for full citation). See also Andrzej Korbonski, "The Warsaw Pact," *International Conciliation*, May 1969 (No. 573), and Korbonski's contribution to this volume.

[14]Isebill Gruhn, *Functionalism in Africa: Scientific and Technical Cooperation* (unpublished Ph.D. dissertation, University of California, Berkeley, 1967). W. R. Derrick Sewell and Gilbert F. White, "The Lower Mekong," *International Conciliation*, May 1966 (No. 558); Carl G. Rosberg, Jr., with Aaron Segal, "An East African Federation," *International Conciliation*, May 1963 (No. 543). Abdul A. Jalloh, *The Politics and Economics of Regional Political Integration in Central Africa* (unpublished Ph.D. dissertation, University of California, Berkeley, 1969).

[15]In Western Europe the Greek response to the strong condemnation on the part of the Council of Europe's organs confirms this finding. A. B. McNulty, "Stock-Taking on the European Convention on Human Rights," Council of Europe document DH(68)7, 1968. The Inter-American Commission on Human Rights has been active and innovating in the face of governmental indifference and is now presenting the OAS Council with a final draft for a stronger and more permanent hemispheric machinery. L. Ronald Scheman, "The Inter-American Commission on Human Rights," *American Journal of International Law*, April 1965 (Vol. 59, No. 2), pp. 335–343; José A. Cabranes, "The Protection of Human Rights by the Organization of American States," *American Journal of International Law*, October 1968 (Vol. 62, No. 4), pp. 889–908.

Hence new hypotheses concerning future regional integration had best be formulated in the context of common markets. This is the richest fund of data and the most powerful stimulus to actors and provides the largest sample of ongoing efforts from almost all portions of the globe. Much richer findings, moreover, can be culled from the literature dealing with specific regions and regional economic efforts. It is hardly surprising that the empirical generalizations that can be uncovered seem to fall into three groups: findings specific to the Western European setting, conclusions and lessons highly specific to socialist countries, and a large mass of heterogeneous generalizations that seem to characterize the late developing nations and their efforts.

Empirical Generalizations: Socialist Groupings

7. Mutual interdependence and dependence on the regional "core area" is a disintegrative force because the smaller nations resent it with varying degrees of intensity and consistency.
    (a) The differences in the national economic planning systems of the member nations of COMECON hinder the definition of a regional economic policy.
    (b) Resources do not flow readily because of differences in national plans and the absence of a regional price and monetary system accepted by all as fair.
    (c) Ideological differences between Communist parties make themselves felt in trade and investment policy and impede regional efforts.
    (d) Differences in the level of industrialization sharply influence expectations of regional action and make the less developed eager to minimize dependence on the more developed. The same is true among nonsocialist developing nations.

Empirical Generalizations: Industrialized-Pluralistic Nations

8. Economic integration in Western Europe displays these regularities:
    (a) Self-interest among governments and private groups has sufficed to weave webs

and expectations of interdependence and mutual benefits. However, with shifts in economic conditions or in the political climate these expectations are capable of being reversed and reevaluated by the actors. Instrumental motives are not necessarily strongly or permanently tied to the EEC.
    (b) Collective decisions—from coal to steel, to tariffs on refrigerators, to chickens, and to cheese, and from there to company law, turnover taxes, and the control of the business cycle—were made incrementally, based often on consequences not initially intended by the actors (governments and important interest groups). This tendency is summed up in the phrase "spillover in the scope of collective action."[16]
    (c) Spillover in scope is confined to decisions and objectives relating to the realization of full benefits from an existing common market. It has not operated markedly in free trade areas; nor has it been true of all policy or decision sectors in common markets (e.g., energy policy, transport).
    (d) There has been very little spillover in the "level" of action, i.e., little progressive penetration from supranational institutions into the lower reaches of decision-making at the national and local levels (with the exception of the mining and agricultural sectors).
    (e) Nevertheless, groups, contacts, and organizations (trade unions, trade associations, working parties of civil servants, parliamentarians, students, professions) grow and prosper across frontiers.
    (f) The style of bargaining is incremental, subdued, and unemotional and seeks reciprocity of benefits, unanimous agreement, and package deals among issue areas. French behavior to the contrary has not been accepted as legitimate and has not remained fixed or final.
    (g) Collective decisions with an economic substance tend to exhibit most spillover

---

[16]The distinction between "scope" and "level" in the discussion of the spillover mechanism is first made by Philippe C. Schmitter in "Three Neo-Functional Hypotheses about International Integration," *International Organization*, Winter 1969 (Vol. 23, No. I), pp. 161–166.

characteristics when they are mediated by a group of actors with overt or tacit federalist objectives. The pace of integration slows down when this group is lacking, i.e., the EEC after 1963, the European Free Trade Association (EFTA).

(h) Young people in Europe are consistently more favorable to the intensification of the integration process than are older people in part because they are self-consciously "nonnationalistic."

(i) The higher educated and professional layers of the population, of all ages, are consistently in favor of intensified integration. Those most satisfied with their standard of living also tend to be prointegration. In short, prointegration attitudes characterize the most successful and most "modern" segments of the population.[17]

(j) A region of great cultural/linguistic homogeneity, even though its members easily create new ties between themselves, does not necessarily proceed easily to the making of integrative collective decisions when the issues perceived as being most salient by actors involve interdependence with countries outside the region. Hence self-encapsulation easily sets in with respect to practices and organs created previously (e.g., the Nordic Council and the network of Nordic cooperation).

Empirical Generalizations: Late Developing Nations

9. Integration in Africa has been largely symbolic; joint policymaking with economic objectives does not follow the European pattern:

(a) Actor expectations are prematurely politicized, thus preventing incremental bargaining on relatively noncontroversial shared objectives.

(b) Bargaining with reciprocal benefits, especially where payoffs have to be deferred, is all but impossible because of the limits on resources. Since issues cannot be kept separate easily, national differences in size and power become divisive.

(c) The absence of pluralism makes the formation of voluntary groups on a regional basis very difficult. Ideological ties between leaders, where they exist, are helpful to integration; ideological cleavages are most divisive and cannot be overcome by shared economic aims.

(d) Countries which are poorly integrated internally make poor partners in a regional integration process because of the reluctance of leaders to further undermine their control at home.

10. While noneconomic integration in Latin America has been largely symbolic, economic integration efforts share many characteristics with the European pattern:

(a) Countries confident that their size and resource base make them relatively independent of regional partners take a very slight interest in regional integration. Under these specific conditions size and power differentials, therefore, inhibit integration.

(b) Differential rates of economic and social development inhibit the evolution of regional elite responsiveness (LAFTA). But similarity of rates favors elite complementarity and responsiveness (CACM and the Andean Group).

(c) Administrative and organizational diffuseness at the national level in a setting of poor local integration and weak nationalism facilitates regional integration dominated by technocrats (CACM). Strong central government and strong nationalism permit little leeway to technocrats (LAFTA).[18]

---

[17]See especially Ronald Inglehart, "An End to European Integration?" *American Political Science Review*, March 1967 (Vol. 61, No. I), pp. 91–105. Inglehart's analysis received powerful confirmation from a poll of French opinion conducted in 1968; see "Les Français et l'unification politique de l'Europe d'aprés un sondage de la SOFRES," *Revue française de science politique*, February 1969 (Vol. 19, No. I), pp. 145–170.

[18]For examples see Gustavo Lagos, "The Political Role of Regional Economic Organizations in Latin America," *Journal of Common Market Studies*, June 1968 (Vol. 6, No. 4), pp. 291–309.

For an argument that distribution crises (in East Africa and Central America) must be expected to arise in such settings, thus inevitably politicizing negotiations and institutions dealing with economic welfare, see Roger D. Hansen, "Regional Integration: Reflections on a Decade of Theoretical Efforts," *World Politics*, (*d*) The incremental decisionmaking logic and the spillover tendency can operate even among late developing countries which are poorly integrated nationally despite a persistent aura of economic crisis (CACM). This is explained by propositions 10(c) and 11(a).

Empirical Generalizations: The External World

Relations between the regional system (subsystem) and the external world (either an important extrasystem state or a larger regional system of which the subsystem being studied is a part) can be of immense importance in explaining integration.[19] But various configurations—quite distinct in impact—of "the exogenous variable" must be made explicit. (1) The "global system" within which the region perceives itself as struggling may be the major concern of actors, as in the case of economic unions among late developing countries. (2) A single state (or its elite) may be perceived as the extraregional force which aids or hinders integration. (3) A regional countersystem may be the extraregional force which explains integration or disintegration. Thus:

January 1969 (Vol. 21, No. 2), pp. 257–270. This feature, among others, leads Hansen to conclude that the neofunctional approach cannot be used for the analysis of regional integration among less developed countries. Hansen finds the tendency toward distribution crises to be an instance of "instant politicization" even though in Central America it did not occur until the integration process had gone on for seven years. In Europe such a development was avoided, he says, because the dominance of the hidden hand of automatic market forces assured more or less equitable distribution of benefits (an argument also made by Lawrence Krause, *European Economic Integration and the United States* [Washington: Brookings Institution, 1967]). The makers of monetary policy, those who fashion subsidies for miners, railroads, and farmers, and the businessmen who conclude specialization agreements would be interested to learn this! On the contrary, serious distribution crises were avoided because of a consistent bargaining style stressing package deals permitting the continuation of special benefits *not* to be expected if an automatic and general free market were to operate. While Hansen is quite right in calling attention to the limits on the spillover from economic policymaking into political unification (see proposition 5 above), he carries the criticism much too far by downgrading the importance of "expansive" bargaining styles and the institutions in which the styles take shape, whether supranational or not.

11. Perceptions of being victimized by the global system tend to spur integration as a way of "getting out from under."
   (*a*) Economic unions among late developing countries are designed to change a situation in which prosperity depends on commodity exports to developed nations (LAFTA, East African Common Market [EACM]).
   (*b*) But perceptions of dependence on a larger system may be so pervasive as to be a disincentive to regional efforts (Nordic Common Market, efforts at economic union in Asia).
12. The role of extraregional single states (or their elites) is indeterminate in explaining regional integration.
   (*a*) A hegemonic extraregional actor can use his payoff capacity to undermine the will to integrate, as has been alleged of the United States in dealings with LAFTA and CACM.
   (*b*) But economic unions among late developing countries sometimes survive largely as a result of support from an exogenous actor (Union douanière et économique de l'Afrique centrale [UDEAC], Conseil de l'entente, and occasionally CACM).
13. Extraregional counterunions are a definite—but temporary—aid to integration.
   (*a*) Regional groups with a military purpose survive only as long as they face a rival external grouping. The same is true of diplomatic groupings which do not take the form of an alliance.
   (*b*) Economic unions among industrialized countries may survive only because they seek united strength in dealing with another such union (EFTA).

[19]Karl Kaiser, "The U.S. and the EEC in the Atlantic System: The Problem of Theory," *Journal of Common Market Studies*, June 1967 (Vol. 5, No. 4), pp. 388–425, and Karl Kaiser, "The Interaction of Regional Subsystems: Some Preliminary Notes on Recurrent Patterns and the Role of Superpowers," *World Politics*, October 1968 (Vol. 21, No. 1), pp. 84–107. See Etzioni, pp. 44–50, for a related treatment of "external elites." Robert E. Denham, "The Role of the U.S. as an External Actor in the Integration of Latin America," *Journal of Common Market Studies*, March 1969 (Vol. 7, No. 3), pp. 199–216. Nils Andrén, "Nordic Integration," *Cooperation and Conflict*, 1967 (Vol. 1), pp. 1–25.

Much ink has been spilled in debates between students of integration as to whether the exogenous variable is really *the* most salient one: For scholars still attached to some version of Friedrich Meinecke's dictum on the *Primat der Aussenpolitik* the military and diplomatic force of the larger system should always be considered as the weightiest influence on the fortunes of the regional subsystem. The failure of the EEC to spill over into political union among the six is explained sometimes in this fashion.[20] The resolution of this conundrum—an entirely unnecessary one conceptually and empirically—is linked to the discussion of "high" as against "low" politics. This takes us, more generally, to a consideration of conceptual problems which remain ill defined and unresolved in the study of regional integration despite the wealth of empirical generalizations which have been generated.

Gaps and Problems Remaining

It is clear by now that the truth conveyed by these summary statements is, to say the least, multilayered in meaning and implication. Only a few of these propositions rise above the level of verifying simple hypotheses based on readily observed behavior or trends rendered in terms of variables. Some, however, do: The propositions dealing with various kinds of spillover involve an act of conceptual evaluation on the part of the observer which is several steps removed from the actual variables. Conclusions about what spills over into which institutional vessel are *analytical*: They are deduced from facts arranged into variables, paired in the

form of hypotheses. I am arguing that such analytical steps are highly desirable, if not imperative, if we wish to avoid simple empiricism. But from where do we get the leading ideas, the metaphors, the inspiration for such a summing up at a higher level of abstraction?

One of the major problems implicit in this list of findings is the dependence of most propositions on a number of explicit and implicit assumptions made prior to the initiation of research; there is a theoretical basis to the mere listing of relevant variables. The findings are as strong as the assumptions, and the assumptions cannot be made evident without looking at the theories which inspired them. The same is true of the measures and indicators embedded in various assumptions.

Another problem with this list is the indefinite nature of the end state or the terminal condition to which regional integration is supposed to lead. Integration appears to be both a process and an outcome. This confusion between process and outcome, appealing though it may be because it sidesteps the definitional problem, simply will not help us unless we know which mix of which variables results in a qualitatively new state of affairs. It is not only a question of whether we wish to explain the process, necessarily stressing a time dimension, whereby relationships change between nations and actors or to describe the terminal condition (which could be conceived in static terms) to which the process is likely to lead. The job is to do both; but the task of selecting and justifying variables and explaining their hypothesized interdependence cannot be accomplished without an agreement as to possible conditions to which the process is expected to lead. In short, we need a dependent variable. The list alone is insufficient for systematic explanation because it merely describes interregional variation in the importance attributable to single independent variables. It says little about the mix of variables to be considered optimal in general or optimal for specific regional settings.

Finally, I shall list four major gaps in factual and conceptual knowledge which began to oppress me after working with the findings I considered established. These gaps involve measurement, assumptions, theories, and a concern with the future on normative grounds. (1) Do variables explaining the initiation of a union also explain its maintenance, as we seem to have assumed? (2) Must we assume—as we have—that decisionmaking styles at

---

[20]For the classic statements of this position see Stanley Hoffmann, "Discord in Community: The North Atlantic Area as a Partial International System," *International Organization*, Summer 1963 (Vol. 17, No. 3), pp. 521–549, and Stanley Hoffmann, "Obstinate or Obsolete? The Fate of the Nation-State and the Case of Western Europe," *Daedalus*, Summer 1966 (Vol. 95, Nos. 3–4), pp. 862–916. Hansen treats the exogenous variable in this fashion, considering it the most "compelling" of all and using it as the most salient for predicting a reasonably rosy future for economic unions of less developed countries. He also explicitly accepts the dichotomy of "high" versus "low" politics, treating economic welfare issues in the third world as an instance of "high" politics. Hansen, *World Politics*, Vol. 21, No. 2, pp. 268–271, 246–250.

the national level must be congruent with those at the regional level? What if the two styles evolve at different rates? (3) Are processes of integration in the underdeveloped world so different from those in the West that we need two different theories or models? This raises the important issue of the relative weight to be given to the variables in each geographical setting. (4) How do actors learn? Do perceptions of benefits from changing transactions affect the definition of interests? Is there some other process of socialization at work? Answers to each of these will have tremendous importance in the construction of a more adequate theory of regional integration, especially if the relative weight of each variable and process can be specified with respect to *each* of various postulated outcomes in *each* major geographical or cultural setting.

III. THREE PRETHEORIES OF REGIONAL INTEGRATION

The task of clarification of findings and filling of gaps bears some of the burdens of the fifteen years of work already done. Three separate theoretical conventions—federalism, the communications approach, and neo-functionalism—have not only shaped the fuzzy conceptions of the outcome of integration but have also been influential in defining independent variables. Students within each convention have postulated causative links between variables. Furthermore, each convention has brought its own methodology into the fray, illustrated especially by the heavy reliance on aggregate and survey data on the part of the communications school and on conceptually focused case studies of integrative efforts on the part of the neo-functionalists. Hence an agreement on a common research strategy or a new focus of study cannot be a matter of choosing between rival approaches or of simply adding them. Variables bear the burden of their ancestry, as do methods, measures, and indicators. Before an agreement on a set of dependent variables can be ratified in terms of a common agenda on hypothesized causes, modal action paths, and a common methodology, the main contours of these "theories" must be thrown into relief and their contributions summarized.

Generous borrowing from other disciplines and subject matters inspired and informed the three theoretical approaches which I shall call "pretheories" because they do not now provide an explanation of a recurring series of events made up of dimensions of activity causally linked to one another. Some pretheorists used as basic building blocks certain assumptions which are relationships demonstrated to be true empirically in the contexts from which they were borrowed; other pretheorists proceeded on the basis of knowledge taken to be self-evidently "true" though based on intuition rather than cognition. In any event, the status of these theories is of tremendous importance because it is they rather than the nature of things which lead students to postulate the relationships between variables; it is they, not the nature of things, which lead us to the specification of what is an independent and a dependent variable.

The *federal* approach assumes the identity of political postulates concerning common purpose and common need among actors irrespective of level of action. It also assumes the transferability, again on the basis of identical postulates, of institutions from the national to the regional level. The *communications* approach proceeds on the basis of the logic of isomorphisms. It transposes laws from cybernetic theory to the relations between groups of people, using the volume of transaction as its major indicator. All social processes are assumed to follow identical laws borrowed from cybernetics; these laws are applied isomorphically by expecting that the logic of the causal pattern is replicated in relations between nations and the regions. The *neo-functional* approach rests its claim to fame on an extended analogy rather than relying on isomorphisms or identities between phenomena. It borrows the postulates of actor perception and behavior which are said to explain the character of a pluralistically organized national state; it notes that certain of these seem to coincide with behavior at the regional level and therefore holds that the rest of the behavior is also explicable in terms of the pluralistic national model. The major point requiring emphasis is that these pretheories are located at varying levels of abstraction, thus giving rise to behavioral postulates which are not symmetrically related. This alone should give rise to doubts as to whether the postulates are additive in terms of a unified theory.

The Federalist Approach

Federalist theorists actually can be divided into two quite distinct groups: an ideological group concerned with developing a theory of action designed to realize a regional federation (mostly in Western Europe but to some extent in Africa immediately before and after the attainment of independence by most African states and in the Malaysian nexus) as opposed to a group concerned with tracing and observing patterns of federal integration. The second group, however, has also been active in the drafting of constitutions for potential federal unions.[21] The two groups agree on many things. They share a concern with the primary importance of institutions and institution building; hence the efforts devoted to the writing of constitutions and to research on the actual history of such federal entities as the United States, Switzerland, and West Germany. They are preoccupied with the merits of rival methods of representation and elections; they devote much attention to the proper division of powers between the federal, the "national," and the local authorities; and they are concerned with checks and balances between organs of government. Moreover, they are both inspired by the dual character of federalism: It can be used to unite hitherto separate jurisdictions but it can also be applied to breaking up overly centralized national governments. Federalism, in short, seeks simultaneously to meet the need for more effective governmental action in some domains (through centralization) and the democratic postulate of local control and local autonomy (through decentralization).

The style of the activist group has been more consistently ideological. The major component of its theory is the imputed need of peoples and nations; these needs will (must, ought to?) result in a federal regime. In short, it is not always clear whether the assertions are normative or descriptive. They are certainly not explanatory. Granting these basic building blocks the theory provides (at least in the words of its major European and African spokesmen) descriptive postulates about necessary strategies and requisite behavior patterns for building regional institutions and solidarities. The main building blocks are normative assertions based on the faith of the asserters. The remainder is illustrative material chosen from the historical experience of federal nations. Undoubtedly it is this feature which has stimulated a recent commentator to consider neofunctional and federal theorizing as next-of-kin.[22] Events since 1954 in Europe and since 1960 in Africa have effectively contradicted these federalists' descriptions, explanations, and predictions. This approach, in its pure form, is probably discredited.[23]

Even though they stress the importance of institutional and constitutional questions somewhat more than do neo-functionalists, the theorist/ observers among the federalists have tended to lose their identity as a clear-cut approach to questions of regional integration. First, federalist theorists do not share the activists' cavalier assumptions about popular needs or imminent

[21] Illustrative of this practice is the massive work by Robert R. Bowie and Carl J. Friedrich (ed.), *Studies in Federalism* (Boston: Little, Brown and Co., 1954), which contains research and theorizing done on behalf of the then functioning European ad hoc Parliamentary Assembly.

[22] Paul Taylor, "Concept of Community and the European Process," *Journal of Common Market Studies*, December 1968 (Vol. 7, No. 2), pp. 83–101. This argument misses the essential distinctions between ends and means and between activist/actor and theorist/observer. To illustrate: Jean Monnet and Walter Hallstein are "federalists" in the sense that they hope to create a united Europe with more or less federal institutions; they are "functionalists" in the sense that they do not believe in constitutional conventions and elaborate institutional schemes because they prefer to initiate common policies and arouse new client groups which will *eventually* result in a federal regime. Federalist theorists believe in the federal end but may be willing to use functional means; federalist activists despise the recourse to functional means. Neo-functionalist theorists are concerned with the end postulated by the actors only to the extent that they are preoccupied with understanding why and how actual integrative outcomes occur. Neo-functional theory and federal theory, therefore, are by no means similar.

[23] As examples of ideological federalists we cite the names of Denis de Rougemont, Hans Nord, Henri Brugmans. See also Alexandre Marc, *Europe: Terre décisive* (Paris: La Colombe, 1959). Another group of federal activists, in disappointment, has turned to a species of neo-functionalism for ideological sustenance; see Bino Olivi, *L'Europa difficile* (Milan: Edizioni di Communitá, 1964), and Altiero Spinelli, *The Eurocrats: Conflict and Crisis in the European Community* (Baltimore: Johns Hopkins Press, 1968). A new twist is given to this complex relationship by the emergence of a young group of federalists anxious to work with functional institutions to achieve the radical democratization of European society. They publish the monthly journal *Agenor*.

and necessary events. Even though attached to federalism for normative reasons they do not push their preoccupation to the extreme of equating all of society's ills with dispersion or concentration of power and of identifying the federal formula as the royal remedy. Therefore, they are less inclined to talk about popular needs than about an optimal distribution of tasks among units of government in a setting of growing popular participation. Second, federalist theorists have shown more and more interest in questions of process, leading the main federalist theorist, Carl J. Friedrich, to speak ·of the "federalizing process" in terms difficult to distinguish from the medley of demands, expectations, rational bargaining, and ad hoc growth of institutions which neo-functionalists seek to trace.[24]

The Communications Approach

Communications theory suggests—it does not assert or prove—that an intensive pattern of communication between national units will result in a closer "community" among the units if loads and capabilities remain in balance. Associated with this suggestion are a number of familiar additional postulates regarding trust, friendship, complementarity, and responsiveness. The units being considered by this theory are nations and only incidentally physical persons or groups. It should be made clear that the character of the suggestions takes the form of very specific hypotheses. "If the rate of transaction is such and so, under conditions of balanced loads and capabilities, then elite responsiveness increases. If elite responsiveness increases then a security community, will arise. . . ." The hypotheses are certainly falsifiable. But even if they are found to correlate positively with the emergence of a security community, can we then assign causes that are clearly associated with human perceptions and motives? Communications theorizing rests content with the demonstration of covariance among variables at the systemic level. It hypothesizes that certain relationships between relationships, ratios between ratios in the case of some clusters of variables, result in a terminal condition, i.e., a security community. The systemic approach thus assumes either of the following: It may assume that transactions *measure* some human quality, a human perception of self-interest, and that the change in the magnitude of the measure records a change in the human behavior to be measured; in this case the indicator becomes a proxy variable for perception that leads to behavior. Alternatively the systemic approach assumes that transactions *are* a type of behavior summing up more mundane, humanly experienced facts and making it unnecessary for the investigator to concern himself with the human element. In brief, are factor scores of ecological variables really measures of actor behavior?[25] It is as if theorists of the balance of power need only worry about the application of the principles of mechanics to international politics and need not worry about how foreign ministers perceive themselves in this supergame.

The communications approach has sought to explain retroactively rather than to predict. The approach does not tell us the content of the

---

[24]This passage from Friedrich's most recent work speaks for itself:

> The review of selected issues in contemporary federal relations has . . . shown that federalism is more fully understood if it is seen as a process, an evolving pattern of changing relationships, rather than a static design regulated by firm and unalterable rules. This finding ought not to be misunderstood as meaning that the rules are insignificant; far from it. What it does mean is that any federal relationship requires effective and built-in arrangements through which these rules can be recurrently changed upon the initiative and with the consent of the federated entities. In a sense, what this means is that the development (historical) dimension of federal relationships has become a primary focal point, as contrasted with the distribution and fixation of jurisdictions (the legal aspect). In keeping with recent trends in political science, the main question is: What function does a federal relationship have?—rather than: What structure?

Carl J. Friedrich, *Trends of Federalism in Theory and Practice* (New York: Frederick A. Praeger, 1968), p. 173. For a similar treatment of federalism in Africa, Malaysia, and the West Indies see Thomas M. Franck (ed.), *Why Federations Fail* (New York: New York University Press, 1968).

[25]The work of Donald Puchala, as represented by his contribution to [*International Organization*, Autumn 1970], though part of this approach, is not based on all of these assumptions and makes a number of allowances to the judgments expressed here.

messages and their imputed relationship to the evolution of capacity on the part of regional institutions. It does not explain when and how trust and responsiveness among actors, elites as well as masses, are to occur. Who are, or what is, to handle the load? Politics, in the sense of demands, negotiations, institutionalization, evolution of tasks, is not really part of the approach since the content of messages is not always treated. Deutsch suggested that future Western European integration is in doubt because of an ebbing in the increase of rates of transaction, as measured by trade, mail, and tourist flow indicators and by the rate of supranational group formation.[26] Only certainty on the *causative* significance of these indicators can justify such a conclusion.

Yet the suspicion remains that transactions *must* have something to do with expectations and therefore with actor behavior. The successful prediction of the neo-functionalists with respect to negotiating behavior in the EEC can be fully explained only on the basis of the transactionalist's finding concerning trade. But whether the resulting ties are based on trust or greed remains an open question. Is the effect of transactions similar in late developing regions? Certainly there is a very good correlation between nontrade and noncommunity formation in LAFTA and an equally good one between the relative success of CACM and the spectacular increases in regional trade. In Africa, on the other hand, UDEAC continues to exist despite the absence of trade increases between the members while the East African Common Market was endangered because the high level of trade between the members was not associated, in their minds, with equitably distributed benefits. But then, perhaps, it is not trade or other kinds of transactions that are crucial in our judgment so much as the *perception* of present and future benefits in the minds of the actors. In that case this type of data is not a good indicator unless it is reinterpreted in terms of actor perceptions.

[26]See Karl W. Deutsch, and others, *France, Germany and the Western Alliance: A Study of Elite Attitudes on European Integration and World Politics* (New York: Charles Scribner's Sons, 1967), especially p. 218.

The Neo-Functional Approach

Neo-functionalists have their own troubles. True, neo-functional theorizing is consistently phenomenological; it avoids normative assertion and systemic generalization. Neo-functionalism stresses the instrumental motives of actors; it looks for the adaptability of elites in line with specialization of roles; neo-functionalism takes self-interest for granted and relies on it for delineating actor perceptions. Moreover, neo-functionalists rely on the primacy of incremental decisionmaking over grand designs, arguing that most political actors are incapable of long-range purposive behavior because they stumble from one set of decisions into the next as a result of not having been able to foresee many of the implications and consequences of the earlier decisions. Ever more controversial (and thus system-transforming) policies emerge, starting from a common initial concern over substantively narrow but highly salient issues. A new central authority may emerge as an unintended consequence of incremental earlier steps. Most neo-functionalists have not explicitly recognized, however, the crucial question of whether even this incremental style is not "foreseen" and manipulated by certain heroic actors (Jean Monnet, Sicco Mansholt, Walter Hallstein, Raúl Prebisch)—and eventually checked by certain equally prescient national actors (Charles de Gaulle).

The neo-functional theory is therefore a highly contingent one. One limitation is embedded in the source of the approach—the modern pluralistic-industrial democratic polity. That source offers a rationale for linking the separate variables found in the neo-functional model in Western Europe; but application to the third world has so far sufficed only to accurately predict difficulties and failures in regional integration while in the European case some successful positive prediction has been achieved. Another limitation, however, involves the very question of what constitutes a successful prediction. Neo-functionalist practitioners have difficulty achieving closure on a given case of regional integration because the terminal condition being observed is uncertain: Neo-functionalists do not agree on a dependent variable and therefore differ with each other on the point in time at which a judgment of "how much successful integration" is to be made.

Thus, specific processes, specific cases of spillover, specific styles of accommodation and increasing mutual responsiveness among actors have been successfully predicted. But whether this adds up to achieving closure or the attainment of some kind of "community" in the region remains a matter of how we define the dependent variable. As of now the theory has not been falsified in the sense that a successful community has been achieved by virtue of processes not contained in the theory; if East Africa or the Association of Southeast Asian Nations (ASEAN) were to attain functioning supranational communities in their respective regions, such an event would falsify the theory. Nor has the theory been fully validated as long as it cannot explain how and why a postulated condition is attained.

Overlap between Communications and Neo-Functional Approaches

Both approaches share a commitment to a certain number of independent variables considered of great salience: regional transactions and the gains or losses associated with them by actors; verbal and symbolic communications between crucial elites; mutual expectations of elites; mutual responsiveness between elites; the adequacy of institutions to handle the transactional and communicational load. But they differ in the way in which they treat the load: Communications theorists consider all types of transactions equally salient and therefore measure whatever the statistics permit to be measured; neo-functionalists, however, argue that welfare-related and foreign· or defense policy issues are most salient for actors. The load related to such transactions thus becomes crucial for studying particularly salient regional "tasks." Hence neo-functionalists prefer to observe bargaining styles and strategies as their basic data rather than to stress the volume and rate of transactions or the ebb and flow of public opinion. Moreover, they prefer to study cases of organizational growth or decay rather than the aggregate data preferred by the followers of the communications approach. In both cases data and measures are determined by initial theoretical assumptions. So are crucial organizing concepts for the data, such as the notions of responsive-

ness and spillover. The strength of communications theory is its generality, its systemic character. The strength of neo-functional theory is its closeness to the actors. But individual strength may turn out to be collective weakness when propositions derived from one fly like eagles through the ethereal heights of systems while those derived from the other burrow like moles through the mud of experience.

None of the major pretheories is very strong. True, only the federal approach has been falsified in the sense that none of its assertions-predictions have proven to be true. The neo-functional and communications theories have neither been falsified nor have they demonstrated positive predictive prowess outside Western Europe: They have been better in predicting failures. Moreover, they cannot be easily compared or added since they address different levels of abstraction. The looseness of the axioms of which they are made up does not help matters. What is clear and crisp at the national level comes close to assumption, or assertion, in the regional context to which the neo-functional theory seeks application. What is a simple hypothesis of great plausibility in the communications theory becomes question-begging when the assumptions underlying the hypotheses are made explicit.

Both theories have been accused of neglecting "high politics," especially in the form of hiding such obviously important matters as international power and prestige, war and peace, arms and alliances under such mundane labels as "interaction," "task expansion," or "welfare maximization." The thrust of world politics and of the superpowers on regional unions is sometimes mentioned as some special instance of "high politics" that cannot be treated or accommodated by either theory. Those who stress the unique qualities of high politics provide an important critical qualifier to both theories without advancing a theory of their own. They hold that all political decisions are either important or routine, that propositions seeking to relate political activity with economic or social objectives err intrinsically by assuming that human conduct in both spheres is identical. The devotees of high politics are thus forced to conclude that while common markets may flourish because of some men's grubby and greedy minds, such mundane arrangements will never lead to political union because that status demands that the pride and fury associated with nationalism be eliminated first. This, clearly, is argument by definition alone.[27] In neo-functional theorizing the existence of special "high political" motives can be discovered by studying the perceptions of actors when they react to external pressures and threats or when they link (or fail to link) extra-regional ambitions with regional decisionmaking. Whether "politics" is more important than "economics" is an empirical question, not a dichotomy given by nature. In communications theorizing the potency of high politics would be suggested when events take a turn sharply counter to what is indicated by the trends of growing interdependence. But General de Gaulle—not "France"—remains the only exception that has amended, but hardly destroyed, the consensus among students of integration that what we analyze are trends and decisions—without defining which are the most important and without arguing that economic questions are "routine."

IV. TOWARD A DEPENDENT VARIABLE

Our reflections have led us to two somber conclusions: First, the lessons we have learned from the study of regional integration have been imperfectly "integrated" because they coexist at several levels of abstraction, thus making it difficult to engage in conceptually focused evaluation and projection; moreover, a primary cause of imperfect conceptual integration is the nonadditive character of the pretheories which have inspired our research. Second, one major reason for the lack of fit between the major theories is disagreement on what constitutes the dependent variable. A giant step on the road toward an integrated theory of regional integration, therefore, would

be taken if we could clarify the matter of what we propose to explain and/or predict.

Ideal Types and Terminal Conditions

Federalist theory has been the least ambiguous in telling which end product it seeks to explain or predict: The terminal condition of the process of integration is the achievement of a federal union among the units being studied, nation-states. Communications theorizing has used the construct of a security community as its terminal condition, recognizing the possibility that such a condition may be of the "amalgamated" or the "pluralistic" variety. This terminal condition, of course, is wider in scope than the federalists' though it is able to subsume the notion of a federal union. Neo-functionalists have worked with the idea of a political community or a political union, a concept which also subsumes a federal union but is less sweeping than a security community because it makes specific assumptions about central institutions and the progressive centralization of decisionmaking among the members. One of the more bothersome aspects of these efforts at specifying a dependent variable was the tendency to mix its imputed characteristics with those of independent and intervening variables.[28]

The nagging thought persists that we lack clear dependent variables because we have followed the practice of erecting these terminal states by treating them as ideal types reconstructed from our historical experience at the national level and then of observing the types of behavior that contribute—or fail to contribute—to the attainment of that condition. These ideal types are not true dependent variables since they cannot yet be

---

[27]See the suggestion by Karl Kaiser that the distinction has relevance only to the attitudes of actors, not to the intrinsic character of the issue area or policy. Actors can shift back and forth as to the importance they attribute to any given issue area—with obvious implications for integration theory. The empirical problem for us is to be able to specify when and how much attitudinal shifts occur, an aspect of a theory of "learning" we shall discuss below. This is quite different from the eternally mystic qualities Hoffmann sees in these distinctions. Kaiser, *Journal of Common Market Studies*, Vol. 5, No. 3, pp. 401–402.

[28]But we have learned, too. Scholars are less prone to circular definitions between independent and dependent variables than they were a decade ago when a "community" was held to require a "sense of community" as a precondition and an integrating region was thought to demand a preexisting propensity to integrate. Still there are more indeterminate variables now than desirable. We certainly should discourage the tendency to add "fudge variables" whenever the standard ones do not seem to do the explanatory trick. This means that we ought to stop talking about "functional equivalents," "catalysts," "federalizers," "compellingness," "high politics," and similar mythical animals.

observed or measured in nature: The postulated conditions have not yet come about anywhere, at least in the contemporary world. At best we have a putative dependent variable.[29]

It is sobering to take a glance at some real-life dependent variables. The European Economic Community in 1962 seemed on the point of a breakthrough to a political community de facto because of an attempted expansion into the scope and level of its decisionmaking capacity; instead it settled down into the uneasy equilibrium state of continuing its established role until 1969. The East African Community moved from healthy exuberance to near-death between 1960 and 1965 only to revive, phoenixlike, after 1967; the Central American Common Market slips from one major crisis into another, always on the point of seeming collapse, but in the aggregate seems to do better than retain a state of equilibrium. The examples could be multiplied. They suggest that the variety of possible outcomes is considerable, that unions may settle down into a stable system without reaching any of the stages we defined in the earlier phases of our research. Yet these stages will represent higher degrees of "integration" than was true of the member states at an earlier point in time.

Scales as Dependent Variables

But why the insistence on a single ideal type as the terminal condition? The terminal condition envisaged could very well be more than a pluralistic security community and less than a political community, defined as the successful pluralistic-democratic state writ large; in fact, this is likely to be the case. Hence I suggest that we follow the approach of deliberately positing end states that could reflect extensive system transformation leading toward centralization or decentralization or the achievement of a new integrative plateau. The verbally defined single terminal conditions with which we have worked in the past—political community, security community, political union,

federal union—are inadequate because they foreclose real-life developmental possibilities.

Efforts have indeed been made to get away from the ideal definition of end states. They have taken the form, predominantly, of specifying separate dimensions or conditions which would constitute a higher degree of integration as compared to a previous point in time. In addition, scales are provided in some instances to observe and measure how far a given union has moved along the specified dimension. The end state, then, is a quantitatively specified "point" on a scale; when several scales are used for several salient dimensions, the end state is a specified convergence of separate curves.[30]

But the quantitatively phrased multidimensional definition—usually rendered as an "integrated community"—also presents problems. It suggests that if the union being studied scores "high" on a number of salient dimensions, particularly if it scores progressively "higher" over time, some theoretically relevant outcome is being attained; yet the total shape of the outcome is not given. This approach has the virtue of papering over the disagreement over the appropriate mix of independent and intervening variables that are embedded in the various theoretical approaches to regional integration studies. It recognizes that we do not know what the mix is,

---

[29]Possible exceptions are the (mostly unsuccessful) noncoercive unions of new states attempted in the last two decades, as analyzed in Franck and in Etzioni. At best, these experiences help to falsify certain theoretical postulates without explaining how a successful federal union can be achieved.

[30]For examples of such efforts see Nye, *International Organization*, Vol. 22, No. 4; Philip Jacob and Henry Teune, "The Integrative Process: Guidelines for Analysis of the Basis of Political Community," in Jacob and Toscano, pp. 1–45.

A similar approach is suggested in the quantification of twelve variables, which in the aggregate are expected to yield an outcome called "automatic politicization," that could be considered a proxy variable for political community. See Mario Barrera and Ernst B. Haas, "The Operationalization of Some Variables Related to Regional Integration: A Research Note," *International Organization*, Winter 1969 (Vol. 23, No. I), pp. 150–160; also the response by Philippe C. Schmitter, "Further Notes on Operationalizing Some Variables Related to Regional Integration," in *International Organization*, Spring 1969 (Vol. 23, No. 2), pp. 327–336. How politization is sequentially linked to other developments during the integration process is set forth by Schmitter, *International Organization*, Vol. 23, No. 1, pp. 161–166. If interdependence along some highly salient dimension is considered a proxy variable for the outcome, the work of Reinton is most suggestive. See Per Olav Reinton, "International Structure and International Integration," *Journal of Peace Research*, 1967 (No. 4), pp. 334–365.

nor whether it is the same for all situations. But it stresses simple observation for the careful development of hypotheses justifying and linking various independent variables—which in turn requires some kind of theory. Nor does this approach overcome the difficulty of foreclosing the future to a variety of possible integrative outcomes since it posits progressively "higher" scores instead of making a disciplined effort at imagining various future conditions. In short, the quantitative definition of progressive integrative developments is best seen as a methodological help in making accurate observations and at limiting recourse to overly restrictive verbal definitions; but it cannot alone provide the dependent variable. Scales of separate dimensions of integration are useful descriptively because they capture a process; but without hypothetically linked variables they are not explanatory of an outcome which, itself, remains unspecified.[31] When used in lieu of descriptive or schematic images of end states they substitute premature operationalization for theory and vision.

This truth is firmly recognized by Leon Lindberg and Stuart Scheingold. They posit three possible outcomes: The *fulfillment* of a postulated task on the part of practices and/or institutions created for integrative purposes; the *retraction* of such a task (i.e., disintegration); and the *extension* of such a task into spheres of action not previously anticipated by the actors. Models are provided for explaining the sequence of action made up of events created by actors. These three terms sum up and interpret independent variables into recurrent patterns yielding one of the three possible outcomes.[32]

In their treatment Lindberg and Scheingold make these outcomes specific to the European community and the stipulations of the treaties establishing the EEC and the European Atomic Energy Community (Euratom). To avoid EEC-tricity the same scheme of analysis could be applied to the collectivity of organizations and transactions characterizing the links between a given group of nations though one particular salient organization (such as the EEC) could be taken as the nucleus of the analysis. In the case of Europe one would then bring in the work of the Council of Europe, NATO, the Organization of Economic Cooperation and Development (OECD), the European Launcher Development Organization (ELDO), etc., with respect to the fulfillment, retraction, or extension produced in relations between the six members of the EEC. To get a total picture one would have to strike a balance among all these issues and issue areas because retraction may have occurred in one and fulfillment in others. In short, one would need a master concept under which all the various functionally specific issues and tasks can be grouped and summed up. This master concept, moreover, would have to provide scores so that we could recognize whether overall fulfillment or retraction has taken place.

Such a master concept is the notion of "authority-legitimacy transfer" or "sharing," a formulation I would myself prefer to the stress put on elite loyalties in my own earlier formulations. Specific indicators for both authority and legitimacy could be provided; these have the advantage

---

[31]See Nye, *International Organization*, Vol. 22, No. 4, pp. 864–875. I disagree with Nye's argument that the notion of integration ought to be "disaggregated" into economic, social, and political components without making any premature judgments as to how these separate ranges relate to each other causally. To avoid making causal assumptions and positing hypotheses merely sidesteps once more the difficulty of finding a dependent variable. Political integration, if that is what we are concerned about, is more important than economic and social trends; these are important because we think they are causally connected with political integration. Disaggregation helps in the attainment of operational accuracy but it hinders the removal of fuzzy dependent variables unless orders of causal priority are thought through. Humpty-Dumpty must be put together again, too, as it is in Nye's contribution to [*International Organization*, Autumn 1970].

[32]Leon Lindberg and Stuart Scheingold, *Europe's Would-Be Polity: Patterns of Change in the European Community* (Englewood Cliffs, N.J.: Prentice-Hall, 1970), chapter 4. For a most complete and perceptive list of possible measures and indicators of progress toward the achievement of any one of these three conditions (or of regress) see Lindberg's contribution to [International Organization, Autumn 1970]. It should be stressed, however, that these specifications still do not add up to the definition of one or several dependent variables in the sense of my argument. They have the enormous merit of providing measures specifically related to a series of independent and intervening variables while being pinpointed in one causative direction. In short, these measures do *not* substitute disaggregation of a fuzzy dependent variable for more sophisticated reaggregation.

of being *ex hypothesi* relevant to all geographical settings. One such measure is the notion of "institutionalization." It could be considered a proxy variable for the notion of political community, and some have so used it. It would be more defensible to elaborate the items and dimensions considered involved in "institutionalization" and define them as indicators of authority and legitimacy transfers, as summed up from activity in specific functional and organizational sectors and as observed in elite and mass perceptions.

Multiple Dependent Variables

We appear to be approaching a dependent variable through a series of evasive movements, laterally rather than frontally. We need a definition which avoids the overly simplistic ideal typical of past efforts while aiming at a more sophisticated goal than measurement alone. The terms "fulfillment," "retraction," "equilibrium," and "authority-legitimacy transfer" introduced above do not constitute a definition of a dependent variable either; they are merely concepts evaluating a process at a somewhat higher level of abstraction than that of verified hypotheses. Without the help of such concepts we can hope neither to combine and make intelligible the separate lessons we have learned about integration nor to fill the gaps in knowledge-which have been uncovered.

I am using the master concept "authority-legitimacy transfer" as an evaluative tool, much as Joseph Nye uses the term "political integration." We ought to be clear that indicators of political integration are *not* conceptually and sequentially on the same level of abstraction as are indicators of economic and social integration because these ought to refer to earlier points on the action paths. Political integration is simply another evaluative term for observing progress along a path of action—leading toward what?

I should like to propose three different dependent variables, all of which are heuristic in the sense that they do not have any real-life counterparts. They provide orienting terminal conditions on which our thoughts and efforts can focus. Nor are they really "terminal"; we can posit them as provisional points in the future on which we fix our analytical attention. But as students of

political life we know that even if the postulated conditions are attained, they are unlikely to remain terminal for very long. Nor are the three dependent variables exhaustive of possibilities. They provide rather an invitation to imagine still different outcomes which involve a higher degree of unity among the participating units than existed at a previous time. In short they are *illustrations of possible temporary results* of the processes we sum up under the label regional integration, so designed as to stretch our imagination of what the future may hold. I shall label the three "regional state," "regional commune," and "asymmetrical regional overlap." The processes associated with all of our pretheories could, in principle, result in the attainment of any of these terminal conditions.[33] Minimally, they all must meet the attributes of a security community. The three differ in how the main resource —legitimate authority—is diffused. Hence normative questions of some moment are implied.

A regional state is a hierarchically ordered arrangement resembling states familiar to us. Political authority is concentrated at the center; resources are marshalled and distributed from it. The centralized authority is legitimate in the eyes of the citizens, voluntary groups, and subordinate structures. To the extent that the political culture of the region is "participant" in character the legitimacy bestowed upon the central authority represents a sense of "regional nationalism."

There is nothing unfamiliar about this construct. But its opposite, a regional commune, is a much stranger beast. It assumes the kind of interdependence among the participating units which does not permit the identification of a single center of authority or perhaps of any clear center. It is an anarchoid image of a myriad of units which are so highly differentiated in function as to be forced into interdependence. Authority is involved primarily in the sense of having

---

[33]These types were suggested by, and correspond to, certain constructs in organization theory, particularly by the literature on organizational complexity. Moreover, each type is derived from set theory and is capable of mathematical manipulation, thereby perhaps contributing to possibilities of computer simulation. Thus, regional state corresponds to a set-theory tree, regional commune to a full matrix, and asymmetrical overlap to a semilattice. I am greatly indebted for these ideas to Todd LaPorte and John Ruggie.

been taken away from previous centers without having found a new single locus. Legitimacy, however it can be imagined, would not take the form of a loyalty akin to nationalism.

Asymmetrical overlapping involves a much more complex arrangement. Many units depend on many others but the pattern of interdependence is asymmetrical: For some purposes all may be equally interdependent, but for others a few of the units cohere closely with a few others while for still other purposes the pattern may again be different without involving all units equally. In short, while authority is certainly withdrawn from the preexisting units, it is not proportionately or symmetrically vested in a new center; instead it is distributed asymmetrically among several centers, among which no single dominant one may emerge, though one might imagine subtypes of this dependent variable involving various degrees of centralized authority. The ensemble would enjoy legitimacy in the eyes of its citizens though it would be difficult to pinpoint the focus of the legitimacy in a single authority center; rather, the image of infinitely tiered multiple loyalties might be the appropriate one. Perhaps the now existing Western European pattern approaches this image.

What about the vexing question of dependence on extraregional centers of influence, if not authority? How significant is it to talk about such end states of regional integration processes when the resulting structure may be autonomous in a rather fictitious sense? It is possible to describe a variant of each type which locates the regional cluster within a larger system and specifies the degree of subservience to it. Moreover, other variants or subtypes will readily come to mind. I emphasize again that nothing exhaustive is being attempted at this stage: My concern is to provide some generalized images of outcomes before we get lost in operationalization.

One final advantage of using heuristic multiple variables is the emancipation thereby provided from our pretheories. Neo-functional efforts stress case studies of decisionmaking within a region and in regional organizations, an interest justified by the neo-functionalist assumption that decisionmakers are the true heroes and villains of the integration process. Transactionalists counter that a great deal of relevant activity goes on outside of organizations and decisional encounters,

an argument based on the assumption that anybody who "transacts" or "communicates" anything is potentially relevant to the creation of integrative/disintegrative trends. Obviously, these two approaches are far from mutually exclusive. Linking them, however, requires articulate hypotheses about presumed relationships between decisional outcomes and communication patterns. Since the multiply defined dependent variable, in turn, implies different scopes of collective decisionmaking and varying strength of interunit dependence, such hypotheses can be usefully linked with the presumed attainment of one or the other of these outcomes. This, in turn, requires a specification of what mix of which independent variables is likely to lead to a given outcome—something clearly not achieved by our pretheories or our empirical generalizations—and raises questions as to what kinds of studies ought to be tackled next.

V. TOWARD A THEORY?

A Plethora of Independent Variables and How to Link Them

What yardstick is there for choosing and justifying ways to explain the arrival of various degrees of regional unity? One extreme is to list every conceivable variable, from the length of the shoreline of the member nations to the proportion of the national budget devoted to veterans' pensions, so that the resulting list of 250 can be reduced by factor analysis. Such a generous and comprehensive approach really implies that we do not know enough on the basis of common sense and immersion in the factual details of regional integration to select variables more economically. It also begs the old question of whether the variable exists "autonomously" at the systemic level or is reflected in the cognitive processes of actors, i.e., whether it merely acts as an indicator (of what?) or accounts for behavior.

Moreover, there is an enormous difference between codifying empirical findings—as I sought to do above—and assessing the significance of specific variables as explanations of outcomes. The empirical generalizations discussed above do not tell us which of several independent variables is the more (or the most) powerful in propelling a given unit toward a specified end state. Nor does the possibility of positively correlating certain trends with an independently assessed growth in integrative institutions settle the question of causation or explanation. In short, several things remain to be done before we even approach an inductive theory. The independent variables with which we propose to work must be specified and operationalized. The hypotheses linking them must be made explicit. And a way must be found to evaluate conceptually the significance of the verified hypotheses in terms of their contribution to explaining an outcome.

The specification of independent variables, their operationalization, and the establishment of clear links between them is advancing rapidly. Several contributors to [*International Organization*, Autumn, 1970] are engaged in this process . . . Nye's list is comprehensive and well chosen in reflecting what we already know about the experiences of various regional efforts on the basis of descriptive case studies. Phillippe Schmitter's list, though somewhat different in inspiration, is equally comprehensive, and it self-consciously incorporates presumed links between variables and explicit hypotheses, equally general in their inspiration and mindful of research already completed. Donald Puchala is careful to specify expected correlations between transactional and conflict-resolution data, thus linking the communications and the neo-functional stands as well as jumping the gap between approaches relying on aggregate data and the behavior of elites. Variables are most explicitly specified and justified.

But one cannot *link* independent variables into some kind of explanatory scheme without recourse to concepts or ideas at a higher level of abstraction than the variables themselves, the facts they comprehend, and the empirical generalizations which sum them up. In short, an external source for *linked* variables is necessary; pretheories do have the virtue of providing such sources. Still, we do not wish to accept pretheories as final; we wish to do better than simply arrive at more empirical generalizations of the type summarized above. Hence we must draw our inspiration for identifying and linking variables from some intellectual constructs that command general acceptance for their utility without being fully

validated and without having found a clear and final niche in some as yet to be formulated theory.

I label such constructs evaluative concepts. Appropriately scored concepts associated with the explanation of one of our postulated outcomes constitute an "action path." We expect the recurrence of particular relations between independent variables. In order to explain a sequence of events, say from background to the initiation, maintenance, slow growth, and eventual pressure, the substitution of one type of leadership for another, and the creation of new groups of actors, especially nongovernmental ones. We would sum up the particular experience by talking about such things as spillover, spillaround, learning, socialization, elite responsiveness, or institutionalization. In short, these terms are empirically grounded evaluations, not simple facts. They can be inferred from observed variables if one is clear about how and why variables are linked. But once they have been inferred they can be used to sum up many ranges of activities and interconnected variables in many places. If our objective is the sketching of action paths leading to one of our postulated outcomes, we must evaluate patterned events with concepts summing up processes.[34]

We are now in a position to summarize and rearrange the various strands of the argument. The act of judging whether a concrete regional set

---

[34]This way of seeing concepts and data involves a change in perspective on my part as to what constitutes a variable and a method of linking variables, as distinguished from a validated summary of a recurring process expressed by a conceptual label such as "spillover." In short, I no longer accept as sufficiently well-explicated and "placed" the "variables" that appear in Ernst B. Haas and Philippe C. Schmitter, "Economics and Differential Patterns of Political Integration: Projections about Unity in Latin America," *International Organization*, Autumn 1964 (Vol. 18, No. 4), pp. 705–737, and in Barrera and Haas, *International Organization*, Vol. 23, No. I, pp. 150–160.

A given action path is characterized by a certain kind of learning, a certain pattern of responsiveness, a certain degree of spillover, whether in scope or level. Michel Crozier has suggested a new term which seems appropriate for summing up the kind of process that we ought to use more as a device for linking variables: *apprentissage institutionnel*. It can be used to light up the interconnections between a pattern of transaction, disappointment, declining responsiveness, bargaining, and the eventual redefinition of common or converging interests.

of trends and decisions approaches one or the other of the three terminal conditions involves a series of evaluative steps on the part of the observer. After specifying the independent variables he expects to be important, observing their operation over time, and after verifying hypotheses involving these variables, several valuations then become necessary:

1. What is the mix of recurrent behaviors which accounts for a given trend in a given sector? This involves the use of such evaluative concepts as spillover, elite responsiveness, and bargaining style.
2. What is the mix of all integrative and disintegrative trends in all sectors for the region (or the sum of the separate organizational transactional experiences)? This calls for the application of the evaluative concepts we labeled fulfillment, extension, and retraction. We could discover, for instance, that fulfillment occurred in the field of agriculture, extension tariff negotiations with third countries, and retraction in defense policy, as associated with differential patterns of spillover, elite responsiveness, and bargaining styles in each.
3. What is the sum of all the processes described under these labels? This calls for the application to the region as a whole of the master concept we have called authority-legitimacy transfer.

The multiple dependent variable we have devised enables us to specify to whom the authority and legitimacy have been transferred. The indicators of institutionalization described elsewhere in [*International Organization*, Autumn 1970] would facilitate the evaluation.

Action Paths and Some Unsolved Problems

When we evaluated the empirical generalizations offered earlier, we noted four major gaps in our knowledge which were in no sense resolved even if we assumed the descriptive accuracy and modest analytical significance of our generalizations. The questions were: (1) Can forces which explain the initiation of a movement toward regional union also be used to explain the maintenance of progress of that union? (2) Is it useful and defensible to use a political model in the study of regional integration which postulates the congruence of national and regional political styles? (3) Is it necessary or desirable to have a special model in the study of regional integration applicable to late developing countries? (4) What should we know about social learning as a way to link various variables? I now wish to reexamine these questions in the light of our discussion regarding dependent variables and the notion of action paths linking independent variables and tying them sequentially to the attainment of a terminal condition. This reexamination should serve the dual purpose of illustrating the notion of action paths and give a few indications of some useful next steps to be taken in research. If regularly observed—and properly evaluated—processes can act as organizing and explanatory concepts for further empirical observations, we ought to be in a position to incorporate them into new research efforts and thus to advance theorizing.

Initiation versus Maintenance of Integration

Actors change their minds, redefine their interests, see new opportunities, and respond to new institutions at home and regionally. Many of these new stimuli arise as a predicted result of what goes on in the integration process and can be evaluated conceptually without introducing new variables at a later point in an integrative/disintegrative sequence. This would argue in favor of assuming the constancy of the explanatory power of a set of variables over time. On the other hand, one could also argue that either of two sets of possibilities can upset this assumption. First, political or social forces internal to the union or common market may arise after initiation and deflect (or strengthen) the initial forces without having been included in the explanation of the origin. This is discussed further when we turn to congruence of national and regional processes. Second, the international environment may change after the initiation of the process and produce an external stimulus for (or against) continued integration not included in the explanation of origin. In either case the assumed linearity between initially programmed impulses and eventual outcome is disturbed.

If we accept the formulation of the dependent variable(s) offered above, a solution to this problem seems possible. Our task is to specify the action paths, i.e., the particular combination of independent variables that most accurately describe the attainment of any one of the postulated outcomes *and* the sequence describing which combination comes to prevail. The list of variables will then remain constant; but the score of each variable will not. The plotting of an action path can then take the form of a scale of progress toward each outcome, made up of the same variables scored differently at various points in time. And the recognized fact of possibly simultaneous integration and disintegration in the same region —depending on task and issue—can then be captured by adding negative and positive scores. Note, however, that such a procedure would still call for the revision of the initial list of independent variables to account for the possibility of the later introduction of the deflecting forces sketched above. This requires the kind of hindsight on the part of the observer which can only arise as a result of assimilating the lessons learned from a considerable number of descriptive case studies of given regional integration experiences. The standard list of conceptually linked variables provided by Joseph Nye and Phillippe Schmitter is particularly useful for enabling us to specify which forces remain of equal importance during the early and the later phases of the integration process and which forces drop out of the picture as the process goes forward.

National-Regional Congruence

We would do better if, in our tailoring of empirical generalizations to selected dependent variables, we kept our minds open to a neglected possibility: Rates of change at the national and regional levels may not be congruent. The Western European model has assumed that changes making for pluralism, incrementalism, and instrumental behavior at the national level are wholly congruent with the same characteristics at the regional level. Neo-functionalists use an implicit congruence model to select and link variables. Efforts in the Latin American and African settings, by contrast, have relied on the lack of congruence between national and regional structures as an important organizing concept. There impatience with immobilisme at the national level was treated as a positive expectation with respect to regional movement. Both perspectives are time-bound.

A congruence model suggests a different set of intervariable links than a noncongruence model does. Furthermore, a strong case could be made that the notion of noncongruence should in the future inspire the search for links between variables no matter which terminal condition we seek to explore. Some of us have assumed that in the initial period of a union the causal influence would run from the nations to the central institutions and in the subsequent period in the reverse direction—national outputs would dominate first, regional outputs later. The example of the EEC since 1965 suggests that this pattern is unwarranted as a general inspiration. Certain national outputs continue to dominate—very strikingly!—but in other issue areas the regional outputs assert their potency as well. National systems are changing at a different rate than the regional system; new national stimuli stressing demands for change with a consummatory quality strike Brussels while the national arena continues to be struck with EEC outputs that correspond to the earlier incremental-instrumental style. National actors and political styles are being re-ideologized, but the regional system holds its pragmatic own; it maintains itself, though stagnating in terms of earlier ambitious objectives. By focusing on a noncongruence model of national-regional interaction we capture this seemingly paradoxical reality; we sensitize ourselves to a two-way flow of inputs and outputs, and we keep in mind that the environmental conditions that made a given pattern possible initially keep changing and therefore produce new—and perhaps qualitatively different—inputs. Evaluative concepts which sum up such trends realistically are thus useful in pinpointing *different* action paths toward a postulated outcome.

Donald Puchala's contribution to [*International Organization*, Autumn, 1970] is particularly useful in establishing this perspective for future studies . . . He shows why the communicational hypotheses create a presumption in favor of increasing elite responsiveness as a result of increasing transactions. If, therefore, a *lack* of responsiveness on some ranges of interdependence is shown to be correlated with growing transactions and more favorable attitudes toward one's partners, a sharply noncongruent feature will be thrown into relief. This would force us to alter a number of poorly validated propositions. Such linked variables as the Nye and Schmitter lists contain could then be pressed into service to explain the lack of congruence and thus give us propositions explaining one of the postulated outcomes. For example, the list contains linked variables which suggest:

> initial converging but instrumental actor motives→ disappointment→ exogenously furnished rewards (or threats)→ revalued actor motives→ larger task and increasing institutionalization of decisionmaking power

An investigation sensitive to noncongruence, however, could detect and explain why increasing institutionalization might *not* occur because, for example, the exogenous impulses are so powerful and so diverse as to inhibit revaluation within the region by turning the attention of the actors to arenas outside.

A Special Model for the Third World?

The pretheoretical efforts have mostly started with a set of universal assumptions and hypotheses which had to be shored up and rescued by recourse to various extraparadigmatic devices. The corrective for this practice is not to reify it by claiming a special status for the exogenous variable and turning it into a deus ex machina capable of reviving a floundering common market in Pago Pago. Nor should we expect a charismatic leader or an ideology with consummatory qualities to ride to the rescue.[35] Rather, the answer is to make the range of independent variables

---

[35]Etzioni, Nye, Haas, and Schmitter have all indulged in this practice. It is raised to a point of faith in Hansen, *World Politics*, Vol. 21, No. 2, pp. 270-271. To those who argue that comparative studies of integration could still proceed if we had one model for industrialized and one for underdeveloped regions it must be pointed out that our findings suggest a different mix of variables at work in explaining the maintenance of regional economic arrangements in Central America, South America, East Africa, and Equatorial Africa, not to mention Eastern Europe.

broad, keep in mind the possible variations of their mix depending on which outcome is being investigated, and experiment with weights for each variable that seem appropriate for given regional settings. But as long as political actors are sufficiently rational to calculate their interests and seek accommodations on that basis, our ingenuity ought to be great enough to devise observational techniques, concepts, and indicators to catch the interregional variation in their modes of calculation. What matters most for the task of systematic study is that there be reasonable agreement on which variables are considered causatively important and on their links with other variables. The specification of action paths leading to each of several postulated outcomes is a capping device for keeping the theory "whole" while recognizing various roads to salvation within it.

Transactions, Attitude Change, and Learning

How can we link variables that describe the rate of transaction between units with variables that describe the attitudes of masses and members of the elites? Some causal link must be imputed or established if the transactional approach to integration is to be blended with generalizations about attitudes. Further, how can the empirical generalizations we have established with respect to changing bargaining patterns and styles, institutional evolution, and the predictable resolution of conflicts between actors be linked with data on transactions and on attitudes? We can say that only when actors perceive and evaluate the events that are summed up by such findings as "changes in the rate of transaction" and "evolution of attitudes" is such a link established causally. But before the cause is established it would be useful to know what the sheer statistical relationship between the three rates of change might be.

In other words, even the magic of action paths will not suffice to tell us *how* different types of actor experiences combine to produce a given trend. The linking of independent variables through articulate hypotheses, even if we allow for the points raised under our discussion of noncongruence and the addition of new forces after the initiation of a trend, will not quite do the trick of adequate explanation. Action paths toward each of the postulated terminal conditions would also have to include explanations of who learns from whom in producing elite responsiveness, how institutions induce or retard learning, and who communicates what to whom when channels of contact open up. It is not good enough simply to note that various independent variables are associated in a given mix in a given action path toward a federal state or an asymmetrically overlapping system.

One very major link would be the notion of social learning. The enterprise of regional integration studies would be improved enormously if we knew when, how, and why actors "learn" to behave differently than they did in the past—either in an integrative or a disintegrative direction. Is it a function of cross-national contact and familiarity, as the psychotherapist would have us believe? Is it the result of ever more complex patterns of intergroup loyalties and of social roles that require a single individual to cater to many patterns simultaneously? Is it related to education and informal socialization practices? Some scholars link interpersonal trust and responsiveness, as a hypothesis, with progressively rewarding experiences derived from the activities of common markets. Thus:

> progressively rewarding experiences→ learning→ trust

Others seek to press simple stimulus-response theory into service in suggesting that the intensity and the frequency of the regional interaction pattern will explain a given integrative outcome. Still others assume a more cognitive style of social learning for explaining the kinds of increasing responsiveness in which we are interested and therefore prefer the lessons of formal decision and coalition theory to discover how and when actors redefine their utilities in bargaining with each other. This approach, of course, differs sharply from the study of emotive forces, affect, and the manipulation of symbols as agents of social learning.[36]

The truth is that we simply do not know enough about the forces and processes which mediate between the various independent variables we consider salient. Moreover, we do not yet know how to conceptualize—or ask questions of—the forces which presumably do the mediating. I suggest as a high order of priority that the notion of social learning be included in new studies of integration in order to make our action paths more than highly intercorrelated scores. Such studies should include not only the investigation of who "learns" what from whom. It must include the meaning of the messages sent through the expanding channels of communication, i.e., with what results in terms of attitude change. Moreover, studies of social learning can easily be linked with the investigation of organizational dynamics in terms tracing the evolution of institutionalized behavior for defining goals, resolving conflict, and persuading actors to live up to their commitments. More abstractly, the application of organization theory to integration studies can tell us more about how the perception by actors of an increasingly complex environment leads them to redefine goals and mechanisms of accommodation so as to increase either adaptiveness or the capacity to control the environment. My own preference in the study of social learning is the application of decision and coalition theory so as to trace modal patterns of redefinition of utilities by actors and the inclusion of this kind of material in the elaboration of a given action path.

---

[36]Donald J. Puchala, "The Pattern of Contemporary Regional Integration," *International Studies Quarterly*, March 1968 (Vol. 12, No. 1), pp. 38–64. Among social psychologists there are exceedingly few whose assumptions and methods can be readily related to the study of social learning as mediated through experiences in bargaining, defining, and redefining interests because the bulk of the psychological literature is organized around the trust-love-friendship-peace versus distrust-hate-enmity-war dichotomy. For notable and important exceptions see Daniel Katz, "Nationalism and Strategies of International Conflict Resolution," in Herbert C. Kelman (ed.), *International Behavior: A Social-Psychological Analysis* (New York: Holt, Rinehart and Winston [for the Society for the Psychological Study of Social Issues], 1965), as well as Kelman's own work, as summarized by himself in ibid., chapter 16. For a discussion of stimulus-response theory in this context see Henry Teune, "The Learning of Integrative Habits," in Jacob and Toscano, pp. 247–282. The work of Chadwick Alger on United Nations diplomats illustrates the same set of assumptions. Fred Iklé with Nathan Leites discusses the modification of actor utilities in "Political Negotiations as a Process of Modifying Utilities," *Journal of Conflict Resolution*, March 1962 (Vol. 6, No. 1), pp. 19–28. In purely game-theory term the work of John Harsanyi is the most suggestive with respect to the exploration of this area.

THE NEXT STEPS

The main utility of the studies of regional integration completed so far has been the systematic investigation of certain potentially crucial independent variables and the search for verification of the assumptions embedded in the pre-theories which led to the positing of the independent variables in the first place. Thus, the accumulation of figures on major trends in transaction and communication has served to map important ties between nations and their evolution over time. The completion of a modest number of decisional case studies has taught us a lot about the limits on the cognitive abilities of leaders and elites to define their own and their colleagues' interests. But I suspect that the utility of these types of studies has been exhausted. We now have our list of major independent variables, and we know enough to correct earlier false assumptions about congruence and the linear projection of variables found to have been causatively significant at the beginning of a given regional integrative process. We must now do systematic comparisons of regional experiences and national behavior patterns clustering around the evaluative concepts posited above in order to delineate the action paths which presumably recur.

Computer simulation is one of the most exciting possibilities open to students of regional integration. It forces them to reduce their multi-layered and nonadditive generalizations to a common denominator, to agree on likely—but verifiable and testable—sequences of action. The possibility of simulation has both a sobering and an intellectually explosive impact: sobering because of the standardization of variables, of links between variables, and of measures that is demanded; intellectually explosive because the standardization also requires subordination to concepts which seem to summarize observed processes and which can thus become branching points on the flow chart. Finally, the most exciting possibility inherent in computer simulation is the chance it affords to go beyond the very limited number of actual historical cases from which our pretheorizing has sprung. While seeking to replicate these cases, the practice of simulation can also imagine new combinations of concepts and variables which have not yet occurred "in nature" and play them out. In short, computer simulation can show us action paths which have not yet been followed or imagined. But it is made more powerful by the availability of heuristic end states.

Concurrently, the possibility of simulation further enhances the need for a methodological synthesis and gives it a special urgency. If the simulators wish to replicate known decision sequences of organizations and groups active in regional integration, they must find ways of grouping and summing the variables from which concepts summarizing recurring processes are deduced. If they wish to replicate and predict integrative outcomes with the help of ecological and/or attitudinal variables, they must achieve agreement on their definition and on the imputed causal links between them. This would incidentally compel students of integration to settle the question of which weights ought to be attached to such variables. In short, progress in theorizing depends on the acceptance of the discipline which computer simulation implies; but computer simulation, in turn, depends on further progress along the lines of resolving the four issues raised by the gaps in our knowledge.

But why do we need a theory? Why can we not continue to follow our individual inclinations and study the phenomenon of regional integration according to the predilections implicit in the existing pretheories? Because the stakes are too high! The systematic links demanded by computer simulation add up to a whole which at least resembles a theory. And simulation can help us explore the question of a future world order.

Mankind may well be taking steps which could lead to a more multi-layered, more complex, less "integrated" world that would permit much local violence but bar global conflict because of its very fragmentation. But regional integration may lead to a future world made up of fewer and fewer units, each a unit with all the power and will to self-assertion that we associate with classical nationalism. The future, then, may be such as to force us to equate peace with nonintegration and associate the likelihood of major war with successful regional integration.

This is possible, not certain, and perhaps not likely. But we ought to inquire about the degree of possibility or likelihood. In short, one major normative utility of the study of regional integration is its contribution as a conceptual, empirical, and methodological link between work on the future of the international system and the future of the nation-states whose interrelationships make up the system. Suppose that local national movements in Wales, Scotland, Bavaria, Brittany, Nagaland, West Irian, Biafra, the Ogaden desert, Quebec, and in dozens of other ethnically complex places succeed in obtaining cultural and linguistic—and much political—autonomy. Suppose further that the same states enter into tighter economic relationships with their regional neighbors. Suppose further still that they ally themselves militarily and diplomatically with states other than their economic partners. Not only will the state decline as an autonomous decision-maker, but the power to make decisions will be given to many other units, some smaller and some larger than the present state. This, I believe, would be a wholesome development for world peace whereas the concentration of all power in a few regional units would endanger it. Simulation would be enormously helpful in enabling us to play out the possible trends at the subnational, the national, the regional, and the global levels of political action. Simulation would truly stretch, if not blow, our minds and give us a purchase on the future. But such an adventure first demands a more systematic theory. Our groping has enabled us to ask the questions that the theory should answer; it has also given us some concepts for refining the questions. But much work needs to be done to realize the potential of these achievements.

Discussion and Questions

1. For recent discussions on operationalizing some of the variables involved in integration, see the following articles: Mario Barrera and Ernst B. Haas, "The Operationalization of Some Variables Related to Regional Integration: A Research Note," *International Organization*, vol. 24, no. 1 (Winter 1970), pp. 150–60 (and note Haas's statement to the effect that he no longer accepts as "sufficiently well-explicated and 'placed'" these variables, in note 34, p. 124 of this volume); Kenneth A. Dahlberg, "Regional Integration: the Neo-Functional Versus a Configurative Approach," *International Organization*, vol. 24, no. 1 (Winter 1970), pp. 122–28; Philippe C. Schmitter, "Three Neo-Functional Hypotheses about International Integration," *International Organization*, vol. 23, no. 1 (Winter 1969), pp. 161–66.

2. Among many efforts to specify the phases of the integration process in systematic detail two are especially worthy of note. Both of these group efforts are heavily influenced by the intellectual leadership of Karl W. Deutsch. (See Karl W. Deutsch and others, *Political Community and the North Atlantic Area* [Princeton University Press, Princeton, 1957]; Philip E. Jacob and James V. Toscano, Eds., *The Integration of Political Communities* [Philadelphia, Lippincott, 1964], especially pp. 1–97, 143–383.)

3. Another suggestive approach to integration is contained in an article by Joseph S. Nye, Jr. ("Comparative Regional Integration: Concept and Measurement," *International Organization*, vol. 22, no. 4 [Autumn 1968], pp. 855–80). For yet another approach, see Fred M. Hayward, "Continuities and Discontinuities between Studies of National and International Political Integration" (*International Organization*, vol. 24, no. 4 [Autumn 1970], pp. 917–941), in which he seeks to establish the usefulness of conceptualizing political integration in a way that might be used for both regional and national studies.

4. Other valuable work by Professor Nye examines subregional integration as the unit of inquiry. (See Joseph S. Nye, Jr., *Pan-Africanism and East African Integration* [Harvard University Press, Cambridge, 1965]; Nye, "Central American Regional Integration," *International Conciliation*, no. 562 [March 1967], pp. 5–66.)

In the latter article, Nye includes a useful analysis of different levels of integration. The lowest level of integration is "token integration" —this is most common in the less developed areas and consists of an "expression of the supra-state sense of community without any significant restructuring of interests." A "security-community" is a higher level of regional integration—here regional institutions and symbols, although perhaps too weak to further economic benefits, are strong enough to produce a sense that recourse to threats or uses of violence in disputes among members is illegitimate. The third level of regional integration is what Nye calls "limited functional cooperation." This signifies a greater interdependence, for example, sharing costs of limited services. The fourth level is "international economic integration," and this "includes a number of means of expanding market size by abolishing discrimination between economic factors belonging to different national states." These means are themselves ranked from lesser to greater interdependence: free-trade area, customs union, common market, economic union, total economic integration. The fifth level is "direct political unification" (See Joseph S. Nye, Jr., "Central American Regional Integration," *International Conciliation*, no. 572 [March 1967], pp. 5–66, at pp. 7–9.)

In "*The Uniting of Europe* and the Uniting of Latin America" (*Journal of Common Market Studies*, vol. 5, no. 4 [June 1967], pp. 315–343), Haas reviews the experience of European integration up through 1957. He contrasts this experience with the predicted course of European integration that he outlined in his influential book, *The Uniting of Europe*, which was written a decade earlier. Haas relies heavily in his essay upon a set of categories developed by Stanley Hoffmann: national consciousness, national situation, and national ideology. These categories help Haas examine the course of regional integration. Haas effectively uses them to compare efforts toward integration in Latin America with those in Europe. Several factors are isolated by Haas as

significant, including the stage of industrialization and the degree of political autonomy enjoyed by the constituent units. Unlike the principal European states, with their long traditions of national unity, many of the most important Latin American countries are mainly occupied with the process of nation-building. To date, as Haas shows, the struggle to achieve strong nations has been regarded as complementary to the efforts to promote economic regionalism of the sort embodied in the idea of the Latin American Free Trade Area. The prospects for political integration in Latin America do not seem very bright so long as the major effort of these countries is to improve their national situation and create a strong sense of national consciousness within their respective societies. The relationship between nation-building and region-building in Latin America gives some insight into the parallel relationship between region-building and the establishment of world order.

The development of Haas' approach to the study of international integration is worth noting. It is more firmly rooted in empirical social science than are the previously given generalizations of Liska which are derived from his reflections upon diplomatic history. Haas' theory has been developing over the years and has culminated, for the time being at least, in the view of integration that he puts forth in the article printed earlier in this chapter. The later Haas differs considerably from the earlier Haas as exhibited in such articles as "International Integration: the European and the Universal Process" (*International Organization*, vol. 15, no. 3 [Summer 1961], pp. 366–92). In an article written with Philippe C. Schmitter, "Economics and Differential Patterns of Political Integration: Projections about Unity in Latin America" (*International Organization*, vol. 18, no. 4 [Autumn 1964], pp. 705–737), Haas already begins to adopt a somewhat less rigidly conceived view of the integration process:

> Integration, to us, means the process of transferring exclusive expectations of benefits from the nation-state to some larger entity. It encompasses the process by virtue of which national actors of all sorts (government officials, interest group spokesmen, politicians, as well as ordinary people) cease to identify themselves and their future welfare entirely with their own national government and its policies.

This conception of integration is psychosocial in orientation, concentrating on expectations prevailing among power-wielders and public opinion.

By 1970 Haas defines integration without explicit emphasis on the loyalties of political actors:

> The study of regional integration is concerned with explaining how and why states cease to be wholly sovereign, how and why they voluntarily mingle, merge, and mix with their neighbors so as to lose the factual attributes of sovereignty while acquiring new techniques for resolving conflicts among themselves. Regional cooperation, organization, systems, and subsystems should not be confused with the resulting condition. . . . [Integration is] a process for the creation of political communities defined in institutional and attitudinal terms. . . . [See p. 105 of this book.]

➤ How does his definition compare with those of Liska and Deutsch?

5. ➤ Wherein lie the basic differences in the three pretheories of regional integration—identified with the federalist, communications, and neo-functionalist approaches? ➤ Are they different in regard to process or variables taken into account?

5. ➤ How do the end-states posited by Haas—regional state, regional commune, asymmetrical regional overlap—compare to Etzioni's 1965 ideas of political communities and unions?

7. ➤ What reasons does Haas give for the necessity for developing an adequate integration theory? ➤ What shortcomings of the existing pretheories does he find particularly disturbing?

8. ➤ How does integration theory relate to world-order theory? ➤ Can integration theory provide a useful tool of analysis with which to approach world-order problems? Note that on a world-order level there is usually an effort to precede economic integration by political integration.

Haas has attempted to apply neofunctional logic to global processes of integration in a book entitled *Beyond the Nation-State* (Stanford University Press, Stanford, California, 1964), which looks at the experience of the International Labor Organization over the years. The ILO is a functional arena within which a certain amount of sovereignty-cutting has taken place as a consequence of an interplay between technical and political pressures. But nothing comparable to "an integration theory" is relied upon by Haas in his study of global processes of interaction. ➤ Would it be useful to conceptualize a planned process of incremental integration on a global basis that involved step-by-step transfer of functions and a gradual unification of standards? ➤Does the United Nations have implicit in its framework a potentiality for stimulating and sustaining global integration? Note the contrast between global integration and second-order integration as world-order strategies for the total system of international relations.

6

Domestic and International Consequences of Regional Integration

STUART A. SCHEINGOLD

I. INTRODUCTION

The purpose of this article is to suggest that the perspective of scholars studying regional integration be broadened to include research expressly concerned with the consequences of integration and to indicate the directions that such efforts might take. To date, the students of integration have been mainly describing, analyzing, and measuring the integration process. This is true of research on the European Communities as well as of studies of integration elsewhere in Europe and on other continents. In our quest for political community we have utilized a number of different research strategies and focused on a broad range of indicators, but our primary concern has been with regional capacities for aggregating political authority.

What has been missing from all this work is some attention to the difference it makes whether or not such regional entities are created. As a result, after more than a decade of research we have only a very limited understanding of the costs and benefits of integration.[1]

Economists who have studied integration provide the major exception to the above generalization. They have tended, right from the outset, to be sensitive to the repercussions of regional integration on world trade and total welfare.[2]

Acknowledgements: The author's intellectual debt extends beyond the contributors to [*International Organization*, Autumn 1970], to his colleague Professor Kenneth M. Dolbeare who first interested him in this article's most basic concerns. He is also grateful to Professor Jack Dennis for his assistance with data analysis.

[1]This article will draw almost exclusively on the experience of the European Communities in specifying the limits of current research efforts and in discussing the kinds of problems that remain to be tackled. Nevertheless, the underlying argument for research on the consequences of integration should be relevant to other regions.

[2]See, for example, one of the standard works: Bela Balassa, *The Theory of Economic Integration* (Homewood, Ill.: Richard D. Irwin, 1961), chapter I.

From *International Organization*, vol. 24, no. 4, Autumn 1970, pp. 978–1002. Copyright 1970, World Peace Foundation, Boston, Mass. Reprinted by special permission. This article was also published in L. N. Lindberg and S. Scheingold, Eds., *Regional Integration: Theory and Research* (Harvard University Press, 1970.)

The internal consequences of integration for patterns of consumption and competition have also been matters of concern for economists.[3] Their focus on consequences in general and concern with welfare in particular stands in sharp contrast to the perspectives of most political scientists. It should, nevertheless, be pointed out that the economists have been more inclined to theory and commentary than to empirical research.[4]

To a limited extent a portion of the work done by political scientists also sheds some light on the consequences of integration. In particular, political scientists working with Karl W. Deutsch have systematically collected and analyzed data which gives us a sense of the changes in attitudes and aggregate behavior (trade, mail, student travel, and tourism) which have accompanied integration. Indeed, they began to study changes in trading patterns well before serious empirical research by the economists was initiated. (Donald Puchala's article in [*International Organization*, Autumn 1970] is the latest in a series of such studies.) Similarly, studies by Ernst Haas and Leon Lindberg, among others, have indicated how integration has given rise to community-wide organization of pressure groups and unprecedented cooperation between national and community bureaucrats, not to speak of institutional innovations that characterize the integrative system.

One might reasonably think of all these changes as the consequences of integration. They are, however, confined to a relatively narrow range of problems. To those who study them these changes are not consequences but *indicators* of integration. Researchers use such data to determine whether or not integration is taking place. For Deutsch, the indicators of social community—transaction flows and elite and mass attitudes—are the defining characteristics of integration while to

Haas, the growth of a pluralist political arena in the context of effective community institutions indicates successful integration. In other words, while this research does yield as a by-product information on the consequences of integration, these consequences are indistinguishable from process concerns having to do with the aggregation of political authority at the regional level.

In contrast, this article will focus squarely on consequences of integration and will broaden the inquiry beyond those considerations which are identifiable with the integration process. Two distinct sets of research questions will be pursued.

The first is to consider the results of integration in terms of the *original incentives* for creating a European community. The integrative process was expected to alter dramatically the relationships between the nation-states of Europe, transform faltering economic systems, and even change continental life-styles. While it is true that the development of the European Communities has been associated with peace, economic growth, and an apparent "Americanization" of life-style, we have little understanding about the extent to which integration is promoting or undermining these trends.[5]

There is also a second set of questions which directs our attention to a range of *distributional issues* transcending the original aspirations of the founders. How is integration affecting the distribution of influence and material well-being among the peoples of the European Communities and what is its impact on other regions of the world?

One can only speculate on the reasons for the rather limited research attention to the consequences of integration. But such speculation is useful if it makes us more sensitive to our own preconceptions and more self-conscious about the limitations of our research paradigms. The preconception in this case was, I believe, that integration was good by definition[6] since it was directed at economic reconstruction and permanent reconciliation between nations whose

---

[3]This was probably first explored by Tibor Scitovsky, *Economic Theory and Western European Integration* (Stanford, Calif.: Stanford University Press, 1958).

[4]An obvious exception is Lawrence B. Krause's excellent empirical study, *European Economic Integration and the United States* (Washington: Brookings Institution, 1968). Krause's book is certainly a big step in the direction favored in this article and will be discussed below. Ingo Walter has also collected a good deal of data in *The European Common Market: Growth and Patterns of Trade* (New York: Frederick A. Praeger, 1967).

[5]The recent outbreak of hostilities between two members of the relatively stable Central American Common Market (CACM) is a case in point—particularly since the conflict seems to have been due at least in part to the absence of regional policies on the free movement of labor.

[6]Again, my reference is primarily to political scientists who have been doing empirical studies of integration.

bloody conflicts had led to major wars engulfing significant portions of the world. A "United States of Europe" seemed almost by definition likely to serve the cause of a peaceful and prosperous future. Under these circumstances the more challenging research problem for social scientists was to describe, explain, and forecast the course of the integrative process. The result has been increasingly subtle paradigms and some very revealing findings, as other articles in [*International Organization*, Autumn 1970] indicate.

At the same time, we have learned very little about the costs and benefits of integration. Europe is prosperous and peaceful, but we do not really know whether, or to what extent, this can be traced to the European Communities. The march toward federal union has been slowed and perhaps arrested. What has emerged is a relatively stable complex of European and national institutions, and the impact of this partially integrated regional system on the European economy—let alone on politics and diplomacy—is not at all clear. Moreover, peace and prosperity do not seem to have insured domestic tranquility. Partisan political conflict over the distribution of wealth and influence seems to be increasing despite affluence—or perhaps because of it. Should we not consider how the growth of the community feeds into these distributional issues? And what of the impact of integration on the rest of the world? What is good for the communities may not be good for nonmembers. Perhaps internal economic growth is being attained at the expense of developing areas. How does peaceful resolution of regional conflict relate to international politics?

In sum, what I am suggesting is a kind of dual perspective for investigating the consequences of integration: (1) actor incentive analysis (to what extent have the initial goals of the European Communities been attained?) and (2) distributional issues (how are the costs and benefits of integration shared within the community and with the world at large?). There is no elaborate rationale for this approach; it has the merit, however, of first allowing us to evaluate the European Communities on their own terms—that is, with respect to the problems which necessarily occupied Europeans at the close of World War II. We will then broaden the investigation to consider issues which do not seem to have figured directly in the plans of the founders. There is a

way in which the first line of analysis relates to the communities' recent past while the second has to do with their proximate future. Certainly, the who-gets-what questions seem likely to intrude themselves with greater insistence into domestic European politics and also into the role of European states in world affairs. To raise questions about the way in which integration impinges upon these problems may then be to focus on issues which will determine the future of the European Communities.

To ask who wins and who loses as a result of integration is also to suggest that we as students of integration should be sensitive to value questions and willing to confront them directly in our research. Such studies could take the form of rigorous critiques of the value premises of integration theory in the classical tradition of political theory. This kind of work would make us more aware of the implications of our own research and would, as well, enhance our understanding of the range of potential consequences of integration. What I have in mind in this article, however, is not exercises in political theory but simply value-sensitive *empirical* research aimed at determining what difference it makes, in fact, whether or not Europe integrates. This kind of work may well be anchored in normative goals and could provide the basis for making informed judgments on the desirability of integration or on future directions that it should take. Nevertheless, personal value preferences are not preconditions to impact research, nor are they obstacles to empirical analysis; and, of course, impact research cannot in any case resolve value conflicts. Thus, my goal in this article is simply to explore an inviting void in the empirical analysis of regional integration and make some tentative suggestions on how it might be filled.

II. THE INCENTIVES TO INTEGRATE

There are at least two reasons why it is relatively easy to identify with some assurance the original goals—economic, political, and diplomatic—of the European Communities.[7] In the first place,

---

[7]The argument here is admittedly simplified with a great many other contributory factors excluded. For a more systematic consideration which places the communities within the general postwar context in Europe

the enormous common problems of postwar Europe suggested a set of obvious priorities. Economic reconstruction and growth, political stability and republican regimes, and peace within Europe, perhaps with restoration of European diplomatic influence, were clearly the goals to be sought—at least by the moderate, governing mainstream parties. Second, political leadership in the nations that were to become members of the community was in the hands of a relatively small and homogeneous group of primarily Christian-Democratic politicians and technocrats. This resulted in a significant agreement on means and ends and, therefore, a relatively coherent set of reasons for choosing integration as a way of coping with postwar problems.[8] The founders tended to see regional integration as the solution to all problems that were pressing in on the states of Western Europe in the decade after World War II. This was an idea rooted in lessons drawn from the thirties by men who were committed to both the productive and consensual capacities of welfare capitalism and pluralist democracy. The communities were to occupy a kind of middle ground which has been characterized as a "pragmatic synthesis of capitalism and socialism in the form of democratic planning."[9] In fact, despite exceptions (in agriculture and regional development, for instance), the treaties—particularly the Treaty Establishing the European Coal and Steel Community—lean more toward a market economy than toward planning. The basic orientation of the communities is toward changing practices by adjustments in the incentives available to entrepreneurs. Planning is to be used only in combination with such adjustments or when the inadequacy of the market is patently clear; hence the exceptions for agriculture and regional development.

This "pragmatic synthesis" was certainly not common ground at the outset of integration. The European Coal and Steel Community (ECSC) was, for example, established in the face of significant distrust on the part of working class parties and major portions of the trade union movement. The consensus that the founders perceived in the ECSC lay in the future. Their economic goal was not simply to utilize integration as an agent of economic reconstruction but also to exploit a single continental-sized market to increase the rate of economic growth which had sagged badly during the interwar period—particularly in relation to the United States.[10] Affluence, in its turn, was to undermine the appeal of extremist ideologies, thus simultaneously insuring political stability and reducing the constituencies of those parties on the Right and Left with expansionist international programs.

Scholars developed the socioeconomic logic of this political program. It involves a kind of chain reaction from the larger market through changes in business practice to new life-styles and political orientations. One of the earliest economic studies of integration developed this line of reasoning:

> Economic union may be expected to change methods of production in two ways. First, it would provide marginal producers with a powerful stimulus to mend their ways and lower their costs; second, it would provide manufacturing industry at large—at least in the competitive markets—with some inducements and new opportunities for the greater use of mass-production methods.[11]

Standardization and mass production would replace the old pattern of product differentiation which would, in turn, bring "a typical middle class item of consumption within the reach of working-class budgets."[12] The logical conclusion of this argument is that to bring the item within

---

see Leon N. Lindberg and Stuart A. Scheingold, *Europe's Would-Be Polity: Patterns of Change in the European Community* (Englewood Cliffs, N.J.: Prentice-Hall, 1970), chapter I. See also Stanley Hoffmann's analysis, "Obstinate or Obsolete? The Fate of the Nation-State and the Case of Western Europe," reprinted in Joseph S. Nye, Jr. (ed.), *International Regionalism: Readings* (Boston: Little, Brown and Co., 1968), in particular, pp. 185–198.

[8]It is interesting to note that where other parties were in power and/or the effects of the war did not seem so crushing, the integration option was not so appealing —in particular, in the United Kingdom and Scandinavia.

[9]Ernst B. Haas, "Technocracy, Pluralism and the New Europe," in Stephen R. Graubard (ed.), *A New Europe?* (Boston: Houghton Mifflin, 1964), p. 68.

[10]See Angus Maddison, *Economic Growth in the West: Comparative Experience in Europe and North America* (New York: Twentieth Century Fund, 1964), p. 37.

[11]Scitovsky, pp. 31–32.

[12]Ibid., pp. 27ff.

reach is tantamount—with some judicious promotion—to establishing a market for it. This, of course, implies that the working class will readily adopt the values and the life-style of the middle class and presumably their moderate political preferences as well.

One can thus think of the purposes to be served by integration on two rather distinct levels. Most obviously and directly, integration was to be an agent of economic reconstruction and a vehicle for creating among the member states permanent institutional ties. At another level integration was related to a general social theory which saw productivity and affluence as a kind of universal problem solvent. There is considerable dispute about the contribution of integration, if any, to either of these objectives. Given the paucity of data and the divergent speculations about the impact of the communities there is no way in which these differences can be resolved in this article. What can be done is to present the available findings together with some of the questions which have been raised and in this way indicate the most promising possibilities for further research.

Economic growth was perhaps the most generally accepted immediate goal of the founders, at least those of the ECSC and of the EEC. Professional economists, however, differed about the effects of integration on growth: Would it induce growth at all? If so, would growth stem from the economies of scale, specialization, competition, etc?[13] The impressive growth rates of member states, particularly since 1958, have not really stilled the controversy since it has been argued that the spurt in growth rates was under way prior to integration.[14] The implication of this line of thought is that the progress of integration is more a consequence than a cause of economic growth.[15]

In this setting of controversy we must be grateful for Lawrence Krause's efforts to cut to the heart of the matter with actual measurement of the impact of integration on the income levels of the member states. It is beyond the scope of this article to consider his measurement techniques or even his results in detail. Krause concluded that the "income of member countries has been stimulated" by integration.[16] He calculated the increment with precision, determined the portion attributable to increases in efficiency and investment, and supported his findings with reasoned argument. All told, this surely adds up to the most impressive effort to come to grips with the consequences of integration.[17]

Still, it is not clear just what the implications of the Krause study are, since the growth attributable to integration seems to be rather modest. The compound annual rate of growth in gross domestic products varied between 5.1 percent and 7.1 percent for the member countries of the EEC during the period between 1958–1959 and 1964 (see Table 1), but the annual income increments induced by economic integration during the transitional period varied between .18 percent and .22 percent.[18] Integration would thus seem to be responsible for only 2 to 3 percent of the annual increase.[19]

What can we conclude from a comparison of the relatively well-integrated Common Market with that of the European Free Trade Association (EFTA)? According to Krause:

> The median increase for the Common Market was at a compound annual rate of 0.19 percent (Netherlands and France) while the median for EFTA was 0.16 percent (Switzerland and the United Kingdom). The lowest estimate for an EEC country was above the EFTA median.[20]

---

[13]See Balassa, chapters 5–8.

[14]One of the most persistent skeptics has been Alexandre Lamfalussy. See his *The United Kingdom and the Six* (London: Macmillan & Co., 1963).

[15]For a rejoinder see Richard Mayne, "Economic Integration in the New Europe," in Graubard, pp. 174–199.

[16]Krause, p. 73.

[17]Ibid., see particularly pp. 35–45. The book ranges well beyond a consideration of these income effects for the member states. Indeed, the basic concern is, as the title suggests, with the impact on the United States. Incidentally, the above conclusions on income are based on manufactured products. Agriculture is treated separately since it has been subjected to a program which has tended to promote self-sufficiency rather than the most efficient allocation of resources. See chapter 3.

[18]Krause, p. 44.

[19]This rough estimate would presumably have to be adjusted for the exclusion of agricultural products from Krause's calculation of annual income increments attributable to integration, but this adjustment would not seem likely to change the total picture appreciably.

[20]Krause, p. 44.

Table 1
Growth of Gross Domestic Product

Country	Compound Annual Rate of Increase in Percentages		
	1953 to 1958–1959	1958–1959 to 1964	Change in Growth Rates
EEC			
Belgium-Luxembourg	2.7	5.1	2.4
France[a]	4.7	5.6	0.9
Germany	6.9	7.1	0.2
Italy	5.2	6.0	0.8
Netherlands	4.5	5.6	1.1
EFTA			
Austria	6.7	4.8	−1.9
Denmark	2.9	5.8	2.9
Norway	2.9	5.3	2.4
Portugal	4.0	6.7	2.7
Sweden	3.9	5.1	1.2
Switzerland	4.6[b]	5.7	1.1
United Kingdom	2.4	3.8	1.4
UNITED STATES	2.1	4.1	2.0

Source: Krause, p. 37.
Note: This table lists gross domestic product growth for each country in the EEC and EFTA, plus the United States, before and after integration in terms of 1958 prices at factor costs.
  [a]At market prices.
  [b]1954 to 1958–1959.

The differences may be distinct and measurable but do they not amount to a rather small return for the heavier commitments made by the member states to the European community? Krause may have demonstrated generally that integration can serve as an agent of economic growth. His analysis still raises questions about whether the constraints imposed by membership in the EEC can be justified on economic grounds alone.

This theme is explored by J. J. Servan-Schreiber in his provocative study, *The American Challenge*.[21] Servan-Schreiber's thesis is that the only meaningful gauge of European economic performance is the United States, and he argues that European firms have not made the necessary changes in general business practice which are required if the European corporate culture is ever

[21]J. J. Servan-Schreiber, *The American Challenge*, trans. by Ronald Steel (New York: Atheneum, 1968).

to compete technologically and financially with its American counterpart. His is not a study heavy in data, but the information which is presented suggests weaknesses in scale, research expenditure, and profit margins. The direction of change is positive; the scale of European business does show signs of increasing, for example. But either the American firms are moving ahead at a better pace or else the European gain is too small to promise any significant narrowing of the gap in the near future.

Servan-Schreiber's case for using American performance as a standard of European achievements is compellingly simple:

Fifteen years from now it is quite possible that the world's third greatest industrial power, just after the United States and Russia, will not be Europe, but *American industry in Europe*. Already, in the ninth year of the Common

Market, this European market is basically American in organization.[22]

It is not just that America continues to offer an object lesson in technocracy and affluence as it did to the founders of the European Communities. Now, the influx of American investment threatens the independent existence of European industry. Servan-Schreiber's conclusion is that the European Economic Community which he characterizes as a "tariff union" can never be expected to induce the changes which are prerequisites to really dynamic growth. Only a European federal system with its own "industrial policy" can stimulate the necessary commitments to research, flexible management, and large-scale production, Servan-Schreiber argues.

Both the problems and the solutions, in all likelihood, are a good deal more complex than are implied in *The American Challenge*. Take the issue of American investment, for example. Is it really an obstacle to growth and innovation among European firms? Krause suggests that this capital may be inducing just the kind of changes that Servan-Schreiber advocates:

> The implications of the growing opposition to American direct investment could be far-reaching. The immediate reaction of European business has been a movement towards mergers among companies in order to reach a scale of operation closer to that of the American firms with which they compete. . . . Mergers in the past have been mainly among firms of the same nationality or between national firms and the large international firms—usually American based. But recently with the Common Market there have been some faint signs that the transnational mergers that have long been expected are finally beginning.[23]

Indeed, one might wonder whether the influx of American capital is not responsible at least indirectly for a portion of the income increment which Krause attributes to integration. It is true that the total flow has been relatively small, but these investments have been concentrated in the most dynamic "research-intensive" sectors.[24] Were

Servan-Schreiber's federal system to answer the American challenge by reducing or reversing the flow of American capital, the results might be counterproductive—at least in the short run.

But all this is mere speculation. What Servan-Schreiber does is direct our attention to handicaps that *may* be inherent in operating through what can be termed a partial political system. At present we *know* very little, if anything, about the extent to which weaknesses in the community political system have stood in the way of an industrial policy and/or the projected transformation in business practice. This problem takes on added importance since—Servan-Schreiber's plea to the contrary notwithstanding—dramatic changes in the character of the current system are unlikely in the foreseeable future. Here then is a neglected area where further research might pay significant dividends.

A European community was to bring peace as well as prosperity to Europe. Certainly, the relationships between the nations of Western Europe have been peaceful in the two decades since World War II. It is, of course, particularly satisfying that Franco-German relations have been so free of conflict. But again we may well ask whether integration is a cause or primarily a consequence of this relatively tranquil period. And how do the communities relate to the continuing tensions with Eastern Europe? Obviously, these are questions of more than passing importance, yet we are without any answers. Or perhaps it is more accurate to say that a number of answers have been proposed but none of them has been validated. Indeed, those who have commented on the impact of regional integration on questions of peace and war have tended to use quite different styles of analysis and often have raised the issues rather obliquely. While I sense competing hypotheses in the various positions taken, they are rather like arguments passing in the night.

David Mitrany asserts that the EEC is increasingly a "closed" system that pursues exclusivist policies and is likely to generate a parochial brand of regional patriotism.[25] It is, he contends, aggregating economic power and diplomatic influence, and consequently its exclusivist policies tend to increase tensions and conflict in Europe

---

[22]Ibid., p. 3.

[23]Krause, p. 146.

[24]Ibid., pp. 144–45. See also Christopher Layton, *Trans-Atlantic Investment* (The Atlantic Papers) (Boulogne-sur-Seine: Atlantic Institute, 1966).

[25]David Mitrany, "The Prospect of Integration: Federal or Functional?" as reprinted in Nye, pp. 43–74.

and elsewhere. For evidence in support of Mitrany's argument we need look no further than the division in Western Europe between EFTA and the EEC. That the EEC is still composed of six members is not due to a lack of applicants. The failure of the United Kingdom's bid for membership so far is due, at least in part, to a fear of watering down that which has already been achieved, just as Mitrany suggests.[26] Moreover, Krause provides us with quantitative evidence of the trade-diverting effects of commercial competition between the blocs.[27]

While the conflict between EFTA and the EEC is real, there are those who doubt that the resultant tensions are likely to ripen into anything approaching armed struggles. Raymond Aron, for example, considers the differences between the EEC and EFTA as

"a conflict of internal policy more than a dispute between sovereign states. By the fact of being allied for better or worse, the adversaries were deprived of the supreme recourse. . . . None was in a position to employ military force; none could employ the threat of commercial war: such threats were resented by public opinion because the reprisals would not be in accord with the spirit of the fundamental alliance among the adversaries and because no violation of the GATT charter by the Six would have justified it. The foils had to remain buttoned. The fencers were debaters, the winners more skillful and determined.[28]

For Aron, the North Atlantic alliance of sovereign states is the relevant policy arena for "political questions." In his analysis of the blocs the European Communities are discussed as "economic organizations" and hardly enter at all into the subsequent consideration of "intra-bloc conflicts."

Aron's assertion could be taken at face value as a kind of empirical observation: The European Communities have been preoccupied with their economic mission and have thus not been a factor in major foreign policy problems.[29] The recent announcement that the foreign ministers of the six had agreed to work toward a joint foreign policy would then suggest that a change was imminent.[30] The communities' marginal role in matters of war and peace can, however, be seen as inherent in their economic orientation. The root assumption is that there are significant discontinuities between economic and political problems—or between what Stanley Hoffmann refers to as "high" and "low politics."[31] Functional theorists resist such distinctions and see major foreign policy implications in the operations of the European Communities. Haas, for example, has argued that German reunification is inconsistent with a viable European community.[32] Similarly, there is a body of opinion, which by all accounts included President Charles de Gaulle, that believed British membership would in all likelihood entail a radical realignment of relations within the North Atlantic area. According to functional theorists the potential linkages for building a foreign policy inhere in problems generated by the communities as now constituted. Hoffmann, on the other hand, sees little if any likelihood of a common will emerging in matters which fall outside the realm of economic policy and, of course, does not find the notion of intrinsic linkages very convincing.

---

[26]"The more fields of activity it actively enters, e.g., agriculture, the more acquisitive it tends to become; and in the degree to which it is rounded out it also hardens into a segregated entity." Mitrany, in Nye, p. 69. Of course, Mitrany's concern is not with the EFTA/EEC split, per se, which he sees as symptomatic of the federalist approach to integration. The confusion of terminology among students of integration is suggested by this characterization of the community. Servan-Schreiber, of course, stigmatizes the community for its failure to adopt a federalist approach. One way out of this confusion is to distinguish between the neofunctional approach of the European Communities and Mitrany's functional ideas—both separable from federal schemes. For details see Lindberg and Scheingold, chapter I. Chapter 7 of the same study analyzes the problem of British entry.

[27]Krause concludes, somewhat surprisingly, that "the loss inflicted on the EEC by EFTA is almost twice as great as the reverse loss." Krause, p. 72.

[28]Raymond Aron, *Peace and War* (New York: Frederick A. Praeger, 1967), pp. 462–463.

[29]On the basis of a very unsystematic sampling it is reasonable to conclude that the policymakers share his view. See, for example, Dean Acheson, "Europe: Decision or Drift," *Foreign Affairs*, January 1966 (Vol. 44, No. 2), pp. 198–205, or an earlier piece in the same journal: Heinrich von Brentano, "Goals and Means of the Western Alliance," *Foreign Affairs*, April 1961 (Vol. 39, No. 3), pp. 416–429.

[30]*New York Times*, March 7, 1970, p. 3.

[31]Stanley Hoffman, *Gulliver's Troubles, or the Setting of American Foreign Policy* (Atlantic Policy Studies) (New York: McGraw-Hill, 1968), chapter II.

[32]Haas, in Graubard, p. 78.

The matter at issue is, of course, not whether the communities as presently constituted have a foreign policy; clearly they do not. On this all the commentators cited would presumably agree. The problem is rather whether there is any way in which the economic tasks of the communities impinge on the more general issues of diplomacy and security within the North Atlantic area or beyond it. Aron and Hoffmann argue in somewhat different ways that integration has no such effects while Haas and Mitrany imply that it does—albeit, perhaps in a covert or indirect fashion. No matter, for the extent to which the communities relate to "high politics" and whether they are increasing or easing political tensions is in the final analysis an empirical question. Yet it is a question that has not been confronted directly in research on integration. We have theories and commentary but very little in the way of empirical research.

There is, on the other hand, some suggestive data which bears on Mitrany's concern that the EEC is nurturing a parochial brand of patriotism. Attitudinal data indicates increasingly favorable orientations toward the goals and institutions of the European Communities.[33] Donald Puchala . . . sees in French and German attitudes "evidence of mutual identification—i.e., some hint of a 'we feeling'" characteristic of community.[34] Of particular relevance to Mitrany's argument is his finding that Frenchmen tend to see the six current members of the European Communities as those which in the long run "must participate."[35]

Puchala's findings are not conclusive, however, since other data suggests that the shifts in loyalty that would seem to be a precondition to regional chauvinism are not developing. Among elites in the Federal Republic of Germany (West Germany) and France there is a strong ad hoc or expediential element in the support for integration. As Robert Weissberg writes,

> among the elite sampled here there are "internationalists" (or integrationists), "nationalists," and many who may lean one way on one issue and another way on a different issue.[36]

[33] See Lindberg and Scheingold, chapter 2; also Ronald Inglehart in [*International Organization*, Autumn 1970].
[34] Donald Puchala in [*International Organization*, Autumn 1970], p. 744.
[35] Ibid., Table 2, part 3, p. 746.

Moreover, preliminary analysis of a recent study of European youth in France and West Germany does not indicate that those committed to a single European government are more strongly attached to the present Europe of the six than are those young people who favor looser forms of cooperation or integration (see Table 2).[37]

Trying to draw general conclusions on the basis of the rather meager data which is available is hardly an inviting task. Some of the objectives of integration have been realized at least in part. A Franco-German rapprochement certainly seems to have been effected, and West European economic growth has been impressive. But whether all this adds up to peace and prosperity within Western Europe is more difficult to determine, as is the role of integration in whatever developments are taking place. Krause assures us that at least a portion of the economic gains of the postwar period are attributable to integration, but Servan-Schreiber warns that these gains are rather modest and that the EEC as it is now constituted is an obstacle to more dynamic and dependable patterns of growth. Opinion data does not indicate clearly whether or not committed "Europeans" are turning inward, but the European Communities do seem to have engendered conflicts and schisms within Western Europe. In any case, much more work must be done if we are to answer even these relatively straightforward questions.

Oddly enough, it is easier to speak with conviction about the more grandiose aspirations of the integrators: the communities' mission to promote beneficent and stabilizing trends. These were to be the fruits of an affluent continental-sized economic union. It now seems clear, however, that the association of affluence with moderation and stability which initially inspired the European Communities is, at the very least,

[36] Robert Weissberg, "Nationalism, Integration, and French and German Elites," in *International Organization*, Spring 1969 (Vol. 23, No. 2), p. 347. The data considered by Weissberg is that collected by Karl Deutsch, and others. See Karl Deutsch, and others, *France, Germany and the Western Alliance: A Study of Elite Attitudes on European Integration and World Politics* (New York: Charles Scribner's Sons, 1967).
[37] Given the rather small number in the sample and the uneven distribution, the German and French figures have been combined. Consideration of each country individually would not, however, alter the above conclusion.

Table 2

Attitudes of German and French Youth about a United States of Europe

Type of European System[a]	Size of the European Systems[b]					
	Europe of Six	Six and Great Britain	All Western Europe	All Europe Except the Soviet Union	All Europe Including the Soviet Union	Total
No European government, regular cooperation among national governments	6	27	18	18	30	99
European government dealing with the most important questions, national governments handling particular problems	6	13	26	26	29	101
European government, no national government	4	12	4	32	48	100

Source: European Youth Study conducted by Jacques-René Rabier, director of information for the European Economic Community, together with Jack Dennis, Ronald Inglehart, Leon Lindberg, and Stuart Scheingold.

Note: The attitudes polled are on the countries to be included in a United States of Europe according to preference for the type of European system. Undertaken in 1969, the results are expressed in percentage figures and N = 184, with sixteen respondents in the sample failing to respond to one or both (of the following) questions:

[a.] As far as bringing about the unification of Europe is concerned, which of the following three formulae would you prefer?
   A. "There is no government at European level, but the governments of each country meet regularly to try to adopt a common policy."
   B. "There is a European government which deals with the most important questions, but each country retains a government to handle its own particular problems."
   C. "There is a European government which deals with all questions and the member countries no longer have a national government."

[b.] Which countries in your opinion must form part of a United States of Europe. I mean the United States of Europe which has been proposed. Would you choose a statement from this list to tell me how you feel about this?
   Statement A: Europe of the Six
   Statement B: The Six plus Great Britain
   Statement C: All Western Europe
   Statement D: All Europe except Russia
   Statement E: All Europe including Russia

too simplistic a perspective to guide policymakers or to describe adequately current trends. This essentially nonpolitical, no-conflict, technocratic model does not explain the world we see around us in which political conflict coexists with affluence and in which the old problems of redistributing material welfare and influence remain salient. Nowadays, it seems just as reasonable to expect the changes that community was supposed to generate to breed dislocation, discontent, and instability—at least in the short run. What we need then are some orienting concepts and researchable questions which will aid us in discovering how the communities relate to the changing patterns of demands that seem to be emerging in postindustrial societies.

III. THE NEW POLITICS

Let us begin by trying to get some idea of the dimensions and nature of this new pattern of demands. I have already referred to them as distributive, and Haas [in the preceding article] uses the term consummatory. Insofar as these words suggest concern with the way in which material welfare and political influence are shared, they are appropriate but somehow too narrow. The diffuse, eclectic, and value-sensitive spirit of the "new politics" is better captured in the following assertion from the European review, *Agenor:*

New Politics

—critical and continuing education, self management, the right to information, and the problems of our natural and man-made environment
—these themes are more immediately relevant to the quality of the life of the individual citizen than tranditional (sic) political issues
—and they are going to be increasingly the object of citizen and political action throughout Europe.[38]

At the very least, the lesson of the new politics is that affluence is no longer its own justification. Affluence perhaps—but for what, for whom, and at what cost?

To read *Agenor* is to be constantly confronted with the full range of objectives to which the European Communities might aspire. It is not the kind of reading likely to evoke complacency among the supporters of European integrations. *Agenor* differs from other critiques in that its emphasis is less on the failure to aggregate authority than on the inability to relate to the emerging problems of the latter decades of the twentieth century. The journal is, then, rather like the conscience of European community; if its forecasting is accurate, a failure to relate to these issues may imperil the integrative process. As Haas sees it,

> new national stimuli stressing demands for change with a consummatory quality strike Brussels while the national arena continues to be struck with EEC outputs that correspond to the earlier incremental-instrumental style.[39]

Such developments undermine the initial congruence between the European and the national systems. They also suggest that the European system will be increasingly vulnerable either because it is an obstacle to changes being pressed upon the national systems or simply because it slips further outside the political mainstream and thus becomes quite dispensable.

The demands of the new politics, therefore, provide standards for assessing the consequences of integration—standards which are much broader than those implied by the initial incentives to integrate and which at the same time may reveal a great deal about the future success of European integration. Although we once again have a good many theories about the way in which the communities do now or will in the future relate to the new politics, there is not much data. Moreover, even the theories do not really cover the full range of problems to be found in the pages of *Agenor*. The discussion which follows will, therefore, be introductory and illustrative and will focus on those aspects of the new politics which are entangled, albeit marginally, with the work of the European Communities. With respect to the member states let us consider whether the communities are likely to promote, or be responsive to, demands for more egalitarian and participatory systems. Internationally, let us consider briefly the impact of integration within Western Europe upon developing areas.

One student of integration, Amitai Etzioni, argues that regional integration in general and the European Economic Community in particular may well be the agent of a participatory or "active society."[40] Etzioni sees regional systems as one of a number of possible "new action units" for transforming unresponsive societies. The active society is, in his words, "a society in charge of itself rather than unstructured or restructured to suit the logic of instruments and the interplay of forces that they generate."[41] The secret of the "active society" is that it is responsive to the needs of all its members, and this calls for a sustained and concerted effort to induce these members to articulate their needs and to mobilize for their realization. In

---

[38]*Agenor*, October 1969 (No. 12). p. 34.
[39]Ernst B. Haas in [*International Organization*, Autumn 1970], p. 641.

[40]Amitai Etzioni, *The Active Society: A Theory of Societal and Political Processes* (New York: Free Press, 1968). Regional integration is, it should be pointed out, at most tangential to the concerns of this elaborate and imposing tome.
[41]Ibid., p. 6. The precise role of regional communities is that of "a 'middle' tier in an evolving world-community consensus-formation structure." Not all regional schemes are suitable, but integrative projects along the lines of the European Communities have significant potential. They serve "central" rather than "marginal" societal functions; they are not directed at "countervailing" other regional bodies as are the North Atlantic Treaty Organization (NATO) and the Warsaw Pact; and finally they are "welfare" communities rather than defensive trading blocs like the European Free Trade Association. See p. 596.

particular, it requires the authorities to enhance "the political power of collectivities whose social power is rising."[42] Were it true that European integration is responding to these ideals, the new consummatory demands would certainly be met: Indeed, there would be no noncongruence problem. But can we realistically expect the communities as they are now constituted even to move in the consummatory direction?

The available evidence, while once again inconclusive, suggests that the European Communities are not presently structured to promote a more active society. Their technocratic orientation and indirect institutions imply limited participation. It is not simply that these institutions are dependent on elites; it is difficult to imagine a political system of any size that is not dependent on elites. Nor can it be said that the communities have not been instrumental in mobilizing or activating societal groups. The more fundamental problems are that: (1) the institutions are designed to minimize rather than maximize participation; (2) integration has been associated primarily with *established* elites; and (3) such mobilization which has occurred has been confined largely to already influential groups.

All of these tendencies are, it seems to me, closely associated with certain aspects of the integrative process. In the first place technocratic decisions designed to maximize wealth call for expertise, not participation. Andrew Shonfield argues that the technocrat

> is normally called in to deal with the type of problem whose solution cannot be precisely defined in advance, and where the area of administrative discretion is therefore recognized as being very large. In practice such a person combines a large part of the lawmaking function with the executive function. He is the embodiment of the principle which is the opposite of classical separation of powers.[43]

Second, resources for generating consent are relatively limited. The result is a heavy dependence on established governmental elites with efforts to mobilize groups restricted to influential collectivities which are in a position to thwart integrative schemes. Jean Monnet's Action Committee for a United States of Europe is prototypical: It is the most unique mobilizing agent associated with integration, and it draws entirely upon established elites. The committee seldom if ever goes outside the mainstream and prides itself on the collection of notables that it has assembled. Consider also the following rather typical assessment of the European Parliament:

> But the European Parliament is not the mother of parliaments. It makes no policies, passes no legislation, appropriates no money, brings down no governments. Nor does it even represent, as the treaty intended it should. None of the appointive delegations has thus far included a communist, even though the French and Italian communist parties have regularly polled 20 and 25 percent of the total vote.[44]

In sum, these nonparticipatory tendencies may be more than peculiarities of the process that has unfolded in Europe; indeed, they may be among the predictable costs of regional integration. At the very least, if Etzioni's vision of a "middle tier action unit" is to take shape at the regional level, these obstacles to participation will have to be overcome.

Of course, the "active society" is not necessarily an end in itself. Were the community committed to the equal distribution of the benefits of integration and to other goals of the new politics, then participatory values might be less important. But the materialistic orientations of the communities are suspect, and given the nature of integration it seems clear that certain groups will be disadvantaged:

> Not all groups are destined to participate in prosperity. As a matter of fact, the process by

---

[42]Ibid., p. 514.

[43]Andrew Shonfield, *Modern Capitalism: The Changing Balance of Public and Private Power* (New York: Oxford University Press, 1965), p. 408. For a discussion of the participatory implications of technocracy within the European community see Lindberg and Scheingold, pp. 266–269.

[44]J. L. Zaring, *Decision for Europe: The Necessity of Britain's Engagement* (Baltimore, Md.: Johns Hopkins Press, 1969), p. 70. Zaring's discussion extends well beyond the parliament and devotes considerable attention to the problem of representation. For a consideration of the community's rather limited and uneven contribution to mobilization, see Lindberg and Scheingold, pp. 75–80.

which prosperity is being created is squeezing some groups viciously—mostly the self-employed and those at the bottom of the service class. The former group include most notably small farmers, artisans, and shopkeepers, who are destined to be replaced by their large-scale counterparts. The emergent new society does not have a high tolerance for inefficiency.[45]

Even the established ideology of the communities is that of the modified market economy with no real commitment to egalitarian values.

This problem of distribution is raised more concretely by the French left-wing intellectual, André Gorz, in his book *Strategy for Labor: A Radical Proposal.* Gorz believes, contrary to Servan-Schreiber, that the EEC has been successful in promoting the changes in business practices that both authors see as prerequisites to more effective growth. That is to say, he believes that European corporations have been willing and able to take advantage of the opportunities for expansion provided by the Common Market. Gorz, however, denies that corporate initiative can promote balanced economic growth. His argument is for planning and his fear is that the market approach to growth will cause as many problems as it will cure; he predicts a failure to develop depressed regions and a growing disparity between these regions and those which are better endowed. More specifically, he argues that the agricultural policy of the EEC will promote overproduction and irrational population shifts which will depopulate agricultural areas "below the threshold of economic viability."[46] Gorz thus challenges the theory of welfare capitalism on which the communities are based and foresees major dislocations stemming directly from their modified laissez faire, *laissez innover* orientation. This is, of course, a neo-Marxist critique, but its relevance and interest lie not so much in its Marxist implications as in its reintroduction of political conflict—whether among groups, classes, or parties—into the analytic framework. Gorz, in other words, directs our attention to the possibility that affluence, technology, and the acquisitive instinct will not necessarily sublimate political conflict. Moderate

two-party or multiparty systems may yet emerge, but clearly there is ferment, and Gorz directs us toward the impact of regional integration on the politics of the member states. He argues that integration may catalyze a major realignment of political forces—specifically, that community policies will tend to generate three distinctive political coalitions:

1. The Atlantic coalition: This would be the neo-liberal or free trade bloc which he identifies as a declining group, composed of a significant portion of European bankers and West German and Dutch (and ultimately British) big business, with tactical support of American corporate enterprise throughout the Common Market.
2. The nationalist coalition: This would be based on precapitalist and what he refers to as "paleo-capitalist" enterprises (in other words: family business, small shopkeepers, medium and small peasants) and perhaps portions of the labor movement.
3. The European coalition: Included in this grouping would be the European technocracy, the Social-Democrats. and what he refers to as neo-capitalist big business.[47]

One may well have doubts as to whether the communities will soon become such a pivotal factor in domestic politics, but since community policies are so integrally linked to the future of such key groups as the farmers and corporate enterprise, is it unreasonable to assume that integration will have an impact on the patterns of political conflict?

---

[45]Lindberg and Scheingold, p. 273.
[46]André Gorz, *Strategy for Labor: A Radical Proposal* (Boston: Beacon Press, 1967), p. 162.

[47]Ibid., p. 149. These coalitions are not, it should be pointed out, perceived to be the normal and necessary consequence of integration, per se, but rather part of a scenario which stems directly from Gorz's mistrust of the communities' essentially market approach to integration. Thus the coalitions will form in periods of recession, brought on by the overproduction which Gorz does perceive as a necessary consequence of integration. As such recessions become the salient political issue, the above groups would tend to crystallize around distinctive solutions: The Atlantic coalition would choose an Atlantic free-trade response; the Nationalist coalition would opt for dismantling the European Communities; and the European coalition would put their faith in planning, intervention, and stabilization at the supranational level.

If the patterns of party conflict change and new coalitions form while others break up, it stands to reason that the quality of political life will be affected. One could argue, for example, that the divisions that Gorz foresees might promote reactionary politics by splitting the forces of liberal capitalism between Atlantic and European blocs. This is, of course, entirely speculative and would in any case depend on whether or not these divisions tended to congeal into long-term alliances. The fact remains that variations in parliamentary coalitions may well facilitate certain tendencies and undermine others, thus significantly affecting the kind of policy outputs that emerge from the national political systems.

Finally, let us consider a distributional issue relating to the international consequences of regional integration in Europe—the impact of integration on the developing areas. Once again questions can be posed, but data bearing on these questions is not really available. Another echo from the earlier analysis is the significant potential for discontinuity between initial expectation and actual impact. Recall that, to the extent that general international relations were considered, regional integration in Europe was perceived as part of a generally expansive trend in world trading patterns—an expansion from which all would gain, if not necessarily in equal shares. This seems to remain the official position of the European Communities which stresses their trade with developing areas, the special concessions granted to those less developed countries (LDCs) that are linked by agreements of association, etc. But if we do not accept at face value the notion that a general expansion in world trade necessarily represents a net gain for all or that what advances the interest of certain LDCs necessarily advances the interest of all, then we might want to probe more deeply and ask some additional questions.

The basic grounds for concern about the impact of European integration on the economic growth and diplomatic influence of developing nations were discussed some years ago by Ellen Frey-Wouters.

1. Do the association agreements indicate a new willingness on the part of European states to assume part of the burden and responsibility for the welfare of developing nations or is it simply a subtle new version of the old colonial relationship?

2. Do the association agreements benefit the associated states at the expense of the other developing areas, thereby reducing the chances of coordinated development and dividing the developing nations against one another?[48]

As she sees it, the answer to the first question is to be found in whether or not the association agreements promote indigenous industrial development by permitting the developing states to protect their infant industries, restrict the entrée of European corporations, encourage the establishment of processing facilities for raw materials in the developing nations, etc. The crucial facets of the second question are more difficult to specify. Certainly, they would include an investigation of trade- and aid-diverting effects which would permit certain developing states to benefit at the expense of others and might at the same time not really encourage development since protected access would not be likely to stimulate industrial efficiency. It would also be significant to learn whether the association agreements were obstacles to regional plans in Africa or whether, in world trading conferences, the associated states regularly broke with the developing states on EEC-relevant issues.

These are the kinds of problems that must be explored if we are to assess the impact of the European Economic Community on developing nations and, more generally, if we are to begin to evaluate the likelihood of regional integration as an agent of upward transfer in the process of world community consensus building. Even without research we can be reasonably sure from statements made that association agreements are perceived as a threat by nonassociated states in both Africa and Latin America.[49] Similarly, efforts have been made within the General Agreement on Tariffs and Trade (GATT) and the United Nations Conference on Trade and Development (UNCTAD) to unite the developing nations in

[48]Ellen Frey-Wouters, "The Progress of European Integration," *World Politics*, April 1965 (Vol. 17, No. 3), pp. 472–476.

[49]See, for example, Ali A. Mazrui, "The Common Market and Non-Member Countries: African Attitudes to the European Economic Community," in Lawrence B. Krause (ed.), *The Common Market: Progress and Controversy* (Englewood Cliffs, N.J.: Prentice-Hall, 1964), and Sidney Dell, *Trade Blocs and Common Markets* (New York: Alfred A. Knopf, 1963), pp. 186–193.

defense of such principles as the most-favored-nation clause.[50] But while there is some rather impressionistic evidence that the EEC is often perceived as disruptive rather than as an agent of development and welfare, more evidence is obviously necessary if we are to assess the accuracy of that perception.

The foregoing analysis raises a good many questions about the way in which the European Communities relate to the demands and values of the new politics. My own impression is that the communities, at least as they are now constituted, entail a significant sacrifice of participatory and egalitarian values. Etzioni would apparently disagree. Again, what is needed is empirical research directed at determining just how integration feeds into national political processes and impinges upon relations with the third world. Such research would be useful in assessing the future prospects of the European Communities—particularly if it focused on the way in which the costs and benefits of integration are tabulated within nation-states.[51] But above and beyond what this work would reveal about the future, it would add an important dimension to our understanding of regional integration by making us sensitive to both its burdens and its benefits.

IV. ALTERNATIVE RESEARCH STRATEGIES

The simple sum of the arguments presented in this article is that our understanding of what is at stake in integration tends to be confined to the member states as such. I am, of course, not arguing that research on integration has focused exclusively or primarily on national units. On the contrary, the tendency to conceptualize integration in terms of interpenetration of the national and the supranational units has directed attention

to the attitudes and/or behavior of bureaucrats, politicians, trade unionists, etc. But what *cost-benefit analysis* there has been has focused primarily on the national units. Political science research on the aggregation of authority, for example, sheds some light on what, if anything, the member states have to lose in terms of legitimacy and independence of action. Similarly, economists tell us how the material gains are being distributed among nation-states.[52] What I am suggesting is that the calculation of gains and losses be extended in a number of ways. Within the communities let us ask about distribution among groups and social classes and let us also consider the costs of increased consumption and technological advance in terms of the quality of life in an affluent society. In addition, more attention should be devoted to the impact of integration on outsiders: Are regional peace and material satisfaction being purchased at the expense of "third countries" in general and developing areas in particular?

At this juncture, given the paucity of empirical information bearing on these issues, I would propose a rather eclectic approach to research. The initial goal should be to accumulate detailed information on individual policy areas or on discrete problems. Rather than attempting, right at the outset, to answer sweeping questions about the impact of integration per se, let us try to understand the variety of ways in which integrative processes impinge on national policies and world politics. Such pilot projects could, like Haas's study of the European Coal and Steel Community, generate tenable hypotheses based on a solid empirical foundation.

It should be noted in passing that my priorities would tend to exclude, for the present, survey research and aggregate data projects. The survey data currently available offers, at best, only some clues to the kinds of problems which will have to be investigated—whether or not, for example, a parochial regional loyalty is to be one of the costs of integration. New data to serve these purposes directly will have to be collected, and this raises questions of time and money. Aggregate data on income, employment, and regional discontinuities is, no doubt, available, but projects to determine

---

[50]Frey-Wouters, *World Politics*, Vol. 17, No. 3, p. 476.

[51]Without research we can only speculate about the costing process. It seems safe to say, however, that it is a good deal more complex now than it was when Europe lay in ruins at the close of World War II and when there were fundamental doubts about the economic potential and political viability of the European state system. Bargains which have to take into account the kinds of expectations voiced in the new politics will surely be more intricate and perhaps more delicately balanced than those of the 1950's in which peace and affluence were the controlling values.

[52]In addition to Krause, see on this point Bernard Heidelberger, "La ventilation des dépenses communautaire," unpublished manuscript.

whether lifestyles are changing or patterns of mobility and stratification are being altered would require large-scale data processing. Moreover, these projects would be best carried out, it seems to me, by sociologists, political scientists, and economists working together. Such interdisciplinary possibilities are attractive and should be encouraged but will take time to develop and could be rather costly. In any case, it is difficult to get at causal relationships or account for opportunity costs with survey and aggregate data. We would, that is, not be likely to get beyond uncovering correlations between general trends and would not be able to determine what would have happened without integration. For all these reasons—time, expense, causal problems, and opportunity costs—I would suggest deferring more elaborate studies until we were better prepared to make these heavier investments wisely.

Accordingly, in the discussion that follows, the emphasis will be on rather modest research strategies that can be undertaken by individual scholars with limited research support. Moreover, since it would, in my judgment, be premature to hypothesize on the basis of the meager data now available, the discussion will be discursive rather than analytical. That is to say, no attempt will be made to conceptualize and operationalize variables or to develop formal propositions. Instead, I shall, within the context of two possible strategies, offer some concrete suggestions about just which policies and processes warrant investigation. In this inquiry we need no longer be concerned with the distinction between the original objectives of the communities and the aspirations suggested by the new politics since the important thing is that we remain sensitive to the full range of costs and benefits as well as to the manner in which they are distributed.

The first strategy calls for an assessment of the impact of given community policies in areas like agriculture, antitrust, medium-term planning, regional development, association agreements, and general commercial policy. The goal of such studies would not be to determine whether or not policies were emerging but rather to evaluate these policies in terms of the changes they are making in the distribution of, for example, welfare and influence. Are antitrust policies frustrating increases in the scale of production or simulating competition? Are regional development policies effectively attracting private capital to depressed areas or is more extensive planning necessary to avoid increasing disparities between regions? Is medium-term planning effectively coordinating investments or is European economic space, as Gorz charges, increasingly laced together by a "multiplicity of private plans" engineered by transnational mergers, cartels, subsidiary arrangements, etc., which are too broad to be confined by national plans and too powerful to be affected by the community's incipient programs?[53] What kinds of displacements are being wrought by the EEC's agricultural policies in terms of unemployment, migration, and regional disparities? Are some people being put out of work? Who are they and what are their prospects for reemployment? We must also learn more in these terms about the process itself: Which groups have effective access and which are excluded? In dealings with nonmembers on questions of commercial policy, for example, we might want to learn about the relative influence and avenues of access of the developing nations, the United States, the associated territories, the states of Eastern Europe, etc. It is not important which policy area is chosen since we know virtually nothing about channels of influence and/or the impact of any of them. What counts is the making of a thoroughgoing intensive investigation of the manner in which burdens and benefits are distributed so that we will understand more about the nature of the change that can be attributed to European integration.

The second line of inquiry would be to begin with interesting changes and recognized problems which appear as if they might be related to the growth of the European Communities and then attempt to determine whether or not this is, in fact, the case. Thus, one could work backward, so to speak, from worker discontent in the German Ruhr; from the long-standing complaints of certain groups of French farmers; from regional problems in Belgium or Italy; or from the rise of extremist-nationalist parties like the National Partei Deutschland. Picking up on Gorz's thesis about changing coalitions, one could check parliamentary votes and debates bearing on community questions and seek to determine whether or not "normal" political alignments are altered on some or all of them, not necessarily to test Gorz's idea, but simply to spot signs of significant polit-

---

[53]Gorz, pp. 144–153.

ical shifts, assess the role of integration, and evaluate the significance for the quality of political life. The goal would once again be to assess the gains and losses of various political groupings and the impact of these changes on the character of political activities. Investigations of this sort could also be made by individual scholars with relatively limited resources, and they could be sufficiently detailed so as to reduce the difficulty of identifying causal relationships.

All the approaches that I have suggested are basically inductive and atheoretical, and the root assumption of this strategy is that it is just as well to avoid theorizing until more data has been accumulated. It is possible, however, that some of the questions posed in this article will not be answered without theory. How, for example, are we to assess Mitrany's thesis that supranational systems (or federal systems, as he terms the European Communities) tend to heighten conflict and endanger world peace? We can uncover some relevant information and probably gain partial insights with a pragmatic approach which raises certain obvious questions. Do the European Communities regularly resolve internal quarrels at the expense of outsiders? Do outsiders have an opportunity to influence decisions which affect them? Such questions would lead to the study of negotiating sequences with outsiders and to multilateral arenas in which the communities are involved. In this way we might be able to learn whether the communities were exerting a moderating influence on interblock relations or contributing to the creation of an international environment which was more responsive to the needs of developing areas. While useful, the information obtained from this ad hoc agenda would fall short of providing a calculus for assessing the net impact of the European Communities on world security. Obviously, imaginative theorizing would be more likely to permit us to design research projects which would answer the big questions posed by Mitrany, Gorz, Etzioni, and others and should be encouraged along with the kind of intensive field research which I am inclined to believe constitutes the most sensible first step.

V. CONCLUSIONS

Regional integration in Europe is a complex process linking nations together through mutual involvement in collective decisionmaking mecha-

nisms and institutions. It is potentially of great significance to both domestic and international politics. In professional terms it thus defies or straddles the standard divisions of the field of political science, in particular, those of comparative politics and international relations. It presumably has implications for both. The fact remains that most members of the profession probably perceive it primarily as a significant subfield within international organization. One of the consequences of this relative isolation is an intensive and highly rewarding pattern of collegial relationships which . . . is beginning to yield the kinds of cumulative research findings which seem likely to result in a real understanding of the nature and the many possible permutations of the process of regional integration. On the other hand, it is difficult to engage the attention and energies of students of comparative politics and international relations whose knowledge of domestic politics and the international system might add a great deal to our understanding of the integrative phenomenon. In other words, the consequence of isolation may be the sacrifice of breadth for depth.

One way to break out of this circle is to develop analytical techniques which by their sophistication and analytic power command the attention of researchers in other areas like organization theory and political behavior. Clearly, this process has already begun, but one of the purposes of this article is to suggest that, in addition, attention to the consequences of integration will make integration more meaningful to other political scientists.[54] These consequences are, after all, the inputs into "their systems" and the obvious point where our interests converge. As Joseph Nye . . . indicates, as we move away from the simpler neofunctionalist model, it becomes increasingly clear that whether feedback is positive or negative depends more on the state of the national systems than on the character of regional outputs per se.[55] Haas alludes to the same point in stressing the importance of noncongruence models whereby "we

---

[54]That portion of Leon Lindberg's article in [*International Organization*, Autumn 1970] which is concerned with outputs and feedback opens the same kinds of opportunities.

[55]Joseph S. Nye in [*International Organization*, Autumn 1970].

sensitize ourselves to a two-way flow of inputs and outputs. . . ."[56]

I have done little more than scratch the surface with my proposals. If, however, these and other leads are followed, if a systematic set of propositions is formulated, and if data collection and testing begin, will we not necessarily be dealing with problems which will be relevant to comparative politics and international relations? In this way we can increase the chances of enlisting the expertise and understanding which are vital to grasping the domestic and international implications of the process of regional integration. To date, we have very little concrete evidence on which to stake a claim to such general relevance.

In closing let me simply underscore the gains that can be expected from a full consideration of the consequences of integration. These gains include: (1) challenging research opportunities; (2) the possibility of engaging more political scientists in our inquiry; and (3) through feedback analysis, a better understanding of the determinants of the success of regional integration. I would not, however, rest my case on any or all of these grounds. The more fundamental justification for this kind of research is that it turns our attention to the product of politics and makes us sensitive to the values by which this product must be judged. More specifically, in the case of the European Communities we are led to ask what difference it makes whether Europe integrates. And in answering that question we cease taking for granted either the goodness of integration or the desirability of the communities' initial goals.

Discussion and Questions

1. ➤ How would you assess the desirability of the European Communities' original goals? ➤ Can they indeed be classified as goals, or should they rather be considered as conditions that had to be satisfied before integration could proceed further? ➤ How does Scheingold suggest separating causes from results of integration?

2. ➤ What issues that became important later on did not figure in the plans of the founders of the communities? Why not? ➤ Were the issues considered at the outset not thought through sufficiently? ➤ Were the unconsidered issues ignored by oversight or to avoid difficulties? ➤ Why have so few studies been made of the domestic effects of integration?

3. ➤ How does what Scheingold calls "the changing patterns of demands that seem to be emerging in postindustrial societies" bear on the

integration process? on the goals of integration? ➤ Does Scheingold think that more participatory and egalitarian systems are likely to be furthered by the communities in the future as demand patterns change?

4. Strongly nationalist societies may participate in integration schemes within certain limits. (See Stanley Hoffmann, "Obstinate or Obsolete? The Fate of the Nation-State and the Case of Western Europe," *Daedalus*, vol. 95, no 3 [Summer 1966] pp. 862–915). Hoffmann argues against the position that economic integration tends to trigger political integration. In this sense, his argument lends itself to the generalization that the form and density of integration varies with the characteristics of each subsystem, the upper limit of integration being set by strength of nationalistic feeling within the principal societies in the region.

5. The selections by Haas and Scheingold illustrate the methods and ideas of American social science. Concepts are clearly delimited,

---

[56]Haas in [*International Organization*, Autumn 1970], p. 641.

variables are specified, and inquiry is organized around a series of hypotheses that are testable by data-gathering and processing. This approach can be contrasted with an essay by Jan J. Schokking and Nels Anderson, "Observations on the European Integration Process" (*Journal of Conflict Resolution*, vol. 4 no. 4 [December 1960], pp. 385–410). This essay represents a less rigorous series of speculations about the integration process as it has been unfolding in Europe, and gives an example of a mode of analysis that continues to be influential in Europe. Special attention to the experience with European integration seems appropriate because it represents the most ambitious and successful experiment in regional integration. Unlike Etzioni, Anderson and Schokking do not assess integration in relation to any ultimate goal of political community at the global level. Their view of integration is broad—encompassing all aspects and phases of "merging interests" and "systematic cooperation between governments on a permanent basis."

6. Ernst Haas rejects what he calls "the teleological aspects" of the assertion by Schokking and Anderson that "The effort toward European integration reflects this need of industrial urbanism for wider organization." Haas writes that,

> In terms of a social process based on rational human perceptions and motives, no mere concept "calls for" or "needs" anything: a discrete set of group motives, converging with motives of cognate groups from across the border, results in a certain pattern of policy; the aims and the policy reflect demands born from the environment, and the later policies may well change the environment in a wholly unintended fashion. Only in this sense, then, does industrial urbanism favor integration. [Haas, International Integration: The European and the Universal Process," *International Organization*, vol. 15, no. 3 (Summer 1961), pp. 366–392, at p. 375.]

➤ Is this line of criticism by Haas persuasive? (See also E.B. Haas, "Technocracy, Pluralism, and the New Europe," in Stephan R. Graubard, Ed., *A New Europe?* [Houghton Mifflin, Boston, 1964],

pp. 62–88; and in Nye, Ed., *International Regionalism* [Little Brown, Boston, 1968], pp. 149–176.)

7. ➤ Does the evidence bear out the conclusion of Schokking and Anderson that volitional, as distinct from coercive, integration is a "slow process"? ➤ Might it not appear, in retrospect, that the world (or regions of it) had been experiencing various "preparations" that might support rapid, abrupt steps toward integration at the present time? After all, the process of decolonization took place rapidly.

8. One important distinction made by Schokking and Anderson is between "integration at the government level" and "integration at the organization level." If one is working out the implications of interdependence, then the *form* by which integration occurs may be less significant than the *extent* and *depth* of integration. Also, the resistance to integration associated with attachment to national sovereignty may be lessened if integration, especially during its early stages, is inter-organizational rather than intergovernmental. The emergence of superunits, and the consequent formation of the symbols of supranationality, might also be postponed, especially if the region is one where strong nationalist traditions combine with a persuasive functional case for integration.

9. ➤ To what extent has the European experience with integration been influenced by the subsystemic factors? Among such factors are the following: common experience of costly intra-European warfare, defensive umbrella of American military power, common perception of the Soviet Union as an external "enemy" capable of dominating any single European country, relatively homogeneous economies and political systems, common cultural heritage. Note the interaction of incentives for security and economic cooperation in the European context. NATO has produced considerable cooperation on the vital matter of European security without significant integration. Indeed, efforts at integrating national military capabilities in the so-called Multilateral Force (MLF) proved totally unsuccessful. ➤ Why?

7

Theory and Practice of Regional Integration: The Case of Comecon

ANDRZEJ KORBONSKI

I. INTRODUCTION

It is generally recognized that the last decade or so witnessed a proliferation of studies dealing with different aspects of regional integration. While most of them discussed the origin and history of various international organizations, some, especially those of a more recent vintage, ventured into the thicket of theory building in an effort to engage eventually in some kind of comparative analysis.

Up to this time the focus of research on integration was clearly centered on Western Europe which offered not only a wealth of relevant data but also afforded the opportunity to test various hypotheses developed in the course of multifaceted attempts at theorizing. It was inevitable that sooner or later the deeply rooted yearning for comparative analysis would lead to research on regional integration in other parts of the world, mainly in Africa and Latin America. To be sure, this horizontal expansion was dictated by more considerations than merely simple desire for comparative study. The widespread dissatisfaction with the ethnocentric, Western Europe-oriented research which made its appearance earlier in the field of comparative politics was bound to spill over into other fields, including that of international relations. The same applied to the process of "model building" which utilized almost exclusively the Western European experience. Finally, the growing amount of available data forthcoming from other areas permitted the initiation of research in non-European integration processes similar to that done previously for Western Europe.

One notable omission in this impressive array of integration studies was Eastern Europe, despite the fact that, formally at least, integration efforts there began twenty years ago and thus largely antedated similar attempts elsewhere. Whether one looks at the recently published anthologies of regional integration studies, at the volumes of periodicals devoted wholly or partially to research in that particular area, or at individual articles claiming to present a comprehensive picture of regional integration throughout the world, one is struck not only by the relative dearth of studies analyzing the Eastern European situation but also by the almost total lack of reference to that situation in works concerned with constructing a universalistic paradigm of integration processes. When and where such references do crop up they are usually either somewhat superficial or are treated as deviations from the norm due to the peculiar character of Communist politics.

There are, indeed, a number of reasons for treating Eastern Europe as a special case. First of all, it is probably correct to say that until very recently the so-called Communist studies could be described as parochial and traditional. Protected by the great wall of "special expertise" from the modernizing tendencies in various fields of social sciences and basking in the light of "expert knowledge" which implied that ordinary research methodology did not apply to their areas of interest, Sovietologists have been rapidly falling behind those of their counterparts in other fields of political science who did not claim such privileges. As a result, Communist studies, including those concerned with Eastern Europe, have over the years become cliché-ridden, stagnant, and plainly dull.

Within the subfield of Communist international relations the study of integration—political, economic, and military—was clearly the villain of the piece. It is true that various books and monographs devoted chapters to the problem of integration in Eastern Europe, but these were chiefly characterized by their concentration on historical analysis, on legal and institutional arrangements, and on policy "outputs," with little or no attention being paid to "inputs" and to decisionmaking processes. Above all, there was a total absence of even the slightest attempt at postulating working hypotheses which might lead to broader generalizations.

This absence of a theoretical bent could be excused on several grounds. To begin with, for a long time the concept of integration in Eastern Europe was firmly rooted in the "model" of the Stalinist monolith so ably presented by Zbigniew Brzezinski who applied to it the notion of "for-

mal" and "informal" linkages.[1] Just as it took a number of years before political scientists began to question the validity of the totalitarian syndrome for the study of Communist internal politics, a similarly long interval elapsed before the idea of the monolith was replaced (with considerable hesitation) by the concept of the "Socialist commonwealth." It should be added, however, that conceptually the latter was never as fully elaborated as its predecessor, and the 1968 events in Eastern Europe, which threw a monkey wrench into a number of assumptions and near-dogmas, probably delayed indefinitely the task of creating a new model of interstate relations in Eastern Europe.

The transformation of the Moscow-controlled colonial empire into a much looser configuration necessitated the revival of the "formal" linkages which hitherto have been overshadowed by the "informal" ones. This meant that the Council of Mutual Economic Assistance (Comecon) had to be taken out of mothballs and elevated to the status of one of the major props supporting the new edifice. This rather sudden resurrection of the previously dormant Stalinist creation remained largely unnoticed until the early 1960's when its existence was finally rediscovered by both Western and Eastern social scientists. Paradoxically, it was precisely at that time that Comecon, having reached its apogee, entered a stage of crisis from which it has still not fully recovered.

The rediscovery of Comecon was followed shortly thereafter in both the East and the West by a number of monographs and studies. As was to be expected, Communist and particularly Soviet writers tended as a rule to glorify the achievements of the organization, pointing to various statistical indicators that showed the growth of intrabloc trade, industrial cooperation, and the like.[2] The Western studies were essentially historical monographs attempting for the first time

---

[1] Zbigniew Brzezinski, *The Soviet Bloc: Unity and Conflict* (Rev. and enl. ed; Cambridge, Mass.: Harvard University Press, 1967), pp. 107–124.

[2] A. D. Stupov (ed.), *Ekonomicheskoe sotrudnichestvo i vzaiimopomoshch sotsialisticheskikh stran* (Moscow: Izdatelstvo Akademii nauk SSSR, 1962); N. Faddeev, *Sovet ekonomicheskoi vzaiimopomoshchi* (Moscow: Ekonomika, 1964); L. Ciamaga, *Od wspolpracy do integracji: Zarys organizacji i dzialalnosci RWPG w*

to get a clear picture of what had been happening in the realm of East European economic integration.[3] As such they performed the indispensable task of accumulating basic factual economic data which filled a number of empty boxes then in existence. Once the boxes were filled they became transformed into an assemblage of building blocks ready to be used by someone either to construct some kind of a theoretical edifice or at least to come up with a series of hypotheses which might be empirically tested. It should be kept in mind, however, that the boxes and the blocks were of economic hue only. While they enlarged our horizon significantly, they still fell far short of the kind of data available in other regions.

Not that useful studies were totally absent. By and large, however, they were still confined mostly to the collection of facts—thus extending simply in time the work initiated in the early 1960's. As additional data became available, it was possible to probe more deeply into such problems as trade patterns, trade composition, price discrimination, balance-of-payments difficulties, and so on.[4] Despite these refinements the research was still predominantly descriptive. Relatively little effort was devoted to analyzing various processes connected with integration in the area and where such

analysis made its infrequent appearance it was confined to a discussion of narrow, discrete problems such as currency convertibility or industrial specialization. All of these were analyzed in a vacuum created by the absence of even a rudimentary theoretical framework.

There was still another reason for the lack of progress in advancing the state of knowledge in this particular area. It is one which, interestingly enough, has up until now delayed such progress but is likely in the near future to advance it significantly. It appears that in the most recent period the emphasis in Communist studies began to shift in a twofold fashion: first, from the international to the domestic arena; and second, within the domestic sphere, from concentration on the "total" domestic system to an analysis of its component parts in both the static and the dynamic contexts. The first approach, as pointed out earlier, was due to the need to elaborate further the new concept of interstate relations in the bloc by starting, so to speak, from the bottom up. The second came about through the attempts to replace the totalitarian syndrome with other concepts.[5]

A similar change seems to have been occurring in the field of East European economics. On the one hand, after years of looking at the "total" process of economic development in the area, the economists began to pay greater attention to microeconomic problems. At roughly the same time the appearance of economic reforms in a number of East European countries forced the Western (and Eastern) economists to concentrate less on total performance of the entire system and more on its components and processes such as the behavior of enterprises, managerial and bureaucratic decisionmaking, interplay of economic groups, etc.[6]

Thus what we have been witnessing in the most recent period was a sort of convergence between political scientists and economists in the field of

---

latach 1949–1964 (Warsaw: Ksiazka i wiedza, 1965); A. Bodnar, *Rozwoj gospodarczy krajow RWPG i problemy miedzynarodowego podzialu pracy* (Warsaw: Panstwowe wydawnictwo ekonomiczne, 1966); J. Novozamsky, *Vyrovnavani ekonomicke urovne zemi RVHP* (Prague: Nakladatelstvi politicke literatury, 1964); Bohuslov Maly, *Mezinarodni ekonomicke vztahy ve spolecenstvi RVHP* (Prague: Svoboda, 1968).

[3]Andrzej Korbonski, "Comecon," *International Conciliation*, September 1964 (No. 549); I. Agoston, *Le marché commun communiste: Principes et pratique du COMECON* (2nd ed; Geneva: Droz, 1965); Heinz Köhler, *Economic Integration in the Soviet Bloc* (New York: Frederick A. Praeger, 1965); Michael Kaser, *Comecon: Integration Problems of the Planned Economies* (2nd ed; London: Oxford University Press [under the auspices of the Royal Institute of International Affairs], 1967); Michael Kaser (ed.), *Economic Development for Eastern Europe: Proceedings of a Conference Held by the International Economics Association* (London: Macmillan & Co., 1968), pp. 125–159; P. J. D. Wiles, *Communist International Economics* (Oxford: Blackwell, 1968), pp. 306–342.

[4]For a good example see Alan A. Brown and Egan Neuberger (ed.), *International Trade and Central Planning: An Analysis of Economic Interactions* (Berkeley: University of California Press, 1968).

[5]A. G. Meyer, "USSR Incorporated," *Slavic Review*, October 1961 (Vol. 20, No. 3), pp. 369–376, and "The Comparative Study of Communist Political Systems," *Slavic Review*, March 1967 (Vol. 21, No. 1), pp. 3–12; H. G. Skilling, "Interest Groups and Communist Politics," *World Politics*, April 1966 (Vol. 18, No. 3), pp. 435–451.

[6]A recent example is Gregory Grossman (ed.), *Money and Plan: Financial Aspects of East European Economic Reforms* (Berkeley: University of California Press, 1968).

East European studies and a move from "high" to "low" in politics and economics. Such an important step is sooner or later bound to make its impression on the study of East European integration, for it could provide the missing link without which it would be virtually impossible not only to utilize integration paradigms constructed earlier but also to formulate hypotheses that could be tested. Much remains to be done and many empty or half-empty boxes have yet to be filled, but there is little doubt that a threshold has been reached.

Thus for the first time since the beginning of integration efforts in Eastern Europe there are enough building blocks for us to erect if not a model then at least a paradigm which would explain and possibly even forecast integration processes in the area. In addition to statistical data and a considerable amount of macroeconomic information we are beginning to accumulate an impressive reservoir of micropolitical and economic data. At long last a kind of parity with other parts of the world is being reached.

II. THE CONCEPT OF INTEGRATION: THE CASE OF EASTERN EUROPE

The confusion surrounding the concept of integration has been pointed out by a number of writers, including those in [*International Organization*, Autumn 1970].[7] Most of the generally accepted definitions run in terms of a process of bringing or combining parts into a whole, with the final product or dependent variable being gradually less and less rigidly determined. The three conventional pretheories of, or approaches to, integration—the federalist, the communications, and the neofunctionalist—have been rather thoroughly ventilated, amended, reformulated, and adjusted in the span of the last fifteen years or so. A number of models, paradigms, and syndromes have been constructed with varying degrees of explanatory and predictive success, always with an eye on their universal applicability to all systems.

As far as Eastern Europe is concerned, integration can be looked upon in a variety of ways. Since, as suggested by Philippe Schmitter, "the

integration of formally independent political entities engages—in the contemporary world—basically the same variables and processes,"[8] the integrative processes in Eastern Europe should lend themselves to the kind of analysis practiced with regard to other regions. However, before such a task can be attempted one is compelled either to choose one of the available definitions of integration or to develop a new one in order to achieve the three major objectives: first, to be able to test the actual progress of integration with respect to the "ideal" final model; second, to be able to forecast the future of integration in the area; and third, to attempt some comparison with integration processes elsewhere in the world.

At the risk of proliferating the number of definitions, an adaptation of Morton Kaplan's definition of integration is suggested here as the most suitable and convenient for the East European context. Thus integration is defined as "a process by which separate systems develop a common framework which allows for the common pursuit of some goals and common implementation of some policies."[9]

Since "the real test of a definition is its utility for research and theorizing,"[10] it appears that there are several advantages associated with this particular definition. To begin with, it permits us to approach integration from a variety of viewpoints: political, economic, military, and ideological without creating a presumption favoring any one of them. It is also a "parsimonious" definition in the sense that it does not require the presence of such ambiguous concepts or conditions as "common behavioral norms," "sense of community," "mutual obligations," "collective capacity," or "authoritative allocation of values," all of which are subject to controversy and are difficult if not impossible to operationalize. This definition also seems "neutral" in the geographic and systemic sense, enabling us to compare integration processes in various regional subsystems regardless of location and regardless of respective levels of political and economic development. Finally, by

---

[7]E.g., Fred N. Hayward.

[8]Philippe C. Schmitter in [*International Organization*, Autumn 1970], p. 837.

[9]Morton A. Kaplan, *System and Process in International Politics* (New York: John Wiley & Sons, 1957), p. 98.

[10]Fred M. Hayward, draft revision of the paper prepared for the Conference on Regional Integration.

being "low-key" it permits us to study integration processes in the absence of significant data which otherwise might reduce or even eliminate the chances of conducting meaningful research. Hence this definition appears particularly suitable for the study of integration in Eastern Europe.

The focus of this article is the economic integration in Communist Europe. Restricting the discussion to the economic sphere was to some extent motivated by the suggestion advanced by Joseph Nye who felt that the disaggregation of the concept of integration would avoid a number of pitfalls associated with many of the usages currently in vogue.[11] The point is well taken even though it carries some pitfalls of its own.

It is clear that the distinction between "economic" and "political" or between "economic" and "ideological" is nebulous in all systems and especially so in the Communist nations. The separation of economic from political integration in this case is therefore highly artificial and hence unsatisfactory. There are, however, at least two good reasons for limiting the discussion to the economic arena. First of all, there is the problem of data. While economic statistics are now not only relatively plentiful but also, by and large, reliable, the same does not hold true for the political sphere. Furthermore, it is much easier to gather information with respect to national economic policies or strategies of development than with regard to political decisionmaking on a national or bloc-wide basis. The perils of kremlinology are too well known to be discussed here. Finally, economic integration in Eastern Europe today can be studied more or less "rationally" with reference to the "objective" economic laws or theories whereas political integration in the area cannot be quite divorced from either the leading personalities or ideology, or both.

In a similar fashion political integration cannot be fully separated from military integration. Is the Warsaw Treaty Organization (WTO) mainly a political or a security community? Applying our definition to the military sector once again confirms the suitability of that definition for the study of various types of integration in Eastern Europe —viz., as a separate defense system developing a common framework (the Warsaw Treaty) for the common pursuit of at least one goal (defense against the West) and common implementation of some policies (training, weapons standardization, unified command structure). The fact that, as suggested elsewhere, the WTO cannot easily be conceived as either a political or a defense community, its greatest value being most likely a symbolic one, does not detract from the definition.[12]

Thus economic integration in Eastern Europe has been for all practical purposes a multidimensional process in which economics plays a major role but in which political, military, and ideological considerations intervene with varying intensity at various stages.

Here again the selected definition offers some advantages. The conventional definitions of economic integration as applied to Eastern Europe are clearly unsatisfactory. As pointed out by Nye, the textbook definition commonly in use has little relevance to planned economies.[13] According to J. M. Montias,

> few subjects of interest to economists are as soft, or "mushy," as the economics of East European integration; there is no recognized methodology for analyzing problems in this field; the problems themselves have not been rigorously formulated or put down in precise language.[14]

In order to get out of the definitional impasse and for the purpose of providing some standard for comparison with various integration systems, Nye postulated two subtypes of economic integration: trade integration measured by the proportion of intraregional exports to total exports of the region; and services integration measured by the share of the expenditure on jointly administered services in gross national product of the region.[15] Regarding the latter indicator, its useful-

---

[11]Joseph S. Nye, "Comparative Regional Integration: Concept and Measurement," *International Organization*, Autumn 1968 (Vol. 22, No. 4), p. 858.

[12]Andrzej Korbonski, "The Warsaw Pact," *International Conciliation*, May 1969 (No. 573), pp. 67–73.
[13]Nye, *International Organization*, Vol. 22, No. 4, p. 861.
[14]J. M. Montias, "Obstacles to the Economic Integration of Eastern Europe," *Studies in Comparative Communism*, July–October 1969 (Vol. 2, Nos. 3–4), p. 38.
[15]Nye, *International Organization*, Vol. 22, No. 4, p. 861.

ness for Eastern Europe is practically nil because of nonavailability of data. The former measure, though easily derived, can be highly misleading and can actually distort the real extent of integration.

If it could be assumed that the relative increase in the volume of Comecon trade was the outcome of the recommendations made by some common institutions, then that particular index could be considered as a more or less correct measure of economic integration in the region. It appears, however, that this was not quite the case. Montias has shown, for example, that the fluctuations in the volume of intra-Comecon trade hinged primarily on the changes in the rates of growth and the economic policies of member countries rather than on their mutually concerted actions.[16] It is also true that the strategic embargo imposed by the West at the outset of the Cold War was greatly responsible for the increase in intra-Comecon trade. The growing differentiation of the economic systems within Comecon clearly played a role as well. Consequently, the trade indicator as a true measure of economic integration must be considered as less than perfect, especially when treated in isolation.

In light of this, economic integration in Eastern Europe will be defined as a process by which separate economic systems have been developing a common framework—the Council of Mutual Economic Assistance—for the common pursuit of some economic goals (industrialization and a high rate of economic growth) and for the common implementation of some economic policies (coordination of national plans, specialization in production, and maximization of regional trade). Obviously, other goals and policies could be considered here but the history of Comecon seems to indicate that these were agreed upon if not by all then at least by the majority of the member states.[17]

What follows is an examination of various problems connected with the progress of economic integration in Eastern Europe since 1964. The choice of this year is not accidental. It coincides with the ouster of Premier Nikita Khrushchev whose fortunes seemed to be closely tied with

those of Comecon. Khrushchev was, in a sense, an evil genius in the affairs of the organization, for it was he who in fact put Comecon on the map in the mid-1950's and it was also he who contributed largely to its decline in the early 1960's. The analysis that follows will concentrate on the reasons for that decline.

III. THE COMECON EXPERIENCE: ECONOMIC FACTORS

One possible way of analyzing the progress of economic integration in Eastern Europe would be to look at Comecon's performance in the implementation of the three major policies mentioned above: coordination of planning, production specialization, and intraregional trade.[18] It is suggested that this approach appears much more promising than the study of the volume of transactions, however defined, or the analysis of the legal-institutional development of the organization. Both of these were undoubtedly important and both had a bearing on the progress of integration. Nevertheless, it is felt that the three major functions spelled out above represented the heart of Comecon's activities and thus provided the major basis for the economic integration of the area.

Coordination of Planning

Coordination of national plans, especially in the field of industry, began in the mid-1950's. The actual coordination was attempted by a number of standing commissions for every major branch of economic activity. In the initial period the commissions examined the plans for the years 1958–1960 and 1961–1965 and made recommendations with regard to the allocation of outputs of selected commodities among the member countries. Currently, national plans for the period 1966–1970 and long-range (perspective) plans up to 1980 are being discussed by the commissions.

---

[16]J. M. Montias, "Problems of Integration," *World Politics*, July 1966 (Vol. 18, No. 4), p. 725.

[17]Cf. United Nations Document ST/CID/7.

[18]The section that follows is a revised version of a paper, "Recent Developments in the Comecon," presented at a meeting of the University of California Project on Comparative Study of Communist Societies, Berkeley, April 21, 1966.

The coordination procedure, initiated in 1954 and continued without major changes for the last fifteen years, has been widely criticized by a number of member states. The major drawback of the whole process of coordination was the fact that the national plans have been examined post facto, i.e., after their approval by the party and government authorities in individual countries. This has meant that for all practical purposes it was next to impossible to make any adjustments in the plans without disrupting the whole precariously balanced economic edifice throughout the area. One remedy might be to compare draft plans rather than the final versions, but so far this suggestion has not made much headway.

As a result the coordination of plans existed mostly on paper and consisted basically of minor adjustments in nonessential sectors where the pressure of domestic requirements left room for some surpluses. For all practical purposes Comecon members continued preparing their annual and five-year plans very much as if Comecon did not exist, save for areas subject to specialization agreements endorsed by the organization. It was this lack of cooperation which apparently prompted Khrushchev in 1962 to come out with his proposal for a Comecon planning body with supranational powers to enforce coordination of plans and outputs.

Judging by the available evidence, Khrushchev's insistence on closer integration had, if anything, the opposite effect from that originally intended. If East European sources are to be believed, during the past several years coordination of plans has been conducted almost entirely along bilateral lines, even though lip service has been paid to the needs for, and advantages of, multilateral collaboration. The move to bilateral coordination which followed the shelving of Khrushchev's proposal received the official imprimatur of Comecon in 1963 and has not been challenged by Khrushchev's successors. Indeed the silence of both Leonid Brezhnev and Alexei Kosygin on the entire subject of Comecon until recently might be interpreted as still another sign of the lack of interest in the organization.

Up to now coordination of plans was conducted by bilateral commissions of economic cooperation set up by Comecon members and Yugoslavia to provide an instrument of mutual collaboration between themselves.[19] These commissions, which appear to have met fairly frequently, were entrusted primarily with comparison of individual plans covering both outputs and foreign trade. The mutually agreed-upon plans were then reported to the standing branch commissions which could make further recommendations for the purpose of achieving some degree of optimization of plans within the organization as a whole. What was involved here was a kind of successive approximation which, hopefully, might result in a mutually advantageous quasi-Comecon plan.

While the abandonment of multilateral coordination in 1962–1963 can be traced primarily to the refusal of the Comecon members to subject their own interests to the decisions of a supranational body, other factors contributed to the lack of progress in this area. One of them is that since 1964 various Comecon countries have been either undertaking or contemplating more or less comprehensive reforms of their economic systems. It is clear that the main focus of the reforms is to reduce the impact of central planning and of all its ramifications in favor of strengthening the market mechanism.

These reforms would clearly have a far-reaching effect on the future of Comecon. The availability of rational cost and price data would permit member states to engage in proper economic calculations. This, in turn, would make it possible for the various countries to improve the efficiency of their foreign trade, utilizing the principle of comparative cost. In this fashion some more rational, areawide distribution of resources could theoretically be achieved.

At the end of the sixties all of this was still a long way off. The fact that various Comecon countries found themselves at different stages in their reformmaking meant that it was virtually impossible for them to engage in a meaningful cooperation. As long as any two countries maintained a highly centralized planning system, the least they could do was exercise some degree of control over the physical volume of output and, though considerably less so, over the volume of trade. Today and in the near future this may no

---

[19]For a list of these commissions see Kaser, pp. 257–261.

longer be true. With the central planning machinery either scrapped or severely restricted, it would be difficult for the respective governments to force individual producers to deliver the quantities of exports agreed upon beforehand or to impose upon the industry a certain product-mix which the planners considered preferable when bilateral coordination was first initiated. It must be kept in mind that until now not only multilateral but also bilateral cooperation has been conducted on an ad hoc basis. The yardstick of comparative advantage was taken into account only in the most obvious cases where it was hardly necessary to go through a process of complex calculation.[20] Otherwise there was a tendency to stick to the product-mix established in the past, often a long time ago, and any adjustments resulting from bilateral negotiations were of a marginal character.

The picture drawn so far is, however, incomplete. For the sake of focusing more sharply on the question of integrated planning in its narrowest sense, two rather interesting and important elements were left out: (1) specialization and (2) joint production and investment.

Product Specialization

Specialization in production, decreed some ten years ago, was eventually embodied in an agreement entitled "Principles of International Socialist Division of Labor."[21] The rationale here was essentially the same as in the case of coordination of plans—namely, to obtain a better allocation of resources by way of avoiding duplication of productive capacities; to expand the volume of output and thus gain benefits of internal and external economies; to increase intra-Comecon trade and to raise the economic level of the less developed member states. In this respect specialization agreements were likely to achieve much more than output coordination via the plan. The national plans were normally considered taboo and could not

easily be tampered with. On the microeconomic level, however, there was usually some room left for maneuver, i.e., specialization. Thus some degree of international division of labor was agreed upon by at least the majority of the member states.

According to the opponents of rigid specialization, the decision to allocate outputs of individual commodities among member countries was based on purely static assumptions.[22] The fact that Czechoslovakia or the German Democratic Republic (East Germany) enjoyed comparative advantage in, say, the engineering industry, was to some extent a historical accident. There was no sound economic reason why other Comecon countries should not produce similar products just as, or even more, cheaply, given a chance to develop similar industrial capacity. The less developed countries were being deprived of that chance as long as Comecon was asked to retain the current profile of production. If one considers also the fact that it was the producer country which reaped the advantages of specialization (growth of monopoly power through restriction of the number of producers, economies of scale due to larger outputs, etc.) the opposition of the less developed countries becomes understandable.

Another type of opposition to specialization reflected the unwillingness of the member countries to scrap existing capacities for a number of reasons. First, many of the plants to be scrapped or adapted were of a fairly recent vintage, thus containing a sizeable amount of frozen resources. In general, various countries might perhaps be willing to abandon producing certain commodities—but not before recovering their investment.[23] The overall scarcity of investment funds meant also that the conversion of existing plants from one line of production to another could not easily be undertaken without some compensatory payment from the other member countries.

In the same context no country was likely to abandon a certain line of production unless it

[20]E. Neuberger, "International Division of Labor in CEMA: Limited Regret Strategy," *American Economic Review,* May 1964 (Vol. 54, No. 3), p. 515.
[21]Full text in *Pravda,* June 17, 1962.

[22]For an interesting Romanian exposition of this view see J. M. Montias, "Background and Origin of the Rumanian Dispute with Comecon," *Soviet Studies,* October 1964 (Vol. 16, No. 2), pp. 131–132.
[23]Personal interviews in Prague and Warsaw during the spring and summer of 1967.

could be assured of obtaining sufficient supplies of a given commodity from outside sources.[24] It is common knowledge that foreign trade plans as well as output plans were seldom if ever fulfilled. This meant that individual importers were more often than not shortchanged. Once a rigid specialization agreement was reached, resulting in concentrating nearly the entire output of a particular commodity in one or, at most, two countries, the importers were at the mercy of the exporters and the only alternative was to turn to the capitalist world. The recent increase in East-West trade may be a partial reflection of this phenomenon.

The same applied to the problem of quality. Member countries asked to forsake the production of commodities in which they were efficient would consent to a specialization agreement only if in return they received goods of equal or higher quality. This, however, was not usually the case. The example of Hungary abandoning production of radios in favor of clearly inferior Bulgarian sets speaks for itself.[25] In addition, the growing competition and availability of higher quality West European imports has been making Comecon specialization less and less attractive.

Furthermore, closing down plants or switching to other branches of production was resented by countries with severe unemployment problems. While no Comecon member admitted it openly, there were indications that considerable slack in labor force did exist, particularly in the less industrialized countries. Yet these were the very countries which were expected to carry the main burden of specialization. Actually, opposition to rationalization was not confined to the less developed countries. Recent attempts to streamline certain industrial branches in Czechoslovakia by eliminating inefficient plants met with fierce resistance of the workers employed in the affected plants, and the attempt had to be temporarily abandoned.[26]

In a somewhat different vein the whole problem of allocation of industrial outputs was still being solved largely on an ad hoc basis. Without proper cost accounting and meaningful exchange rates any distribution of particular outputs was still based, by and large, on the traditional or historical pattern of resource allocation which made it difficult to enforce adjustments. The Comecon countries stated openly that so far it had proved impossible to determine the economic efficiency of specialization for Comecon as a whole. All attempts either to work out an appropriate methodology or to calculate directly the most efficient allocation of outputs have met with failure.

Finally, one must not underestimate the strength of the perennial bias favoring maximum gross output regardless of cost. As long as national plans at various levels of activity were calculated in physical terms, there was likely to be a reluctance on the part of industry to close down inefficient plants and concentrate on the efficient ones. There were still abundant examples forthcoming from the Comecon countries which reflected general unwillingness to abandon unprofitable lines or to introduce technological progress if it meant a loss of bonus for both management and labor.[27] Though this argument is bound to lose its force once economic reforms are put into effect, for the time being it remained a significant obstacle on the road to specialization.

Some of the recent actual cases of specialization provide an example of the existing difficulties. Thus in the field of agriculture, Bulgaria was chosen as the major producer of oilseed, wool, and vegetables, supplying the northern members of Comecon. As it turned out, the increased Bulgarian output, thanks to the aid received from the other countries, was partly consumed at home and partly exported to the West, especially to the Federal Republic of Germany (West Germany). Bulgaria, on the other hand, resented the fact that it was obliged to export wool to countries which were in the process of reducing their own herds or to supply vegetables to countries such as Czechoslovakia which processed them and then reexported them also to the West.[28] The example of

[24]A. Bodnar, "Rok 1962—przelomowy w rozwoju RWPG," *Gospodarka planowa* (Warsaw), January 1963 (Vol. 18, No. 1), p. 15.

[25]Personal interviews in Prague and Warsaw during the spring and summer of 1967.

[26]Personal interviews in Prague during the spring of 1967.

[27]For an excellent treatment of this problem see Alec Nove, *The Soviet Economy: An Introduction* (Rev. ed; New York: Frederick A. Praeger, 1966), chapter 6.

[28]Personal interviews in Prague during the spring of 1967.

Bulgarian radios, mentioned above, fell into the same category.

There is little wonder then that specialization has progressed slowly with the participating countries much more preoccupied with reforms of their systems or with expanding trade with the West than with the allocation of specific types of output. Nevertheless, in the last five years some degree of specialization was achieved in engineering and shipbuilding industries and, according to official communiqués issued periodically by the Comecon Executive Committee, discussions are continuing with the aim of increasing the number of branches and products subject to specialization agreements.

The entire question of international specialization came under severe criticism at a conference of Comecon industrial experts held in Moscow in February 1966. The conference represented a watershed in the long-standing discussions concerning industrial specialization within Comecon. Various members submitted far-reaching proposals aimed at a fairly fundamental departure from the current practice and reflecting a considerable difference of opinion on how to proceed.[29]

The proposals submitted by a majority of members at the Moscow conference and confirmed the following year called, first of all, for abandonment of the current practice of extending specialization agreements over the largest possible assortment of products. From now on specialization was to be restricted above all to goods which were either not produced at all within Comecon or which were in short supply. Even then specialization was not to be considered as permanent, and only short-term agreements were to be concluded.

The emphasis on specialization in the production of final products was to give way to stressing the need for enlarged international cooperation and subcontracting. This was not only to lead to a better utilization of capacity, greater technological progress, and higher quality but also to a closer and more permanent cooperation among enterprises in different countries. The new approach was intended also to solve the problem of

a given country's being told to concentrate on the production of goods which were either expensive or without prospects for future growth. Specialization in the production of subassemblies and parts was to spread the cost more evenly among interested parties.

The majority of conferees agreed that the monopolistic tendencies resulting from allocating the output of a given commodity to a single country should be reduced by accepting the Hungarian suggestion which called for at least two countries producing a given commodity within Comecon. While suggestions concerning specialization might be made on a multilateral level, concrete specialization agreements were in general to be concluded bilaterally. The former "administrative" approach to specialization was to be replaced by an economic approach. This meant that agreements were to take into account all possible parameters in each of the interested countries.

In the final analysis each country was to be the ultimate judge of the benefits accruing from specialization. These benefits for both the producers (exporters) and buyers (importers) were to be calculated in world market prices. In anticipation of the changes to be introduced by the economic reforms, stress was laid on the economic rather than administrative character of specialization. The emphasis on the market as the final determinant of the product-mix produced in a given country spoke for itself, as did the concern with costs, profits, and prices. The need for flexibility, coupled with the assertion of the primacy of national over international interest, underlined the new approach.

The proposals also envisaged that specialization would be undertaken whenever at least three member states showed an interest in it. This meant that the principle of unanimity, long advertised as an example of Comecon's respect for its members' national sovereignty, was no longer to be adhered to. The emphasis on enterprises rather than governments as partners in specialization agreements spelled the further decline of Comecon as a coordinating agency.

It is clear that some of the proposals were not likely to generate much enthusiasm among the participants. The most controversial idea appeared to be that of specialization in the production of subassemblies and parts. Although economically

---

[29]This summary is based on A. Bodnar, "Podzial pracy w przemysle maszynowym krajow RWPG," *Zycie gospodarcze* (Warsaw), 1966 (Vol. 9, No. 11), p. 8.

justified the suggestion must have been approached with a healthy dose of skepticism, taking into account the perennial difficulties with subcontracting in the domestic economies throughout Comecon. To be dependent for essential parts on domestic producers was bad enough, and the extension of cooperation to foreign suppliers made the dependency worse still. On the other hand, the insistence on making individual enterprises signatories to specialization agreements attempted to eliminate one of the major drawbacks of the old system, namely, the total lack of interest on the part of individual producers in specialization. The involvement of enterprises combined with greater freedoms granted to managers was intended to make specialization mutually profitable.

There were other major differences of opinion among the member countries. Thus, there was disagreement concerning the duration and extent of specialization agreements. While Poland, and to some degree Romania, favored short-term agreements covering a narrow range of products, Czechoslovakia, East Germany, Hungary, and Yugoslavia called for a more permanent allocation of outputs.[30] To some extent the conflicting viewpoints reflected existing differences in individual countries. Poland and Romania had a less developed engineering industry than most of their opponents, and, in addition, Poland appeared to be most advanced in some of the most capital-intensive and slowest growing branches such as railroad equipment and shipbuilding. Neither country wanted to be permanently saddled with declining or slow-growing industries. On the other hand, countries such as Czechoslovakia and East Germany, currently enjoying supremacy over a wide range of engineering products, favored long-term arrangements which would permit them to retain their advantageous position for as long as possible.

For the same reason the more advanced countries called for the reintroduction of the market as the regulator of international exchange. The higher level of productivity of their industries would guarantee them benefits of specialization based on purely economic criteria. Because of this at least one country, Bulgaria, voiced opposition

to purely commercial specialization agreements between enterprises and demanded that main emphasis be put on intergovernmental agreements.[31] Such agreements would have the virtue of safeguarding Bulgaria's share in the Comecon division of labor.

Perhaps the only real progress in the entire field of economic cooperation in recent years was made in the area of joint production and investment. Here again, with few exceptions, most of the tangible results came into being prior to Khrushchev's ouster. Such joint projects as the "Friendship" pipeline, the freight car pool, and the electric power grid began operating prior to 1964. The only significant exceptions were the establishment of new joint enterprises in the field of metallurgy and chemicals under the names of *Intermetal* and *Interchem* and the creation of a ball-bearing cartel. Thus far these organizations have proved to be something less than successful. Their proclaimed purposes (full utilization of capacities, rationalization of production, coordination of investment, area-wide sales and purchasing agencies) were not achieved.[32] Once more the reason was the unwillingness of the members to commit their resources fully, thus risking further exposure to the vagaries of Comecon trade characterized by the persistent lack of sanctions for nonfulfillment of obligations.

This, then, was the way in which economic cooperation proceeded within Comecon in the past few years. The progress, with minor exceptions, was meager, and the future looked bleaker still. This picture, however, was not quite complete without taking into account intra-Comecon trade which was to have played a crucial role in the integration process.

Trade Policies within Comecon

Perhaps the major task which confronted the rejuvenated Comecon in 1956 was the need to expand intra-Comecon trade. During the first few years of the organization's existence trade among its members did not reach significant proportions

---

[30]Ibid; Z. Keh, "Kierunki prac," *Zycie gospodarcze*, 1966 (Vol. 9, No. 17), p. 1.

[31]Radio Prague, March 29, 1966; *Figyelo* (Budapest), May 11, 1966 (Radio Free Europe Hungarian Press Survey, No. 1714).

[32]Personal interviews in Prague and Warsaw during the spring and summer of 1967.

for a variety of reasons. The most important among them were the belief in autarky and the distrust on the part of the planners who feared the consequences of possible import deficiency on the fulfillment of plans.

The emphasis put on the expansion of intra-Comecon trade went hand in hand with the new policy of coordination and specialization. It was trade which permitted the initial adjustments in national plans when available surpluses were exchanged among member countries, reducing pressure on existing capacities and releasing resources to other priority sectors. Moreover, the whole concept of international division of labor was based on the assumption that intra-Comecon trade would play an ever-increasing role in relations among member countries.

As in the case of integration, the progress has been disappointing. Not that considerable expansion in turnover did not take place: Comecon statistics show a fairly high annual rate of growth and the share of Comecon countries in total value of trade of individual members remained high.[33] Nevertheless, judging by the tenor of various pronouncements, there was a good deal of dissatisfaction. The grounds for complaint may be treated under the headings of relatively narrow range of traded and tradable goods, incorrect prices, and payments difficulties.

Ever since the beginning, intra-Comecon trade has been a barter trade involving a bilateral exchange of goods, with prices serving mainly as units of account. It soon became clear that this procedure was not very successful in expanding trade. Despite the fact that the former autarkic bias has been severely restricted, the effects of the past policy have still been felt, meaning that with some exceptions the industrial outputs of individual Comecon countries reflected the same or similar system of priorities. Scarce commodities, whether raw materials or manufactured goods, were likely to be in high demand both in the producing country and in Comecon as a whole, and the opposite might well be true for the surplus goods. In other words, the range of commodities which have been surplus in some and in short supply in other Comecon countries tended to be narrow, limiting the possibility of

trade. In the presence of fixed prices the trade consisted usually of exchanging raw materials for raw materials, machinery for machinery, and so on, always aiming to achieve as perfect a balance as possible, especially in the case of the so-called "hard" or deficit goods.[34]

The hard bargaining which usually accompanied trade negotiations among Comecon countries concerned also the quality of traded goods. As part of an agreement trading partners tried to sell to each other goods of inferior quality as a condition for the delivery of "hard" goods. Czechoslovakia, for example, was forced to acquire Hungarian trucks which had a tendency to overturn; this promptly earned them the sobriquet "Rakosi's revenge." Bulgarian radios and Romanian trucks came into the same category. Bulgarian battery-operated trucks were imported by Czechoslovakia principally as a means of obtaining the batteries which were then taken out and used elsewhere.[35]

This state of affairs was to be remedied by the specialization agreements. By concentrating on some lines of production and relinquishing others the Comecon countries were expected to expand trade rapidly, reaping the benefits of the division of labor. But, as shown, progress in specialization was painfully slow, and according to Comecon statistics even the volume of trade in categories of goods covered by specialization agreements did not look especially impressive.

It is not surprising, then, that one by-product of the slow expansion of intra-Comecon trade was a substantial increase in trade with the non-Communist world.[36] This trend, one must add, was provoked not only by the scarcity and low quality of available goods but also by the imperatives of an expanding economy throughout Comecon. These led to a growing demand for more sophisticated products which the member countries either did not produce at all or which were still in short supply. In time, member states were openly urged to acquire modern technology in

---

[33]*Economic Survey of Europe* 1966 (New York: United Nations, 1967), chapter 3, pp. 2–7.

[34]S. Ausch, "Mezinarodni delba prace a ekonomicky mechanismus," *Planovane hospodarstvi* (Prague), December 1965 (No. 12), p. 66.

[35]Personal interviews in Prague during the spring of 1967.

[36]For a good discussion see *Economic Survey of Europe 1967* (New York: United Nations, 1968), chapter 2, pp. 71–79.

the West instead of trying to devleop it at home in order to accelerate the process of development.[37]

One of the two measures which might well contribute to the expansion of intra-Comecon trade would be a comprehensive reform of foreign trade and domestic prices. This was perhaps one of the most interesting, albeit most controversial, aspects of Comecon policy.[38]

Intra-Comecon trade, at least since 1956, is said to have been conducted at world market prices.[39] In fact most of the time there has been a sizable discrepancy between the "world prices" used by Comecon and the actual prices on the world market. No great difficulty has arisen so long as world prices did not exhibit any sudden and/or substantial movements. Once this happened, however, Comecon prices began to bear little resemblance to actual world prices except in name, and any attempt, however primitive, to calculate comparative advantage both between Comecon and the rest of the world, and within Comecon itself, was therefore made difficult, if not impossible.

One possible remedy, more frequent price adjustments, has not been applied in view of the attitude of the planners who have abhorred price changes and who have been essentially status quo oriented. Moreover, any price reform has had a tendency to drag itself into infinity and a number of years usually passed before the new price lists were ready. By that time the new prices would often have been again out of line with the actual world prices. Finally, were prices to have changed frequently, this would have affected the balance of payments, creating surpluses and deficits for the trading partners. The debtor countries in particular would have found themselves in a difficult position since inelastic supply conditions fixed by the plan would have made it next to impossible to eliminate the deficit by exporting additional quantities of goods.

The major drawback of fixed prices has been that they served to conserve the existing product-mix and the division between "hard" and "soft" goods. Comecon trade prices have not reflected the average cost of production within Comecon, nor the prices in the world market, nor supply-demand conditions in the Comecon market. For example, despite the chronic shortage of raw materials and relative abundance of certain categories of machinery within Comecon, the prices of raw materials in Comecon trade exceeded the level of world prices of raw materials much less than was the case with machinery.[40] Fixed prices also discouraged technological progress since producers received the same prices whether they introduced improvements or not.

It must be added, however, that in many instances the fixity of prices was more apparent than real. The "fixed" prices were, as a rule, adjusted during annual negotiations, with the result that one country was sometimes selling the same product to different countries at different prices. The annual price adjustments depended on the relative strengths of the negotiating partners and added more confusion to the already complex picture.

Interestingly enough the latest country to take issue with Comecon price policy was the Union of Soviet Socialist Republics, supported to some extent by Bulgaria.[41] Soviet complaints concerned the terms of trade within Comecon which apparently favored the smaller East European countries. The Soviet Union as the major supplier of raw materials to the member countries felt that the application of world market prices in intra-Comecon trade benefited the importers and penalized the exporters of raw materials. Since the real cost of developing new sources of raw materials in the Soviet Union has been going up, the Soviets felt that if the cost could not be

---

[37]W. Berger, "The Technological Revolution and Economic Cooperation among Socialist Countries," *World Marxist Review*, April 1965 (Vol. 8, No. 4), p. 17.

[38]B. Csikos-Nagy, "Currency and Price Problems in Socialist Economic Integration," *Gospodarka planowa*, August 1969 (Vol. 24, No. 8).

[39]For an excellent treatment of foreign trade pricing see United Nations, *Economic Bulletin for Europe*, 1964 (Vol. 16, No. 2), pp. 42–44.

[40]Ausch, *Planovane hospodarstvi*, No. 12, p. 66. See also P. Marer, *ASTE Bulletin*, Fall 1968 (Vol. 10, No. 2), p. 8.

[41]Cf. O. Bogomolov, "Khoziaistvovny reformy i ekonomicheskoe sotrudnichestvo sotsialisticheskikh stran," *Voprosy ekonomiki* (Moscow), 1966 (No. 2), pp. 76–86, and "Aktualne problemy ekonomicheskogo sotrudnichestva sotsialisticheskikh stran," *Mirovaia ekonomika i mezhdunarodnye otnoshenia* (Moscow), 1966 (No. 5), pp. 15–26; and V. Ladygin and Y. Shirayev, "Voprosy sovershenstvovania ekonomicheskogo sotrudnichestva stran SEV," *Voprosy ekonomiki*, 1966 (No. 5), pp. 81–89.

shared by all members, then either the price level of raw materials should be raised or the ruble should be revalued.[42] At the same time the Soviet Union, which imports a large amount of engineering products from its East European partners, complained that the prices charged for machinery were too high, especially when quality was taken into consideration. Taking its cue from recent emphasis on the primacy of national interest, the Soviet Union implied that unless its terms of trade improved it may have to introduce some changes in its trade pattern.[43]

Thus far the response of the other countries has been mixed. Czechoslovakia agreed to provide development capital while Hungary felt that the problem could be solved on a purely commercial (price and quality) basis. Hungarian spokesmen pointed out that no one had suggested that Italy, a major importer of Soviet oil (for which, by the way, it has been paying less than the Comecon countries), should help in developing Siberian oil fields.[44] Whatever the final result may be, this conflict represents another blow against Comecon.

The second measure which would likely result in the growth of intra-Comecon trade was the reform of the payments system. Until recently the payments system was based on bilateral settlements, with each partner trying hard to achieve balanced trade. Surpluses of deficits, if any, were not convertible into another currency. This lack of convertibility provided a powerful brake on trade expansion. In the final analysis it was the weaker of the two sides which determined the volume of trade. The creditor country found itself often at the mercy of the debtor and frequently had a long wait before the debt could be settled.

It was in order to introduce limited convertibility and thus contribute to an expansion of trade that the International Bank of Economic Cooperation began operating on January 1, 1964. The bank's main function was to provide an instrument for multilateral settlement of outstanding debts with the aid of the so-called "convertible rubles." Each of the eight member states was also required to put in a certain share of the bank's capital, thereby acquiring drawing rights on other members' currencies.

Even though on paper the bank represented an important step forward in the direction of facilitating trade expansion, it was a far cry from being a true bank of multilateral settlements comparable to the Bank of International Settlements which acted as a settlement agency within the European Payments Union. First of all, intra-Comecon trade was still conducted mainly along bilateral barter lines and there was little scope left for multilateral settlements which, moreover, had to be agreed upon by all interested parties. Furthermore, the penalty for nonsettlement of debts was so low as to make it almost worthwhile for the debtors to delay repayment, thus changing a short-term debt into a long-term credit. Since the creditor had to obtain the approval of the debtor before using the latter's debt in settling his own obligations, the whole procedure was slow and cumbersome, and there was no incentive to expand trade and build up surpluses which were essentially worthless.

As a result of strong criticism by certain countries, especially Poland, the bank's members have recently been required to contribute part of their shares in gold or convertible currencies.[45] Nevertheless, this alone is not likely to result in significant trade expansion. On the contrary, intra-Comecon trade may in fact decline still further

[42]*New York Times,* January 7, 1968; A. Shonfield, "Changing Commercial Policies in the Soviet Bloc," *International Affairs* (London), January 1968 (Vol. 44, No. 1), p. 11.

[43]Bogomolov, *Voprosy ekonomiki,* No. 2, p. 85; Wiles, pp. 248–250.

[44]Personal interviews in Prague during the spring of 1967.

[45]E. Babitchev, "The International Bank for Economic Cooperation," in Grossman, pp. 148–152.

Since the completion of this article there were further developments in the Comecon banking field. Following a series of discussions regarding the ways and means of strengthening the organization, culminating in a Comecon "summit" meeting in April 1969, a Comecon investment bank was formally established in July 1970. Its basic purpose is to finance investment projects in the various member countries which would benefit the organization as a whole. The bank began operating in 1971. Henry Schaefer, "What Role for Comecon?" *Radio Free Europe Research Reports in Economics,* April 1970 (No. 1), and "Recent Developments Involving the Comecon Investment Bank," ibid., July 30, 1970 (No. 5); Harry Trend, "The Comecon Investment Bank," ibid., June 15, 1970 (No. 2); Hertha W. Heiss, "The Council for Mutual Economic Assistance—Developments since the Mid-1960's," in United States Congress, Joint Economic Committee, *Economic Developments in Countries of Eastern Europe* (Washington: Government Printing office, 1970), pp. 528–542.

since member countries would not want to be caught with deficits which would have to be settled in dollars or gold and would be likely to limit their trade to the amounts that could be balanced.

It was difficult to be optimistic about the future of multilateral payments within Comecon. The payments question formed a link in the vicious circle which included intra-Comecon trade, specialization, and coordination of production. Any change in one of them had to affect the others, and the prospects in each were slim. Some East European sources saw great potential for improvement of the payments problem in the economic reforms under discussion at the present time. While in the long run they might very well be right, the uncertainty surrounding the reforms and the confusion which inevitably would follow them (as well as the need for a lengthy period of adjustment) might be expected to make the hoped-for solution an uncertain prospect. In the meantime, the tug-of-war was likely to continue between debtors and creditors and true multi-lateralism might be a long way off.

IV. THE COMECON MILIEU: REGIONAL AND INTERNATIONAL ENVIRONMENTS

The preceding discussion concentrated almost entirely on economic factors hindering economic integration in Eastern Europe. While clearly important, they alone could not fully explain the difficulties encountered in the integration process in the area. The analysis of the situation would not be complete without some discussion of the political changes in the individual member states and, to borrow James Rosenau's terms, in the "regional" and "cold-war" environments.[46]

The three major changes in individual polities were: the persistence of factionalism within ruling oligarchies, the emergence of new political elites, and the growing importance of pressure groups. The extent of these changes varied from one national system to another but elements of each of them were present in every country and all of them undoubtedly had an impact on integration processes.

The last six years witnessed a change in top leadership in three member countries (the Soviet Union, Czechoslovakia, and Romania) and a major challenge to the existing leadership in a fourth country (Poland). Everywhere, with the possible exception of the Soviet Union, the ruling elite was subjected to increasing pressure from below which in some cases necessitated major reshuffling in the highest echelons of the party and government bureaucracy. Only in the Soviet Union did the ruling gerontocracy manage to escape unscathed.

In addition to personnel changes it was becoming increasingly clear that most of the member countries have been undergoing a crisis in their decisionmaking apparatus. The process of the disintegration of the decisionmaking structures had been under way for some time and it became accelerated some six years ago, following the ouster of Khrushchev. As far as the Soviet Union alone was concerned,

> the fragmentation of the decisionmaking process combined with the erosion of Soviet ideology has produced a new element of both instability and uncertainty in Soviet behavior, an institutionalized irrationality, particularly in crisis situations.[47]

The erratic Soviet behavior in the months preceding the intervention in Czechoslovakia is a case in point. Except in emergencies Soviet actions are likely to be rational and cautious and characterized by a persistent immobilisme. The latter appears to be the result of a precarious interfactional consensus on the basis of the lowest common denominator.

There is evidence that junior Comecon partners have experienced similar difficulties. The split within the Czechoslovak leadership which antedated the "Prague spring" of 1968 has continued ever since, even after the ouster of Alexander Dubcek and the return of conservatives to power in the spring of 1969. The right-wing challenge to Wladyslaw Gomulka in Poland, accompanied by the virulent antisemitic campaign and temporarily deflected by the events in Czechoslovakia, has not been fully eliminated.

---

[46]James Rosenau (ed.), *Linkage Politics: Essays on the Convergence of National and International Systems* (New York: Free Press, 1969), pp. 49–56.

[47]Vernon V. Aspaturian, "Soviet Foreign Policy at the Crossroads: Conflict and/or Collaboration?" *International Organization*, Summer 1969 (Vol. 23, No. 3), p. 598.

In East Germany Walter Ulbricht, forced to admit some young technocrats to the party's top leadership, has been under pressure to abandon his traditional policies, as, for example, in the case of negotiations with West Germany. Only in Romania, and to some extent in Bulgaria and Hungary, has the leadership been united.

The inertia resulting from continuing factionalism among top national elites did not augur well for the future of integration in Eastern Europe. The tendency to sweep problems under the rug, the inclination to postpone decision-making for as long as possible, and the propensity to avoid making drastic solutions, so characteristic of the current regimes, were not likely to speed up the process of integration.

Another factor contributing to either the slowdown or to the maintenance of the status quo was the emergence of the "new middle class" in each of the member states, but especially in the smaller East European countries.[48] The new elite, better educated, more pragmatic, and, above all, often highly nationalistic, appeared to be much more interested in establishing closer economic links with the West than in fostering integration in their region. The young technocrats, especially the economists, were increasingly concerned with the growing technological gap between East and West, the gap which Comecon was simply unable to narrow. Their pragmatism was further reflected in greater emphasis on rational economic calculation at the expense of ideological considerations. Their nationalism which burst out in the late 1950's continued unabated, also militating against closer ties with their immediate neighbors.

The emergence of the "new middle class" was tied in with the growing influence of pressure groups. The problem of pluralism in Eastern Europe has not been dealt with in the literature until recently, and there is today still no agreement on such issues as the actual presence, power, influence, and scope of activity of interest groups.[49] Additional research is needed before anything definite can be said about the role of groups in the integrative processes. Judging from fragmentary data on group behavior in at least two Comecon countries, Czechoslovakia and Poland, one important group, the managers of the nationalized enterprises, has been divided on the issue of intrabloc economic relations. While some members of this group were strongly opposed to the continuation of close links with other Comecon countries, others favored it since this type of trade guaranteed them a more or less steady market for their low quality products which otherwise could not be sold elsewhere.[50] On the other hand, there is also evidence that various groups have been participating more and more frequently in major policy formulation in an advisory capacity for some time. Their influence was particularly visible in the preparation and implementation of economic reforms which, as suggested earlier, were hardly conducive to improved chances of successful integration.[51] Moreover, the leadership of the groups shared similar characteristics with the new political elites. Both exhibited a healthy dose of pragmatism and nationalism, and both were relatively well educated even by Western standards.

The changes in the "regional environment" have been ably analyzed elsewhere and need not be discussed here.[52] Suffice it to say that disintegration rather than integration characterized the developments in Comecon and the Warsaw Treaty Organization during the period under discussion. The top elites, although still meeting periodically if only to maintain a facade of unity for outside consumption, have been known to be frequently divided on a variety of issues, be it the Sino-Soviet conflict, the Middle East crisis, the situation in Czechoslovakia, or the rapprochement with West Germany.

The "new middle class" in individual countries felt it progressively harder to find a common language with their counterparts elsewhere in Comecon which made communication more and more difficult. Elite complementarity, fairly strong until the early 1960's and considered crucial for the success of integration, has been eroding rapidly. Even if the national political elites

---

[48]K. Jowitt, "Revolutionary Breakthroughs and National Development: The Case of Romania 1944-1965" (unpublished Ph.D. dissertation, University of California, Berkeley, 1970), pp. 231-240.

[49]Skilling, *World Politics*, Vol. 18, No. 3; and A. Korbonski, "Bureaucracy and Interest Groups in Communist Societies: The Case of Czechoslovakia," *Studies in Comparative Communism* (forthcoming).

[50]Personal interviews in Prague and Warsaw during the spring and summer of 1967.

[51]See p. 963 [of *Regional Integration*].

[52]Brzezinski, pp. 433-455.

in Communist Party leadership strata and high-level bureaucracies occasionally tended to think and act alike, the same did not hold true for the economic elites. In the early days of Comecon the economists from different countries, educated with the aid of Soviet textbooks and speaking the same pseudo-Marxist economic jargon, had at least a common standard of reference.

Today the situation is quite different. The economic reforms in various countries were in some cases accompanied by reforms in the curriculum, especially in the field of economics. As a result the young economists in Czechoslovakia and Hungary began to pay more attention to John Maynard Keynes, Paul Samuelson, and Milton Friedman than to Marx while their counterparts elsewhere probably considered Yevsei Liberman the greatest innovator since Adam Smith. While the Czechs and the Hungarians spoke in terms of value-added, free price formation, and comparative costs, others still adhered to the old concepts of central plan, price control, and gross output regardless of cost. It can only be presumed that in many instances the partners in trade negotiations simply talked past, rather than to, each other.

The lack of a common standard of reference negatively influenced the chances of integration by making it difficult to agree on an objective yardstick with which to measure and distribute the benefits accruing from integration. As pointed out earlier, none of the Comecon countries has been able to calculate real benefits derived from international transactions. All such calculations have been hitherto conducted on an ad hoc basis without real grounding in both static and dynamic cost analysis. Of course, what mattered here was the *perceived* rather than *real* benefits. Thus the Romanian policy makers saw the various specialization agreements as detrimental to their country's economic future even though, at least in the long run, some type of a division of labor in Comecon would be beneficial to all countries.[53] Similarly, the Soviet Union saw itself being "exploited" by the smaller East European countries without actually being able to prove it satisfactorily.[54] Similar problems have been encountered with regard to the distribution of real

or alleged benefits, thus hurting the chances of integration.

The changes in the "cold-war environment" also had an impact on East European economic integration. Here again the developments have been discussed in some detail and the main arguments are generally familiar.[55] The chief factor was the decline in the intensity of the Cold War, followed by the change in the attitudes of the two superpowers and their respective clienteles. The idea of "peaceful coexistence" began to compete with that of "peaceful engagement" and the outcome was a rapprochement between the two camps which showed no signs of diminishing despite occasional lapses.

In practical terms the consequences of the détente proved almost identical on both sides. Perhaps the most striking were the parallel developments in the two military alliances—the North Atlantic Treaty Organization (NATO) and the WTO. Initially established as defense measures against an outside threat—imaginary rather than real—both organizations lost their raison d'être once the danger was perceived as rapidly disappearing. France's behavior was matched by that of Romania and there was a good chance that if the restiveness, particularly among the junior members, was permitted to continue unabated, both alliances would be reduced to the role of talking shops. For Eastern Europe the weakening of the cohesion of the WTO meant that one major prop capable of sustaining and justifying economic integration was showing signs of fatigue.

Perhaps a more important consequence of the continuing détente was the rapid expansion of East-West economic contacts which reinforced rapprochement through a snowballing effect. The impact of the growing East-West trade on integration was discussed earlier. Here one may venture a prediction that in the final analysis the revival of the traditional economic links in Europe, spearheaded by West Germany and aided and abetted by other countries in the European Economic Community (EEC) and by the United Kingdom, may mean a kiss of death for the chances of integration in the East. The realization of the growing technological gap between Eastern and Western Europe appeared to convince even the most die-hard champions of

---

[53]For the best treatment of Romania's attitude see J. M. Montias, *Economic Development in Communist Rumania* (Cambridge, Mass: M.I.T. Press, 1967), pp. 187–230.

[54]See p. 960 [of *Regional Integration*].

[55]Korbonski, *International Conciliation*, No. 573, pp. 71–73.

Comecon that the only way of overcoming the persistent economic difficulties in the area was to import modern technology and know-how from the West.[56]

To a large extent it was a reversal of the situation that existed twenty years before. There is little doubt that Comecon, created in 1949 for the purpose of laying the foundations for economic integration of the Communist camp, was the stepchild of the Cold War. The embargo imposed by the West at that time was largely responsible for the increase in the intra-Comecon trade which in turn had a spillover effect in other areas of common interest, thus contributing greatly to the progress of economic integration at least until the early 1960's. It was only when the trade barriers were lowered once again that the process of integration began to show signs of slowing down.

It may also be speculated that the difficulties encountered by the Common Market in the most recent period had some repercussions on Comecon although their magnitude cannot be easily ascertained. The whole question of the "demonstration effect" of the EEC on Comecon is a moot one. It can be presumed that the early successes of the Common Market, realized rather late by Comecon leaders, affected East European integration in at least two ways: First, the genuine fear of the effects of a common EEC tariff, especially on agricultural products and raw materials, might have forced Comecon countries to seek common solutions; second, the impressive performance of the EEC might have helped to reduce the resistance to closer cooperation. To say this, however, is not to imply, as Marshall Shulman seems to do, that the success of the EEC was *the* factor responsible for the noticeable increase in Comecon activities in the early 1960's.[57] It can be assumed that closer integration in the bloc would have taken (or not taken) place regardless of the success or failure of the Common Market. If, on the other hand, the atmosphere of early successes in the EEC did in fact prove contagious east of the Elbe, the present impasse in the West might have some impact on the developments in Eastern Europe.

In the light of the foregoing discussion the question should now be raised about the extent of economic integration in Eastern Europe 21 years after the first step was made in that direction. Keeping in mind our original definition it can be said that the common framework managed to maintain itself in one form or another throughout the entire period and that it did provide for the mutual pursuit of some goals and common implementation of some policies. However, it can also be said that the past six years or so showed hardly any progress in the three variables. On the contrary, some of them reflected growing decay.

The institutional framework has remained roughly unchanged since 1964 even though the creation of the Comecon bank and the establishment of some cooperative ventures might be interpreted as a functional expansion of the organization. On the other hand, there has been a visible decline in the area of common pursuit of goals and execution of policies. While the ultimate goal of every polity remained industrialization, there was much less agreement regarding the other goals such as the achievement of the maximum rate of growth, rapid development of heavy industry, or full (or overfull) employment. While some countries (Soviet Union, Poland, Bulgaria) still seemed to adhere to these goals, others preferred to think in terms of optimum allocation of resources and/or improvement in consumption patterns of the population (Czechoslovakia and Hungary), in terms of expanding commercial ties with the West (Romania), or in terms of improving the old economic system by eliminating its worst features (East Germany).

There seems to be also little agreement on the implementation of economic policies. Growing differentiation in the national economic systems made it virtually impossible to coordinate domestic and foreign economic policies, and competition rather than cooperation seemed to become the prevailing form of intra-Comecon relations.

Departing for a moment from a strictly definitional standpoint, it can be stated that Comecon as an instrument of integration in 1970 was a far cry from what it was ten years earlier. Stripped of its function as a coordinating agency, Comecon also appeared to be deprived of its role as an instrument of allocation. Its competence as a promoter of intra-Comecon trade was also seriously challenged not only by the continuing

[56]*Economic Survey of Europe 1967*, chapter 2, pp. 79–84.

[57]Marshall D. Shulman, "The Communist States and Western Integration," *Problems of Communism*, September–October 1963 (Vol. 12, No. 5), pp. 47–54.

stress on bilateral agreements but also by the increase in East-West trade and growing demands for participation in the worldwide rather than the Comecon division of labor. More and more, Comecon seemed to act primarily as a clearing house for ideas and suggestions, providing an institutional umbrella for bilateral and occasionally multilateral agreements; serving as a forum for the exchange of economic and technical information; conducting research; and acting as an arbiter in cases of disagreement or nonfulfillment of contracts. However important and useful, all these functions could be seen as a terminal rather than an initial stage in the East European integration process.

V. COMECON WITHIN THE THEORETICAL ENVIRONMENT

Until now the question of integration in Eastern Europe was discussed in largely nontheoretical terms. It was also limited to the analysis of the various factors hindering economic integration in the area. Such a discussion, however interesting and enlightening, has one major drawback in that it does not permit meaningful comparisons with integration processes in other parts of the world. As suggested above, the absence of any theoretical studies of East European integration was a reflection of the peculiar character of the so-called Communist area studies which until now abhorred theorizing, considering it inappropriate and downright harmful.

It is thus not without some irony that the first systematic attempt at including Comecon in a broader theoretical framework was made by scholars whose interest lay well beyond the boundaries of the area. In their pioneering 1964 article Ernst Haas and Philippe Schmitter included Comecon among the seven integration schemes they tested, and on the basis of their investigation they concluded that the "chances of automatic politicization" of Comecon, i.e., the chances of the economic union being transformed into a political one, were "possible-doubtful."[58]

This is not the place to discuss in detail the ranking assigned to Comecon by the authors. My own verdict, based on the Haas-Schmitter paradigm, would have been considerably less optimistic. Nevertheless, keeping in mind the fact that the above-mentioned article was written in 1964 when no one else even attempted to present a comprehensive *factual* history of Comecon, the courage and imagination of the authors in undertaking this task can only be admired, even if today their interpretation has lost some of its earlier glitter.

The criticism of the Haas-Schmitter paradigm induced Joseph Nye to construct what he calls "a revised neo-functionalist model," intended to remedy the major deficiencies of the earlier approach.[59] There is no doubt that Nye's model represents a significant advance in the field of comparative integration studies. From a parochial East European point of view it appears to overcome a number of problems associated with the Haas-Schmitter model even though it still leaves some issues unresolved. Space does not permit a full discussion of the various "process forces" and "integrative conditions" which form the core of the model, especially as some of them were mentioned earlier. Thus only a few variables will be briefly commented upon.

Perhaps the two most important or strategic variables are the *involvement of external actors in the process* and the *perception of external compellingness*. The peculiarity of the Comecon situation lies in the position of the Soviet Union. Although a founding member of Comecon, the Soviet Union easily could (and perhaps should) be treated as an external actor since its influence upon and involvement in the affairs of the organization are of paramount importance.

It is probably correct to say that the Soviet attitude toward Comecon has been highly ambiguous over the years. As mentioned below, the reasons for creating Comecon in the first place are still obscure. It also appears that the Soviet Union, or more correctly Stalin, effectively destroyed the chances of an economic union in Eastern Europe by permitting the then satellites to retain a semblance of political independence and control over their economies. There is also little doubt that a political union could have

[58]Ernst B. Haas and Philippe C. Schmitter, "Economics and Differential Patterns of Political Integration: Projections about Unity in Latin America," *International Organization*, Autumn 1964 (Vol. 18, No. 4), p. 720.

[59]J. S. Nye in [*International Organization*, Autumn 1970].

been formed with the use of force. No such attempt was made, however, and instead Comecon never got off the ground as long as Stalin was alive.

It is also clear that the perception by the national decisionmakers of the Soviet attitude vis-à-vis Comecon was (and is) of considerable importance for at least some of the junior partners. Thus a strong Soviet commitment to the organization would most likely induce the smaller members to move in the same direction, and vice versa. The decline in Comecon activities after 1963 could be attributed to a reduction of Soviet interest in East European economic integration which was correctly interpreted as such by some of the countries.[60] On the other hand, a revival of Soviet concern about integration might also influence some of the member countries in the opposite direction, as witnessed by Romania's resistance to closer integration in 1963 and after.

The sheer economic size of the Soviet Union does not in itself present any inherent problems.[61] In the case of Comecon the huge size of the Soviet economy might actually be considered as a catalyst which, *ceteris paribus*, could be instrumental in maintaining and expanding the scope of integration. The presence of an immense market for manufactured goods as well as the existence of large raw material reserves puts the Soviet Union in a highly favorable role as the potential economic federalizer. Once the *ceteris paribus* clause is removed, however, the importance of this particular factor is considerably reduced.

Another condition to be commented upon, *low (or exportable) costs of integration*, is of some relevance to the Comecon situation. To be sure, even the limited degree of East European integration was said to be quite costly in terms of foregone alternatives. Seen in this light the process of economic integration in the area might have already gone too far.[62] While there was

clearly a diminution in the welfare on the part of the East European population, it was much larger than a corresponding decline outside the region due to trade diversion, as the share of East European trade in the total volume of trade in the non-Communist world was much smaller than the share of Western trade in total Comecon trade.[63]

There is, however, another aspect of the exportability of costs within Comecon. It concerns the problem of the so-called "exploitation" in intra-bloc trade. Space does not permit a full discussion of this interesting question but it appears that a number if not all of the Comecon members have been engaged in exploiting each other by charging higher prices for their exports than those paid by non-Communist buyers of identical commodities and by being forced to pay similarly higher prices for their imports from other Comecon countries.[64] The extent of this "exploitation" varies in time and between different partners in the exchanges, and the fact that all members participate in this "beggar my neighbor" policy goes a long way in sweetening the potentially bitter pill of integration.

When the "exploitation" becomes too one-sided or when it persists for a long period of time, it may develop into a threat to the integrative process. In the last few years, for example, there were several indications that the Soviet Union was less than happy with the conduct of intra-Comecon trade, claiming among other things that it had to pay too high a price for the low quality manufactured products imported from its junior partners while at the same time the prices it received for its exports of raw materials were below world market prices.[65] In other words, the Soviet Union de facto charged price discrimination on the part of the other Comecon members, and it demanded some sort of compensation for its worsening terms of trade. It is quite possible that these charges and the lack of enthusiastic response to them by the rest of the membership were responsible for the lack of progress in Comecon in recent years.

[60]For a somewhat different interpretation of the role of the Soviet Union See Karl Kaiser, "The Integration of Regional Subsystems: Some Preliminary Notes on Recurrent Patterns and the Role of the Superpowers," *World Politics*, October 1968 (Vol. 21, No. 1), pp. 99ff.

[61]Kaser, pp. 202–205.

[62]J. M. Montias, "Obstacles to the Economic Integration of Eastern Europe," paper prepared for the Semaine de Bruges, College of Europe, Bruges, Belgium, 1969, p. 5.

[63]For details see *Economic Survey of Europe 1966*, chapter 3, sections 2 and 4.

[64]Cf. F. Holzman, "More on Soviet Bloc Trade Discrimination," *Soviet Studies*, July 1965 (Vol. 17, No. 1); Wiles, pp. 222–248; Marer, *ASTE Bulletin*, Vol. 10, No. 2, pp. 6–7; and Kaser, pp. 182–185.

[65]See p. 960 [of *Regional Integration*].

Nye's "expected national response" in the case of Comecon is the maintenance of status quo. This could be perceived as the most likely outcome in the short run although the possibility of disintegration cannot be completely ruled out. My own judgment of the strength of process forces and favorability of integrative conditions is somewhat less sanguine than that of Nye, and my own verdict as to the chances of integration in Eastern Europe would be even less optimistic.

Another interesting attempt at defining the scope of integration in the area was made by Michael Gehlen who utilized the communications approach for that purpose.[66] Gehlen tested the progress of integration in Eastern Europe with reference to ten types of transactions of which the most important seemed to be the interpersonal contacts among top national elites, bilateral and multilateral treaties, other interpersonal contacts such as educational exchanges and tourism, and finally trade. On that basis Gehlen then proceeded to rank the seven East European countries in terms of high, medium, and low levels of integrative activity and in terms of their dependence on the Soviet Union. The two divisions did not parallel each other so that in a number of cases countries which showed a low degree of integrative behavior had a high level of dependence on the Soviet Union. Gehlen saw this discrepancy as the result of the lack of agreement by the partners to establish a regulatory, coordinating mechanism and of the different appreciation of the intraregional relationships by the Soviet Union and its junior partners. Thus,

> for the latter they are economically vital but for the former such relationships seem to be largely a question of commercial partnership enabling the USSR to obtain certain resources for its own advantage.[67]

The appropriateness and usefulness of the communications model for the study of integration has been debated for a long time and there is no need to restate the arguments here. In Gehlen's case it appears that in the final analysis the overall judgment regarding integration in Eastern Europe hinges on the volume of intra-Comecon trade. This, as was suggested above, is not a very useful index of integrative process, especially when considered in isolation. Moreover, Gehlen's explanation of the discrepancy between each country's integrative behavior and its dependency on the Soviet Union is not convincing. It can be argued that with the exception of Bulgaria, by far the least economically developed member of Comecon, for no country including the Soviet Union were the intraregional relationships "economically vital," especially in the second half of the last decade.

In the end Gehlen appears to discard the communications approach and explains the meager results of integration processes in Eastern Europe with reference to "operational problems within the system making it difficult for a resolution of conflict over goals to be attained within the official organs of Comecon."[68] This seems to be the crux of the matter and confirms the judgment that emerged from the earlier discussion in this article.

Two other recent articles by David Finley and R. J. Mitchell also deal with theoretical aspects of integration in Eastern Europe.[69] Neither of them attempts to explain its progress or predict its future, but both seek rather to develop a theoretical framework for study and research. Thus Finley uses four indices of integration—scope, institutional structure, authority, and extent—to compare three supranational institutions in Communist Europe: Comecon, the Warsaw Pact, and the Joint Institute for Nuclear Research. His conclusion is that while the latter two organizations appeared to reach a higher plateau of integration, Comecon had a better chance to maintain itself in the long run mainly because it relied more on consensus than on coercion. This may well be true although one could argue that a comparison between the three organizations is not very meaningful in view of the striking differences in their respective areas

---

[66]Michael Gehlen, "The Integrative Process in East Europe: A Theoretical Framework," *The Journal of Politics,* February 1968 (Vol. 30, No. 1), pp. 90–113.

[67]Ibid., p. 112.

[68]Ibid.

[69]D. Finley, "Integration among the Communist Party-States: Comparative Case Studies," and R. Mitchell, "A Theoretical Approach to the Study of Communist International Organizations," in J. Triska (ed.), *Communist Party States: Comparative and International Studies* (Indianapolis, Ind.: Bobbs-Merrill Co., 1969), pp. 57–105.

of concern, institutional structures, and sheer volume of transactions.

Mitchell in turn applied both coalition theory and organization theory to the study of Comecon, claiming that each of the theories taken separately has only partial explanatory, and no predictive, value. He concludes by saying that

> it seems beyond question that quantification and other behavioral study can yield predictions with far greater accuracy than any guesswork based upon impressionistic conclusions about the communist system.[70]

This statement is as vague as it is meaningless. Mitchell does not make clear what kind of "quantification" he has in mind and thus it is difficult to say anything about his conclusion. Not every piece of statistical data necessarily improves our understanding of integrative processes; and Mitchell's effort, while suggestive, does not contribute much to advancing the theory of integration.

Another recent effort to discuss obstacles to economic integration in Eastern Europe was that of J. M. Montias.[71] Looking at Comecon as an integrative vehicle, Montias distinguishes four factors which played (and continue to play) a major role in obstructing the path toward closer integration in the area. The four factors are: political restrictions on the movement of labor and other resources, obstacles due to the strategy of development of individual member states, impediments to trade inherent in the economic mechanism of member states, and obstacles arising from the institutional arrangements for trade in goods and services among members.

It can be seen that Montias's discussion runs in terms comparable to those used in the analysis of economic factors hindering integration in part II above. The only major difference between the two discussions lies in the varying interpretations of the importance of political restraints on integration.

In discussing the political and strategic restrictions on integration in Eastern Europe, Montias emphasizes the point that it was in effect the Soviet Union which lost its chance of integrating the area economically in the early postwar years when it had the power to do so. By retaining, at least formally, the system of independent East European states, Stalin "laid the foundations of economic nationalism" which has since haunted the Soviet leadership.[72] In Montias's view the reasons for the formation of Comecon in 1949 are still shrouded in obscurity, and it is not at all certain that Comecon was ever seriously intended as an instrument of genuine economic integration of the Soviet bloc.

There is nothing basically wrong with this interpretation except that it seems to provide only a partial explanation of the lack of progress in East European integration. To be sure, Stalin appeared opposed to any form of international cooperation in this area as evidenced by his criticism of the attempted Balkan federation of the late forties, and it may be assumed that he did not seriously contemplate Comecon becoming an efficient tool of integration. But why limit the discussion to Stalin?

Undoubtedly, by not insisting on total absorption of individual countries into the Soviet Union Stalin allowed the former to retain a modicum of sovereignty and notion of national interest as well as some control over the movement and utilization of resources. Montias might conceivably be right in claiming that this single act destroyed any chances of meaningful economic integration, yet one may wonder whether this was really the case. Comecon was clearly imposed on Eastern Europe from above and had little chance of success as long as it remained part and parcel of the Stalinist system. Yet there are strong indications that after Stalin's death and Khrushchev's accession to power, Comecon did have some chance of success. Thus, as suggested elsewhere,

> the main reason for its failure in the early sixties was the inability or unwillingness of the Soviet leadership to make the final break with the Stalinist *modus operandi*, and its determination to continue imposing its own preferences on Comecon.[73]

---

[70]Mitchell, in Triska, p. 103.
[71]J. M. Montias, *Studies in Comparative Communism*, Vol. 2, Nos. 3–4, pp. 38–60.

[72]Ibid., p. 41.
[73]A. Korbonski, "Some Random Thoughts on Economic Integration of Eastern Europe," paper prepared for the Conference on Regional Integration, Madison, Wisconsin, April 1969, p. 13.

Also, while in the initial stages of Comecon's existence the Soviet Union was guilty of a lack of commitment, in the latter stages it tried to do too many things too fast without realizing that its earlier inaction did little to prepare the junior members for what was to come later.

Montias's conclusion is that the key role in the liberalization and expansion of exchanges, i.e., integration, will be played by the economic reforms now under way in some of the countries. He also feels, however, that chances of such a liberalization are slim until and unless the Soviet Union abandons its policy of high-cost autarky in raw materials and agricultural products which would lead the relative scarcities (and prices) of commodities in Comecon to coincide with those in the world market. Only then will the individual countries be able to depart from irrational trading practices and to expand multilateral trade. Furthermore, the uneven pace in reformmaking is not likely to bring about that expansion for reasons spelled out earlier in the article. Thus, according to Montias, the overall prospects for closer economic integration in Eastern Europe are not very bright.

Montias feels, however, that the so-called "Brezhnev Doctrine," justifying the Soviet intervention in Czechoslovakia, might be used by the Soviet leadership to impose "integration from above."

> Putting teeth into Comecon by fiat would, as a matter of fact, be much simpler and more consonant with the working style of communist bureaucrats than the patient search for solutions agreeable to every member of the organization in the framework of liberalized institutions.[74]

While Montias's prognosis concerning the economic obstacles to East European integration is highly plausible, the same cannot be said about the possibility of politically inspired and Moscow-enforced integration. The meaning of the "Brezhnev Doctrine" is still a subject of controversy and its full impact on the future of Eastern Europe cannot be easily predicted.[75] Moreover, there is no evidence that the Soviet

Union is strongly interested in the speed-up of integration and in the revival of Comecon as an instrument of Moscow's control. With overall Soviet foreign policy becoming gradually more pragmatic and conventional, Russia's interest and involvement in Comecon are becoming more and more a function of the short- and long-run usefulness of the organization for the achievement of Soviet policy objectives. As long as Comecon proved helpful in providing an instrument of control over Eastern Europe, the Soviet Union was actively concerned with maintaining and even strengthening it. Today, however, it is clear that Comecon's performance in that particular sphere was and is a disappointment. As long as the organization served as a channel for economic exploitation and regulation it did perform a useful task. At the present time, however, Comecon may have already become an economic burden for Moscow and this would tend to explain a decline in Soviet involvement manifested, for example, in the lukewarm support for the East European convertibility scheme.

To be sure, the events preceding the invasion of Czechoslovakia seemed to confirm Montias's hypothesis. References to Comecon cropped up with increasing frequency in the various Soviet-sponsored official statements made public during that period. The need for continuing close mutual economic relations, reaffirmed in the Dresden declaration of March, in the Warsaw letter in July, and the Cierna and Bratislava communiqués in August 1968, underscored the seeming importance of this particular problem. It apparently reflected the apprehension on the part of Czechoslovakia's partners within Comecon that that country might in the near future reduce its participation in that organization and turn instead to the West, following the path chosen by Romania. The evidence of Czechoslovakia's intention to withdraw from Comecon is hard to come by, however, and in the final analysis it is hard to imagine that the intervention of August 1968 was undertaken in order to keep the country in Comecon. Moreover, the large expansion in East-West contacts following the invasion would indicate that economic rapprochement with the West was no longer considered anathema by Moscow.

Except for sporadic attempts to breathe some new life into the Warsaw Pact, Soviet international behavior seems to reflect continuing in-

[74]Montias, p. 60.

[75]Aspaturian, *International Organization*, Vol. 23, No. 3, p. 595.

terest in maintaining political détente with the West, as evidenced by the recent revival of the idea of the conference on European security. As a rule, political rapprochement tends to sustain and expand economic rapprochement. Thus Montias's prediction about the possibility of "integration from above" does not appear to be well founded, at least not at present. On the other hand, the erratic behavior of the Soviet oligarchy so well demonstrated during the events of 1968 may yet manifest itself in some sudden tightening of the reins of economic control in Eastern Europe.

What then is the future of integration in Communist Europe? The overall consensus that emerges from the writings of Nye, Gehlen, and Montias would indicate that the most likely tendency, at least in the short run, is going to be the maintenance of the status quo. My own feeling is that while the latter appears plausible there is also a good chance of economic disintegration in the area. In the final analysis the outcome will be dictated by the combination of endogenous and exogenous factors. Changes in the political, social, and economic systems, as well as developments in the regional and "cold-war environments" which are hardly predictable, cannot help but make any hypothesis highly tentative.

VI. EAST EUROPEAN INTEGRATION: PROSPECTS FOR FUTURE RESEARCH

The final issue to be considered is the agenda for future research in the area of East European integration.

The priority should be assigned above all to microtheories in both the political and economic arenas. Western scholars seem to have a pretty good knowledge of the workings of the national economic and political systems. What is needed is a switch in emphasis from the macro- to the microtype of analysis. We still know relatively little about the behavior of some key individuals and groups such as party and government bureaucrats, managers, and planners. We have even less

knowledge about the processing of "inputs" and the process of decisionmaking in Comecon countries. The same applies to such problems as negotiating techniques and style, ways and means of solving disputes, formal and informal arrangements for consultations among strategic actors, and so on.

As far as a more general type of theorizing is concerned, one possible approach might be the linkage theory made popular recently by Rosenau.[76] The concept of direct and indirect linkages and of policy and environmental inputs and outputs may well be applied to the study of integration in Eastern Europe. To be sure, the concept of linkages per se has been used by Nye and other students of integration but only as one of the variables in the model. On the East European scene the linkage analysis was applied by R. V. Burks to the study of leadership selection, policy formulation and implementation, and ideological community.[77]

What might be done in the case of Eastern Europe is to utilize more extensively the matrix of national-international linkages developed by Rosenau. This may permit us to establish a linkage network which, in turn, might bring to the surface some unfamiliar (latent) linkages that heretofore played little or no role in the process of integration. Also linkage research might bring into focus other interesting problems such as the duration, flexibility and stability of various linkages, linkages between various environments, fused linkages, and others. To quote Rosenau,

> such research would focus on the interdependence of polities and their environments, and would thus be of special interest to students of international institutions and to those concerned with the prospects of supranational integration.[78]

The point is well taken and it is worth pursuing.

---

[76]Rosenau, pp. 44–63.
[77]R. V. Burks, "The Communist Politics of Eastern Europe," in Rosenau, pp. 275–303.
[78]Rosenau, p. 59.

Discussion and Questions

1. ➤ Why doesn't the adherence by members of COMECON to a common ideology greatly facilitate the integration of Eastern Europe? ➤ Does this experience suggest the persisting strength of the sovereign state as the organizing center of human affairs? ➤ Or does it just suggest the particular geopolitical vulnerability of East Europe to Soviet exploitation and domination?

The Soviet Union has been an active participant in East European integration efforts, thereby raising directly the issue of economic exploitation and political dependence disguised as support for regional integration. If the socialist countries of Europe could be "integrated" into a Soviet dominated grouping, then Moscow would have effective, reliable, and subtle levers of power. Each lesser state would have an economy that was totally dependent on interaction with the larger socialist whole. Disaffiliation would be virtually impossible, and a permanent loss of political autonomy would seem to follow from carrying regional cooperation across thresholds of economic integration. For instance, if the modern sector of the smaller participants is dependent on spare parts from the main supplier country, a virtually irreversible relationship of subordination is established. Certainly the desire for political autonomy in East Europe has worked against regional autonomy. ➤ Do socialist economies necessarily resist supranationalization more than capitalist economies? ➤ Is there any explanation for this? John Pindar has argued that centrally planned economies are not able to merge their economic activities on a gradual basis as well as market economies. (See John Pindar, "EEC and COMECON," *Survey*, no. 58 [January 1966], pp. 101–117, in Nye, Ed., *International Regionalism*, pp. 22–42.)

2. As many scholars of Latin American regionalism have pointed out, in contrast to integration in Europe, integration in Latin America would serve to strengthen the political autonomy of constituent states by making them less vulnerable to direct hegemony and penetration by the United States. The Latin American sociologist Gustavo Lagos looks toward integration as a means by which Latin American countries can jointly and severally improve their status within the international system. "The Political Role of Regional Economic Organizations in Latin America" (*Journal of Common Market Studies*, vol. 6, no. 4 [June 1968]) is a sequel to Lagos' earlier important book, *International Stratification and Underdeveloped Countries* (University of North Carolina Press, Chapel Hill, 1963), which argued that international society is hierarchically structured in such a way as to deny status and proportionate participation to the less developed countries. In his 1968 article, Lagos sees integration as an ideology suitable for the Latin American setting, both with respect to achieving greater autonomy vis-à-vis the United States and with respect to enabling Latin American countries to do better as a group within the world system. In essence, he is arguing that Latin American countries are, by and large, too small to uphold their national interests so long as they act individually, but that their cumulative weight and position will be felt if they learn to act collectively. It should be useful to compare this line of inquiry, designed to upgrade the capabilities of weaker states, with the presentation of a multibloc model of world order outlined by Roger Masters in Part I. More recently, however, Latin American voices have expressed concern that regionalist movements, if captured or dominated by the economic forces fostering growth of multinational corporations, will provide the main capital-exporting countries with new organizational forms to perpetuate their dominion over less industrial and less prosperous countries. This tendency is accentuated to the extent that leading governments within the region are captured by elites whose interests are associated with

dominant extraregional forces rather than with the welfare of the general population internal to the region. In this respect, the United States' membership in the OAS amounts to the penetration of the region by "a nonregional" country.

3. ➤ How would you analyze the prospects for the over-all integration of the European continent? ➤ Would such integration be a positive development in terms of world order? ➤ Why? ➤ Why not? ➤ What factors govern your response? In this connection, it is useful to compare the achievements and potentialities of the all-European Economic Commission for Europe (ECE) with the more tightly organized regional movements that have developed in East and West Europe. (For an analysis of the ECE, see Jean Siotis, "ECE in the Emerging European System," *International Conciliation*, no. 561 [January 1967], pp. 5–66.)

4. ➤ Can the encouragement of a "regional consciousness" be reconciled with the effort to stimulate a "global consciousness"? ➤ Is there a natural harmony or contradiction between these two types of supranational political identification? ➤ What factors control the degree of compatibility among regional movements? ➤ Is it possible to think in terms of staged growth culminating in an eventual world community after a period of experience with regional political communities? ➤ Or can there occur parallel and mutually reinforcing lines of political consciousness? ➤ Is there a need for an appropriate strategy of reeducation in the values and symbols of "citizenship"?

5. W. Warren Wagar poses the question "who will integrate the integrators?" His concern is more with the separate approaches to global integration taken by world thinkers situated in distinct cultures than with the unification of regionally integrated communities. But the idea of integrating integrators is relevant to the whole idea of moving toward a world commonwealth after an interim period of experience with regional communities. (See Wagar, *The City of Man* [Penguin, Baltimore, 1967], pp. 239–58.)

6. It is plausible to contemplate a heterogeneous world system of the 1990's constituted by continental-sized states. One of the trends in international society is toward the proliferation of *kinds*, as well as *numbers*, of actors. Medieval international society, which was moderately stable so far as basic structure was concerned for long periods of time, was also constituted by a variety of actors, ranging from the Catholic Church and the Holy Roman Empire to miniscule principalities. Carl J. Friedrich envisions "Such a polycentric world . . . in the making." Its constituent parts would be "Europe, . . . Africa, Arabia, China, Great Britain and the Commonwealth, India, Latin America, the United States, and the Union of Soviet Socialist Republics" (Friedrich, *Europe: An Emergent Nation?* [Harpers, New York, 1969], p. 18).

REGIONAL ACTORS:
SPECIFYING AND SELECTING UNITS

Part III focuses on two distinct topics. Selections 8 and 9 are concerned with variations on the central question: what is a "region"? Selections 9, 10, and 11 are concerned with some qualitative aspects of the regional unit.

As indicated in Part I we are using the term "region" as a comprehensive term covering any unit in international society that is composed of two or more sovereign states and is not a global political international institution; blocs, limited international institutions, subsystems, alliances—all qualify as "regions."

In Part III we continue our concern, first of all, with the integration potential of units "larger" than the nation-state, of units already integrated to some extent on a regional scale. Larger is used only to denote the multinational scope of operations. In terms of political influence, military capability, or even size, regional groupings are often "smaller" and less highly structured than principal sovereign states. There is, of course, also a growing interest in subnational regionalism, that is, in delegating authority to regional units within a state.

Issues bearing on second-stage integration can only be considered after we have a fairly clear understanding of what kind of unit has emerged from the first stage. In this connection there are some questions that should be considered. Would large federal states or empires or regional organizations provide the best political base for global integration? Is the mix of political units—their degree of homogeneity or heterogeneity—a critical variable? Is the degree of correspondence between formal political units and systems of culturally determined beliefs and values of great significance? These questions all bear on whether or not regional units are terminal or transitional stages in the processes of economic and political integration.

We are also concerned with regionally constituted global systems of world order of the sort that Roger Masters described in his selection in Part I. Most thinking about world-order has been devoted to various proposals to mobilize the integration potential of interacting nation-states. The goal of such a mobilization effort has been the direct transition to some form of world government. Here, in contrast, we are only interested with whether the nation-state might be transformed into a global system constituted by regional units of participation. Such a line of utopian thinking is relatively rare in world government literature, although a strong regional emphasis is found in proposals for a world constitution put forward after World War II by a diverse group of scholars headed by Robert Hutchins at the University of Chicago. The project was further developed at the Center for the Study of Democratic Institutions. See *A Constitution for the World,* reprinted in Part VI.

In selections 10, 11, and 12, we raise some questions bearing more directly on regionalism as a base for strengthening the capacity of the world order to provide for social justice, peace, and human dignity. The available literature does not put a sharp focus on these normative concerns. Most intellectual energy has been devoted to analyzing first-stage integration potential (see especially Part II). Our hope in Part III is to enable serious consideration both of issues of second-stage integration and of whether a regionally constituted system of world order would be an improvement upon a world of states.

Selection 8 consists of some extracts from Bruce Russett's *International Regions and the International System: A Study in Political Ecology* that illustrate the complex process of identifying a "region." Russett relies upon behavioral methods of data analysis to present material on degrees of relatedness that persist between countries. He emphasizes the following variables in identifying the existence and boundaries of a region: cultural similarity, common political orientations, institutional memberships, transaction flows, and proximity. A proposed region is accepted as such if it attains a certain minimum score when measured quantitatively against these criteria. Russett's approach to the delimitation of regions can be compared with Oran Young's delimitation of subsystems in Part I. Russett relies much more heavily upon quantitative indicators of regional boundaries than does Young. For an exchange of criticisms, see Oran Young, "Professor Russett: Industrious Tailor to a Naked Emperor," *World Politics,* vol. 21, no. 3 (April 1969), pp. 486–511; Bruce Russett, "The Young Science of International Politics," *World Politics,* vol. 22, no. 1 (October 1969) pp. 87–94.

It remains necessary to determine the first-stage integration potential of a "region" once it has been delimited according to Russett's criteria.

Selection 9 is "What is the Commonwealth?" by Hedley Bull. The reason for including this essay is mainly to indicate the range of actors that is embraced by the rubric "region." The British Commonwealth may not qualify very well as a "region" in Russett's terms, but it exists as a center of interrelatedness for a group of states, and represents one form of relatively weak post-imperial integration. The degree of interrelatedness, of "regionality" in our terms, of the Commonwealth, as with other political entities, has varied with time. There are other special kinds of groupings with rather vague referents such as "the Atlantic Community" or "the Communist International System." It is evident that the critical dimension of cohesion for these groupings is in some cases a common historical or cultural legacy, in other cases an ideological movement of either expansionist or defensive character, and in still other cases a tacit bargain (for example, the Commonwealth) in which one side (the United Kingdom) receives a measure of deference, and the other side (ex-colonial members) receives certain material or political gains. Each of these groupings exhibits differing degrees of both first-stage and second-stage integration potential. As compared with more conventional regional actors these special groupings exhibit very unstable patterns of integration.

SOME QUALITATIVE ASPECTS OF THE REGIONAL UNIT

In selections 10, 11, and 12, we shall explore some of the issues raised in the notes following Hedley Bull's article (selection 9), especially the consideration of George Ball's ideas on the Atlantic Union and George Modelski's depiction of the Communist international system. Our purpose is to enable a fuller theoretical grasp of the varieties of regional structure and their distinct relationships to the world system. In particular, a closer look will be given to the relationship between *de jure* formations of regional groupings (for example, the Atlantic Union) and *de facto* formations (for example, spheres of influence). The power base of first-stage and second-stage regionalism is also examined to improve our understanding of the conditions under which superpower participation helps or hinders regional integration.

In selection 10, Ronald Yalem's analysis, drawn from his book *Regionalism and World Order*, represents an effort to consider the main lines of theorizing about a regional basis for world order. In this endeavor, Yalem examines small-state regionalism (no principal state among the membership), hegemonial regionalism (a principal state among the membership, spheres of influence), and the relationship between regionalist and universalist ordering efforts in international society.

This initial emphasis is further developed in an extract from George Liska's book *International Equilibrium: A Theoretical Essay on the Politics and Organization of Security*, which analyzes the political deficiencies of *de facto* and *de jure* forms of small-state regionalism. Liska's basic argument is that no regional unit is stable unless it can assume the existence of intraregional security; in this respect, a sphere of influence arrangement tends toward greater stability.

Liska's traditionalist emphasis on power relationships as the basis of order in international society stands in contrast to the belief that the prospects for a just and durable world order depend on voluntary arrangements that embody some form of cultural synthesis. Cultural identity provides the outer boundary of regional units in this more voluntaristic view. To unify the world politically becomes feasible and desirable only after a successful prior experience with cultural unification. Some of the most suggestive thinking along these lines has been done by F. S. C. Northrop who believes that a system of world law cannot become viable until it is first purged of Western cultural bias. Subsequently it might be reconstituted so as to bring to bear all of the living law traditions of the great world cultures. (See, for example, F. S. C. Northrop, *The Meeting of East and West* [Macmillan, New York, 1946]; Northrop, *The Taming of Nations* [Macmillan, New York, 1952].) This more universalist kind of thinking is illustrated in this chapter by a selection from W. Warren Wagar's *The City of Man*.

8

International Regions and the International System

BRUCE M. RUSSETT

WHAT IS A REGION?

The notion of a region, either within a single country or a region of the world embracing a number of nations, has provided a venerable tool in the workshed of political and social research. Like most ancient implements, originally designed for specific purposes by their inventors, it fairly soon was discovered to be an instrument useful for a wide variety of tasks—chopping, splitting, shaving, and smoothing diverse bodies of sociological data. In time different workers refined the tool for particular tasks. While they usually kept the basic name "region" for what they were working with, the implements became so specialized that, like the innumerable breeds of *Canis familiarus*, one would hardly know that they all belonged to the same species. The tool for splitting a political body into various groupings became so different from that for smoothing the edges of economic aggregates that to refer generally to the "region" tool was to invite confusion and to risk producing a botched job. Use of an inappropriate version of the implement in otherwise skilled hands has furthermore often unjustly discredited the tool itself.

Some of the results can be seen in a proverb which many Frenchmen enjoy citing to the fury of their southern neighbors: *L'Afrique commence aux Pyrenées*. Actually, though most Spaniards surely take umbrage, the search for a cultural (rather than a geographic) definition of Europe is not a simple one. In "Western Europe" and "Africa" we have two regions which seem, in matters of political and social consequence, to be relatively homogeneous within themselves but different from each other. But how would we draw the boundaries so as to maximize the similarity within each group and minimize that between them? In the words of a recent article, "Where is the Middle East?"[1] Does it extend from Morocco to Pak-

From Bruce M. Russett, *International Regions and the International System: A Study in Political Ecology*, © 1967 by Rand McNally & Company, Chicago, pp. 1–7, 167–190.

[1]Roderic Davison, "Where is the Middle East?" in Richard Nolte (ed.). *The Modern Middle East.* New York: Atherton Press, 1964.

istan, or should the line be drawn somewhere between? What do we do about Israel which, though right in the middle of any geographic delimitation of the region, still does not fit by any cultural criterion? Or Turkey, which in part is physically on the European continent? Or within a country like the United States: Where is the South? Does it include Texas? Kentucky? And what difference does it make to the politics of a state if it is more, or less, "Southern"?

There is, of course, no simple answer to these questions. Different definitions and different criteria will often produce different regions, and no two analysts may fully agree as to what the appropriate criteria are. This is a problem which has vexed social scientists, both students of international relations and observers of national social and political systems, for decades. In the late 1930's, very substantial research was done on the matter within the United States, under the sponsorship of the Social Science Research Council and the National Resources Committee, with sociologist Howard Odum probably the principal contributor to the body of theory and data which grew up. Yet the various questions involved were never fully answered for the United States even by the distinguished and sophisticated laborers of the time, and nothing comparable to their effort has been devoted to delineating regions of the world. Since the problem is a major one, both in its theoretical and its policy implications, it demands further conceptual clarification and extensive empirical research.

SOME CRITERIA

First we must face certain problems. What definitions of a "region" have been offered in the past, and how can we choose among them? Clearly we want something more satisfactory than the traditional and often nonoperationally defined geopolitical or geostrategic regions long familiar to students of international politics.[2] One possibility is simply to identify an area divided from another by barriers, perhaps geographic ones, producing thus a definition by *isolation* or separateness. One might find a natural region, such as a river valley or plain. But virtually all social scientists, including geographers, would reject this definition. A region, they might say, must be composed of units with common characteristics. Regions should be areas of relative *homogeneity*. This might still be defined in physiographic terms: "any portion of the earth's surface whose physical characteristics are similar," for example.[3] More common, however, is the demand for a homogeneity of economic and social structure. Or, the composite social region might combine "a relatively large degree of homogeneity measured by a relatively large number of purposes or classifications. This means it must comprehend both the natural factors and the social factors."[4]

A perceptive critic of the regionalism concept replies, however, in terms akin to those of our opening paragraph: "Regionalism is not one thing, but many things. The failure to discriminate the many distinct factors that underlie the emergence and persistence of regions is a serious fault of present-day research. Areas of homogeneity have been mistakenly represented as areas of integration."[5] Rupert Vance quotes a geographer's reference to "an *ensemble de rapports* between man and the natural milieu." Therefore regions are sometimes explicitly defined by *interdependence*, as areas within which a higher degree of mutual dependence exists than in relationships outside that area, nodes where people are bound together by mutual dependence arising from common interests.[6] This easily leads to a definition of a region according to *loyalties* or patriotism, "an area of which the inhabitants instinctively feel themselves a part," for example.[7]

Nor is this the end of the possibilities. A region may also be an areal unit defined by an *ad hoc problem*. One suspects that "Southeast Asia's"

[2]For example, Halford J. MacKinder, *Democratic Ideals and Reality*. New York: Henry Holt, 1919.

[3]Rupert B. Vance, "The Regional Concept as a Tool for Social Research," in Merrill Jensen (ed.). *Regionalism in America*. Madison, Wis.: University of Wisconsin Press, 1951, p. 123.

[4]Howard W. Odum, and Harry Estill Moore. *American Regionalism: A Cultural-Historical Approach to National Integration*. New York: Henry Holt, 1938, p. 30.

[5]Louis Wirth, "Limitations of Regionalism" in Merrill Jensen (ed.). *Regionalism in America*. Madison, Wis.: University of Wisconsin Press, 1951, p. 392.

[6]Hawley (1950, p. 260) distinguishes between a homogeneous "region" and a functionally interdependent "community area." (Amos H. Hawley *Human Ecology: A Theory of Community Structure*. New York: Ronald Press, 1950, p. 260.)

[7]Vance, "The Regional Concept," p. 123.

principal claim to regional status with many Americans is simply the threat posed to the whole area by Communist China. This leads to yet another definition, "a device for effecting *control*." The term "Middle East" seems to have been originated by the British in the late Nineteenth Century to refer to an area with common implications for Her Majesty's strategy.[8] According to the analysts of the S.S.R.C. project referred to above, "regionalism provides an economy for the decentralization of political power."[9] A region can therefore be an area of administrative convenience. Perhaps the baldest usage of the latter pragmatic sort is contained in the following statement about regions:

> There is no particular mystique about identifying them and working with them as units of analysis. They are ordinary, common, practical, geographic areas for which social and economic improvement programs have been conceived, planned, and undertaken. Sometimes these regions are defined by natural features such as river basins, agricultural zones, forest districts and the like. Sometimes they find their identity in terms of trading areas within which economic transactions and flows are numerous and dense as compared to their economic relations with outside areas. In some instances, a metropolitan region is the focus of primary concern. . . . In still other instances, a region will be characterized by relative cultural similarity; for example, a tribal region, an ethnic or traditional area with a high degree of self-consciousness, a remote and backward district, or a distinct political jurisdiction such as a province or republic. . . . In other words, the regional concept . . . [has] been found useful and reasonable under a variety of circumstances.[10]

We thus find a combination of description and prescription in the approach of some regionalists. This certainly was true of Odum and Moore, who advocated the delegation to regional authorities —especially one for the Southeast—of political functions which they thought could properly be carried out neither by the federal nor state governments. The same prescriptive orientation is evident in many international relations writings. Much talk, both by scholars and premiers, about regional (e.g., Latin American, Arab) political integration is based upon a presumed homogeneity, or interdependence, or loyalties, which may exist only in the mind of the beholder.[11] The United Nations Charter explicitly allows for security arrangements under regional agreements; NATO is often described as coming under a rather loose interpretation of "regional" in this context.[12]

Even once we finally settle upon a definition or group of definitions—perhaps homogeneity, or homogeneity plus interdependence plus geographical separateness[13]—the problem of finding suitable methods for *delineating regions* remains. The task, in effect, is one of making the definition operational; at best the concept of region is but an analytical device for separating certain areal features thought relevant.[14] If separateness is a primary criterion, physiographic indices might be included. Crop and manufacturing areas might be relevant. The ethnic composition of the populace could be taken into account, as could the level of

[8]Davidson, "Where is the Middle East?"

[9]Odum and Moore, *American Regionalism*, p. 27.

[10]Resources for the Future. *Design for a Worldwide Study of Regional Development*. Baltimore: Johns Hopkins Press, 1966, pp. 3–4.

[11]See the criticism of George Lundberg of Nicholas Spykman and others. George Lundberg, "Regionalism, Science, and the Peace Settlement." *Social Forces*. 21, 2 (1942) pp. 131–37; Nicholas Spykman, *America's Strategy in World Politics*. New York: Harcourt, Brace, 1942.)

[12]The term *regional* is not defined in Article 51 of the Charter. When the Charter was drafted an Egyptian attempt to define it was defeated. Egypt's proposed amendment was, "There shall be considered as regional arrangements of a permanent nature grouping in a given geographical area several countries which, by reason of their proximity, community of interests or cultural, linguistic, historical or spiritual affinities make themselves jointly responsible for the peaceful settlement of any disputes which may arise between them. . . ." (United Nations Conference on International Organization. *Documents of the United Nations Conference on International Organization, San Francisco*, 1945, 12. London and New York: UN Information Organization, 1945.

[13]As for example in the suggestion of Ackerman that one should be concerned with the "compage," the community of features that depict the human occupancy of space. (Edward A. Ackerman, "Regional Research—Emerging Concepts and Techniques in the Field of Geography." *Economic Geography*, 29 (1953), pp. 188–97.)

[14]William, Bunge, *Theoretical Geography*. Lund, Sweden: G. W. K. Gleeruys, 1962.

economic development, the history of the area, and its religious divisions. Frederick Jackson Turner, in discussing possible ways of dividing the West into sections, suggested looking at the way business houses divide up the "territory."[15] Emphasizing the political aspects of regionalism, he once defined a section as a group of states contending with other groups of states. As measures he suggested homogeneity of votes by Congressmen in their role as national legislators, or areas defined by relative homogeneity of vote in presidential and state elections.[16] Perhaps if interdependence is to be a major criterion, the patterns of newspaper circulation (To the papers of which central city do outlying regions subscribe?) or mail, trade, or rail traffic patterns would be good indicators. Or if patriotism or loyalty is considered the key, one might, perhaps through survey research, simply ask a large number of residents, especially of the presumed border areas, of what region they considered themselves to be members.

Most of the large-scale empirical efforts to delineate regions have in fact made use of a wide variety of indices, though they have chiefly emphasized that class of indices which might be expected to measure homogeneity rather than one of the other aspects mentioned above. In using a number of variables one can take advantage of the fact that "cultural traits" are correlated among themselves. If no cultural characteristic were related to any other, a region would have to be determined by a single trait and would have no meaning except in terms of that trait.[17] On the other hand, "while the natural and cultural landscape often coincide they also often clash."[18] And, in addition, different *measures* of the cultural landscape will, though they may frequently correlate, also often clash. "The continental United States cannot be divided into a single set of sizeable regions which meet perfectly all the standards of hypothetical regionality. Compromise is indi-

cated. . . . A region may be delineated upon the basis of many factors, and its extent varies with the factor or factors selected for generalization."[19] In the Appendix to its report the National Resources Committee gives over 100 maps for what it describes as "proto-regions"; i.e., single-factor regions. The factors in this case are the definitions applied by Federal administrative agencies—virtually all are differently delineated. Again according to Louis Wirth,[20]

Various purposes require different areal scope, and it is difficult to find any single criterion that will satisfy the multiple demands of adequacy. . . . Short of considering the whole world as a single region . . . there is no other regional arrangement of lesser scope that will fully satisfy the many interests that clamor for recognition. The best we can do is to make the most reasonable compromises we can invent, which means weighting some functions more heavily than others, and to keep our lines of demarcation flexible enough so that they can be adjusted to changing needs and possibilities.[21]

Odum and Moore conclude, "The mere grouping together of facts and indices does not give us an organic regional entity, but simply gives us a description, an inventory of what has happened and what *is* under the given forces, which must of course be duly analyzed." They add, furthermore, "Many of the cultural factors, such as personality, folkways, motivation, handicaps, are not measurable in terms of our present objective methods."[22] In the end, the criteria "must be chosen not by chance, but in close relation to the definition of

[15]Cited in a letter by Turner. (Fulmer Mood, "The Origin, Evolution, and Application of the Sectional Concept," in Merrill Jensen (ed.). *Regionalism in America*. Madison, Wisconsin: University of Wisconsin Press, 1951, p. 95)

[16]Frederick Jackson Turner, *The Significance of Sections in United States History*. New York: Henry Holt, 1932, p. 288.

[17]Vance, "The Regional Concept," p. 129.

[18]Wirth, "Limitations of Regionalism," p. 392.

[19]National Resources Committee. *Regional Factors in National Planning and Development*. Washington, D.C.: Government Printing Office, 1935, pp. 123, 145.

[20]Wirth, "Limitations of Regionalism," p. 389.

[21]A partially dissenting view is expressed by Walter Isard who, though he recognizes that at present different indices will identify different regions, hopes their proximity, community of interests or cultural, linguistic, historical or spiritual regions on which all the important indices will agree. (Walter Isard, "Regional Science, the Concept of Region, and Regional Structure." *Papers and Proceedings of the Regional Science Association*. Cambridge, Mass.: Regional Science Association, 1956.)

[22]Odum and Moore, *American Regionalism*, pp. 447-448.

the region as a functional unit."[23] Perhaps we return to some idea of interdependence.

If there is no agreement about indices for delineation, even more clearly there is no consensus on the *proper magnitude* of a "region." Again according to the National Resources Committee,[24]

> The term "region" is not commonly applied to small areas, but there seems to be some disagreement as to whether it should be applied to very large sections such as the Middle West, the South, etc., or to smaller subdivisions of these, as for instance, the Corn Belt, the Industrial Piedmont, the Chicago metropolitan area, etc.

If states (or nations) are taken as the basic subunit from which regions are to be built up there is clearly a lower limit to the size of a region. Most often some such political unit is used as the building block, not necessarily because such a course is theoretically most desirable, but because satisfactory data are not readily accessible for smaller units. Even so no consensus on size exists. The size criterion might in large part determine whether "Latin America" emerged as a single region or was divided into several groups like Central America, tropic South America, and temperate South America. Ackerman[25] and Berry and Hankins[26] emphasize an alternative to any attempt to specify a "correct" size for a region: the construction of a *hierarchy* of regions, with several levels of regions and, with progressively tighter criteria, sub-regions.[27] Simon[28] takes a similar position with regard to what he describes as "nearly decomposable systems," defined by a very high ratio of transactions within sub-systems to those between sub-systems.

Finally, there is the sticky problem of *identifying the boundaries* of various regions. If one uses separateness or isolation as a major element in the definition of a region this problem may not be difficult, but otherwise it is. "It seems to be agreed that regional boundaries are usually indefinite, being zones rather than lines. In the majority of instances, therefore, any boundaries which may be drawn will be necessarily arbitary."[29] "The world does not in fact break easily along neatly perforated lines."[30] "It is quite absurd and illogical to seek to establish regional boundaries in detail. They must remain vague, for they are boundaries of a generalization. If, for practical purposes, one finds that he must draw boundaries, then he should do so in a frankly arbitrary manner."[31] Actually, many researchers would contend that the final decision need not be quite so arbitrary, though neither is it likely to be clear-cut. "The characteristics of a region should be most pronounced in its interior. . . . Regions end in transition, seldom in definite boundaries. The areal complex is substantial, it is only its boundary that is inclined to be capricious."[32] Hence we are sure that France is in Western Europe, however defined, but it is hard to know where to put Finland.

All this will sound more than vaguely familiar to students of general systems theory, who have wrestled with the boundary delineation problem for many years and in a variety of empirical domains. These problems are also highly relevant to

[23]Svend Riemer, "Theoretical Aspects of Regionalism." *Social Forces,* 21, 3 (1943), p. 279.

[24]National Resources Committee, *Regional Factors,* p. 145.

[25]Ackerman, "Regional Research."

[26]Brian J. L. Berry, and Thomas D. Hankins. *A Bibliographic Guide to the Economic Regions of the United States.* Chicago: University of Chicago, Department of Geography, 1963.

[27]Berry and Hankins provide an extremely useful bibliography of the literature on regions of the United States. Donald Bogue takes up this suggestion for a hierarchy of regions and urges such an ordering for homogeneous areas of the world, *ignoring both national and provincial boundaries.* For analytical purposes this would have great utility (Brazil is not well described as an average of the industrialized south and the impoverished north) but would, as Bogue recognizes and advocates, require an enormous data-collecting effort. (Donald J. Bogue, "The Need for an International System of Regions and Subregions." *Proceedings and Papers, Regional Science Association,* I [1955], pp. 1–11.)

[28]Herbert A. Simon, ("The Architecture of Complexity." *Proceedings of the American Philosophical Society,* 106, 6 [December 1962], pp. 467–82.)

[29]National Resources Committee, *Regional Factors,* p. 145.

[30]Inis L. Claude, *Swords Into Plowshares.* New York: Random House, 1959, p. 113.

[31]National Resources Committee, *Regional Factors,* p. 147; quoting the reply of Preston E. James to a questionnaire.

[32]V. C. Finch, "Geographical Science and Social Philosophy." *Annals of the Association of American Geographers,* 29, 1 (1939), p. 14.

the efforts of international relations scholars to define and analyze subsystems of the international system. There is no consensus on what constitute the characteristics of an international subsystem, though geographical contiguity, interaction, and perception of belonging to a distinctive *community* are frequently offered. Perhaps a boundary criterion of "differences in the quality or frequency of communications and interactions"[33] is most common. The subsystems hypothesized by various authors are, however, almost invariably geographic regions: Western European or North Atlantic;[34] Middle Eastern;[35] Western African;[36] and South or Southeast Asian.[37] The usage of system and subsystem in many of these cases is much less rigorous than would be demanded by general systems theory—which would require, for instance, that a variety of operations be carried out, preferably by several disciplines, to establish the existence of a specific system.[38] Our approach [here] is not solely a general systems one, yet the definition of regions by multiple criteria that we shall undertake will be important to all who do wish to apply such an approach.

REGIONS AND SUBSYSTEMS

"Peace by pieces" is a well known functionalist aphorism. It could as well be the slogan of an enthusiast for regional integration, whether that advocate sees regionalism as a step in the creation of "building blocks" for worldwide institutions, or as a plateau for the development of a multibloc international system. Whatever the purpose, the emphasis on piece work is widespread. Given such an outlook, just what potential pieces can be identified from the various aggregates examined here; what clusters of countries, or regions, exhibit the characteristics required for integration or seem to have a significant potential to become integrated blocs?

We shall in this [discussion] be strict constructionists, asking what aggregates show essentially the same *boundaries* as identified by different criteria. That is, in the general systems sense, what groupings can properly be termed subsystems of the international system; what clusters include the same nations, and only those nations, whether aggregated according to socio-cultural similarity, common political orientations, institutional memberships, transactions, or proximity? Are there indeed *any* such aggregates where the boundaries consistently coincide from one characteristic to the next? Such an area would, by definition, be one that was relatively homogeneous and showed . . . [not only] high interaction but clear distinctiveness from the rest of the world and low rates of transaction with its neighbors.

The traditional nation-state best typifies such a unit, with a clearly defined political boundary that marks the boundary of a monetary system and a set of customs and currency controls which provide a barrier to foreign trade, a cultural and often a linguistic dividing line, and perhaps a distinct change in popular political values as well. These boundaries may be extremely divisive and impermeable, such as those between Israel and Jordan or Egypt, or divide less distinctive and more interacting units such as those of the new Western Europe. But whether the boundary is an iron curtain or merely a white picket fence, it is likely to coincide for all these characteristics. Where it does not, such as the enclave of German-speaking people in the Italian Alps, or those parts of Canada that are tied especially tightly to the United States economy, stresses arise and there may be demands either that the boundaries be brought into coincidence (the German-speaking areas be returned to the Austrian political and economic unit) or, under other circumstances, sometimes for the removal of the boundary alto-

[33]F. K. Berrien, "Homeostasis in Groups." *General Systems: Yearbook of the Society for General Systems Research,* 9 (1964), p. 207.

[34]Stanley Hoffmann, "Discord in Community: The North Atlantic Area as a Partial International System." *International Organization,* 17, 3 (1963), pp. 521–49.

[35]Leonard Binder, "The Middle East as a Subordinate International System." *World Politics,* 10, 3 (1958), pp. 408–29.

[36]Thomas Hodgkin, "The New West African State System." *University of Toronto Quarterly,* 31 (1961), pp. 74–82.

[37]Michael Brecher, "International Relations and Asian Studies: The Subordinate State System of Southern Asia." *World Politics,* 15, 2 (1963), pp. 212–35; George Modelski, "International Relations and Area Studies: The Case of South-East Asia." *International Relations,* 2 (1961), pp. 143–55.

[38]O. R. Young, "The Impact of General Systems Theory on Political Science," *General Systems: Yearbook of the Society for General Systems Research,* 9 (1964), p. 239.

gether and the political unification of the entire area. While there will nevertheless always be examples of fuzzy or incongruent boundaries between nation-states, those boundaries are virtually certain to be sharper and more consistent than those delineating international subsystems or regions. A second question relevant to finding areas of integration concerns the *absolute level* of capabilities—homogeneity, economic interdependence, etc.—that is achieved within the area defined by a given boundary. We shall postpone examination of that question . . .

There is *no* region or aggregate of national units that can in the very strict sense of boundary congruence be identified as a subsystem of the international system. . . . such a subsystem must be identified empirically by the agreement of several different criteria. Trade interdependence could establish one set of limits, but these would have to match closely with others.[39] Inclusion in any of our regions always marks a rather arbitrary point on a continuum, not something that can always be identified as the simple presence or absence of a characteristic.[40] This is a common enough problem in social research where for our intellectual convenience we often convert problems of "more-or-less" to ones of "yes-or-no," and we can bear in mind that our cut-offs, though presented as lines, must be remembered also as shaded zones. Even allowing for this arbitrariness, however, there is in our findings no area where the inclusions and exclusions are the same over all criteria.

[39]See, for example, Talcott Parsons' identification of a system as marked by a high level of interactions and also some degree of complementarity of expectations. Etzioni uses the term merely to refer to interdependent units, emphasizing that a *system* need not be *integrated*. (Talcott Parsons, "Order and Continuity in the International Social System," in James N. Rosenau [ed.]. *International Politics and Foreign Policy*, New York: Free Press, 1961, pp. 324–325; Amitai Etzioni, *Political Unification*. New York: Holt, Rinehart & Winston 1965, p. 6]. I, of course, agree with the latter, since common membership in a system is necessary for integration but not sufficient.

[40]In the most rigorous general systems usage, however, one would expect to find boundaries marked by step-level changes in the quantity of information transmitted (James G. Miller, "Living Systems: Cross-Level Hypotheses." *Behavioral Science*, 10, 4 (1965), p. 385). Perhaps this would, however, be true of national systems, emphasizing once again how loose or "open" are our regional approximations to subsystems.

COMMUNIST EASTERN EUROPE

Searching one's knowledge of world politics for an example of a group of states marked by high intra-group homogeneity, clear qualitative differences from nearby states outside the group, and especially distinct transaction boundaries, brings quickly to mind the "Soviet Bloc," or, less anachronistically, the Soviet Union and its allies of Eastern Europe. But political events of the past several years . . . show how far even that area is from deserving, in the rigorous sense, a label like "Sino-Soviet Bloc" or "Communist International System."[41] We shall study this and several other aggregates which have at least some of the characteristics of a subsystem with the aid of a graphic presentation illustrated in Figure 1.

[In the previous chapters of *International Regions and the International System,*] each of the factor analyses . . . (for homogeneity, similar political behavior, institutional ties, trade transactions, and proximity) was compared with the others for approximately the same point in time (trade in 1954, U.N. behavior in 1952, and international organizations in 1951 are compared with each other, as are trade and U.N. voting in 1963, and international organizations in 1962). Each of these is also compared with the cultural homogeneity and proximity analyses, which were done for only one point in time.[42] For each of these sets of analyses we have a total of ten paired comparisons. By finding a factor which is more or less closely identified with an area that we hypothesize may have some of the characteristics of a subsystem, and following it through one comparison after another for the factor or factors which it most closely resembles in other analyses, we can discover the degree to which the boundaries do indeed coincide over different criteria. A group which fell *between* factors (e.g., Latin America in the late 1963 UN) will not match well with a

[41]If "system" is defined differently, of course, the term may still apply (e.g., Modelski, "*International Relations.*")

[42]Unless one is prepared to engage in rather finer geological measurements than could be carried out on a table-model globe, proximity is unchanging anyway. Cultural homogeneity is of course not static, but problems of the accuracy and availability of ecological data are still too serious to permit confident assessment of any but the most gross changes over a period as short as a decade, and it was not attempted.

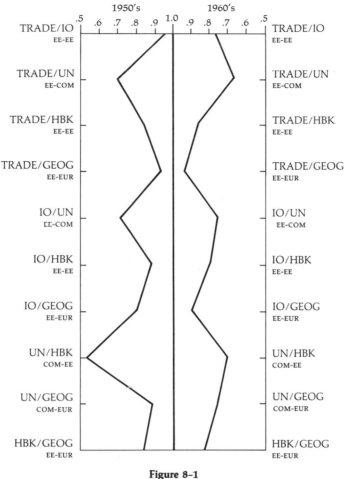

Figure 8–1
Communist Eastern Europe.

group which was closely identified with a *single* factor in another analysis—as is appropriate because of the former's indistinct boundaries.

The graph shows, for Communist Eastern Europe, the two sets of comparisons, on the left for the early 1950's and on the right for the early 1960's, divided by the center line. Each paired comparison is marked off at the margin, and the names of the two factors being matched are given just below the labels identifying the empirical domains being compared. The center line indicates the value of 1.00 for the index of agreement between two factors, and this tapers off on either side toward an index of 0.50. The points marking the actual agreement scores are connected by the jagged lines running down the figure. Thus if

there were an Eastern Europe factor that coincided exactly with another factor in each of the other analyses for that time period, its continuity would be marked by the center line at 1.00. The amount of actual deviation from such an ideal is measured, over all ten comparisons, by the area between the jagged line and the center.[43]

---

[43]All indices of agreement of 0.50 or higher between factors are listed . . . [in Table 1.] The graphs are limited to illustrating those matches that seem to trace a single cluster. For trade, only the Chooser analyses were used in the comparisons, since addition of the Chosen factors would have complicated the presentation and discussion without adding substantial information. (The Chooser and Chosen analyses correlated an average of 0.90 with each other for 1954 and 1963. As indicated

There is a core group of states, made up of the U.S.S.R., Poland, Czechoslovakia, Romania, Bulgaria, and Hungary, that are always found together. In no case, however, do the boundaries encompass only these nations. For the early 1960's Albania is usually present also, but for the United Nations voting cluster, and for international organization memberships (IO) as well, it is distinctly marginal, and entirely absent for trade. Its recent independent pattern of behavior, in fact, has served to bring Albania's overall pattern into greater consistency, since it was even in the 1950's very poorly tied into the East European group by the interactional and structural bonds of trade and organizational membership. Had those links been stronger in the early years either the desire or the ability to pursue such an independent policy later might have been prevented.

Not only is China the mainstay of Albanian defiance of Moscow, in structural and behavioral terms its relationship to Eastern Europe is much like Albania's, only more. Institutionally it is aloof from the European communist organizations, and has always been so. For a while it carried on a fair volume of trade with the Soviet Union and, to a lesser extent, with other communist states, but its size has always permitted a high degree of economic self-sufficiency. As a very poor and Asian nation, its socio-cultural profile from the *Handbook* (Hbk) shows much more clearly some of the tendencies exhibited by Albania. Distance, and Mao's historical accession to power without Soviet military support, provide further bases of independence. It was not during the period analyzed a member of the United Nations, but its other behavior in international politics indicates that it would hardly have been more conforming with the bloc than was Albania in 1963. China's ties to the other communist countries have never been as strong as those of the East European states, hence its recent behavioral independence is not surprising.

---

earlier, the Chooser factor gives a better indication of preference, though not of impact.) Because of difficulties in data gathering the years measured for each criterion are not always the same, especially for the early 1950's. The high agreement between each of these and the corresponding analysis for as much as a decade later, however, strongly indicate that little noise is introduced by this necessity.

. . . Yugoslavia is not notably different in culture or social organization from the other communist states; it is geographically proximate and carries on a high level of commercial transactions with them. But the Yugoslav government has chosen neither to tie itself intimately to its neighbors by a large number of institutional bonds, nor to behave too much like them in international politics. Actually the close economic association is a fairly recent phenomenon, for during the years while Yugoslav political independence was being established Belgrade either cut off, or had terminated by the bloc, the bulk of its normal trade with the East. Only with the improvement in political relations over the past decade has the trade level returned to something approaching the original volume, at the same time without diminishing notably the commerce that had been established with the West during the interim. Finland, Austria, Egypt, and a number of other states of Central Europe and the Mediterranean carry on substantial trade with the communists but are not otherwise closely associated with them.

In most respects East Germany does not differ greatly from the other communist states. It is not a member of the United Nations, but if it were it surely would vote no more independently than Poland or Czechoslovakia. But in institutional ties at the level of formal governmental organizations it is, like China and much more than Albania, very isolated indeed. Much of this is in the communist system compensated by a functional equivalent, the formally non-governmental but politically most relevant ties among communist parties. The presence of 20 Red Army divisions also provides a unique "bond." Nevertheless the lack of broad intergovernmental organizations linking East Germany with other communist states might some day make a difference to a government that wanted to find an extra degree of freedom.

Cuba is of course geographically very distant from the other communist nations, and is but loosely connected with them in some other ways too. The socio-cultural data from the *Handbook* were largely for the late 1950's and so did not take account of the changes introduced by Fidel Castro. Had they done so, Cuba's factor loadings in that analysis probably would not have been very different from, say, such a semideveloped East

European state as Romania. By a combination of choice and the United States-directed embargo, Cuba's trade has become heavily directed toward Eastern Europe, and in international politics Havana acts like a good communist capital. However, it is not yet a member of many of the purely communist organizations, and given the irrelevance to it of many of the purely East European institutions is not likely to develop many. This, plus distance, plus the partly forced and artificial character of its current foreign trade pattern, plus the social and cultural subtleties that would not fully show up on the gross *Handbook* dimensions in any event, provide much of the potential for a future independent course by Cuba. Yet the longer current bonds are maintained, the stronger they are likely to become. With spill-over into the cultural and organizational realms, the accretion of ties over the years probably makes a completely independent course less likely the longer it is delayed.

Even for the communist "subsystem," therefore, the term *subsystem* is inexact and the boundaries are indistinct. For some purposes Yugoslavia, Cuba, China, East Germany, and Albania are in, for others one or more of them are not. It is not, in precise sense, a bloc. Nor is this entirely a phenomenon of the post-Stalin thaw and the surfacing polycentrist tendencies. Examination of the graph shows that the fit among the factors was only slightly tighter in the 1950's than since. Yugoslavia's political independence was very evident even then, as were the weak institutional ties of China, Albania, and East Germany to the rest of the bloc. The admission of a number of reliable East European states to the United Nations has perhaps disguised, on the measure of voting, some increases in behavioral independence and compensated for the maverick activities of Albania. The entry of mainland China, which would hardly be more docile, would make these disparities more evident.

Still, much of the evidence of polycentrism in the 1960's can be seen as the natural and even expectable result of the failure to create more bonds, across a number of dimensions, in the previous decade. What remained latent during the period of Soviet military occupation of Eastern Europe, and was suppressed by strategic factors and the atmosphere of military tension in the 1950's, has since become manifest. Under Ro-

mania's leadership efforts to weaken the controls exerted by institutions have spread from the economic sphere (COMECON) to the military (Warsaw Pact). Unless force, in substantial quantities, is employed to reunify the bloc, the prospects for a return of the wayward are poor.[44] There has been some trend among the communist states for the patterns of cultural relationship, transaction, behavior, and institutional structure to be brought into agreement, and this is to be expected since each of these promotes the other. But the opposite side of the coin is that the absence of several contributes to the atrophy of those that are present. The prospects for retaining the long-term allegiance of Cuba and East Germany are suspect, and will require, by the other communist states, assiduous cultivation over a wide range of activities.

LATIN AMERICA, WESTERN COMMUNITY, AND ASIA

Latin America is another region of common parlance, and one where, in the 1950's at least, the congruence of differently defined boundaries was quite high, in most instances exhibiting an index of agreement above 0.90. Institutional structure, behavior, transactions, cultural homogeneity, and geographic proximity all gave much the same patterns. As Figure 2 shows, the major discrepancy was for trade, where the hemisphere was split into two components, a North and Central American aggregate, and one for South America. The North and Central American group provides the closer fit, but a second jagged line, farther from the 1.0 mark, is included to identify South America's fit as well.

Recall the pattern of clustering in previous chapters and it will be apparent that not all of Latin America is equally involved in this potential subsystem, but rather that the core group is to be found in Central America and other continental states bordering on the Caribbean, with the nations in the lower half of South America, and of

---

[44]Note the very interesting proposition of Etzioni (*Political Unification*), that the relationship between coercion and successful unification is curvilinear; i.e., some force can help, but much creates strains that will result in eventual dissolution.

Table 1
All indices of Agreement Exceeding .50 Among Factors at Approximately the Same Point in Time, 1950's and 1960's

1960's	Geography				Handbook				IO							UN					
	Africa	Asia	Europe	West. Hem.	Afro-Asia	East. Eur.	Latin Am.	West. Com.	Asia	Arabs	French Aft.	British Aft.	East. Eur.	Latin Am.	West. Eur.	Cons. Arab	Afro-Asia	Communists	Braz. Aft.	Iberia	West. Com.
Trade																					
N. & C. America				.95			.93							.98							.79
S. America				.64			.70							.85					.66		
West. Eur.								.74							.84						.53
East. Eur.			.94			.87							.77		.51						
British Carib.	.55			.75				.77				.78									
British Com.	.78				.62							.85									
French Com.	.90				.88						.96								.79		
Arabs					.57					.75						.84					
Asia		.97			.96				.97								.52				.64
UN																					
West. Com.			.75					.96						.74	.71						
Iberia			.50	.79			.98						.76								
Braz. Afr.				.59			.72				.93			.57							
Communists	.79		.76	.55		.71		.55	.81			.83	.80								
Afro-Asia			.64	.53	.99				.76				.50					.50			
Cons. Arabs				.56	.67					.84											

UN		West. Com.	Latin Am.	Communists	Afro-Asia
	West. Com.		.68	.83	.51
	Latin Am.	.92	.69		.73
	Communists		.70		
	Afro-Asia	.59		.84	.96

Correlation matrix comparing regional delineations across five classification schemes (Trade, UN, IO, Handbook, Geography), 1950's.

Scheme	Region	Trade N. & C. America	S. America	N. Atlantic	East. Eur.	British Com.	French Com.	Mid. East	Asia	UN West. Com.	Latin Am.	Communists	Afro-Asia	IO West. Eur.	Latin Am.	East. Eur.	White Com.	Mid. East	Arabia	S. E. Asia	Handbook West. Com.	Latin Am.	East. Eur.	Afro-Asia
IO	West. Eur.			.88						.85											.99			
	Latin Am.		.98 .81								.97											.97		
	East. Eur.				.95							.71											.90	
	White Com.					.74		.50 .92		.92		.53									.78			
	Mid. East							.50													.73			
	Arabia						.62						.99								.91 .78			
	S. E. Asia								.58				.70								.53 .96			.96
Handbook	West. Com.									.80				.97			.76							.78
	Latin Am.										.97				.97							.96		
	East. Eur.		.84				.80 .65 .94			.62			.98			.88							.83	.60
	Afro-Asia	.99	.85	.74		.87					.95	.88 .63	.62				.80	.50 .67	.56 .94	.87 .98 .75			.69	
Geography	West. Hem.	.99								.80				.92 .96			.86 .65	.50 .65	.56		.78			
	Europe			.93							.95													
	Asia				.63	.90			.95				.62											
	Africa				.67	.90 .66							.69											.60 .69

1950's

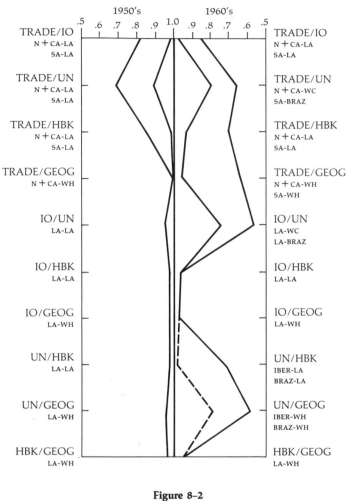

Figure 8–2
Latin America.

course the United States and Canada, very much more marginal. The group of socio-culturally homogeneous states, as defined by the *Handbook* variables, excluded Haiti, the British colonies, Argentina, and, on the whole, Uruguay, Chile, Puerto Rico, and Cuba. The latter were appreciably more developed economically, and hence characterized by a more urban or industrial culture than the less-developed majority. The highest loadings on the Western Hemisphere factor from the analysis of geographical proximities were also for Central American states, with the North American nations and Chile-Uruguay-Argentina about equally far down the list.

Some of these divisive tendencies were reaffirmed in the analyses for the 1960's, to the point that most of the agreement scores are lower for the right-hand half of the graph. Cuba and the Dominican Republic were no longer identified with the Central American trading group, Cuba of course becoming heavily involved with Eastern Europe instead. Cuba, the Dominican Republic, and Uruguay also had by then slipped quite far down the list of states who belonged to large numbers of Latin-American oriented international organizations. Haiti had always been very marginal. And Cuba's behavior in the United Nations was emphatically not that of a Latin American nation, but of a communist (East European) state. Haiti, Bolivia, and Uruguay had, by 1963, reinforced earlier tendencies to vote often with the Afro-Asian neutralists, and the Latin Americans in general did not show a high degree of cohesion. By noting their fairly high loadings on two different factors we were able . . . to identify a general Latin American group, but the dispersion was substantial with some members absent and some, like Argentina, quite closely identified with the Western Community. By some, but hardly all, criteria, the Iberian mother-countries were more like Latin America as a whole than were some of the states physically located in the hemisphere.

In sum, Latin America in the 1950's possessed many of the attributes of an international subsystem, especially if one looked not at the 20 republics in toto, but most closely at the group of nations in Central America and the area once known as Gran Colombia. But by the beginning of the 1960's some of this had disappeared. North America, which had always been so distinct culturally, was not less so, and in United Nations voting behavior, trade, and international organization membership, there had been a distinct falling off of several states from the Caribbean and the southern half of South America. Of all the world's geographic regions, Latin America as a whole exhibited the sharpest decline in intra-regional trade as a proportion of its total income over the decade. . . . The Latin American Free Trade Area experienced very little success in correcting the situation, though trade among the *Central* American states, with their common market, did rise substantially; hence the finding . . . of a more distinct split into *two* Latin trading groups. There is, perhaps, a rising degree of coherence in mainland Central America on several counts, but the area is not yet sufficiently distinct from its neighbors by most criteria to constitute a subsystem by itself. Extrapolating the trends of the past decade, prospects for the next few years seem to be possibly for rising unity in Central America, but not elsewhere, either in the sense of an all-encompassing Latin American system or of a competing center in the southern continent. In the entire Western Hemisphere the composition of various clusterings (by homogeneity, trade, etc.) differs too greatly, and varies from smallish subgroups to encompassing the entire two continents, to constitute the boundaries of a tight subsystem.

Many of these same general comments apply to the *Western Community* which, like the previous major aggregates, includes a core group of countries who are included by any criteria, but for which the other exclusions and inclusions vary widely. For trade, international organizations, and geography a group readily identifiable as Western Europe constitutes this core. (The agreement between the trade and geography factors, however, was so poor as to be less than 0.50, as is indicated by the arrows pointing beyond the 0.50 line on the graph.) At its heart are the countries of the Common Market, plus Austria, Switzerland, Denmark and surprisingly, the United Kingdom. These are to be found in each of the Western Community or Western Europe clusters. By the criteria examined here, this group of countries does possess the minimal requirements for political integration. Whether the present degree of integration will grow, or whether the needs for political unification can be met, is a question we cannot answer from this general overview. But this cluster of ten nations is the largest aggregate to be found over all five criteria in the entire analysis. The strength of Britain's ties with the continent is especially notable, and may hold a major portent for the future.

Except for the fairly tight trading group of the 1960's, the other clusters include most or all of the remaining non-communist states of Europe. Spain and Portugal are absent from the socio-cultural and United Nations clusters, and marginal geographically and institutionally as well. Turkey's cultural differences are profound, and it is also linked but weakly by commercial bonds to Europe. Its continued association with the European nations in international organizations, and the maintenance of its very pro-Western orientation in international politics and the United Nations, is open to doubt since these orientations draw only limited reinforcement. Cyprus was found to be fairly Western in culture, but not joined with many European states by trade, institutions, or political behavior.

The strongly European characteristics of this grouping are shown by the in-and-out nature of some non-European states' relations to it. The

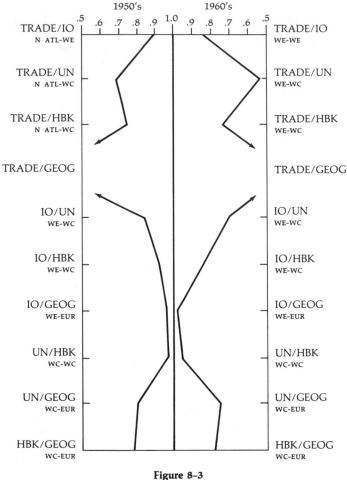

Figure 8–3
Western Community.

United States and Canada share a common Western culture with their European allies, and generally agree with them on most of the issues of international politics which are posed in the United Nations General Assembly. Their physical distance, however, is reflected in, and reinforced by, only a limited degree of association in international organizations and a limited commercial dependence upon them. The same remarks apply, with greater force, for Australia and especially for New Zealand, whose current institutional and transactional bonds with the rest of the Western Community are indeed tenuous. Israel, and more surprisingly Japan, however, belong with the European countries on every criterion except proximity (and Israel is not really so distant). For international organization membership they rank low in the Western Community list, and strictly speaking Israel's United Nations voting pattern looks more like that of a Latin American country than of a European. But despite its location Israel was one of the small group of countries identified as Western Europe on the 1963 trade analysis, and while Japan was outside that group it nevertheless fell only just below the cut-off mark employed. If the world of the next several decades is to see a very general kind of agreement and common interest among the Western industrialized countries, with interests that come increasingly into conflict with the non-Western underdeveloped nations of Asia and Africa, Israel and Japan, now "have" states,

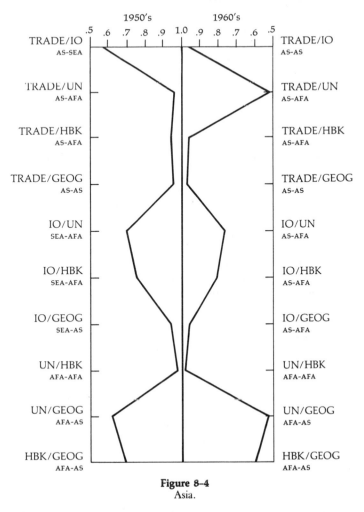

Figure 8-4
Asia.

are much more likely to be aligned with their rich developed fellows than with their geographic neighbors.

Yet these results suggest that the prospects for widespread co-operation and presentation of a common front should not be exaggerated. In the ideal-type sense defined for this book there is no Western or North Atlantic subsystem, and though there is a core area of Western Europe, its edges are too inconsistent to constitute boundaries in any strict sense. Nor has there been any identifiable trend toward sharpening these boundaries. The differences among the clusters identified by the various criteria were, on the average, every bit as great in the 1960's as in the 1950's.

We shall look at a number of other regional subgroups in the following pages, but only one, *Asia,* has sufficient continuity from one criterion to another in both periods to warrant serious consideration as a possible international subsystem. The level of agreement here actually is not better than for the Western Community, and appreciably lower than for either Eastern Europe or Latin America. The closest fit is obtained for the broadest groupings—the Afro-Asians from the United Nations, and the Afro-Asians as defined by a broad sort of cultural homogeneity. These are not *just* Asian groupings, but ones that include a substantial number of Arab North African states as well. A more limited Asian group showed up in each of the trade, international organization, and, naturally, the geographic analyses. They agree rather well with each other, but usually not at all well with the all-encompassing clusters from the UN and *Handbook* studies.

In any case these are very large aggregates which hide considerable diversity, and once more there are substantial variations in the inclusions and exclusions. Japan is pretty regularly absent; it is Asian in hardly more than the strict geographic sense, plus substantial commercial involvement with its Southeast Asian neighbors and, especially, former colonies. The Afro-Asian cluster of states who vote together regularly in the General Assembly is certainly broad enough in geographical terms, but it omits a large number of countries that vote with the West at least on Cold War issues. Such states include some Arab and Southeast Asian states, and the very pro-U.S. voting records of Japan, Taiwan, and the Philippines. South Korea and South Vietnam would surely, had they been UN members, also not have behaved as cold war neutralists. The Philippines was absent from the Asian socio-cultural group, primarily because of the strong differentiating role that religion took on in that inductive analysis. The international organization cluster for Asia included most non-communist Asian nations except for politically untouchable Taiwan and Afghanistan and Nepal, whose geographic isolation has permitted them to remain as aloof from international trade and world politics as almost any modern political unit. China is absent from all of these Asian clusters except for geography and modest commercial ties; the same would doubtless have been true for North Vietnam and North Korea had we possessed enough data to include them formally in the analyses.

Aside from the boundary problem, there is not even any major Asian cluster that simply can meet the demand of inclusion in the same group over all five criteria. Seven states cluster together on at least four: socio-cultural similarity, trade, international organization membership, and proximity. They differ greatly, however, in their orientations in international politics. On many issues, especially cold war ones, Malaysia, Pakistan, and Thailand have voted with the developed Western nations, to the point where in 1963 their United Nations voting patterns were about the same as most Latin Americans. India, Indonesia, Burma, and Ceylon, however, were leaders of the Afro-Asian neutralist group. Possibly governmental changes in some of these states (as in Indonesia) or the rise of China to complicate the simple cold war divisions of the original United States-Soviet conflict (as it has affected the original alignments of both Pakistan and India) will mitigate the division between these two sub-groups. The effect so far, however, has been moderate, and the split continued to be manifested on issues like seating Communist China in 1966. And the bonds would still be highly tenuous; for instance by our indices India and Pakistan do not differ notably, but it is perfectly obvious that their antagonisms are more profound than their current, relatively minor, and perhaps temporary variations in cold war outlook.

REGIONS AND INAPPROPRIATE COMPARISON

Thus there is no sharply identifiable Asian or Southeast Asian system either, even less than could be found for other areas. There is a real danger, in the facile use of regional labels we all employ when discussing international relations or comparative politics, of comparing the incomparable. In so many respects Japan is *not* an Asian country, nor Haiti a Latin American one, nor Turkey either a European or an Asian state, that to expect them to behave like their geographic neighbors, or to have political and social systems like them, is often extremely misleading. Similar strictures apply, with only a little less force, to treating Argentina or Uruguay as typical Latin Americans, Spain and Portugal as Western Europeans (Latin America begins at the Pyrenees), or even the Philippines as an Asian state.

These distinctions naturally are well-known to an area specialist on Latin America or Southeast Asia, and he may not find many new insights here for considering the particular intellectual problems of his specialty. The firm evidence of these differences may nevertheless surprise him, since comparative data to document and sharpen his more intuitive perceptions are not always readily available. Also, it is sometimes possible to become so engrossed with one's particular tree as to forget to ask systematically how it is similar to, and differs from, the adjoining flora. And for the analyst with more general interests and lacking a regional specialization, or for the regional specialist when he wants to go beyond the geographic area of his expertise, these findings may be more instructive. To assume uncritically that the kind of general program for economic development and political stability that worked well in Chile would have equal success in, say, Honduras, would be extremely unsound. Similarly, to treat Spain as potentially like France, only poorer, might be very unwise. Note that this argument is not that no use can be made of cross-national comparisons, or that the experiences of one state cannot suggest the prospects for another, or that every case is unique and must be considered as a *tabula rasa*. The whole methodological approach of this volume is just the contrary. It is always an empirical question as to when and under what circumstances one can generalize from one nation's experience to another's. But some cautions and general guidelines are required to suggest where such comparisons may be most fruitful and where there is a special risk that they will be misleading. I would suggest that they can most successfully be attempted between countries within the same group as defined by *all* criteria of this volume. Whatever the incomparabilities and risks in analysis, the most valid results should arise with countries that cluster together by all or at least most of the criteria.

For there is indeed, for each major aggregate, a core, a limited number of states found in each of the clusters. Nor is the disagreement from one criterion to the next so violent that we cannot expect, in a general sense, to find the same states associated from one analysis to the next. The Philippines and Pakistan are absent from one or two, but they are more likely to be found with an indentifiable Asian grouping than not. The *majority* of states grouped with Asia on trade will be there for international organizations, and vice versa. Thus in a general sense the regional labels we use when discussing international relations or comparative politics do hold. There is in the strict meaning of the term no all-purpose region, but for many purposes Asia or Latin America correctly connotes the same cluster of states by most criteria. One primary danger is of being too confident that this general observation will hold in the particular case. The other is in employing the *geographic* labels carelessly. Our moral is that for purposes of generalization one should not refer to Asia unless one specifically means to refer to countries with a certain *physical* proximity to each other and distance from the rest of the world. For

some types of strategic analysis, perhaps, such a usage is proper. But the political systems of Asia form a much less valid subject for generalization. It would be far safer, and productive of more accurate propositions, to discuss "the political systems of the non-communist underveloped states of Asia." While inelegant, the precision obtained by excluding such very deviant cases as Japan and mainland China should bring its own rewards.

SMALLER REGIONAL GROUPINGS

There are several other aggregates of nations that do not have overall boundaries even as sharply delineated as those of the above four groups, and thus cannot be considered promising candidates for the label of subsystem or "all-purpose" region. They are clusters of states that agree very substantially over two or three criteria, but fall within a much larger grouping, with poor internal differentiation, for the others.

One of the most important such groups is the Arab or *Middle East* cluster. . . . it did not stand out as separate from the other Afro-Asian states, but the addition of other variables to that analysis might well have brought out the distinctive character of this relatively compact and identifiable geographic area. It emerged clearly from the analysis of international organization membership as a predominantly Arab group except for the absence of Yemen and the marginal inclusion of Iran and Israel. Much the same group, but without Iran and Israel, was found in the trading patterns, save for the absence of the former French North African territories—Morocco, Tunisia, and Algeria—which carried on the bulk of their commerce within the franc area. Both of these were more clearly Arab groups (rather than general Middle East) in the 1960's than in the 1950's, indicating *some* progress toward Arab unity. All the members of the trading cluster shared the further historic bond of inclusion, in the relatively recent past, within the Ottoman Empire, though Turkey itself was consistently outside any current Arab aggregate.

In international politics, however, there was another division that did not coincide with these. Most of the Arab countries voted with the Afro-Asian states on the great majority of issues in 1963, and they were helped to do so by the virtual absence of Palestine-related issues from the 18th

Session agenda, the one policy dimension on which the Arabs unite and can be readily distinguished from other Afro-Asians. But a minority of the Arabs, three of the remaining monarchies plus Mauritania and democratic Lebanon, hived off to form an identifiable Conservative Arab grouping. While this separate group was larger than it had been in previous sessions, its roots nevertheless go back at least to 1957, shortly after Libya and Jordan were admitted. Saudi Arabia balances somewhere between the two groups.

Arab unity is still a myth and perhaps an aspiration, not yet a reality. If one is looking for clusters that emerge by all of the criteria we set, it requires at least three to account for most of the Arab states. One can perhaps be called the radical or revoluntionary Arabs of the geographic heartland: Egypt, Syria, Iraq, and Sudan. A second is Algeria, Morocco, and Tunisia of the Maghreb, and the other comprises the geographically dispersed states of Jordan, Libya, Lebanon, and Kuwait. This last is especially tenuous, since important political and economic characteristics of Lebanon make it marginal, and, as of 1963 at least, Kuwait had not yet obtained membership in too many of the international organizations of the area. Saudi Arabia, and much more so Yemen, cannot readily be placed with either, and Yemen's situation is unlikely to change before its problems of political regime are settled. The governments of the radical states have at various times made moves, serious or half-hearted, toward political unification, but, except for the brief union of Syria and Egypt, nothing has come of it. Their experiences of the past few years do not encourage much confidence in their prospects for the immediate future. Yet except possibly for the Maghreb states, their potential is greater than it is anywhere else in the Middle East. That alone is sufficient commentary on the likelihood that a strong and wide-ranging Arab nation will emerge during the lifetimes of the area's present rulers.

Possibly better prospects lie in black *Africa*, especially among most of the former French colonies there. Excluding the Arabs, all the ex-French African territories except the radical states of Guinea and Mali vote together (with others) in the cluster we labelled Brazzaville Africans. These same nations (again with Guinea absent) belonged to the Former French Africa cluster we identified in the international organization analysis. And except for some of the smallest and/or landlocked states, they again appear together

(with France, North Africa, and former Indo-China) as a distinctive trading group. . . . Altogether they form a group with sufficiently distinct boundaries in 1963 that we should illustrate the congruence with another graph, Figure 5. No comparisons are given for the 1950's because too few French African territories were included in the analyses for the matchings to be instructive.

Remember the presence of the former *Belgian* Congo in each of these groups. Congo (Leopoldville) was not a part of the former colonial empire, yet it trades substantially with the French Africans, votes with them in the General Assembly, and belongs to most of the same international organizations. While it is sometimes a marginal member of these clusters (especially for interna-

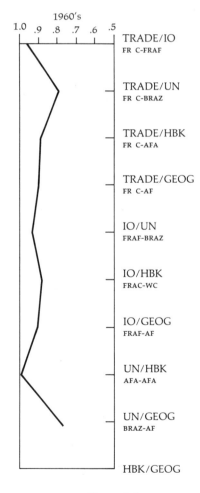

Figure 8–5
Former French Africa.

tional organizations) its presence here at all is instructive, indicating that this French African group is an association chosen by the leaders of independent nations, not a hang-over from the past. It seems even more a case of voluntary choice when one recalls the Congo's geographic position. The country is substantially to the south of most of the French territories. It borders on two, but is not at the center of French Africa, thus providing the opportunity for an association without compelling it. Perhaps this aggregation, particularly the Congo's inclusion, is made possible only by the presence of French-speaking elites in power everywhere, and will not outlast the eventual politicization of the speakers of different African languages and dialects. But for the moment these governments do seem drawn together for at least limited purposes in a way that is not wholly accounted for by their colonial past.

Although it included the Belgian Congo, and did not incorporate France or the former French territories of Asia or North Africa, the lineage between the preceding group and the French Union was quite apparent. No such clear lineage exists for the British Commonwealth, which is split into many, sometimes overlapping, subgroups. The states predominantly settled by Europeans (Canada, Australia, New Zealand, and the United Kingdom itself, but not South Africa) vote together regularly in the United Nations, carry on substantial mutual trade, and certainly have very similar socio-cultural profiles. These links are not, however, bolstered by a substantial number of common international organization memberships, with New Zealand's bonds to the others being especially weak in this regard. And of course these four nations are dispersed across the face of the earth. The Western Hemisphere states of Trinidad, former British Guiana, and Jamaica share similar broad socio-cultural profiles, trade some with each other (though British Guiana's ties were weak), and vote much the same way in the General Assembly (again omitting British Guiana, which was not then a member). Yet even this small group is not joined by many institutional bonds, and the failure of the West Indian Federation is still a recent memory. Among the ex-British colonies of Asia there is also no very notable unity except among quite small groups. As we showed during the broader Asian discussion above, Malaysia, Pakistan, India, Ceylon, and Burma share some common links, but their behavior on issues of international politics splits them

into a pair and a triplet, and even then the bonds are not overly numerous or strong.

Already we have found that French Africa is distinct from the former British and Italian colonies and from the long-time independents (Liberia and Ethiopia). Nor is the division so simple as, for the major clusters, merely French and British. We did identify a cluster of Former British African states in the international organization analysis, and on the whole these states (except Sierra Leone) voted together pretty regularly in the United Nations. But East and West African states split up in their trading patterns, with Uganda, Tanganyika, and Kenya going with the larger Commonwealth group, and Ghana and Nigeria more heavily involved with the cluster that included the former British colonies in the Caribbean. So again, any attempt to discover a Commonwealth aggregate would succeed in finding no more than two or three countries per group, with over the entire world at least five such small clusters. This confirms the impression we gained while looking at one attribute at a time: the Commonwealth, as a worldwide association bringing together many nations of diverse characteristics, is an extremely amorphous and fractionated group. The divisions and differences within it are so great, and the bridges so few and narrow, that it is hard to see how it has the potential for any significant upgrading or reunification. Quite the opposite—its divisions have become deeper and more numerous over the past decade, and as the reality of the Commonwealth has become more amorphous, many Britons' ardor for it has wandered toward Europe.

Much of the world therefore remains fragmented, and this is especially true of the separate nations which were part of the former colonial empires. Only in West Africa among the French colonies has the legacy of colonialism included the bequest of many widespread and congruent ties among the once dependent territories. Elsewhere in Africa, Asia, and the Middle East one finds at most three or four nations that cluster together on all the criteria we have assembled. In the world at large, the divisions throughout the underdeveloped areas make the emergence of a big semi-continental have-not power, with great influence in international politics, a negligible prospect.

The situation is somewhat different in Latin America, where perhaps as many as nine states in Central and northern South America are consistently found together, and three more (Chile, Argentina, and, more tenuously in the UN, Uruguay) in the southern part of the Hemisphere. The size of the Central American group is impressive, and it will bear watching.

A half dozen countries in Eastern Europe always cluster together, with several others often with them, and no rival clustering in sight. The origin of this aggregation is obvious—Red Army occupation at the end of World War II, with the subsequent imposition of communist governments in each state. Yet Soviet armed forces have now been withdrawn from most of these nations (they remain stationed in Poland and Hungary, and very substantial in East Germany) and many of the rigid controls of the Stalin era have been relaxed or removed. The consequence has indeed been greater but still limited national independence on the part of virtually all these states, with Albania and Romania the most dramatic current examples. But force was not the only cement for these nations, or if it was it has now been replaced by other bonds of institutions, similarity, interaction, and common interests vis-a-vis the international system. Though it will never return to the monolith which we saw in public during the Stalin years, the unity of Eastern Europe is based on real ties and has a strength that must not be ignored. Under the impact of new strategic conditions the bloc has moved from a coercive attempt at semi-amalgamation to a more pluralistic effort. The new structure is likely to produce higher mutual responsiveness than could the old one.

Western Europe's original unity was the product not of military occupation and externally imposed force, but of common needs for co-operation in reconstruction and protection against a common threat. That unity was already sufficient for the threat indeed to be perceived as a *common* one rather than providing a potential external ally whose help might be used by one European state against another. That in itself is most significant. The unity has been fostered by many consciously and semi-consciously constructed bonds over the past two decades, with the result that there is now a total of about ten nations who consistently are clustered together. No doubt this unity has its limits and cannot uncritically be projected into a probability of political unification—past difficulties between France and her partners surely are not simply passing squabbles. No doubt too the degree of integration is higher for the Six of the Common Market than it is between them and the states on their fringes—Denmark, Switzerland, Austria, and the United Kingdom—which go to make up the ten countries mentioned. But even allowing for both these weaknesses, Western Europe makes up the largest aggregate of states which group together in the entire world. No other area can claim so many states joined by even the network which cements the most separate of the ten.

Nor is there likely to be any such group within the next few decades. In every instance in the preceding chapters [of *International Regions and the International System*] where we had information on the agreement of clusterings over time, we dwelt at length on their stability and continuity (indices of agreement exceeding 0.90 for all the ten-year comparisons).[45] The cases where trade, organizational memberships, or even voting behavior changed radically were few indeed. This vividly illustrates what we should already know, that the growth of such ties is a slow process of accretion, not something that can be expected to occur over the course of only a few years. Political integration must be built up bit by bit, as the achievement of one bond creates the possibility of constructing another. If Western Europe still has far to go, other areas of the world have a yet longer road before them. It will be many years before even Western Europe's limited present achievement is surpassed elsewhere.

Neither does there seem to be much prospect for the re-integration of the two areas where the most notable fault-lines have appeared in recent years. The differences between the Soviet Union and Eastern Europe on the one hand, and mainland China on the other, are numerous and profound. They are very likely to continue to pursue divergent policies, with at best a limited military alliance or tacit agreement for defense *in extremis*. Similarly if less drastically, the divisions in the Atlantic Alliance have become somewhat more pronounced, and are reflected not merely in the political behavior of France or a few other European countries, but in some of the background conditions as well.

[45]Incidentally, this finding of very high continuity argues strongly for the basic accuracy and reliability of the data used in the analyses. Whatever difficulties in measurement, reporting, and recording doubtlessly exist, these indices of agreement, for data gathered independently, greatly circumscribe the problems of data error which must worry us.

Discussion and Questions

1. The recent book by Louis J. Cantori and Steven L. Spiegel, *The International Politics of Regions,* and Lynn Miller's two articles reprinted in Parts I and V of this book offer other definitions of "region." F. S. C. Northrop's consideration of "What is a Nation?" raises the problem of unit delimitation by reliance on a method of inquiry that is quite different from that used by Russett. What follows is a rather extended extract taken from Northrop's over-all presentation. This presentation may appear somewhat obscure taken out of its full context, but it will be discussed further in the second section of this Part (Selections 10, 11, and 12), and it does reveal a quite definite contrast with Russett, since it stresses what Northrop calls "philosophical anthropology." It should also be appreciated that Northrop's discussion was published in 1960.

It may be said: "But everybody knows what a nation is. There is the United States. There is the Soviet Union. There is Free India. There is, or there was, Free Pakistan." This seems to be the case. But the necessary qualification "there was" with respect to Free Pakistan suggests that the matter is not such a simple and empirically self-evident thing as at first appears. Is Pakistan under a military dictatorship the same nation as Pakistan under a free, democratic, modernized Islamic theory of goal values? To be sure, the concrete people are bodily the same, the two widely separated geographical terrains in which they reside are the same and their military power is the same, but does this suffice to make the nation the same before and after the military coup? Also, the bodies of the people are concrete and the two geographical areas are concrete, as are the military weapons, but in what does the concreteness of the nation consist? Clearly, the bodies of the people and the geography are not enough to answer this question. Nor is the answer empirically self-evident. Hence our query, "What is a nation?" is not merely a real question, but also a difficult one to answer.

This becomes more evident if we consider another aspect of the recent military coup in Pakistan. Some say that this marks the beginning of the breakdown of Pakistan as a nation. Whether this is the case or not is irrelevant to our present concern. That such might be the eventuality is, however, most relevant. Any theory of what a nation is must provide meaning for a nation passing out of being when the concrete people, the concrete geography and the concrete military soldiers and weapons with which it was previously associated remain.

In the case of Pakistan, there is physical power. Certainly a military leader is not devoid of that. Yet with all of these three physical things—the people's bodies, the geographical terrain and the physical power—Pakistan as a nation may, nevertheless, disappear. Obviously, therefore, whatever a nation is, it is something apparently very abstract and empirically very elusive.

These considerations mean that when we, or our "experts" in international relations, suppose that we know what a nation is, we are guilty of confusing abstract nouns such as "nation," "national interest" or "national power" with concrete entities. This occurs when one puts the word "the" before such abstract nouns to produce expressions such as "the nation," "the national interest" or "the major powers" and then supposes, without further reduction of these abstract expressions to empirically verifiable concrete entities, that one knows what one is talking about.

The word "the" is meaningless unless it refers to an empirically observable or indirectly or experimentally confirmable scientifically designated particular entity, but the words "nation," "national interest" and "major powers" by themselves do not refer to concrete entities. Thus when taken by themselves as the elementary concepts in foreign policy or international relations, as is done by Professor Morgenthau and Mr. Kennan, instead of being realistic or scientific concepts such expressions are abstract words that are confused with concrete things. Until a reduction of such otherwise meaningless abstract nouns to empirically verifiable concrete entities is given, the expertness of present professors of international relations and of other similar foreign policy decision makers is spurious.

At this point we of the older generation can learn something very important from the younger generation of Anglo-American analytic philosophers. This something is to be exceedingly suspicious of abstract nouns unless statements containing them are reduced to at least indirectly testable empirical statements about concrete entities and events. To confuse an abstract noun with a concrete entity by putting the word "the" before it and then supposing that one is talking about something realistic and meaningful is what Whitehead called the "fallacy of misplaced concreteness." This does not mean that abstract nouns like "nation," "culture," "the living law," "legal system," "pattern of a culture," "a great power" or "national interest" must be thrown away. It does mean, however, that, before we can know what we are talking about when we use them, we must translate them into theoretically precise and direct or indirect empirically confirmable statements about concrete entities and find the specific concrete entities in terms of which such a translation can be made. Until this occurs, we shall do well to trust our domestic and foreign policy to our most experienced diplomats and domestic politicians, probably also to those who do not theorize too much about foreign policy, rather than to professors of international relations or of "social science," or to the graduates of our traditional law schools where only the positive law of one particular nation is taught.

Even so, the crucial question remains, What is a Nation? In other words, What are the concrete entities and events in terms of which the abstract noun "nation" is to be analyzed? It is unlikely that even politicians with lengthy experience or career diplomats can avoid self-defeating decisions involving other nations unless they, as well as we, become clear about the answer to this question. Is there any clue?

A more concrete understanding of the difficulty which the question raises will become evident if we compare the unity of the group of concrete human bodies making up a nation with the quite different anatomical unity of any one of these concrete individual human bodies. Looked at comparatively in this manner, the existence of a nation appears as almost a miracle. In the case of any individual man or woman, the anatomical parts are physically held together by physical bones, nerves, muscles and tendons. Consequently no person with all his or her anatomical parts intact can move one part of his or her body without that anatomical part physically pulling all the other parts along. The unity of the concrete people who make up the nation which is the United States of America or the Soviet Union is, however, something quite different from this. There are no material wires, bones, muscles or tendons physically connecting all the bodies of the individual American people in such a manner that, if one of the bodies responds in a certain way, the bodies of all the others must do the same. Nevertheless such a unified response is what occurs when any people form a nation or when a majority of them or any group of them respond with a common domestic or foreign policy. How is this possible? This is our question. . . .

Stated as briefly as possible, *a "nation" is any group of concrete, particular human beings who possess in the hierarchically ordered neural nets of their brains a similar set of elementary trapped impulses* (which are the physiological epistemic correlates of consciously or unconsciously memorized elementary ideas and postulates) *for firing or inhibiting their motor neurons and thereby mechanically causing a similar cognitive behavioristic living law response to any given stimulus.* . . . what is trapped, as the neurological epistemic correlate of any particular directly introspected or unconsciously held idea, is an impulse that is passed around a circular neural net or some neural physiological formal equivalent of such a persisting impulse. The entire hierarchically ordered system of such neurophysiological surrogates of a particular person's immediately conscious or covertly retained idea is, like the events of any other theory of mathematical natural science, not directly sensed. Instead, it is known only by theoretically constructed imageless theory and its existence is confirmed only indirectly by way of epistemic correlations or epistemic rules of correspondence with the directly experienced meanings, ideas and other data of awareness and introspected consciousness that are denoted by concepts by intuition.

The advantage of supplementing the bare data, ideas and theories of radically empirical introspective psychological consciousness with such a concept by postulation theory of neurophysiological events, only some of which possess directly inspectable epistemic correlates in the domain of immediate conscious experience, is identical with the advantage of mathematical chemistry over merely sensed chemistry or of mathematical electromagnetic theory with its spectrum of electromagnetic waves, extending far beyond the so-called visible range. The psychology of the unconscious and the anthropology of the covert, as well as the psychology of the immediately conscious and the anthropologically overt, arc thereby given public logically realistic neurological and behavioristic psychological meaning. . . .

Furthermore, in dealing with domestic or international political questions we must avoid confusing the objective description of what the philosophical properties of a given nation are, or what the complex of philosophical properties of that nation is, with the quite different question of evaluating what we have thus described. The unfortunate fact is that politicians, laymen and many social scientists corrupt their descriptive judgments because their descriptive method is so intuitive and nebulous that they surreptitiously and frequently quite unconsciously smuggle in evaluative judgments of their own political party or nation or school of "social science" when they are purporting merely to be describing another party or nation. We cannot be too careful, therefore, in specifying in further detail the descriptive method of philosophical anthropology as applied to politics. Only if it is made clear and then distinguished from the evaluative method can any social scientist's or politician's judgments be based on objective evidence concerning what the other nations or his own nation is, rather than on what he feels or thinks it ought to be. [Reprinted with permission of the Macmillan Company from *Philosophical Anthropology and Practical Politics* by F. S. C. Northrop.© F.S.C. Northrop 1960. Pp. 74–88.]

➤ What is the difference between Northrop's empiricism and Russett's behaviorism? Both approaches are strongly committed to the verification of their presentations by "scientific methods."

2. There is a continuing debate about whether or not the nation-state is losing its capacity to control human affairs. On one level the debate stresses the diminishing capability of even powerful governments to provide for the security and welfare of their populations. Nuclear weaponry, the deterioration of the environment, the character of modern industrial operations, and the dependence of the national economy upon the world economy are among the factors contributing to a loss of confidence in the capacity of national governments to meet successfully either domestic or international challenges. The doctrine of sovereignty and the idea of a territorial state corresponded with social and political reality only so long as there was an overriding internal need to establish domestic order through a centralization of the instruments of violence. The rise of the nation-state in post-medieval Europe was, in part, a means of drastically disarming feudal centers of power and concentrating military capabilities in a single national center of authority. External expressions of sovereignty also seemed acceptable so long as governments could plan their defense effectively and at a reasonable cost. (For an incisive analysis of the rise and fall of the nation-state as a functional basis for international order, see John H. Herz, *International Politics in the Atomic Age* [Columbia University Press, New York, 1959].)

Other specialists stress the depth of nationalist sentiment and contend that, at minimum, there is a long period of lag between the objective obsolescence of a political form and the subjective appreciation of this fact. High levels of international cooperation can be evolved to deal with the manifest interdependencies of the modern age without any real shift of loyalty or power to supranational institutions. Thus, it is argued, the nation-state is at once more durable and more adaptable than had been generally supposed. In this regard the capacity of the nation-state to transform its operations and its ideologies to meet the needs of the day is a point worthy of careful examination.

Another quite different argument is that the nation-state is becoming more benign precisely because it has lost the pretensions of the prenuclear age. As a consequence, there is now no longer any particular need to suppose that the future of world order is contingent upon building new, more inclusive centers of political authority. The awareness that territory is not coincident with power, the inhibiting effect of nuclear weaponry on the use of military capabilities, the rise of multinational corporations, and the emergence of a more cosmopolitan ideology among various social and vocational classes, are some of the factors that are alleged to be helping reshape the state to satisfy the new needs of the age.

An aspect of the idea of the transformed nation-state is the notion expressed by Max Beloff:

That the process of decision-making within national systems of government is becoming increasingly dependent upon the outcome of agreements reached or decisions taken within the framework of international institutions and that the old contrast between a fully sovereign state on the one hand and a mere component of a wider political union on the other is no longer as important as it was fifty or a hundred years ago. [Beloff, "Federalism as a Model for International Integration," *Yearbook of World Affairs,* vol. 13 (1959), pp. 188–204.]

As Mr. Beloff points out, it is necessary to investigate this proposition by specific observation of how decisions are actually being made by various national governments on matters of political importance.

Another form of argument stresses that whether one wishes it or not, the hard evidence supports the persistence of nation-states as the dominant political unit in the world for a long time to come. National governments may engage in all sorts of cooperative enterprise, but there is a great reluctance by governments to commit themselves to any international effort that becomes part of a nonreversible process. It has been argued that nation-states will cooperate, especially in the face of a serious common external threat (for instance, in time of war), but that there are systemic limits on forms of cooperation that threaten the integrity and autonomy of the state.

A special dimension of this speculation on the future of the state arises from national efforts in the less developed parts of the world to build up modern states. In such national circumstances, the nation-building focus actually gives a functional role to nationalist thinking that is comparable to the modern state in Europe several centuries earlier. Many of the governments of Asia and Africa are devoting their energies to welding their various ethnic, tribal, and local subunits into coherent wholes. The symbols of sovereignty provide a unifying image, mainly directed at domestic issues. These Afro-Asian countries are inner-directed, concerned above all with the stable tenure of their own rulership; in these circumstances world-order issues only receive marginal attention.

At the same time, and with opposite effect, these states are often subject to significant levels of interference from more powerful industrial states and from multinational corporations. The impulse toward establishing national autonomy, especially for recently independent or ex-colonial states, has prompted an awareness of common, community-wide interests. This impulse helps to explain, as Gustavo Lagos suggested in the article mentioned in Part II, why regional integration has been an attractive complement to nationalism in the Latin American setting. That is, regionalism (up to a certain point) may be a *shield* (not a *substitute*) for developing strong nation-states in some areas of the world. Also, small, overspecialized economies may have many practical reasons to pool resources through the encouragement of region-wide arrangements without in any sense seeking to pursue an integrationist path when it comes to political identity.

There is also the problem of discovering ways for weaker governments to achieve meaningful participation in the global system. Poorer, smaller states with certain common interests can often develop a more effective voice by acting in concert. The various Afro-Asian meetings of nonaligned states, the formation of UNCTAD, and bloc voting in the United Nations all exhibit a high degree of solidarity that manages to coexist with intense nationalism. ➤ Is it possible to sustain a nationalist identity for purposes of modernization and a regionalist or bloc identity for purposes of foreign-policy making?

In Africa, Asia, and the Middle East the logic of integration has often been thwarted by intraregional differences arising from antagonistic political orientations. Governments, jealous of their independence, are suspicious of efforts by ambitious and strong neighbors to establish new patterns of domination. There are also big differences among ruling groups with regard to private capital formation, foreign investment, rate of economic growth, type of political system, linkages to the global system, and domestic social policy.

In general, then, the international system exhibits various contradictory tendencies as to the nature and future of the sovereign state. There are also widespread disagreements as to the extent to which the erosion of the nation-state is an essential part of any adequate effort to build a stronger system of world order. The status of the nation-state seems further complicated by the quite distinct values and roles that appear to attach to nationalism in industrial and postindustrial societies of the Northern Hemisphere and in the preindustrial societies of the Southern Hemisphere. Globalist generalizations about the future of the nation-state seem misleading. Subsystemic levels of generalization can be more safely made. Given our normative concerns these inquiries should seek to clarify the circumstances under which various kinds of nationalist ideologies facilitate or obstruct the transition to a safer, more valuable system of world order. ➤ In particular, does the nation-state as it is evolving in the principal subsystems of the world obstruct the creation and development of regional political communities (that are to be preferred for world-order reasons over national political communities) and, if so, how? We need to know more clearly under what conditions and in what forms regional communities are to be preferred. We also need to know how the nation-state, as it presently operates, interferes with the pursuit of these goals.

Stanley Hoffmann in his well-known article, "Obstinate or Obsolete? The Fate of the Nation-State and the Case of Western Europe" (*Daedalus*, vol. 95, no. 3 [Summer 1966], pp. 862–915), develops the case for attributing persisting vitality to the nation-state even in the most industrial parts of the world, where the appeals of integration are strong and the deficiencies and dangers of nationalism are obvious. Hoffmann emphasizes the obstacles to further integration in Europe. He argues that the divergent situations and backgrounds of each state within Europe lead to a different weighting of costs and benefits that impedes each further step in the integration process, and that the European experience suggests that success with economic integration and the adoption of common defense policies does not assure political integration. In this sense, Hoffmann disagrees with integration theorists such as Ernst Haas, who regard integration as a cumulative process that gradually erodes the status and function of the sovereign state. Hoffmann also argues that sovereign states have adjusted their ideology and behavior to the constraints of the nuclear age, and are much more cautious and restrained in the execution of foreign policy.

Johan Galtung, in contrast to Hoffmann, argues in an article "On the Future of the International System," (International Peace Research Institute, Oslo, Publication no. 25-6, 1967) that on the basis of certain trends, mainly associated with various transnational forms of functional activity, the nation-state is destined to play a steadily diminishing role in human affairs. Galtung emphasizes the growth of specialized organizations of an intergovernmental and nongovernmental character as one important sovereignty-cutting trend. He also places stress on cross-national patterns of identification—by which individuals who are, for example, young or black or businessmen form transnational reference groups that are, in aggregate, comparable to or even stronger than their bonds with their own national societies. The transnational movement to oppose the American intervention in the Vietnam War is also regarded by Galtung as evidence of an emerging cosmopolitan consciousness. Tourism, trade, communications, and culture all help to erode national boundaries and to make political facts of separate sovereignties less central to life circumstances. The emergence of new patterns of loyalty along with the functional imperatives of the neomodern world point toward a gathering momentum for integration in developed countries. The type of integration anticipated is not clearly indicated, nor are subsystemic variations other than degree of industrialization given much emphasis. For Galtung it appears to make little difference whether the emphasis is upon the relatively centralized and planned economies of the Soviet bloc or upon the relatively decentralized and market economies of Western Europe. The crucial variable is the stage of socioeconomic development.

Galtung expects nationalist trends to intensify in the less developed portions of the world. Whether the exploitation of the poor by the rich will lead to accomodation-by-compromise or catastrophe-by-confrontation is one of the great imponderables of the future. Galtung is among those social scientists who think that knowledge and the techniques of "peace research" can increase "the growth rate of the more peace-productive courses."

The implicit debate between Hoffmann and Galtung raises the following questions: ➤ To what extent, in what circumstances, does the nation-state obstruct transition to regional political communities? ➤ Can the international role of the nation-state be modified so as to make it compatible with the development of a more effective and just system of world order? ➤ If reform of the nation-state is possible, then will

it come about by the cumulative impact of indirect trends or by a direct transfer of functions
and shifts of loyalties away from the national
level? ➤ Is the North-South distinction central
to an assessment of the future of the nation-state
and the doctrine of national sovereignty? ➤ Is it
necessary to conduct a separate inquiry for each
set of subsystemic conditions? ➤ Is the nation-
state more able to participate in regional communities than in global communities?

3. There are increasingly rich sources of data
about distinct national characteristics. The availability of these data should enable more informed
predictions about potentialities in various regions.
It also becomes possible to appraise actual integration progress as compared to hypothetical integration potential. For some studies that provide
a national data base, see, for example, Arthur S.
Banks and Robert B. Textor, *A Cross-Polity Survey* (MIT Press, Cambridge, Mass., 1963); Russett
and others, *World Handbook of Political and
Social Indicators* (Yale University Press, New
Haven, 1964); Gabriel Almond and Sidney Verba,
The Civic Culture (Princeton University Press,
Princeton, 1963). The most systematic study of
regional developments appraised on a comparative basis is by Louis J. Cantori and Steven L.
Spiegel, *The International Politics of Regions: A
Comparative Approach* (Englewood Cliffs, Prentice-Hall, 1970); this book combines a coherent
textual interpretation with a carefully selected set
of readings by regional specialists.

4. Walker F. Connor in "Myths of Hemispheric, Continental, Regional, and State Unity"
(*Political Science Quarterly*, vol. 84, no. 4 [De-
cember 1969], pp. 555–582), contends that geographical contiguity does not necessarily lead to
unity: "*If distance is a meaningful consideration,
then two points connected by water are closer
than two points equally distant but separated by
land*" (p. 570).

Note that Russett's approach also does not
make geographical proximity an essential attribute of a "region." No single variable is crucial to
assure that a group of states might or might not
qualify as a region. Note also that a unit of interaction can be formed by conflict and antagonism
without there being any implicit potential for
first-stage integration. To affix the term "region"
does not imply actual or potential integration,
and certainly does not suggest the existence or
possibility of an integration movement. ➤ Is it
possible that second-stage integration potential
exists in some "regions" that have a very low
first-stage integration potential?

9

What is the Commonwealth?

HEDLEY BULL

The association of states known as the Commonwealth of Nations has received little attention from students of international politics. Outside the Commonwealth the association has, on the whole, been ignored;[1] alongside other institutions and alliances, its significance is not great; and the foreign policies of the ten states that now belong to it can to a large extent be accounted for, except in the case of Britain, without reference to the fact of their membership. Within the Commonwealth there has been study of it, but the impulse behind this has been provided less by intellectual curiosity than by the desire to see it prosper: British students have been themselves in the grip of the myth of the Commonwealth, which has become in Britain, along with much else, a totem which it is scarcely good form to examine with an innocent eye. Of these two attitudes, that of the foreigner is, I believe, the less unsound. Nevertheless the Commonwealth does require study, for it is a fact which has to be accounted for within the categories of a science of international politics.

The central idea of the Commonwealth myth is that the Commonwealth combines the liberty of many states with the unity of one. That, in the event of a conflict between them, the unity of the Empire must give way to the liberty of its parts has been accepted in broad principle by British governments for the colonies of European settlement since the 1840's, and for the Asian and African dependencies since 1947. The idea of the Commonwealth took shape as it came to be held that this liberty of the parts did not prejudice the unity of the whole, but provided it with a new basis in a common will. The Balfour Report of 1926 gave expression to this doctrine when it held that "Though every Dominion is now, and must always remain, the sole judge of the nature and extent of its co-operation, no

From *World Politics*, vol. 11, no. 4 (copyright©1959 by Princeton University Press), pp. 577–587. Reprinted by permission of Princeton University Press.

[1]The recent publications of Duke University's Commonwealth Studies Center are a notable exception.

common cause will, in our opinion, be thereby imperilled."[2] This idea carries with it two corollaries: that the Commonwealth is "unique"; and that it is a model for other and wider international associations.

Together, these ideas constitute an affront to that theory of international relations according to which sovereign states have a prime concern for the maintenance of their own power and therefore an inherent antagonism. They confront the description of international relations as a "contest for power" with the claim that Commonwealth relations are an exception, and the skeptic about the future of leagues of nations with the claim that the Commonwealth is "the League in practice" (General Smuts), "the United Nations in miniature" (Lord Attlee). They are offensive, in particular, to Turgot's comparison of colonies with fruit, according to which the former, as they mature, come to obey the laws of power politics as inevitably as the latter, as they ripen and grow heavy, are torn by gravitation from the parent tree.

It is the myth of the Commonwealth, not the doctrine that international relations are power politics, that is more clearly at fault. In the past, the foreign skeptic has been prone to question the element of liberty; and a long tradition of misunderstanding and misrepresentation has dismissed the Commonwealth relationship as a new form of British domination. Today he is more likely to question the element of unity, and here he is on more solid ground. The Durham Report of 1839, which made the first great concession of liberty by recommending responsible government for Canada, held the unity of the Empire to reside in the powers of the Imperial government over the form of the constitution, the disposal of waste lands, external trade, and foreign relations. By the First World War only the control of foreign policy remained. During the war, though the Empire retained its diplomatic singularity, the Imperial government came to share this control with the Dominion and Indian governments. In the interwar period, the Dominions came to assume international personalities and to conduct

foreign policies of their own; the Empire was no longer a single state, and its unity consisted in the substantial concurrence of different policies differently arrived at, in the existence of a "British Entente."[3] Since the Second World War, this entente has ceased to be recognizable. The entry of India, Pakistan, Ceylon, Ghana, and Malaya into full membership has introduced a division on the central issue of international politics, between those who adhere to the neutralist bloc and those who adhere to the Western: and it has brought into the sphere of Commonwealth relations two antagonisms characteristic of international politics, between India and Pakistan, and India and South Africa. And although Britain, Canada, Australia, New Zealand, and Pakistan each belong to one or more of the Western alliances,[4] their identity as a Commonwealth group has become submerged in the wider Western system, and the source of their military unity is much less their Commonwealth relationship than the attraction exerted upon them all by the power of the United States; if a part of the Commonwealth marches in step, the beat is called by a country which is outside the Commonwealth.

The history of the Commonwealth, then, is one of continuous disintegration. Close in the wake of these changes have come changes in the mythology of the Commonwealth; for that mythology, always abreast of the times, has sought to account for the disintegration, and even to turn it into a kind of triumph, by means of an elaborate terminology of "development," "decentralization," and "increasing flexibility." But it has kept alive the idea of the unity of the Commonwealth, only by diluting, at each turn of the screw, the criterion of Commonwealth unity. Nor, on the basis of past evidence, would it be safe to say, with L. S. Amery,[5] that the centrifugal process has now worked itself out, or that the ever-thinning elastic of "unity" can stretch no further. Today, this unity is said to consist not in any concurrence in substance of Commonwealth members' foreign policies, but in their consultations with one

---

[2]Report of the Inter-Imperial Relations Committee, Imperial Conference, 1926, in A. B. Keith, *Speeches and Documents on the British Dominions, 1918–1931*, London, 1936, p. 162.

[3]Cf. Sir Alfred Zimmern, *The Third British Empire*, London, 1926.

[4]Britain—NATO, SEATO; Canada—NATO; Australia and New Zealand—SEATO, ANZUS; Pakistan—SEATO.

[5]L. S. Amery, *Thoughts on the Constitution*, London, 1953, p. 170.

another in the framing of them: the flow of secret information between the Commonwealth Relations Office and the overseas Commonwealth governments, the meetings of Commonwealth diplomatic representatives at the United Nations and in major capitals, and the Conferences of Commonwealth Prime Ministers in London are held to express a latent unity. But the reliance of newly independent governments on British advice and sources of information is manifestly a temporary phenomenon which will pass with the acquisition by these states of their own diplomatic machinery, and has already passed in the case of some of them. Furthermore, close consultation and the exchange of secret information cannot go on in isolation from substantive issues of policy; how close is that consultation which occurs between countries pursuing conflicting policies? Even the most negative test of the unity of the Commonwealth, the absence among its parts of a disposition to war, is invalidated by the case of India and Pakistan.

The formal basis of Commonwealth relations is that they are not strictly international relations at all, but the relations of a community whose parts are "not foreign": these countries exchange High Commissioners, not Ambassadors; the dealings of the overseas members are with the Commonwealth Relations Office, not the Foreign Office; they recognize at least the shadow of a common citizenship; they accept the Sovereign of Great Britain as the Head of the Commonwealth. But what the form of Commonwealth relations suggests, their substance seems to belie; and if this is so, then the main basis of the claims that Commonwealth relations are unique, and a model for the rest of the world, is undermined. Even if it were true—which, as I have suggested, it is not—that the Commonwealth has combined the liberty of many and the unity of one, it would not follow that it provided a precedent for the rest of the world: as an American writer[6] has pointed out, such unity as the Commonwealth has displayed has been the unity of the parts of a single state in process of decomposition: about the amalgamation of previously independent units, it has no lessons to offer.

It is true that the relations of Britain, Canada, Australia, New Zealand, and South Africa appear to lack, or to contain only in an unimportant sense, the element of international politics. War between any two of them, for example, is "unthinkable": they are an interlocking series of what Karl W. Deutsch and his colleagues have called "pluralistic security-communities."[7] More than that, their governments are not competitors for power, and their dealings with one another are largely technical or administrative: even cessions of territory, as in the case of the cession by Britain of Newfoundland to Canada and the Cocos Islands to Australia, are non-political acts, remote from any consideration of the ratio of power between these countries. In the image which an inhabitant of these countries has of the world, they are not seen as being related in such a way that the inflation of the stature of one is the deflation of the stature of the others. Indeed, it is even the case that vocal sections of public opinion in at least Britain, Australia, and New Zealand regard the inflation and deflation of each other's position as essentially bound up with their own. But international relations of this sort are not characteristic of Commonwealth relations as such, even if they find in them their most striking illustration, and they have their analogues outside the Commonwealth—for example, in the sets of North Atlantic states (United States-Canada; United States-Britain; Norway-Sweden, etc.) which Deutsch and his colleagues have studied. The existence of states whose mutual relations are not characteristically political needs to be explained, and to be reconciled with the generalizations of the Realpolitiker; this is a very important general problem of the theory of international relations, but not especially a problem of Commonwealth studies.

We have not accounted for the Commonwealth, however, simply by noting that it is not what its mythology claims it to be. The Commonwealth exists: ten sovereign states belong to it, and their persistence in membership requires an explanation. These nations have a common memory of organic union within the British Empire, and have inherited many of their institutions from it, some more, some less; and they

---

[6]Inis Claude, *Swords into Ploughshares*, New York, 1956.

[7]Karl W. Deutsch *et al.*, *Political Community and the North Atlantic Area*, Princeton, N.J., 1957, Introduction.

have a wide range of overlapping interests, economic, military, and cultural. In the absence of these factors, the Commonwealth would not exist: yet it is not in itself explained by them. None of these common institutions or common interests organically depends upon the Commonwealth connection. The economic links between these countries consist in the fact that all the overseas members, except Canada, trade more with Britain than with any other country, have Britain as the main holder of their overseas investment capital, and belong to the Sterling Area. The military and political links arise either from regional pacts (NATO, SEATO, ANZUS) or from special agreements between Britain and one or more of the other members, like ANZAM (Britain, Australia, New Zealand, and Malaya) and the now-defunct British agreements with South Africa and Ceylon for the use of bases. "The imperishable empire of our arts, our morals, our literature and our laws" rests on no Commonwealth connection, and substantially includes the United States. Think away the Commonwealth and most of these links remain, as, indeed, most of them have remained in the case of Eire, which does most of its trade with Britain, belongs to the Sterling Area, and even has its citizens in the United Kingdom accorded the same rights as Commonwealth citizens and its relations with Britain handled by the Commonwealth Relations Office. The institutions of the Commonwealth—its Head, its Prime Ministers' Conference, its diplomatic machinery—have no special tangible tasks to perform—i.e., while they find such tasks to perform, there are none which only they can perform. The one function which only they can perform is not a tangible one, but that of providing evidence of the existence of the Commonwealth. The essential service with which the Commonwealth provides its members, its one great indispensable, is a set of symbols. To provide these symbols, the Commonwealth must be kept alive, its membership, if possible, undiminished.

At each of the crises in the history of the Commonwealth, when the question is raised, "What purpose does it serve?", "What form shall it take?", the continued existence of the Commonwealth in its widest membership has been preferred to its serving any particular purpose or taking any particular form. It has been successively judged more important that the Commonwealth should persist unimpaired than that it should be based on the indivisibility of the Crown, than that its citizens should all acknowledge allegiance to the Crown, than that it should have a common strategy, than that its members should all be parliamentary democracies, than that none of them should practice racial discrimination, than that they should have any distinctive ideals beyound the truisms that are the stock-in-trade of all governments. So far is the Commonwealth from being an association which has consistently pursued any particular purpose that those who write about it often appear, *post hoc*, to cast about for purposes which might provide it with a *raison d'être*: thus its mission has been discovered to be to provide a prop to the League of Nations, to set an example in race relations, to develop backward countries, to undertake an experiment in international co-operation, to form the nucleus of a Third Force. Seeley's *Expansion of England*[8] saw the secret of the Empire as residing in the fact that its self-governing parts felt themselves to be a single nation, Greater Britain: today its unique character is held to reside precisely in its being a "bridge" between widely different nations, its essence to be diversity, not homogeneity.[9] So long as the Commonwealth has some formal existence (the minimum would appear to be that certain governments must declare that they belong to it), then it is a symbol, and its essential purpose is served.

The effect, in part contrived, in part unconscious, of this symbol is to disguise the disintegration of the British Empire, to prolong the spirit after life has departed from the body. By no means is it the case that it is only in Britain that this symbol has the power of attraction. It has a direct appeal to large sections of the populations of Canada, South Africa, Australia, and New Zealand, each of which countries has become exposed and insecure as the Pax Britannica has waned, and each of which knows the yearning for the comfort of the Imperial womb—the last two, the most strategically exposed, and the most avid consumers of British security in the past, as well as the most homogeneously British, sometimes expressing their yearning, their wish to escape from their Asian environment, in assertion that they are British first, and, if at all, Australian and

---

[8] J. R. Seeley, *The Expansion of England*, London, 1883.

[9] Cf. e.g., Lord Listowel, *Commonwealth Future*, Fabian Tract 308, London, July 1957.

New Zealand second. For the governments of each of these countries, then, even South Africa, some minimum of deference to the Commonwealth symbol is, quite apart from considerations of foreign policy, an elementary necessity of electoral tactics. In the Asian and African Commonwealth countries, the Commonwealth symbol attracts (as it repels) only sections of the ruling elites, and deference to the symbol, far from being conducive of mass domestic support for the governments, can be positively damaging to them. But here, too, the Commonwealth symbol is basic to the understanding of their membership in the Commonwealth: if the symbol does not attract the masses of African and Asian citizens and voters, it does attract the masses of British voters, and its preservation is a major interest of British governments. To this extent the leaders of African and Asian Commonwealth countries, holding in their hands, as they do, the power to leave the Commonwealth, and thereby weaken the effectiveness of the Commonwealth symbol, have derived a great bargaining counter in relation to the British government, albeit one that is kept discreetly in the background of their policies. By remaining in the Commonwealth, the Asian and African members have conceded to Britain the enjoyment of the symbolic prolongation of the British Empire: in return, they have secured conveniences and services, the good will of the British government, and an influence over British policy accruing to them from the knowledge in Britain that they might leave.

It is in Britain, however, that the Commonwealth symbol exerts its most powerful influence on the shaping of policy. Britain, though constitutional form takes no account of this, is the center of the Commonwealth; the strongest links between the Commonwealth countries—economic, military, cultural, emotional—are not multilateral, but are the bilateral ones between Britain and each of the other members; it is true only of Britain that her fortunes, and those of the Commonwealth as a whole, are closely connected in the public mind, both in Britain and abroad; and Britain is the member whose attention is most fixed on the Commonwealth as a whole, each of the other countries tending to think of the Commonwealth simply as its link with Britain. It is true only of Britain, furthermore, that the preservation of the Commonwealth with its present wide membership is a major interest of policy.

What is the source of British interest in the preservation of the Commonwealth? First, the Commonwealth symbol has enabled British governments to preserve, at home and abroad, the image of their country as a great Power. The idea of the importance to Britain of the unity of the Empire became strong only in the 1870's, when the preponderance of Britain in industry and trade was first challenged, and when the unification of Germany and the survival of the American Union in civil war had suggested to British writers and statesmen that a new dimension was arising in international politics, in which a small island state could no longer remain in the first rank. In the mid-Victorian high noon of British industrial supremacy, the Empire was thought to be as unimportant to the maintenance of British world power as its eventual disintegration was certain; the ideas of pride of empire, and of the importance of Imperial solidarity, came in response to the beginning of a decline in the power of Britain herself, and served to provide a substitute for it. "If the United States and Russia hold together for another half century," wrote Seeley in 1883, "they will completely dwarf such old European States as France and Germany, and depress them into a second class. They will do the same to England, if at the end of that time England still thinks of herself as simply a European State, as the old United Kingdom of Great Britain and Ireland, such as Pitt left her." Seeley's remedy was Imperial federation, the state of Greater Britain. "It would indeed be a poor remedy," he said, "if we should try to face these vast states of the new type by an artificial union of settlements and islands scattered over the whole globe, inhabited by different nationalities, and connected by no tie except the accident that they happen all alike to acknowledge the Queen's authority."[10] It is indeed a poor remedy, and to the extent that some of the parts of the Commonwealth do not acknowledge the Queen's authority, it is poorer still, but it is today the only one available. The Empire, as a prop, has gone, and only the Commonwealth, its symbolic continuation, remains.

If there is any one state in relation to which the ideas of Imperial and Commonwealth solidarity have been most asserted, that is the United States. America and the countries of the Commonwealth

---

[10]Seeley, *op.cit.*, p. 88.

(including, so far as their ruling minorities are concerned, the Asian and African ones) form the wider community of the English-speaking world. The natural leader of this community in terms of English-speaking population, power, wealth and, increasingly, cultural and scientific attainment is not Britain, but the United States: and one of the chief threats to the coherence of the Commonwealth is the gravitation of the Commonwealth countries, including Britain herself, as yet partial and gradual, toward the United States, looking to it for security, capital, and ideas. The idea of the English-speaking community was once held, in Britain, to be prior to that of the solidarity of the Empire; when Sir Charles Dilke took pride in the community of English-speaking cultures which England had bequeathed to the world, this was a community which included the United States, "a truer colony of Britain than is Canada."[11] Writers like Dilke and Goldwin Smith,[12] indeed, sought the severance of the connection between England and Canada, so that Canada might join the American Union and the over-all harmony of the English-speaking world come to fruition. But once it became clear that the natural leader of this English-speaking community was not Britain, but the United States, the idea of Imperial solidarity came to be preferred to it—as in the later writings of Dilke himself.[13] Britain must gather the lesser members of the English-speaking community to herself; she must attract them to a specifically British sub-culture, within the wider Anglo-Saxon culture. As if to assert this, the branches of the English-speaking Union in the Commonwealth countries today are organized as "The English-Speaking Union of the Commonwealth." The Commonwealth has to be understood, I believe, to be an incident, or a theme, in the history of Anglo-American relations: the theory that was to underlie the Commonwealth relationship was first defined by Burke during the revolt of the American colonies; it has been Canada, caught between Britain and America, that has to the greatest extent provided the pattern of the modern Commonwealth; and it is America, today, who is the main competitor with Britain (though the competition, restrained by the alliance of the two countries in the global conflict, is a mild one) for influence in the overseas Commonwealth countries. It may be that all the overseas Commonwealth countries are tending to follow the Canadian precedent that has so far eluded them, that of falling primarily into the American sphere of economic and cultural influence.

Secondly, the existence of the Commonwealth provides a moral reply to the critics of imperialism. The principle of national self-determination to which the British government during the First World War declared its adherence is corrosive of the moral foundations of empire: since that time, the British Empire has stood in need of justification, and the definitions of the Commonwealth relations that have been produced since the Imperial Conference of 1926 have gone toward meeting this need by showing that the Commonwealth is not, in the ordinary sense, an empire at all. There are two not wholly consistent lines of argument by which this position is arrived at. According to one, the characteristically left view of the Commonwealth, the association represents a sharp break with the tradition of the Empire, a disavowal of what it stood for, perhaps even an atonement for what was done in its name. According to the other, the characteristically conservative view of the Commonwealth, it is essentially continuous with the Empire, and is its culmination and vindication; the principle of the Commonwealth was always immanent in the Empire, the Empire was simply the period of preparation for the Commonwealth which is its teleological definition. The second view, because it provides a vindication of past as well as present British policies, is now the more widely accepted: ". . . fundamentally," writes Professor Mansergh, "the British people did not believe in colonial rule at all. They believed in the government of men by themselves; and because of that faith in self-government they regarded colonialism as a stage necessary for the bringing of backward peoples to political maturity, but of its very nature transient."[14] The Commonwealth symbol assuages the guilt-feelings of Englishmen about their Imperial record, and pro-

[11]Sir Charles Dilke, *Greater Britain*, London, 1868, 11, pp. 153–54.

[12]Goldwin Smith, *The Empire*, Oxford, 1863.

[13]Cf. Sir Charles Dilke, *Problems of Greater Britain*, London, 1890.

[14]Nicholas Mansergh, *Survey of British Commonwealth Affairs: Problems of External Policy, 1931–1939*, London, 1952, p. 7.

vides them with a defense in the councils of the world: the willing membership of the African and Asian states strengthens both these effects by suggesting that the former Imperial subjects themselves accept one or the other of these arguments.

Finally, the Commonwealth symbol enables the British nation to avoid, or at least to dull, the sense of historical defeat. If something remains of the Empire, and it conforms to the moral fashions of the times, then not all of Britain's efforts in the past have been in vain. By throwing a cloud of ambiguity over the loss of power which is in fact suffered when independence is granted to subject territories, it has enabled the British public to accept gracefully what they otherwise might not have accepted at all. More than that, it has enabled the claim to be made that what is apparently defeat is really victory, that the disintegration of the Empire is the fulfillment of a deliberately willed policy of constructing a great association of free peoples. For some enthusiasts—as remote, I believe, from the present mood of the British people as they are from the realities of the situation—it even proffers great new goals for the future, no less grand than those of the past, "a task for giants" that affords new outlets to the enterprise of the nation.[15]

If the myth of the Commonwealth presents a distorted picture of reality, it also contains elements of truth; it may be that the picture it presents is no more distorted than the one I have suggested by emphasizing facts which, though they are well known, are usually not emphasized or mentioned at all. Furthermore, all political institutions contain myths and depend upon them for their working; to have shown that the Commonwealth is a myth, therefore, is not to have shown that it is not a reality. Nor is it in any sense to have "attacked" the Commonwealth: the activity of supporting and opposing political policies and institutions is different from the activity of political inquiry, and, in my view, incompatible with it. Nevertheless, political inquiry does have practical effects, however unintended these may be; and it may be that the explosion of the myth of the Commonwealth, to which any serious inquiry into that institution will lead, has the effect of damaging the Commonwealth itself. If one believes that the Commonwealth myth serves useful, though modest, purposes in the world, one may shrink from carrying out a thorough investigation of it. But it is just this prostitution of inquiry to practical ends that is the foremost obstacle to the development of the science of politics.

Discussion and Questions

1. ➤ Could the British Commonwealth qualify as a region in Russett's sense? as a "political community" in Etzioni's sense or in the sense of the Deutsch group?

2. ➤ What are the bargaining trade-offs that maintain the British Commonwealth? ➤ Would the Commonwealth be stronger or weaker without the participation of states that had been colonies until after World War II? ➤ Does the

Commonwealth have any second-stage integration potential? ➤ Can one postulate a plausible system of global order in which principal states formed "commonwealths" with a series of lesser states and in which a series of commonwealths joined together to form a global confederal system?

3. There is considerable support in the United States for the idea of an Atlantic Union, i.e., for eventual economic, military, and political integration of the United States and Western Europe. ➤ Is such an objective beneficial from the per-

---

[15]Cf. The Hon. Patrick Maitland, M.P., *Task for Giants: An Expanding Commonwealth*, London, 1957.

spective of global stability? Would a successful Atlantic Union movement create second-stage potential by developing a more globalist orientation in some of the most sovereignty-conscious countries beyond the nation-state? See "Atlantic Union" Hearings (House Committee on Foreign Affairs, 89th Cong., 2nd Sess., August 30, 31 and September 1, 8, and 20, 1966). For exposition of the "Atlantic Idea" see Clarence K. Streit, *Union Now: A Proposal for a Federal Union of the Democracies of the North Atlantic* (Harper, New York, 1939). Note especially the testimony of George Ball, then Under Secretary of State, who regards the encouragement of "a federal union of the North Atlantic countries" as not in "accord with the political realities of the mid-20th century." Mr. Ball goes on to say: "It is our experience that the pursuit of unrealistic goals distracts from rather than assists, the achievement of the useful and the possible" (p. 165). Is such an admonition persuasive in this instance? in general? Mr. Ball suggests a two-stage conception of his own: first, European unity; then, greater coalescence of United States-European relations. As for the present situation, Mr. Ball says that "the fact of disparity of size [between the United States and the individual states of Europe] is, it seems to me, the central and inescapable impediment to serious movement toward Atlantic Union at the present time" (p. 166). ➤ Why should a disparity in size and resources be an obstacle to integration? See Selections 10 and 11 (by Yalem and Liska); consider the role of the United States in the inter-American system in this light. Mr. Ball expanded his views on the issue of disparity as follows:

> Quite frankly, I find little evidence of any strong interest among Europeans for any immediate move toward greater political unity with the United States. We Atlantic nations are of different size and the Europeans are sensitive to this disparity. They fear the overwhelming weight of U.S. power and influence in our common councils. They fear the superior resources of U.S. industry in their economic life. They are concerned that, in their relations with the United States, they may tend to lose their identities and become simply passive ancillaries to American policy" (p. 167).

Does this reasoning suggest the importance of excluding predominant states from regional integration movements? What Mr. Ball has said about disparity in Europe would appear more applicable to the relations between the United States and Latin America. ➤ Are there counter-considerations that diminish the bad effects of disparity? ➤ What are they? For Mr. Ball's own conception of the proper condition of international society, as distinct from his statements as an official of the United States Government, see Ball, *The Discipline of Power* (Little, Brown, Boston, 1968). In this book Mr. Ball proposes that world order be based on somewhat benignly animated spheres of influence. A sphere of influence is an expression of quasi-dominance. It is, in many ways, a pattern of influence and organization that is analogous to a bloc, except possibly that the subordinate members of a bloc *might* participate as virtual equals; the Soviet bloc, the tightest sphere of quasi-dominance, has, on occasion, denied subordinate bloc members even the option of domestic liberalization. Military intervention in Hungary (1956) and Czechoslovakia (1968) are demonstrations of Soviet insistence on "bloc cohesion." Certainly, the Soviet bloc could also be analyzed as "a sphere of influence." (See Zbigniew Brzezinski, *The Soviet Bloc: Unity and Conflict* [Harvard Press, Cambridge, rev. and enl. ed., 1967]; Brzezinski, "The Organization of the Communist Camp," *World Politics*, vol. 13, no. 2 [January 1961], pp. 175–209.)

➤ How does the idea of an "Atlantic Union" compare with the late President Charles de Gaulle's proposal for "a Europe from the Atlantic to the Urals" in terms either of desirability or attainability? ➤ What is the proper timetable and geographical scope for first-stage integration efforts? ➤ What kinds of units are most easily and most effectively combined? ➤ To what extent do answers to such questions depend on distinctive attributes of a particular international subsystem? There are arguments for and against seeking either a homogeneous or a heterogeneous integration base, whether a single variable such as culture, language, level of development, ideology, proximity, shared experience, common enemy or a combination of variables is considered.

4. George Modelski has described the Communist international system. He takes issue with

the orthodox view that the Communist system could be adequately described "as primarily an expansive empire, an array of satellite governments dominated from one, and later possibly from two, centers" or "a bloc of states assuming a place in a world system of bipolarity." Modelski rather suggests that the Communist international system is "a potentially global political system" whose constituent units might nevertheless retain a measure of national identity and autonomy. In this spirit, Modelski is attributing to the Communist international system a serious capability for second-stage integration potential, the main concern of Selections 10, 11, and 12. The attributes of second-stage integration potential mentioned by Modelski as descriptive of the Communist international system are as follows: (1) an ideology that claims universal validity, and is espoused by aligned political parties throughout the non-Communist world; (2) the segmentation of authority among prominent Communist states that has given to the system an international character that is useful for further expansion; (3) the clarity of the boundary that differentiates Communist states from non-Communist states; (4) the capacity of Communist states to sustain the solidity, leadership, and authority of the cohesive elements of the Communist world movement; and (5) the capacity of the Communist system to confine conflict within its systemic boundaries and to prevent penetration by non-Communist states. Modelski also

argues that Communism as a movement possesses "a world political party" that operates in international arenas (such as the United Nations). Finally, Modelski suggests that in the future "possible transformations are (1) a monolithic bloc, (2) dissolution, and (3) entry into a 'normal' world party system." The considerations bearing on whether any of these transformations is likely, are complex; among the more obvious of these considerations are, in Modelski's words, "the inevitable disintegration of the Communist monolith and the gradual dissipation of revolutionary fervor." (See George Modelski, "Communism: The International System," *International Encyclopedia of the Social Sciences*, vol. 3 [Crowell, Collier, and Macmillan Co., Inc., New York, 1968], pp. 126–32; see also Modelski, *The Communist International System*, Princeton University, Center of International Studies, Research Monograph no. 9, 1960.) As with other complex actors, the dynamics of growth make analysis at a given point in time emphasize factors that may not persist indefinitely; generalizations about the British Commonwealth or the Communist international system often imply an identity that is seriously altered by subsequent, unanticipated developments. Therefore, any description of a "regional" actor should be understood to contain an invisible superscript notation of date (as, for example, "the Communist international system^{1960}").

10

Theories of Regionalism

RONALD YALEM

Characteristics of Regional Solidarity. Thus far [in *Regionalism and World Order*] we have been chiefly concerned with the external aspects of regionalism. Although regional cooperation is affected by the strength or weakness of the universal organization and by inter-regional relationships, regional politics also determines the solidarity of member states. Inquiry into the nature of intra-regional politics requires an analysis of two basic questions: (1) what are the elements which make up a stable regional system and (2) what conclusions may be drawn with regard to the efficacy of small-state regionalism and regional associations clustered around one or more great powers?

Earlier [in *Regionalism and World Order*] some characteristics were presented that account for the cooperation that is theoretically possible among states within a specific region. In addition to geographic proximity, the existence of a similar political, ideological, social, and cultural background were cited as unifying elements.

Perhaps the most comprehensive attempt to analyze the elements that comprise a "stable" regional system is the study by B. Bhoutros-Ghali.[1] Approaching the study as a political sociologist, he draws on the insights of both disciplines to enlighten our understanding of the substructure of regional associations. While the principles presented are normative in character and somewhat idealistic, they constitute a major contribution to an appreciation of the interrelated aspects of regional solidarity.

Regional groups are said to be composed of a mixture of necessary and sufficient elements. The following necessary elements include: (legal) a treaty for the maintenance of peace; (sociological) a treaty based on a particular sociological solidarity embracing racial or ethnic affinities, economic cooperation, mutual defense; (geo-

From Ronald Yalem, *Regionalism and World Order.* © 1965, Public Affairs Press, Washington, D.C., pp. 17–37. Reprinted by permission of Public Affairs Press.

[1]This discussion is based on B. Bhoutros-Ghali, *Contribution a L'Etude Des Ententes Regionales* (Paris, 1949).

graphic) contiguity of member states and (institutional) an international agency of a permanent character.

In addition to these necessary elements, regional groups require for their success the following: legal equality of member states; free adhesion; and more than five signatories.

Necessary and sufficient elements are interdependent and mutually reinforcing since regional systems that depend upon a single element of solidarity "will be condemned to failure to the extent [that] they are not based on different elements which are interconnected."[2] While this is an assumption that has not yet been verified by empirical research, there is increasing acceptance of its validity among scholars. The persistent internal conflicts within NATO, for example, have frequently been attributable to a juridical structure too narrowly based on military solidarity.

According to Bhoutros-Ghali, the various elements of sociological solidarity constitute the substructure upon which are superimposed provisions for pacific settlement, use of force, juridical structure, and economic and social cooperation. Regional solidarity is further defined in terms of three aspects: a series of primary elements existing prior to any human will such as the belief in a bond of imaginary race, belonging to a similar complex history, the existence of a given geographical situation, and certain consciousness of group sentiment that dominates in time of crisis.[3]

In the discussion of geographical contiguity as a prerequisite for regional cooperation, a distinction is made between direct contiguity and interposition in which a number of states have a common interest in a region but are themselves not contiguous with each other.[4] For example, Argentina and the United States are not geographically contiguous but both have a common interest in the Western Hemisphere which is realized by their membership in the Organization of American States. The earlier cited example of the association of geographically separated states in the SEATO is also illustrative of interposition.

If some degree of geographic contiguity is a basic element of a regional system, the region itself is not susceptible to geographic precision. Ultimately, regions are defined politically according to the power capabilities of states, for while natural barriers may separate one region from another they have not prevented states from establishing spheres of influence far removed from the home territory.

Political relations among the members of regional groups often pose difficult problems of dependency as suggested earlier.[5] One view is that "the only basis upon which regional arrangements can be made to function . . . is that of mutual respect for the sovereignty and independence of all members . . ."[6]

Although legal equality is mentioned by Bhoutros-Ghali as necessary to perfect a regional system, he does recognize the disparity between legal equality and political inequality in those systems dominated by one or more great powers. These elements are relatively balanced only in those small state regional systems which, unfortunately, have not demonstrated much durability or strength.

Whether the discrepancy between political inequality and legal equality that is characteristic of Western regional systems will bring about their dissolution is debatable. Coalitions under the domination of a great power, according to Bhoutros-Ghali, "will [lead to] . . . a restricted union provoking the dislocation of the general union; soon the general union will disengage itself; each small state taking refuge in its former independence."[7] Although disintegrative tendencies are visible in the Western coalition systems of NATO, OAS, and SEATO, they have not been powerful enough to bring about their termination. If the threat of Soviet and Chinese aggression were to recede, it is unclear whether NATO and SEATO would survive. The answer would seem to depend on whether other bonds of cooperation could be developed in which the member states could channel their energies.

---

[2]*Ibid.*, p. 228.
[3]*Ibid.*, p. 32.
[4]*Ibid.*, p. 42.

[5]See p. 13 [of *Regionalism and World Order*].
[6]Padelford, "Regional Organizations and the United Nations," *International Organization* 8 (1954), p. 211.
[7]Bhoutros-Ghali, *op. cit.*, p. 79.

On the basis of the preceding description of the elements comprising a successful regional system, Professor Bhoutros-Ghali defines regional understandings (ententes) "as organisms of a permanent character, grouping in a geographically determined region of more than two states which by reason of their proximity, their communities of interests or their affinities, . . . [establish] an association for the maintenance of peace and security in their region and for the development of their economic, social and cultural cooperation with the final purpose of forming a distinct political entity."[8]

The advantage of such a theoretical formulation of the ingredients of regional solidarity is that it focuses on the anatomy if not the institutional structure of regional systems. By probing the foundations that serve to unite nation-states, we are in a better position to understand what is often vaguely referred to as the greater homogeneity of regionalism in contrast to the world at large. However, there is a danger in overstressing similarities and understressing differences and antagonisms that exist within regional groupings. Geographically proximate states may not be friends but enemies as in the classic case of France and Germany. Moreover, despite the presence of a certain sociological solidarity or unity, Western Europe was fragmented into competitive and autonomous units until quite recently. In the Middle East a common Arab heritage has not proved to be a sufficiently adequate basis for regional cohesion for a loosely formed Arab League organization. Thus, despite social and cultural similarities, nations and regions may be susceptible to disassociative forces engendered by mutually competitive foreign policies that may nullify all of the preexisting necessary and sufficient elements for successful regionalism.

Secondly, while the sociological approach to regional solidarity is useful, it neglects to explore the interaction between those elements that predispose states to seek cooperation and the institutions created to fulfill such cooperation. Too little attention is devoted to the importance of the institutional factor in retarding or accelerating regional integration. Fortunately, this gap has been partially filled by Professor Ernst Haas, who has developed two suggestive hypotheses regarding the influence of regional institutions on economic and political integration in Western Europe:[9]

1. A central institution will affect political integration meaningfully only if it is willing to follow policies giving rise to expectations and demands for more—or fewer federal measures. If it fails to arouse strong positive or negative responses, its impact is apt to be minimal.

2. Regional integration involves a complex interaction among international institutions, national governments, national and supranational parties, and national and supranational pressure groups in which "major interest groups as well as politicians determine their support of, or opposition to, new central institutions and policies on the basis of a calculation of advantage."

Haas believes these conclusions are valid not only for Western Europe but for other areas in which there is a similarly high level of industrialism, parliamentary or presidential democracy, identifiable elites, and articulate and literate masses mobilized for political action.

Though Bhoutros-Ghali acknowledges the significance of economic factors for regional cooperation, he seems to view regional economic cooperation as less desirable than universal economic cooperation. Yet if the latter ideal is unattainable states may be disposed to initiate regionalism in the economic sphere. The desire for economic advantage has proven to be a powerful stimulus to the creation of regional unity in Western Europe since 1945. With less economic justification, the European experience is being imitated in many non-European areas. This is not to imply that the basis of regionalism is primarily economic or to deny that regional economic unity may indeed be discriminatory toward non-regional states, but only to indicate that regional economic cooperation has been of such importance that it is necessary to emphasize that of all of the elements undergirding regional solidarity the expectation of economic advantage is increasingly significant.

Should the object of regional groups include the eventual formation of a political union? In reply to the question of whether it is not harmful

[8]*Ibid.*, p. 101.

[9]Ernst B. Haas, *The Uniting of Europe* (Stanford: Stanford University Press, 1958), pp. xiii–xiv.

to indicate in advance to states that the final purpose of their association is to lose their independence, Bhoutros-Ghali asserts that a study of the various elements of a regional understanding reveals:[10] "that there . . . is a natural tendency [for regional groups] to tighten their ties. History teaches us . . . that this tendency has been helpful several times in making evolution of several of these communities from an anarchial or weakly organized state to a federal state. [It is an evolutionary goal which] does not necessitate a formal acceptance by members; nevertheless, the latter are presumed to recognize this purpose as one of the elements of regional life and should adapt themselves to it."

Examination of these assumptions, however, may result in somewhat different conclusions. The experience of the American colonies and the Swiss cantons does reveal tendencies that culminated in an amalgamation of previously separate units as discussed in a recent study on the formation of political community.[11] But this does not necessarily warrant analogy with contemporary regional agencies. The two cases involved the expansion of community within essentially national settings not the integration of a number of states into a regional community. Also, the period involved the 18th and early 19th centuries before the rise of industrialization and mass political movements. However, it is conceivable that future studies may demonstrate that those factors which precipitate the unification of national states also operate internationally.

Conversely, certain factors may affect international integration that do not affect national integration. What are such factors? It is still premature to be scientific, but intuitive examination of the process of European integration since 1945 suggests that a certain disillusionment with traditional nationalism coupled with an appreciation of the economic and political advantages of regional unification were instrumental in launching regional unity. Until more is known about the differences and similarities between national and international integration, however, it should not be assumed that there is an inevitable evolution of regional groups toward centralized or federalized structures. There are too many variables that may impede a process of regional integration well under way. [12] The French veto of Great Britain's admission into the European Common Market in January, 1963, provides a recent illustration. Regional groups may have the potential to expand into supranational political communities, but they may also be vulnerable to disintegrative forces.

Small State Regionalism and the Theory of Great Power Orbits. An inquiry into the internal dynamics of regionalism would be incomplete if it were limited only to an appreciation of the factors predisposing independent states to merge in cooperation. A vital aspect of all regional groups involves not only the strength of the interests which bind but an understanding of the relative political influences of the member states. These influences may be integrative (centripetal) or disintegrative (centrifugal); they may involve large and small states.

The case for small state regionalism has been stated in terms of an antipathy toward great power domination and with a frank contempt for their qualities:[13]

"International regionalism favors in the spiritual interest of the world, the survival of small and middle powers, in the midst of which a qualitative civilization can develop through opposition to the quantitative civilization proper for the great modern powers, and if the regional arrangements complete only that mission, that would be sufficient to justify their existence. . . ."

In his analysis of the dynamics of small state regional organizations, however, Professor Liska expresses grave doubts about their viability as summarized below:[14]

1. Small state regionalism is impractical because of the inadequacy of weak powers to ensure regional security and welfare.
2. While small states value participation in a world organization, they are attracted to regional

---

[10]Bhoutros-Ghali, *op. cit.*, p. 107.

[11]See Karl Deutsch et al, *Political Community and the North Atlantic Area* (Princeton: Princeton University Press, 1957), pp. 1–21.

[12]The chief impediment would appear to be nationalistic tendencies by one or more member states.

[13]J. M. Yepes, "Les Accords Regionaux et Le Droit International," *Recueil Des Cours* 71 (1947), p. 256.

[14]Liska, [*International Equilibrium,*] pp. 142–148.

groups where their national security may be guaranteed by great powers.

3. Study of the Arab League and the Little Entente reveals a number of inherent disadvantages of small state regional cooperation.

Specifically, study of the Little Entente and the Arab League reveals some of the limitations of small-state groups:

—Both brought together minor states formerly belonging to large empires situated in strategic areas but with inadequate defensive power.

—The incentive to association in both instances was negative—the Arab states to offset Israel the Little Entente to check Hungary and Bulgaria.

—While both groups desired to expel great power influence (France from the Middle East and Russia, Italy, and Germany from the Balkans) they needed the aid of outside powers for stability: France to support the Little Entente and the United States and Britain to aid the Arab League.

Liska concluded that the lack of a centralized structure, an exacting security commitment to repel aggression, and the absence of positive goals militated against the achievement of a closer unity despite a common cultural and historical tradition. The fact that both systems could not isolate their policies from the wider world distribution of power, especially the activities and pressures of the major powers, was another cause of their failure.

Do these conclusions, drawn from an examination of only two small-state regional groups, constitute sufficient evidence to condemn such associations as ineffective? The answer would appear to be affirmative if such agencies are assessed in terms of their record of deterring aggression since the Little Entente and the Balkan Entente failed to preserve regional security. On the other hand, while these groups achieved only token economic and social cooperation, the possibility of such cooperation among small states cannot be excluded. In fact, the emergence of customs union arrangements recently in Latin America, Africa, and the Middle East is based on the feasibility of partnership among smaller nations for economic and social development, including eventual elimination of

abnormal economic dependence on the wealthier states. The difficulties should not be minimized in view of the fervent nationalism that envelops these areas and the considerable economic and social improvements necessary. It is premature to evaluate the success of such efforts, but it is possible that they may be useful especially if the participating nations recognize that national integration is an important precondition for effective regional cooperation.[15]

More difficult and more controversial than small state regionalism is whether "a more promising alternative might be regional groupings anchored in the superior resources of a nuclear Great Power."[16] As this has been the most common type of regional arrangement, a thorough examination of the merits and defects of such groupings is required.

The intrusion or participation of one or more great powers in a regional complex is the strongest factor in altering its narrow geographic scope since the interests of such states are increasingly global. As a result the regional body tends to ". . . lose its geographic sense as well as its assured emancipation from involvement in the unwelcome complexities of the wide world."[17] An interesting example may be found in the recent history of the inter-American system of which the Organization of American States is the political and juridical expression. In spite of the increase in hemispheric solidarity expressed in the Rio Pact and the consolidation and extension of informal pre-war cooperation through the OAS, that agency was hampered in its formative period because the United States as the dominant great power relegated Latin America to a relatively low priority in its foreign policy and concentrated on Western Europe and the Far East where it was involved in balance of power politics against the Soviet Union.

The aftermath of this policy of polite neglect produced intra-regional resentment and criticism of the United States for its abandonment of earlier stated proposals to strengthen inter-American solidarity. Between 1948 and 1960

---

[15]For an informed discussion of the problem of economic regionalism in the underdeveloped areas see Lincoln Gordon, "Economic Regionalism Reconsidered," *World Politics*, January, 1961, pp. 231–254.

[16]Liska, *op. cit.*, p. 148.

[17]Claude, [*Swords into Ploughshares*,] p. 114.

Latin America provided a classic illustration of a region in which a great power's global responsibilities undermined the cohesion of a regional system with which it had long been identified as the leading state. The Castro-led Cuban revolution of 1959 and the ensuing instability it created within Latin America may have served as a healthy antidote to the period of relative neglect by redirecting the attention of the United States to the difficult problem of containing the spread of communism to other parts of the hemisphere. Whether its heightened interest in the region as expressed by the Alliance for Progress program will be able to revitalize the inter-American system is not clear. In any event the motivation for increased great power concern was not precipitated by humanitarian consideration for the welfare of Latin America, but was inextricably linked with the world wide ideological struggle between communism and democracy.

A much more common criticism of regional systems geared to great powers is that the increment in national security gained by the participation of small states in such systems is often more than offset by the gradual erosion of their independence.[18] Another common indictment of regionalism is that rival regional groups degenerate into competing "spheres of influence" that lead to international instability rather than to international equilibrium.

To see the problem in clearer perspective, it is necessary to study the theory and practice of great power orbits. Theories contemplating a world order of regional superpowers were developed during World War II by Walter Lippmann and E. H. Carr and need to be studied separately from their pragmatic application brought about by the disintegration of the World War II alliance system.[19]

The theory of great power orbits is based on the premise that "regional groupings of small states ought to cluster around the local Great Power and pool military, economic, and other resources in peace and war."[20] The arrangement would help the great power by supplying it with additional facilities and give to the smaller powers aid, protection, and a degree of independence thereby enhancing intra-regional and inter-regional security.[21]

Regional orbits managed by great powers may be justified on the basis of three additional assumptions: the ability of great powers to insure regional security; the compatibility of interests between the regional great power and small states; and the disposition of great powers to develop policies of restraint toward their lesser allies. Empirical analysis, however, casts doubt on the validity of each of these premises. In an era of nuclear stalemate, great powers are unable to guarantee the security of their satellites against surprise attack; there is often conflict between the great power and its associates who tend to resent their power inferiority; and the necessity of maintaining regional solidarity may dispose the great power to exert periodic pressure or even coercion on recalcitrant smaller powers.

An elaboration of the theory of great powers postulates the coexistence of a number of regional systems controlled by great powers that would undergird and strengthen world order. Winston Churchill, for example, believed that a universal order based on the general concept of collective security had proved to be too ambitious during the inter-war period and needed to be replaced by regionalized security systems. Early in World War II he supported the idea of a regionalized world organization:[22]

> It is the intention of the Chiefs of the United Nations to create a world organization for the preservation of peace, based upon conceptions of freedom and justice and the revival of prosperity. As a part of this organization an instrument of European government will be established which will embody the spirit but not be subject to the weakness of the former League of Nations.

---

[18]The obvious illustration is the Soviet dominated Warsaw Pact, but it may also be visible in lesser degree within the inter-American and North Atlantic defense systems. It is a moot point, however, as to whether the Warsaw system represents a genuine regional association inasmuch as the legal independence and sovereignty of the East European satellites is more fictional than real.

[19]See E. H. Carr, *The Twenty Years Crisis* (London: Macmillan, 1946), pp. 228–231 and Walter Lippmann, *U.S. War Aims* (Boston: Little, Brown and Company, 1944), pp. 80–85.

[20]Liska, *op. cit.*, p. 149.

[21]*Ibid.*

[22]Winston Churchill, *The Hinge of Fate* (Boston: Houghton-Mifflin, 1950), pp. 711–712.

The units forming this body will not only be the great nations of Europe and Asia Minor as long established, but a number of Confederations formed among the smaller states, among which a Scandinavian Bloc, a Danubian Bloc, and a Balkan Bloc appear to be obvious. A similar instrument will be formed in the Far East, with different membership. . . .

Thus under the theory "a general international organization is reduced to a secondary role or renounced altogether."[23]

Insofar as the politics of great power orbits are concerned, the tendency is for fluctuation between domination of the smaller power and a reconciliation of "the legitimate regional interests (of the great power) with the rights of the smaller nations."[24] But in the absence of external countervailing pressures, it is difficult for even a liberally oriented major power to avoid periodic interference.

Within the British Empire and the Western Hemisphere a pattern of intra-regional power originally based upon satellitism has progressively evolved to near partnership primarily because of the liberal values and ideologies of the dominant powers—the United States and Great Britain.[25] Yet the problem of developing coequal partnership rather than domination has been difficult. The inter-American system has been weakened not only because of extra-regional problems demanding the attention of the United States; the enormous disparity between the economic and political power of the United States and the other Latin American nations precludes the emergence of political equality which the concept of partnership presupposes.

While the establishment of the Commonwealth of Nations was a pragmatic attempt by an imperial power to perpetuate its influence among former dependencies and thereby offset "the end of empire," this unique association has also experienced disintegrative forces that jeopardize its cohesion. The decline of Great Britain as a major power undermined the protective foundation upon which the solidarity of the "old" Commonwealth was based, causing Canada,

Australia, and New Zealand to seek new security ties with the United States. Expansion of the membership to include non-white and non-western states in Africa and the Far East further eroded the family-like atmosphere that prevailed among the older and more homogenous Commonwealth members. But the potentially most divisive factor confronting the Commonwealth is the possible entry of Britain into the European Common Market and with it the abandonment of the traditional British policy of aloofness from continental European politics. Though it may be possible for Britain to work out some pattern of compromise of her emerging loyalties to Europe with her traditional ties to the Commonwealth, it is unlikely that the latter will ever be as viable an association as in the past.

As a result of the imperfections of the great power orbits described above, the smaller nations within the inter-American system and the Commonwealth have sought a counterweight to their dependency by active participation in the United Nations. The Latin American nations especially have displayed a curious fluctuation between regionalism and universalism. Dependent upon the United States for military and economic security, they are fearful of the effect of such dependency upon their independence and paradoxically disgruntled whenever the United States becomes preoccupied with the problems of other regions. They seek solace for their insecurity in the United Nations which they value as "a forum for their own extra-hemispheric self-affirmation" and utilize as "an additional potential check on the Colossus of the North."[26]

With regard to the Commonwealth and the inter-American system, it is possible that the major powers and their lesser allies may find participation in the universal and regional organizations mutually beneficial depending upon the circumstances of the moment. . . . the flight to regional security agencies after 1945 developed as a result of uncertainty regarding the efficacy of the collective security mechanism of the United Nations. Although membership in the general organization for the United States and its Western European allies still proves useful and indeed

---

[23]Liska, *op. cit.*, p. 150.
[24]*Ibid.*, p. 152.
[25]*Ibid.*

[26]*Ibid.*, p. 154.

necessary, there is a greater security advantage within the more limited association of NATO whose collective security obligations are automatic rather than conditional. Similarly, regional agencies may prove advantageous as dispute-settling mechanisms as in the success of the Organization of American States in quelling minor regional disputes before they could be exploited by the Soviet Union.

Contrarily, outright incompatibility between regionalism and universalism is symbolized by the policies of the Soviet Union. It considers participation in the global organization a tactical necessity while working constantly to weaken the United Nations as a peace-keeping agency. Efforts to strengthen the solidarity of the Warsaw Pact organization have been given greater emphasis in recent years.

Plausible though the theory of great power orbits may be, it is fraught with numerous defects when applied in practice. The basic difficulty is the tendency of great powers to manipulate and control their lesser allies unless ideology serves as a restraint against interventionism. The theory assumes self-restraint but does not provide any defense for small nations in the event that the great power displays expansionist proclivities. Possible defenses include the utilization of the general organization to focus world opinion on great power machinations, solicitation of assistance from an extra-regional great power, or ultimately secession from the regional system. Resort to one or more of these techniques would not only be indicative of the lack of compatibility between the great power and its smaller allies but also potentially dangerous to the solidarity of the regional system.

These observations may serve to heighten our awareness of the difficulty of regional isolation in the contemporary international system. In a system in which there is likely to be a continuous and changing interaction among three types of actors—powerful extra-regional states, the United Nations, and the regional system itself—the difficulties of sustaining regional groupings apart from the wider system appear obvious.

Does this necessarily lead to the conclusion that the theory "stands for the enlargement of the vertical power of the nuclear state typical of imperialism?"[27] Although this tendency was discernible in the early phase of the NATO system because the European nations were peculiarly dependent on the United States for military and economic assistance, it has been reversed by the gradual economic and political unification of Western Europe and the possible possession of nuclear weapons by small states within the alliance.

Within the other regional agencies headed by the United States, a comparable reduction of power disparity has not developed, but this does not necessarily mean that the gap in power that now exists is destined to continue. As the weaker members of these coalitions make a successful transition to economic and political modernization, they may be able to reduce their overwhelming contemporary dependence upon the great power.

A second limitation of the theory pertains to the alleged cohesion which a great power may stimulate within regional groupings by virtue of its superior economic and military resources. Yet it is doubtful that the interests of such powers can be centered exclusively within one region. This may lead to a neglect of the smaller powers as reflected in the American policy toward Latin America before 1960. Also, because of the tendency of security zones to overlap, increasing pressures may be generated on the great power to solidify control over its allies in an effort to compete with rival regional systems for the allegiance of intermediate smaller states.[28] The uncommitted states that interpose themselves between the Western and Soviet blocs are an obvious example of the overlapping of security zones.

As mentioned earlier, insofar as there is a tendency of great powers toward imperialism, it may be counteracted by a restraining ideology, the external pressures of the general organization, or by the intrusion of a rival great power. Using the NATO and OAS systems as models, we may perceive that the intra-regional dynamics of these great power orbits appear to be governed by fluctuations ranging from expansionism of the great power toward a more progressive sharing of responsibilities with the smaller powers.

---

[27]*Ibid.*, p. 160.
[28]*Ibid.*, p. 159.

Finally, the theory of great power orbits is open to criticism if viewed as a panacea for international stability. It assumes that an inter-regional equilibrium is facilitated by regionally dominated great-power systems. But this is hardly possible unless regional blocs are headed by powers of a similar ideology. Moreover, even if such a constellation of ideologically compatible blocs could be developed, there would still be the possibility of inter-regional conflict arising out of the extra-regional interests of major powers unless the regional blocs were equilibrated and reconciled within the framework of a universal international organization. In turn this would require the relinquishment of great power regional hegemony for equilibrium between the global organization and a series of regional blocs through the subordination of the latter to the former. How could such an arrangement be managed if the organization of peace and security was centralized among a number of regional blocs and decentralized at the universal level?

A more effective approach to world order than a series of unregulated regional blocs is one in which regional systems are subordinated and controlled by the universal organization. Such an approach, however, would require the revitalization of the United Nations as a peace enforcement agency. As long as the major powers entrust their security to regional bloc systems rather than to the United Nations, that organization will be impotent as a collective security mechanism and the global-regional equilibrium posited by the United Nations Charter inoperative.

Furthermore, the contemporary trend toward regional integration may slow down universal integration if the consolidation of regions and their coexistence within the general organization accentuates their identities and interests.[29] The universal system will then remain what it is now: an arena for minimizing conflict and maximizing common interests in deference to a minimum common denominator.[30]

A more optimistic view of the contemporary situation, however, is presented by Professor Inis Claude:[31]

It should be emphasized that the United Nations is irrelevant to the security issue posed by great-power conflict only in a very partial and limited sense. The Organization is incapable of exercising coercive control over a great power. It cannot prevent or suppress aggression by major powers; it cannot prevent war among them; hence, it cannot promise protection to any state against the ravages of war launched by a great power. However, the rules of the Charter prohibiting the aggressive use of force are assuredly applicable to the rival great powers, despite the fact that their enforcement cannot under present conditions be institutionalized; the Charter excused the United Nations from the effort to enforce these rules against the great powers, but it does not excuse the latter from the obligation to respect them. Moreover, the United Nations is relevant in the sense that it possesses a variety of resources which may be used . . . to influence the behavior of the major powers toward each other and toward lesser states, to promote the moderation of conflict. . . . The regional groupings are the organizations of force relevant to the crisis in great-power relationships. The relevance of the United Nations is of a different, but not necessarily inferior, order.

It is by no means certain, however, whether the United Nations would be able to play such a definitive role in the case of direct confrontation of the superpowers as in Berlin. As Professor Claude himself admits, the United Nations has been effective mainly in those conflicts where the confrontation is indirect such as in the Suez Crisis of 1956 and in the Congo Crisis of 1960.[32] In such conflicts United Nations peace forces have functioned as agencies of interposition sealing off the area in dispute from the direct clash of the superpowers. But this is a much more modest role for the United Nations than was contemplated in the Charter inasmuch as these international forces have been utilized only after first obtaining the consent of the states involved in the dispute rather than exercising an independent coercive power.

---

[29]Ernst B. Haas, "European and International Integration," *International Organization*, Summer, 1961, pp. 391–392.

[30]Ibid., p. 392.

[31]Inis L. Claude, "The United Nations and the Use of Force," *International Conciliation*, March, 1961, pp. 367–368.

[32]Inis L. Claude, "The Containment and Resolution of Disputes," in Francis Wilcox and H. Field Haviland (editors), *The United States and the United Nations* (Baltimore: Johns Hopkins Press, 1961), p. 116 and ff.

A Theory of Isolation and Collaboration. To conclude this discussion of theories of regionalism, we will now examine a recent theoretical model constructed by Professor Harold Guetzkow that further explores the complex interrelationship between regionalism and universalism.[33] The distinctiveness of his contribution arises from the fact that it illuminates two variables that are crucial in the life of nations—isolation and collaboration—and attempts to predict future trends toward isolation or collaboration on the basis of the past experience of states. His conclusions may be applied to the behavior of regional groupings in two ways: (1) collaborationist tendencies of individual nations result in efforts toward the integration of a group of nations; and (2) as regional entities emerge they may exhibit tendencies of inward isolation or outward collaboration toward the universal organization.

The model postulates the opposition of isolation and collaboration factors said to influence the behavior of certain types of groups such as the labor union, city council, and the nation-state. Following are some of the factors that operate to direct the behavior of groups inward, other things being equal:

1. Experience with self-reliance has been favorable to solve needs.
2. Ideologies of the group are oriented toward isolation.
3. Self-reliant means to achieve goals are more advantageous and practical than collaborative means.
4. The tasks of the group permit it to pursue its goal or goals in isolation.
5. Members feel collaboration interferes with successful self-reliance.
6. The leadership of the group fears collaboration will undermine its position.

To the extent that these factors are reversed, the direction of behavior will turn outward into collaboration.

It is not necessary to reproduce the model in its entirety here but rather to extrapolate those features of it that clarify the theoretical aspects of the interaction between universal and regional organizations.

In determining the behavior of groups certain past experience factors are influential in predicting how new demands will be met. As might be expected, the greater the satisfaction of needs through internal or self-reliant measures, the greater the tendency for internal solutions as new needs arise; conversely, to the extent that such needs have been previously solved through intergroup relations, the more likely will collaboration with other groups be sought in the future.[34]

Some additional hypotheses of the model are:

1. If new demands arise (to meet certain political or economic needs) or members believe that their existing demands are not being met satisfactorily, the following responses may occur: (*a*) members may try to satisfy their demands self-reliantly by making internal changes in the group itself, acting in isolation from other groups; and/or (*b*) members may try to satisfy their demands through cooperation with other groups by collaboration.
2. If the needs of group members are relatively constant and relatively well satisfied, there will not be any significant impulse for change.

The direction of behavior of groups toward isolation or collaboration is determined by the following factors:

1. The relative strengths of the factors of isolation and collaboration and their components "determine the direction of behavior."
2. The direction of behavior may be thus complicated by equally strong pressures for isolation and collaboration thereby producing conflict within the group as to which direction to move. (Applied to regionalism, this hypothesis envisages a situation in which a regional organization may be pressured by forces tending toward exclusivism or toward cooperation with other regional agencies or the universal organization.)
3. Stalemates will be produced when there is equilibrium of opposing factors of isolation and collaboration.

---

[33]The following discussion is based on Harold Guetzkow, "Isolation and Collaboration: A Partial Theory of Inter-Nation Relations," *Journal of Conflict Resolution*, March, 1957, pp. 48–68.

[34]*Ibid.*, p. 51.

Do regional organizations hinder or support the development of universal agencies? On the basis of the preceding hypotheses, the model predicts "that the development of partially inclusive groups would tend to delay the growth of more inclusive universal organization, to the extent that partial arrangements are successful in meeting their members' goals."[35]

Is it possible, however, that this prediction neglects a crucial variable operative in the real world of international politics? Some needs will be satisfied only by simultaneous cooperation at both the regional and universal level rather than on the basis of mutually exclusive alternatives. For example, United States membership in the United Nations and in various regional agencies may be logically justified as consonant with the promotion of national security objectives at dual levels; small powers, too, may utilize a dual pattern to maximize their influence which may be weak in a regional agency dominated by a major power but stronger when acting as a member of a regional bloc in the General Assembly of the United Nations. On the other hand, many of the newly emerging nations have favored universalism over regionalism in their desire to maintain maximum maneuverability vis-a-vis the superpowers and thereby escape the domination which would ensue through participation in regional alliance systems.

Contemporary utilization of universalism may be the result of inadequate regional integration in the Western Hemisphere, Africa, Asia, and the Middle East. To the extent that regional agencies are not successfully satisfying the needs of individual states in these areas, they will seek assistance from the universal organization. Unable to supply the capital and technical experts necessary for economic development and industrialization, the underdeveloped nations turn to the United Nations and its specialized agencies for support as well as to individually prosperous nations outside of their regions.

If regional economic and political integration is realized in the underdeveloped regions, attention of national states would probably shift inward and away from the universal organization as Guetkow's model predicts. As such integration has only developed significantly within Western Europe, it is not surprising to find that the behavior of states within the non-Western regions is collaborative toward the universal organization. They frequently use the latter in order to compensate for their political and economic weakness through various bloc voting tactics designed to extract from the major powers the maximum commitments for economic development concerns; gradually, however, an incipient recognition of the utility of regional cooperation is emerging and may evolve into institutional arrangements of a multifunctional and transnational character.

In Western Europe, France, and to a lesser extent Belgium and Portugal, have adopted a semi-isolationist attitude toward the United Nations not only because burgeoning European economic and political unification is more satisfying to their needs but also because of the vehemence of criticism from the Afro-Asian bloc in the General Assembly for their colonial records. This may indicate that a corollary should be added to the model: the relationship between regionalism and universalism is conditioned not only by the degree of success with which regional communities satisfy the demands of their component member states but also by the nature of the experiences of individual nation-states in the universal organization.

One final example reinforces this observation. The threats of the Soviet bloc to leave the United Nations usually occur whenever its aims have been frustrated by United Nations action as for example in the defeat of their "troika" proposal to reorganize the administration of the Secretariat. Secession from the organization, however, would not be compensated by any tangible gain for the bloc. Nevertheless, the Soviet Union still cherishes as an ideal the goal of transforming the United Nations into a Communist controlled organization.[36] In the absence of the attainment of this goal, the universal organization may serve as a useful mechanism for Soviet propaganda but the bloc relies primarily on its own regional system, the Warsaw Pact, to serve its security needs.

Although there may be tendencies toward isolation from the universal organization as regional communities become integrated, it is unlikely

---

[35]*Ibid.*, p. 64.

[36]Alexander Dallin, "The Soviet View of the UN," *International Organization*, Winter 1962, p. 27.

that such tendencies will ever be absolute. The problems of regional systems cannot be totally isolated from the world community. In practice, it is impossible to exclude regional politics from world politics because of the pull of extra-regional interests affecting great power orbits. Similarly, while regional problems often require regional solutions, the impact of such problems upon other regions or the difficulty of solving them without some assistance from the universal organization militates against an automatic replacement of universalism as regional integration progresses. In matters involving disarmament, economic development, the control of outer space, and the expansion of international trade, a concerted effort by the entire international community is necessary. While the wider divergences of culture and economic and political policies at the world level may inhibit such cooperation, they do not make it any less vital or necessary.

Aside from the preceding observations, the various hypotheses advanced by Professor Guetzkow may invite certain objections. Can the nation-state or a regional system be classified as a group in common with entities of a more restricted character? If the theoretical model purports to explain the behavior of inter-group relations, does not the state possess certain attributes such as sovereignty that make it unique? In anticipation of such an objection, Professor Guetzkow declares that:[37] "The facts of international life indicated that states, like other groups, are circumscribed in their behavior by political, social, cultural and economic realities both within themselves and in their external environment. The leaders of nations, just like the leaders of other groups, are dependent for their very positions upon a complex structure of power within the group."

Acceptance of the assumption that the nation-state is a group exhibiting behavior characteristics not wholly dissimilar from other less inclusive and complex groups in regard to the variables of isolation/collaboration does not obscure the fact that there are basic differences among and within group structures. The interchangeability of nations, trade unions, city councils and political parties needs to be qualified by structural, socio-psychological, quantitative and qualitative distinctions. The nation-state operates in an environment of greater complexity than subnational groups because the former is subject to the peculiar influences of the international environment of states and regional and universal institutions in addition to the customary domestic political and nonpolitical influences. Unlike the state, the trade union, family, church, and city council function in a more restricted and hence less complex milieu. Until we know more about the variety of factors that impinge on the state as distinguished from less inclusive groups, it would be premature to accept without qualification the assumption that there is a basic similarity between the isolation/collaboration behavior of the nation and other less complex groups. The behavior of the nation is a composite of infinitely more variables than the behavior of even a major political party or trade union which represents only a limited segment of the nation. These qualifications seem to be recognized by Professor Guetzkow in citing three limitations of his model:[38]

1. The model does not enumerate all the factors which play an important part in determining the direction of national/or subgroup/behavior.

2. The need to explore the socio-psychological mechanisms which underlie isolation/collaboration behavior more adequately than developed in the model. For example, how do we measure or arrive at or define the members' satisfaction that the group is meeting their needs and/or demands? How can we determine that there is dissatisfaction? Are these mechanisms more complex for the nation than for the trade union?

3. The model is only concerned with group policy; it does not predict the form in which isolation/collaboration behavior will take place. For example, should problems be solved bilaterally or multilaterally or both with regard to trade cooperation? Will collaborative behavior be official or unofficial? The trend of behavior may be predicted by the model but the important question of form is left vague.

Summary. The preceding survey of various theories of the regionalist approach to peace and security has attempted to delineate five central

---

[37]Guetzkow, *op. cit.*, p. 62.

[38]*Ibid.*, pp. 62–63.

aspects: the theoretical assumptions underlying regionalism as a basis for international cooperation; the tangible and intangible elements upon which regional systems are based; the internal political dynamics of regional groupings involving the interaction of large and small powers and its effect on regional cohesion; the difficult problem of promoting global-regional equilibrium; and a theoretical consideration of the factors that influence isolative and/or collaborative behavior of individual nations and regional alignments.

The purpose of this theoretical introduction has been to reveal both the advantages and limitations of the regional approach to peace and security, and especially to indicate the difficulty of divorcing regionalism from universalism in the real world of international politics. No attempt was made to suggest practical solutions for reconciling contemporary regionalism and universalism since the international system is so rigidified by ideological conflict as to preclude a reconciliation. In this connection, however, the author agrees with those scholars who believe that global-regional equilibrium can best be promoted by the subordination of regional agencies to the universal organization. Yet while in theory it may be possible to effect such a harmonization, in practice the contemporary disequilibrium does

not appear susceptible to reversal in the fore-seeable future.

The question of what is meant by the subordination of regional agencies of the United Nations does require some attention. It involves in the opinion of the author a return to the constitutional theory of the Charter of the United Nations which legitimized regional arrangements but provided for their control by the Security Council through Articles 52, 53, and 54. Yet the problem of effecting such a subordination is hardly constitutional but inherently political. In all likelihood the political prerequisite would be the emergence of a lasting consensus among the permanent members of the Council regarding the international status quo to be enforced. This would in turn imply an end to the ideological and power conflict between the United States and the Soviet Union that has gripped the world for nearly twenty years. Under such circumstances, regional agencies such as NATO and the Warsaw Pact organization would cease to operate as instrumentalities of conflict between the superpowers, and they and other security agencies could be more properly controlled in a revitalized United Nations system. Political equilibrium between universalism and regionalism would then be restored. . . .

Discussion and Questions

1. ➤ How do you assess the difference between the views of Bhoutros-Ghali and Liska on the issue of "disparity" between the legal equality of states and their political inequality? ➤ Is this the same kind of "disparity" that George Ball identified as the decisive obstacle to the present creation of Atlantic Union? ➤ Does the relevance of "disparity" to first-stage integration depend on various other subsystemic variables? For instance, if external encroachment is feared

more than internal domination, the hegemonial regionalism may be actively encouraged by smaller states. Or if the national governments of smaller states were unpopular and vulnerable to rebellion and revolution, then the hegemonial presence of a principal state might be sought by unpopular incumbent governments to maintain power. The relations between the Soviet Union and the compliant governments of Eastern Europe illustrate the use of regional mechanisms to validate the imposition of Soviet hegemony; similarly, the United States has, in conjunction with compliant governments of South Asia and Latin America, tried to develop regional arrangements both to maintain and disguise the actualities of hegemony. Therefore, one motive for hegemonial regionalism is to thwart processes of internal change in the units that make up the region. Recall the idea that a political community is one in which conflict is generally resolved by nonviolent means; in the context of hegemony, the supranational political community is subordinated both to the national need for social control in the form of rigid domination and to the imperial need to exert control over foreign societies. To the extent that human rights in both a *collective* sense of self-determination and in an *individual* sense of dignity are part of a valued system of world order, these forms of hegemonial regionalism represent regressive trends in regard to building international political community.

2. ➤ What are the shortcomings of "great-power orbits"? ➤ Does an answer depend on the characteristics of a particular subsystem? ➤ Does "active participation" in the United Nations compensate in any way for inadequate forms of *de facto* regionalism?

3. ➤ What factors determine whether a regional entity will collaborate with or work against global organizations of peace and security? ➤ Can these factors be manipulated in constructive directions by efforts at social engineering? ➤ How do we identify which directions are "constructive"? ➤ By what criteria of value and performance?

11

Geographic Scope; The Pattern of Integration

GEORGE LISKA

Reprinted by permission of the publishers from George Liska, *International Equilibrium*, Cambridge, Mass.: Harvard University Press, Copyright, 1957, by the President and Fellows of Harvard College.

GEOGRAPHIC SCOPE

Types of Regionalism

To what extent are regional associations fit to adjust an intraregional equilibrium among unequally powerful states, improve the position of the relatively weaker states in the balance of power, and promote institutionally a multiple equilibrium within the region? There are different types of situations and responses. A relatively trusted Great Power may extend regional protection to not too resentful lesser associates; smaller states may have to pursue security and welfare in an area exposed to many conflicting pressures; and finally, such states may either accept active involvement or try to preserve a neutral position.

Smaller states exposed to the pressures of several major Powers find it most difficult to reconcile regionalism with membership in a general organization, national security, and genuine independence. This has been the situation of most smaller countries in Europe and, increasingly, in the Middle East and South Asia.

Weaker states ready or impelled to participate actively in the quest for national and international security value the greater independence and dignity of membership in a general organization; they are also attracted by the promise of more certain security from a regional alliance, based on concrete interests and backed by one or more Great Powers. They both desire and resent the need for alliance with a major state and seek to lean on a remote rather than a local Power. They would wish to receive the intervention of the powerful ally only when claimed and then with certainty; the Great-Power ally is likely to prefer the exact opposite. From the respective advantages of general and regional organization the smaller states wish, not unnaturally, to retain both. Only doubts about the effectiveness of the general system will tip the balance toward the regional pattern. But smaller nations that are anxious to avoid absorption in a Great-Power-centered alliance will wish for the regional pact to stay related to the general system of collective security and underpin rather than supersede it.

A new situation arises when the general system is discredited. Then even formerly activist smaller states may prefer to become buffers between contending Great Powers rather than participate in a regional pact. After 1933, Poland chose to be a "barrier of peace" between Germany and Russia instead of joining an Eastern Locarno; Belgium resumed her neutrality after the unpunished breach of Western Locarno and the Covenant. Or, for domestic as well as external reasons, neutralism may be elevated into a creed and generate a corresponding conception of regionalism.

Contemporary Asian neutralism typifies the preference of smaller states for regional organization without Great Powers. According to this school of thought, the global character of security requires a global approach through a general collective security system. It is there that the Great Powers should perform their functions and counterbalance each other in the process. Regional arrangements around a Great Power are merely disguises for domination over weaker associates; they could not enforce sanctions against another Great Power if they conformed literally with the Charter. Instead, regional organizations should be set up among states with approximately equal resources and development, certain to respect each other's sovereignty and independence. They should concentrate on socio-economic and cultural tasks and stay aloof from Great-Power conflicts.[1]

Such a doctrine cannot but appeal to youthful nationalism anxious for both economic development and political independence. The influence of the Asian-African bloc in the United Nations makes it safe to emphasize general organization as the principal instrument of security, forum of mediatory activities, and agency for economic assistance. Consistently enough, India and a number of other Southeast Asian countries, with the exception of the Philippines and Thailand, refused to join the security pact for the area sponsored by the Western Powers. But the implementation of the alternative program has run into difficulties, too. Among them are insufficiency of local resources, divergent orientations in regard to the "cold war" intertwined with mutual territorial and other conflicts, and distrust of real or suspected leadership aspirations on the part of regionally prominent states like India, the Philippines, and, increasingly, Communist China. It is a sad fact that all areas of any scope comprise states with highly unequal resources and corresponding claims to influence; and that the exclusion of Great Powers, local or remote, is not always possible (even supposing it were always desirable) since most countries are unable to ensure regional security and welfare with their limited resources alone. The Bandung Conference produced chiefly verbal results; the Colombo Plan is inseparable from British and American support; and a "Marshall Plan" for South Asia would be sure to vitalize the languid SEATO into more than literal resemblance to NATO.

Convenient and strikingly comparable examples of the virtues and the limitations of small-state regionalism are the Little Entente and the Arab League, emerging from the First and the Second World War respectively. It is worth while to look at the similarities and limitations, without denying the differences and accomplishments.[2]

The similarities are many. Both associations brought together relatively minor communities

[1]See K. M. Panikkar, "Regionalism and World Security," in Panikkar, ed., *Regionalism and Security*, p. 4 and *passim*; K. Santhanam, "A Regional Authority for South-East Asia," *Regionalism and Security*, pp. 26–27; P. Talbot, "South and Southeast Asia," *Regional Arrangements for Security and the United Nations*, pp. 126–130; L. A. Mills and associates, *The New World of Southeast Asia* (1949), pp. 376, 379 ff., 412; and A. Appadorai, "The Bandung Conference," *India Quarterly* (July–September 1955), pp. 207–235.

[2]See Howard, "The Little Entente and the Balkan Entente," in Robert J. Kerner, ed., *Czechoslovakia* (1949), pp. 368–386; Paul Seabury, "The League of Arab States: Debacle of a Regional Arrangement," *International Organization* (November 1949), pp. 633–642; M. Khadduri, "Regional and Collective Defense Arrangements in the Middle East," *Regional Arrangements for Security and the United Nations*, pp. 100–117; Charles Malik, "The Near East Between East and West," in R. N. Frye, ed., *The Near East and the Great Powers* (1951); Halford L. Hoskins, *The Middle East: Problem Area in World Politics* (1954); and Dankwart A. Rustow, "Defense of the Near East," *Foreign Affairs* (January 1956), pp. 271–286.

formerly belonging to large empires, situated in contested geopolitical areas with considerable strategic importance and resources but inadequate local power for successful defense. The decisive incentive to association was a negative one, opposition to revisionist neighbors—Hungary and to a lesser extent Bulgaria in the case of Yugoslavia, Rumania, and Czechoslovakia; the Jews in Palestine in the case of the Arab countries. Beyond this, the partners desired to keep down Great-Power interference in the region: the founders of the Arab League were anxious to expel first the French and then the others, and to create a self-contained Arab world in the Near East; the Little Entente statesmen were chiefly concerned about Germany, Italy, and Russia. Both groups needed, however, the aid of friendly Powers as a means to stability and development. At the outset, all the Little Entente countries found a unifying safeguard against their local antagonists in France's blanket support for the *status quo*. The Arabs depended, however resentfully at times, on Great Britain and, more recently, the United States for revenues, welfare, and security, using in the latest phase both the overt advances and the latent threat of the Soviet Union as a counter to a too exclusive Western sway. The positive, if vague, inspiration of both associations was the desire to build from the fragments of a "balkanized" area the nucleus of a larger union.

Attempts to cope with a critical regional position engaged all aspects of the international equilibrium. The coördinate structure of both organizations rested on the postulate of undiminished national sovereignty under the international law; neither of them possessed internal constitutional homogeneity; but both leagues displayed on many occasions considerable diplomatic unity. The Little Entente states sought deliberately to integrate their particular system into the League in order to reinforce it and demonstrate its defensive character; the paramount object of the Arab League seemed to be less consistent with the principles and purposes of the charter. Both groups increased their international weight and internal cohesion by common action in global institutions. The Little Entente acquired a permanent representation in fact on the League Council and frequently had one member express a concerted view in the Assembly; it was described as a virtual diplomatic federation, an organic union, and the most perfect form of a regional understanding on record; at times it might fancy itself as constituting something like a collective Great Power with respect to external relations. There were attendant dangers. The group's institutional influence depended greatly on France's backing and did not rest on effective military-political and socio-economic regional integration; the disparity between the position in the institutional equilibrium and the balance of power gave rise to ambiguities and to eventually disappointed expectations. Much the same applies to the disparity between the weight of the Arab bloc in the United Nations General Assembly, the Arab League as a military force, and the Middle East as an economically lopsided area.

The level of the mutual-security commitment was low in both instances. The Little Entente rested on only a gradually consolidated network of bilateral treaties of mutual assistance providing for joint defense against Hungary and, in the case of Yugoslavia and Rumania, against Bulgaria. All members had a treaty with France, but only the Franco-Czechoslovak Treaty had a convincingly military character. No mutual-security provisions adorned the original Arab League Pact, and the lack was remedied only reluctantly after the conflict with Israel. Neither of the two associations developed an integrated collective force which would sustain their position in the region and in the global security system. In regard to the latter, the Little Entente supported collective enforcement in both principle and practice, whereas the Arab League states—with the exception of Lebanon—adopted a neutralist attitude to the United Nations action in Korea and to collective security generally.

In the actual military-political balance, the Entente could assert itself successfully against the largely disarmed Hungary, particularly as long as she lacked the backing of a determined Power; the Arab League states failed to tip in their favor even the local balance of power with regard to Israel. In 1948 they placed themselves very much in the position of aggressors under the collective-security system and had to be saved by that system from a still greater defeat. Since then, they have gone to great lengths to improve their relative military posture. The Little Entente was in a worse position in relation to the local Great Powers; perhaps characteristically, it was not meant to operate against them in the first place. Among the local Powers, Czechoslovakia feared most Germany, Rumania's main apprehensions were focused on Soviet Russia, and Yugoslavia was at odds with Italy. Centrifugal anxieties were translated into divergent orientations when the Hungarian threat had passed and Germany again emerged into the position of power and influence; by that time the initial unifying basis was eroded by France's changing policies toward Italy and Soviet Russia, and by her own growing dependence on a Great Britain opposed much too long to Central-Eastern European commitments. The Arab states have been no more effectively united in matters of regional defense. Under the jealous if contested leadership of nationalistic Egypt, the Arab League did anything but complement the various Middle Eastern defense schemes put forward by the far from harmonious Anglo-Saxon Powers. Torn by conflicting rights and competing demands of intra- and interregional balance of power, the Middle Eastern area beyond the Turkish borders of NATO would fare no better than Central-Eastern Europe in case of an unfavorable shift in the global equilibrium.

Both the Little Entente and the Arab League pacts provided for many-sided functional coöperation through appropriate organs; but accomplishments were limited by subjective attitudes as well as by actual inadequacy of resources. The predominantly agricultural economies of Yugoslavia and Rumania could not be adequately complemented by industrialized Czechoslovakia alone; in the most favorable conditions the entire Danube area would hardly be a sufficient basis for self-sustaining economic integration and development among politically sovereign states. As for the Arab states, they are patently unable to overcome on their own the many economic, socio-political, and cultural obstacles to the growth of their one-sided, underdeveloped economies; Israel's industrial potential is completely dependent on outside assistance; and plans for a joint Jordan River Valley development languish in the absence of a political settlement.

In both areas, indecisive and rival gestures toward political and economic integration have been frustrated by divisive separatisms. In the Arab Middle East as well as in Central-Eastern Europe, separatism has been fed by vested interests of the élites, dynastic and personal feuds, and the overcompensating nationalism of plural societies split along cultural and social lines and confused rather than fused by various pan-movements; the Little Entente and the Arab League states were kept from closer ties with their neighbors by additional interrelated conflicts over national minorities, irredentist revisionism, and claims to regional leadership, all residues of the shifting tides of historic empires. In such a situation, a judicious combination of Great-Power intervention and aid may be decisive. France, however, was unable to induce a larger association of the Danubian states. Her own economic structure barred other than financial backing for immediate and chiefly military requirements; and no scheme for Central-Eastern European integration could overcome the contradiction of a political orientation against the German Reich and economic dependence on the German market and product. In the critical period following the Second World War, the United States had more means but no more consistency and success with a parallel socio-economic and military-political approach to Middle Eastern problems; and the Soviet Union is now bestirring itself in both respects to end the Anglo-American monopoly and succeed Germany in the Middle East as well.

On the whole, despite more hopeful isolated signs, seemingly imperative preoccupations of the moment militated in both instances against a concerted attack on long-range regional problems, thus perpetuating conditions inimical to internal as well as external security and welfare.[3]

It would appear that a loose regional grouping of smaller states has but limited merits. In matters of security and the military-political balance, the addition of small-state weights must be qualified by a drastic deduction on account

---

[3] Cf. V. Reisky-Dubnic, "The Idea of a Central and Eastern European Regional Federation," *Regional Arrangements for Security and the United Nations*, pp. 133 ff.; Hugh Seton-Watson, *Eastern Europe Between the Wars 1918–1941* (1945), pp. 35 ff.; Khadduri, "The Scheme of Fertile Crescent Unity: A Study in Inter-Arab Relations," in Frye, pp. 168, 173; A. E. Ebban, "The Future of Arab-Jewish Relations," *Commentary* (September 1948), p. 206; and Don Peretz, "Development of the Jordan Valley Waters," *Middle East Journal* (Autumn 1955), pp. 397–412.

of insufficient coördination and divergent purpose. Only still weaker states of the region can be contained. The Little Entente was not really put to a conclusive test, but the evidence is not encouraging; the Arab League has been anything but a convincing success militarily and otherwise. Neither of the two organizations was in equilibrium with respect to sufficiently centralized institutional structure, exacting mutual-security commitment, and functionally and geographically extensive scope. They did not realize for their members, let alone the respective regions as a whole, closer integration in terms of a favorably adjusted multiple equilibrium. The desire to contain Great-Power contests for a monopoly of regional sway came to naught over the apparently irresoluble conflicts among the revisionists and the anti-revisionist smaller states. Yet for ultimate success any comparable organization must transcend its original negative impetus in a broader community. In the final analysis, the fortunes of the Little Entente were tied to the fate of the general organization; and any Arab regional system will depend on a favorable configuration of global factors at least as much as on closer ties of language, religion, and shared past.

In no way are, of course, these limitations peculiar to the two regions: they apply to Western Europe almost as much as to Central-Eastern Europe, and the similarities of the latter with Southeast Asia are even more pronounced than those with the Middle East.

The Theory and Practice of Great-Power Orbits

Smaller countries are hardly able to contrive regional integration and stability on their own; a more promising alternative might be regional groupings anchored in the superior resources of a nuclear Great Power. This idea was worked out during World War II in theories contemplating a world order based on such regions; the vision has been realized since in some places. It is therefore both necessary and fair to distinguish between the intrinsic validity of the conception and its deformation in the Soviet and to a lesser extent Chinese orbits, between its ideological roots in the experience of British and American

dominion over lesser communities and its derivation from the circumstances of the wartime alliance.[4]

According to the idea, regional groupings of small states ought to cluster around the local Great Power and pool military, economic, and other resources in peace and in war. Such an arrangement would implement the fact of interdependence and the need for integration of resources and advance planning for defense. The smaller communities would extend to the focal Great Power facilities and amicable coöperation, and receive in return a realistic measure of independence, aid, and protection. They stand to gain by transferring into stronger hands the chief responsibility for organizing regional security; and the Great Powers would also profit from having dependable allies within their strategic area. There would be more security and prosperity both intra- and interregionally.

Among the more or less explicit premises is a gloomy view of the "mirage" of collective security, its feasibility and implications. Instead of a general and abstract commitment there should be a realistic balance between national power and commitments confined to areas of vital interests.[5] There should be no more all-out application of the principle of national self-determination generating insecure and insecurity-producing small national states. Instead, diversified self-determination should satisfy the needs for intimate cultural life of an ethnic community on the one hand, and for larger association for economic and military purposes on the other. Within a Great-Power-centered area of regional integration, modified collective security and modified self-determination would produce a more realistic pattern of organization. Logically enough, the theory is informed by skepticism about smaller

---

[4]The following synthesis is based on Carr, *Conditions of Peace*, esp. pp. 7–8, 51–52, 56–58, 67–69; Carr, *The Twenty Years' Crisis*, pp. 228–231; Lippmann, *U.S. War Aims*, pp. 80–85; Cobban, *National Self-Determination*, esp. pp. xi, 167 f., 171–172, 178; Fox, *The Super-Powers*, pp. 95–96; and F. L. Schuman, "Regionalism and Spheres of Influence," in Morgenthau, *Peace, Security and the United Nations*, p. 105.

[5]Cf. Lippmann, *U.S. War Aims*, pp. 187, 193, 194, and *U.S. Foreign Policy: Shield of the Republic*, pp. 7, 9, 71 ff., 149.

states. Their validity, viability, and capacity to conduct independent foreign policy, defend themselves, or maintain their neutrality is questioned; their obsolete practices of economic nationalism and balance-of-power politics are condemned. By contrast, assumptions concerning the Great Powers are favorable. The authors of the idea emphasize the primacy of Great-Power strategic interests, their special ability and responsibility to ensure general security, and the ultimate dependence of the smaller states on their behavior. The legitimate interests of the major Powers and the legitimate rights of the lesser states are held to be compatible; so is national independence with strategic and economic interdependence. To concede bases to the protecting Great Power in no way infringes national independence and state equality. A cardinal assumption is that in their own interests the Great Powers will pursue liberal and non-aggressive policies toward the smaller states and each other. There is a connection: without self-restraint and respect for the rights of smaller states there can be no enduring accord among the Powers. Yet a nuclear coalition of the Great Powers must sustain the global order as necessarily as a nuclear Great Power must provide the magnetic core for regional integration.[6]

A general international organization is reduced to a secondary role or renounced altogether. It is pronounced "forever dead," not mentioned at all, or half-heartedly restored to life as a framework for globally ramified socio-economic functions and, somewhat illogically, the regulation of relations between the smaller and the greater states. A general system of collective security could hardly be admitted. A commitment which might require the intervention of an associated smaller country against the nuclear Great Power or another regionally associated state could not be honestly undertaken in law and honored in fact. There could be no organic connection between the global organization and the regional pattern even if the former were admitted to inferior coexistence. The Great-Power protectors interpose themselves in varying degrees between

their dependents and the organization. This is more than a reasserted international hierarchy of the Concert type; the League's ideal of international democracy is replaced by international feudalism, a system of bilateral duties and rights rooted in territorial relationships, without the moral climate requisite for an equitable functioning of the system.[7]

On the one hand, the theory represents a deliberate concession verging on surrender to geopolitical determinism in world affairs; on the other, it half-consciously attempts to liberalize elements of the *Wehrwirtschaftsraum* doctrines of Nazism and the coprosperity-sphere slogan of the Japanese in the light of British and American experience. Unwittingly, the Western writers returned the compliment of the Nazi and Japanese apologists who had appealed to the admired and supposedly legitimizing precedent of the Monroe Doctrine; their reservations and inconsistencies show also how hard it is to reconcile liberal and totalitarian precepts in international politics. The difficulties did not seem insuperable in the glow of wartime alliance with the Soviet Union; but no attempt to extrapolate the "Good Neighbor Principle" and the idea of the Commonwealth from their particular contexts and elevate them into a general principle of international organization can assign due weight to a fundamental point which disqualifies the Anglo-American precedent from broader application.

The point is that international politics, being power-normative, comprises the interaction of power and purpose. The former has its rules and "laws" which no Power may and dare disregard; but the latter is affected by the projection into foreign policies of a nation's value system, ideology, social and governmental structure, and other variables. These influence objectives, methods of dealing with other nations, and the evaluation of the outside world in the same way as the nature of a nation's international involvement reacts on its domestic order. There are thus obvious differences in the type of control "natural"

---

[6]Cf. Wolfers, "The Small Powers and the Enforcement of Peace," pp. 12 ff.; Lippmann, *U.S. Foreign Policy*, p. 73; and Fox, pp. 153–154.

[7]See Schuman, p. 90, for the quoted phrase; Carr, *Nationalism and After*, pp. 54–57, 61–67, for a guarded return to general organization; and Cobban, pp. 163–165, for deliberate attempt to combine the regional pattern with global organization.

to different systems. A major difference between the totalitarian and the liberal Powers is the latter's capacity for transcending in an evolutionary fashion the coercive origins and aspects of control over weaker communities into a more consensual type of relationship. A totalitarian system seems unable either to maintain control on the basis of consent alone or still less to relax coercion without seeing its pattern of control disintegrate. If a liberal Power can rise above the limitations of domestic politics, it is in a better position to combine self-restraint based on more sensitive moral propensities with self-control derived from a pragmatic calculation of long-range advantage. A totalitarian system, with its haunting concern with survival, and equation of survival with expansion, prefers the absolute and immediate certainties of complete domination. In that sense it is always to some extent irrational.

Thus relations among unequal countries depend not only on the existing power situation; they are greatly influenced by the structure and purpose of the greater Powers as well. Each Power within its sphere faces the choice between the crude combination of imperialism and satellitism, and a more subtle reconciliation of its legitimate regional interests with the rights of the smaller nations. Even for a nontotalitarian Great Power the tendency to dominate rather than strive for consent will be difficult to resist in the absence of external countervailing restraints.

Accordingly, the unique evolution of the British Empire and the transient character of American imperialism in the Western Hemisphere were due in large part to the predominantly liberal values of the two societies. Both imperial systems avoided the self-aggravating momentum of deepening coercion, peculiar to their situation; instead, they have evolved in a process of self-determination for the smaller countries toward a new basis in consent, equality of status, and interdependence. In its imperialistic phase, the Monroe Doctrine embodied the major traits of the Great-Power-zone species: isolation of a regionally dominant nation's security area from the outside world and the maintenance therein of greatest possible political and economic conformity. Yet the more galling corollaries and uses of the Doctrine, notably in the Caribbean, were overcome in the Good Neighbor Policy as recip-

rocal pledges of nonintervention and mutual assistance for security and welfare extended outward the principles of American colonial and constitutional tradition; the growth of the Inter-American system is the tale of gradual multilateralization and institutionalization of North American hegemony into pan-American solidarity. Similarly, the originally coercive British Empire was progressively liberalized into the Commonwealth in an outward projection of British conventional constitutionalism with its aptitude for organic growth and adjustment. In both instances, although not with equal consistency, the greater Powers have shouldered ever more of the duties and retained less of the privileges of the association; by the same token, the smaller communities have been moving toward a position which is almost the reverse of a satellite's.[8]

The peculiar liberal ethos of the two English-speaking nations was not the only factor favorable to self-restraint; another was their geopolitical situation, in many respects unique. A deliberately manipulated balance of power in Europe freed the extra-European spheres of control of the insular Great Britain and the remote United States from large-scale competitive interference. If the United States was the incidental beneficiary of British balancing, it was also its occasional if secondary object—when Canning extended the technique into the New World to shield the young Latin American republics; and its opponent—when the senior North American Republic frustrated the attempts of the British as well as those of other non-American Powers to counterbalance its sway in the Western Hemisphere. By that time, however, the preponderance of the United States could not be really challenged from within the region and it could soon afford to be generous. Basically the same was true of

---

[8] Cf. especially *The British Empire*, A Report on its Structure and Problems by a Study Group of Members of the Royal Institute of International Affairs (1937); Ernest Barker, *The Ideas and Ideals of the British Empire* (2nd ed., 1951); Dexter Perkins, *The Evolution of American Foreign Policy* (1948), pp. 58 ff., 117 ff., and *Hands Off: A History of the Monroe Doctrine* (1946); Duggan, *The Americas: The Search for Hemisphere Security, passim*; and Carter, *The British Commonwealth and International Security*, pp. 94–95 and *passim*.

Great Britain when she relaxed her control over the white settlements at the height of her nineteenth-century power and let them reinforce theirs by helping them federate. Factors of distance, too, favored moderation by making rigid control either unnecessary or too onerous; and the naval character of both nations' power called for only a limited claim on the resources and facilities of dependent communities.[9]

In neither case has all been sweetness and light. Both leading nations have tried with varying intensity and success to promote regional partnership rather than reinforce their own predominance. In the case of the Americas, the task has been impeded by the very economic and political superiority of the United States—not always wisely employed; in that of the British Commonwealth, by the decline in the resources and power of the mother country. In both instances, common ties of interest and sentiment have been strained by divisive pulls for greater independence or rival predominance in the Americas, for neutrality in Britain's wars or outright secession in the Commonwealth and Empire. Ireland and more than one Latin American republic gave the Anglo-Saxon Powers an opportunity to show unique self-restraint during the Second World War; they continue to demonstrate the failures of liberalized association between greater and smaller nations joined by geography but separated by nationality and the feelings of grievance. Argentina tried to find counterweights in hostile European Powers; outlying Dominions such as Canada and Australia could not but gravitate into the sphere of the United States, trying to keep in balance their relations with Washington and with the mother country. On the whole, it has been often difficult and sometimes impossible to span the many political, cultural, economic, and strategic divergences among geographically and racially differentiated segments within the Western Hemisphere and the Commonwealth.[10]

In the face of such shortcomings and maladjustments, both particular systems have found in global organization a useful means for a larger equilibrium.

The ambivalence of the smaller members of the Inter-American system in regard to general and regional organization reflects their attitude toward the United States, and is an inverted replica of this country's own dualism as a regional and a global Power. On the one hand, Latin Americans rely on the United States for security and welfare, and are jealous of its commitments outside the hemisphere; hence they sought at San Francisco to strengthen regional organization in relation to the global body. On the other hand, they continue to be uneasy about unilateral intervention by the United States within the hemisphere and value the general organization as a forum of their own extra-hemispheric self-affirmation. The regional collective-security pact of Rio, the Bogotá Charter's repudiation of even collective intervention in internal affairs, and the weight of the Latin American states in the United Nations constitute a coherent institutional basis for the resolution of their dilemma. Their massive collective vote provides the Latin American states with an additional potential check on the Colossus of the North. Washington's frequent dependence on this vote offsets at least partly in the eyes of the Latin Americans their real dependence on this country for their physical security and much of their welfare. In this fashion a not unimportant psychological equipoise is promoted in a situation surcharged with the familiar manifestations of rankling inferiority feelings.

Broadly comparable are the attitudes of the lesser members of the British Commonwealth. They, too, have sought to reconcile regional interests, association with a global Power, and the desire for independent status in world affairs by way of a favorable adjustment of the privileges and obligations which go with participation in both the general and the more restricted system. Membership in the League implemented internationally their independence; their stature grew further in the United Nations. For some smaller countries, like Ireland, membership in the general organization could serve to counterbalance the British connection; for all it provided an additional source of security, a

---

[9]Cf. Spykman, *America's Strategy in World Politics: The United States and the Balance of Power* (1942), pp. 62 ff.

[10]Cf. Frank Tannenbaum, "An American Commonwealth of Nations," *Foreign Affairs* (July 1944), p. 581; W. K. Hancock, *Survey of British Commonwealth Affairs* (1937), Vol. I, pp. 67–68, 276 ff.; and Eric A. Walker, *The British Empire* (1947), p. 192 and *passim*.

framework for economic welfare larger than the imperial preference system and the sterling bloc, and a formal basis of resistance to undesired imperial entanglements. Conversely, the flexible Commonwealth tie gave the lesser members a higher standing in the world bodies; it preserved for them the more concrete safeguards of Britain's might as supplementary and if need be substitutive to general collective security; and, before SEATO, when British power was at a particularly low ebb, it even allowed that the regional ANZUS pact associate Australia and New Zealand with the United States under the aegis of the United Nations Charter, without including Great Britain herself.[11]

There is thus a definite interrelation between regional and global organization. Depending on policies and predispositions, it may be turned into mutual reinforcement advantageous to all parties; into merely one-sided advantage, for instance when regional systems keep the general organization out of some intra-regional affairs and purge themselves of others by passing them on to the world body; or into outright incompatibility. The Inter-American and the British Commonwealth systems cover mainly the first two possibilities; the Soviet bloc is a glaring instance of the fundamental conflict between self-contained territorial regionalism and the structure and spirit of global institutions. A less shocking incompatibility may be revealed in a specific event involving the application of collective security. In this respect the United States collaborated unwittingly with the Soviet Union to provide a striking illustration.

It revolves around the relevant features of the Korean and the Guatemalan cases. The two constitute a kind of inverted parallel. It may not be too far-fetched to say that the Communist-infiltrated Guatemalan government in the Western Hemisphere meant about the same to the United States as the pro-American South Korea

on the mainland of Asia to Communist China and Soviet Russia. The common denominator was the existence in a small country of a political regime antagonistic to the local Great Power, which regarded the area as part of its geopolitical and historical orbit. It might be argued that the United States by its position in Japan was a local Power with regard to Korea, too; the argument would hardly be admitted by the Communist Powers. If anything, the ambiguity highlights the theoretical weakness and the political dangers inherent in the unavoidable overlaps of the Great-Power-zone pattern. In both instances, the desire for ideological and political homogeneity within its security sphere induced the regional Great Power to look favorably, to say the least, on a forcible attempt to eliminate the discordant feature. The local Great Power interpreted as civil war what the remote Great Power, desirous of maintaining its foothold, described as international aggression. When the two breaches of the peace were brought before the United Nations, both the United States and the Soviet Union adopted in each case an attitude to collective enforcement almost diametrically opposite to that taken in the previous case. The only consistency in the situation was that the remote Great Power in both instances favored action, and the local Power inaction, on the part of the United Nations.

In both contrast and opposition to the complexities of the groupings around the United States and Great Britain stands the would-be monolithic unity of the Soviet bloc. There the question of an interaction between the smaller countries and the dominant Great Power as members of regional and world organization does not even arise. Instead, the Soviet system raises the issue, and the spectre, of the satellite as the typical status for smaller states in a Great-Power zone of the totalitarian variety.

An order based on satellitism is at the opposite pole to the premises of flexible equilibrium. Its fundamental principle is preponderance on one side and subjection on all others. A satellite cannot exert even vestigial political self-direction and international codetermination. Its nominal independence and sovereignty are revocable conveniences of the dominant Great Power and a concession to the principle of national self-

---

[11]Cf. Carter, p. 314, and *passim*, and the same author's "The Commonwealth in the United Nations," *International Organization*, (May 1950), pp. 247–260; Lionel Gelber, "The Commonwealth and the United Nations," *Regional Arrangements for Security and the United Nations*, pp. 49–64; and Evatt, "Australia's Approach to Security in the Pacific," in Panikkar, pp. 15, 17.

determination inimical to outright annexation. The Great Power has absolute control without corresponding responsibility; the small states retain duties without correlative rights, the liabilities without the assets of international status. Satellitism has transposed into modern Europe the most reactionary manifestations of colonialism, including a perverted form of "indirect rule." The dependent community is an instrument for the dominant Power's security, prosperity, and expansion. At best, it can hope to collect the incidental perquisites of its ancillary status.

Institutionally, the relationship finds expression in a more or less enforced alliance—a *foedus iniquum* constituting a *societas leonina*—which is further reinforced by a "supranational" apparatus of party and secret police as the out-reaching tentacles of the controlling totalitarian body politic. A two-level approach is facilitated by the very nature of the "dual state": a kind of federation between the Great Power and the small-state satellites on the party level, and the continuation of separate international status—far from unprofitable to the hegemonic Power—on the formal institutional plane. Actual federative strengthening among the satellites themselves is vetoed. In the socio-economic sphere, the techniques of exploitation will differ according to whether the Great Power practices private or state capitalism and places itself in the posture of creditor or debtor. Whatever the specific method, the captive economies will be anything but balanced internally, and regional coördination will be governed by immediate or long-range military needs of the imperialistic taskmaster. Any incidental industrial development of the satellite will be used to increase its economic, military, and political dependence. Finally, in the military-political security zone of the dominant state, the satellite will function as an expendable armed buffer, "ally," or proxy aggressor.

Being itself largely the result of previous global imbalance of power, the enforced satellite status of smaller countries will perpetuate global instability. A malaise settles over international affairs as majorities in the captive communities strain away from the local totalitarian to the more cognate remote Great Powers, who in turn contest the legitimacy of the local Power's coercive control. The interplay of power and con-

science as the essence of politics reaches an agonizing climax.

As long as it lasts, the character of Soviet regional hegemony in Eastern Europe illustrates the *telos* of the Soviet concept of the balance of power, while the global picture reflects the ideologically tolerated temporary acceptance of military-political equilibrium, pending the destruction of all "hostile" forces and the real peace of Communist utopia. The Soviet doctrine of the balance of power does in its essentials little more than explicitly radicalize the drive for preponderance, always implicit in the balancing process, by the Marxist-Leninist postulates of necessary conflict and ultimate Communist domination. Consequently, the widespread failure in the West generally and among the American military in particular to apply any balance-of-power thinking at all to the Soviet ally in a single-minded campaign against the Fascist Powers was much more serious than the ignorance of the not at all startling peculiarities of the doctrine. The Soviets found it relatively easy to establish their regional hegemony; and, when the Soviet ally had to be branded as an enemy before it was countered as an unbalancer, the shift of Western policies from concessions to counter-offensive must have appeared to the more ideologically minded among the Soviet policy-makers as a delayed manifestation of only temporarily subdued "necessary" anti-Soviet hostility, vindicating *ex post facto* Soviet expansionism in the first place.

In the perspective of history, the tendency of local Powers to assert regional control appears as natural and the freedom of exposed smaller countries as a compound of fiction and accident. The United States eliminated progressively all outside interference in its orbit; so did or tried to do Germany and Soviet Russia more recently. This country escaped on the whole the need for satellite control; the two totalitarian Powers did not. Yet, however recurrent the pattern, the satellite technique has never been permanently successful in the modern state system.[12]

---

[12]See C. C. Abbott, "Economic Penetration and Power Politics," *Harvard Business Review,* (July 1948), pp. 411 ff.; Seton-Watson, *The East European Revolution* (1951), pp. 254 ff.; Bedrich Bruegel, "Methods of

In pronouncing on problems of international organization, it is thus necessary to take into account not only the actual or desired balance of power among states, and the balance between the several nations' power and commitments, but also the likely balance between the power of the principal Great Powers and their sense of responsibility and self-restraint. If a great nation's ideology does not counteract the expansionist and coercive tendencies implicit in superior power, but stimulates them instead, the smaller communities within its reach are doomed to extinction or to satellite status unless otherwise protected.

Such protection is certainly not provided for in the theory of Great-Power orbits. Smaller countries, by being irrevocably assigned to regional power blocs, are denied even the measure of safeguards they may derive from the balance of power. Henceforth, only an interregional balance makes sense. A puzzling question is against whom are regional defenses organized if the Great Powers are expected to exercise self-restraint and respect their separate preserves —an assumption more "utopian" in a regional configuration of power than in the conceptual universe of the United Nations Charter. Security zones are practically certain to overlap, making contests over intermediate smaller countries at least as likely. This will increase the pressure on the nuclear Powers to tighten control over "their" allies, and to consolidate intraregionally a fusion of power rather than implement a diversified pluralism. To expect the spontaneous adherence of the smaller nations to such a scheme is to mix would-be realism with considerable blindness to any organism's natural response to the threat of extinction. There is thus no need to invoke moral considerations or special factors, such as historical and ethnic antagonisms among neighbors, to invalidate the proposition that regional zones

Soviet Domination in Satellite States," *International Affairs* (January 1951), pp. 32-37; Adam B. Ulam, *Titoism and the Cominform* (1952); Dana Adams Schmidt, *The Anatomy of a Satellite* (1952); Crane Brinton, "The Pattern of Aggression," *Virginia Quarterly Review* (Spring 1949), pp. 172-173, and Raymond L. Garthoff, "The Concept of the Balance of Power in Soviet Policy Making," *World Politics* (October 1951), pp. 85-111.

are desirable as a general principle of international organization, and that they would freely coalesce and remain cohesive without being made exclusive.

Moreover, it is fallacious to assume that Great Powers with mutually alien social ideologies, which have to organize regionally their military-political defenses, would coöperate globally in socio-economic matters. The reverse proposition is more plausible. As an alternative to global coöperation, the several groupings would have to contrive a socio-economic equilibrium from limited intraregional resources and even more limited, if any, interregional exchanges. But regionalism came too late to catch up with the sudden leap from national to global economic interdependence; it cannot supply the basis for a balanced economy, planned or free. Complementary resources and diverse functional needs, constituting not a few self-sufficient but many overlapping regions, might weave together existing communities into larger ones if they were left to spontaneous organic growth; they confound attempts at coördination in overlapping institutions; and they are the source of unrest when they cut across the boundaries of reciprocally hostile security areas. Interregional needs tear then at the concentric pull of regionally organized power systems. Results will vary depending on the geographic scope and degree of self-sufficiency of the region, the expansionist or conservative phase and ideology of the regional Great Power, and the pressure applied to the region from outside.

Three main types of responses are possible. First, the Great Power may let the horizontal relationships of interdependence dissolve, as it were, the regional power structure and pursue the objective of a larger equilibrium. It will do so more easily if its potential is such that the relationships will serve as channels of influence abroad rather than as avenues of encroachment from the outside. Great Britain and the United States came closest to adopting this course. Or, as in the case of Nazi Germany and Imperial Japan, a Great Power may set out to conquer the interdependence pressing beyond too narrow regional confines, disrupt an already badly shaken global equilibrium, and be defeated by the world-wide reaction. Finally, a Great Power may attempt to seal off interdependence within a larger region organized against other Powers. In the effort to repress global interdependence it will depress the small states of the region into the position of tributary dependence. This has been the case with the Soviet Union. Thus if any determinism is involved, war and satellitism are much more the necessary consequence of integral regionalism than such regionalism is the necessary and enduring pattern of world organization.

In its implications, the theory as well as the practice of Great-Power spheres is essentially illiberal. It stands for the enlargement of the vertical power structure of the nuclear state, typical of imperialism, rather than for the release of institutional, socio-economic, and military-political forces and relationships into the equilibrium interplay of reciprocal adjustment and restraint, which constitutes the nearest equivalent of constitutionalism in the international community. By the same token, regional compression of broader interdependence will put a premium on dictatorial rationing of security, welfare, and prestige among dependent satellites; it will not allow international exchange and communications to dissolve local restrictions and sustain an equitable distribution of these values among independent parties to authoritative general institutions.

This does not mean that the theory is all wrong. In the first place, the organization of security around several Great Powers is a recurrent if objectionable makeshift in international relations. And in the second place, the theory is correct in emphasizing the need for economic and military integration to counteract nationalistic fragmentation, the primary role of major states in any security scheme, and the dangers of neglecting particular facts of geography and power in an abstract system. As an alternative to the fusion of power in the focal state, however, intraregional relations between major and minor states should at least be multilateralized in an institutional equilibrium extending into a complementary global organization. Moreover, the relatively smaller states within the region should be free to strengthen themselves by means of federative integration rather than be kept in separate dependence.

It is not intended to examine in detail the extent to which the Soviet system realizes the illiberal potential of Great-Power spheres. Instead, . . . [we shall now] explore the application of the remedial features in the Western regional association.

THE PATTERN OF INTEGRATION

According to the density of institutional, functional, and communal ties, patterns of international organization can be distributed along an integrative continuum from an unorganized congeries of isolated states to a unitary global superstate. . . . the hitherto implied pattern of integration will now be explicated and exemplified in relation to the North Atlantic Treaty Organization as a framework for different levels of integration and a potential balancer in the Western European federalizing process. . . .

Security through Regional Community

If the North Atlantic Treaty Organization is the main framework for the integration of the North Atlantic Community, it is in the first place an institutionalized regional coalition for the maintenance of the global balance of power, formally related to the United Nations as an agency for collective self-defense. As such it illustrates the fusion of security, community, and welfare in the revised idea of collective security as a "community security system," pooling national resources in an integrated defense effort against a suspected aggressor. A drastic departure from the early League ideals attempts to adjust to the contemporary schism the integrative approach of the Charter; effective collective security is now coterminous with an integration area and expands or shrinks with the latter.[13]

NATO displays a particular kind of integration and institutional equilibrium. As an organization

[13]On the "federalizing process," see Friedrich, "Federal Constitutional Theory and Emergent Proposals," in Arthur W. MacMahon, ed., *Federalism: Mature and Emergent* (1955), pp. 514 f. See also Kunz, "Supranational Organs," *American Journal of International Law* (October 1952), p. 697, and Briggs, "The Proposed European Political Community," *ibid.* (January 1954), pp. 114–115.

of sovereign states, NATO is located at a relatively low point on the integrative continuum. It has no supranational organs and shows no federative tendencies; yet a noticeable organic growth has been stimulated by the interacting responses to specific functional tasks within a "two-chamber system" of expert and political bodies. The Council is the seat of national representation and multilateral high policy. In the Permanent Organization, the International Secretariat is the central fortress of the collective NATO spirit. Between the nationalist and the internationalist extremes of the institutional spectrum, the Permanent Representatives of the member-states constitute an intermediary link. But the balance is uneven because the Secretariat—the most highly integrated civilian organ—is endowed with only advisory and mediatory powers, and the authority delegated to the Representatives is scant. On the other hand, the Permanent Organization is an effective civilian counterweight to the more tightly integrated military structure of NATO headed by a Supreme Commander. This enables the Permanent Organization to coördinate the economic and military aspects of security and give continuity to the sporadic action of the national Ministers, who constitute the ultimate check on the military.

NATO's integration is thus primarily operational. First, delegation of authority has gone to the standing operational organs rather than to political organs. Second, integration has resulted from the actual operation of the national and international organs rather than from a unique constituent act establishing a supranational authority. Interallied relations have been greatly institutionalized by the so-called "NATO method" of multilateral consultation aiming at unanimous recommendations without resort to vote. A rather progressive structural equilibrium

---

[13]The principal collective-security provisions of the North Atlantic Treaty are in Article 5, the community provisions in the Preamble and Articles 2 and 3. Cf. Appendix I in *Atlantic Alliance: NATO's Role in the Free World*, A Report by a Chatham House Study Group, Royal Institute of International Affairs (1952). See also Fox, "NATO and Coalition Diplomacy," *The Annals of the American Academy of Political and Social Science* (July 1953, "NATO and World Peace," ed. by E. M. Patterson), pp. 114–118; Alfred J. Hotz, "NATO: Myth or Reality," *ibid.*, pp. 126–133; and Dulles, "Policy for Security and Peace," pp. 353 ff.

between the military and civilian standing organs has stimulated the growth of NATO's modest powers; another factor for increased efficiency has been the continual adjustment between the "supra-national NATO view" and the "national views." This informal interplay has kept in bounds the imbalance between the limited jurisdiction of the integrated organs and the extensive domestic jurisdiction of members assembled in the Council. On the whole, NATO shows that any closely coördinated military and economic undertaking among materially interdependent nations will result in *de facto* supranational character of the joint organs and some derogation of effective national sovereignty.[14]

Such as they are, NATO institutions have served as a coactive framework for military-political and, to some extent, economic integration. Integration and balance were the watchwords of NATO's first concern, joint equitable rearmament. Among allies with greatly disparate resources, contributions must be properly adjusted to "politico-economic capabilities"; a balance must be evolved between joint military needs and the requirements of economic, social, and political stability of member-nations. The aim was to develop "balanced collective forces" and later "an integrated force under centralized command." The "community power" of jointly trained and strategically directed national units is to replace separate national potentials as the foundation of security; and a measure of integration is to narrow within NATO's regional scope the fatal gap between a collective-security commitment and the actual ability and willingness of states to perform. Anticipation of performance should strengthen the community of tradition and interests among the allies. Thus, a *casus foederis* should find NATO in equilibrium with respect to the mutual-assistance commitment of its members. Yet final evaluation depends on NATO's fitness to implement its long-range community function.[15]

In this respect, the organization has been subject to a number of limitations. Treaty provisions

---

[14]The quoted phrases are from *Atlantic Alliance*, pp. 82, 84, 126–127.

[15]See *Atlantic Alliance*, pp. 52–54, 65 (note 2), 121; Dulles, "Policy for Security and Peace," p. 356; and McGeorge Bundy, ed., *The Pattern of Responsibility* (1952), pp. 74–75.

and statements of intention must be distinguished from actual means and accomplishments. The provisions are broad enough, but their implementation has lagged. Military-political equilibrium has been established more effectively against the Soviet bloc than internally: it is not easy for unequal partners to develop integrated, balanced forces, and international specialization is not favored by continued sovereignty; furthermore, military integration is still not matched by correspondingly intimate coördination of foreign policies. It has proved no less difficult to adjust the organization's short-range and long-range purposes. The initially legitimate concentration on the military-defense problems has grown one-sided as NATO passed from the emergency stage into the "long haul." It is difficult to strike the right balance. On the one hand, the primary task of NATO was to redress the "serious imbalance of military strength" in Europe into a balance or even "preponderance of power." This contributed to general stability and a sense of community in the West. In that sense "economic measures are not enough." But, on the other hand, neither is military balance or preponderance. And as international tensions relax, even reduced burdens of military preparedness are borne with growing reluctance by societies which have a narrow margin of expendable economic resources and social peace.[16]

NATO's limitations have been also geographical. In spite of the vast resources and overseas connections of its members, NATO lacks scope for a diversified equilibrium and flexible defensive strategy in depth. It has had to be extended beyond the North Atlantic region proper, and inter-allied relations have suffered from larger needs, chiefly economic and strategic, and wider problems, mainly colonial. Since the regional alliance has not been able to relate itself organically to the world organization, it looked at times as if it would supersede the United Nations under the impetus of expanding pressures.

Hence, if NATO may be presumed to be in fair equilibrium with respect to the commitment to military assistance, it is not in that position with respect to its functional and geographic scope, and to the global organization. Today, the idea of the Atlantic Community is alive primarily in the method and the spirit of the quest for a fair ratio of burdens and advantages flowing from the alliance. Yet there is a growing feeling, most recently taken up by the United States, that the alliance must develop more positive and extensive nonmilitary activities. Otherwise, it will become brittle, the equilibrium will be lopsided, and the tissues of regional community will not grow. The very existence of the alliance might be jeopardized as an all-out war of annihilation comes to be considered less likely; "massive retaliation" yields in popularity to "graduated deterrence" and limitation of peripheral conflicts; and strategic thinking catches up with the revolution in weapons and long-range delivery systems.[17]

One factor that has hitherto obstructed more extensive delegation and integration is the problem of a "balance of influence between the small and the large countries." In bare outline, the present compromise consists of the exclusive representation of the three Great Powers in the authoritative military Standing Group, and an equal vote and formal veto for even the smaller nations in the ultimately decisive NATO Council. An informal play of pressures and influence assures the requisite supremacy for the major Powers and the equally necessary safeguards for the lesser states within this arrangement. It may be argued that structural equilibrium as well as further integration would benefit from a political standing group where fewer members with higher average power could properly exert greater powers. Yet the smaller states, far from disposed to abdicate more authority, wish to compensate for the predominance of the Great Powers in the military organization by retaining the greatest possible role in multilateral policy-making. They, like Great Britain and France when bypassed by the United States, insist on consultation prior to irrevocable decisions that might have equally irrevocable consequences for all in the age of nuclear weapons. Conversely, the Great Powers wish to preserve some of the advantages of bilat-

---

[16]Cf. Ambassador Warren Austin's statement in the *North Atlantic Treaty Hearings*, 81st Congress, 1st Session, 1949, pp. 92, 97; Dean Acheson's statement in Bundy, p. 68; and Dulles, "Policy for Security and Peace," p. 363.

[17]See *Atlantic Alliance*, pp. 33, 100, and also for the so-called Pearson Report on the Atlantic Community; and Kaufmann, ed., *Military Policy and National Security* (1956).

among themselves. They do not wish to be exposed to too many "organizational pressures." The situation is reflected in the uneven employment of the NATO Council, ranging from consultations of all or only the major members to their unilateral decisions, not least so by the United States.[18]

In the long run, the internal equilibrium of the alliance would be served best by' moves toward equalizing resources among its component units.

---

[18]See *Atlantic Alliance*, p. 94, and Elliott, et al., *United States Foreign Policy*, pp. 170–171, for the quoted phrases.

American aid is to mutual advantage and is partly compensated for by the strategic and other facilities made available by others. But it cannot redress the imbalance of strength among the allies and, when combined with greatly unequal contributions, tends to upset the vital psychological equilibrium. It might be argued that a federatively integrated Western Europe together with Great Britain would constitute a desirable counterpart to the United States within the alliance, improve relations among partners, and increase the security and welfare of all concerned. For a time NATO seemed to be assisting the process.

Discussion and Questions

1. ➤ How would you assess Liska's suggestion that "Asian neutralism typifies the preference of smaller states for regional organization without great powers"? In this period following decolonization, many governments have accorded priority to the values of national autonomy. ➤ Does such a priority schedule suggest that efforts to promote "cooperation" are normally more realistic than projects that involve "integration"? But consider Lagos (page 176) who associates some degree of integration with the acquisition of genuine national autonomy by smaller states. ➤ Under what conditions will a national government gain greater independence by relinquishing a portion of its former sovereignty?

2. ➤ To what extent does Liska give weight to changes in the international environment, such as the new global scope of political participation and the development and proliferation of nuclear weapons? ➤ Is it essential to have nuclear weapons to be a great power? ➤ Does a state necessarily become a great power as a consequence of

possessing nuclear weapons? What about the status of "nuclear" states such as Great Britain and France compared with "non nuclear" states such as Japan and West Germany? ➤ Is a great power the leader of some group of lesser states? ➤ Would India or Japan acquire or lose regional status through the acquisition of nuclear weapons? ➤ Does a response depend on the extent of the nuclear capability or merely on its existence?

3. ➤ Is Liska's presentation of "the socialist community of states" too one-sided in its depiction of negative features? ➤ Does the role of the United States in various regions suggest the exercise of a more beneficial influence within its spheres of domain? ➤ What of the affiliation between the isolated and reactionary elites of Asia and U.S. military power, culminating in the American role in the Indochina War?

4. ➤ What are the implications for second-stage integration potential of the selections from Yalem and Liska?

12

The Concert of Cultures

W. WARREN WAGAR

From Warren W. Wagar, *The City of Man,* 1967, pp. 129–154. Copyright © 1963 by Warren Wagar. Reprinted by permission of the publisher Houghton Mifflin Company. (This book as been reprinted by Penguin Books Inc.)

THE ORGANIC SOCIETY

One generalization holds good for nearly all recent attempts to anticipate the over-all structure of the world civilization proclaimed in meta-historical prophecy. Whether a prophet stresses the spiritual, the intellectual, the economic, or the political aspects of cosmopolis, he is likely to contend that healthy societies, and the civilizations that sustain them, are "organic"; hence the world civilization must also be "organic." The term is generally used loosely and analogically, rather than strictly and literally. Analogies to life may seem more apt than analogies to natural or man-made machinery if only because living organisms—somewhat like human societies—have unpredictable destinies, in which the whole and its parts work together for the same internally determined ends. The machine, on the other hand, is purposeless, futureless, inert, and un-self-willed; its parts have only an external, utilitarian relationship to the whole, and there is so little *esprit de corps* that the breakdown of the smallest part can send the whole machine grinding to a stop. An organic unity perseveres through thick and thin. The tendency, then, is to look on the coming world civilization as a kind of superorganism. But, of course, the question is, how much organicity? Must men become Man, the "Great Being" in Comte's phrase, a human coral reef of one blood, flesh, mind, and spirit? Or will something less titanic do?

Thinkers have compared societies to organisms since the earliest recorded essays in social philosophy. Ancient Indian, Greek, Roman, and medieval Christian thought bristles with organic analogies. During the Enlightenment, it became popular, following Hobbes and Locke, to think of societies and states more as mechanical contrivances created by individuals to serve their mutual interests than as organisms. This theory, the logical corollary of Enlightenment individualism, led to the dismantling of the *ancien régime* in

France in 1789; but the passions generated by the French Revolution swept up the individuals involved and ironically fused them into a national organism, *la France*, which tried with limited success to reproduce on a smaller scale the organicity of medieval Christendom. Nevertheless, most liberal thought still adheres to the Enlightenment idea of society as an inorganic contractual arrangement, a machine built by individuals to serve their individual ends: life, liberty, and the pursuit of happiness. The United States is expressly founded on this mechanical principle. A hopeless contradiction yawns between Enlightenment liberalism and organic nationalism, which sometimes divides a man even against himself in modern Western countries. Witness the liberal patriot, forced to choose between the national interest and civil rights.

But organic theories have not been rare in the past century and a half. Comte and Spencer both used elaborate organic analogies in the nineteenth century, and Spencer at least was simultaneously a fervent individualist, which has puzzled his readers no end. Toward the close of the century, a number of professional sociologists especially on the Continent worked hard to rejuvenate organic theory. Most of them, like von Lilienfeld, Worms, Novicow, and Cooley, are now more or less forgotten. Even the great organic nationalists, like Treitschke and Barrès, seem remote in the Europe of NATO and the Common Market.

But the world crisis has forced a reopening of the whole question of whether cultures, societies, and civilizations must be, in some sense, organisms—in order to thrive and survive. Spengler looked on his cultures as organisms with life-histories. Most of the exponents of a world civilization, even those firmly attached to the liberal gospel of the existential uniqueness and freedom of the person, argue that the person cannot realize his potentialities except in a civilization that coheres organically, through the sharing of commonly agreed upon values, goals, symbols, and institutions. That is to say, fullness and wholeness of life in the person requires fullness and wholeness in the common life. Some prophets emphasize the need for synthesis in philosophy and science, others in religion and ethics, others in the arts, others in economic and political life; and there is a vast literature, in particular, on

the ultimate question of East-West cultural synthesis. The common denominator throughout is the demand for organicity, in some measure, with formulas running all the way from loose-spun arrangements for cooperation and continuous dialogue to highly unitary schemes for a world brain and a world state. In all events, scarcely any thinker committed to the idea of world integration believes in a world simply of individuals each going his separate way like the golfers in a country club. The goal is a union of the liberal philosophy and the organic quality of nationalism in a durable, viable world order of free men freely united.

Recall, for example, Lewis Mumford's diagnosis of the disintegration of the historic cultures. They have all collapsed, he writes, because their guiding theme, the pattern of meaning in which they grew to maturity, wore threadbare and lost the power to attract creative genius to its message. Our task now is to conceive "a new drama, in which elements of the human personality that have been repressed or mutilated by older institutions will form the core of a new synthesis." The requirement is for "a deep organic transformation in every department of life. . . . The field for transformation is not this or that particular institution, but our whole society."[1]

Then, too, Sorokin's "cultural supersystems" by definition are characterized by "sociocultural integration." The personalities, cultural life, and social institutions of a thriving supersystem, including the new "ideational" or "integral" supersystem he sees on the horizon for mankind, must be meaningfully related and united in order to exist. Sorokin also anticipates that the coming world order will be built more on "familistic" than on "contractual" or on "coercive" relationships. Familistic systems are "permeated by mutual love, devotion, and sacrifice." What success the Soviet Union and other twentieth-century totalitarian societies achieve they owe to the familistic quality of some of their institutions, the creation of a "we" feeling that warms the soul and makes men willingly sacrifice personal gain for "higher" causes. "The new rising sociocultural order," he concludes, "promises to give a spontaneous unification of religion, philosophy,

---

[1]Lewis Mumford, *The Conduct of Life* (New York, 1951), 223–24.

science, ethics, and fine arts into one integrated system of supreme values of Truth, Goodness, and Beauty."[2]

Toynbee also embraces the organic theory. "A growing civilization," he points out, "can be defined as one in which the components of its culture. . . are in harmony with one another; and, on the same principle, a disintegrating civilization can be defined as one in which these same elements have fallen into discord." The unity of purpose and direction necessary to the spiritual health of a society is achieved by coordinating all the elements in its culture "in a harmony such as is maintained by the various instruments in an orchestra when the musicians are playing a symphony under the leadership of a conductor." An integrated culture is also like "a flint that has been compacted by the age-long pressure of enormous forces."[3]

For F. S. C. Northrop, a culture is the product of "a basic philosophy in terms of which the economic doctrine, the political doctrine, the legal theory, the religious theory and the artistic forms of that culture are defined."[4] His hopes for the "meeting of East and West" and the "taming of the nations," to quote the titles of his two most important prophetic books, rest on the possibility that through a fundamental re-examination and organic synthesis of the ideological premises of all living cultures, a world civilization can gradually evolve, with a single integrated world ideology.

At least two prophets of world order seem to use even what might be called "organismic" analogies: they anticipate the emergence of a collective human organism, not simply with organic properties, but with a literal biological unity difficult to describe in ordinary prose. Teilhard de Chardin ingeniously combined . . . a sincere personalism with a faith in the approaching development of a "hyper-person," "the birth of some single centre from the convergent beams of millions of elementary centres dispersed over the surface of the thinking earth," "an organic

super-aggregation of souls," thinking and living as one being.[5] And Oliver Reiser writes of "the birthing of a Planetary Being . . . in very fact a biological-social entity" with a Wellsian World Brain uniting East and West.[6] But genuinely organismic concepts are always too ecstatic to reduce to plain language. . . .

WORLD PHILOSOPHICAL SYNTHESIS

Most contemporary prophets of world order agree that no lasting concert of nations, no true world commonwealth, is possible without a concert of cultures. The United Nations or an arms control commission acting under its supervision could conceivably hold back the deluge for some time, but men must think and feel as one, before they can make the leap to cosmopolis.

As Toynbee points out, in discussing contracts between civilizations, when a culture reaches the "radioactive" stage and begins penetrating another, its economic techniques move most rapidly and penetrate most deeply, whereas the systems of thought and faith at its core arrive last and take the longest time to sink in.[7] So, in the modern world, Asian countries influenced by Western civilization have adopted Western technological know-how most readily, Western political ideas and institutions with much difficulty, and Western philosophy and religion hardly at all, except in communist China, and there only by ruthless totalitarian tactics quite alien in their dogmatic thoroughness to Asian traditions. The West is similarly unsympathetic, on the whole, to Eastern thought, although it responds warmly to Eastern cuisine, dress, and *objets d' art*. As a result the world is growing together most rapidly on the level of technics and trade, and least rapidly on the more fundamental level of belief, outlook, and value. The failure of modern technics to give the world more than a superficial physical unity is precisely what we should expect. Technics pave the way for communication and exchange of ideas, but they cannot alone create a world culture or even a world state. The only permanently viable

[2]Pitirim A. Sorokin and Walter A. Lunden, *Power and Morality* (Boston, 1959), 134–35.

[3]Arnold J. Toynbee, *A Study of History* (London, 1934–61), VIII, 7, 495, 498.

[4]F. S. C. Northrop, *The Logic of the Sciences and the Humanities* (New York, 1948), 4.

[5]Pierre Teilhard de Chardin, *The Phenomenom of Man*, tr. Bernard Wall (New York, 1959), 248, 259.

[6]Oliver L. Reiser, *The World Sensorium* (New York, 1946), 15, 48.

[7]Toynbee, *A Study of History*, VIII, 7.

societies are founded, in the final analysis, on a common spiritual and intellectual culture, which in turn makes possible unity and fraternity in the sphere of practical politics.

The problem of world cultural synthesis may be attacked at several different levels, and although some prophets operate on all of them equally well, the more typical prophet of world integration in mid-century tends to focus on one and ignore the rest. Philosophy suggests one approach, theology and ethics another, science and education a third, and there are even speculations here and there on the role in cultural synthesis of the arts. If we adopt the undramatic but common-sense point of view that an organic world culture will hardly be able to get along without philosophy, religion, ethics, science, education, and art, all tending toward organic unity, there is not much point in trying to figure out which department of culture has "priority" over all the others. They all hang together.

In any event, one major approach to world integration favored by many prophets is the synthesis of the world's great cultures and civilizations through a unification of their basic habits of thought. Most often, this amounts to a proposal for world philosophical synthesis. The premise here is that "a man is what he believes,"[8] that cultures are the products of their philosophies, and that only by a fusion of the philosophical underpinnings of cultures can the people in those cultures feel members of a common family of man. Japanese and Americans, for example, may both play baseball, both eat sukiyaki, and both build steamships, and still go to war and treat one another as vicious animals. Only when Japanese and Americans, and all othe peoples, look at the totality of things from the same philosophical point of view, or from points of view considered complementary, will they create a true world civilization and enjoy lasting peace. This is a thesis impossible to prove except by trying it out in the real world. The relative philosophical homogeneity of the nations of Western Europe did not prevent them from springing at one another's throats for centuries. On the other hand, although ideological differences are clearly not the only cause of war, harmony of thought and culture is just as clearly a major asset to a people in process of building a new civilization or even a single nation, as history suggests time and again. Even the great American "melting pot" might have cracked and shattered generations ago, if there had not been a hardy core of Protestant North European settlers in possession of a distinctive American way of life and willing and able to initiate immigrants into its mysteries. The immigrants have made their contribution, but within the framework of traditional American culture.

A genial, brilliant descendant of those same Protestant North European settlers, F. S. C. Northrop—his ancestor Joseph Northrop founded the town of Milford in Connecticut in 1639—has done more than any other single Western Philosopher in recent years to advertise and elaborate the idea of a concert of cultures through world philosophical synthesis. He is that philosopher rarely encountered nowadays who still adheres to the classical textbook definition of philosophy as "a reflective and reasoned attempt to infer the character and content of the universe, taken in its entirety and as a single whole, from an observation and study of the data presented by all its aspects."[9] He moves about with equal sureness of touch in metaphysics, epistemology, ethical and legal theory, the philosophy of science, Oriental thought, and political philosophy, and for many years until his retirement in 1962 occupied a chair at Yale which straddled the department of philosophy and the school of law. The present writer remembers with much pleasure auditing a "seminar" of his in the Yale Law School with an enrollment of nearly a hundred students. The meeting place had to be changed twice, to accommodate the overflow.

Northrop's formula for world cultural integration begins with a flat statement he seems to take on faith. "The presuppositions of a culture determine its empirical manifestations and institutions."[10] A culture does not develop out of pure whim or chance: every part of it is organically related to its fundamental assumptions about nature, man, and ultimate reality. The first step to synthesis, then, is the purely scholarly job of

---

[8]Charles A. Moore in Horst Frenz, ed., *Asia and the Humanities* (Bloomington, Ind., 1958), 79.

[9]B. A. G. Fuller, *A History of Philosophy*, rev. ed. (New York, 1945), I, 1.

[10]Northrop, *The Logic of the Sciences and the Humanities*, 293.

determining exactly what are, in fact, the presuppositions of a given culture. This requires painstaking analysis. Glib generalizations based on styles of art, for example, or tour guide information, or positive law codes, or historical descriptions of "national character," will not get to the heart of the problem. A congenial desire to compromise is not good enough either. Philosophical analysis comes first. If analysis discloses that the basic assumptions of the cultures being studied are compatible and even complementary, then the total ideology on which they are founded can simply be enlarged to incorporate the new insights. Nothing need be lost. The total cultures of East and West are complementary in just this way, and Northrop's technique for East-West philosophical synthesis is described in some detail below.* If incompatible elements exist, as obviously do exist between, say, North American, Nazi German, and Soviet Russian culture, they must be tested against the only objective criterion available to man—nature itself. Quite often one or more of the incompatible elements will be found to derive from a false interpretation of naturally given facts, as, for example, the Nazi assertion that white Nordic Europeans constitute a biologically superior race. When natural science has corrected these errors in the interpretation of nature, and when a new and more catholic set of assumptions has been worked out true to our best currently available scientific knowledge of man and nature, all the elements of all cultures concerned can be harmonized, and the cultures themselves will gradually unite. Northrop looks forward to a world order "in which the diverse basic conceptions and resultant valuations" of East and West will be "combined into a single world civilization, the richer and better because it includes in complementary harmony with balanced emphasis the most profound and mature insights of each."[11]

Not many prophets of world integration would agree with Northrop on the role of the Western natural science in the forming of a world culture; and of course Northrop himself would not suggest that a conference of philosophers could assemble and unify the world in one blow by sheer brain power. But his fundamental argument seems solid. And his view of a world culture as a balanced synthesis rather than a patchwork quilt or a lopsided cultural imperialism reflecting the basic assumptions of only one parochial culture, is quite typical. Modern prophets of world order want unity and diversity in dynamic equilibrium. "We should not aim," writes Sir Julian Huxley, "at the spread of one uniform type of culture over the entire globe, but at what has been well described as a world orchestration of cultures."[12] And in the words of India's Aurobindo Ghose, written over forty years ago, although "the unity of mankind is evidently a part of Nature's eventual scheme and must come about," it must be achieved "with safeguards which will keep the race intact in the roots of its vitality, richly diverse in its oneness.[13]

Aurobindo worked much of his long life for a reconciliation of East and West, and for exponents of world culture this, of course, is the ultimate challenge. An integration of Western civilization with its centers in Europe and the American hemisphere, and the Eastern civilizations of India and East Asia would bring most of the world's peoples together and prepare the way for an authentic world commonwealth.

As if following Northrop's advice, scores of Easterners and Westerners alike have been trying for many years to fathom, by philosophical and historical analysis, the basic, underlying ideational differences between Eastern and Western culture. Some have decided that the problem is insoluble because falsely stated. Sorokin, with his theory of cultural supersystems passing through all possible phases in endless succession, cannot accept the idea of a permanent, thorough-going distinction between East and West at all. A good many professional scholars of Eastern history and cultures also dismiss the whole concept of the "Orient" as antiquated, in view of the deep gulf between the cultures of India and East Asia: a gulf hardly noticed by earlier generations out of sheer ignorance. In a telling attack on Northrop's *Meeting of East and West*, for example, Arthur F. Wright

---

*See pp. 253–254.

[11]Northrop in Charles A. Moore, ed., *Philosophy—East and West* (Princeton, 1944), 234.

[12]Julian Huxley, *A Touchstone for Ethics* (New York, 1947), 140. Sir Julian's phrase is borrowed from Lawrence K. Frank, *Society as the Patient* (New Brunswick, 1948), 392–93.

[13]Aurobindo Ghose, *The Ideal of Human Unity* (New York, 1950), 23.

maintains there is no such thing as a traditional culture of the whole Orient. Nor can either "Eastern" or "Western" cultures be taken in three-thousand-year doses, in the Northrop manner, missing all the immense changes in orientation through the centuries.[14] This is clearly only one more episode in the perennial struggle between the erudite specialist who sees nothing but trees and the high-flying generalist who prefers forests; neither is infallible. But "East" and "West" can and have been distinguished in general terms, even if each is less monolithic than each once supposed. Also, in recent centuries, Western technical progress has had the effect of neatly dividing the world economy in two, its Western half prosperous, its Easter half poor. Under the circumstances, the Eastern peoples have drawn more closely together than ever before, not only because of reawakened interest in such ancient historic ties as Buddhism, but also for the practical reasons made very plain at the Bandung Conference in 1955. The immediate political and economic problems of the Asian nations are all painfully similar; they run a common race against time, in light of which the famous Cold War seems even more imbecile than it is.

Taking into due account the broad differences between the various parts of Western culture, and between India and East Asia, what marks off the "East" from the "West"? What basic attitudes will have to be harmonized in the ultimate synthesis? Each thinker who has accepted the problem as legitimate has solved it somewhat differently. The most ambitious collective efforts to uncover the "real difference" between East and West have been made at the three East-West Philosophers' conferences held under the auspices of the University of Hawaii at ten-year intervals since 1939. Northrop's widely discussed book, *The Meeting of East and West,* published in 1946, grew out of a paper he presented at the first conference. Other important contributors have included Charles A. Moore, William Ernest Hocking, George P. Conger, E. A. Burtt, Charles Morris, and John Wild, all American philosophers; and such Oriental scholars as Chan Wing-tsit, Junjiro Takakusu, and Daisetz Suzuki.

Most of the papers read at the Hawaii conferences have agreed that significant basic contrasts can be drawn between Eastern and Western thought, and as a rule the scholars participating have also been able to reach agreement on the areas where East-West differences are most clear-cut. Eastern metaphysics, they argue, incline almost always to monism. For the Eastern cultures, the cosmos is a single, undivided, harmonious reality, whereas the Western religions and philosophies tend to carve the cosmos into two or three distinct realms of being, such as Descartes' mind, matter, and deity, or the conventional Judeo-Christian contrast between creation and creator. In habits of thought, the East prefers intuition, synthesis, the pointing out of similarities; the West prefers closely reasoned analysis, exhaustive fact-finding, the drawing of precise and minute distinctions. Eastern ethical philosophy stresses the search for inner peace and harmony with the cosmos; Western moralists stress the active and practical life.[15]

Most of these same contrasts reappear in recent prophetic literature on the prospoects for world order. Erick Fromm, for example, sees the great differences between Eastern and Western thought in the Eastern preference for a logic of "paradox" and the Western for a logic of "identity." The Western mind classifies and organizes reality, whereas the Eastern mind rejects isolable, articulated, objective truths in favor of the ineffable Whole, of which all specific things are manifestations. "Various cultures have emphasized various aspects of the truth, and the more mankind becomes united culturally, the more will these various aspects become integrated into a total picture."[16] Denis de Rougemont, taking India as representative of the East, and Western Europe as representative of the West, finds that the Eastern way is "excarnation," absorption into the cosmos through concentrating on the spiritual dimension of reality, whereas the West seeks "incarnation," a this-worldly life centered in the person and marked by ceaseless adventure and anxiety. The Eastern idea of society is a magical

---

[14]Arthur F. Wright, "Professor Northrop's Chapter on the Traditional Culture of the Orient," *Journal of the History of Ideas,* X (1949), 143-49.

[15]See the papers in Charles A. Moore, ed., *Philosophy —East and West* and *Essays in East-West Philosophy* (Honolulu, 1950).

[16]Erich Fromm, *The Art of Loving* (New York, 1956), 72-80; Fromm, *Man for Himself* (New York, 1947), 239.

body held together by ageless tradition and in harmony with the cosmos. The Western is of a society of persons forever seeking new meanings and new hazards.[17] Lancelot Law Whyte discovers in Western thought a perpetual dualism between mind and matter, intellect and instinct, which keeps Western man forever at war with himself. Eastern man, on the other hand, accepts intuitively the unitary nature of the world-process. In the coming world civilization, Asia will borrow the West's most distinctive achievements, but the West will also accept from Asia her "deeper aim of harmony as proper to all men. . . . A new type of man emerges combining the unity of the East with the differentiation of the West. The separation of East and West is over."[18]

But, again, perhaps the most elaborate and careful analysis of East-West differences comes from F. S. C. Northrop. His formula for East-West philosophical and cultural integration has attracted, in its field, the same kind of broad public interest as Toynbee's *Study of History*, even to the extent of an article in *Life*;[19] and it explains, ingeniously, how the Western mind can be both dynamically this-worldly and yet highly abstract and theoretical, whereas the Eastern mind can focus simultaneously on concrete experience and undifferentiated ultimate reality. Northrop himself is a perfect example of the Western penchant for abstract theorizing and classifying. He helps prove his own theory, by the very methods he uses to arrive at it.

Northrop's argument recalls in places Sorokin's entirely independent theory of the phases of a cultural supersystem.[20] His starting point is the distinction between what he calls the "aesthetic" component of knowledge and the "theoretic" component. Aesthetic knowledge is reached by immediate experience, which includes what is commonly called intuition. Knowledge in the theoretic component is reached through concepts by postulation, as when a Western scientist, studying the history of forms of life through the fossil record, formulates the theory of evolution; or looking at man and nature in general, suggests the theory of the divine Logos. The Eastern philosophies, and all Eastern cultures necessarily, are founded on a very high development of the aesthetic component of knowledge. The Western specialty, of course, is the concept by postulation, which runs through our monotheistic religions, Greek philosophy, and all later thought evolved from these Judeo-Hellenic starting points. Western knowledge tends, therefore, to be abstract, determinate, dogmatic, and precise. Not surprisingly, our chief system of logic, the Aristotelian, holds that each "kind" of "thing" is separate and distinct from each other "kind." The concept by postulation, reached inductively by empirical observation and followed through all its logical consequences by rational deduction, is the secret of the West's amazing success in the natural sciences. It gives man a way to scrutinize nature objectively, with a minimum of interference from the investigator.

There is more to the aesthetic component of knowledge, however, than may meet the eye at first glance. Knowledge in the theoretic component is always highly determinate, which is to say, expressed in certain exact words and/or mathematical symbols, which tend to shut it off from other similar bits of knowledge and from reality as a whole. A concept by postulation, one might say, taking a few liberties with Northrop, mentally slices the cosmic pie and tears pieces out of their existential context. Still other concepts by postulation slice the pie other ways. The world is thus mentally slashed into an infinity of sometimes overlapping, sometimes entirely isolated tatters of knowledge. Moreover, such knowledge is always indirectly verified. A theory cannot be seen, touched, or tasted. It cannot be scanned existentially by the inner eye of intuition. It is, so far as the living mind goes, "abstract." Knowledge in the aesthetic component, on the other hand, is always vibrantly direct, and it ranges anywhere from the sensuous experience of sound, smell, and color common to all men everywhere, to the Eastern mystic's intuitive absorption in total reality. In explaining the latter, Northrop argues that even Western science, with the advent of field theory in physics, has come around to the recognition that the entire universe can be regarded as a single continuum. This total continuum can be

---

[17]Denis de Rougemont, *Man's Western Quest*, tr. Montgomery Belgion (New York, 1957), chs. 1–2.

[18]Lancelot Law Whyte, *The Next Development in Man* (New York, 1950), 244.

[19]"The Mind of Asia," *Life*, December 31, 1951, 38–42.

[20]Sorokin, *Social Philosophies of an Age of Crisis* (Boston, 1950), 145–58, 244–59, 275–322 *passim*.

studied through theoretical differentiation, as in Western science, or as in Eastern philosophy and religion, it can be felt in its entirety, undifferentiated and inexpressible in any kind of language: hence, Northrop's much debated phrase, the "undifferentiated aesthetic continuum," symbolized by such Oriental terms as Brahman-Atman and Tao, but knowable aesthetically only through the direct Eastern experience not of communion but of actual self-equation with the world continuum. In the Hindu formula, *tat tvam asi*: "that thou art." The genius of the East lies in its profound, direct cultivation of this sense of the unity of all being.

Clearly, Western culture has much to offer the East, but Eastern art, religion, and formal thought can also greatly enrich the West, which has been notably sluggish in developing the potentialities of the aesthetic component of knowledge. Northrop feels that both components are worth exploiting. Each is irreducible into the other, but a set of basic assumptions can be devised more catholic than either, asserting the validity of both. An integral knowledge of reality requires the "epistemic correlation" of both components, which can lead not only to a deeper sense of reality in East and West alike, but also to the foundations of a world civilization uniting them both in a higher synthesis. On the Indian subcontinent, for example, an acceptance of the complementarity of theoretic and aesthetic knowledge would make Muslims less fanatic and Hindus more scientific—the Muslims with their dogmatic monotheism representing an eastward migration of Western culture, the Hindus with their lack of enthusiasm for the theoretical articulation of the aesthetic continuum illustrating the lopsidedness of Eastern culture. The result would be peace and prosperity for the whole subcontinent. And India is, in this sense, the planet in microcosm.[21]

Northrop has not escaped severe and able criticism. Sorokin and Radhakrishnan object vigorously to the sharpness of his contrast between Eastern and Western modes of thought. As Northrop himself has always conceded, but never stressed, the West has its mystics, its monists, its existentialists, its artists and musicians deeply skilled in plumbing and communicating purely aesthetic experience. The East has its logicians, its theorists, its concepts by postulation. "Almost all the main concepts of Indian thought," Radhakrishnan writes, "are more concepts by postulation than concepts by intuition." Not all Westerners are dogmatic, as the history of Western science and exploration shows plainly, whereas the East has had its share of quarrelsome pedants and furious fanatics. The difference is a matter of degree. "The truth," Radhakrishnan concludes, "which is somewhat exaggerated in Northrop's analysis, is that in the East there is greater preoccupation with the richer and less determinate facts of existence than with the abstract and determinate facts of essence."[22]

Exaggerated or not, Northrop's formulas for East-West synthesis have given wide publicity to the problem of East-West differences, and they contain more than a few grains of useful truth. The main thing, again, is a passionate conviction of the complementarity of cultures. The very act of synthesis will have to be a joint East-West project, if Northrop's analysis is at all sound: Western philosophers are best qualified by their traditional methods to analyze the problem, Eastern philosophers to supply the conviction of cosmic harmony without which no attempt at synthesis could expect organic results.

Of course the need for painstaking analysis of differences can itself be challenged by Eastern thinkers, leading to a more characteristically Oriental formula for synthesis. Radhakrishnan prefers to emphasize the broad areas of agreement between East and West. All cultures, he writes, ask much the same questions and search for much the same things, each in its own way. Western culture is no morass of materialism, nor is Eastern culture so profoundly spiritual as many of its modern apologists like to think. Enough links exist between the two worlds of thought to bring them into fruitful union. All that is needed is tolerance and mutual sympathy. And since "great spiritual revivals occur through the fusion of different traditions," he expects a mighty spiritual renaissance to emerge from the true meeting of Eastern

[21]Northrop, *The Meeting of East and West* (New York, 1946).

[22]Sir Sarvepalli Radhakrishnan in Paul Arthur Schilpp, ed., *The Philosophy of Sarvepalli Radhakrishnan* (New York, 1952), 823, 828. But see Northrop's "Methodology and Epistemology, Oriental and Occidental," in Charles A. Moore, ed., *Essays in East-West Philosophy*, 151–60.

and Western minds. "The separation of East and West is over. The history of the new world, the one world, has begun. It promises to be large in extent, varied in colour, rich in quality." Men must bend every effort to forge a "unitary world culture," which is "the only enduring basis for a world community."[23]

Along somewhat similar lines, Jaspers calls for free and limitless communication between East and West, suspecting that "we are on the road from the evening-glow of European philosophy to the dawn of world philosophy."[24] Denis de Rougemont even predicts that by the turn of the century the debate between communism and capitalism will be replaced by a great and sober dialogue between East and West. "And I mean a real dialogue, at the level of religions and philosophies; that is to say, at the level on which civilizations and cultures are created." Whether one will absorb the other, or a transcending principle will be discovered uniting both, he cannot say; but he hopes at least for the "sincere alliance" Minerva negotiated between Ulysses and his foes at Ithaca.[25]

Meanwhile, East and West go on meeting—and colliding. Through the United Nations and its affiliated agencies, through trade and tourism, through the exchange of students and films and books and art, through conferences such as the series in Honolulu, the conferences on Oriental-Western literary relations at Indiana University, the annual Eranos symposia on Lago Maggiore in Switzerland, the Salzburg congress on comparative civilizations, and many others, the two cultural hemispheres of the world slowly coalesce. Perhaps, as Toynbee suggests, the final synthesis will be, in outward appearance, a "Westernization" of the world accompanied by profound Easternizing counter-tendencies within the West proper. East-

ern acceptance of Western science and technology has gone a long way toward homogenizing the two sets of civilizations, if only because, as Gandhi foresaw, it is hardly possible to industrialize an Eastern country without also, in the long run, bringing in all the rest of the Western way of life. The East throws off the chains of Western imperialism, but "the formerly subject non-Western peoples . . . are all using their newly won power of self-determination to Westernize their social structures and their cultural configurations of their own accord. In doing this, they are laying the foundations for a single world-wide society and for a uniform world-wide culture that will take its first shape within a Western-made framework—though, no doubt, it will become less specifically Western in complexion as all the cultural heritages of all the extant societies come to be the common possession of the whole of mankind." Toynbee hopes with fervor that "the ex-Western oecumenical civilization" will assimilate "all that was best in all the heritages of all the civilizations that . . . preceded it."[26]

Of course this over-all question of total East-West synthesis far from exhausts the problems involved in the concert of cultures. It is probably the gravest challenge before us in the long run. If the two worlds do not permanently fuse, an exasperated, hungry, overpopulated Orient armed with nuclear and bacteriological weapons may turn on the West some day and overwhelm it, counting its casualties as blessings in disguise and eager to even the score with its thriving ex-conquerors. This might be poor justice, but the Occident would not go to its grave entirely guiltless. And there are other problems. Within the West proper, the Latin American cultures clash with the North American way of life. The English-speaking world is not entirely at harmony with Continental Europe, and perhaps the German question is not yet solved, in spite of two world wars. The Islamic West remains at loggerheads with the Christian West, after thirteen hundred years of conflict. Within the Orient proper, no one could imagine the cultures of such disparate areas as India, Indonesia, China, and Japan in perfect harmony with one another, in spite of a certain vague fellow feeling, and many ties of blood and outlook and history. Negro Africa must also

---

[23]Radhakrishnan, *East and West* (New York, 1956), 121, 131; *The Philosophy of Sarvepalli Radhakrishnan*, 73. Northrop objects that Radhakrishnan is actually guilty of provincialism here, since toleration is one of the cardinal virtues in Hindu thought, and Radhakrishnan, therefore, is asking all other peoples to behave like Hindus. Northrop urges union through tough-minded reconception, rather than through sympathy and tolerance alone. Northrop, in *The Philosophy of Sarvepalli Radhakrishnan*, 647.

[24]Karl Jaspers in Paul Arthur Schilpp, ed., *The Philosophy of Karl Jaspers* (New York, 1957), 83–84.

[25]Rougemont, *op. cit.*, 187–88, 196–97.

[26]Toynbee, *A Study of History*, XII, 309, 529.

be reckoned with: a whole continent neither Eastern nor Western in cultural origins.

Finally, there is the formidable issue of communism, a Western cult now in possession of half of Europe and most of East Asia. As the other Western social philosophies and creeds become noticeably more flexible and tolerant, and even anxious to win Oriental friendship, communism sets out to conquer the world with genuine nineteenth-century Western verve. But dressed as it is in Russian sheep's clothing, it can somehow detach itself from the "real West" and appeal to the East as an almost Eastern creed.

. . . In its growth and expansion, communism has undeniably created a new kind of culture, bringing the West proper into a strange new union with traditional Russian Orthodox culture, and into an even stranger alliance with traditional Chinese culture. The meeting of East and West, then, is by no means confined to the encounters and collisions of the Euro-American West with the non-communist East. For practical political and military reasons, it is clearly imperative to persuade the new Eurasian communist cultures to enter into a serious and frank dialogue with the rest of the world. Now that Moscow is no longer the unrivaled capital of world communism, and there is a wider variety of contacts between East and West, the prospects for such a dialogue are no doubt improved.

A number of plausible solutions can be imagined, if both camps in the Cold War manage to avoid a suicidal global exchange of intercontinental ballistic missiles. Except for the extremists on either side, the most hopeful possibility is a gradual growing together under the impact of technology: as the two systems become less different, their missionary ardor may wear off, and they may little by little join forces. It is also conceivable that both will go on indefinitely, distinct from one another, but able to cooperate in keeping the peace for practical reasons. Or communism may—to use a famous phrase—wither away altogether, as the Soviet people, at least, outgrow their need for it.

From the point of view of the new science of economic development, capitalism and communism are only two different ways of reaching much the same economic goal. As Robert L. Heilbroner notes, communism is a substitute for capitalism, accomplishing for stagnant and backward econo-mics in countries without a tradition of vigorous free enterprise what capitalism did, more gradually, in the nineteenth century for the West.[27] Walt Rostow strongly suspects that when Soviet Russia enters the era of high mass-consumption already reached by the West, communism "is likely to wither" and Russia is likely to fall prey to that notorious but not necessarily fatal affliction of all families and nations once they have achieved prosperity and want to enjoy it in peace: like the Buddenbrooks in Thomas Mann's early novel, they no longer care for empire-building. Rostow is hopeful that "the Buddenbrooks' dynamics will operate in Russia, if given time and a strong Western policy that rules out as unrealistic Soviet policies of expansion." The new generation will demand a higher standard of living, more personal freedom, a richer cultural life, and no part of messianic communism.[28]

Of course capitalism is changing, too. The graduated income tax, public welfare programs, social insurance, government controls, public ownership in many sectors of the economy, collective bargaining, and the cooperative movement have totally transformed the old laisser-faire capitalistic system of Marx's time. The individual entrepreneur counts for much less, just as his Soviet counterpart already counts for much more. Lewis Mumford hears the death knell of Economic Man in the steady movement of capitalist countries toward the welfare state and of communist countries toward many of the virtues of individual initiative. In the change from "a money economy based on power and productivity to a life economy based on participation and creativity," the long-drawn-out industrial crisis in civilization will finally be resolved, and "instead of maintaining their ideological purity," capitalist and communist regimes "will tend to take on more of the diversified attributes of living systems."[29] Economics will give place, at last, to life itself, and goods will be produced in accordance not with economic laws, but with human desires and needs. William Ernest Hocking insists that even now the dichotomy between capitalism and communism is

---

[27]Robert L. Heilbroner, *The Future as History* (New York, 1960), 75–101.

[28]Walt W. Rostow, *The Stages of Economic Growth* (Cambridge, 1960), 133–34.

[29]Mumford, *The Transformation of Man* (New York, 1956), 214.

wholly fictitious. "All actual economies of developed nations are *mixed economies*." Capitalism, whether of the public or private variety, has turned out to be the best way of mobilizing resources for maximum production; the socialist or communist principle is everywhere applied to some extent for equitable distribution of the goods so produced.[30]

But differences do and will persist between the total culture and ideology of the West and of Soviet Russia, even if the economic issue no longer really divides them or will not divide them in the near future. Northrop sees Soviet culture dogmatically committed to the Hegelian-Marxian concept of the individual as merely a part of a social organism which fits into a vast historical process, and as having merely set physiological needs, which can be satisfied by planned production. Since all this goes along with a typically Western conviction of absolute rightness, a familiar failing of ideas in the theoretical component of knowledge, Soviet culture is dynamically aggressive. It cannot be reconciled with the liberal democratic ideology of the West derived from Locke and Bentham unless its fundamental presuppositions, and those of the West, are enlarged and purged of the "nothing but" fallacy, so as to create a new ideology embracing the insights, compatible with each other and true to human nature, of both. Obviously both rest, for example, on pitifully thin psychological assumptions: Soviet culture on the idea that men are bodies, the liberal-democratic West on the idea that men are simply consciousnesses which seek pleasure and avoid pain, in the famous formula of Jeremy Bentham. The nature of man is much fuller and deeper than either capitalism or communism would have us believe. In China, Northrop similarly hopes that communism will be able to achieve a higher synthesis in union with the rich culture of Confucian-Buddhist-Taoist tradition. If such a synthesis proves impossible, then he sees no alternative but the total extirpation of one or the other, communism or Sinism, since the two cannot coexist peacefully. The Red regime's massacres of monks and destruction of family life are ominous strides in the direction of the de-Sinicization of China. But the whole communist bloc must be politically quarantined by the rest of the world, through collective military action, until a true meeting of minds can produce a true reconciliation of the deep ideological differences separating communist cultures from those in the so-called free world.

Jaspers is still less optimistic about the possible role of communism in the coming world civilization. He accepts the need for a measure of socialism and for democratic planning, but he sees no compromise possible between the Soviet idea of total planning and the Western idea of freedom. A world totally planned would be a world totally despiritualized, closed to transcendence, reduced to insecthood. "Either . . . we have confidence in the chances of the free interplay of forces, notwithstanding the frequency with which they give rise to absurdities . . . or we stand before the world planned in its totality by man, with its spiritual and human ruin."[31] Toynbee sees some possibility of partial reconciliation in a democratic socialism that accepts but constantly strives to minimize the inevitable tension between the equally essential values of personal liberty and social justice. He looks on the new West European welfare states with their mixed economies as the most promising sign for the future. But at the level of the purely human, he admits that freedom and equality are basically incompatible abstractions. Only spiritual forces greater than the forces of this world can make them work together: in the Christian symbols, the brotherhood of man and the fatherhood of God.[32]

Perhaps, in another hundred years, the Cold War between capitalism and communism will be a dead issue, as de Rougemont prophesies. Or, perhaps, of all the obstacles in the path of world cultural synthesis, communism will prove the highest. It is certainly a most formidably tough nut at the present writing. Charles Moore makes the point that the philosophical attitudes of the traditional Orient and the traditional Occident are in fundamental harmony, even though emphasizing different things, whereas communism, with its materialism, determinism, totalitarianism, economic obsessions, ethics of crass expediency, and rejection of all spiritual or divine power, is

---

[30]William Ernest Hocking, *Strength of Men and Nations* (New York, 1959), 35.

[31]Jaspers, *The Origin and Goal of History*, tr. Michael Bullock (New Haven, 1955), 180.
[32]Toynbee, *A Study of History*, IX, 577–604.

basically incompatible with both.[33] This may be a harsh and extreme judgment born of Cold War hysteria, but there are times when the most cheerful observer cannot help but agree with it.

Still, no man can predict what changes may overtake communism in succeeding decades. Its program has not remained strictly consistent even over the past forty-five years. In the case of both Russia and China, revolutionary messianism has already been displaced to a very marked degree by old-fashioned great-power chauvinism, which may be just as dangerous to world peace in the long run, but at any rate is not the same thing. Nothing absolutely rules out the possibility that the Eurasian communist cultures will some day take their place in a unified world civilization, if the will for harmony exists on both sides.

Even assuming that all living creatures will eventually and freely flow into the common stream of humanity, the prophets leave us somewhat in the dark, as they must, on the total ultimate shape of the world culture. It may be one uniform culture, an alloy blended from all the best in the contributing historic cultures. Or the separate regional cultures may continue to flourish on a reduced scale, as Welsh or Basque culture persists in Britain or Spain today, with the true world culture limited to a few authentic cosmopolitan centers located here and there around the planet, analogous to the role of Paris in modern France. Or each regional culture may become the nucleus of its own particular independent version of world-synthesis, making the world a confederation of "globalized" Brazils, Germanies, Indias, Chinas, and so forth. Or finally, it may be a world of mishmash.

This last prospect seems to bother a good many people. Anyone familiar with the extensive critical literature on Toynbee will remember, for example, Hugh Trevor-Roper's maliciously witty lampoon of the Toynbeean world civilization. Toynbee himself will be its divinely inspired prophet, he says, and his *Study of History* its only

sacred book. Western civilization will disappear and "all that is good in it, and in other civilizations" will be "preserved and pickled in the universal world-state with its universal world-religion of Mish-Mash."[34] This is the usual quarrel of critics fond of the status quo with the coming world civilization, after mishmash, are "syncretism," "eclecticism," and "hodgepodge." If the prophets of world integration may be believed, this is a pseudo problem. No world culture, unitary, federate, confederate, or what not, is going to hang together in tomorrow's world unless it is growing in the direction of organicity at a convincing speed. But this is only the historical process. Roman culture was outrageously syncretic, no doubt, in the second and third centuries AD., but out of it flowered the medieval synthesis. Christianity itself is a fantastic potpourri, if broken down into its constituent bits. No one looking at the agony of fifth- or sixth-century China, overrun by barbarians and invaded by alien religions, might have anticipated the incredible syntheses of T'ang and Sung culture. Synthesis is never born fully formed out of the brain of Jove. It arrives by degrees, from hodgepodge and confusion; and if it comes to the whole world in the centuries ahead, it can only come the same way.

But the prophets of world integration have investigated some special features of a world culture in more detail, which deserve separate treatment. Two essential ingredients, for prime examples, are religion, which will link Eastern and Western insights, and science, which the world civilization will have to borrow principally from the West. In both instances, especially the first, integration at several levels is urgently needed, if World Man is to think, feel, and act in creative harmony. Many prophets would argue that religious and intellectual integration may even, to some extent, have to precede the sort of philosophical synthesis surveyed above, although all three are intimately interrelated.

---

[33]Moore in *Asia and the Humanities*, 93–94.

[34]H. R. Trevor-Roper, *Men and Events* (New York, 1957), 314.

Discussion and Questions

1. F. S. C. Northrop writes, as of 1950, that "there are seven major cultural political units in the contemporary world." He describes them thus:

(1) The Asian solidarity of India, Ceylon, Tibet, Burma, Thailand, Indo-China, China, Korea and Japan rooted in the basic philosophical and cultural similarity of non-Aryan Hinduism, Buddhism, Taoism and Confucianism. (2) The Islamic world rooted in the religious and philosophical faith and reconstruction of a resurgent Islam. (3) The non-Islamic, non-European African world rooted in its lesser known culture. (4) The continental European Union grounded in a predominantly Roman Catholic culture with a secular leadership that has passed through the liberalizing influence of modern philosophical thought. (5) The British Commonwealth with its predominantly Protestant British empirical philosophical traditions combined with the bond of unity derived through classical education, English law, the Church of England and its Royal Family from a Stoic Christian Rome that has passed through Hooker, the Tudors and Cromwell's versions of the Protestant Reformation. (6) Pan America rooted in the liberal constitutionalism of the common law of the United States on the one hand and the modern equivalent of Cicero's liberal Stoic Roman legal universalism on the other hand as expressed in governments, and even education, under secular leadership. (7) The Soviet Communistic world comprising the U.S.S.R., her Eastern European satellites, mainland China and North Korea.

This leaves out of account the Scandinavian countries of Norway, Sweden, Denmark, and Finland; Ireland, apart from North Ireland; Spain and Portugal; Switzerland; and the future of East Germany, Poland, Yugoslavia, Czechoslovakia and the other Russian satellites.

Ireland is, of course, an untamed maverick. Like Pat himself, if there is a government anywhere, she is "agin it." Sooner or later, however, the meaning of his Roman Catholic faith with its lawful universalism should catch up with even Irish intuition. When this occurs Pat may find it possible to get the regiment into step with himself.

All four of the Scandinavian nations are predominantly Protestant in their religious traditions and British empirical in their liberal parliamentarian economic and political theory. In this respect they belong naturally with the United States and the nations in the British Commonwealth. The North Atlantic Charter and NATO show that this cultural tie has come very close to producing a political bond. To be sure, Finland and Sweden, because of their proximity to Soviet Russia, find it necessary and probably wise to remain neutral in the present rather demoralized world situation when the effectiveness of police action under international law is so uncertain. The moment, however, that international law becomes strong enough . . . the movement to political unity on cultural lines will undoubtedly be so strong that it will embrace these two nations also.

The extent to which Great Britain, Canada and the United States work together politically for all practical purposes in a spontaneous way is equally evident. Any suggestion for the United States and Canada to enter into a treaty guaranteeing that one will not launch a military attack upon the other within the next twenty-five years is so unrealistic as to be absurd. There are no guns from one end to the other of the Canadian border because the people of both Canada and the United States know that the governments of each country are operating from the standpoint of common cultural, moral, political and legal principles. Such spontaneous unity of faith and outlook is worth a thousand written treaties. Already, therefore, we find the contemporary world has taken what may be termed a second step toward world unity and law by binding together two or more of the seven cultural political units indicated above. [Reprinted with permission of the Macmillan Company from *The*

Taming of Nations by F. S. C. Northrop. Copyright 1952 by F. S. C. Northrop. Pp. 286–288.]*

2. Premier Chou En-Lai of China delivered an address at the Bandung Asian-African Conference of nonaligned powers in 1955. His presentation of the goals of Chinese foreign policy should be compared with Liska's perception of the Communist international system. Despite the lapse of time and change of posture, Premier Chou's speech seems appropriate to insert at this point because it presents an early statement of the need for "third world" solidarity, and it exhibits a side of Chinese diplomacy that has not been sufficiently noticed. In the context of our concerns, it sets forth a basis for "regionalist" identifications that might, if implemented, lead to more formal efforts. ➤ Do these interests take precedence over the sort of cultural unities that Northrop stresses? ➤ Is Chou En-Lai's stress on "unity" persuasive? We publish here an excerpted version of this speech.

SPEECH BY PREMIER CHOU EN-LAI TO THE POLITICAL COMMITTEE OF THE ASIAN-AFRICAN CONFERENCE, APRIL 23, 1955.

Yesterday and today I have heard the views of many delegations and I would like now to put forth proposals of the delegation of the People's Republic of China.

The present world situation is indeed tense but we have not lost hope of peace. As a matter of fact, there are more and more people who stand for peace.

Twenty-nine countries of Africa and Asia came here to this conference and have called for peace. This proves that more than half the world's population which we represent here wants peace and unity.

This manifestation which proves our desire receives support from the majority of nations and peoples of the world. It further proves that it is possible to stop the danger of war.

Therefore, in this conference when we discuss the question of promotion of world peace and cooperation, we should take the following stand: We should leave aside our different

---
*Cf. Friedrich, *Europe: An Emergent Nation* (Harper and Row, New York, 1969).

ideologies, our different state systems and the international obligations which we have assumed by joining this side or that side. We should instead settle all questions which may arise amongst us on the basis of common peace and cooperation. . . .

Secondly, if we talk about cooperation then we, the twenty-nine countries assembled here, should be united in promoting international cooperation and in seeking collective peace. Such a collective peace is not for the purpose of opposing any countries outside Asia and Africa. We are merely starting with Asian-African countries in promoting peace and opposing war.

As far as China is concerned, we are a country led by the Chinese Communist Party. We are against formation of ever more antagonistic military alliances in the world because they heighten the crisis of war.

For instance, we are against NATO, the Manila treaty and other similar treaties. However, if antagonistic military treaties continue in the world, then we would be forced to find some countries to enter into [with] and sign a similar, antagonistic military alliance in order to safeguard and protect ourselves against aggression.

It is for this reason, basically, that we are against antagonistic military alliances, and now that we have assembled here to discuss problems of common concern and the question of peace we should abandon the idea of such alliances, because they are to nobody's good and also it is to no one's good to publicize these treaties.

Let us first have unity among us. . . .

When the Prime Minister of China visited India and Burma they put forward these five principles. They accepted these five principles and made commitments on them. We have done this together with the Indian premier to alleviate doubts which many countries have as regards China. Ever since we entered into these five principles there are more and more countries who are in favor of them. Prime Minister Nehru told me Mr. Edén, now the Prime Minister of Britain, even agreed to the five principles. I am very glad to hear that. If Prime Minister Eden was prepared to issue a statement with the Prime Minister of China, I think the Prime Minister of China would be the first to sign that statement giving support to the five principles.

Of course, every delegation here could not agree to the wording of these five principles or agree to all five principles. Therefore, we can reformulate these five principles to make them agreeable to all the delegates. We can add to these five principles or we can subtract from them. In this way we can on the basis of common desire establish these principles with a view to safeguarding collective peace.

There have been some references to some international organizations. The delegate from Iraq mentioned the Cominform. But there are a great number of other international organizations in the world. We are ourselves displeased, for instance, with the network of the United States Intelligence Agency because we have been the victims of that agency. Unfortunately, we cannot raise this question at this conference because although these organizations might have some connection with some of our Asian-African countries, we cannot reach any agreement at this conference on these questions. Besides, this is outside our agenda. This should not be raised at this conference.

On what basis are we going to do all that? The points on which we all agree are no longer five. They are seven. I hope we can all agree. With this basis of seven points we on our part would like to give our assurances here that we will carry them out. China is a big country and China is led by the Chinese Communist party. So some people feel that we will not carry them out. So we give you our assurances and we hope that other delegations will do likewise.

The first point. We respect each other's sovereignty and territorial integrity. We will adhere to this principle. Our relations with Burma have proved that we have respected the sovereignty of Burma. As to respect for territorial integrity, it is stated that China will not and should not have any demand for territory. We have common borders with four countries. With some of these countries we have not yet finally fixed our border line and we are ready to do so with our neighboring countries. But before doing so, we are willing to maintain the present situation by acknowledging that those parts of our border are parts which are undetermined. We are ready to restrain our government and people from crossing even one step across our border. If such things should happen, we would like to admit our mistake.

As to the determination of common borders which we are going to undertake with our neighboring countries, we shall use only peaceful means and we shall not permit any other kinds of methods. In any case, we shall not change this.

The second point is abstention from aggression and threats against each other. We shall also abide by this principle. There is fear of China on the part of our neighbors, Thailand and the Philippines. Since we lack mutual understanding, it is quite natural that they have this fear. But during our contacts this time, we have made assurances to Prince Wan of Thailand and General Romulo of the Philippines that we will not make any aggression or direct threats against Thailand or the Philippines. We also told Prince Wan of Thailand that even before diplomatic relations are established between our countries, we welcome a delegation from the Philippines to visit our coastal regions, especially Fukien and Kwangtung provinces, and to see for themselves whether we are carrying out any activities for purposes of directing threats against the Philippines.

The third point. Abstinence from interference or intervention in the internal affairs of one another. This is a question with which the Indochina states are most concerned. During the time of the Geneva conference we made assurances to Cambodia and Laos. We have also told Mr. Eden, the then Foreign Secretary, and Mr. Molotov about our assurances. Later we also told Prime Minister Nehru and Prime Minister U Nu about our assurances. This time again we make our assurances to the delegations of Cambodia and Laos. We earnestly hope that these two countries will become peace-loving countries, peace-loving countries like India and Burma. We have no intention whatsoever to interfere or intervene in the internal affairs of these two neighboring states of ours. This is our policy toward all countries. We are merely mentioning these two countries as examples.

The fourth point. Recognition of equality of races. This point needs no explanation: we have always regarded that different races are equal. New China has not practiced any discrimination.

The fifth point. Recognition of the equality of all nations, large and small. We attach special importance to this question because we are a big nation. It is easy for big nations to disregard small nations and have no respect for small nations. This is the result of tradition. We are constantly examining our behavior towards small nations. If any delegation here finds a representative of China does not respect now any of the countries which are represented here, please bring this point out. We will be glad to accept the criticism and rectify mistakes.

The sixth point. Respect for the rights of the people of all countries who [to?] choose freely a way of life as well as political and economic system. We think that this is acceptable to all. The Chinese people have chosen a way of life as well as political and economic systems in new China. We will not allow any outside interference.

We on our part respect the way of life as well as the political and economic systems chosen by other people. For instance, we respect the way of life and political and economic systems chosen by the American people. We have also told the delegation of Japan that we respect the choice made by the Japanese people. When the Japanese people chose the Yoshida Government we recognized that Government as representative of the Japanese people. The Chinese Prime Minister said the same thing to all the delegates when they visited China.

Point Seven. The abstention from doing damage to each other. Our relations should be mutually beneficial to each other, and one side should not do damage to the other. For instance, in our trade, it must be equally and mutually beneficial to one another; neither side should ask for privileges or attach conditions. China can give the assurance that in its dealings with the countries represented here and other countries which are not represented here, when entering into peaceful cooperation with all countries, when having economic and cultural intercourse with those countries, she will not ask for privileges or special conditions. We will go on an equal basis.

It is our belief that with these seven points as a basis it is possible to have peace and cooperation among us; it is possible to safeguard peace. And, first of all, to start with peace among us. In fact, in these seven points we have said in our draft proposal that we Asian-African countries advocate settlement of international disputes by peaceful means and support all measures that are being taken or may be taken to eliminate international tension and promote the growth of peace. In our view this is acceptable. . . . [Reprinted from George McT. Kahin: *The Asian-African Conference, Bandung, Indonesia, April 1955.* © 1956 by Cornell University. Used by permission of Cornell University Press.]

➤ Do such views suggest a basis for first-stage integration? for second-stage integration? ➤ Are they merely concerned with the formation of a regional bargaining coalition vis-à-vis other centers of influence in international society? or are they mainly concerned with establishing suitable conditions for intraregional cooperation and peace within the traditional system of sovereign states?

3. ➤ Is it easier to proceed beyond cooperation to political unification if the wider community shares common cultural traditions and values? How are the boundaries of a culture to be identified? ➤ Would Russett's method of delimitation of a region work within the framework of Northrop's thought?

4. ➤ Is it important to maintain a clear distinction between international cooperation among units in a region and international integration in which there is a fusion of national units for certain economic, political, and cultural purposes? The potentiality for cooperation is a test, in the sense of reform prospects within the state system, whereas the potentiality for regional integration is one test of the prospects for limited transformation of the international system by voluntary means.

PART IV

REGIONALISM AND GLOBALISM (THE UNITED NATIONS): SOME CONTRADICTORY TENDENCIES AND TRENDS

A great deal of intellectual energy has been expended in the past on the questions: are regional organizations impeding or facilitating the work of the United Nations? is the promotion of regional integration a help or a hindrance to the growth of adequate global institutions? Joseph Nye has written that "too often the issues have been discussed in the general terms of regionalism v. globalism in the security field in terms of the bureaucratic and political debate during World War II and the immediate, post-war period." (Joseph S. Nye, Ed., *International Regionalism* [Little, Brown, Boston, 1968], p. vi). Nye calls for more careful inquiries into the specific experience of regionalizing tendencies. He also argues that ideological debate about the relative virtues of regionalism and globalism are pointless exercises.

The debate has been particularly confusing because it frequently lumps together the following quite distinct issues:

1. Under what circumstances and conditions is the exercise of authority at the regional level a contribution to rather than an interference with the exercise of authority at the global level?

2. What sorts of capabilities is it desirable for various regional institutions to possess? what sorts of global restraint should be placed upon their use?

3. In the present international system, what is the proper "mix" between regional action and global action? Is the proper "mix" decisively dependent—

   (a) on the character of the subsystem?
   (b) on the character of the issue area or subject matter?
   (c) on the general condition of the over-all international environment at a particular time?

4. What is the best means of stabilizing the relationship between regional and global spheres of action? By formal treaty provision? by clear lines of procedural authority? by *ad hoc* decisions based on political majorities? by third-party procedures and determinations?

5. In terms of the present international system, what is the map of interaction between regional and global patterns of authority and practice? Does this map reveal any characteristic weaknesses in the present relationship between regional and global levels of supranational authority?

6. Is the present apportionment of energies and resources between the promotion of integration at the regional level and at the global level appropriate?

7. What uses can global institutions make of regional units *within* or *outside* of their own organizational framework to achieve various kinds of goals and objectives?

There are two points of conceptual confusion that need to be considered.

First, the term "regional" in this discussion refers to formal organizational units, and thus does not include blocs, alliances, or subsystems. There is, however, especially in the security area, a rather blurred boundary between the role of an alliance like NATO and the role of a regional organization like the OAS (especially since the expulsion of Cuba in 1962). This boundary cannot be firmly established by pointing to the provisions of the United Nations Charter, which prefigure a "collective security arrangement" in Chapter VII and a "regional organization" in Chapter VIII. It would be helpful to clarify the consequences of the differing juridical status enjoyed by these two kinds of entities, but the functional role of each needs to be studied by reference to practice as well as by attention to Charter provisions. The NATO-OAS comparison is also rendered more difficult by broadening the substantive concerns of NATO to include nonsecurity challenges, such as those associated with environmental decay. A useful article devoted to both the constitutional provisions and to the early period of related practice is Gerhard Bebr's, "Regional Organizations: A United Nations Problem," *American Journal of International Law*, vol. 49, no. 2 (April 1955), pp. 166–184).

Second, there is a basic distinction between (*a*) the formation of regional units by the main organs of the United Nations as a way to accomplish its tasks and (*b*) the formation of regional units outside of the United Nations as a consequence of subsystemic activity. When the United Nations forms a regional unit, as it has by organizing the regional economic commissions, which will be examined later in Part IV, there is really no reason to anticipate a conflict between the two levels of operation. Such a regional unit is an agent situated at a lower level of a hierarchical network joining together many separate centers of organizational activity. Of course, such regional units may evolve in such a way as to emphasize their relative autonomy or may develop regional constituencies outside the UN framework, and may even uncover a direction of conduct at variance with preferences that are dominant in the parent organization.

A second distinction that should be made is between the growth of regional-security mechanisms and various arrangements for economic and social cooperation and integration. The maintenance of international peace and security is the prime, overriding responsibility of the United Nations; efforts to organize regional security almost always encroach upon this role by establishing organizations with more partisan goals and orientations. Although economic and social issues also give rise to organizations outside the scope of the United Nations, there is much less evidence that they undermine UN organizations. Part of the reason for this difference seems to be the general feeling that the UN was established to prevent war and that any dispersal of this role weakens whatever small potentiality exists to build a basis for universal peace.

This difference between economic and war-peace subject matter undoubtedly reflects, in part, the effort of global organizations to limit the discretion of national governments to use force in resolving their international disputes. The Charter contains a prohibition against national use of force except for purposes of self-defense [Articles 2(4), 51]; no comparable restrictive norms exist with respect to economic and social policies, although a line of prescriptive development has emerged to give some substance to the vague obligation to promote human rights. Regional security arrangements may have as their *raison d'être* the option to use military force in circumstances other than those contemplated by the Charter, or, put differently, to carry out the Charter mission under circumstances of political stalemate within the United Nations. There are many motives of varying significance for world order hidden behind such a purpose. If regional action results from procedural inability to mobilize a consensus within the political organs of the United Nations, the interpretation of regional initiatives would tend to be more positive than if regional action conflicts with the Charter (for example, by being undertaken for purposes other than the fulfillment of reasonable claims of individual or collective self-defense). A regional grouping also enjoys a somewhat better world-order rating if it is a genuine instrument of community consensus, and not just a cover for the foreign policy initiatives of a powerful sovereign state or an ideologically allied group of states. The use of the OAS as a legitimating fig leaf for the imposition of the will of the United States Government in certain situations of conflict in Latin America illustrates a less than convincing attempt to reconcile statist action at the regional level with participation in the United Nations system. For a major study of the United States in the OAS and its relationship to the UN, see Minerva M. Etzioni, *The Majority of One: Toward a Theory of Regional Compatibility* (Sage, Beverly Hills, 1970), especially pages 90–218. In addition, the reliance upon the SEATO arrangement to justify American involvement in the Vietnam War during the Johnson period was intended to mobilize public support for military action by supporting respect for Charter obligations and establishing a supranational basis for waging war.

In the language of earlier chapters, it also seems useful to consider issues of integration potential in the context of linkages between regional and global actors. The integration activities of regional actors organized outside the United Nations framework raises the issue of first-stage integration already considered in Part II. However, the actors emerging out of regionally implemented globalism pose a new set of questions about first-stage integration. There are also questions raised by the overlapping and interrelated efforts to achieve first-stage integration inside and outside the global framework. Under what circumstances are these strategies of first-stage integration at cross purposes with or complementary to one another?

Broad areas of inquiry about second-stage integration potential also exist. Has the formation of regional alliances and regional organizations with security functions impeded the prospects for sec-

ond-stage, or global, integration? By raising this question, we do not mean to imply that the growth of a centralized world-order system needs to proceed along the path set by the two stages of integration, but simply that it would be helpful to investigate the effects of regionalism in the security area upon such a two-stage model of the transition process. Certain forms of first-stage integration may not only diminish second-stage integration potential more than do other forms, but may as well diminish whatever prospects do exist for "giant-step," or more direct, approaches to world order. See, for example, David Mitrany, "The Prospect for Integration: Federal or Functional?", *Journal of Common Market Studies*, vol. 4, no. 2 (December 1965), pp. 119–149.

It is also plausible to suggest that first-stage integration at the regional level, carried on *within* the framework of the United Nations greatly increases the second-stage integration potential of that organization.

The preceding discussion is not meant to suggest that world order and integration are synonymous. It is important to assess the relative ordering potentialities of various political systems and to consider alternative possibilities, including both a continuation of high degrees of decentralization and a sudden shift to a relatively stabilized system. The integration process, especially if conceived of as a gradual evolution toward world unification, is by no means the best and is certainly not the only course of development worth considering. There may be natural limits that curtail the potential for regional integration. Beyond these limits, integration may do more to build stronger adversary units of interaction than to create the basis for transforming problems of adversary relationships into issues of community concord.

Finally, it is important to consider the potential for disintegration arising from various developments at the intersections of regional and global organization. The future of world order does not necessarily entail a trend toward larger units of control and an eventual pattern of political unification at the global level. There are contradictory tendencies at work, indications that atomizing forces are exerting considerable influence in dispersing authority more widely. The emergence of ministates, subregional groupings, militant subnational movements, secessionist uprisings; the instability of larger states; and the periodic assaults of governments upon the activities of the United Nations—all are part of the counter-drift to centralized world political authority that needs to be understood by a student of world order. It is possible to interpret any shift of emphasis from the United Nations to regional organizations as itself indicative of disintegrative tendencies at work in the center of international society. The futility of achieving consensus at the global level as a consequence of intense rivalries in world politics has induced governments to seek new international settings that are more likely to be capable of effective action. In a sense, then, the emergent spirit of partisan regionalism in the decade of the 1950's signified a shift from the politics of reconciliation to the politics of confrontation. Organizational evolution—detached from sociohistorical circumstances—does not by itself predicate anything about the quality of world order. It is only when regionalism is appraised in relation to various sociohistorical settings that a judgment can be made as to whether regionalism is a regressive or a progressive factor in world affairs (see the General Introduction).

THE SECURITY LINKAGE: MAINLY REGRESSIVE TENDENCIES

We shall use Selection 13 ("The OAS, the UN, and the United States" by Inis L. Claude, Jr.) to explore the relationship between regional-security organizations and the United Nations. The overall orientation for inquiry (for which some introduction is found in Lynn Miller's article in Part I) is provided here by some general questions:

1. What conception was embodied in the United Nations Charter of the role of regional-security undertakings?
2. What factors in the international environment have generated regional action in the security area?
3. What patterns of practice have evolved with respect to the relations between the United Nations and regional-security operations?
4. To what extent have regional-security operations been juridically consistent with the Charter obligations and to what extent have regional-security operations been means by

which to execute the will of the political majority in the United Nations?
5. Has the growth of regional-security organizations exhibited any long-term first-stage integration potential and is this growth relevant to our analysis of second-stage integration potential?
6. Are there any structural reforms that might be proposed to strengthen the linkage between regional and global actors in the security field so as to assure a fuller realization of Charter ideals or to create greater integration potentialities?

These inquiries need to be undertaken in such a way as to be sensitive to subsystemic and sociohistorical variables. That is, we need to explore the distinctive subsystemic variables that affect the security operations and mission of formal regional actors, such as OAS, the Arab League, and OAU; of formal, coherent alliances, such as NATO and the Warsaw Pact; and of quickly contrived and superficial alliances, such as CENTO and SEATO. We also need to adjust these variables for changes in the subsystemic and systemic environment (see Oran Young's article in Part I) such as might occur as a consequence of (a) the proliferation of nuclear weapons, the establishment of nuclear guarantees, or the extension of nuclear free zones, (b) shifting international alignments, or (c) through reductions or intensifications of tensions at the strategic level of great-power relations.

It is impossible for us to deal with all of these questions here.

We begin Part IV with an influential article by Inis Claude that is devoted to American diplomacy as conducted within the OAS framework. Claude describes the main issues of procedure and substance that come up when a regional organization purports to be acting in the area of security, especially when regional action involves the application of "sanctions" against intraregional dissenting states. It is helpful while reading Claude to bear in mind the distinction that Lynn Miller introduced in Part I between an outward-looking regional arrangement, such as NATO, which has the purpose of organizing a defense against an external threat, and an inward-looking regional organization, such as the OAS, which has the purpose of preventing undesired developments from taking place within the region. One of the controversial issues in regard to the OAS is the effort to characterize "inward-looking undertakings as efforts to thwart external penetration."

ECONOMIC LINKAGE: AN EXPERIMENT IN REGIONAL FORMS

Selection 14 ("The UN Regional Economic Commission and Integration in the Underdeveloped Regions," by Robert W. Gregg) will be the basis of our inquiry into economic regionalism. The relation between economic regionalism and the United Nations Charter causes no apparent difficulties. There is no Charter obligation to refrain from participation in whatever regional organization appears to promote the interests of a national society. Economic regionalism is a matter of national or sovereign discretion. However, it is clear that patterns of integration have been shaped by political rivalries. This influence is most manifest in the economic division of European regionalism between the effort of the socialist countries and those of the Western democracies. Thus, economic regionalism appears to reinforce the geopolitical conflicts that exist in the world today. First-stage integration potential is carried on within the bloc (or sphere) boundaries set by geopolitical rivalries. Second-stage integration is virtually inconceivable so long as these rivalries persist.

Are there strategies to achieve first-stage integration that erode rather than reinforce bloc boundaries? Are such strategies preferable? One such strategy is functional integration as a complement (or as an alternative) to spatial integration. The specialized agencies of the United Nations attempt to integrate behavior on a global scale, bypassing the normal patterns of first-stage integration. One major approach to functional integration, associated with the writing of David Mitrany, argues that the technical character of the subject matter, the professionalization of an international civil service, and the nonsalience of functional activities build an integrationist momentum that can develop in the interstices of geopolitical struggle. For a seminal presentation of this analysis first formulated in the 1940's, see David Mitrany, *A Working Peace System* (Quad-

rangle Books, Chicago, 1966). Haas has argued against Mitrany's position by gathering evidence to demonstrate that the basic functionalist dynamic depends on geopolitics, that partisan causes build up precedents that could never be created on the basis of mere technical cooperation. For exposition of this neofunctionalist line of analysis in the setting of the ILO, see Ernst B. Haas, *Beyond the Nation State: Functionalism and International Organization* (Stanford University Press, Stanford, 1964); see also James P. Sewell, *Functionalism and World Politics* (Princeton University Press, Princeton, 1966).

Another way to mitigate the impact of geopolitical factors upon the regional movement is through the use of the United Nations framework itself. This is the device we examine here by looking at the activities of the principal regional economic commissions formed under UN auspices: ECE (Europe), ECLA (Latin America), ECA (Africa), and ECAFE (Asia). ECE includes the countries of Eastern and Western Europe and ECLA includes Cuba. Cuba's participation in ECLA is particularly notable in view of her exclusion since 1962 from standard forms of economic regionalism in the Western Hemisphere.

The overlapping membership of countries in a variety of international organizations creates new centers of policy-making activity that take on functions previously discharged by national governments. This process, if it continues and expands, may eventually diminish the role of states in international society. See the discussion of both Beloff's and Galtung's position in the introduction to Part III.

We are concerned here, especially, with an assessment of the experience of the United Nations in sponsoring regional developments within its own organizational framework. Can this experience with economic commissions be extrapolated to the area of peace and security? If not, why not? This is the central question linking the two selections in this chapter.

In this discussion we have chosen to emphasize the regional economic commissions in the less-developed areas primarily because it is our belief that they are likely to be more significant than those in the developed regions of the world. At the same time the activities of the UN regional economic commissions in developed areas are significant.

In "The UN Regional Economic Commissions and Integration in the Underdeveloped Regions," Robert Gregg looks very carefully at the activities of ECLA, ECA, and ECAFE to assess their first-stage integration potential and performance. The examination of ECLA is particularly interesting because it shows that the United States is much less able to play a hegemonial role within this setting than in relation to other forms of economic regionalism in the Western Hemisphere. Does this experience with ECLA suggest a strategy for containing the influence of predominant states upon the action of regional organizations? Note also the definition of integration relied on by Gregg ("transformation of an international sub-system in a direction in which more weight is accorded to decisions and actions in the name of the aggregate of actors") and compare it with the various definitions found in the introduction to Part II.

13

The OAS, The UN, and the United States

INIS L. CLAUDE, JR.

From *International Conciliation*, no. 547, March 1964, pp. 3–67. Reprinted by permission of the publisher.

REGIONALISM IN THE UN CHARTER

Theoretical debate as to the superiority of the regional or the universal approach to international organization for the handling of political and security problems is a rather sterile exercise, for experience suggests that statesmen need not, and do not, choose one of these approaches to the exclusion of the other. In its original design, and even more in its actual development, the post-World War II system of international organization has combined regional elements with the basic universalism of the United Nations. It might be argued that the real question is not which approach to adopt, but which to emphasize; in these terms, the international decision in 1945 was clearly to assign predominance to general international organization. In practice, however, even this question proves rather too abstract. The decision of the San Francisco Conference to make the United Nations the primary agency in the sphere of international politics provided no precise indication of the contemplated division of competence and responsibility between it and regional agencies, much less a firm basis for predicting the nature of the relationships that would emerge in the dynamic interplay of the United Nations and regional organizations during the next two decades. In the final analysis, the problem of the relationship between general and regional international institutions involves a set of specific questions posed by developing political circumstances, rather than a single issue of principle that can be settled in the abstract.

This study represents an attempt to develop an understanding of the evolving relationship between the Organization of American States and the United Nations in the political and security sphere. While the OAS is merely one of many regional agencies on the contemporary scene, it stands out as the only one that has been significantly involved in formal controversies concerning the interpretation and application of the provisions of the United Nations Charter bearing upon the role of such agencies in relation to the world organization.[1] Making due allowance for the unique features of the OAS case, we may hope that an examination of the interplay between that organization and the United Nations in the political-security realm will contribute to an understanding of the general political process whereby the working relationships of universal and regional bodies are determined and progressively altered.

Moreover, the preponderance of the United States in the OAS and the prominence of the region embraced by that agency in foreign and defense policy concerns of the United States indicate that the relationship between the OAS and the United Nations is something more than a test case in the admixture of regionalism and universalism. It is an issue of prime importance in United States foreign policy, and the very considerable influence of the United States upon the shaping of the OAS-United Nations relationship has been exercised less for the purpose of promoting an ideal pattern of international institutional arrangements than for the achievement of more immediate national policy objectives. Hence, this study should provide some insight into the particular aspects of international political rivalry which affect the evolution of regional-global organizational patterns. It is at once a study of international organization and of United States foreign policy, and, in the nature of the case, it cannot successfully deal with the former topic without dealing with the latter.

In the initial phase of wartime thought regarding the international political structure that should be erected after World War II, the regional theme assumed great prominence. Winston Churchill placed particular emphasis upon the potential role of regional councils as vehicles for the leadership of the great powers and appeared to assign distinctly secondary importance to a world organization. President Franklin D. Roosevelt had not clearly committed himself to a scheme of postwar organization, but, perhaps under the influence of Sumner Welles, he tended to agree with the Churchillian conception. Secretary of State Cordell Hull waged a vigorous battle against this view, arguing that dominant regionalism might recreate a competitive balance-of-power system conducive to war, and that emphasis upon regional organization might provide "a haven for the isolationists, who could advocate all-out United States cooperation in a Western Hemisphere council on condition that we did not participate in a European or Pacific council."[2] Hull insisted that a general international organization should have supreme responsibility for political and security questions, and that regional agencies should function as subordinate and supplementary bodies. In the course of 1943, Hull's arguments prevailed. The official planning mechanism in the United States adopted the proposition that postwar organization should rest upon a universal rather than a regional basis, and Hull succeeded in incorporating this principle in the Moscow Declaration, signed on 30 October 1943 on behalf of the governments of China, the Soviet Union, the United Kingdom, and the United States. This agreement provided the essential impetus for the process that resulted in the creation of the United Nations.[3]

Thenceforward, United States officials adhered to the general position that regional arrangements were unavoidable in some instances and might serve as useful supplements to the global institution, but that it was vitally important to ensure their subordination and control by the projected United Nations.[4]

The attitude toward regionalism that had crystallized within the United States government found expression in the Dumbarton Oaks Proposals, formulated in the autumn of 1944 by

---

[1] The most relevant provisions of the United Nations Charter are to be found in Articles 33 and 51–54. For texts of these articles, see Appendix B [at the end of this discussion.]

[2] *The Memoirs of Cordell Hull* (New York: Macmillan, 1948), II, p. 1645.

[3] The material in this paragraph was drawn largely from ibid., pp. 1639–48.

[4] See Ruth B. Russell, and Jeannette E. Muther, *A History of the United Nations Charter* (Washington: The Brookings Institution, 1958), pp. 121, 255, 398–99. For provisions relating to regional agencies in various drafts developed within the United States planning mechanism, see *Postwar Foreign Policy Preparation 1939–1945*, U.S. Dept. of State Pub. 3580 (Washington: GPO, 1949), pp. 482, 531, 586–87, 596, 600.

the same powers that had produced the Moscow Declaration.[5] This preliminary version of the Charter provided that the existence of regional bodies for dealing with peace and security matters should not be precluded, if their arrangements and activities were consistent with the purposes and principles of the general organization. This rather negative and conditional endorsement was followed by more positive provisions: the Security Council should encourage such agencies to promote the peaceful settlement of disputes among their members and should, in appropriate cases, utilize them for enforcement action under its authority. Finally, the draft reverted to the negative tone in stipulating that regional enforcement action should not be taken without authorization by the Security Council, and that the Council should be kept fully informed of activities undertaken or contemplated by regional bodies in the peace and security sphere. In summary, the authors of the Dumbarton Oaks draft conceded that regional agencies might be useful, but considered that they might be dangerous if not effectively subordinated to the Security Council.

This triumph of universalist ideology was short-lived. "Regionalism Resurgent" was emblazoned on the banner hoisted at the Inter-American Conference on Problems of War and Peace in Mexico City, which culminated in the signing of the Act of Chapultepec on 3 March 1945. At this gathering, representatives of the Latin American states expressed their misgivings about the universalist bias of the Dumbarton Oaks Proposals, affirmed the value of the Inter-American system, proclaimed the intent to refurbish and strengthen that system, and insisted that the constitution of the new world organization should leave the way open for the functioning of a politically active and largely autonomous Inter-American agency. The United States, in signing the Act of Chapultepec, virtually acknowledged its responsibility for helping to secure the alteration of the Dumbarton Oaks draft in a pro-regionalist direction, and accepted the necessity of collaborating to some degree with its Latin neighbors in their

projected campaign to make the United Nations Charter safe for regionalism.

The battle over the role of regional agencies which had been foreshadowed at Mexico City took place as scheduled at San Francisco, centering in Committee 4 of Commission III of the Conference.[6] Senator Arthur H. Vandenberg dealt with the regional problem for the United States. He pressed the cause of the Latin Americans in negotiations with other delegations and within the United States delegation; at one point he warned his United States colleagues who were resisting a pro-regionalist move "that if this question is not specifically cleared up in the Charter, I shall expect to see a Reservation on the subject in the Senate and . . . I shall support it."[7] The major task at San Francisco was to achieve a compromise between those spokesmen for the United States who stressed the primacy of the world organization and those who shared the Latin American concern for regional autonomy. Once this was accomplished, the United States succeeded in having its formula incorporated in the Charter.

The crucial issue related to the anxiety aroused by the Dumbarton Oaks clause prohibiting enforcement action under regional auspices without the authorization of the Security Council: the apprehension that regional response to aggression might be paralyzed by this requirement, particularly in view of the fact that the veto formula dictated by the great powers would enable any permanent member of the Security Council to prevent the authorization of regional action. The interests of various groups of states converged on the point that the requirement of Security Council approval of enforcement action, which was to be incorporated in Article 53 of the Charter, should be liberalized. The European great powers were accommodated by a provision, inserted in Article 53, which emancipated their anti-Axis mutual assistance pacts from this requirement for an indefinite period. In turn, the advocates of the autonomy of the Inter-American

---

[5]For the text of the relevant provision, Chapter VIII, Section C, see Appendix A [at the end of this discussion].

[6]*Documents of the United Nations Conference on International Organization, San Francisco, 1945*, Vol. XII (London and New York: UN Information Organizations, 1945). This collection is hereinafter cited as UNCIO.

[7]*The Private Papers of Senator Vandenberg*, ed. Arthur H. Vandenberg, Jr. (Boston: Houghton Mifflin, 1952), p. 189.

system were satisfied by the introduction into the Charter of Article 51, acknowledging a right of collective as well as individual self-defense, in the exercise of which a group of states might respond to armed attack, report their action to the Security Council, and continue it until and unless the Council should itself undertake to deal with the situation. This provision, applicable only in cases involving armed attack, reversed the significance of negativism in the Security Council; an unfriendly veto could not be used to block regional action, but a friendly veto could be used to prevent Security Council interference in regional action. While Article 51 was couched in terms of general applicability, it was proclaimed by Latin American delegates and acknowledged by others as a prescription designed primarily to remove the regional organs of the Western Hemisphere, existing and projected, from the sphere of Security Council control in the most critical cases. The Latin Americans were not particularly concerned to fight for regionalism in general; indeed, some of them proposed that the Charter should single out the Inter-American system as an approved regional arrangement enjoying a high degree of autonomy.[8]

The United States delegation was distinctly unhappy at the prospect of the emancipation of all and sundry regional groups under the terms of Article 51. Those members of the delegation who had posed difficulties for Senator Vandenberg in his development of the formula had not been so much opposed to autonomy for the Inter-American system as worried about the generalization of regional autonomy. The Senator himself regarded with considerable distaste the necessity of generalizing the privileges of Article 51. He had toyed with the idea of attempting to secure an explicit exception from the rule of Article 53 in favor of the Western Hemispheric organization, and he tried hard but vainly to develop a formula which would have the effect of legitimizing autonomous operations by that agency without giving equally free rein to other regional groups whose activities, he feared, would be detrimental to world order.[9] In later years, the

United States has found unexpected uses for Article 51, but it supported the inclusion of that provision in the Charter in spite of, not because of, the fact that the article weakened the control of the Security Council over collective self-defense arrangements other than those contemplated in the Act of Chapultepec.

In addition to the urge to secure the emancipation of their regional system from the requirement of Security Council authorization for enforcement action, the Latin American states expressed a strong demand for recognition of the primary jurisdiction of Inter-American organs in promoting peaceful settlement of intraregional disputes. Considering the attitude toward external intervention in the affairs of the Western Hemisphere which had long been associated with the Monroe Doctrine, it is surprising that United States plans for a world organization had not dealt with this point. But the influence of the universalist viewpoint had been so dominant that regional contributions to peaceful settlement had received no special emphasis.

There was no reversal of policy in the endorsement by the United States of the Dumbarton Oaks Proposals, which provided that the Security Council should encourage settlement of local disputes through regional machinery, but in no sense conceded to regional agencies a peculiar status with regard to the handling of disputes among their members. Indeed, regional methods were not even mentioned in the list of alternative approaches to peaceful settlement in Chapter VIII, Section A, of the Proposals, which disputants were adjured to explore before resorting to the Security Council.

At San Francisco, several Latin American delegations urged the adoption of provisions that would have assigned the function of promoting the peaceful settlement of intraregional disputes to regional organizations, permitting the Security Council to intrude only if the regional body handling a given case should so request, or if a dispute should threaten to spread beyond the boundaries of a single region.[10] As a result of this pressure, Committee III (4) recommended, and the Plenary Conference approved, the incorporation in the Charter of the stipulation that members of regional organizations should attempt to

---

[8]See UNCIO, Vol. XII, pp. 771, 773, 779.

[9]*The Private Papers of Senator Vandenberg*, op. cit., pp. 187–92.

[10]See Doc. 269, UNCIO, Vol. XII, pp. 764–84.

settle their local disputes at the regional level before referring them to the Security Council (Article 52[2]), and the addition of resort to regional agencies to the list of recommended methods of peaceful settlement which states should explore before turning to the Security Council (Article 33[1]). Thus, the Charter went significantly beyond the Dumbarton Oaks Proposals in stressing the role of regional bodies as agencies of the first resort for dealing with disputes among their own members. Behind the generality of these provisions lay the particular intent of acknowledging the primacy of Inter-American institutions in matters pertaining to the Western Hemisphere.

This Latin American victory was neither complete nor clear-cut. Under Article 33, resort to regional mechanisms of peaceful settlement was treated as only one of several options for disputants in their preliminary efforts to find a solution for their difficulties. Article 52 (2) was stronger, in that it appeared to oblige members of regional agencies to exhaust the pacificatory resources of those bodies before turning to the United Nations, but this provision was qualified and perhaps confused by the addition of Article 52 (4), stipulating that the Article did not impair the application of Articles 34 and 35, which recognized the competence of the Security Council to investigate disputes or situations to determine whether they might endanger international peace and security, and authorized states to bring such cases to the attention of the Council or the General Assembly. Moreover, under Article 36, the Security Council was authorized, at any stage of a dispute, to recommend methods of peaceful settlement. Considering this entire complex of provisions, one can conclude that the framers of the Charter intended to assign to regional agencies a primary role in the solution of local problems, while retaining the principle that the Security Council should have overarching responsibility and unrestricted competence to intervene in any case at any time.

At the meeting of Committee III (4), which approved the package of proposals designed to meet the pro-regionalist demands of the Latin Americans, a Peruvian spokesman articulated his concern that the changes did not clearly preclude the Security Council from asserting jurisdiction over intraregional disputes at any stage; he was disappointed that the exclusiveness of regional responsibility for dealing initially with local disputes had not been recognized and safeguarded.[11] The president of the Committee, speaking for Columbia, offered reassurance. He saw no problem of double jurisdiction, but believed that the newly adopted provisions established the rule that the Security Council must leave initial efforts at peaceful settlement of local disputes to regional agencies; the Council might investigate to determine whether such disputes threatened international peace, but it could not intrude upon the regional settlement process unless and until the latter had failed. His government believed that the revised formula constituted "a statute for regional arrangements, entirely satisfactory to the American nations, which are linked together by an almost perfect system of peace and security."[12]

The Peruvian comment was more accurate than the Colombian, but it is perhaps fortunate that the latter was convincing to the Latin American bloc, since this permitted the issue to be closed. An ambiguous compromise had been reached, allowing champions of regionalism to assert that they had won a clear victory for the autonomy and primacy of regional agencies, and universalists to congratulate themselves that the supremacy of the Security Council in matters affecting peace and security had not been impaired.

Spokesmen for the United States tended to insist that complete success had been achieved in reconciling the competing viewpoints concerning the relationship of the United Nations and regional organizations. Senator Vandenberg declared:

> We have found a sound and practical formula for putting regional organizations into effective gear with the global institution. . . . We have infinitely strengthened the world Organization by . . . enlisting, within its over-all supervision, the dynamic resources of these regional affinities. [In supporting the Pan-American regional system] we are no less faithful to the world ideal and to the dominant supremacy of the United Nations in the maintenance of peace and security.[13]

[11]UNCIO, Vol. XII, p. 685.
[12]Ibid., p. 687.
[13]UNCIO, Vol. XI, p. 52-53.

Secretary of State Edward R. Stettinius, Jr., interpreted the provisions introduced into the Charter at San Francisco pertaining to peaceful settlement as simply a formula to "make more clear that regional agencies will be looked to as an important way of settling local disputes by peaceful means."[14] In similar vein, he reported to the President that the changes made at the Conference had indicated that the procedures of regional systems would be utilized to the fullest possible extent, but had maintained the basic principle of the ultimate authority of the world organization.[15] In analyzing the Charter for the Senate Committee on Foreign Relations, Stettinius commented that it "encourages the use of regional arrangements and agencies in the peaceful adjustment of local disputes."[16]

Leo Pasvolsky, Special Assistant to the Secretary of State for International Organization and Security Affairs, interpreted the Charter as providing that regional agencies "should be used to their utmost" in facilitating settlement of local disputes.[17] John Foster Dulles, who had served as an adviser to the United States Delegation at San Francisco, presented this summary of the Charter's impact upon the position of regional organizations:

> Without the Security Council and the new world organization we could have had in this hemisphere a regional organization which was wholly autonomous and which could act on its own initiative to maintain peace in this hemisphere without reference or regard whatsoever to any world organization. As it results from the Charter at San Francisco, the world security organization is given the first opportunity to maintain peace everywhere, using presumably regional organizations which it is invited to do but not absolutely compelled to do.

If, however, the Security Council fails to maintain peace and despite the existence of the Security Council there is an armed outbreak, then the regional organization moves in without regard to the Security Council.[18]

None of these statemente by leading participants in the work of the United States Delegation supported the view that the Charter had assigned to regional agencies, and denied to the Security Council, the task of initiating efforts at peaceful settlement of local disputes. All of them emphasized the basic value of the supremacy of the United Nations, and reflected the view that the virtue of the compromise worked out at San Francisco lay in the fact that it had accommodated the demands of regionalists and provided for the utilization of the potential contributions of regional agencies without sacrificing that fundamental value. The United States, which had started with a universalist premise, was happy with the result of the negotiations at the Conference.

The basic Latin American urge, on the other hand, had been to establish the autonomy of the Inter-American system—and, so far as necessary, that of other regional arrangements. In contrast to the United States, most Latin American states had hoped to deprive the Security Council of competence to deal with local disputes until regional agencies had completed efforts to achieve a solution, and, in espousing the interpretation stated by the Colombian representative, they purported to believe that this had been accomplished. This belief was incompatible with the understanding of the United States as to what had been decided at San Francisco concerning the role of regional agencies in the quest for solution of disputes among their members.

To provide for the utilization of regional bodies in promoting peaceful settlement of local disputes is one thing, but to establish the exclusive jurisdiction of regional bodies over such cases in their initial stages is quite another. It appears that the United States was correct in the view that the framers of the Charter should be understood as having attempted the former, not the latter. This interpretation rests ultimately upon the implications of Article 52 (4). As Stet-

---

[14]See his statement for the press, 15 May 1945, No. 25, reproduced in *Hearings Before the Committee on Foreign Relations. U.S. Senate, 79th Cong., First Sess., on The Charter of the United Nations* (Washington: GPO, 1945), p. 306. Hereinafter cited as *Charter Hearings.*

[15]See *Report to the President on the Results of the San Francisco Conference by the Chairman of the United States Delegation, the Secretary of State,* U.S. Dept. of State Pub. 2349, Conf. Series 71 (Washington: GPO, 1945), pp. 101–108.

[16]*Charter Hearings,* p. 210.

[17]Ibid., p. 302.

[18]Ibid., p. 650.

tinius put it, this paragraph "insure[d] the paramount authority of the Council and its right to concern itself if necessary with disputes of this [intraregional] character."[19] It reserved the right of the Security Council to deal with any dispute—local or not—whenever it should decide that its primary responsibility for the maintenance of international peace and security so required. For better or for worse, this attribution of fundamental responsibility to the Security Council was the keystone of the Charter.

In summary, the San Francisco Conference retained the broad principle of universalism as the fundamental basis for the new system of international organization, while making significant concessions to the demands of champions of regional organization. With regard to the issue of enforcement action, the Conference produced the ambiguous combination of Articles 51 and 53. This ambiguity favored regional autonomy; the emancipation of regional agencies from meaningful Security Council control over their responses to armed attack tended to reduce United Nations supremacy in this vital area of activity to a doctrinal fiction. With regard to the issue of jurisdiction over disputes at the pacific settlement stage, the Conference produced the ambiguous combination of Article 52 (2) and Article 52 (4), with Articles 34 and 35 linked to the latter. This ambiguity, in contrast to the one noted above, favored United Nations supremacy; despite the stipulation that regional efforts should have priority, the clauses safeguarding the discretion of the Security Council as to how it should exercise its world-wide authority and responsibility tended to reduce regional agencies to subordinate bodies whose role might be determined by the Council.

Given this pair of ambiguities—each pushing in a different direction—it is difficult to sustain the view that a "clear" delineation of the relationships between the general and regional organizations was written into the Charter. It was "clear" only that the United Nations and regional agencies would coexist, and that political controversy concerning their proper relationships was likely in the actual operation of the system. The United States hoped that the provisions of the Charter would "mesh into the system of international

security established on a universal basis such existing or future regional instrumentalities as might serve to further its objectives without detracting from its authority and effectiveness," and, more concretely, that the projected organs of the Inter-American system would constitute "an integral and valuable element of an effective collective security system on a world-wide basis . . . without establishing a precedent which might engender rivalry between regional groups at the expense of world security."[20] These official comments reflected the continuing bias of the United States toward the principle of universalism in matters of peace and security.

THE REGIONALIST CHALLENGE TO UN SUPREMACY

Many close observers of the actual performance and development of the postwar system of international organization have pointed out that the Charter scheme for relating regional agencies to the United Nations has been drastically altered. Regionalism has come back into its own, producing agencies that have figured more prominently in world affairs and functioned more independently of the United Nations than was foreshadowed in the Charter. Edgar S. Furniss, Jr., expressed the view that "In the name of regional arrangements the United Nations has been placed in a position of inferiority, so that now the links between the regional arrangements and the world organization exist at the practical pleasure of the former."[21]

Concerning contemporary regional organizations in general, one can say that they have been more active in the security sphere and less active in the field of peaceful settlement than the framers of the Charter appeared to expect or intend. The principle laid down in Article 53, that regional agencies should not take enforcement action without the authorization of the Security Council, has been overshadowed by the exceptions stipulated in that Article and in Article 51; for the maintenance of international peace and security, states have come to rely not

[19]*Report to the President . . .* , op. cit., p. 105.

[20]Ibid., pp. 101, 108.
[21]"A Re-examination of Regional Arrangements," *Journal of International Affairs,* Vol. 9, 1955, p. 84.

upon the Security Council, nor upon agencies subject to its control, but upon alliance systems that have been created for the explicit purpose of functioning autonomously. With respect to the principle laid down in Article 52 (2–3), that members of regional agencies and the Security Council itself should emphasize the role of those agencies in the settlement of local disputes, the general experience has been quite different; the existence of regional bodies has not, by and large, tended to reduce the case load of United Nations organs by facilitating solutions at the regional level.[22] In short, both of the fundamental concepts of the Charter pertaining to the role of regional agencies have broken down. Neither the negative control nor the positive utilization of such agencies by the Security Council has become a significant feature of recent international relations.

These developments can be explained by the circumstances that have occasioned the creation and development of most of the regional bodies functioning in the political-security field. These bodies are primarily *external* in their orientation; they exist to provide joint security against potential enemies on the outside. Hence, their members are wary of subjecting them to possible immobilization by the Security Council, in which the influence or voting power of the external enemy may be effective. The North Atlantic Treaty Organization, for instance, would be meaningless if the Soviet veto could be used in the Security Council to deny its authority to act. In short, alliances would wither under Article 53 —but they flourish under Article 51. Moreover, the external orientation of the regional agencies helps to explain their relative insignificance as promoters of local peaceful settlement. Their preoccupation with external threat implies the neglect of this internal concern, although this need not be the case.[23] More importantly, the provisions of Article 52 do not emancipate re-

gional agencies from the Security Council's control in the clear-cut fashion of Article 51. As already noted, the ambiguity of the scheme regarding peaceful settlement leaves large opportunities for Security Council intrusion into intraregional difficulties, and an unfriendly outsider with a seat in that body—particularly a permanent seat involving veto power—may be both eager and able to promote such intrusion. On the whole, regional organizations have had greater incentive and ability to eliminate effective Security Council control over their collective self-defense policy than to prevent the Council's involvement in the handling of disputes among their members.

To some extent these generalizations fail to fit the case of the postwar Inter-American regional system, the OAS. This regional agency is, of course, designed to promote collective resistance to armed attack from outside its zone, and, like other such groupings, it relies upon Article 51 as the legal basis for emergency action unencumbered by the requirement of Security Council authorization. However, the OAS is also characterized by a significant degree of *internal* orientation. As is indicated by its basic documents—the Inter-American Treaty of Reciprocal Assistance (the Rio Pact, 1947) and the Charter of the Organization of American States (formulated at Bogotá, 1948)—the OAS is concerned with the settlement of disputes and the suppression of conflicts within its ranks. It is in some sense a collective security system on the regional level, as well as an externally oriented defensive alliance. The relationship of the OAS to the United Nations therefore is not reducible to the relatively simple terms of Article 51, but involves also the complexities of Articles 52–54. Unlike such agencies as NATO, which simply capitalize upon Article 51 to remain separate from the United Nations, the OAS finds itself linked to the world organization because of the breadth of its role in political and security matters. This is a unique relationship; only the experience of the OAS provides a thorough test of the practical application of the Charter's formula for the meshing of regional and global political activity.

The problem of working out an acceptable relationship between the United Nations and the OAS can be reduced to two central issues, both of which were foreshadowed in the controversies that raged at San Francisco: (1) the "Try OAS

---

[22]See Inis L. Claude, Jr., *Swords Into Plowshares* (2nd ed.; New York: Random House, 1959), pp. 121–22.

[23]In a news conference on 22 May 1956, Secretary of State John Foster Dulles described NATO as essentially a military alliance—a collective defense association under Article 51 of the Charter, rather than a regional association. He said it had no "policy or jurisdiction to deal with disputes as between the members," although he recognized that it might be given such a function. *New York Times*, 23 May 1956.

first" issue and (2) the issue of the autonomy of the OAS in imposing sanctions upon its members.

The first of these issues relates to the interpretation of the provisions of Articles 33–35 and 52 bearing upon institutional efforts to promote peaceful settlement of intraregional disputes. Following their success at San Francisco in securing reference to the principle of priority for regional modes of settlement in Article 33, and more prominently, in Article 52 (2), the American states took pains to insert formal commitments to use the mechanisms of the OAS before resorting to the United Nations in both of the fundamental instruments of their new organizational system.[24] Ignoring the question of the legal effectiveness of these articles within the context of the United Nations Charter, one can readily see that these formulations represented an attempt to reinforce the Charter's ambiguous recognition of regional priority in pacific settlement, and even to give the OAS the clear-cut jurisdictional monopoly of the preliminary stage of pacific settlement that some Latin American delegations had advocated at San Francisco. These OAS provisions laid the basis for a political struggle to interpose the OAS as a barrier to Security Council consideration of Inter-American disputes whenever regional privacy might be particularly desired. The other side of the "Try OAS first" coin reads, "Security Council, stay out!"

The issue of the autonomy of the OAS in imposing sanctions upon its members relates to the interpretation of Articles 53 and 54. Contention on this point has involved the problem of defining the "enforcement action," which the OAS is forbidden to take except with the authorization of the Security Council. As we shall see, a persistent effort has been made to shake off the restraint imposed upon the OAS by the terms of Article 53, leaving that agency only with the obligation, stated in Article 54, of keeping the Security Council informed of its activities and plans.

The most striking fact about this struggle to enhance the status of the OAS is that leadership was belatedly taken over by the United States. At San Francisco, the United States with mixed emotions followed along in the Latin American drive to minimize the universalist bias of the Charter, and, at Rio, it was conspicuous among the states submitting draft proposals for the Inter-American Treaty of Reciprocal Assistance in its failure to suggest explicit expression of the "Try OAS first" principle.[25] Nevertheless, the great power of the Western Hemisphere has subsequently assumed the captaincy of the battle, with the political forces of Latin America lending support in imperfect and uncertain array.

This shift can only be understood as one aspect of the development of the United States policy of resistance to Soviet expansionism. The United States has led the fight for OAS jurisdiction in certain cases, not because it regarded them as local matters, but precisely because it believed they involved communist intrusions into hemispheric affairs; for the United States, the campaign on behalf of the OAS has been, in reality, a struggle against the Soviet Union.

It should be clear that the following analysis of the cases in which the issues pertaining to the role of the OAS have figured prominently is at once a study of the interplay of regionalism and universalism, and an investigation of the conflict between the Soviet Union and the United States which provides the political dynamics for that interplay.

THE "TRY OAS FIRST" ISSUE

The first occasion for the application of the Charter provisions concerning the role of regional agencies in relation to the United Nations arose on 19 June 1954, when the government of Guatemala alleged that it was the victim of aggressive attacks launched from Nicaragua and Honduras with the support of the United States, and urgently requested that the Security Council take measures to halt the aggression.[26]

---

[24] Inter-American Treaty of Reciprocal Assistance, Article 2; Charter of the OAS, Article 20. For text of these articles, see Appendices C and D [at the end of this article].

[25] *Inter-American Conference for the maintenance of Continental Peace and Security, Quitandinha, Brazil, August 15–September 2, 1947: Report of the Delegation of the United States of America*, U.S. Dept. of State Pub. 3016 (Washington: GPO, 1948). Cf. the United States proposal, p. 82, and those of Brazil, p. 77; Chile, p. 78; Guatemala, p. 79; Mexico, p. 81; Panama, p. 82; Bolivia, p. 112.

[26] UN Security Council, Official Records (SCOR): 9th Yr., Suppl. for April, May and June 1954 (S/3232, 19 June 1954).

The Guatemalan Case

Although Guatemala simultaneously appealed to the Inter-American Peace Committee, it requested suspension of consideration of its complaint by that OAS agency on the next day, and complete withdrawal of the case on 21 June.[27] By thus proposing to bypass the OAS in favor of the Security Council, Guatemala precipitated a full dress debate on the "Try OAS First" issue.

The Guatemalan government, headed by Jacobo Arbenz Guzmán, was regarded by the United States as substantially communist. The invasion of which Guatemala complained had been launched by a small band, predominantly Guatemalan in composition, and led by an exiled officer, Colonel Carlos Castillo Armas. In brief, the course of events after 19 June was as follows: The Security Council, on 20 June, was prevented by the Soviet veto from passing a resolution to refer Guatemala's complaint to the OAS, but it then voted unanimously to call for termination of the invasion and to request states to refrain from giving assistance to the attackers.[28] During the next few days, the Inter-American Peace Committee, at the behest of Honduras and Nicaragua, developed a plan to send a subcommittee to investigate the situation, and sought to obtain the consent of Guatemala. The latter, however, rejected this move on the ground that the Security Council was handling the case, and devoted itself to urging the Council to meet again to consider alleged violations of its resolution of 20 June. This insistence brought about a meeting of the Security Council on 25 June, but that body failed to adopt the agenda, and thus left the case to the OAS.[29] At this point, the OAS developed a dual approach to the problem. The Inter-American Peace Committee continued its effort to arrange an investigatory mission, and Guatemala, as a result of the rebuff administered by the Security Council, agreed to cooperate. Additionally, the OAS Council decided to call a meeting of the Ministers of Foreign Affairs of the American States for 7 July

to consider the case.[30] However, the invading forces achieved rapid success in Guatemala. The Arbenz regime was ousted, and within a few days Castillo Armas was installed as head of a new government. The subcommittee of the Inter-American Peace Committee, which had reached Mexico City, turned back; the projected meeting of foreign ministers was cancelled; and Guatemala officially informed the Secuirty Council that the case was closed.

The meetings of the Security Council on 20 and 25 June (675th and 676th meetings) provided the setting for full discussion of the jurisdictional issue. At the first of these sessions, Guatemala, strongly supported by the Soviet Union, asserted that Honduras, Nicaragua, and the United States had conspired to sponsor and support the invasion, making bases available to Castillo Armas and supplying him with arms and equipment. Guatemala denied that it was obligated to rely upon the OAS in such a situation. Technically, the "Try OAS first" provisions of the Rio Pact and OAS Charter did not bind Guatemala, since it had not ratified those instruments. However, Guatemala made little of this point, arguing instead that the United Nations Charter entitled it to invoke the protection of the Security Council, particularly since the case involved an act of aggression, not simply a dispute. It requested that the Council send an observation mission to the scene, and warn Honduras and Nicaragua against continuing to support the invaders.

"The Soviet Union both agreed with Guatemala's contention that it had, under Articles 34 and 35, "an unchallengeable right to appeal to the Security Council," and insisted that the Council had a clear responsibility to deal with the matter. More explicitly than Guatemala, the Soviet Union argued the political case for rejecting reference of the issue to the OAS. The latter body was dominated by the United States, which manifestly intended to use the regional machinery to cover and support its scheme to replace the Arbenz government: "Guatemala can expect nothing good from that body."

On the other side of the issue, spokesmen for the Western Hemisphere rallied behind a draft resolution submitted by Brazil and Colombia

---

[27]"Report of the Inter-American Peace Committee on the Controversy between Guatemala, Honduras, and Nicaragua, 8 July 1954." *Annals of the Organization of American States*, Vol. VI, 1954, pp. 239–41.

[28]SCOR: 9th Yr., 675th Mtg., 20 June 1954.

[29]Ibid., 676th Mtg., 25 June 1954.

[30]*Annals of the Organization of American States*, Vol. VI, 1954, p. 160.

which would have referred the case to the OAS, and asked for a report to the Council on the measures taken by the regional agency.[31] Representatives of Honduras and Nicaragua, who had been invited to participate as interested parties without vote, took the legal position that only the OAS could properly assume jurisdiction at that stage of the case and, consistently with that view, declined to enter into substantive discussion of the charges. Colombia also resorted to legal argument, insisting that under Article 52 (2) —and ignoring Article 52 (4)—members of the OAS had "the duty to apply first to the regional organization, which is of necessity the court of first appeal."

Otherwise, the advocacy of reference to the OAS was based upon nonlegal arguments. The draft resolution itself did not stipulate that such action was mandatory under the Charter, but referred to "the availability of Inter-American machinery which can deal effectively with problems. . . ." Brazil noted that regional settlement of disputes was a *tradition* in the Inter-American system, and cited Article 52 (3) as inviting the Security Council to encourage use of the regional forum. France, Britain, Lebanon, and New Zealand supported the move to request OAS intervention, but explicitly asserted the jurisdiction of the Security Council and justified use of the OAS on practical grounds. Finally, the United States held that it was a question of "where the situation can be dealt with most expeditiously and most effectively," and maintained that the "draft resolution does not seek to relieve the Security Council of responsibility; it just asks the Organization of American States to see what it can do to be helpful." Even Honduras turned to a pragmatic argument: "The Council is not in a position to deal with these difficulties in Central America. We have Pan-American organizations which are described as perfect. . . ."

France proposed, and the sponsors accepted, an amendment to the Brazilian-Colombian draft, calling for cessation of the invasion and abstention of members of the United Nations from lending it support. When the amended draft was defeated by the Soviet veto (the vote was 10-1-0), France reintroduced its proposal as a

separate resolution, and the Council adopted it unanimously. Thus, all the members of the Security Council favoring submission of the case to the OAS voted *twice* at the 675th meeting in favor of the French text, which clearly implied an assertion by the Security Council of its competence and responsibility for dealing with the case. Indeed, in submitting the proposal for a separate vote after the defeat of the more inclusive draft, France explicitly described it as a means by which the Council should "give expression to its authority and bring the blood-letting to an end." The unanimous passage of this resolution indicated that not even the most avid champions of the OAS among the members of the Council were prepared to press the legal argument that the regional body had sole claim to jurisdiction over the case. The Council did not refer the case to the OAS, but neither did it prohibit the entry of that agency into the case.

At the 675th meeting, the United States had acknowledged the jurisdiction of the Council and argued for reference to the OAS on pragmatic grounds. This mild position had been tinged with political color at only one point when the United States Ambassador to the United Nations, Henry Cabot Lodge, Jr., asserted that the anticipated Soviet veto of the Brazilian-Colombian draft would show "that the Soviet Union has designs on the American hemisphere," and addressed himself directly to the Soviet spokesman in these terms: "Stay out of this hemisphere and do not try to start your plans and your conspiracies over here."

Two days later, Lodge issued a statement in which he combined more explicitly the legal, pragmatic, and political bases of the United States position.[32] Referring to the 675th meeting, he said that the Council had voted by ten to one

> that the right place to go to get peace in Guatemala is the Organization of American States, where there is both unique knowledge and authority. The one vote against this was that of the Soviet Union. In the face of this action, . . . those who continually seek to agitate the Guatemalan question in the Security Council will inevitably be suspected of shadow boxing—of trying to strike attitudes and issue statements for propaganda purposes.

[31]SCOR: 9th Yr., Suppl. for April, May and June 1954 (S/3236, 20 June 1954).

[32]U.S. Dept. of State *Bulletin*, 5 July 1954, p. 28.

He asserted that Guatemala, in seeking Council action, appeared "to be a cat's paw of the Soviet conspiracy to meddle in the Western Hemisphere." Lodge interpreted the vote on the Brazilian-Colombian draft as demonstrating that the Council "emphatically believed that the Organization of American States was the place to try to settle the Guatemalan problem. To fly squarely in the face of this recommendation would raise grave doubts as to the good faith of those who make such requests."

Lodge's statement was remarkable in several respects. It assumed that the Security Council had, in effect, passed the resolution in question, even though it recognized that the resolution had been vetoed, and it incorrectly implied that the defeated draft denied the jurisdiction of the Council. It ignored the resolution that had actually been adopted, with United States support, in which the Council had asserted its jurisdiction. It suggested that Guatemala was acting improperly in reporting, and demanding that the Council react to, violations of the appeal for cessation of the invasion which that organ had unanimously adopted. Finally, it treated Soviet advocacy of Security Council action in response to Guatemala's complaint of aggression as a hostile and conspiratorial policy. Clearly this was not the statement of a government which was concerned merely to discover "where the situation can be dealt with most expeditiously and most effectively," as Lodge had said in the Security Council.

As this statement indicates, Lodge, who was then President of the Security Council, was not eager to respond to Guatemala's insistent pleas for another meeting to consider the evidence that the resolution of 20 June had proved ineffective. Nevertheless, the Council was called for the 676th meeting on 25 June for that purpose. On this occasion, the issue of adopting the agenda provided the framework for a renewed debate on the jurisdictional question. Brazil and Colombia combined legal and pragmatic arguments for leaving the matter to the OAS. On behalf of the United States, Lodge presented an elaborate statement of opposition to the Council's consideration of the case. In contrast to the previous meeting, Lodge now relied heavily upon legal argument. He no longer defined the problem in pragmatic terms, but held that the issue was the maintenance of the Charter's formula for balancing regionalism and universalism—which he interpreted as establishing the "Try OAS first" principle. He warned that the failure of the Council to "respect the right of the Organization of American States to achieve a pacific settlement of the dispute between Guatemala and its neighbours" would produce "a catastrophe of such dimensions as will gravely impair the future effectiveness of both the United Nations itself and of regional organizations such as the Organization of American States." He alleged that Guatemala's "effort to bypass the Organization of American States is, in substance, a violation of Article 52, paragraph 2, "and that the United States had a legal duty to oppose Security Council consideration of the case until the OAS had first dealt with it. In political terms, Lodge made Guatemala and the Soviet Union the defendants in the case; the former was attempting to violate the Charter and acquire "a veto on the Organization of American States" by invoking the protection of the Security Council, and the latter was, by supporting the Guatemalan plea, trying to produce the organizational catastrophe of which Lodge warned.

The United States succeeded in preventing the adoption of the agenda; only Denmark, Lebanon, New Zealand, and the Soviet Union voted for its adoption, while China and Turkey joined Brazil, Colombia, and the United States in opposition, and Britain and France abstained. This closed the case so far as the United Nations was concerned. In effect, the Security Council handed the matter over to the OAS.

However, this does not mean that the "Try OAS first" principle won the endorsement of the Security Council. In the debate at the 676th meeting, the two states which abstained on the adoption of the agenda—Britain and France—explicitly asserted the competence of the Council. The British spokesman said "there is a state of affairs to which the Security Council certainly cannot remain indifferent. . . . For the Security Council to divest itself of its ultimate responsibility would be gravely to prejudice the moral authority of the United Nations. . . ." France welcomed the prospect of a factual report from the Inter-American Peace Committee, which would enable the Council "to take all decisions which may then seem proper." Moreover, of those states that opposed adoption of the agenda,

Brazil suggested that the Council should simply await a report from the OAS body, with the implication that it might then take action, and China, while accepting the view that members of the OAS were legally obliged to seek regional settlement first, considered that rejection of the agenda at that meeting would not mean elimination of the item from the continuing agenda of the Council. At this meeting, only Colombia, Turkey, and the United States failed to express or intimate in some way the conviction that the Security Council could or should regard the Guatemalan complaint as falling within its realm of responsibility. As we have noted, even these states had voted at the previous meeting for a resolution whose language implied, and whose sponsor declared, that it represented an assertion of the Council's competence to deal with the case. One finds in all of this no endorsement by the Security Council of the position that Guatemala had a duty to go to the OAS, or that the OAS had a right to assert exclusive jurisdiction over the case, or that the Council had a duty— or even a right—to refrain from dealing with it.

Indeed, at the 676th meeting it was already too late to establish the proposition that only the OAS could properly consider Guatemala's complaint, for the Council had, at the previous meeting, adopted the agenda and acted on the case. Guatemala correctly asserted that this constituted assumption of jurisdiction,[33] and the Secretary General subsequently included the case in official lists of matters of which the Security Council was seized.[34]

Behind the facade of legal and pragmatic arguments as to the proper roles of the OAS and the Security Council in this affair lay the decisive political considerations, which, as we have seen, occasionally obtruded into the debates. An examination of these will illuminate the real meaning of the case.

The government of Guatemala was reluctant to entrust its problem to the OAS because it recognized that, under the leadership of the United States, the regional body was more inclined to promote than to prevent its overthrow. The evidence for this viewpoint, most explicitly stated in the Security Council debates by the Soviet Union, was overwhelming. At the Tenth Inter-American Conference, held in Caracas in March 1954, the United States had pressed for a resolution asserting that the establishment of communist control in any American state should be treated as a threat to the peace, calling for counteraction by the OAS. While the Caracas Declaration, as adopted, was somewhat weaker than the United States draft, it was interpreted by Washington as a collective commitment to support or condone action directed at ousting the Arbenz regime. President Eisenhower later said, "This resolution formed a charter for the anti-Communist counterattack that followed."[35] On 10 June 1954, Secretary of State Dulles publicly declared that the Caracas Declaration applied to the case of Guatemala, and stated, "I hope that the Organization of American States will be able to help the people of Guatemala to rid themselves of the malignant force which has seized on them."[36] For some weeks before the invasion of Guatemala, Dulles had indicated in news conferences that plans were developing for an OAS foreign ministers' meeting to deal with the threat posed by what he described as the Communist-dominated regime in Guatemala.[37] Finally, on the day before the Security Council took up the case, the State Department commented that:

> The latest outbursts of violence within Guatemala confirm the previously expressed views of the United States concerning possible action by the Organization of American States on the problem of Communist intervention in Guatemala. The Department has been exchanging views and will continue to exchange views with other countries of this hemisphere

---

[33]SCOR: 9th Yr., Suppl. for April, May and June 1954 (S/3241, 23 June 1954).

[34]See United Nations, *Repertory of Practice of United Nations Organs*, Vol. II (New York, 1955), p. 457.

[35]Dwight D. Eisenhower, *Mandate for Change*, 1953–56 (Garden City: Doubleday, 1963), p. 424. See also Richard P. Stebbins, *The United States in World Affairs*, 1954 (New York: Harper, for the Council on Foreign Relations, 1956), pp. 371–77.

[36]Speech to the Rotary International Convention, Seattle, U.S. Dept. of State Press Release No. 316, 10 June 1954.

[37]U.S. Dept. of State Press Releases Nos. 279, 285, 25 May 1954; No. 310, 8 June 1954; No. 323, 15 June 1954.

. . . regarding action needed to protect the hemisphere from further encroachment by international Communism.[38]

These statements were surely pointed enough to convince the government of Guatemala that the advice of the United States to take its troubles to the OAS was motivated by something other than the urge to assist it in finding the forum "where the situation can be dealt with most expeditiously and most effectively." If that government suspected that the United States was not wholeheartedly devoted to securing its protection against the invasion, the suspicion must have been strengthened on the day after the Security Council decided to leave the case to the OAS, when the United States joined with nine other American states in requesting a meeting of foreign ministers to deal with "the demonstrated intervention of the international communist movement in the Republic of Guatemala and the danger which this involves for the peace and security of the Continent."[39] Two days later, the Council of the OAS approved that request, scheduling a meeting in Rio de Janeiro on 7 July,

> for the purpose of considering all aspects of the danger to the peace and security of the Continent resulting from the penetration of the political institutions of Guatemala by the international communist movement, and the measures which it is desirable to take.[40]

Thus, it appears that the transfer of the case from the Security Council to the OAS was not simply a matter of having the latter substitute for the former as a peaceful settlement mechanism, but a device for reversing the terms of the case. The OAS was prepared to treat Guatemala as the defendant, not the plaintiff. Whereas the Security Council had appealed for the cessation of the attack, the OAS declared its intent to consider means for expediting the demise of the government of Guatemala. In insisting that the

government of Guatemala should resort to the OAS, the United States was recommending what it hoped and intended would prove a suicidal act. As it turned out, the invasion accomplished its purpose without the assistance of the OAS, but United States officials subsequently confirmed that the ouster of the Arbenz regime was the business with which the OAS would otherwise have had to concern itself.[41]

However, the hostility of the United States toward the Arbenz regime was not expressed solely or even primarily through insistence that the OAS take over the case. The United States was significantly involved in the invasion; it was acting positively, along with Honduras and Nicaragua, to unseat the Guatemalan government, and it was at least as much concerned to keep the Security Council out as to bring the OAS into the affair. It hoped that the OAS would at least condone its activity, and perhaps lend support. It feared that the Security Council might impede the operation and thought that, at best, the Council might be induced to look the other way.

Although the United States, Honduras, and Nicaragua hotly denied the charge of complicity in the attack upon the Arbenz regime when it occurred and insisted that the problem was purely one of civil war, this version of the event won little credence. As early as 22 June 1954, Joseph C. Harsch wrote in the *Christian Science Monitor*:

> The only question seriously at issue is whether the United States can manipulate an operation of this kind skillfully and successfully. . . . If there were no native revolutionary movement to encourage and support, then some other . . . remedy would have to be found. Fortunately, there was a bona fide native movement; and, fortunately, Honduras was willing to let it be launched from Honduran soil. . . .[42]

---

[38]Statement of 19 June 1954, U.S. Dept. of State *Bulletin*, 28 June 1954, pp. 981–82.

[39]U.S. Dept. of State Press Release No. 351, 26 June 1954.

[40]*Annals of the Organization of American States*, Vol. VI, 1954, p. 160.

[41]See U.S. Dept. of State Press Releases, No. 378, 10 July 1954, and No. 412, 28 July 1954; speech by Secretary of State Dulles in General Assembly Official Records (GAOR): 9th Sess., 475th Plenary Mtg., 23 Sept. 1954, p. 23.

[42]Cited in Philip B. Taylor, Jr., "The Guatemalan Affair: A Critique of United States Foreign Policy," *American Political Science Review*, Vol. L (Sept. 1956), p. 806.

In the next few years, United States commentators on the case increasingly asserted, and even came to take it for granted, that the United States and Guatemala's neighbors had been heavily involved. In 1958, C. L. Sulzberger stated flatly that "when a regime sympathetic to our opponents was installed in Guatemala we ousted it," and in 1960, James Reston declared that

> every official who knows anything about the fall of the Arbenz government . . . knows that the United States Government, through the Central Intelligence Agency, worked actively with, and financed, and made available the arms, with which the anti-Arbenz forces finally "threw him out."[43]

After his retirement, President Eisenhower wrote frankly that the anti-Arbenz force had invaded Guatemala from Honduran territory, and that he supplied the force with aircraft during the invasion, through a third country, thus cooperating "in providing indirect support to a strictly anti-Communist faction."[44]

The conclusion is inescapable that the United States was implicated in the invasion which provoked Guatemala's appeal to the Security Council, and that it preferred reference of the case to the OAS rather than the Council because it hoped thereby to prevent the raising of any obstacle to the success of the invasion. Guatemala and the Soviet Union at least surmised that this was the situation and consequently attempted to keep the case before the Security Council. At bottom, the Guatemalan case was not a local affair of the OAS region, but a duel between the Soviet Union, which was sympathetic to the development of communism in Guatemala, and the United States, which was engaged in an effort to eliminate this intrusion. For the latter, escape from the Security Council was a means of depriving the Soviet Union of the capacity to protect its foothold in the Western Hemisphere. In this instance, the Soviet veto was a device not for paralyzing the Security Council, but for preventing the United States from reducing that body to inactivity by invoking the pretext of regional jurisdiction.

In a narrow and literal sense, the United States succeeded. However, as noted, it did not secure the establishment of the principle that the "Try OAS first" concept overrides the right of an American state to appeal to the Security Council whenever it feels threatened, or the duty of the Council to assume responsibility in such circumstances. The reaction against this implication was almost immediate, as many members of the United Nations reached the conclusion that the organization had been maneuvered into the role of an accomplice in the external attack upon Guatemala. The Secretary-General made a thinly veiled criticism of the handling of the case:

> The importance of regional arrangements in the maintenance of peace is fully recognized in the Charter and the appropriate use of such arrangements is encouraged. But in those cases where resort to such arrangements is chosen in the first instance, that choice should not be permitted to cast any doubt on the ultimate responsibility of the United Nations. Similarly, a policy giving full scope to the proper role of regional agencies can and should at the same time fully preserve the right of a Member nation to a hearing under the Charter.[45]

At the ninth General Assembly, in the autumn of 1954, several Latin American governments entered their protests and disavowed the notion that their membership in the OAS should be taken as restricting their right to have immediate recourse to the United Nations; even Brazil, which had played a prominent role in pushing the case to the OAS, denied that it had intended

---

[43] For the Sulzberger and Reston quotations, see the *New York Times,* 28 July 1958 and 24 Oct. 1960, respectively. See also Daniel James, *Red Design for the Americas: Guatemalan Prelude* (New York: John Day, 1954), pp. 297–98, 316; Donald Grant, "Guatemala and United States Foreign Policy," *Journal of International Affairs,* IX, 1955, pp. 64–72; Richard P. Stebbins, op. cit., pp. 382–83; John C. Dreier, "The Organization of American States and United States Policy," *International Organization,* XVII (Winter 1963), pp. 44–45; Herbert L. Matthews, "Diplomatic Relations," in the American Assembly, *The United States and Latin America* (2nd ed.; Englewood Cliffs: Prentice-Hall, 1963), pp. 132, 141–43, 151, 164.

[44] Eisenhower, op. cit., pp. 425–26.

[45] *Introduction to the Annual Report of the Secretary-General on the Work of the Organization, 1 July 1953 to 30 June 1954,* GAOR: 9th Sess., Suppl. No. 1 (A/2663), p. xi.

"to imply that the Security Council could not deal with the matter."[46] Sir Leslie Munroe, who had represented New Zealand in the Security Council proceedings, subsequently drew the conclusion from the case that:

> The Council's jurisdiction . . . should not be limited by the initiation of concurrent action in a regional organization. . . . The principle of the universal and overriding authority of the Security Council is one which seems to my government well worth maintaining against the happier day when it may be less affected by the stresses and strains of great Power conflicts of interest. . . .[47]

In the final analysis, the victory of the United States was Pyrrhic, as well as incomplete. The United States had its way in Guatemala, but instead of establishing a precedent that the United Nations would be inclined to follow, it stimulated a persistent wariness against allowing the recurrence of such episodes.

The Cuban Case

On 11 July 1960, the Cuban government requested a meeting of the Security Council to consider charges of interventionist policy and conspiracy to commit aggression which it lodged against the United States.[48] The situation was quite similar to the Guatemalan case, in that it involved friction between the United States and a regime which it regarded as giving communism a foothold in the Caribbean area. In this instance, the "Try OAS first" issue was raised even before

the Security Council met. The Cuban note anticipated the issue by citing Articles 52 (4) and 103 of the Charter; the United States rejoined in a note to the President of the Security Council, denying the charges, indicating that the Inter-American Peace Committee had begun investigation of Caribbean tensions under a mandate from the meeting of OAS foreign ministers, which had convened in Santiago in August 1959, and declaring that Cuba should deal directly with the United States or "bring the matter to the attention of the proper organ of the Organization of American States." Cuba was not, according to the United States, "resorting to the methods which the American States have established for the solution of such problems."[49]

The Council of the OAS decided, on July 18, to schedule a Meeting of Consultation of Ministers of Foreign Affairs "for the purpose of considering the requirements of continental solidarity and the defense of the regional system and of American democratic principles against possible threats,"[50] and, on the same day, the Security Council began a series of three meetings on the Cuban case.[51]

In the Security Council, Cuba began with an emphatic assertion of its right to choose the Council in preference to the regional forum, buttressing its case by citation of the Latin American affirmations of this principle made in the wake of the Guatemalan affair, at the ninth General Assembly. The Cuban spokesman then came quickly to the political point: the United States was intent upon repeating its Guatemalan tactic, covering its projected action against the Castro regime with the mantle to be provided by an obedient OAS. Cuba was being asked "to allow ourselves meekly to be led away, like a docile beast, to the slaughterhouse."[52]

In reply, the United States offered formal assurance that it had no aggressive designs against Cuba, and argued for OAS jurisdiction over the case both on legal grounds and on the ground that the OAS was already planning a foreign ministers' meeting to deal with it. "In these circumstances, the United States believes that

---

[46] For the Brazilian statement, see GAOR: 9th Sess., 486th Plenary Mtg., 1 Oct. 1954, p. 150. See also the statements of Uruguay, 481st Plenary Mtg., 28 Sept. 1954, p. 98; Ecuador, 485th Plenary Mtg., 1 Oct. 1954, p. 148; and Argentina, 488th Plenary Mtg., 4 Oct. 1954, p. 174. For a Mexican comment in similar vein, see Jorge Castañeda, *Mexico and the United Nations* (New York: Manhattan Publishing Co., for the Carnegie Endowment for International Peace, 1958), p. 126.

[47] "The Present-day Role of the Security Council in the Maintenance of Peace," *Proceedings of the American Society of International Law*, 49th Annual Mtg., 1955, pp. 134, 135. See also the statement of New Zealand, in GAOR: 9th Sess. 482nd Plenary Mtg., 28 Sept. 1954, p. 104.

[48] SCOR: 15th Yr., Suppl. for July, August and September 1960 (S/4378, 11 July 1960).

[49] Ibid. (S/4388, 15 July 1960).

[50] Ibid. (S/4399, 20 July 1960).

[51] SCOR: 15th Yr., 874th and 875th Mtgs., 18 July 1960; 876th Mtg., 19 July 1960.

[52] Ibid., 874th Mtg., 18 July 1960, p. 24.

the Security Council should take no action on the Cuban complaint, at least until . . . such discussions have taken place in the Organization of American States."[53] This position was expressed in a draft resolution submitted by Argentina and Ecuador, which asked the Council to state its concern about the situation, take note of the fact that it was being considered by the OAS, adjourn consideration of the matter pending receipt of a report from the OAS, invite members of the OAS to assist in promoting peaceful settlement, and urge other states to avoid exacerbation of the tensions between Cuba and the United States.[54]

Britain and France joined the United States in asserting that Cuba had a legal obligation to "Try OAS first,"[55] but no other state did so. Italy cited the tradition of regional action in the Western Hemisphere, and China offered no comment on the jurisdictional issue in support of reference of the case to the OAS.[56] Both Ceylon and Tunisia endorsed Cuba's right to have recourse to the Security Council, but judged it expedient for that body to make use of the OAS.[57]

Even the Latin American sponsors of the draft resolution refrained from supporting the legal doctrine of OAS priority. Argentina declined to enter into legalistic argument, but conceded that "no country can be denied access to organizations of which it is a member," and held that adoption of the draft would not imply renunciation of jurisdiction by the Security Council; it would simply recognize that the OAS was dealing with the case, and that the Council should await the result.[58] One might speculate that Argentina evaded the legal argument for fear of losing it; knowing that its case was weak, Argentina sought to win the victory without fighting the battle—by persuading the Council, on pragmatic grounds, to act as if it had rejected Cuba's claim of right to choose the global, in preference to the regional, forum. Ecuador, however, clearly did not *want* to win the legal battle for OAS priority; it not only conceded but vigorously espoused the doctrine that members of the OAS had no obliga-

tions restricting their right to resort to the Security Council. Having thus agreed with Cuba's legal position, Ecuador insisted that, as a practical matter, the Council should make use of the OAS. In approving the draft resolution, the Council would be exercising, not relinquishing, its competence.[59]

The Soviet Union rejected this interpretation of the draft resolution, insisting that it was an evasive device to have the Council repudiate its proper responsibility. "From the political standpoint . . . the effective purpose . . . is to prevent the Security Council from taking the requisite effective measures to protect . . . Cuba, a purpose that suits the convenience of the United States." It was not true that the OAS was dealing with Cuba's complaint; Cuba had filed no complaint with that body, and, in any case, it was evident that the OAS was about to consider complaints *against* Cuba in order to develop plans for supporting the anti-Castro campaign of the United States. In effect, the United States was maneuvering to keep the Cuban case confined to the OAS, where it "could quietly deal with Cuba as it pleased."[60]

The Soviet Union proposed amendments to the draft sponsored by Argentina and Ecuador, deleting all reference to the OAS. This effort to have the Council keep the case entirely to itself was roundly defeated, with only Poland supporting the Soviet position, and Tunisia abstaining. Thereupon, the Council voted 9 to 0, with Poland and the Soviet Union abstaining, in favor of the original draft.[61] Thus, the Council effectively handed the case over to the OAS—but without renouncing its own jurisdiction or denying Cuba's right of uninhibited recourse to the United Nations. Again, the United States had won its case, but had failed to secure general endorsement of the "Try OAS first" principle.

A new phase of the Cuban case began in the autumn of 1960, at the fifteenth General Assembly. Speaking in the general debate, Fidel Castro emphasized that Cuba's pessimistic expectations in regard to the treatment it would receive in the OAS had been confirmed by the proceedings of

[53] Ibid., p. 28.
[54] United Nations Doc. S/4392, 18 July 1960.
[55] SCOR: 15th Yr., 875th Mtg., 18 July 1960, pp. 4–5, 13.
[56] Ibid., pp. 1–2, 14.
[57] Ibid., pp. 6–9.
[58] SCOR: 15th Yr., 874th Mtg., 18 July 1960, pp. 34–35.

[59] Ibid., pp. 38–39.
[60] SCOR: 15th Yr., 876th Mtg., 19 July 1960, pp. 2–20.
[61] Ibid., p. 24. For the Soviet amendments, see SCOR: 15th Yr., Suppl. for July, August and September, 1960 (S/4394, 19 July 1960); for the resolution as passed, see ibid. (S/4395, 19 July 1960).

the Seventh Meeting of Consultation of Ministers of Foreign Affairs at San José, Costa Rica, in August. Cuba's charges against the United States had been brushed aside, and the Soviet Union, not the United States, had been censured.[62] Castro's analysis was essentially correct. The foreign ministers of the OAS had been preoccupied with the threat to hemispheric security posed *by* the Castro regime, viewed as an instrument of communist intrusion, not with the threat *to* that regime of which it had complained before the Security Council.[63] Since the OAS had insisted upon treating Cuba as the defendant, rather than the plantiff, Cuba turned once more to the United Nations.

On 25 October 1960, Cuba appeared in the General Committee to urge the addition to the agenda, for urgent attention in plenary session, of its renewed charge of acts of intervention and plans for aggression by the United States.[64] The Cuban representative evidently feared another "Try OAS first" episode, for he asserted his country's right "to decide to which organ to submit any complaint it might have to make," and warned against permitting the United States to repeat its Guatemalan tactic—a warning that was echoed by Bulgaria and the Soviet Union.

The United States did observe that Cuba should have brought its case to the OAS, "to which under its treaty obligations it was required to submit such complaints first," and even suggested that Cuba should have resorted to the Security Council rather than the Assembly if its sense of urgency was genuine. However, this point was for the record only. The United States approved the inscription of the item—perhaps because it sensed the lack of support for the pro-OAS line (Costa Rica and Haiti both declined to contest the competence of the United Nations), or because Cuba had already resorted to the OAS in accordance with the July resolution of the Security Council. However, the United States waged a successful fight to have the item referred routinely to the First Committee, rather than slate it for urgent consideration by the plenary Assembly.

The Assembly subsequently approved the allocation of the item recommended by the General Committee, after a debate marked by the accusation, stated by Romania, that referral to the First Committee was a device to enable the United States to complete its projected action against Castro, à la Guatemala, before the United Nations could intervene.[65]

Although Cuba continued to proclaim that its own invasion was imminent, it made no move to have the First Committee shift its charge to the top of the agenda—a move which the United States had promised not to oppose. Instead, Cuba invoked the consideration of the Security Council, which took up the case again in January 1961.[66] The United States did not formally object to this action, although it declared that the Cuban fear of attack was both mistaken and fraudulent; if Castro's concern were genuine, he should not have refused the services of the Ad Hoc Committee of Good Offices which the foreign ministers of the OAS had created at their San José meeting in August 1960. The British spokesman was even more emphatic in insisting that Cuba, having disregarded the Council's earlier advice to seek a solution through the OAS, had no claim to the renewed attention of the Council. The Council dropped the matter without taking formal action, but it is significant that the Latin American members, Chile and Ecuador, advanced a proposal for a resolution which would have had that body urge peaceful settlement without making the slightest reference to the regional forum.[67] The "Try OAS first" line was clearly losing ground.

On 15 April 1961, the First Committee of the Assembly began a series of meetings on the item pertaining to Cuba, which had been allocated to it the preceding autumn.[68] During these meetings, the Committee was confronted not with the

[62]GAOR: 15th Sess., 872nd Plenary Mtg., 26 Sept. 1960, p. 125.

[63]For the text of the Final Act of the San José meeting, see SCOR: 15th Yr., Suppl. for July, August and September, 1960 (S/4480, 7 Sept. 1960).

[64]GAOR: 15th Sess., General Cmte., 131st Mtg., 25 Oct. 1960.

[65]GAOR: 15th Sess., 909th Plenary Mtg., 31 Oct. 1960. The Assembly rejected a Cuban move to mark the item for plenary action. See ibid., 910th Plenary Mtg., 1 Nov. 1960.

[66]SCOR: 16th Yr., 921st and 922nd Mtg., 4 Jan. 1961, and 923rd Mtg., 5 Jan. 1961.

[67]SCOR: 16th Yr., Suppl. for January, February and March 1961 (S/4612, 4 Jan. 1961).

[68]GAOR: 15th Sess., 1st Cmtte., 1149th to 1161st Mtg., 15-21 Apr. 1961.

Cuban contention that an attack was being planned, but with the actuality of the Bay of Pigs invasion, an abortive attempt to topple the Castro regime in which the United States first denied, and then admitted, complicity. It was the Guatemalan story again, but with crucial differences: the United States did not succeed in eliminating the communist-oriented regime, or in persuading the United Nations to hand the matter over to the OAS. The latter failure may well have been attributable to the memory of the Guatemalan affair.

The debate in the First Committee centered on a set of competitive draft resolutions. The United States backed a proposal introduced by seven Latin American states, which had the familiar pro-OAS ring: it characterized the situation as disturbing to "the American Continent," recalled the Security Council's handing over the case to the OAS and the latter's action at the San José meeting of foreign ministers, exhorted the states belonging to the OAS to promote a settlement in accordance with the charters of the United Nations and of the OAS, and requested other states to abstain from action that might aggravate tensions.[69] Sudan proposed amendments to this draft that would have the effect of reversing its meaning, taking out all regional emphasis and treating the Cuban case as a world problem to be handled by the United Nations.[70] Mexico submitted what might be called a renegade Latin American draft, implicitly condemning United States intervention in Cuba and calling for peaceful settlement without reference to the OAS.[71] Romania introduced a draft which, without naming names, called upon the United States and its confederates to desist from attacking Cuba. The Soviet Union then proposed that the Assembly condemn these states as aggressors and call upon members of the United Nations to assist Cuba, if it should so request, in repelling the agression.[72]

To a considerable extent, debate focused on the joint Latin American draft, the chosen instrument of the champions of the OAS. However, the argument that legal propriety required the United Nations to respect the jurisdictional priority of the OAS was virtually absent from the speeches. The United States was too much on the defensive to lead the battle. Italy appeared to substitute for the United States in asserting that "the Cuban crisis was the concern of the American hemisphere. . . ." and that the OAS was "the forum chosen by the American Republics themselves to deal with their problems."[73] Among the sponsors of the joint draft, only Uruguay clearly took the "Try OAS first" line and suggested that adoption of that proposal would transfer the case to the OAS.[74] Otherwise, Latin American spokesmen in the Committee tended to accept without question the proposition that it was legitimate for Cuba to bring its case to the United Nations, and proper for the world organization to deal with it—while supporting, in most instances, the view that the United Nations should rely primarily upon the American states to solve the crisis. Mexico argued most sharply against the "Try OAS first" doctrine.[75] Venezuela spoke for the sponsors of the joint draft in rejecting the view that they denied the competence of the United Nations, saying that they "considered it preferable to solve the problem within a regional framework, but each one of them reserved the right to appeal directly to the United Nations, for the two bodies, far from being mutually exclusive, were complementary."[76]

It was left for the Soviet Union to argue that the joint Latin American draft represented an effort to push the United Nations aside in favor of the OAS, even though its sponsors claimed to respect the jurisdiction of the United Nations. In the Soviet view, the draft "sought to refer the question to the OAS, thus removing it from the jurisdiction of the United Nations. The effect would be to postpone action indefinitely, since the United States exercised a preponderant influence in the OAS."[77]

As the First Committee neared the voting stage, the sponsors of the joint draft accepted a Sudanese amendment that transformed a preambulary reference to the Cuban crisis as disturb-

---

[69]GAOR: 15th Sess., Annexes, Agenda item 90 (A/4744, 21 Apr. 1961, para. 7).

[70]Ibid. (para. 9).

[71]Ibid. (para. 6).

[72]Ibid. (paras. 5 and 8).

[73]GAOR: 15th Sess., 1st Cmtte., 1158th Mtg., 20 Apr. 1961, p. 94.

[74]Ibid., 1156th Mtg., 19 Apr. 1961, pp. 83–84.

[75]Ibid., 1154th Mtg., 18 Apr. 1961, pp. 75–76; and 1159th Mtg., 20 Apr. 1961, pp. 97–98.

[76]Ibid., 1158th Mtg., 20 Apr. 1961, p. 96.

[77]Ibid., 1159th Mtg., 20 Apr. 1961, p. 99.

ing "the American Continent" to one which treated the case as a "world" problem. They balked, however, at Sudan's proposal to delete all regional references from the operative part of the resolution, and this amendment was defeated, 31 to 43, with 23 abstentions.[78] In this crucial vote, which involved the issue of whether the United Nations would, in any sense, turn the case over to the OAS, Mexico joined Cuba in supporting the anti-OAS position, and the Dominican Republic and Ecuador abstained. These Latin American states maintained the positions of opposition and abstention when the Committee voted (61-27-10) to adopt the joint draft. This substantial victory for the United States was immediately spoiled by the Committee's adoption (42-31-25) of the Mexican draft resolution, which was implicitly critical of United States intervention in Cuba and utterly devoid of reference to the OAS as an appropriate agency for dealing with the Cuban problem. Ominously, five Latin American states joined Cuba in supprting this draft, and one abstained.[79]

This mixed pattern of success and failure for the United States in its drive to have the United Nations leave Cuba to the OAS persisted in the plenary meeting at which the Assembly considered the recommendations of the First Committee.[80] The Mexican draft failed for want of a two-thirds majority, but so did the first operative paragraph of the joint Latin American resolution —the provision that, in essence, assigned to the OAS the task of solving the Cuban problem. Four members of the OAS, in addition to Cuba, failed to support this provision. The modified joint draft was adopted as General Assembly resolution 1616 (XV), by a vote of 59 to 13, with 24 abstentions, but the deletion of the first operative paragraph emptied the text of most of its pro-OAS content. In its final form, it referred to the Security Council's resolution of 19 July 1960, and the peaceful means of settlement that had been made available by the OAS. However, its single operative paragraph exhorted all members of the United Nations to promote peaceful settlement, without recognizing a special role for the OAS in the Cuban case. The reduction of the resolution to these terms was at least a partial victory for the USSR, which deplored the possibility that the case "would be referred to an organization in which the aggressor had a decisive influence and which had already taken up a hostile position towards the Cuban revolution."[81]

On balance, the handling of this case by the United Nations represented a setback for the doctrine that the OAS has a jurisdiction over local disputes that its members are bound to accept and United Nations organs to respect. Most notably, Latin American states tended to shy away from this position, which they had previously advocated. The Cuban case suggested that Guatemala had not provided a precedent, but had produced a reaction.

The Haitian and Panamanian Cases

The "Try OAS first" issue has excited no major contention since the Cuban case. In May 1963, the Security Council devoted two meetings to consideration of a dispute between the Dominican Republic and Haiti at the latter's request.[82] Although a serious jurisdiction controversy might have developed, Haiti averted this by agreeing that the Council should defer to the OAS, which had already begun efforts to promote a settlement. Using the consensus procedure, the Council dropped the matter, while retaining it on the agenda.

Similarly, the Council took up a complaint by Panama against the United States in January 1964.[83] It found both parties willing to rely primarily upon the OAS, and confined itself to authorizing—without vote—an appeal by its President for moderation and restraint on both sides. The crucial factor in these instances was the willingness of the complainants to accept the pacifying role of the OAS, in sharp contrast to the situation that prevailed in the Guatemalan and Cuban cases.

---

[78]Ibid., 1161st Mtg., 21 Apr. 1961, p. 108.
[79]Ibid., p. 109.
[80]GAOR: 15th Sess., 995th Plenary Mtg., 21 Apr. 1961.

[81]Ibid., p. 493.
[82]See the discussion at the 1035th and 1036th Mtgs., 8 and 9 May 1963, in *Report of the Security Council 16 July 1962–15 July 1963*, GAOR: 18th Sess., Suppl. No. 2 (A/5502), pp. 15–18.
[83]United Nations Doc. S/PV. 1086, 10 Jan. 1964.

However, the jurisdictional issue was clearly visible beneath the surface of both these recent cases. Haiti was prepared to deal with the OAS only if it were understood that the Security Council would remain seized of the case, and the consensual move in the Panamanian case depended upon the same understanding. Significantly, in both cases, Latin American members of the Council were emphatic in declaring the necessity for recognizing the unrestricted right of members of the OAS to resort to the Security Council at any time. In the Haitian case, Venezuela cited Article 52 (4) of the United Nations Charter and Article 102 of the OAS Charter in repudiation of the "Try OAS first" principle; in the Panamanian case, it was Brazil that suggested the informal appeal by the President as a means of asserting the legitimate concern of the Council. In short, these cases reveal a Latin American urge to destroy the last vestiges of the proposition that membership in the OAS impairs in any way the rights derived from membership in the United Nations.

As in previous cases, the Soviet Union emphasized not only the competence but also the responsibility of the Security Council to deal with disputes within the Western Hemisphere, and displayed a skeptical attitude toward the OAS, viewing the latter as an instrument by which the United States effectuates the domination of its sphere of influence. While the Latin American states denied the legal necessity but affirmed the political propriety of the Council's standing aside in favor of OAS action, the USSR was evidently inclined to deny the latter as well as the former. The position the Soviet Union took in the Panamanian debate indicates that its acquiescence in reference of the matter to the OAS must have been very reluctant; it could tolerate the move only because the right of the Security Council to re-enter the case was fully recognized.

If the Soviet Union could barely consent to the use of the OAS, the United States had equal difficulty in acknowledging the competence of the Security Council. The fact that the Council exercised its competence in these cases only to endorse the work of the OAS no doubt minimized the disposition of the United States to challenge its jurisdiction; had it acted otherwise, the Council might have stimulated a spirited restatement of the "Try OAS first" thesis by the United States. In contrast to the Latin American members of the Council, which *asserted* the competence of that body, the United States *conceded* the point. It was willing to recognize the jurisdiction of the Security Council; so long as there was no challenge to the utilization of the OAS; most other states were willing to accept the utilization of the OAS, so long as there was no challenge to the jurisdiction of the Council.

The "Try OAS first" doctrine, interpreted to mean that the American states are bound to treat the OAS as the international agency of first resort and that the organs of the United Nations are obligated to respect the jurisdictional priority, has been generally discredited and discarded. Aware of this, the United States has found it pointless to continue advancing the argument. Nevertheless, its political implication, "Keep the Security Council—and, thereby, the Soviet Union—out of Western Hemispheric affairs," remains important for the United States. In routine cases, the Council may continue to defer to the OAS on pragmatic rather than legal grounds. However, if new versions of the Guatemalan and Cuban cases occur, the effort of the United States to prevent the Soviet Union from impeding anti-Communist activity in Latin America again will conflict with the effort of the Soviet Union to deprive the United States of freedom of action against communism in Latin America. As before, this substantive struggle will doubtless take the form of a jurisdictional conflict.

THE ISSUE OF THE AUTONOMY OF THE OAS IN IMPOSING SANCTIONS

The second major aspect of the struggle for the autonomy of the OAS vis à vis the Security Council relates to its role in applying sanctions to states adjudged guilty of threatening or violating the peace, or committing aggression. Article 53 of the Charter prohibits regional enforcement action without the authorization of the Security Council; Article 51 lifts this restriction so far as response to armed attack is concerned, but the restriction holds with respect to other violations of peace and security. In the present era, when aggression so often takes subtle forms, the prohibition stated in Article 53 imposes a significant limitation upon the work of regional organizations. Hence, it is understandable that champions of the OAS have striven to escape from the implications of Article 53 and that this effort has provoked controversy in the United Nations.

The effort to emancipate the OAS from Article 53 has been manifested in the advocacy of a restrictive interpretation of "enforcement measures," excluding from this category all non-military measures and thus eliminating the requirement of Security Council approval for OAS sanctions of that type. Beyond this, proponents of an independent OAS would undoubtedly move to escape the necessity for Security Council authorization of military sanctions by insisting upon a generous interpretation of Article 51—making "armed attack" include indirect aggression. Such an interpretation was foreshadowed in the Report of the Senate Committee on Foreign Relations on the North Atlantic Treaty, on 6 June 1949: "Obviously, purely internal disorders or revolutions would not be considered 'armed attacks. . . .' However, if a revolution were aided and abetted by an outside power such assistance might possibly be considered an armed attack."[84] It is hardly conceivable that the United States, which balks at the subjection of OAS diplomatic and economic sanctions to Security Council control, would tolerate such control over regional military measures. As we shall see, the effort to minimize the impact of Article 53 upon the OAS represents an urge to achieve the total autonomy of the regional organization.

The Dominican Case

On 20 August 1960, the foreign ministers of the OAS meeting at San José as an Organ of Consultation, formally condemned the Dominican Republic for "acts of intervention and aggression," not involving overt military attack, against Venezuela, and resolved that other members of the OAS apply diplomatic and partial economic sanctions to their errant colleague. In accordance with this resolution, the Secretary-General of the OAS reported the action to the Security Council as required by Article 54 of the Charter.[85]

In the view of the United States, this should have been the end of the matter so far as the United Nations was concerned. The Soviet Union, however, thought differently. It requested a meeting of the Security Council to consider the question of authorizing the OAS enforcement measures, under Article 53, and submitted a draft resolution whereby the Council would express its approval of the regional action against the Dominican Republic.[86]

This was a shrewd tactical move. The Soviet Union proposed to establish the competence of the Security Council to control the application of enforcement measures by the OAS, by advocating the *approval*, not the rejection, of OAS action in the initial case. The legal implication was clear: the Council would be asserting its authority to disapprove as well as to approve, and the Soviet Union would enjoy the right to veto Council decisions in such matters. Moreover, the political meaning of the move was apparent: Soviet initiative in promoting Council approval of OAS sanctions in the Dominican case was designed to lay the groundwork for Soviet obstruction of Council approval—that is, for Council *disapproval*—of possible OAS enforcement measures against China. The timing of the move supports this interpretation. It came less than two months after the Council's resolution of 19 July 1960, referring Cuba to the OAS. The Soviet Union had charged that the regional agency would prosecute rather than protect Cuba, and developments had borne out that prediction; the foreign ministers at San José had no sooner concluded their Sixth Meeting of Consultation, dealing with the Dominican Republic, than they had gone into sessions as the Seventh Meeting, producing a declaration treating the Castro regime as an instrument of intolerable Sino-Soviet intrusion into the OAS region.[87] Both the Soviet Union and the United States regarded the Dominican case as a prelude to a possible new phase of the Cuban case.

The Security Council considered the Dominican case on 8 and 9 September.[88] The Soviet

[84]*American Foreign Policy, 1950–1955, Basic Documents,* U.S. Dept. of State Pub. 6446 (Washington: GPO, 1957), Vol. I, p. 835.

[85]SCOR: 15th Yr., Suppl. for July, August and September 1960 (S/4476, 1 Sept. 1960).

[86]Ibid. (S/4477, 5 Sept. 1960, and S/4481/Rev. 1, 8 Sept. 1960).

[87]Ibid. (S/4480, 7 Sept. 1960).

[88]SCOR: 15th Yr., 893rd to 895th Mtgs., 8 to 9 Sept. 1960.

Union, backed by Poland, invoked the rule of Article 53 as unquestionably applying to the case. As the Soviet representative put it:

> The Security Council is the only organ empowered to authorize the application of enforcement action by regional organs against any State. Without authorization from the Security Council, the taking of enforcement action by regional agencies would be contrary to the Charter of the United Nations.[89]

In opposition to this literal interpretation of Article 53, the United States took the equally firm and dogmatic position that the requirement of Security Council authorization applies only to forcible measures, not to such diplomatic and economic sanctions as the OAS was putting into effect against the Dominican Republic. Actions of the latter sort could legitimately be taken by any state in exercise of its sovereignty; hence, it was inconceivable that Article 53 could be taken to restrict the right of a group of states to apply such measures. Additionally, the United States pointed out that the OAS foreign ministers had considered that the Charter required them only to inform the Security Council of their action, not to seek its approval. Accordingly, the United States proposed, in conjunction with Argentina and Ecuador, that the Council merely acknowledge receipt of the OAS report and "take note" of the fact that sanctions were being employed on a regional basis.[90]

It should be noted that this conviction that the phrase "enforcement action" as used in Article 53, referred only to military measures was of recent vintage. In two draft plans for the Charter, including the one used as a working paper at Dumbarton Oaks, the United States had explicitly included economic, commercial, and financial measures within the category of enforcement action.[91] At the San Francisco Conference, Bolivia had proposed a text requiring that neither economic nor military sanctions be undertaken by regional agencies without the authority of the Security Council, and Venezuela had interpreted the Dumbarton Oaks provision for Council control over regional enforcement action as applicable to "penalties of a military, economic or other character."[92] The proposals submitted by the United States for the Rio Pact had clearly provided that the imposition of sanctions of either a military or nonmilitary character would require the authorization of the Security Council, as stipulated in Article 53.[93] Similarly, Bolivia, Chile, Ecuador, Guatemala, and Mexico had presented drafts for the Rio Pact, which treated nonmilitary sanctions as enforcement measures within the meaning of Article 53.[94] Finally, at San José, Secretary of State Christian Herter had intimated that such sanctions as were adopted in the Dominican case might fall under the rule of Article 53. He argued against the immediate adoption of these measures, stating his case "without entering into any debate over questions of whether such action would be affected by the provisions of the Charter of the United Nations with respect to enforcement action by regional agencies. . . ."[95] Herter thereby seemed to imply that he *might* legitimately raise the point that the proposed action required authorization by the Security Council; at the least, his statement acknowledged that the point was debatable—an acknowledgment that did not appear in the position of the United States when the Council took up the Dominican case.

In the Security Council, only the United Kingdom, China, and Venezuela (the latter participating in the debate by invitation, as an interested party) expressed clear and complete agreement with the interpretation of Article 53 espoused by the United States, and only Poland fully endorsed the Soviet interpretation. Other states displayed varying degrees of uncertainty as to the meaning of the crucial provision.

Particularly significant is the fact that both Argentina and Ecuador, the Latin American cosponsors of the United States draft resolution, admitted that the applicability of the rule of Article 53 to the Dominican case was an open

---

[89]Ibid., 893rd Mtg., 8 Sept. 1960, p. 4.

[90]SCOR: 15th Yr., Suppl. for July, August and September 1960 (S/4484, 8 Sept. 1960).

[91]*Postwar Foreign Policy Preparation, 1939–1945*, op. cit., pp. 583, 596.

[92]UNCIO, XII, pp. 767, 783.

[93]*Inter-American Conference for the Maintenance of Continental Peace and Security*, op. cit., pp. 103, 121.

[94]Ibid., pp. 89, 113 (Bolivia); 92 (Chile); 95 (Ecuador); 97 (Guatemala); 98–99, 119 (Mexico).

[95]U.S. Dept. of State *Bulletin*, 5 Sept. 1960, p. 356.

question. These states appealed to the Council to avoid the effort to settle the legal question and to approve the joint draft—in effect, to rule against the Soviet position without considering the legalities of the matter. Evidently feeling that the United States interpretation of Article 53 was untenable, they suggested that the Council ought to base its position on the general principle of regional autonomy rather than the literal text of that article.[96]

Of the remaining members of the Security Council, France, Italy, and Tunisia leaned toward the United States view, and Ceylon toward the Soviet view, without taking dogmatic stands. In the end, all members of the Council voted to adopt the resolution proposed by the United States and its Latin American cohorts, except for the Soviet Union and Poland, which abstained.[97] The Soviet Union thereupon withdrew its proposal without a vote.

The United States took this vote as a clear vindication of its legal position, and of its political position as well. Shortly before the vote, the representative of the United States had asserted: "The Soviet request for Security Council action in this case was a bald effort to seek a veto over the operation of the inter-American system. In our opinion, it is malicious meddling and will not succeed."[98] More objectively, one might say that the USSR was taking the position that Article 53 conferred upon the Security Council the right to disallow OAS sanctions of the type under review, and that most members of the Council had not been prepared to declare that the Soviet reading of the article was clearly incorrect. Nevertheless, the resolution demanded by the United States was overwhelmingly adopted, and the United States proclaimed, both then and subsequently, that the Council had thereby definitively asserted that OAS sanctions not involving force were exempt from the requirement of its authorization and, most importantly, from the range of the Soviet veto power.

The USSR, on the other hand, attempted to snatch victory from the jaws of defeat. Its own resolution had been dropped, not rejected. It read the United States-sponsored resolution as a mild victory for the Soviet view; in "taking note" of the OAS action without expressing disapproval, the Council had implicitly approved the action and thus established its competence to give or withhold approval. For this reason, the Soviet Union had refrained from exercising its veto power. Moreover, it interpreted the views of members who had advocated evasion of the legal issue as indicating that they had not intended to set a precedent, but that they wished instead to leave the door open for future determination of the meaning of Article 53. In short, the Soviet Union claimed victory at least in the sense that its position had not been clearly and conclusively defeated.

If the Soviet Union slightly understated its defeat, the United States vastly overstated its victory. Eight states had voted with the United States for the resolution, but six of them had expressed doubt as to the proper interpretation of Article 53, and one of those—Ceylon—had stated that its vote was intended to express agreement with the Soviet view.[99] Adding Poland and the Soviet Union to these six, we find that eight members of the Council either denied or expressed skepticism concerning the United States position. This hardly represented a decisive endorsement of the proposition that the authorization of the Security Council is not required for OAS sanctions falling short of military force.

Cuba Revisited

In the most recent stages of the Cuban case, the issue of OAS autonomy in undertaking enforcement measures has superceded the "Try OAS first" issue. At the Eighth Meeting of Consultation of Ministers of Foreign Affairs, held at Punta del Este in January 1962, this organ of the OAS suspended Cuba from the regional system by the device of declaring that Cuba had placed itself outside the pale, and imposed partial economic sanctions upon it.[100] Under these circumstances,

---

[96] For the elaborate statements by Argentina and Ecuador, see SCOR: 15th Yr., 893rd Mtg., 8 Sept. 1960, pp. 5–12.
[97] SCOR: 15th Yr., 895th Mtg., 9 Sept. 1960, p. 5.
[98] Ibid., p. 2.

[99] SCOR: 15th Yr., 894th Mtg., 9 Sept. 1960, p. 5.
[100] For text of the Final Act, see SCOR: 17th Yr., Suppl. For January, February and March 1962 (S/5075, 3 Feb. 1962).

it became difficult, as well as futile, to insist that Cuba should resort to the OAS in preference to the United Nations. Henceforward, the United States complained that Cuba appealed to the United Nations not prematurely, but too frequently, too repetitiously, and with malicious propagandistic intent. Cuba complained of the OAS sanctions. Interestingly enough, it protested vehemently against its virtual expulsion from the OAS, the agency from whose grasp it had previously fled to the United Nations. The worm had indeed turned; now the United States insisted that Cuba *stay away* from the OAS, and Cuba demanded its right to go there!

A Cuban charge of intervention and aggressive intent on the part of the United States was debated in the General Assembly in February 1962.[101] Although the agenda item did not refer to the sanctions initiated at Punta del Este, they figured prominently in the discussion. Members of the OAS voted solidly against any formal action. Neither the First Committee nor the Assembly approved resolutions on the charge.

The Security Council met on 27 February 1962 to consider a Cuban accusation that the Punta del Este sanctions constituted illegal enforcement measures forced by the United States upon the OAS; "The United States has thus converted the Organization of American States into an instrument for aggression."[102] However, the agenda failed of adoption when only Ghana, Romania, the Soviet Union, and the United Arab Republic voted in favor, and the other seven members of the Council abstained. Opposition to the agenda was based upon the argument that Cuba's charge was substantially the same as that which the Assembly had just considered, and, more fundamentally, upon the contention that the precedent established in the Dominican case indicated that it was not within the province of the Council to approve or disapprove the non-military measures instituted against Cuba by the OAS. Britain and Chile joined the United States in the explicit invocation of the latter argument.

The Soviet Union not only denied this interpretation of the Council's action in the Dominican case and insisted that the OAS sanctions were invalid without the authorization called for in Article 53, but also introduced a warning against the generalized emancipation of regional agencies from United Nations control reminiscent of the strictures against regionalism voiced by United States officials in the formative period of the world organization:

> If today the Security Council fails to nullify the unlawful decisions thus taken against Cuba, then tomorrow similar action may be taken against any other country of Latin America, Africa, Asia or any continent whose neighbours, upon some pretext or other, having assembled at a regional meeting, arbitrarily decide to apply to it the machinery of coercion in the form of enforcement action, thus usurping the prerogatives of the Security Council.[103]

These arguments were reiterated and elaborated at a series of Security Council meetings extending from 14 to 23 March 1962,[104] which dealt with a Cuban request that the Council seek the advisory opinion of the International Court of Justice on a number of questions relating to the OAS sanctions, and, pending receipt of the Court's opinion, call for suspension of those sanctions.[105] Cuba's list of questions to be put to the Court mixed two issues, which were similarly combined in the Council's debate: whether the OAS sanctions were subject to Council action, and whether they were worthy of approval. In effect, Cuba proposed to ask the Court to affirm the competence of the Security Council to rule on the propriety of the sanctions, but then to undertake that function itself.

In this instance, the Council adopted the agenda without debate and invited Cuba to participate in its proceedings. Cuba, Romania, and the Soviet Union argued that the measures undertaken by the OAS were invalid without Council approval and should be invalidated by the Council by its refusal to confer approval upon them.

[101]GAOR: 16th Sess., 1st Cmtte., 1231st to 1243rd Mtgs., 5 to 15 Feb. 1962; 1104th to 1105th Plenary Mtgs., 19 to 20 Feb. 1962.

[102]SCOR: 17th Yr., Suppl. for January, February and March 1962 (S/5080, 22 Feb. 1962, p. 82); SCOR: 17th Yr., 991st Mtg., 27 Feb. 1962.

[103]SCOR: 17th Yr., 991st Mtg., 27 Feb. 1962, p. 10.
[104]Ibid., 992nd to 998th Mtgs., 14 to 23 Mar. 1962.
[105]SCOR: 17th Yr., Suppl. for January, February and March 1962 (S/5086, 8 Mar. 1962, and S/5095, 20 Mar. 1962).

They challenged their opponents to let the Court decide on the correctness of this position.

The United States asserted that the question of the Council's competence had been closed by the resolution adopted in the Dominican case, when the Soviet initiative had been recognized "as a prelude to a later effort to employ its veto against the Organization of American States, and in defense of its base of operations in the Western Hemisphere: Cuba."[106] The Soviet Union claimed that the outcome of the Dominican case had implicitly supported its view of Article 53, and Ghana developed an elaborate rebuttal of the United States analysis of that case, contending that the issue of the meaning of enforcement action under Article 53 had been left unsettled and should now be settled by reference to the Court. France and China invoked the Dominican precedent—as did the United States—while Britain, Chile, Ireland, and Venezuela indicated agreement with the interpretation of Article 53 established, according to the United States, by the Dominican resolution. This represented a significant increase of support in the Council for the position that Article 53 clearly did not require that body's authorization of nonmilitary sanctions undertaken by the OAS; now, only four members denied or questioned this interpretation. Thus the victory that the United States had proclaimed at the close of the Dominican case became belatedly a fact.

However, controversy as to the meaning of Article 53 was not the primary feature of the Council's debate in March 1962. The focus of debate shifted instead to the broader issue of the proper relationship between regional organizations and the United Nations. Not the technical legal problem of interpreting a particular provision, but the general political question of the role of regional agencies dominated the discussion.

The United States, picking up the point introduced by the Soviet Union at the 991st meeting of the Council, treated the case as one affecting the fate of *all* regional agencies, not merely the OAS. But whereas the USSR had warned against the impairment of the United Nations as a protective bulwark of all states that would result if regionalism were allowed to flourish without restraint, the United States warned against the stultification of all regional organizations that would result if they were subjected to the overriding authority of the Security Council.[107] This position was strikingly inconsistent with the United States' position in 1945, which emphasized the necessity of preserving the supremacy of the world organization while fitting regional agencies into its framework. It is doubtful, however, that the United States had actually been converted—as it now appeared—to the general philosophy of regionalism; the United States was not supporting the OAS in order to strengthen the cause of regionalism, but was invoking the support of all states having a stake in regional organizations in order to establish the autonomy of the OAS. This was a triumph of policy over principle. The intensity of the determination of the United States to ensure the freedom of action of the OAS against communist intrusions in the Western Hemisphere was demonstrated by its willingness to espouse the principle that regionalism should reign unchallenged in international politics.

The United States also generalized the argument in the sense that it contended for an autonomous status for the OAS that, at least by implication, went well beyond the establishment of its right to initiate nonmilitary sanctions without regard to the will of the Security Council. It appeared to advocate a virtually unlimited independence for the OAS; in short, the argument demanded the elimination, not merely the restrictive interpretation, of Article 53. The heart of the matter was the Soviet veto power in the Security Council. The United States was unwilling to tolerate the use of this instrument to embarrass or inhibit the anti-communist activities of the OAS or its own anti-communist activities, for which it sought the support and legitimizing cover of the OAS. The United States denounced the Soviet invocation of the rule stipulated in Article 53 as an effort to extend its veto power over the OAS. In fact, the position asserted by the United States represented an attempt to abolish the veto power over the OAS that Article 53 assigned to the Soviet Union.

---

[106]SCOR: 17th Yr., 993rd Mtg., 15 Mar. 1962, pp. 23–24. See also ibid. 998th Mtg., 23 Mar. 1962, p. 15.

[107]Ibid., 993rd Mtg., p. 14, and 998th Mtg., pp. 14–15, 29.

The case against permitting the Soviet veto to interfere with the operation of the OAS was also stated by several other members of the Council in such broad terms as to cast doubt upon their willingness to consider Article 53 a valid part of the Charter. Chile asserted, "We are considering whether the Council should approve or disapprove of those decisions [taken by the OAS foreign ministers at Punta del Este] or of *any others* which may be taken in the future,"[108] and replied in the negative. It conceded that Article 53 gave the Council competence to rule on regional military sanctions, but the logic of its argument was inimical to this as to any other impairment of the autonomy of the OAS. Similarly, China gave broad expression to the view that the Security Council must not be given the capacity to negate the activity of regional organizations.[109]

France went so far as to characterize the OAS sanctions against Cuba as "a matter of collective protection which is justified under *Article 51* of the Charter."[110] This ally of the United States thus seemed to be saying that the OAS was free to undertake enforcement measures of any variety without the approval of the Council; a restrictive interpretation of Article 53 and a broad interpretation of Article 51 would support the complete autonomy of the OAS vis à vis the Security Council. As for the United States, it did not deny that the restrictive interpretation of Article 53 it supported left the Soviet Union a residual veto power over the validation of regional military sanctions. It simply ignored this fact, and argued that the veto power should not operate against regional autonomy. This implied the necessity of the total elimination, not just the restriction, of the Soviet veto in matters affecting the OAS.[111]

On the specific issue of submitting questions relating to the case to the International Court of Justice, Cuba gained little support. The seven states that had expressed confidence that Article 53 did not give the Council competence to rule on the OAS sanctions voted solidly against resort to the Court, first in a separate vote on the paragraph dealing with that particular issue, and then on the remaining portions of the Cuban draft.[112] Although they presented various reasons for opposing this move, one may speculate that their central objection lay in the fact that they could not be certain of the Court's agreement with their position. The Court might be expected to base its opinion upon an analysis of Article 53, which could well lead to results favorable to the position stated by Cuba and the USSR. As a judicial body, it was unlikely to derive its opinion from the general political principle of regional autonomy, which formed the real basis of the pro-OAS position. What the United States and its friends required was an interpretation of the competence of the OAS based upon awareness of the political problems posed for them by communist tactics in the cold war, and disregarding the rules that had been formulated in 1945. They had made such an interpretation prevail in the Security Council, but they could have no assurance that the Court would similarly place general political considerations above textual analysis of the Charter. Hence, they prevented resort to the Court.

Far more genuinely than the Dominican case, the Cuban case in its March 1962 phase constituted a substantial victory for the United States demand that the Security Council be debarred from exercising control over the enforcement activities of the OAS.

The Cuban problem reached the crisis stage again in October 1962, when the United States reacted to the clandestine installation of Soviet missiles in Cuba by demanding their immediate removal and instituting a naval blockade directed against the continuation of the Soviet military build-up on the island. The Kennedy Administration secured the prompt collectivization of these unilateral measures by a resolution of the OAS Council calling upon all members of the Organization, in accordance with Articles 6 and 8 of the Rio Pact, to "take measures, individually and collectively, including the use of armed force," in support of the United States move.[113]

In this instance, the United States took the initiative in bringing the Security Council, as well

[108] Ibid., 994th Mtg., 16 Mar. 1962, p. 10. Italics added.

[109] Ibid., 995th Mtg., 20 Mar. 1962, pp. 6–7.

[110] Ibid., p. 13. Italics added.

[111] Ibid., 993rd Mtg., 15 Mar. 1962, pp. 14–15; 994th Mtg., 16 Mar. 1962, p. 6; 998th Mtg., 23 Mar. 1962, pp. 14–15, 29.

[112] Ibid., 998th Mtg., 23 Mar. 1962, pp. 21, 28.

[113] *Annual Report of the Secretary-General on the Work of the Organization, 16 June 1962–15 June 1963*, GAOR: 18th Sess., Suppl. No. 1, (A/5501), p. 44.

as the OAS, into the case; far from invoking the principle of regional privacy, it treated the crisis as essentially a confrontation of the Soviet Union and the United States, and asked that the resources of the United Nations be used to promote a solution that would avert the danger of catastrophic war. For the first time, the OAS had decreed *military* sanctions, but the United States had no thought of conceding that their validity was dependent upon approval by the Security Council under Article 53. If they had to be justified, this might be done by invoking Article 51, with a reading of "armed attack" expansive enough to include threats to peace and security. In fact, however, the United States argument rested upon the principle that the OAS must be considered an autonomous agency, entitled to protect the security of its region without hindrance from the United Nations. This episode provided the ultimate confirmation of the proposition that the real objective of the United States has not been the restrictive interpretation of Article 53, but its virtual repeal insofar as it purports to inhibit the operation of the OAS.

The Soviet Union picked up this point, denouncing the OAS sanctions as "a violation of the prerogatives of the Security Council, which alone could carry out enforcement measures,"[114] but the crisis was too grave to leave anyone an appetite for discussion of jurisdictional questions. The overriding urge to avoid a disastrous showdown took precedence and the meshing of United Nations and OAS involvement in the case facilitated the negotiation of a solution by the great powers. The crisis passed without serious attention being devoted to the ultimate implication of the United States position on the relationship between the OAS and the United Nations.

CONCLUSIONS

This analysis of the episodes in which the status of the OAS has been heated by argument and hammered into shape at the United Nations forge demonstrates above all the malleability of the Charter under the impact of political consid-

erations and political forces. For an understanding of what has happened, the analytical skill of the student of international politics is vastly more relevant than that of the international lawyer. The cold war has prevailed over the Charter; the latest adaptation of the Monroe Doctrine has relegated Article 53 to the ash heap of politically charred legal provisions; the fear of the Soviet veto has taken precedence over the principle that regional agencies should be subordinated to the United Nations.

Most of the political impetus for this transformation of the status of the OAS has been provided by the United States, which lagged behind and held back its fellow members of the Inter-American system in their drive for regional autonomy during the formative stages of the United Nations. The record shows a mixed pattern of victories and defeats for the United States in the pro-OAS campaign. The effort to establish the mandatory "Try OAS first" principle came to naught and was abandoned, in part because of the gradual diminution of Latin American support; after the Guatemalan case, the United States could find few friends, in the OAS or elsewhere, willing to endorse the view that American states were prohibited from appealing to the Security council, and the Council was barred from heeding their appeals, until the OAS had completed its action or inaction on their complaints. On the other hand, the United States succeeded, thanks largely to the steady growth of Latin American support, in emancipating OAS enforcement activity from United Nations control; after the Dominican case, the United States found an increasing number of friends, both in the OAS and outside, willing to endorse the view that Article 53 should not be so construed as to inhibit OAS activities against communist intrusions in the hemisphere. In the one case, the Latin American states refused to accept the restriction of their rights; in the other, they rallied to support the expansion of their rights as a regional group.

Fundamentally, this entire struggle over the OAS must be regarded as but a chapter in the larger volume of the cold war. A major feature of the general history of the United Nations is the persistent effort of the United States to deprive the Soviet Union of an effective veto power and of the Soviet Union to retain that power. In this

[114]Ibid., p. 42. The Security Council considered the Cuban crisis at its 1022nd to 1025th meetings, 23 to 25 Oct. 1962.

instance of the conflict over the veto, as in many others, the United States has succeeded. It may well be that the United States was able to attract greater support for releasing the OAS from the restriction of Article 53 than for expanding its jurisdictional rights under Article 52, precisely because the former did, and the latter did not, involve an attack upon the Soviet veto power. The Soviet Union's position in regard to the "Try OAS first" issue supported the competence of a majority in the Security Council to take action; its position with respect to Article 53 represented its claim of competence to veto action by the Council, and implied that all regional organizations were subject to the paralyzing impact of the veto power. Hence, it is not surprising that the Soviet Union was rebuffed in the latter case, rather than the former.

Throughout these cases, the Soviet Union appeared in the unusual role of champion of the rights and competence of the United Nations, while the United States was cast, in equally significant deviation from normal character, as the prime opponent of a strong and active world organization. No more striking demonstration can be found of the inexorable subordination of principle to policy in the operations of statesmen than was revealed by the United States in this set of cases. The United States did not repudiate the principle of the paramountcy of the United Nations in the international system, but it subordinated that principle to the necessity of gaining a free hand for combating communist infiltration in the Western Hemisphere. It did not renounce the principle of nonintervention, or of nonviolence except in self-defense, but it made these yield to what is regarded as vital policy considerations. It did not deny the principle of truthfulness and good faith, but, under the pressure of policy commitments, it misstated both its acts and its intentions with respect to communist-oriented regimes in the Caribbean area. It did not renounce the principle of the rule of law, but it protected its policy by constricting the provision of Article 53 that expressed the authority of the Security Council over the OAS, and insisted upon avoiding a judicial inquiry into the meaning of that provision.

The development of the relationship between the OAS and the United Nations confirms the proposition that the original project of per-

mitting and encouraging regional agencies to operate within a framework of United Nations supervision and control has broken down. The OAS has failed to achieve a monopolistic jurisdiction over disputes within its area, but, more importantly, the Security Council has lost any meaningful capacity to regulate or restrict the enforcement operations of the OAS. Broadly, these observations apply as well to other regional organizations dealing with political and security problems. These organizations have exhibited little interest in establishing jurisdictional priority over local disputes, and their members would probably resist any effort to restrict the right of access to the United Nations, just as the Latin Americans have done. With regard to enforcement measures, however, members of all regional agencies have an interest in escaping the control of the Security Council, and it is unlikely that the superior authority of the Council can be effectively applied to any regional body. In the era of the cold war, regional organizations are the chosen instruments of the great antagonists locked in political conflict. Those antagonists will not permit their instruments to be held in check by the United Nations.

Note: Only those sections of articles that are relevant to this study are reproduced in the appendices.

Appendix A

THE DUMBARTON OAKS PROPOSALS

Chapter VIII.
Arrangements for the Maintenance of International Peace and Security Including Prevention and Suppression of Aggression.

Section C: Regional Arrangements

1. Nothing in the Charter should preclude the existence of regional arrangements or agencies for dealing with such matters relating to the maintenance of international peace and security as are appropriate for regional action, provided such arrangements or agencies and their activities

are consistent with the purposes and principles of the Organization. The Security Council should encourage settlement of local disputes through such regional arrangements or by such regional agencies, either on the initiative of the states concerned or by reference from the Security Council.

2. The Security Council should, where appropriate, utilize such arrangements or agencies for enforcement action under its authority, but no enforcement action should be taken under regional arrangements or by regional agencies without the authorization of the Security Council.

3. The Security Council should at all times be kept fully informed of activities undertaken or in contemplation under regional arrangements or by regional agencies for the maintenance of international peace and security.

Appendix B

CHARTER OF THE UNITED NATIONS

Chapter VI.
Pacific Settlement of Disputes.

Article 33

1. The parties to any dispute, the continuance of which is likely to endanger the maintenance of international peace and security, shall, first of all, seek a solution by negotiation, enquiry, mediation, conciliation, arbitration, judicial settlement, resort to regional agencies or arrangements, or other peaceful means of their own choice.

2. The Security Council shall, when it deems necessary, call upon the parties to settle their dispute by such means.

Chapter VII.
Action With Respect to Threats to the Peace, Breaches of the Peace, and Acts of Aggression.

Article 51

Nothing in the present Charter shall impair the inherent right of individual or collective self-defense if an armed attack occurs against a Member of the United Nations, until the Security Council has taken the measures necessary to maintain international peace and security. Measures taken by Members in the exercise of this right of self-defense shall be immediately reported to the Security Council and shall not in any way affect the authority and responsibility of the Security Council under the present Charter to take at any time such action as it deems necessary in order to maintain or restore international peace and security.

Chapter VIII.
Regional Arrangements.

Article 52

1. Nothing in the present Charter precludes the existence of regional arrangements or agencies for dealing with such matters relating to the maintenance of international peace and security as are appropriate for regional action, provided that such arrangements or agencies and their activities are consistent with the Purposes and Principles of the United Nations.

2. The Members of the United Nations entering into such arrangements or constituting such agencies shall make every effort to achieve pacific settlement of local disputes through such regional arrangements or by such regional agencies before referring them to the Security Council.

3. The Security Council shall encourage the development of pacific settlement of local disputes through such regional arrangements or by such regional agencies either on the initiative of the states concerned or by reference from the Security Council.

4. This Article in no way impairs the application of Articles 34 and 35. . . .

Article 53

1. The Security Council shall, where appropriate, utilize such regional arrangements or agencies for enforcement action under its authority. But no enforcement action shall be taken under regional arrangements or by regional agencies without the authorization of the Security Council, with the exception of measures against any enemy state, as defined in paragraph 2 of this Article, provided for pursuant to Article 107 or in regional arrangements directed against renewal of aggressive policy on the part of any

such state, until such time as the Organization may, on request of the Governments concerned, be charged with the responsibility for preventing further aggression by such a state.

2. The term enemy state as used in paragraph 1 of this Article applies to any state which during the Second World War has been an enemy of any signatory of the present Charter.

Article 54

The Security Council shall at all times be kept fully informed of activities undertaken or in contemplation under regional arrangements or by regional agencies for the maintenance of international peace and security.

Appendix C

THE INTER-AMERICAN TREATY OF RECIPROCAL ASSISTANCE

Article 2

As a consequence of the principle set forth in the preceding Article, the High Contracting Parties undertake to submit every controversy which may arise between them to methods of peaceful settlement and to endeavor to settle any such controversy among themselves by means of the procedures in force in the Inter-American System before referring it to the General Assembly or the Security Council of the United Nations.

Appendix D

CHARTER OF THE ORGANIZATION OF AMERICAN STATES

Chapter IV.
Pacific Settlement of Disputes.

Article 20

All international disputes that may arise between American States shall be submitted to the peaceful procedures set forth in this Charter, before being referred to the Security Council of the United Nations.

Discussion and Questions

1. Elsewhere Claude has written that the choice between global and regional action depends upon "the nature of the problem to be dealt with":

> The advocacy of regionalism can be, and often is, as doctrinaire and as heedless of concrete realities as the passion for all-encompassing organization. It should be stressed that the suitability of regionalism depends in the first place upon the nature of the problem to be dealt with. Some problems of the modern world are international in the largest sense, and can be effectively treated only by global agencies. Others are characteristically regional, and lend themselves to solution by correspondingly delimited bodies. Still others are regional in nature, but require for their solution the mobilization of extra-regional resources. Thus, the control of armaments is pre-eminently a problem demanding global action; the interlocking of national railway systems is a proper subject for an organization of merely continental scope; and the economic development of Asia requires not simply the pooling of Asian poverty but the fertilization of Asian resources by vital contributions from the West.

The nature of a problem is significant not only for the determination of the most appropriate means of solution, but also for the measurement of the range of its impact. A problem may be regional in location, and susceptible of regional management, and yet have such important implications for the whole world as to make it a fit subject for the concern of a general organization. The world-at-large cannot be disinterested in such "regional" matters as the demographic problem in South Asia or the status of forced laborers in the Soviet bloc. Thus, the question of the ramifications of a problem as well as that of its intrinsic quality affects the choice between regional and universal approaches. [From *Swords into Plowshares: The Problems and Progress of International Organization*, 4th edition, revised, by Inis L. Claude, Jr. Copyright © 1956, 1959, 1964, 1971 by Inis L. Claude, Jr. Reprinted by permission of Random House, Inc.]

➤ In the OAS context, what is the nature of the linkage problem? Do problems vary with the particular circumstances of each region? ➤ Is the exclusion by force of Soviet missiles from the Western Hemisphere a regional problem? ➤ How about the carriage of Soviet missiles in the high seas of the Western Hemisphere? ➤ How about the exclusion of the United States missiles from Europe? ➤ Does it facilitate inquiry to allocate competence between regional and global actors by reference to the nature of the problem? ➤ What kind of decision process should govern this allocation of competence?

2. ➤ What are the special factors that characterize the operations of the OAS and differentiate it from other regional organizations? Certainly one special factor is the long tradition of United States hegemony over Latin American affairs and the struggle by Latin American diplomats to achieve political independence for their separate countries and for their region. It is important to appreciate that more is involved in this tradition than the preponderant power of the United States in hemispheric affairs; there is the self-serving presumption of "a special responsibility" exercised by the United States. This aura of quasi-legitimacy associated with the U.S. role in the hemisphere has a long history dating back to the unilateral enunciation of the Monroe Doc-

trine in a Presidential address by James Monroe in 1823. (For a full account of American practice under the Monroe Doctrine including its quasi-imperialistic aspects see Dexter Perkins, *A History of the Monroe Doctrine*, Little, Brown, Boston, 1955.)

Note that the original formulation of the Monroe Doctrine included an American gesture of reciprocity in the form of an undertaking to refrain from interference in European affairs as an exchange for the expectation (or insistence) of European noninterference in Latin American affairs. The high-water mark of quasi-legitimacy for the Monroe Doctrine was the approving reference to it in Article 21 of the Covenant of the League of Nations. In the 1930's the United States under the leadership of President Franklin Delano Roosevelt initiated the era of the Good Neighbor Policy. This policy was proclaimed by Washington as involving a rejection of earlier American policy and prerogative, an acceptance of the doctrine of nonintervention in intrahemispheric affairs, and the evolution of machinery for collective action on behalf of hemispheric defense. (For an official American account of the shift from unilateral to collective intervention, see the statement by Assistant Secretary of State Edward G. Miller, "Nonintervention and Collective Responsibility in the Americas," *U.S. Department of State Bulletin*, vol. 22, no. 567 [May 15, 1950], pp. 768–770.)

A critical account of the diplomacy of collective defense in Latin American affairs is provided by the careful and restrained comments of Jorgé Castaneda, a distinguished Mexican diplomat, in his article, "Pan Americanism and Regionalism: A Mexican View" (*International Organization*, vol. 10, no. 3 [August 1956], pp. 373–389). He maintains that the Rio Treaty states are losing sight of the original purposes of the collective-defense principle in two important respects. First, the enforcement measures provided in the treaty for use against external aggression and in collective defense are now being used as a means of pressure on regimes that offend the reactionary majority of Latin American republics. Second, recent regional action under United States leadership has been principally motivated by the "extra continental objectives" of the United States. Consider in this context Oran Young's analysis

(Part I) of the relationship between systemic and subsystemic behavior. ➤ Is Casteneda's critique persuasive? (For an exposé of the regional facade used to disguise unilateralism in relation to the overthrow of the Arbenz regime of Guatemala by CIA intervention in 1954, see Philip B. Taylor, Jr., "The Guatemalan Affair: A Critique of United States Foreign Policy," *American Political Science Review*, vol. 50, no. 3 [September 1956], pp. 787–806.)

Consider also Soviet diplomacy in East Europe. Note that both the intervention in Hungary in 1956 and the invasion of Czechoslovakia in 1968 rested on regionalist patterns of justification. In fact, the Czechoslovakian invasion was presented to the world as a collective undertaking of Warsaw Pact countries, with troops from Poland, East Germany, Bulgaria, and Hungary participating along with Soviet forces. But note, further, that the debates in the Security Council of the United Nations ignored the regional pretension and treated the invasion as a consequence of decision-making in Moscow. First enunciated in a *Pravda* commentary by Sergei Kovalev (September 26, 1968), for which an excerpt of the English version can be found in *Problems of Communism* (vol 17 [November–December 1968], p. 25), and then reiterated by Foreign Minister Andrei Gromyko before the United Nations General Assembly on October 3, 1968, the Brezhnev doctrine in effect denies the sovereignty and independence of any socialist country within reach of the Soviet Union by asserting Russia's region-wide right of intervention. The vital weakness of the Warsaw Pact as a partnership of independent states was underlined by the 1968 armed invasion of Czechoslovakia. The Pact was a mere formality, although Poland, East Germany, and Bulgaria each had its own statist reasons for supporting the Soviet initiative.

In an article entitled "The Johnson and Brezhnev Doctrines: The Law You Make May Be Your Own" (*Stanford Law Review*, vol. 22 [May 1970], pp. 979–1014), Thomas M. Franck and Edward Weisband point out that "virtually every concept of the Brezhnev Doctrine can be traced to an earlier assertion of identical rights by the United States vis-à-vis Latin America" (p. 980). ➤ Is there symmetry of treatment by the United Nations of "regional" uses of force in Soviet-dominated spheres of influence (or subsystems) and in United States-dominated spheres? ➤ Does the Western preponderance in the United Nations lead to asymmetry? ➤ Did the long period of exclusion of China from the United Nations (and the nonparticipation of North Vietnam) discourage serious debate on the Vietnam War from being heard before UN organs? ➤ Was the U.S. claim, especially in the 1965–67 period, to be fighting in Vietnam as a consequence of SEATO commitments persuasive?

3. Elaborate attempts were made after the Cuban missile crisis of 1962 to demonstrate the legality of the United States' action to interdict shipments of Soviet missiles by reference to regional instruments of authorization. Regional justifications and roles were developed by United States officials to vindicate a decision process that was notably unilateral and centered in Washington, D.C. (For a detailed account of this decision process, see Elie Abel, *The Missile Crisis* [Lippincott, Philadelphia, 1966]. This actual pattern of decision needs to be contrasted with regional patterns of justification. One formulation of the official contention that the interdiction of Soviet missiles represented a valid claim of regional security was developed by Leonard C. Meeker, then Deputy Legal Adviser to the Secretary of State of the U.S. Government, in "Defense Quarantine and the Law" (*American Journal of International Law*, vol. 57, no 3 [July 1963], pp. 515–524, at 516–518).

4. ➤ How would you propose dealing with security at the regional level? ➤ What are the "rights" of the Arab League against Israel, of the OAU against South Africa? ➤ Can the United Nations authorize a regional organization to use coercive means on its behalf? ➤ Does the prospect for improved coordination between regional and global efforts to achieve international security depend upon better procedures for authorization? ➤ Does improvement depend upon delegitimizing the claims of hegemonial regionalism to be reflective of the will of the regional community? ➤ Can we make a useful distinction between genuine and spurious regionalism? ➤ By what criteria would such a distinction be drawn? What organs should be authorized to draw the distinction? Is such a change in the status of regional action feasible given the present character of

international society? ➤ What social and political changes would make it feasible? ➤ Is there any reason for juridical reform, for example, amending the relevant provisions of the United Nations Charter?

5. It seems clear that there are positive roles for regional organizations in the security area, especially as agencies for the peaceful resolution of intraregional disputes. The OAU's contribution, for instance, to the resolution of some intra-African boundary disputes illustrates the positive potentialities for regional actors. (For an account of African boundary disputes, see Robert O. Matthews, "Interstate Conflicts in Africa: A Review," *International Organization*, vol. 24, no. 2 [Spring 1970], pp. 335–360, at pp. 339–344; Patricia Berko Wild, "The Organization of African Unity and the Algerian-Moroccan Border Conflict: A Study of New Machinery for Peacekeeping and for the Peaceful Settlement of Disputes Among African States," *International Organization*, vol. 20, no. 1 [Winter 1966], pp. 18–36.)

6. Johan Galtung has proposed that the United Nations create regional security commissions that would operate in roughly parallel fashion to the regional economic commissions that we will consider below. We print here a substantial extract from Galtung's paper, "Regional Security Commissions under the United Nations," for your consideration:

> . . . we now propose a *United Nations' system of regional security commissions,* standing in the same relation to the Security Council of the UN*, as the regional economic commissions (ECE in Geneva for Europe, ECLA in Santiago de Chile for Latin America, ECA in Addis Ababa for Africa, and ECAFE in Bangkok for Asia) have to ECOSOC, the Economic and Social Council. Thus, we are suggesting an SCE, SCLA, SCA, and SCAFE. However, to develop the argument further we shall proceed here only discussing the Security Commissions

for Europe, SCE, and later return to the other commissions and put them in a more global perspective.

To start with the arguments just discussed in connection with ENDC: it is obvious that a major reason for establishing a UN security commission for Europe would be that it would give a UN setting to the discussion of intra-European problems, thus permitting Europeans to arrive at a solution to their problems without necessarily having to adjust formulae to the conditions prevailing in other parts of the world. At the same time it will neutralize long-time tendencies towards the formation of an all-European super power by launching security cooperation solidly within the UN context. There would of course be a system of reporting procedures to the UN and coordination with the security commissions in other parts of the world, but this coordination would take place at a higher level and consequently constitute less of an impediment to efforts to arrive at intra-European agreements.

A fundamental point in this connection would be that the *launching* of a security commission could take place without the least threat to the existing power alliances. SCE would be a meeting ground for discussion, for the elaboration of technical background papers and position papers, and for highly gradualistic and often very implicit moves that may some time in the future lead to the abolition of the alliances. Thus, SCE would not in any sense in the beginning constitute any threat to the vested interests, in the East or West power blocs. SCE would constitute the missing setting within which the two power blocs could meet together with the non-aligned countries in Europe (all together ten countries that are not today members of the military alliances), *in other words serve the same function for security matters as the ECE serves for economic matters.* It is hoped that the net outcome will be not only convergence but some type of positive interdependence. The basic factor is only that this type of institution, the umbrella under which the parties could meet to discuss security matters is today missing in Europe.

Any *ad hoc* secretariat for meetings between the NATO powers and the Warsaw Pact powers would not constitute an alternative solution, partly because it would leave out ten European powers, some of them highly important, and partly because meetings of this type

---

*This would, as far as we can see, be in agreement with the UN Charter, Ch. 8, paragraphs 52, 53, and 54. Some consultations with specialists in international law do not seem to warrant the conclusion that any major revisions of the Charter would be necessary. On the contrary, the institutions suggested seem to fit easily into the general pattern of relations between the UN and the regions of the world.

would only play up to the cold war structure and activate fears and antagonisms. It would probably also put in the foreground the more adamant and rigid personalities at the head of either alliance. There is certainly also this danger in connection with SCE, but the tensions would be somewhat alleviated through the presence of the non-aligned countries, and because *countries* would be members rather than *alliances*.

On the other hand, the alliances should probably from the very beginning be invited as observers or as associate members (just as domestic organizations today very often have both individual members and charter members). Here the parallel with the ECE as a meeting ground for OECD and CEV is quite convincing: one could use this mechanism to bring the alliances closer together, and also as a way of bringing West German and East German experts and politicians within debating distance as members of intergovernmental delegations. Moreover, there are precedents for commission members not having to be members of the UN. Neither West Germany nor Switzerland are UN members, yet West Germany is a member of ECE and Switzerland is a consultant to the secretariat.

[Furthermore,] East Germany is not granted any form of ECE membership and it is a telling reflection of some element of Western dominance that the unequal treatment of the two Germanies in the ECE comes out in favor of the Germany aligned to the West. In our opinion it would have been far better if both of them had been given a status corresponding to the status of Switzerland until some more lasting formula for the German problem can be found.

But the point in this connection is of course that both Germanies should be given *some*, and *equal* status in a Security Commission for Europe, otherwise discussions of security in Europe become somewhat less than realistic. One may argue that the percentage DDR makes of the "security budget" for Europe (however that should be measured) is higher than the score on any economic budget—and this should in itself constitute a major reason for finding a more acceptable formula than participation in Warsaw Pact delegations.†

---

†Correspondingly, The People's Republic of China must be given a status within the framework of any Security Commission for Asia and the Far East.

So much about the composition. Precisely what should the Security Commission for Europe do?

First of all, it would have a secretariat, probably in Geneva. This secretariat would obviously draw on the experience, and to some extent also on the personnel of the modest ENDC organization. The secretariat would to a large extent function as a "peace research" or a "security research" institute, investigating past experiences, elaborating present proposals, and opening for future visions–"security" all the time being taken in a relatively broad sense. The experiences accumulated by such organizations as the Pugwash conferences, SIPRI in Stockholm, PRIO in Oslo, and the Institute for Strategic Studies in London would be of significance in this connection because of the international nature of these four organizations. It goes without saying that the whole undertaking would be meaningless unless the secretariat had a fairly international composition, with due representation of the various subregional groupings. As for ECE its Secretary General would have to come from a non-aligned European country or at least be a highly non-aligned person from an aligned country. Also, there is a need for high calibre military and non military expertise, and certainly more of a need for imagination of a very creative kind than usually seems to be acknowledged.

Second, the secretariat would prepare the ground for arms control and disarmament measures between NATO and Warsaw Pact powers in Europe, all the time taking into consideration how intimately such measures have to be related to the transition from a non-war structure to a peace structure in general. This is another reason for tying the discussions to the UN system, since the flow of communication between ECE and SCE is extremely important in this connection. Thus, it may well be that in the SCE secretariat ideas would emerge about the future economic structure of Europe, and be referred to appropriate bodies via the SCE/ECE channel of communications, and also from other organizations security aspects would be referred to the SCE for their consideration.

Among proposals which could be discussed even at earlier stages, are the various plans to freeze, thin out, or empty completely various zones for their military loading in general and their nuclear loading in particular. It would include the exchange of observation posts between two lower blocs, joint manning of inspection systems, etc. The secretariat would be a setting for permanent, technical discussions of such matters, resulting in various types of proposals.

Third, the secretariat would serve as the organization that could and should prepare the ESC, the *European Security* Conference suggested by the socialist countries. One objection against this conference has been that it would mainly serve as a forum for voicing propaganda of one variety or another. Hence, it has been argued, such a conference should be very well prepared, with some agreements reached in advance so that the conference would not just be an empty, top level performance. It has been argued that the socialist countries have a tendency to be somewhat ritualistic in this matter, to confuse the simultaneous presence of a number of heads of government or heads of state around the green table, and the signature of a mutually agreed declaration, with real solid substance.

Although one should not underestimate the psychological importance of having such meetings, this type of argument seems generally to be well taken. Obviously, SCE would be the appropriate organization for the preparation of background papers as well as for providing an informal forum through which agreements could have been reached in advance. At this point experiences from ECE seem to be important: there is no setting where the socialist countries have participated so eagerly and with such willingness, and this seems to a large extent to be due to the fact that there is no other setting in which there has been a built-in symmetry in the participation. Any use of the Western, sub-regional organizations automatically leads to some kind of Western dominance, and this is also to a large extent the case in the more universal UN organizations since the socialist countries, constituting about 1/3 of the European countries, are conspicuously in a minority in that global setting.

There is however, a second objection in connection with ESC that should also be considered: the participation of the United States. The Western countries have by and large maintained that the US presence is a *sine qua non*. The impression from the Eastern countries is that the objection against US participation is less strong than one might have been led to believe, and it does not appear far-fetched to imagine that a solution could be found

along the following lines. USA would be given membership in the SCE, but not full membership. Thus, if thirty European powers agreed that a point on the agenda should be considered an intra-European matter not requiring US presence, then they might well say that US should be considered a non-member where that point is concerned. But if there seems to be general agreement that US military, political, and not to say economic pressure in Europe for all practical purposes makes it a European power, then there is probably little doubt that US should be present for most discussion. Also, one could weight the voting procedure in favor of US presence, for instance requiring a 2/3 majority in favor of excluding US from a point on the agenda. It should be noted that there are some similarities between the structure of Finland's cooperation with the EFTA countries and this proposal.‡

Fourth, it should not be excluded that a security commission for Europe would not only deal with matters of regulation and reduction, in other words with *institutional distrust*, but with matters of *security cooperation*. Small powers in Europe, in the light of recent events, might decide that they have common interests that could be articulated in a common peace keeping force, leaving big powers out. In general one would assume that military cooperation, once political willingness exists, would be more easy than economic cooperation for the simple reason that the military structure is relatively similar all over the world. Such peace keeping forces might also grow out of the experience from joint manning of observation posts.§

---

‡This is developed in more detail in *Cooperation in Europe*, see particularly para. 153. Of course there are also arguments for including Canada in the SCE, which would mean that SCE for all practical purposes would define a region stretching from and to the Bering Strait encompassing most of the industrialized world—with Japan as a noticeable exception. And this is perhaps a much more realistic conception of a region than the classical conception from elementary school geography text books. See Johan Galtung, "On the Future of the International System," *Journal of Peace Research*, 1967, pp. 305-333.

§Of course, the experience with peace keeping forces so far points to important limitations in the use of this instrument, and it tends to freeze rather than to solve any conflict. And it tends to be used only under certain conditions: either in non-aligned nations, or in aligned nations to preserve superpower hegemony. US intervention in the Dominican Republic, with the cooperation

Needless to say, this latter point is for the future. It would probably be a concomitant of the gradual dissolution of the power blocs which is inevitable: so far the world has not seen any eternal military balance. Obviously, such joint capabilities constitute major problems, and some words will have to be added about this.

5. *A system of regional UN security commissions*

In our view the growing interdependence among industrial and post-industrial nations is of such a nature that symbiotic relations will be established in the Northern hemisphere whether these nations like it or not. Scientific and technological cooperation are necessities for nations that want to develop along such roads. Economic cooperation is an almost necessary consequence. Security cooperation is the missing link, and we have been arguing that this is to a large extent due to a faulty organizational network: there is simply no organization dealing with cooperation in this field.

But if this type of interdependence is going to come anyhow, then it is better to assure that the security aspect of the cooperation is from the very beginning placed solidly within the UN network, in order to regulate the type of inter-regional conflicts that we may very easily grow into in the 1970's. Probably, we shall have a number of military regional systems by that time. The OEA system (referred to in the US as O.A.S.) in the Western hemisphere, based on the 1947 Rio de Janeiro treaty, will in all likelihood break up due to excessive U.S. domination. But experiences derived from it, and some of its structure will probably be used to put together an organization of Latin American states with its own security organization. For Africa there is the O.A.U. with headquarters in Addis Ababa and it is not inconceivable

that this organization sometime in the 1970's will have gained sufficient unity and military experience from its fights against the white redoubt in Southern Africa to constitute a power of some significance. Correspondingly, there is the O.A.S. (Organization of Arab States, the Arab League) and the stage is thereby almost set for a violent confrontation between the non-Arab members of the O.A.U. and O.A.S., with the conflict border among other places running somewhere in the Sudan. It is only Asia that so far is deficient in security cooperation, mainly due to the highly pluralistic colonization pattern in that area with most European colonial powers, as well as the United States and Japan having played the role of colonial rulers.

Thus, the stage is set for an extremely dangerous structure, particularly since our experience so far seems to be that *the bigger the units the bigger the wars.* Just as much as regional integration will lead to increased security within the region, it can also lead to increased insecurity between the regions, and the latter may be increasingly catastrophic the bigger the regions. So far the regions we are discussing have devoted much of their energy to discuss, fight, and solve internal conflicts. But that will not last forever, and the more these conflicts are solved, the closer may we come to a new danger point of an even higher order.

For these reasons it is highly to be regretted that the security systems currently found in the West and in the East not only have a non-UN but even an anti-UN character. This was witnessed particularly well in connection with the American intervention in the Dominican Republic, where the O.E.A. was used to monopolize security matters and to keep the UN out,‖ just as the Warsaw Pact was used in connection with Hungary in 1956 and Czechoslovakia in 1968, and an attempt made to use the NATO system in the Cyprus crisis in 1964 and the Greek crisis in 1967. Thus, there is the double danger, both of the emergence of regional super powers, and of the continued feudalization of the international system by means of

---

of the FIP powers (Fuerza interamericana de la paz) and Soviet intervention in Czechoslovakia, with the cooperation of the Warsaw Pact powers, are good examples of the latter; the well-known UN operations of the former. If past experience is a guide this means that peace keeping cooperation of this kind might be adequate as a protection of one non-aligned country against another. But there would be difficulties as soon as aligned powers were involved. A peace keeping force of this kind could not be used to maintain hegemony within a sub-regional bloc, but it could possibly some time in the future be used to resist such hegemonial tendencies. However, many changes in the international system and atmosphere would be needed before such patterns could emerge.

‖ USA uses the same tactics in far more peaceful fields. Thus, there is a tendency to ignore statistics for Latin America, compiled by UN organizations in general, and ECLA in particular, and base reports, policy recommendations and decisions on OEA statistics (Juan Bosch, in a private communication).

superpower or big power manipulation within a security "sphere of interest."

In our mind both are extremely strong arguments for an internationalization of regional security matters, starting with a system of security commissions. Moreover, such a system, which may sound utopian in its ultimate consequences (intra-regional regulation, inter-regional coordination through the UN), nevertheless puts very few requirements on the international system as far as the first few steps are concerned. Thus, the commissions would not be financially costly since they could very well start with relatively small secretariats. Nor would they have to be politically costly since they would not immediately presuppose the dissolution of any power bloc or existing system. E.C.L.A. in Santiago de Chile has had considerable influence on the economic policy of the region by its mere existence, for instance by means of standardization of statistics and economic data in general. The security commissions could have similar influence.

There is of course the problem of how regional UN security commissions could at all be created, given the existence of non-UN security arrangements. However, this is perhaps less problematical than it may seem.

Thus, in *Europe* neither NATO, nor the Warsaw Pact will pretend to be more than sub-regional, and a concert between the two —although extremely powerful—would also have to realize that one cannot solve security problems in Europe without the non-aligned nations. Any effort to do so over their heads may easily lead to a *rapprochement* between these nations and a new, although admittedly interesting, division of Europe. Hence, in Europe a security commission would be peace-building by bridging gaps and bringing in other elements, and already existing alliances are no valid substitutes.

In *Latin America* a security commission would be a completely new creation and in our mind be peace-building not by bridging gaps but by creating more autonomy for the Latin American nations, making them more equal partners to North America thus building up the condition of symmetry. The commission might be located in Santiago, Chile, and stand in much the same relation to ECLA as we have recommended for SCE relative to ECE.

Africa is the only continent where there is already an organization that comes very close to what we have in mind. It is set up by the Africans themselves, but with clear UN attachments. Perhaps the solution in that case would be to ask Africans whether the OAU, or parts of it, as it stands or somewhat modified, could carry out the task of a security commission for Africa. At any rate, to set up a parallel machinery would clearly be a waste of resources so some solution along such lines would have to be found.

In a sense the most problematic region is *Asia* since there is such a complex web of security arrangements in that part of the world and since the major Asian power has been kept outside the UN system. However, we see this as a pro- rather than as a contra- argument for launching an institution where security could be discussed in an egalitarian manner, as free as possible from the machinations of outside powers. Thus, it might be a good idea to stipulate that no power can be a member of more than one regional security commission to avoid multiplication of big power influence through multiple memberships justified by "presence" in the region. This would then serve to keep. . . the US, Soviet Union, Britain and France out since they would all, presumably prefer to be members of the SCE. As already mentioned, some solution to the problem of representation of the People's Republic of China, as well as both Vietnams and both Koreas must be found, and this problem may be given a new start in a new institution. The SCAFE should be located in a non-aligned Asian country.

CONCLUSION

Of course there is admittedly no guarantee that these low political and financial costs would necessarily be coupled with high dividends. It is quite possible that the security commission might develop into discussion forums and relatively academic research institutes, # with little or no impact on decision-making. But even if this were the case in the beginning, they would constitute the logical setting for confrontation between major power

---

The UN is weak on security/disarmament research, partly because there is no strong unit of this kind in the Secretariat and partly because there has not been any agreement so far to use UNITAR for that purpose. The regional security commissions might constitute a new start in that direction.

blocs once the political atmosphere has been created for such confrontations. And it seems in itself to be a sufficiently strong argument to warrant some initiative in this field. And, much further ahead in the future, the world might perhaps be prepared for a global rather than a set of regional security arrangements when the regions tend to wither away and the world society emerges as a web of social, economic, political and cultural interaction tying nations and people much more tightly together than today. [From an article prepared for a conference of research directors of the World Order Models Project.]

14

The UN Regional Economic Commissions and Integration in the Underdeveloped Regions

ROBERT W. GREGG

It is the purpose of this article to examine the role which the three regional economic commissions of the United Nations serving the developing world[1] play, whether consciously or unconsciously, in promoting integration within the regions which they serve. The emphasis is upon economic integration, not because it is more important than political union or federation or because it is a necessary antecedent to political integration. No attempt is made here to establish the thesis that the relationshop between economic and political integration is that of a continuum.[2] Any contribution which the UN regional economic commissions make to regional or subregional integration will almost certainly be in the economic area, given their terms of reference, the nature of their work programs, and the environmental conditions in which they operate. Economic integration resulting from ideas and initiatives originating in the regional commissions *may* contribute to the evolution of political union.

In this context integration may be defined as the transformation of an international subsystem in a direction in which more weight is accorded to decisions and actions in the name of the aggregate of actors. In other words, the nation-state ceases to be an autonomous decision-making unit with respect to certain important policies; the locus of economic problem solving is to some extent shifted from the state to an intergovernmental or supranational body.[3]

---

[1]The Economic Commission for Latin America (ECLA), the Economic Commission for Asia and the Far East (ECAFE), and the Economic Commission for Africa (ECA).

[2]For a recent discussion of this relationship see Ernst B. Haas and Philippe C. Schmitter, "Economics and Differential Patterns of Political Integration: Projections About Unity in Latin America," *International Organization,* Autumn 1964 (Vol. 18, No. 4), pp. 705–737.

[3]This definition is adapted from that employed by Haas, which focuses on political integration. See, for example, Ernst B. Haas, "International Integration: The European and the Universal Process," *International*

From *International Organization,* vol. 20, no. 2, Spring 1966, pp. 208–232. Copyright 1966, World Peace Foundation, Boston, Mass. Reprinted by special permission.

The role of the regional economic commission in this process is difficult to assess. It is only one of several agents which may inspire integrative experiments; what it promotes could often more accurately be described as cooperation, which is clearly a much more modest relationship than integration. However, if the commission has a thrust which is regional in scope and emphasis and if it contributes to a way of thinking about economic problems which permits and encourages the delegation of more authority to some new and larger center, then the commission may be said to have an integrative output.

THE UN SETTING

Article 68 of the United Nations Charter provides for the creation of commissions under the aegis of the Economic and Social Council (ECOSOC) and suggests functional criteria for their establishment. The legislative history of the Charter reveals little interest in spatially as opposed to functionally defined institutions in the economic field.[4] However, it was not long after San Francisco that the UN embarked upon a policy of regionalization in the economic sphere, a step neither invited nor precluded by the Charter. The rationale for the creation of the first commission, the Economic Commission for Europe, was postwar reconstruction. In an early instance of UN coalition politics, however, the Asian and Latin American states engaged in some effective logrolling which led to the creation of commissions for each of those regions over the opposition of Western European and North American Members.[5] Thus,

by March of 1948 the UN had created three regional economic commissions,[6] had laid the foundation for honoring the claims of other regions,[7] and had broadened the mission of these commissions from reconstruction to economic development.

In effect, the regional economic commissions, while subsidiary organs of a universal international organization, are in a very real sense regional organizations with all that that fact implies with respect to relative environmental homogeneity. What is more, they are not regional replicas of the parent organization. They are more limited in purpose, embracing the economic and social tasks of the United Nations but not, in any direct fashion, its tasks in the fields of peace and security, self-determination, or human rights. Whereas the UN itself has been characterized by several historic phases,[8] a manifestation of environmental instability which has militated against integrative precedents, the regional commissions have been buffeted much less directly and obviously by the shifting winds of cold-war and colonial conflict. Although the commissions have not been guaranteed an integrative impact by their locations in the sheltered coves of relatively greater environmental stability, the absence of environmental phases, coupled with the exclusively economic and social content of their terms of reference, has facilitated comparatively stable agreement within the commissions on the tasks which are to receive primary attention.

Furthermore, the commissions enjoy a considerable amount of institutional independence from the parent organization. It is true that in a formal sense they are very much an integral part of the United Nations. Their budgets are a part of the

Organization, Summer 1961 (Vol. 15, No. 3), pp. 366–367. See also the related definition, also derived from Haas, employed by Jean Siotis. "*Integration occurs when consensus formation tends to become the dominant characteristic of relations among actors in a system.*" (Jean Siotis, "The Secretariat of the United Nations Economic Commission for Europe and European Economic Integration: The First Ten Years," *International Organization*, Spring 1965 [Vol. 19, No. 2], p. 178.)

[4]The question is probed in a recent book by Robert W. Macdonald, *The League of Arab States* (Princeton, N.J.: Princeton University Press, 1965), Chapter 1.

[5]For a description of debates and bargaining which led to the creation of ECE, ECAFE, and ECLA, see David Wightman, *Toward Economic Cooperation in Asia: The United Nations Economic Commission for Asia and the Far East* (New Haven, Conn: Yale University Press, 1963), Chapter 2.

[6]ECE was established under ECOSOC Resolution 36 (IV) of March 28, 1947; ECAFE under ECOSOC Resolution 37 (IV) of March 28, 1947; and ECLA under ECOSOC Resolution 106 (VI) of February 25, 1948.

[7]The Economic Commission for Africa was established under ECOSOC Resolution 671 A and B (XXV) of April 29, 1958. Establishment of a commission for the Middle East has been considered and would almost certainly have been accomplished were it not for the enduring schism between the Arab states and Israel.

[8]For a discussion of these historic phases see Ernst B. Haas, "Dynamic Environment and Static System: Revolutionary Regimes in the United Nations," in Morton Kaplan (ed.) *The Revolution in World Politics* (New York: John Wiley & Sons, 1962), pp. 267–309.

UN budget; their staffs are part of the staff of the UN's Department of Economic and Social Affairs, subject to the same rules and regulations; their Executive Secretaries are selected by the Secretary-General. Their terms of reference, which are quite modest in scope, specify that they shall act within the framework of UN policies and under the general supervision of the Economic and Social Council.[9] But these limitations are deceptive. In practice the commissions have more discretion than their terms of reference suggest and consequently more capacity for taking initiatives, independently of New York, appropriate to the needs of the region. This independence should not be exaggerated. But it is an important fact, one which makes it possible to speak of the commissions as agencies which may have an ideology and a thrust of their own, shaped to some extent by their UN connection but not so inhibited by it as to deny them a distinct influence upon the regions they serve.

Although each commission has developed its own distinctive style and carved out its own areas of emphasis, all have experienced an expansion of tasks and a gradual strengthening of their positions within their respective regions. This shifting role was the theme of some remarks by Philippe de Seynes, Under Secretary for Economic and Social Affairs, which are quite revealing of the gulf between the thinking of headquarters and that of the regional centers.

> So far as the regional commissions are concerned, we were more or less dominated, over a long period, by a way of thinking which doubtless originated in a desire to simplify and clarify matters. According to that way of thinking, the regional economic commissions were organs which should devote themselves to research and study and which should be barred from what are termed operational activities.[10]

Intergovernmental study groups, serviced by secretariats performing research and conference machinery functions, would almost certainly not have been in a position to make much of an impact upon their regions. But the commissions, in every case but to varying degrees, have exceeded this minimalist level of involvement in the affairs of their respective regions. There are several explanations for their strength,[11] but in essence ECLA, ECAFE, and ECA have grown and assumed more importance both within the UN system and within their respective regions because they are a product of that system and perform an essential function within it.

This phenomenon is attributable to the environmental changes which have transformed the international system since the Korean War and the comparatively stark bipolarity of the UN's early years. The tacit agreement to encapsulate[12] the more destructive levels of cold-war conflict; the pronounced increase in the number of independent underdeveloped states; the emergence of a crude UN party system which is, to a very considerable extent, a multiregional system; the evolution to paramountcy of the economic tasks on the UN's long agenda; the resultant increase in opportunities for bargaining among the UN's "parties"—all of these interrelated factors have contributed to the strengthening of the regional economic commissions. The recent campaign to decentralize authority for some UN economic and social programs from Headquarters to the regional commissions may be viewed as a natural culmination of these changes in the environment within which the UN system functions.[13] Regional groups

---

[9]Their terms of reference may be found in annexes to the annual reports of the commissions to ECOSOC. For recently amended versions, see Economic and Social Council *Official Records* (37th session), Supplement No. 2, Annex III (ECAFE); Supplement No. 4, Annex III (ECLA); Supplement No. 7, Annex III (ECE); and Supplement No. 10, Annex III (ECA).

[10]UN Document E/CN.12/572, March 5, 1961, pp. 1–2.

[11]One UN official, a long-time observer of the commissions, attributes it to the inclusive character of their membership within their respective regions; their tendency to act by agreement rather than by voting; a self-imposed discipline which induces them to behave in accordance with Charter principles and Assembly and ECOSOC resolutions; and a marked degree of regional consciousness and solidarity. See W. R. Malinowski, "Centralization and Decentralization in the United Nations Economic and Social Activities," *International Organization*, Summer 1962 (Vol. 16, No. 3), pp. 523–524.

[12]The term is Amitai Etzioni's. See his article "On Self-Encapsulating Conflicts," *Journal of Conflict Resolution*, September 1964 (Vol. 8, No. 3), pp. 242–255.

[13]For a more detailed discussion of decentralization, see the author's chapter "Program Decentralization and the Regional Economic Commissions" in [G. J. Mangone (ed.), *UN Administration of Economic and Social Programs* (New York: Columbia University Press, 1966)].

have quite naturally tended to upgrade in importance those UN structures which are most conspicuously their own, whose secretariats have consciously been given a regional coloration, whose announced purposes correspond most closely with their own perceptions of the UN's most important tasks. The commissions have not only acquired a symbolic importance; they have also become vehicles whereby the claims of developing states upon the UN could be articulated with the assistance of a professional secretariat attuned to the interests of the region. They are peculiarly agencies for action of the region, by the region, and for the region.

THE REGIONAL SETTING

What each of the regional economic commissions has sought to accomplish and what it has achieved have been conditioned in large measure by the regional context in which it has had to work. Is there a tradition of thinking about the region as a unit? Is the geographical scope of the region natural or artificial? What are the economic, social, and political conditions which prevail within the region? To what extent is it characterized by industrialization and economic diversification? How much functional similarity exists among units? What conditions prevail with respect to such variables as elite complementarity? All of these considerations enter into any assessment of the prospects for integration.[14]

The Economic Commission for Europe, for example, is distinguishable from the other commissions in that it serves a region which, for all the vicissitudes of European interstate relations, has traditionally been described as a community. As Jean Siotis has noted in a recent and perceptive essay on the role of ECE,[15] the central task for the Commission has been to prevent the disintegration of Europe into two implacably hostile and self-contained regions. The main element in

the organizational ideology of the first Executive Secretary, Gunnar Myrdal, was his belief that ECE should be used as a bridge of functional cooperation between East and West, and that it should strenuously resist all efforts to institutionalize within ECE the rift between the two blocs. The Secretariat's problem was to find specific tasks which could fan the flickering flame of "Europe." The other three regional commissions, which are the primary concern of this article, have had a somewhat different problem. Fragmentation has, of course, accompanied decolonization, especially in Africa; but a sense of community had not been a characteristic of these areas, and so a principal task of the commissions has been to assist in the creation of such a sense of community, rather than to prevent the collapse of a previously existing one.

Moreover, these regions, quite aside from their lack of historical cohesiveness, are to varying degrees artificial in the geographic sense. Much the most arbitrary of the regions is Asia and the Far East. ECAFE's domain extends from Iran to Western Samoa and from Mongolia to New Zealand; Saudi Arabia and Israel have recently requested membership. Surely this is a single region in name only, appropriate perhaps for an administrative subdivision of the UN but not as a candidate for economic or political integration. The Economic Commission for Africa serves a region which looks more logical on the map but which is really an amalgamation of several regions, including the very dissimilar areas separated by the vast expanse of the Sahara. ECLA's domain, extending from the Rio Grande and the Straits of Florida to Tierra del Fuego, is also geographically arbitrary, a fact recognized by the division of the area into two subregions, with a main office in Santiago and a subregional office for Central America in Mexico City.

More significant than either the absence of a regional tradition or the presence of unwieldy regional boundaries are the economic, social, and political conditions prevailing in each region. The environmental conditions necessary for political integration are more exacting than those for economic union, but there would appear to be a relationship between successful economic integration and such factors, identified by Ernst Haas, as comparability of unit size and power and of pluralism plus elite complementarity and the rate of transaction among units. If recent experiences

---

[14]Conditions conducive to integration are discussed, *inter alia*, in Haas and Schmitter, *International Organization*, Vol. 18, No. 4, pp. 705-737; Haas, *International Organization*, Vol. 15, No. 3, pp. 366-392; and the recent book by Haas, *Beyond the Nation-State: Functionalism and International Organization* (Stanford, Calif: Stanford University Press, 1964).

[15]Siotis, *International Organization*, Vol. 19, No. 2, pp. 177-202.

with integration yield any lesson, it is that urban-industrial societies with a relatively high level of economic diversification are better candidates for more rapid progress toward union than are underdeveloped, monocultural societies. Ironically, the integration movements in Europe, where optimal environmental conditions exist, are probably an important factor in spurring experimentation with economic unions in areas which otherwise fail to meet some of the criteria for integration. In spite of this incentive and that supplied by a shared state of underdevelopment and discouragingly slow progress toward overcoming it, the regions served by ECLA, ECAFE, and ECA do not present a profile conducive to economic union or even to very elaborately institutionalized cooperation. Some subregional clusters of states may constitute more promising laboratories for integration, but all are defective on one or more important counts. Although any generalization is differentially applicable among the regions, it is safe to state that the great majority of states within all three regions tend to be economically dependent upon a very few primary commodities and to trade predominantly with states outside the region.[16]

THE REGIONAL ECONOMIC COMMISSIONS

The environmental setting in which each of the three regional commissions exists would appear to be unpromising for economic, much less political, integration. This does not mean, however, that the commissions have not engaged in activities or promoted policies which may be described as integrative. It is the function of the following analysis to identify the integrative output of ECLA, ECAFE, and ECA.[17]

---

[16]For statistical data on these and other indicators, see Bruce Russett and others, *World Handbook of Political and Social Indicators* (New Haven, Conn: Yale University Press, 1964). For useful classification schemes, see Gabriel Almond and James S. Coleman, *The Politics of the Developing Areas* (Princeton, N.J.: Princeton University Press, 1960). For data on trade, see, *inter alia*, Robert M. Stern, "Policies for Trade and Development," *International Conciliation*, May 1964 (No. 548), and the sources cited therein.

[17]Many of the judgments made in the following sections are based upon interviews with UN Secretariat

Integrative output of a regional commission is shaped, to a very considerable extent, by the political and economic forces which operate upon that commission. Governments bring to the regional commissions different perceptions of national interest and different attitudes toward institutionalized forms of regional cooperation. Although a commission may pursue policies at variance with the preferences of some of its members, the integrative output of a commission is not likely to be significantly greater than the receptivity to integration of the commission's members. Integrative output is thus a product of an international secretariat which can articulate nascent interest in the idea of integration, synthesize diverse policies and proposals with an integrative content, and otherwise supply creative leadership. The focus here is primarily upon what the commissions, and more particularly their secretariats, do rather than on the policy inputs of member governments.

Several questions may be asked in order to facilitate judgment of the integrative output of the regional economic commissions.

1. What has been the ideology of the leadership of the regional commission? Has it been significantly oriented toward economic problem solving at a level higher than that of the nation-state?

2. What has been the degree of initiative assumed by the commission secretariat for skewing the work program of the commission in a regional direction?

3. What has been the institutional legacy of the commission's activities? Is there a residue of organizations or programs with regional or subregional outlook which are thriving?

4. What has been the flow of regionally minded commission secretariat personnel into positions of influence within individual states and especially into government posts with planning responsibilities?

5. What has been the centripetal pull of the commission itself as a source of regional pride and purpose? Is there evidence of growth of respect for

---

personnel at Headquarters and in the regional offices of ECLA in Santiago and Mexico City, ECAFE in Bangkok, and ECA in Addis Ababa.

the commission secretariat as a kind of intellectual lodestone for the region?

The terms of reference of none of the regional economic commissions speak specifically of integration of the whole or of portions of their regions as one of their purposes, much less their paramount purpose. However, there is ample latitude for such an interpretation in authorizations to study regional economic and technical problems, to initiate measures for facilitating regional economic and social development, and to help formulate policies as a basis for practical action in promoting country and regional development. The problem is not whether the commission may or should be used as a fulcrum for transferring expectations for growth and development from the state to some larger unit; it is whether such an effort has been made or whether that has been the net result of activities undertaken by the commission.

It is very difficult to identify that component of the work of a regional economic commission which has a regional as opposed to a country orientation. There is very little to be gained by an attempt to factor out of the work program those activities which are concerned with the region as a whole or with some subregional grouping of states. Virtually all of the work carried on by a regional secretariat *may* be infused with the imperative of regionalization or, conversely, none of it. What matters is not the frequency of such phrases as "regional programs of cooperation" or "development on a subregional or regional basis," phrases liberally sprinkled through descriptions of commission projects, but the extent to which the appearance of an integrative mission is supported by the appropriate mix of project significance and timeliness, the commitment of the secretariat, mutual reinforcement of various elements of the commission program, and governmental receptivity (or at least absence of active hostility).

ECLA

Of the three regional economic commissions serving the developing world, the Economic Commission for Latin America has made the most sustained and conscious effort to achieve a manner of thinking about economic problems of individual countries which would result in a shift of emphasis from decision making by and for the state to decision making by a collectivity of states for the economic benefit of the whole as well as each of the parts.

In part this is surely the consequence of a combination of environmental factors which produce a net political input more receptive to integration. There is the frequently cited evidence of comparatively greater cultural homogeneity; there is the fact of a much longer postcolonial history; there is statistical proof of a higher mean gross national product(GNP) per capita;[18] there is the history of common concern for the economic and geopolitical reality of the hemispheric hegemony of the United States; there is the relative absence of intraregional quarrels and of regional diversions from the task of economic growth and development. This does not mean that economic and political differences do not exist and are not reflected within ECLA. The United States has frequently been a dissenting member, taking exception to economic theories which have permeated Commission discussions and actions and occasionally placing a strain upon relationships among the Commission's Latin American members. The Cuban revolution has introduced a new ideological dimension into Commission debates.[19] There have been policy differences arising from different perceptions of advantage and disadvantage in specific ECLA program proposals. The case of Venezuelan reluctance to join the Latin American Free Trade Association (LAFTA) is a well-known example, one which conditioned ECLA's recommendations on the subject.[20]

But it has been the Secretariat of ECLA which has attracted the most attention and made the

---

[18]See Russett, especially Table 44, pp. 155–157, and Table B. 2, pp. 294–298.

[19]Note that the Cuban application for membership in the Latin American Free Trade Association (LAFTA) was rejected. See Sidney Dell, *Trade Blocs and Common Markets* (New York: Alfred A. Knopf, 1963), p. 265.

[20]See the September 1960 statement of the Bank of Venezuela:

> Any common market or free trade area will leave us producing nothing but petroleum and iron ore, and importing everything else. Our textiles cannot compete with Brazilian textiles, our coffee cannot compete with Colombian coffee and our meat cannot compete with Uruguayan meat. For us a free trade area is utopian at the present time.

(Quoted in Dell, p. 274.)

most conspicuous contributions to integration in Latin America. As Albert Hirschman remarks,

> The arresting feature of ECLA is that it possesses attributes not frequently encountered in large international organisations: a cohesive personality which evokes loyalty from the staff, and a set of distinctive beliefs, principles, and attitudes, in brief an ideology, which is highly influential among Latin American intellectuals and policymakers.[21]

ECLA's long-time Executive Secretary, Dr. Raúl Prebisch, supplied the ideology which infused the Secretariat with a sense of purpose and gave the Commission its sense of direction. There are many who will take issue with Dr. Prebisch's economics but none who will dispute the contention that his views have had an impact in Latin America, and indeed beyond that region.

The essence of the Prebisch-ECLA position has been that the economic difficulties of the developing countries are attributable to the prolonged and continuing deterioration in their terms of trade. To remedy this condition and overcome dependence of the periphery (developing state) upon the center (developed states), industrialization via the mechanism of a preferential regional market is proposed. To avoid a situation in which some states within Latin America would benefit from such a market at the expense of others, ECLA has promoted a doctrine of regionally balanced economic growth, with formulas for reciprocity and complementarity "to assure that everybody would be cut in on the deal, that nobody would gain disproportionately.[22]

The institutional embodiments of this philosophy and some of its subthemes are the Central American Economic Integration Program, the Latin American Free Trade Association,[23] and, in a somewhat different sense, the United Nations Conference on Trade and Development (UNCTAD). ECLA-sponsored studies and negotiations, fed by ECLA research, led directly to the creation of the two subregional associations in Latin America. It is interesting to note that ECLA, alone of the four regional commissions, has not established an elaborate substructure of committees and other standing subsidiary bodies for its various fields of work. The only two exceptions are a Central American Economic Cooperation Committee and a Trade Committee, and it is no accident that the former played a key role in the evolution of the General Treaty on Central American Economic Integration (and its predecessors, the Agreement on Central American Integration Industries and the Multilateral Treaty on Central American Free Trade and Economic Integration) and that the latter performed a similar function with respect to the Treaty of Montevideo creating LAFTA.

This is not the place to evaluate either the Central American Economic Integration Program or LAFTA. Either or both may stagnate in the face of conditions which do not appear to be optimal for economic integration, much less politization. Haas argues that LAFTA in particular must experience a "creative crisis" and be blessed with the dynamic leadership of a reform-monger if this now weak and to a considerable extent untested economic union is to develop in the direction of political union.[24] However, the important point to be made in the context of this article is that while LAFTA and the Central American Agreements have now assumed the burden of serving as vehicles for integration, it is ECLA which played the catalytic role, launching both experiments. Moreover, it has the continuing task of supplying creative leadership, indirectly through the force of ideas or directly through ECLA-trained personnel, with which to meet challenges requiring adaptation. The ECLA Secretariat has already displayed some aptitude for creative adaptation. As Hirschman notes, ECLA "has transferred the principal

---

[21] Albert O. Hirschman, "Ideologies of Economic Development in Latin America," in Albert O. Hirschman (ed.), *Latin American Issues: Essays and Comments* (New York: Twentieth Century Fund, 1961), p. 13.

[22] Haas and Schmitter, *International Organization*, Vol. 18, No. 4, p. 730. For a recent, definitive statement of the ECLA-Prebisch theses see *Towards a Dynamic Development Policy for Latin America* (UN Document E/CN.12/680/Rev. 1), December 1963.

[23] The Central American Agreements embrace Costa Rica, El Salvador, Guatemala, Honduras, and Nicaragua. LAFTA includes Argentina, Brazil, Chile, Colombia,

Ecuador, Mexico, Paraguay, Peru, and Uruguay. For a recent study of LAFTA, including the role of ECLA in its creation, see Miguel S. Wionczek, "Latin American Free Trade Association," *International Conciliation*, January 1965 (No. 551).

[24] Haas and Schmitter, *International Organization*, Vol. 18, No. 4, pp. 732 ff.

center of its activity from one area to another as it ran into difficulty or decreasing returns,"[25] but it has managed to do so without sacrifice of identity of its personality. The Commission, for example, spent a number of years urging upon Latin American governments the detailed programming of economic development; the shift to common market studies reflected, in part, frustration with the limited impact of its programming activity.

It may be that the Commission has been guilty on occasion of a utopian cast of mind or, conversely, that it has had more prosaic purposes than integration in mind, as Sidney Dell alleges with his observation that LAFTA was in part the product of a desire to observe General Agreement on Tariffs and Trade (GATT) rules, not to achieve economic integration.[26] In either case, ECLA has nonetheless contributed as has no other agency to a reexamination of economic, and hence political, relationships within and among Latin American states. As one observer remarks, Prebisch has been a "creator of enthusiasms and a destroyer of illusions."[27] He has made ECLA a force to be reckoned with in the western hemisphere. When policy decisions affecting economic development, industrialization, and trade are pending within a state, the outcome is likely to be affected by the Cassandra-like warnings of ECLA's annual reports, by the recommendations of one of ECLA's economic development advisory groups, or by the very existence of an ECLA-fostered free trade machinery. Moreover, such decisions may be influenced by the presence within the government of economists who have held prominent positions on the ECLA staff.[28] More than in any of the other regions there is a significant flow of senior officials between the Commission Secretariat and the governments of member states.

Several years ago, one observer credited Prebisch with the feat of making ECLA into a kind of responsible political opposition in Latin America.[29] It is submitted that ECLA even has one foot in the government in some states. However, as Haas points out, the *técnicos* have an uneven influence throughout Latin America; his observation that they might be able to exert considerable influence in a number of the more advanced countries of the region "*if* their lines of rapport with major political groups were stable"[30] is illustrated by the exile of one of ECLA's more prominent "exports," Celso Furtado, from Brazil.

In spite of the recognized expertise in the ECLA Secretariat and the presence of ex-ECLA personnel in many governments, several UN officials have remarked that ECLA's impact is weakened by the preoccupation of its Secretariat with economic theory. Thus it has been alleged that ECLA underestimates the problems of negotiability; phrased another way, ECLA has been accused of a reluctance to get its hands dirty with operational complexities. As one UN official observed, the ECLA Secretariat is probably the only agency in Latin America that could find the common denominators for implementing economic integration programs but does not possess the bent of mind necessary to do so.

In respects other than ideology, its translation into a work program with institutional results, and the interchange of senior economists, the Economic Commission for Latin America has not performed in a manner conspicuously different from that of ECAFE or ECA. What has distinguished ECLA's activities is that the integrationist ideology permeates the otherwise routine research and advisory services. For example, as a result of ECLA initiatives an Institute for Economic and Social Planning was established with UN Special Fund and Inter-American Development Bank (IDB) support in Santiago; Dr. Prebisch became the Institute's first Director General, and this prospectively influential training organ proceeded to assume responsibility for advisory groups which ECLA had pioneered, for the important economic development training program, and for research with respect to planning. The curriculum will not necessarily produce

---

[25]Hirschman, p. 20.

[26]Dell, p. 264.

[27]Roberto de Oliveira Campos, quoted in Hirschman, p. 27.

[28]Among the more prominent have been Victor L. Urquidi and Carlos Quintana in Mexico, Celso Furtado in Brazil, José A. Mayobre (now Executive Secretary of ECLA) in Venezuela, Hugo Trivelli in Chile, and Regino Boti in Cuba. Similarly, upon Juan Perón's overthrow, the government of Argentina requested Prebisch to make an economic survey of that country, his own.

---

[29]Andrew Shonfield, *The Attack on World Poverty* (New York: Random House, 1962), p. 49.

[30]Haas and Schmitter, *International Organization*, Vol. 18, No. 4, p. 731.

integrationists; but the close historical, physical, and personal links with ECLA suggest that the Institute may become an important training ground for regionally minded economists. Similar institutes have been created in Bangkok for Asia and the Far East and in Dakar for Africa, but while these bodies may relieve the regional economic commissions in those areas of in-service training responsibilities, the possibility is remote that they will in the near future serve as incubators for integrationists.

One final observation should be made concerning the political role of the Economic Commission for Latin America. The recurrent conflict between the UN and the Organization of American States (OAS) in the peaceful settlement and enforcement fields[31] has had an interesting corollary in the competition between ECLA and the Inter-American Economic and Social Council (IA-ECOSOC) of the OAS. Although the Alliance for Progress has fostered formal structures for bringing activities of the two organizations into harmonious relationship,[32] the resultant coordination has been superficial and ECLA and IA-ECOSOC remain distinct and competing entities. It is not an exaggeration to state that the prestige within the region enjoyed by ECLA, an organization in which the United States has usually been a minor and dissenting participant, has been enhanced by the fact that the OAS is widely viewed as a United States-dominated institution. Regional pride in ECLA and a disposition to listen when ECLA prescribes for the region's ills may be inversely related to regional acceptance of the OAS machinery.

ECAFE

If the number of experiments in regional and subregional organization is any yardstick, Asia promises least progress of any of the developing regions

toward economic, much less political, union. Reasons for Asian separatism are not hard to find. The litany of obstacles to cooperation has been cited many times: the region's geographic dispersion; its religious, cultural, and linguistic diversity; its deep political cleavages; the vast disparity in unit size. It is within this milieu that ECAFE operates.

Functional similarity is conspicuously lacking in this sprawling region. Two of ECAFE's territorial members (Australia and New Zealand) are "high mass-consumption" societies with a GNP per capita of more than $1,300; four (Afghanistan, Burma, Laos, and Nepal) are "traditional primitive" societies with a GNP per capita of less than $70; and only a handful, including only one major state, Japan, have a GNP per capita of as much as $200.[33] Clusters of states of roughly comparable size and power are divided by religious, ideological, and other deeply rooted animosities. If civil strife is divided into personnel wars, authority wars, and structural wars,[34] in Latin America such strife has usually been of the first two types, while in Asia it has frequently been structural; thus it has had much wider repercussions and has made it more difficult for the Commission to give undivided attention to economic development problems.

Among other inputs which have inhibited ECAFE's deliberations are the deep-seated suspicion of Japan's leadership, dating back to the days of the Coprosperity Sphere; anxiety about and some resentment of India's claims to leadership within the region and the Commission;[35] dissension introduced into the Asian scene by the creation and continued existence of the Southeast Asia Treaty Organization (SEATO); the presence within ECAFE, alone of the three commissions, of both the United States and the Soviet Union; and the fact that mainland China is within the geographic scope of the Commission but that the

---

[31]See Inis L. Claude, Jr., "The OAS, the UN, and the United States," *International Conciliation*, March 1964 (No. 547).

[32]An *Ad Hoc* Committee on Cooperation was established to guarantee coordination between the OAS, ECLA, and the Inter-American Development Bank (IDB). ECLA is also linked to the Inter-American Committee on the Alliance for Progress (CIAP), a committee of IA-ECOSOC, in an advisory capacity.

[33]Classification and data are from Russett, Table B-2, pp. 294–298.

[34]This typology is developed by James N. Rosenau, "Internal War as an International Event," in James N. Rosenau (ed.), *International Aspects of Civil Strife* (Princeton, N.J.: Princeton University Press, 1964), pp. 45–91.

[35]Figures supplied to the writer on a visit to ECAFE in 1964 revealed that as of that time India had as many professional staff serving on the Commission's Secretariat as Pakistan, Burma, Ceylon, Indonesia, and Iran combined.

Peking government, a brooding presence in all Asian affairs, is not a participant. In such an atmosphere economic progress is difficult, and no better or more enduring example can be found than Pakistan's lukewarm attitude toward the activities of ECAFE, a function of India's leadership of and stake in the Commission's affairs.

ECAFE has had no ideological thrust remotely comparable to that of ECLA. To say this is not to disparage the leadership of ECAFE but to record a fact. The impact of the Commission has simply been quite negligible. ECAFE's early years were characterized by the Commission's domination by non-Asian states. It was not until the Lahore Agreement of 1951 that the Asian states succeeded in converting the Commission into a body which could do what its Asian members wanted it to do without interference, and indeed blocking votes, from outside powers.[36] In the words of David Wightman, the Agreement "affirmed that ECAFE existed primarily to serve the interests of its Asian members."[37] This rudimentary triumph did not, of course, define those interests or guarantee that the Asian states and a secretariat consisting largely of their nationals would undertake a program with integrative purpose or potential.

Although it would be a mistake to underestimate the significance for Asia of the "Asianization" of the only important regional body in the entire continent, it must be noted that the subsequent performance of ECAFE has not created apprehension and dissatisfaction outside of the Commission comparable to that generated by

ECLA. In other words, ECAFE is regarded as a relatively "safe" commission; the Lahore Agreement has not proved to be a Pandora's box. There has been little friction between ECAFE and the UN, which in this case means both the predominantly Western leadership within the Department of Economic and Social Affairs and the influential Western states on the Economic and Social Council and in the Second (Economic and Financial) and Third (Social, Humanitarian, and Cultural) Committees of the General Assembly. ECAFE may fairly be characterized as the most UN-minded of the regional commissions. The assessment implicit in this characterization, and one explicitly voiced by some UN staff members, is that the Secretariats in New York and in Bangkok are both cautious, slow to embrace new ideas, generally satisfied to perform routine tasks efficiently. Furthermore, a capacity for self-criticism, so necessary to continuing redefinition of tasks and the growth of influence, has been conspicuously lacking in ECAFE's leadership. ECAFE may do well those things that it does, but such an organization is unlikely to contribute significantly to the transformation of thinking either of economists or politicians within its member states.

Having stated that Asia is not Latin America and ECAFE not ECLA, it is necessary to scan the performance of the Commission for islands of impact in an unpromising sea. The first Executive Secretary, P. S. Lokanathan, had early indicated his determination not to preside over a mere study group.[38] Yet the Working Group of Experts on Regional Economic Cooperation for the ECAFE Region, in an important report submitted to the third Executive Secretary, U Nyun, in 1963, observed that

> increased regional cooperation as envisaged in this report requires the establishment of decision-making machinery, in contrast to the largely consultative machinery which ECAFE has provided for the past seventeen years.[39]

During ECAFE's long years as consultative machinery/study group, the ground was being laid for "joint efforts to secure the common or integrated development of basic facilities of natural

---

[36]See Wightman, pp. 50–52. A memorandum presented by the Executive Secretary, P. S. Lokanathan, at the 1951 session of the Commission catalyzed support for the following declaration by the Commission:

Member governments feel, however, that the time has come when clearer recognition should be given to the principle that member countries belonging to the region should take their own decisions in the Commission on their own economic problems. . . . In pursuance of this principle the member countries of the Commission not in the region would be willing, as a general rule, to refrain from using their votes in opposition to economic proposals predominantly concerning the region which had the support of a majority of the countries of the region.

(See Economic and Social Council *Official Records* [13th session], Supplement No. 7, paragraph 341.)
[37]Wightman, p. 52.

---

[38]*Ibid.*, p. 286.
[39]UN Document E/CN.11/641, p. 69.

resources" and, hopefully, for "those forms of co-operation which arise from the treatment of the region as a whole, or parts of it, as a single market."[40] The habit of consultation had to be instilled first; the economic map of the ECAFE region had to be charted. Both the map and the habit have been improved by ECAFE's existence and the list of ECAFE-inspired projects of regional or subregional import is beginning to lengthen. The roster includes the Mekong River Project, the Asian Highway, the Asian Institute for Economic Development and Planning, Intraregional Trade Promotion Talks, the Conference of Asian Planners, the Ministerial Conference on Asian Economic Cooperation, and the Asian Development Bank.

These frequently cited evidences of ECAFE's salutary role in that conflict-ridden region fall into two categories. The Mekong Project, the Highway, and the Institute are similar in that discussions have been followed by action in each case and in that they do not involve any sacrifice of the right of member countries to determine their own development and commercial policies. The Institute, as noted earlier, is comparable in form to one established through the initiative of ECLA, but its integrative potential will probably depend upon the development of a curriculum with a self-consciously regional viewpoint. The Asian Highway will no more lift the eyes of planners beyond the boundaries of nation-states than will the ECE-sponsored convention for transport of goods by roads under customs seal in Europe[41] although a comparison of the two projects underscores the rudimentary nature of ECAFE's task. However, the Asian Highway is symbolically important, "a modern revival of the ancient caravan routes along which traveled not only goods but peoples and ideas."[42] Unlike most highway projects, it is not a response to traffic but a promoter of it. The Highway, in other words, *may* in time help to create environmental conditions which are favorable to integration.

The other major project associated with ECAFE initiative is the development of the Me-

kong. Perhaps no other experiment in regional cooperation within the developing regions of the world has received more attention. Much has been made of the fact that under ECAFE's patient nurturing the Mekong Project has gone forward during periods of bitter political and even military conflict in the Southeast Asian subregion. By any standard ECAFE's performance has been a creditable one.[43] The Coordination Committee, a brainchild of the Commission's second Executive Secretary, C. V. Narasimhan, is a unique instrumentality in Asia, a body composed of representatives of the four riparian countries with authority to raise funds and approve programs for implementation. It was not intended to be a supranational body and it has not evolved in that direction, but under "the ECAFE umbrella"[44] the Committee has survived and registered tangible progress. Some of the most critical hurdles lie ahead, and the pattern of cooperation for decisions with respect to surveys and dam construction may not spill over into decision making with respect to costs, benefits, or modes of operation, not to mention other questions involving subregional development. Nevertheless, one is compelled to agree with Wightman that "the tinder of the ECAFE vision has been set alight."[45]

The second category of ECAFE initiatives includes those based upon the assumption

that the purpose of any major measures of intraregional co-operation must be to give the trade and production structure of the ECAFE countries a more regional orientation.[46]

This theme is not new, dating back at least to Lokanathan's aide-mémoire to the heads of delegations at a Tokyo session of the Commission in 1955;[47] but the ECAFE Secretariat approached the area of regional planning circumspectly for many years. Wightman takes the Secretariat to task for its failure to pursue the matter more vig-

---

[40]*Ibid.*, pp. 53–54.

[41]See *Fifteen Years of Activity of the Economic Commission for Europe 1947–1962* (UN Document E/ECE/473/Rev. 1), pp. 16, 81.

[42]Wightman, p. 221.

[43] See *ibid.*, pp. 183–202; and C. Hart Schaaf and Russell H. Fifield, *The Lower Mekong: Challenge to Cooperation in Southeast Asia* (Princeton, N.J.: D. Van Nostrand Co., 1963), especially Part II.

[44]The figure is Wightman's.

[45]Wightman, p. 197.

[46]UN Document E/CN.11/641, p. 57.

[47]See the discussion in Wightman, pp. 104–105, 292–294.

orously, suggesting that "a touch of questing bold-ness on this theme would not have been amiss"[48] as long ago as 1955 and offering in mitigation the Secretariat's new preoccupation with the Mekong. Modest steps in the direction of regional coopera-tion in the field of trade and development were taken with the inauguration of Intraregional Trade Promotion Talks in 1959 and Conferences of Asian Planners, the first of which was held in New Delhi in 1961. Both were instituted only after strong opposition had been overcome and only with the constructive if belated leadership of the Secretariat. But periodic discussion is no substitute for joint action, and of the latter there has been very little to date. The discussions may be moving in the direction of limited action, how-ever. Two groups of experts have rendered re-ports, the first in 1961 and the second in 1963, which not only urge cooperative regional action but also stress the need to establish machinery for the purpose.[49] The Manila Ministerial Conference on Asian Economic Cooperation used the second of these two reports as its principal working paper and resolved to pursue most of its objectives.[50] But except for the important agreement on establish-ment of an Asian Development Bank (which, in the recommendation of the Expert Group, would finance only regional projects), the level of com-mitment has been low, with emphasis still upon further *ad hoc* meetings of representatives and expert groups. The institutional equivalent of LAFTA, not to mention the European Economic Community (EEC), is still over the horizon.

Unlike ECLA, ECAFE has had no appreciable impact upon its member states through the place-ment of regionally minded officials from the Com-mission Secretariat in important government posts. Not only has there been a less coherent gospel of regionalism to carry back to the service of individual governments, but there has also been a much lower turnover among senior officials. There is less enthusiasm for new blood in the

ECAFE Secretariat than in any of the other com-missions. The result has been the perpetuation of the tradition of caution and a failure to build useful bridges between the Secretariat and the ministries concerned with development questions. In general, the recommendations and activities of the ECAFE Secretariat seem to occupy no very prominent place in the discussion of policy within governments.

ECA

The Economic Commission for Africa is still the least developed and hardest to categorize of the commissions, as one might expect of an organiza-tion which is less than eight years old and more than half of whose members have been indepen-dent states no more than six years. Every effort has been made to give the Commission parity with ECLA and ECAFE, however, and in UN circles there are those who insist that the real meaning of ECA is "every cent for Africa." In its relatively brief life ECA has overtaken the other commissions in size of staff,[51] in the volume of UN regional technical assistance projects,[52] and in the number of subregional offices.

In spite of all this activity, and some would say in part because of it, ECA has not yet developed a distinctive style of operation or an identifiable sense of direction. Most of its membership lived until recently as colonies either of France or of the United Kingdom, and economically most ECA members still remain within the orbit of the former metropolitan power. The preferential

---

[48]*Ibid.*, p. 297.

[49]Consultative Group of Experts on Regional Eco-nomic Cooperation in Asia (1961) and Working Group of Experts (1963). See UN documents E/CN.11/615, February 13, 1963, and E/CN.11/641, Appendix V, Annex 2.

[50]The Ministerial Conference's resolution on Asian economic cooperation appears in UN Document E/CN. 11/641, pp. 2–3.

[51]Professional staff as of April 1 in each of several recent years:

	1960	1962	1964
ECAFE	78	75	87
ECLA	87	87	103
ECA	34	70	102

(Figures supplied by the Administrative Management Service of the UN Secretariat and by the individual com-mission secretariats.)

[52]In 1965 the UN was executing agency for regional projects in Africa under the Expanded Program of Technical Assistance (EPTA) and its own regular pro-gram totaling approximately $1,520,000; most of the projects were decentralized to ECA. This is to be com-pared with the figures for Asia ($1,010,000) and Latin America ($1,000,000). (UN Document E/4075, June 14, 1965, p. 24.)

treatment accorded countries in the French Community by the EEC and countries of the British Commonwealth by the United Kingdom is "a disintegrating factor in Africa, and tends to perpetuate the cleavage between the British and French areas of the continent."[53] Furthermore, the political boundaries make even less economic sense on this badly fragmented continent than they do in other areas. The number of states involved in any regional or subregional negotiations looking to economic union would necessarily be large if negotiations are to be economically meaningful, and yet the larger the number of participants the more difficult the task of mutually satisfactory negotiation.

Nor are the fragmentation of Africa and the fact of distinctive areas of residual British and French influence the only significant forces acting upon the Commission. The Pan-African leadership aspirations of some African states are viewed with suspicion by others; there are latent problems in the relationship between the Arab members of ECA, especially the United Arab Republic, and the sub-Saharan African states; there has been competition over the location of subregional offices. Of singular importance has been the continuing struggle for self-determination of the indigenous African population in the southern quarter of the continent. This issue, which unites African states as does no other, has also distracted ECA from its economic tasks. Although ECOSOC "resolved" the problem in 1963 by expelling Portugal from membership in ECA[54] and suspending South Africa until conditions for constructive cooperation had been restored by a change in that country's racial policies,[55] in the larger sense ECA functions at less than full effectiveness because the primary preoccupation of many of its member governments remains the colonial and racial issues.

Another issue which has preempted the attention of the Commission is the Africanization of the ECA Secretariat. ECA is the only one of the three commissions serving the developing world the majority of whose professional staff is not indigenous to the region. But the talent pool in Africa is still shallow, a stubborn fact which has made it difficult to Africanize the Commission's Secretariat. The effort to do so continues, however, with the result that ECA's staff, in spite of some areas of considerable skill, is not yet either particularly effective or stable. Nor was there stable leadership at the top during the critical early years. The first Executive Secretary, Mekki Abbas, had only a brief tenure, and the second, Robert K. A. Gardiner, spent his first year in the post on assignment in the Congo (Leopoldville). Political considerations have dictated that there be a French-speaking African Deputy Executive Secretary, and the result seems to have been to smuggle the continent's divisions into the Secretariat rather than to ameliorate the problem. As a result of uncertain leadership, staff deficiencies, lack of experience, and the imperatives of Africanization, ECA has had to move with "deliberate speed."

Although ECA has been plagued by the existence of barriers not of its making, it has been spared some other problems which could have complicated its efforts to establish itself as an effective force in Africa. In the first place, neither the United States nor the Soviet Union is a member although it was originally assumed that both would be; this has partially removed from ECA the propensity, often noticeable in ECAFE, to substitute ideological argument for more pragmatic discussion of hard issues. In the second place, the Organization of African Unity (OAU) had not yet been launched when ECA was created in 1958. Had the order been reversed, ECA might have failed, its role preempted by another organization, prospectively stronger because its participants are foreign ministers rather than economic and finance ministers. On the other hand, the relatively late establishment of the Economic Commission for Africa meant that the conference habit, dating back to Bandung in 1955, was built into ECA as it had not been in the case of ECAFE.

Like ECLA, ECA has had to compete with other regional organizations; and like ECLA, ECA has benefited in this competition from its "regional purity." ECA's principal strength, however, derives from the simple fact that it has survived while other African organizations have folded. The Organization of African Unity is, of course, very much alive; but the OAU has come

---

[53]Dell, p. 286.

[54]ECOSOC Resolution 974 D III (XXXVI), July 24, 1963.

[55]ECOSOC Resolution 974 D IV (XXXVI), July 30, 1963.

to depend upon the ECA Secretariat to do its economic and social work, a relationship which the Commission has encouraged and which is facilitated by the location of both organizations in Addis Ababa.

In the final analysis, there is probably not now in Africa a disposition to see economic problems as the most critical ones. This takes pressure off ECA, but it also deprives ECA of some of its prospective importance and suggests that African political leaders will probably not for a time tolerate the emergence of strong leaders within the ECA Secretariat. The prospect, therefore, is for a further development of Secretariat strength; continued leadership in such areas as the development of statistical standards through the Conference of African Statisticians; the gradual assumption of more operational responsibilities under the decentralization program; an expansion of advisory and training services through the African Institute for Economic Development and Planning in Dakar; and the further elaboration of an economic profile for the continent. The impact of the EEC, the example of LAFTA, and participation in planning for UNCTAD are making the ECA Secretariat more integration conscious. It has prepared preliminary documentation on the subject of an African common market,[56] helped to launch an African Development Bank, worked with a group of experts in the preparation of a report on an African payments union,[57] organized industrial coordination missions to several subregions in Africa, and laid the groundwork for a standing Conference of African Planners. This list of activities could be expanded. There is obviously a great deal of ferment within ECA, but the fact remains that virtually every one of these programs is still on the drawing board. What is more, the plans are still fuzzy and Commission discussions still deal in generalities, as evidenced by the following excerpt from the summary of discussions during a recent ECA session: "The creation of an African common market was a generally accepted goal. What remained to be determined, was the best way of going about it."[58]

It may be that the most significant impact of the Commission upon national political systems will be registered through the subregionalization of ECA's structure and work program. One UN official likens the subregional aspects of ECA's activity to the submerged portion of an iceberg. Although the iceberg analogy may seem climatically out of place in a discussion of African affairs, it is true that ECA has created subregional offices for West Africa in Niamey, for East Africa in Lusaka, for North Africa in Tangier, and for Central Africa in Leopoldville; that it has curtailed the number of large meetings in favor of small, specialized subregional meetings in such fields as trade, energy, industry, and transport; that many of the regional technical assistance projects proposed and implemented by ECA are organized subregionally (such as the Regional Center for Demographic Research and Training in Cairo, serving Algeria, Libya, Morocco, the Sudan, Tunisia, and the United Arab Republic, and the subregional statistical training centers which serve different clients from such points as Yaoundé, Accra, Rabat, and Addis Ababa). This emphasis upon the subregion is made explicit in a recent statement of the Executive Secretary of ECA, who noted that if there was to be economic progress in the foreseeable future,

> each country would have to determine its development strategy and each subregion its machinery for cooperation. Groups of countries should decide on criteria for sharing out new industries, and conferences should be superceded by closer negotiations between countries.[59]

By focusing its studies increasingly upon subregional groupings of states and giving its industrial coordination missions subregional assignments, the Secretariat has sought to translate this appeal into state policy. The talk of an African common market has a regionwide flavor, and the Secretariat is trying to develop an integrated African telecommunications network with the help of the International Telecommunications Union (ITU) to nationalize African air transport in cooperation with the International Civil Aviation Organization (ICAO), and to promote a trans-Sahara road

---

[56]See UN Document E/CN.14/261 and Corr. 1.
[57]UN Document E/CN.14/262.
[58]Economic and Social Council *Official Records* (37th session), Supplement No. 10, paragraph 234 (c).

[59]*Ibid.*, paragraph 109.

link, all objectives which transcend any one sub-region. However, the principal thrust of ECA is today subregional, suggesting that the Commission is coming to terms with some of the geographical and linguistic realities of Africa.

RECAPITULATION AND SOME TENTATIVE CONCLUSIONS

The foregoing paragraphs constitute a *tour d'horizon*, a necessarily brief and limited inquiry into the nature of the momentum, if any, imparted by ECLA, ECAFE, and ECA to the regions which they serve. Hopefully they offer a few benchmarks for further study of the extent to which the commissions have assumed an integrative function.

Earlier in the article five questions were raised relative to the performance of the commissions. They concerned the ideological leadership of the Executive Secretary; the tangible initiatives taken by the commission, as reflected in the work program; the institutional legacy of the commission at the regional or subregional level; the flow of regionally minded personnel from commission secretariat to positions of influence within states; and the image of the commission within the region. Although it is difficult to measure leadership and initiative or to pin down such an elusive commodity as image, a very rough scale of integrative output can be constructed, ranging from nil through marginal, low, modest, and substantial to high, for each of the five areas A net evaluation should then be possible.

ECLA has had the highest integrative output. Certainly the environmental conditions in that region are more conducive to this kind of thrust

Variable	ECLA	ECAFE	ECA
Ideological leadership	Substantial	Low	Marginal
Tangible initiatives	Substantial	Modest	Marginal
Institutional legacies	Modest	Low	Marginal
Personnel mobility	Modest	Marginal	Marginal
Regional image	Modest	Marginal	Low
Net evaluation of integrative output	Modest	Low	Marginal

than those in Asia or Africa, but ECLA could easily have fallen into the rut of a more limited role. Instead, its leadership has been characterized by an ideology which, while short of supranationalism, has nonetheless been instrumental in focusing attention on regional approaches to problems previously deemed domestic. Its initiatives have given meaning to that ideology, putting it to work in a program which has given to the region several modest but pioneering projects, some of which may yet acquire supranational traits. Alone of the commissions it has a record of senior staff mobility, a phenomenon which spreads ECLA's ideas and prestige and which reflects at least some willingness to entertain some of those ideas. The Commission has a strong image although it is predictably controversial; at least it is paid the compliment of attention.

ECAFE, on the other hand, has been handicapped by the vastness and variety of its region, by the shadow of Communist China, by fear of domination by India and Japan, by a protracted quest for identity, and by an uncritical attitude toward its own performance. No organizational ideology or comprehensive program for regional growth and development has been put forward by the Commission's leadership. In this case, the *ad hoc* initiatives of the Commission have anticipated the development of an ideology, and one or two of these, e.g., the Mekong Project, are monuments to ECAFE's creativity and perseverance. Although the Commission has been called extravagantly an economic parliament for Asia, there is little evidence that this wish, if wish it is, will become father to the fact. ECAFE's integrative output has been low.

The third commission in the developing world, ECA, is even weaker than ECAFE in every respect except image. This is not surprising, given its relative newness and growing pains. That its image in Africa exceeds its accomplishments is due to a variety of factors, including the importance attached to international organization generally on that continent. Otherwise, it is too early to make a judgment about ECA, except to say that to date its integrative output is low, buoyed only by the growing consciousness of a common cause among all African peoples from which ECA benefits and to which it may in time contribute.

In all three cases the judgment as to integrative output is based upon the complete record. If one were to look only at the current situation, it is doubtful if ECLA would stand out so far above ECAFE. Some veteran observers at the UN think they detect signs of stagnation in Santiago, while ECAFE is coming to life. A flurry of excitement has attended the launching of the Asian Development Bank; on the other hand, the slow progress of LAFTA has eroded some of ECLA's enthusiasm, and continued uncertainty about the viability of the Alliance for Progress appears to have contributed to a state of suspended animation in ECLA. But these observations may only suggest that what distinguishes the regional commissions may be less important than what they have in common. If ECLA is in a less creative phase, it may be that it has simply encountered some of the boundaries imposed by environmental conditions, while ECAFE may be discovering in the midst of regional conflict that it can do more, that the very urgency of the political situation may generate pressure for functional cooperation.

The performance of the commissions indicates that each of them, like water seeking its level, will in time but at a differential rate produce some common institutions and policies. ECLA has frequently pioneered, although action by ECAFE and ECA has often had an independent genesis. Thus, the creation of an Asian Development Bank means that each region now has both a regional planning institute and a development bank. Neither is an instance of economic union, of course, but both reflect a capacity to cooperate in launching institutions of continuing utility to the region as a whole. If neither promotes integration directly, they will at least afford an opportunity for nationals of several states from within the region to cooperate in managing programs of regional scope, and they will hopefully contribute to a reshaping of national views about integration and national capacities to approach the subject seriously.

Similarly, recent measures of decentralization from UN Headquarters to the commissions and attendant efforts to strengthen the latter's secretariats should provide more opportunities for the commissions to identify themselves with specific, concrete tasks of regional proportions. Although decentralization is primarily a movement to transfer UN decision making in the economic field from the hands of Europeans and North Americans to persons from the developing countries, not a movement to transfer decision making within the region from the state to some subregional or regional organization, it has the effect of focusing attention upon agencies of regional scope and upon projects of a regional rather than a country-by-country nature inasmuch as it is regional projects which have been decentralized.[60]

Another institutional development in which all three commissions share and one which may have a profound impact upon their direction and function is the United Nations Conference on Trade and Development. The Secretariats of ECLA, ECAFE, and ECA served as research staff for the several groups of developing countries which joined forces to form the surprisingly cohesive and effective "77" at Geneva. There is every reason to believe that they will continue to perform in the capacity of "secretariat for the poor," a role which the commissions have explicitly been invited to play. Dr. Prebisch has carried his economic doctrines from ECLA, where he made Santiago the most vital of the regional centers, to UNCTAD. Just as the commission secretariats helped to make the first Geneva Conference a success, so should the UNCTAD connection logically contribute to a broader, regional outlook within the commissions.

Although the subregional approach has been made most explicit in the case of ECA, all three commissions have been characterized by this kind of pragmatic response to the challenge of political and economic diversity within their regions. In spite of the concern of each commission for a whole region, many of the important instances of commission initiative, such as the Central American Agreements and the Mekong Project, have a subregional focus; the broader scope of LAFTA and the Asian Highway does not conceal the fact that both are primarily programs of a subregional nature, at least for the present. It would seem fairly safe to assert that the commissions will continue to explore the

---

[60]For the most recent official statements on the status of decentralization see UN Documents A/6114, November 23, 1965, and E/4075, June 14, 1965.

possibilities of subregional cooperation. If the commissions are less ambitious with respect to the geographic scope of their projects, they can perhaps afford to be more ambitious with respect to their integrative content.

All of this activity underscores the vitality of the commissions, but it does not mean that economic policy is about to be made at any level higher than that of the nation-state. Certainly the regional commissions themselves have no such mandate or the faintest prospect of acquiring one, and the evidence that ideas and initiatives emanating from the commissions will foster supranational decision making is fragmentary and on the whole disappointing. To date we have only LAFTA and the Central American Agreements as modest examples of economic union. Cooperation, not federation, has been the highwater mark reached by the commissions, and much of the cooperation is still in a rudimentary stage.

Integrative output of the commissions, we may conclude, is related closely to environmental conditions and resultant receptivity of member states to ideas and initiatives of the commissions and their secretariats. One of the principal functions of the commissions has been to increase the awareness of member states of the possibilities for cooperative economic behavior within the limits set by those conditions and to help devise schemes for mobilizing energies which will carry members to those limits. Hopefully, conditions and attitudes will be modified in the process, thereby removing some of the limitations upon cooperative action within the region In any event, whether the commissions will play a role of increasing consequence within their respective regions depends upon their ability to increase their integrative output by overcoming environmental impediments and to sustain their impact by creative adaptation in the face of inevitable environmental changes.

EPILOGUE

In a modernizing society, security means development.

Security is not military hardware—though it may include it. Security is not military force—though it may involve it. Security is not traditional military activity—though it may encompass it.

Security is development.

Without development, there can be no security. . . .

As development progresses, security progress [es]; and when the people of a nation have organized their own human and natural resources to provide themselves with what they need and expect out of life—and have learned to compromise peacefully among competing demands in the larger national interest—then, their resistance to disorder and violence will be enormously increased.

From an address made by Robert S. McNamara, United States Secretary of Defense, to the American Society of Newspaper Editors in Montreal on May 18, 1966. (*The New York Times*, May 19, 1966, p. 11.)

Discussion and Questions

1. The Carnegie Endowment for International Peace has done a valuable service by publishing several issues of *International Conciliation* dealing with regional economic commissions. Among them are the following: Miguel S. Wionczek, "Latin American Free Trade Association," no. 557 (January 1965); Branislav Gosovic, "UNCTAD: North-South Encounter," no. 568 (May 1968); Joseph S. Nye, Jr., "Central American Regional Integration," no. 562, (March 1967); James S. Magee, "ECA and the Paradox of African Cooperation," no. 580 (November 1970).

2. Note the influence of Raul Prebisch on the approach of ECLA. It is especially interesting to note that the stress on deteriorating terms of trade for Latin American exports amounts to a suggestion of United States responsibility for Latin American economic ills and their correction. ECLA has developed an ideology that foreshadows that of UNCTAD. Would this development have been possible in the traditional settings of economic regionalism in Latin America?

3. ➤ Can you envision a major role for ECAFE in the economic reconstruction of Indochina and in the establishment of a more stable Asia? ➤ Can ECAFE play any major role until North Vietnam and China participate actively within the United Nations? ➤ Does the heterogeneity of Asia in terms of ideology, stage of economic development, language and ethnic variation, and national size set special limits on the first-stage integration potential of ECAFE?

4. For a recent analysis of ECA see James S. Magee's article "ECA and the Paradox of African Cooperation" (*International Conciliation*, no. 580 [November 1970], pp. 5–64). Before ECA can teach African nations the importance of ideas such as multinational coordination and cooperation, the nations must have the ability to plan internally and to set up policies that will promote both national and regional development. Even if these capabilities are developed, past suspicions and rivalries among African nations seem to be so persistent as to make prospects for building a strong ECA in the near future very low. The ECA-OAU clash is a case in point. Reinforced by other rivalries and political quarrels, this clash has unhappy implications for African development. ECA's superior financial and technical resources are faced with OAU's theoretical political dominance.

Catherine Hoskyns, in her article "Pan-Africanism and Integration" (in Arthur Hazlewood, Ed., *African Integration and Disintegration*, [Oxford Press, New York, 1967], pp. 354–93), examines the early experience with regionalism in Africa. In Africa, the regional movement took on, from the beginning, a strong ideological and ethnic orientation and involved, at least—and often little more than—an enthusiastic endorsement of Pan-Africanism. (For an important assessment of this ideological impulse so natural as an aftermath to colonial dependence and its susceptibility to manipulation, see Ali A. Mazrui, *Towards A Pax Africana: A Study of Ideology and Ambition* [Weidenfeld and Nicolson, London, 1967].) But in Africa the national energies of principal African countries have been consumed with the struggle to overcome internal divisions and build effective central governments. The tragic civil wars in the Congo and Nigeria, Africa's two largest counties, are characteristic of the region as a whole. Also new national governments in these recently independent states have been jealous of their national prerogatives. At the same time, the functional character of some of the problems called for subregional solutions, and efforts have persisted to achieve some real progress in these terms. In Africa we witness preindustrial states, confronted by immense domestic challenges of poverty, disease, and unemployment, unable to proceed very far along the line of integration except for very specific kinds of cooperative arrangments to secure joint services. The ideology of regional identification does not seem supported as yet in Africa by serious political commitments to overcome the mechanism of the nation-state. The idea of national sovereignty is on the rise in Africa, and it does not seem to be evolving in a form that is very conducive to regional integration in the near future, although the idea of regional sovereignty vis-à-vis intervention by great powers remains politically potent in African affairs, and the possibility of regional action to secure shared goals (for example, in relation to southern Africa) should not be discounted entirely.

Catherine Hoskyns makes three points that deserve special stress: (*a*) that already during the preindependence period, the colonial powers fostered, with varying degrees of success, multinational integration; (*b*) that in the period after independence, an important obstacle to significant integration by African States was "their almost total economic dependence on the outside world;" (*c*) that there have been a variety of subregional experiments with integration in Africa, some of which have enjoyed success.

The Organization of African Unity, aside from helping with the solution of certain intra-African disputes, has been able to present to the world a solid front in relation to anticolonialism and antiracism. The OAU has operated principally as a caucus of black African states that is fully consistent with both the espousal of a strongly nationalistic orientation and the use of the political organs of the United Nations for the implementation of these goals. In Africa more than in other geographical sections of the world, race provides the prime boundary line for organizational efforts of a regional character.

The OAU's espousal of a strongly nationalistic orientation is not necessarily an asset in tackling the problem of African development. We feel that within the UN context ECA with its regional perspective might well have some impact on this problem in the future.

5. ➤ What second-stage integration potential, if any, is possessed by the regional economic commissions of the United Nations? ➤ With regard to the future of world order, is the present balance of effort between economic regionalism within and outside the United Nations framework an acceptable one?

6. Richard N. Gardner has written two very informative articles on UNCTAD: "GATT and the United Nations Conference on Trade and Development" (*International Organization*, vol. 18, no. 4 [Autumn 1964], pp. 685–704); "The United Nations Conference on Trade and Development" (*International Organization*, vol. 22, no. 1 [Winter 1968], pp. 99–130). In the original 1964 conference North-South differences were taken into account rather than East-West differences—indicative of UNCTAD's special character: (*a*) it had a secretariat oriented toward the viewpoint of the poor countries; (*b*) a new decision-making center was available to mobilize the demands to put pressure on the rich; and (*c*) trade, aid, and financial questions related to economic development were brought together in a new form for examination.

7. There have been excellent articles written on the ECE, perhaps the most interesting of which is by Jean Siotis, "ECE in the Emerging European System" (*International Conciliation*, no. 561 [January 1967], pp. 5–70), in which he analyzes in detail the experience of the ECE. Although the detail of his analysis makes it very difficult to summarize, perhaps it would not be unfair to present the main ideas of the article in the following manner: Opportunities for the continued development of ECE abound. The bipolar system is increasingly displaced as political influence becomes more diffuse, and it is within this context that ECE developments must be viewed. The great powers cannot impose their views because the negotiations of ECE's multilateral bodies involves a large number of delegations. Because of this diffusion of power, however, the matter of developing new objectives for the organization becomes increasingly complex.

Siotis indicates that the two principal functional orientations of the Commission are: (*a*) coordination and cooperation between members of the system; (*b*) limited integration of the system in most areas of intra-European economic relations. He maintains that, provided certain structural obstacles are overcome (that is, the question of East German membership; maintaining a high level of professional competence in the

Secretariat; deciding how the Secretariat should define objectives in the context of the changing system; the role of the permanent missions in Geneva; and establishing good working relationships to avoid waste of effort between ECE, UNCTAD, UNIDO, and subregional organizations), the scope for building from the above orientations is virtually unlimited. At present certain results are within the immediate reach of the Commission—tasks such as regulating transport systems through all-European cooperation, coordinating statistical research, regulating exchanges of energy, to name a few. Joint consideration of economic policies by senior advisors, at present chiefly concerned with the tools of policy making, could be expanded to cover substantive policy issues. The ECE also could be instrumental in removing obstacles in the path of East-West trade development, since in the past it has been very effective in keeping channels open and building new bridges between East and West when divisons seemed decisive impediments to interaction.

The dominant practical function of the Commission is cooperation; integration exists to a limited extent in only a few sectors.

Note that both the Soviet Union and the United States participate in the ECE, and that West Germany participates but East Germany does not. Note also that the great Swedish social scientist Gunnar Myrdal served as the first Executive Secretary of ECE and imbued its operations with his own belief in the need for East-West reconciliation. ➤ How does the promotion of European integration relate to the separate integration efforts going on in East and West Europe? ➤ Does the smaller scale or less vital subject matter of ECE operations help explain its apparent success? ➤ Does the experience with ECE suggest the existence of more first-stage integration potential than is generally assumed? ➤ Are there likely to be stabilizing political payoffs arising from dramatic progress toward all-European economic integration? ➤ Can such a pattern of integration facilitate a solution of "the German problem"? ➤ Is United States participation desirable from the viewpoint of ECE, of the United States, of the future of world order? ➤ Why do you suppose that the experience of the ECE has been so neglected by students of world order? ➤ What are the lessons of its experience?

SUBORDINATE INTERNATIONAL SYSTEMS: THE CONTOURS OF REGIONAL INTERACTION

Part V attempts to develop an understanding of international society on the basis of subsystemic units of analysis. A subsystem is a major component of the global system, either a geographical group of states that exhibits "regional" characteristics or a large multinational state such as China, India, the United States, or the Soviet Union. Subsystems are politically determined units of analysis and contrast with the formal structures of regional scope that were dealt with in Part IV.

Oran Young's article in Part I suggested that international society can be viewed as a series of interacting subsystems. We considered two major issues at that point: (1) the manner by which globally dominant political influences are introduced into various political "regions" throughout the world; (2) the different attributes of the principal subsystems and the importance of these differences for the present and future prospects of world order. We are not concerned with the comparative politics of subsystems, but with the extent to which the subsystemic focus—as one type of regional analysis—alters our understanding of central world-order issues.

There are various attributes that seem to differentiate subsystems from one another: (1) the relative homogeneity of actors with respect to size and level of economic and social development; (2) the relative compatibility of actors with respect to internal political ideology and external revisionist goals; the presence or absence of intrasubsystemic forces with political ideologies that are intolerable to others or with irredentist claims that can only be satisfied at the expense of others within the subsystem; (3) the extent of regional consciousness deriving from a common cultural and linguistic heritage, a shared experience of subordination and struggle, and a common set of internal problems and external goals; (4) the orientation of political leadership within the subsystem, whether stressing values of national autonomy or regional unity; (5) the organizational implementation of subsystemic unity through the creation of forms for multinational cooperation, economic integration, and political unification; and (6) the perceived existence (or absence) of an extraregional enemy posing a threat to regional values. These aspects of subsystems deserve careful consideration.

There is also the need to clarify the character of the involvement of global actors in each particular subsystem: (1) the extent to which a subsystem is located within a "sphere of influence" or has been made subject to hegemonial management; (2) the extent to which global patterns of conflict are introduced into a subsystem by external rivals acting to acquire or retain influence or to deny predominant influence to the rival; (3) the degree to which the national societies within a subsystem are dependent for their domestic stability upon the receipt of economic, political, and military assistance from actors external to the subsystem; (4) the expectations and experience of the subsystem with regard to intraregional and extraregional intervention; (5) the perceived relevance of the outcome of subsystemic conflict to the stability and equilibrium of the global system; and (6) the extent to which the logistical circumstances and political attitudes of a subsystem allow the United Nations to play an active role in the confinement, termination, and avoidance of violent conflict. These are among the factors that need to be considered, not only in the *organizational* sense of Parts IV or V but in the *political* sense of comprehending the patterns of interaction between the global system and varying regional subsystems.

What are the boundaries of a particular subsystem? What features should govern its delimitation? How shall this delimitation be explained? Is it more or less permanent than the boundaries identifying the territorial extent of a sovereign state? Some of these issues are dealt with in the following excerpt from an article by Stanley Hoffmann, "Discord in Community: The North Atlantic Area as a Partial International System," *International Organization*, vol. 17, no. 3 (Summer 1963), pp. 521-549, at pp. 523-528:

I will look at the North Atlantic area as a *partial international system*. Despite the fuzziness of its geographical boundaries,* the area meets two of the criteria suggested by Raymond Aron for the identification of subsystems:

1. Its nations "spontaneously live a common destiny and make a distinction between what happens within and what happens outside their geographic-historical zone"†—a criterion which separates the area from Japan or Australia and New Zealand, as well as from the underdeveloped countries (including Latin America).

2. The nations of the area are "a theater of diplomatic operations" in which the relationship of major tension—the Cold War—takes forms different from what it is elsewhere.

3. I would add a third criterion that identifies the North Atlantic area as a subsystem; this characteristic is a revision of another one suggested by Aron and has obvious connections with the second. The area is characterized by a distinctive configuration of military forces. While some parts of the world can be called subsystems because of a regional balance of military power (for instance, the Middle East), the North Atlantic group, like the Soviet bloc, is a subsystem because of the preeminent presence of the military power of one member—in this case the United States.‡

As a partial international system, the North Atlantic area presents the following features:

1. Its inhabitants are predominantly white; the economies of its members are developed; and the area represents the biggest prize in the Cold War, being both the largest developed segment of the non-communist world and the component closest to the Soviets' military might.

2. Its members are linked by a common appreciation of the threat communism represents for their existence or for their social order.§

3. As for their actions, they have established a number of ties among themselves to enhance their common interests. In contrast to other subsystems, they form a zone of peace. Tensions and crises among them have not led to

*We shall assume here that the Atlantic nations are those that are members of either the North Atlantic Treaty Organization or the Organization for Economic Cooperation and Development.

†Raymond Aron, *Paix et Guerre* (Paris: Calmann-Levy, 1962), p. 388.

‡See also Michael Brecher, "International Relations and Asian Studies: The Subordinate State System of Southern Asia," World Politics, January 1963 (Vol. 15, No. 2), pp. 213-235.

§This seems to me true even of those members such as Switzerland and Sweden who are militarily neutral.

the use of force since the end of World War II.|| The same can hardly be said either of their relations with peoples outside the area, or of the relations among members of the Middle Eastern or south Asian subsystems. One of the ties is the "Community-building" experiment of western Europe.

However peace can be a negative word. The absence of war is compatible with a variety of diplomatic constellations among the "peacefully coexisting" groups. Are we in the presence of an imperial peace, of a balance-of-power system, of a "pluralistic security community"? Furthermore, the process of political integration (in Haas' sense) is hard to distinguish from and is one possible product of the interplay of foreign policies of the separate states, i.e., of ordinary international politics. Hence, we must look at the politics of the areas as if we were examining any other international system.

The relations among the North Atlantic nations are far too diverse to be examined all in the course of one article. A selection is necessary, All systems show forms of cooperation as well as forms of conflict. I have deliberately focused on the latter, and, among the latter, on those that involve the United States and the nations of continental western Europe. After some remarks of a theoretical nature about concepts useful for such an approach, I will examine types of contests and tensions (rather than types of cooperation) within the area, and discuss some of the national strategies that make for harmony.

Concepts

We are often misled by the language we use. The same words serve in the diplomatic vocabulary and as tools of scholarly analysis. We must be careful not to let the analysis be distorted by diplomatic practices—for the words that the statesmen choose can be either platitudes that express pleasant hopes, or subtle instruments used to prod and to pry, or veils needed to conceal and disguise. In this respect although the political difficulties encountered by the Atlantic nations are re-

flected in the scattering of metaphors strewn by statesmen in order to describe their states' relations, it would be dangerous to take any one of these expressions at face value. Statesmen talk of the Atlantic *Community*; more recently the idea of partnership has been introduced, and the rather unfortunate image of the *dumbbell* has been used to make partnership more graphic. Livingston Merchant, however, prefers another figure, that of "an inner *circle* [i.e., western Europe] in a larger surrounding circle."# Those who resort to the expression "community" do not always mean the same thing, depending on whether they apply it to the Six or to the whole Atlantic area.

None of these terms, as I will try to show, describes adequately the highly complex set of relations among the Atlantic states. Therefore, before engaging in the analysis, I want to stress certain postulates of a theoretical nature.

1. Within the realm of international relations the word *community* does more harm than good as a tool of analysis. One can distinguish two layers of relations. At bottom, there are the relations between *individuals* or *groups* across borders— let us say, to simplify, the relations that the old expression *jus gentium* brings to mind. This is the sector of *transnational society*. I prefer the word society to community because the latter term brings to mind *Gemeinschaft* that "was particular in membership, diffuse in function, and ascriptive in allocation."** The bulk of transnational relations, however, are much closer to those implied by the term *Gesellschaft*.

Superimposed on this sector we find the area of politics properly so-called—that is, the competition and the cooperation of *states*, in a milieu marked by the fragmentation of mankind into sharply differentiated groups (the nations) without any common power over them. If one defines a political community as "a condition in which specific groups and individuals show more loyalty to their central political institutions than to any other political authority,"†† it becomes obvious

---

||Every rule has its exceptions: there have been incidents between Britain and Iceland over fish, between Britain and Greece over Cyprus. However even those crises have been moderate.

#See his article in [*International Organization*, Summer 1963], p. 627 (italics added).

**Karl Deutsch, "Supranational Organizations in the 1960's," *Journal of Common Market Studies*, 1963 (Vol. 1, No. 3), p. 212.

††Ernst B. Haas, op. cit., p. 5. See also his article, "International Integration: The European and the

that international politics is by definition the negation of political community—and that the Atlantic area is no exception.

Is it therefore absurd to talk about the Atlantic "Community"? No, for two reasons. First, there exists among the individuals and groups involved certain common values, periodically celebrated by politicians and scholars alike, that make it possible to talk about a "moral community;'‡‡ there is also a "distinctive way of life" and a "wide range of mutual transactions," to which William Diebold, Jr., pays close attention.§§ In other words, the transnational society is a particularly intense one which seems to justify the use of the word community in a loose sense. Secondly, the states within the Atlantic area appear to have renounced the resort to force (otherwise the very mark of international relations) as a way of settling differences among them. Furthermore, they have instituted a variety of organizations in which they cooperate. Does not all this give us grounds to believe that the North Atlantic area is a "security-community" in Deutsch's sense?

Nonetheless, from the viewpoint of political analysis the use of the term "community," if not absurd, remains misleading.

(a) The common values and intense relations across borders which exist within the transnational society indicate what the attitudes and interests of the citizens are likely to be but do not determine either the policies of the governments or the nature of the political institutions and legal obligations that the governments may establish throughout the area. Of course, the governments will be influenced by the underlying interests and attitudes.‖‖ However, two caveats must be entered. First, the "moral community" and the range of transactions are rather unevenly distributed over the area, which has its own pockets of underdevelopment in both respects.## Secondly, common values have not in the past always prevented the mutual slaughter of peoples that were divided into separate political units; intense transactions have not always been an effective deterrent to political disputes and wars; and shared values and transactions have not even sufficed to establish similar forms of government over the whole area.

(b) Abstention from the use of force and the setting up of long regional organizations are one thing; a consensus of long duration among states on the procedures for settling disputes and for carrying out various functions in common is quite another. Only if the latter is achieved does it become legitimate to talk of a community in Deutsch's sense. The competition of states can be pursued by means short of violence but still far in excess of those used by even sharply opposed political parties which accept the basic constitutional order of a state. In the absence of such a basic procedural consensus, the Atlantic nations form at best a *potential* community.

2. The rest of this essay will be concerned only with the level of interstate relations. When we consider this level from the viewpoint of *theoretical* analysis, we find an essential difference between the relations among states (even peaceful and cooperative) that are not engaged in the process of integration toward "Political Community" in Haas' sense, and the relations among states that have joined (even partially) in such a process.

The main difference lies in the conceptual framework suitable for study of those two types of situations. Once nations are engaged in political community-building, methods derived from the "group theory of politics" become relevant. Since their borders are not being merely pierced by the very thin holes through which the threads of diplomacy can pass, but to a large extent dismantled, the formation of transnational parties and interest

---

Universal Process," *International Organization*, Summer 1961 (Vol. 15, No. 3), pp. 366–392.

‡‡See *Valeurs de base de la Communauté Atlantique* (Leyden: Sythoff, 1961). Also the statement by Christian Herter, "In New England we say 'community' when we are thinking about a society in which people live together as good neighbors, with a common recognition of the supremacy of law, and, having the benefits of varied economic and political institutions while united by their common cultural heritage and by their feelings of common destiny. In this sense we speak of the Atlantic Community." [Quoted in *Freedom and Union*, Feb. 1963 (Vol. 18, No. 2, p. 16).

§§See his article in [International Organization, Summer 1963], pp. 663–682.

‖‖I am following here the analysis of John Ladd, "The Concept of Community: A Logical Analysis," in *Community*, edited by C. J. Friedrich (New York: Liberal Arts Press, 1959).

##See the negative conclusion reached by J. Godechot and R. R. Palmer, "Le Problème de l'Atlantique," *Atti del X Congresso Internazionale de Scienze Storiche*, Florence, 1956, Vol. V, pp. 173ff.

groups, the birth of a "community viewpoint" that can animate even the separate governments, the development of common institutions with an authority and a legitimacy of their own, the settlement of conflicts by "upgrading the common interest" rather than by "splitting the difference" or by "minimum accomodation" all become possible, although not certain.*** If, on the other hand, one is dealing with a group of states, however friendly, whose statesmen remain in the mental universe of traditional interstate relations, the application of the methods and concepts I have just mentioned will be impossible or misleading. Parliamentary meetings may have an indicative value but no more; parties and pressure groups will try to get their viewpoints endorsed by their respective governments, rather than relying on supranational action; the joint institutions will share the basic ambiguities and weaknesses of general international organizations; and it will be difficult to define a joint rationality or a common interest higher than those of any member. More often than not, those who advocate "upgrading the common interest" really advocate (deliberately or not) the endorsement by all of the interest of one—usually that of the predominant partner. If an agreement on matters in dispute is reached, it will be by acceptance of the demands of the strongest, or by minimum accommodation, or, at best, by "splitting the difference." In other words, we are still in the realm of "strategic diplomatic behavior," with its own rules of the game.

These two theoretical poles are of course ideal types; reality is more complex. However, within the North Atlantic area, I contend that it is the latter that predominates, whereas the experiments among the Six point toward the model of political community. Whoever would apply Ernst Haas' methods to the "Atlantic Community" would waste his time. This is, I believe, the meaning of the distinction Walter Hallstein insists on making between the European "Communities" and Atlantic "partnership."††† A graphic example of the difference is being provided by the thorny subject of agriculture. The negotiations among the Six in December 1961–January 1962 demonstrated that on various points

agreements could apparently be reached by "upgrading the common interests" (for instance, reinforcing the role of the Commission); some of the Six appeared willing to suffer losses because those could be seen as concessions to and progress toward a higher common good rather than as losses to a competitor. The same spirit hardly prevails in the negotiations between Orville Freeman and the Six—within one framework, chickens tend to lose their national tag; in the other, the chicken's national origin makes all the difference in the world.‡‡‡ [From *International Organization*, vol. 17, no. 3, Summer 1963, pp. 521–549, at 523–528. Copyright 1963, World Peace Foundation, *Boston, Mass.* Reprinted by special permission.]

Hoffmann raises sharply two related issues that have been of concern throughout this volume: (1) under what conditions does an interacting group of political units constitute "a community"? and (2) does the particular effort to achieve integration, as distinct from cooperation, alter the character of political relationships within international society?

We also regard it as important to draw up a first-stage integration balance sheet for each subsystem and to assess various indications of second-stage integration potential. The degree of coherence of a subsystem and the dominant conceptions of the future of world order held by principal leaders are also of interest. To what extent and in what respects does each subsystem emphasize national autonomy, regional solidarity, and global stability and justice?

Part V contains some principal studies of subsystemic configurations. The purpose is to provide a substantive base for the conceptual issues discussed in these introductory paragraphs and not to provide any depth of knowledge about the regions themselves. We choose distinct subsystems to give some insight into the discontinuities that become evident in making comparisons among subsystems.

The selections in this part contain rather self-conscious justifications of the methodology used,

---

***See Ernst Haas, "International Integration . . . ," p. 367.

†††See his article in [*International Organization*, Summer 1963], pp. 779–780.

‡‡‡The negotiations in Brussels between the Six and Great Britain (especially over agriculture) had already demonstrated that point.

partly because a certain novelty continues to attach to any analysis of international conduct at a level of analysis intermediate between the national and the global level, especially if it is not associated with a formal organizational entity. None of these authors is especially concerned with world order, except perhaps in the sense of clarifying the conditions for "balance" or "equilibrium."

The first selection in this chapter is an article by Louis J. Cantori and Steven L. Spiegel, entitled "The International Relations of Regions." Their approach is developed further in *The International Politics of Regions* (Prentice-Hall, Englewood Cliffs, N.J., 1970, pp. 1–40) a book co-edited by Cantori and Spiegel. These authors attempt to establish a basis for the systematic study of regions as units of participation in world politics. Their main effort is to delineate clearly the idea of "subordinate system" in relation to the more embracing global system and to provide a series of analytical constructs (especially, "core," "periphery," and "intrusive system") to enable cross-regional comparison. The objective here is to evolve the same kind of disciplined basis of comparison on a regional level as has been developed on cross-national levels of comparison.

In the second selection, Leonard Binder considers "The Middle East as a Subordinate International System." His analysis well demonstrates one general proposition—namely, that the shape of Middle Eastern Politics cannot be understood in terms of the patterns of political conflict prevailing at the global level. It also seems clear, as Binder suggests, that the efforts of global powers to influence Middle Eastern politics floundered as a consequence of their insensitivity to the importance of subsystemic values and forces. Binder seems to suggest that Middle Eastern politics are a subordinate political system both because of subordination (global influences on the subsystem outweigh subsystemic influence on global politics) and because of an identifiable degree of subsystemic autonomy.

In the third selection, "International Relations and Asian Studies: The Subordinate State System of Southern Asia," Michael Brecher makes a comparable analysis of Southern Asia. The Asian setting is made very distinctive by the participation of two enormous states—China and India—within a subsystem that also includes a group of

small states. It would be possible, of course, to regard Southern Asia as a group of subsystems and to treat India and China as separate subsystems. The problems of intraregional hegemony are especially pronounced, and the search for a regional balance of power or equilibrium has been difficult to attain. Brecher, especially, suggests that the definition of subsystemic balance is one of the special preoccupations of intermediate-level analysis of international politics. The Asian subsystem is one in which the global rivals, the United States and the Soviet Union, have played roles that could not have been directly deduced from their position in the global system. For instance, both the Soviet Union and the United States supported India during the violent stages of its conflict with China.

The fourth selection, "Africa as a Subordinate State System in International Relations," is an examination of the African subsystem by William Zartman. This subsystem is characterized by the low military capabilities of the actors, the weakness of the central governments, the low stage of economic development, and the relatively marginal relationship that Africa has to global politics. The bipolar interpretation of the global system bears little relation to the patterns of interaction within Africa. Zartman well describes "the normative characteristics" of the African subordinate subsystem. Such a conception seems a useful supplement to emphases upon the configuration and distribution of power relations and the organization of relations. Despite the marginality of Africa to the global pattern, there are certainly occasions on which East-West rivalries are a significant input into the African subsystem.

In the fourth selection Kay Boals carefully examines the notion of "subordinate international system." She considers both its utility as a tool of analysis and its application to specific regional subject matter by Binder, Brecher, and Zartman. As well, she poses an alternate notion of "potential national system" to deal more responsively with the same material. In a sense, Boals raises for us the whole issue of what kinds of concepts are most useful for this subject matter when our objective is to think clearly and to present a coherent depiction of political developments.

Our final selection in Part V is Lynn Miller's "Regional Organizations and Subordinate Systems." In this article Miller seeks to combine structural analysis with systems analysis to show the "potential relevance of regional organizations to the systemic study of international relations of regions (p. 412)." He begins by classifying regional organizations on the basis of three types of orientation: (1) Cooperative, (2) Alliance, and (3) Functional. This analysis is followed by a section that delineates reasons for combining an interest in systems analysis with an interest in regional organizations. In giving an overview of membership in regional organizations of states participating in subordinate systems, Miller delimits some of the issues that ought perhaps to be considered in any very thorough treatment of particular organizations and subordinate systems.

15

The International Relations of Regions

LOUIS J. CANTORI
STEVEN L. SPIEGEL

It is the purpose of this article to suggest a comparative approach for analyzing the role of the region in present-day international politics. We will consider regions to be areas of the world which contain geographically proximate states forming, in foreign affairs, mutually interrelated units. We will attempt here to provide a framework for studying the region in terms of the shared features of all regions. As a result of these shared features, comparisons become feasible and generalizations are facilitated.

Recently, there has been a good deal of concentration on the region as a subordinate system.[1] This interest has developed simultaneously with studies of integration and international organization both of which have also been largely region-centered.[2] In this article we are concerned primarily with the subordinate system approach,

From *Polity,* vol. 2, no. 4, 1970, pp. 397–425. Reprinted by permission of the authors and publisher.

[1]See for example, Leonard Binder, "The Middle East Subordinate International System," *World Politics,* X (April, 1958), 408–29; Larry W. Bowman, "The Subordinate State System of Southern Africa," *International Studies Quarterly,* XII (September, 1968), pp. 231–62; Michael Brecher, "International Relations and Asian Studies: The Subordinate State System of Asia," *World Politics,* XV (January, 1963), 213–35, and Brecher, *The New States of Asia* (London: Oxford University Press, 1963), Chapters III and VI; George Modelski, "International Relations and Area Studies," *International Relations* (London), II (April, 1961), 143–55; William I. Zartman, "Africa as a Subordinate State System in International Relations," *International Organization,* XXI (Summer, 1967), 545–64. From another perspective, Bruce M. Russett has attempted to examine the possible criteria for regions, using a variety of quantitative methods, *International Regions and the International System: A Study in Political Ecology* (Chicago: Rand McNally and Company, 1967). For an attempt at a "systems approach" to the study of regions, see Oran R. Young, "Political Discontinuities in the International System," *World Politics,* XX (April, 1968), 369–92.
[2]See, for example, Karl Deutsch, *et al., Political Community and the North Atlantic Area* (Princeton, N.J.: Princeton University Press, 1957); Ernst B. Haas, *The Uniting of Europe* (Stanford, Calif.: Stanford University Press, 1958); Haas, "The Uniting of Europe and the Uniting of Latin America," *Journal of Common*

which provides us with a unit of analysis that facilitates comparison and allows us to concentrate on the international politics of a region rather than on particular processes (for example, integration, organization). Since the dawn of the modern era, the present period is the first in which all regions of the world maintain a measure of independence. The present is also a time in which communications and technology permit scholars to become knowledgeable about events that occur simultaneously around the world. The gaining of independence and the increase of communications allow for an unprecedented capacity to compare regions to each other. But we are not interested in comparison for its own sake. Rather, we aim to develop a means of judging the causal factors which are responsible for the particular mixture of cooperation and conflict present among the nations within a particular region. We are interested in the relationship between such factors as culture and stability, power and order, communications and cohesion.

In this article we will attempt to explicate a framework for the delineation of subordinate systems in order to establish a basis for the study of regional international politics.[3] We will begin

---

Market Studies, V (June, 1967), 315–43; Ernst B. Haas and Philippe Schmitter, *The Politics of Economics in Latin American Regionalism: The Latin American Free Trade Association After Four Years of Operation* (Denver, Colorado: University of Denver Monograph, 1965); Karl Kaiser, "The Interaction of Regional Subsystems: Some Preliminary Notes on Recurrent Patterns and the Role of Superpowers," *World Politics*, XXI (October, 1968), 84–104; Joseph S. Nye, "Comparative Regional Integration Concept and Measurement," *International Organization*, XXXII (Autumn, 1968), 855–80; *Pan-Africanism and East African Integration*, (Cambridge, Mass.: Harvard University Press, 1965); and Amitai Etzioni, *Political Unification: A Comparative Study of Leaders and Forces* (New York: Holt, Rinehart & Winston, Inc., 1965). In addition, see the excellent collections of articles in *International Political Communities: An Anthology* (Garden City, N.J.: Doubleday & Company, Inc., Anchor Books, 1966) and Joseph S. Nye, Jr., ed., *International Regionalism: Readings* (Boston: Little, Brown and Company, 1968). Finally, for a criticism of this integrationist approach to regional international relations which calls for an "empirical systems-analysis" approach, a fair label for the present study, see Roger D. Hansen, "Regional Integration Reflections on a Decade of Theoretical Efforts," *World Politics*, XXI (January, 1969) 242–71.

[3]For further elaboration see Louis J. Cantori and Steven L. Spiegel, *The International Politics of Regions: A Comparative Approach* (Englewood Cliffs, N.J.:

with a discussion of some of the problems inherent in the identification of subordinate systems and in explaining regional politics within them. We will attempt to show the relationships between the pattern variables and sectors, and conclude with a brief discussion of intersubordinate system relations.

I. THE IDENTIFICATION OF SUBORDINATE SYSTEMS

Nation-states are delineated by events, political practice, and (at least in part) membership in the United Nations. The dominant system, composed of the most powerful of states in any period of history, is more difficult to discern and its precise membership is a matter of constant conjecture, but there are at least a minimum of contenders for predominant status and therefore a minimum of potential configurations. There is also a degree of consensus among most observers: some form of bipolarity is present. Regional or subordinate systems, on the other hand, do not easily lend themselves to clear-cut identification: there are many alternatives, potential definitions, and groupings. Consequently, the determination of subordinate systems is difficult and complex.[4]

Given the complications of identifying subordinate systems, the authors have attempted nonetheless to identify fifteen subordinate systems (see Table 1).[5] They have done so on the following bases:

Prentice-Hall, 1970), and "Regional International Politics: The Comparison of Five Subordinate Systems," *International Studies Quarterly* (December, 1969).

[4]It is adequate for our purposes to define a system as the total interaction of relations among the autonomous units within a particular arena of international politics (for example globe, region, nation-state). The authors, while aware of the suggestiveness of what they have to say for systems theory in political science, have deliberately sought to avoid using the complicated technical vocabulary of systems theory as it appears, for example, in David Easton, *A Systems Analysis of Political Life* (New York: John Wiley & Sons, Inc., 1965); Morton Kaplan, *System and Process in International Politics* (New York: John Wiley & Sons, Inc., 1957); and O. R. Young, "A Survey of General Systems Theory," *General Systems*, IX (1964), 61–80.

[5]For a virtually identical breakdown, independently arrived at, see G. Etzel Pearcy, "Geopolitics and Foreign Relations," *Department of State Bulletin*, L (March 2, 1964), 318–30. We wish to thank Professor John Sigler for calling this to our attention.

Table 1
Subordinate Systems of the World and Their Subdivisions (Notes appear at the end of the table.)

Region	Core	Periphery	Intrusive System
1. Middle East	United Arab Republic	Israel	US
		Turkey	USSR
	Yemen	Iran	France
	Saudi Arabia	§Afghanistan	Gr. Britain
	Kuwait		W. Germany
	Iraq		Peoples Republic of China
	Lebanon		
	Sudan		
	Jordan		
	Syria		
	South Yemen		
	†Persian Gulf States		
2. Western Europe	France	Northern:	US
	W. Germany	*Gr. Britain	USSR
	Italy	*Ireland	
	Belgium	*Switzerland	
	Netherlands	Iceland	
	Luxembourg	§Finland	
		*Denmark	
		*Sweden	
		*Norway	
		*Austria	
		Southern.	
		*Spain	
		*Portugal	
		§Turkey	
		Greece	
		Malta	
		Cyprus	
3. Eastern Europe	Poland	*Albania	US
	Czechoslovakia	*Yugoslavia	France
	Hungary	Finland	W. Germany
	Rumania	E. Germany	USSR
	Bulgaria		Peoples Republic of China
4. Russia	USSR		

Table 1 (*continued*)

Region	Core	Periphery	Intrusive System
5. *North America*	US Canada	§Trinidad and Tobago §Jamaica §Barbados †§West Indies Associated States	
6. *Latin America*	Argentina Bolivia Brazil Chile Colombia Costa Rica Dominican Republic Ecuador El Salvador Guatemala Honduras †British Honduras Mexico Nicaragua Panama Paraguay Peru Uruguay Venezuela	*Cuba Trinidad and Tobago Jamaica Barbados Guyana Haiti †Surinam †West Indies Associated States	US USSR Gr. Britain Netherlands France Peoples Republic of China
7. *East Asia*	Peoples Republic of China	*Taiwan North Korea South Korea *Mongolia Japan †Hong Kong †Macao	US Portugal Gr. Britain USSR
8. *Southwest Pacific*	Australia New Zealand	†Islands of South Pacific Western Samoa	US France Gr. Britain USSR Japan

(continued)

Region	Core	Periphery	Intrusive System
9. Southeast Asia	I. Maritime S.E. Asia	Singapore	Peoples Republic of China
	Indonesia	†Territory of New Guinea	Japan
	Malaysia	†Territory of Portuguese Timor	Portugal
	Philippines		Australia
	II. Mainland S.E. Asia		US
		Burma	France
	Laos		Gr. Britain
	North Vietnam		USSR
	South Vietnam		
	Cambodia		
	Thailand		
10. South Asia	India	*Ceylon	US
		*Nepal	USSR
		*Bhutan	Gr. Britain
		*Sikkim	Peoples Republic of China
		Afghanistan	
		Maldive Islands	
		Pakistan	
		Burma	
11. North Africa	Morocco	Mauritania	France
	Tunisia	Libya	USSR
	Algeria	‖Spanish Sahara	US
			Peoples Republic of China
			Spain
12. West Africa	Ivory Coast	Nigeria	US
	Dahomey	Liberia	USSR
	Guinea	Sierra Leone	France
	Senegal	Gambia	Gr. Britain
	Upper Volta	Ghana	Portugal
	Mali	†Portuguese Guinea	
	Niger		
	Togo		
13. Southern Africa	South Africa	Malawi	US
	Rhodesia	Malagasy Republic	Gr. Britain
	†Angola		Portugal
	†Mozambique	Lesotho	

Table 1 (*continued*)

Region	Core	Periphery	Intrusive System
	†South-West Africa	Botswana	
		Zambia	
		Swaziland	
		Mauritius	
14. *Central Africa*	The Congo (Kinshasa)	Central African Rep.	US
			Belgium
	Rwanda	Chad	Peoples Republic of China
	Burundi	Cameroon	
		Gabon	USSR
		Congo (Brazzaville)	France
			Spain
		Equatorial Guinea	
15. *East Africa*	Uganda	Ethiopia	US
	Kenya	Somali Republic	USSR
	Tanzania		France
		†French Somaliland	Peoples Republic of China
			Gr. Britain

*Peripheral states with core potential.

†Angola, = colony; only the most important colonies have been chosen for their effect upon the subordinate systems.

§Afghanistan = states which could possibly be members of a second periphery.

Every nation-state (no matter how strong or how weak) is a member of one subordinate system. There are two exceptions to this generalization: the most powerful states are also active in other subordinate systems besides their own, and there are a few states which exist on the borderline between two subordinate systems and may be considered to coexist in some degree in both (for example, Finland, Turkey, Afghanistan, and Burma).

All subordinate systems are delineated—at least in part—by reference to geographical considerations, but social, economic, political, and organizational factors are also relevant. Consequently, members of subordinate systems are proximate, but they need not be contiguous.

Size does not necessarily determine the existence of a subordinate system. It may consist of one nation and be relatively large (the USSR),[6] or may consist of several nations and be relatively compact in area (the Middle East). Where only one nation is a member of a region we can say that the internal (or domestic) and subordinate systems are identical.

Within the boundaries of a subordinate system, there is a complex interaction between political, social, and geographic factors. It is this interaction which is most important in defining the limits of a subordinate system. For example. primarily political boundaries divide East and West Europe; social and political boundaries

[6]The Soviet Union has been considered a region in and of itself because with reference to social, political, and geographic factors it resembles many of the other subordinate systems. While many of the states on the Soviet Union's borders might have been considered as part of its periphery, Soviet relations with these states resemble more closely intrusive relations elsewhere rather than core-periphery relations.

divide Latin America and North America; geographic boundaries help to identify the Middle East and divide North Africa from the rest of Africa.

Indigenous political relationships (antagonistic and cooperative), geographic factors, and social and historical backgrounds help to define a subordinate system. Thus, the authors believe that, despite the Organization of African Unity (OAU), the African continent is fragmented by a variety of local interactions, while in Latin America, despite great differences, the area has shown more frequent interrelated characteristics.[7]

Outside powers play a role in defining a subordinate system. This is particularly the case in East Europe, Southeast Asia, and Latin America.

Although geographic boundaries do not easily change and social factors rarely do, political and ideological factors are fluid. Consequently, the identity of a subordinate system is both tenuous and dynamic. For example, the nineteenth-century writer would probably have suggested the significance of the Central European subordinate system, but he would not have found most of the nation-states which are presently located in the Middle East.

We can thus conclude that a subordinate system consists of one state, or of two or more proximate and interacting states which have some common ethnic, linguistic, cultural, social, and historical bonds, and whose sense of identity is sometimes increased by the actions and attitudes of states external to the system. The seven foregoing basic generalizations, plus this definition,

should be sufficient to enable us, at least tentatively, to identify a subordinate system. It will become clear as we proceed to elaborate the components of our approach that we are at the same time elaborating our definition.

Although the general identification of a given subordinate system is relatively easily established, the specific membership of certain states poses some difficulty. In Table 1, the authors have divided the globe in fifteen subordinate systems, each of which has been determined with reference to the considerations already discussed. (It is, of course, possible that other researchers—even using a similar framework—could come to slightly different conclusions.) Nevertheless, by accepting these delineations for the remainder of this article, the reader will be able to participate in an attempt to provide a methodology for comparing the international politics of diverse subordinate systems.

II. FOUR PATTERN VARIABLES

Granted the identification of a subordinate system in which the preceding generalizations are operative, it is possible to differentiate it further into three subdivisions: the core sector, the peripheral sector and the intrusive system. Before turning to a discussion of these three subdivisions of the subordinate system, we shall first proceed to a discussion of four pattern variables which we believe to be crucial to the demarcation of these subdivisions. These are: (1) nature and level of cohesion, (2) nature of communications, (3) level of power, and (4) structure of relations. These variables are crucial to the comparison of subordinate systems with diverse qualities.

Nature and Level of Cohesion

By cohesion we mean the degree of similarity or complementarity in the properties of the political entities being considered and the degree of interaction between these units. The concept of cohesion plays a similar role in the consideration of regions to that which the concept of integration has played in the analysis of nation-states. In the study of comparative national politics, integration has been used to mean, "The problem of creating a sense of territorial nationality which

---

[7]It is worth noting in this regard that Africa is almost twice as large as Latin America and that its population is also about twice as large. Some readers may be surprised that the authors have not defined such areas as Scandinavia and Central America as separate subordinate systems. It is our position that were political integration to occur among such nations (Benelux and the British West Indies may be added), they would have a similar position in their subordinate systems (for example, as part of the core or periphery) to their present one, even though their power within the system would be increased. For example, a United States of Central America would play a similar role to that played by Mexico or Venezuela as members of the Latin American core, and a United States of Scandinavia would relate to West Europe as Great Britain does at present. Our subsequent analysis of cores and peripheries should further clarify the rationale for these judgments.

overshadows—or eliminates—subordinate parochial loyalties."[8] When applied to the study of international relations the concept of integration can thus represent an assumption that the states being compared will lose their independence as they become more interlocked. Cohesion involves no such assumption. As states become more similar and more interactive, there is no guarantee that they will unite or federate; on the contrary, cohesiveness may as likely lead to disunity as to unity. When the term "integration" is applied to regions it is usually assumed at a minimum that warfare does not exist among the members or that a more encompassing political institution results from the process. "Integration and security community . . . imply stable expectations of peace among the participating units or groups, whether or not there has been a merger of their political institutions," or "Political integration is the process whereby political actors in several distinct national settings are persuaded to shift their loyalties, expectations and political activities toward a new center, whose institutions possess or demand jurisdiction over the pre-existing national states,"[9] There is, on the other hand, no direct correlation between cohesion and absence of warfare or between cohesion and a shift of political loyalty.

The concept of cohesion as discussed here can be further differentiated into its social, economic, political, and organizational elements. Under the rubric of social cohesiveness, attention is focused upon the contributive factors of ethnicity, race, language, religion, culture, history, and consciousness of a common heritage. The contrasts that these factors may present can be seen in the extremes of the Middle East subordinate system's high degree of social cohesion and Southeast Asia's extremely low degree of social cohesion. Under the rubric of economic cohesiveness, the focus is upon the distribution and complementarity of economic resources as well as on the character of trade patterns. The extremes of this factor can be seen in the West European system's high degree of economic cohesiveness and the West African and Middle Eastern systems' low degree. Under the rubric of political cohesiveness we are concerned with the manner in which the pattern and degree of complementarity of types of regime contribute or detract from the cohesion of a subordinate system. In this respect one could compare West Europe, with its multitude of reconciliation or parliamentary-type regimes, and the Middle East, with its contrasting mobilizational and modernizing autocracies.[10]

Finally, under the rubric of organizational cohesion we should note the possible effects upon cohesion of membership in the United Nations and in regional organizations. The analysis of voting behavior in the United Nations has revealed the existence of groupings of states identifiable as Afro-Asian, Latin American, and so forth, all of which contribute in some degree to regional consciousness.[11] As for regional organization, we should note to what extent a regional organization is coterminus with the region's boundaries, contrasting, for example, the European Common Market and the Arab League. If all members of a subordinate system or a sector of a subordinate system belong to a regional international organization, this tends to reinforce cohesion, particularly if the boundaries of the membership coincide with the system's or sector's boundaries.

Nature of Communications

The second pattern variable, the nature of communications, is divisible into four aspects: personal communications (mail, telephone, telegraph); mass media (newspapers, radio, television); exchange among the elite (intraregional education, tourism, diplomatic visits within the region); and transportation (road, water, rail, air). It is

---

[8]Myron Weiner, "Political Integration and Political Development," in *Political Modernization*, ed., C. Welch (Belmont, Calif.: Wadsworth, 1967), 150–51. Reprinted from *The Annals*, CCCLVIII (March, 1965), 52–64.

[9]The first quotation is from Karl Deutsch, "Security Communities," in *International Politics and Foreign Policy*, ed., J. Rosenau, (New York: The Free Press, 1961), 98. The second is from Ernst Haas, *The Uniting of Europe* (Stanford, California: Stanford University Press, 1958), 16.

[10]For this classification of political systems, see David Apter, *the Politics of Modernization* (Chicago: University of Chicago Press, 1965), 28–38, Chapters 9, 11.

[11]For an analysis along these lines, see Bruce Russett, *International Regions and the International System* (Chicago: Rand McNally & Co., 1967), Chapters 4, 5.

evident that literacy rates and differences in language will affect the first three and that geography and technological development will affect all four. Regions will differ from each other with the degree to which these four factors are present and applicable. Southeast Asia is weak in all four, for example, as is West Africa, while West Europe has been able to outweigh linguistic differences by the sheer profusion of channels of communications and other pattern variables.

Level of Power

"Power," the third pattern variable, is defined here as the present and potential ability and the willingness of one nation to alter the internal decision-making processes of other countries in accordance with its own policies. We can isolate three broad aspects of a nation's power: material, military, and motivational. The material elements of power comprise the basis of a nation's capacity: these include its location and resources; the size, quality, and structure of its population; its economy and industrial capacity (particularly to be measured by gross national produce (GNP), per capita GNP, and production and consumption of energy) and the relative efficiency of its administration and government. The military elements of power comprise a nation's ability to wage war: its military techniques, weaponry, manpower, and efficiency. They also include the effect which scientific and technological developments have on the ability of stronger nations to increase their margin of superiority over weaker nations or of weaker countries to overtake the leaders. Finally, the motivational elements of power center on a nation's will to seek prestige and status in international affairs, and on its readiness to sacrifice consumer satisfaction to build its material and military power. Motivation is influenced by such elements as ideology, national character and morale, nationalism, history, the personalities and abilities of particular statesmen, and diplomatic skill.

Because existing and potential[12] national strengths and weaknesses are frequently contradictory, it is difficult to produce a "power calculation" in order to compare states. Given the complexity of the process, the attempt to estimate the power of nations nevertheless produces valuable information about the distribution or balance of power among nations in a subordinate system. This analytical process also facilitates the comparison of the character of various subordinate systems.

It is possible to detect seven types of nation-states in the current period: primary powers, secondary powers, middle powers, minor powers, regional states, micro-states, and colonies. Which category a nation-state belongs in depends on its degree of power, as suggested by the three factors discussed above and its range of influence, as indicated by the number or location of states with which a particular nation is able to exercise its power.

Primary Powers. The primary powers (the US and USSR), together with the secondary powers constitute the great powers, that is nations which influence domestic politics and foreign policies of other countries in several areas of the world and are individually superior to other nations materially, militarily, and in motivation. Primary powers are superior to secondary powers on the basis of these three factors, but both types compose the dominant system in international politics.

Secondary Powers. Compared to primary powers, secondary powers (the United Kingdom, France, West Germany, Japan, and China) have a limited capacity to participate in selected subordinate systems of the world.

Middle Powers. Middle powers (for example, Italy, Canada, Australia, East Germany) are those states whose level of power permits them to play only decidedly limited and selected roles in subordinate systems other than their own.

Minor Powers. Minor powers (for example, Cuba, Algeria, United Arab Republic) are those

---

[12]"Potential" applies to each factor of power (material, military, and motivational). An advanced state may be capable of growing further or may change in motivation as a result of altered international conditions or a new domestic regime. A developing state's potentiality may be long or short-term, depending upon its possible development and rate of growth.

states which play leading roles in the international relations of their own systems.

Regional States. Regional states (for example, Greece, Hungary, Syria) are those states which are able on occasion to play a limited but not leading role in their own subordinate systems. They also tend to have greater flexibility with reference to stronger powers than do micro-states and colonies.

Micro-States. Micro-states (for example, Jamaica, Togo, Laos) are states which have little or no influence in regional international relations because their power calculation leaves them almost totally within the orbit of one or more large powers.

Colonies. Colonies (for example, Spanish Sahara, Angola, Hong Kong) are the few remaining political entities which have little or no independent motivational power.

This categorization allows us to make an estimate of both the distribution and hierarchy of power within a subordinate system. West Europe is distinctive for its prevalence of secondary and middle powers. In Latin America there are only one middle power (Brazil), a few minor powers and a few regional powers, and many micro-states. In the Arab sector of the Middle East congeries of regional and micro-states are all minor powers. The categories also facilitate the comparison of subordinate systems: the predominance of secondary and middle powers in West Europe indicates that its level of power is greater than that of either Latin America or the Middle East.

Structure of Relations

The fourth pattern variable, the structure of relations, refers to the character of the relationships which exist among the nation-states that compose a subordinate system. It is important here to determine: (1) which states are cooperating and which are in conflict (the spectrum of relations); (2) the bases for their amity or antagonism (the causes of relations); and (3) the instruments which they use to effect their relations—for example, types of weapons, ways of ameliorating

Table 2
Spectrum of Relations

bloc		
alliance		
	limited	
	cooperation	
		equilibrium
	stalemate	
	sustained	
	crisis	
direct		
military		
conflict		

conflict, methods of cooperation (the means of relations).

The Spectrum of Relations.[13] The structure of a system's interrelations can be described by reference to the conditions depicted in Table 2, which shows a spectrum extending from the close cooperation of a bloc to the exacerbated conflict of direct military confrontation.

Conditions of amity include: a bloc, in which two or more nations act in international politics as if they were one political entity; an alliance, in which they agree to aid each other in specified ways—usually including military means; and tentative cooperation, in which they coordinate their actions for specific purposes and over a very short period of time (days rather than weeks, weeks rather than months). From the opposite direction, conditions of antagonism include: direct military conflict, in which combat occurs between the troops of two opposing sides; sustained crisis, in which contending parties make persistent attempts, short of direct military conflict, to alter the balance of power between them; and stalemate, in which contention continues while neither side is prepared or able to alter the existing relationship. In direct conflict, the means used to change the status quo are forceful and deliberate, but in sustained crisis the primary means of contention are more subtle: they include political

[13]The concept of power, the seven types of nations, and the spectrum of relations are discussed in greater detail by Steven L. Spiegel in *Dominance and Diversity* (New York: Little, Brown and Company, 1972).

maneuvering among neutral and independent states, arms races, limited local warfare between parties aligned on either side, vituperative exchanges, crises, and in general a chaotic atmosphere filled with tension. In stalemates, contention is at a lower level because both sides decide that, given existing conditions, they would prefer to live with the situation than face the consequences of attempting to upset the prevailing balance of forces.

Only when we arrive at equilibrium do we find a standoff in competitive power between two sides that is mutually acceptable. Whether or not an equality of power exists, the effect is the same: the statesmen of both sides not only accept the situation but prefer it to any foreseeable alternative. The status quo becomes a standard of the acceptable balance of power, and so long as neither side moves to alter it or perceives that it is being altered the equilibrium will continue. The difference between stalemate and equilibrium is that in a stalemate one or both sides would change conditions if they could and are seeking means of doing so; in equilibrium neither side believes that it would alter the balance of power even if it had the means to do so. Equilibrium is a prerequisite to most stages of amity—except the lowest forms of limited cooperation.[14]

The Causes of Relations.   States are, of course, not always consistent in their relations. In any relationship between two or more states there may be elements of conflict on one level and of cooperation on others. Many Latin American states (for example, Peru, Chile, Bolivia) are in a stalemate with reference to border issues while they are allied in economic and diplomatic international organization. Saudi Arabia and the UAR have been in a sustained crisis in regard to Yemen but in an alliance in regard to Israel. It is therefore necessary to consider the relative significance of major issues which cause conflict or cooperation between particular states in a subordinate system. In Latin America, the effect of American influence has been to subordinate local issues

to regional pursuits. Similarly, in the Middle East, intra-Arab disputes are muted by the confrontation with Israel.

When there is conflict, the nature of the disputed issues reveals the intensity of the contention. For example, border and economic disputes are usually less damaging to peaceful international relations in the region than racial, religious, ideological, and historical rivalries. Similarly, when there is cooperation the reasons for collaboration indicate the strength of the cross-national ties. A common enemy is likely to be a stronger tie than mutual economic interest; under present conditions, economics is likely to be a stronger incentive to cooperation than are religious ties.

The Means of Relations.   The spectrum of relations within a subordinate system is further elucidated by reference to the means which are used in such relations. The type of warfare (for example, guerilla versus conventional) being carried on helps to explain the relations which exist. Moreover, the manner in which conflicts are ameliorated and terminated indicates the strength of particular conditions in the spectrum of relations. For example, conditions in Latin America, where an elaborate set of diplomatic devices exists for the settlement of many types of conflict, are very different from conditions in the Middle East, where cease-fires are arranged by intermediaries and there is little or no contact between the Arabs and Israelis. West Europe, where states are also likely in the current period to resort to established means of amelioration, is different from Southeast Asia, where guerrillas either emerge victorious or fade into the interior and where rare agreements are broken freely. Finally, the extent of established consultative devices and the range of ties between cooperating governments not only help to indicate whether a bloc, alliance, or limited cooperation is in progress; they also hint at the durability of these relationships.

These three elements, then, provide a frame of reference for examining the prevailing nature of relationships within a subordinate system. They enable us to make comparisons with other subordinate systems, both with respect to the influence of what we shall call the "intrusive system" and the effect of levels of cohesion,

---

[14]The spectrum we have presented does not include nations which are "neutral" toward each other in the sense of noninvolvement in hostile relations. In current subordinate systems, equilibrium or stalemate in respect to two conflicting sides is frequently either the cause or the effect of neutral policies of individual states.

power, and communication. As we shall see, these four pattern variables, when applied to a given subordinate system, unveil the existence of what we term "core" and "peripheral" sectors.

III. THE CORE AND THE PERIPHERY

The Core Sector

The core sector consists of a state or group of states which form a central focus of the international politics within a given region. It usually consists of more than one state, and when it does the constituent units possess a shared social, political, and/or organizational background or activity. There may be more than one core sector within a given subordinate system.[15]

We can make our definition more specific and useful by examining a hypothetical core sector in terms of our four pattern variables: the level of cohesion, the nature of communications, the level of power, and the structure of relations. The minimal conditions for the existence of a core sector can be determined by its level of cohesion which requires a consideration of the degree of social, economic, and political similarity, complementarity, and interaction within the particular group of states. In addition, the factor of organizational cohesion would have to be considered. Thus, an analysis of the similarity or complementarity of social cohesiveness would take into account ethnic, linguistic, cultural, and historical similarities, while economic cohesiveness would depend upon the complementarity of natural resources as well as the patterns and the degree of trade within the core and within the periphery. Political cohesiveness would be determined by the similarities among regimes

and the manner in which these might contribute to or detract from the cohesiveness of the core sector. For example, in West Europe the regimes of the core sector are relatively similar, while in the Middle East they are not. Organizational cohesion would be revealed by the extent to which an organization (for example, the European common market and the West European core sector) coincides with a core sector. The degree of common membership in international organizations, moreover, would be an indication of the extent of interaction within the core sector. It is evident that a knowledge of the degree of similarity or complementarity of these factors of cohesion will assist us to delineate a core sector. It is also evident that one type of cohesion may be more pronounced than others in a given core sector (for example, the organizational in West Europe and the social in the Middle East), while still other core sectors may be significantly united by all four elements of cohesion, (for example, North America, Southwest Pacific). Most often, however, one or more of the elements of cohesion, but not all of them, are significantly present in a core.

The second pattern variable, the nature of communications, should further inform us about the nature of a core sector in terms of personal communications, mass media, interchange among the elite, and transportation facilities. Striking, for example, is the extent to which the flow of communication within a subordinate system can be restricted to a core sector and fail to penetrate the peripheral sector (for example, the Francophonic core sector of West Africa and the Anglophonic peripheral sector).

An analysis of the core sector in terms of levels of power, our third pattern variable, should inform us of the political capabilities contained within it. As in a region as a whole, the distribution of power within the core reveals the political processes at work. The primacy of France and West Germany in the Common Market, of Australia in the Southwest Pacific, of Algeria in North Africa, and of the Union of South Africa in Southern Africa may be contrasted with the rough equality among the participants in the cores of maritime Southeast Asia and East Africa. The degree of supremacy of the preeminent states of a core (for example, United States in North America versus the UAR in the Middle

---

[15]Generally, the identification of a core sector is assisted by the existence of an easily identifiable culturally heterogeneous peripheral sector. When the peripheral sector is not so heterogeneous, as, for example, in the West African Anglophonic peripheral sector, such factors as degree of cohesion, size or geographical area, population, and economic wealth have to be considered in order to determine the political center of gravity of the subordinate system. In West Africa, the high level of cohesion relative to the periphery and the vastness of the Francophonic area are the decisive factors.

East), can be contrasted with the position of weaker states (for example, Canada in North America versus Jordan, Yemen, and South Yemen in the Middle East), the relative gap between strongest and weakest must also be assessed. Finally, in distinguishing the core from the peripheral sector it is important to note the relative power of each. The Middle East and West Africa are distinctive for the strength of their peripheral states *vis-à-vis* the core, while in Latin America and Southeast Asia the peripheries are particularly weak. In West Europe, the core and periphery come closer to approximating equality than in any of the cases just cited.

The fourth pattern variable, the structure of relations, completes the profile of a core sector. It is closely connected to the third variable, for it informs us of the dynamics of the exercise of power. Differing levels of power within a core sector will have profound consequences on its internal relations. The conflicts between the UAR and Saudi Arabia, Brazil and Argentina, North Vietnam and Thailand, Guinea and the Ivory Coast, among Indonesia, Malaysia, and the Philippines, and between Algeria and her two neighbors, Tunisia and Morocco, are related to power conditions within the core. The means of both conflict and cooperation are, moreover, directly connected to the level of power of the core—except where outside powers intervene and provide their own instruments of contention (for example, jet fighters) or collaboration (for example, international organization). The causes of relations, however, often involve wider issues than mere level of power. Cohesion and communications are especially significant in explaining the reasons for the particular structure of relations within the core. For example, the factor of political cohesion helps to explain the split within the Arab core; improved communications and political and organizational cohesion help to explain Franco-German reconciliation.

It can thus been seen that while the initial delineation of the subordinate system may itself be considered somewhat subjective, the application of the four pattern variables soon reveals the identity of the subordinate system and of the more well-defined core sector as well. In fact, our ability to delineate the core sector so sharply in turn assists us to define the subordinate system itself.

The Peripheral Sector

The peripheral sector includes all those states within a given subordinate system which are alienated from the core sector in some degree by social, political, economic, or organizational factors, but which nevertheless play a role in the politics of the subordinate system. While the core sector tends toward cultural, social, and political homogeneity, the peripheral sector is characteristically heterogeneous, and there is usually little interaction among periphery members. The minimal factor accounting for the inclusion of the member states of the peripheral sector in the subordinate system appears to be primarily geographical, although additional social, cultural, political, and historical factors exist. It follows, then, that the peripheral sector, as compared with the core sector, is characterized by less cohesion, less communication, relatively unrelated levels of power, and much more fluid relations.

There are some exceptions, however, in areas where there tends to be some degree of homogeneity if not also cohesiveness (notably in the Anglophonic periphery of West Africa, groupings in the West European periphery, the Black states of the Southern African periphery, and the Francophonic area of Central Africa). In West Africa, for example, a common British colonial experience and knowledge of the English language among the elite contribute to this comparative homogeneity. Where both the core and periphery are cohesive, it is necessary to assess the relative degree of cohesiveness and the focus of political centrality within the subordinate system before assigning the label "core."

One of the outstanding characteristics of the periphery is that its diplomatic orientation is typically outside of the region; for example, peripheral states usually seek their diplomatic alignments outside of, rather than within, the subordinate system. This can be seen, for example, in the key role played by Nigeria, a member of the West African peripheral sector, in the founding of the OAU and in the membership of Iran and Turkey, members of the Middle Eastern peripheral sector, in the Central Treaty Organization (CENTO). Another characteristic of the peripheral sector is that it often serves as a geographic and diplomatic buffer between external powers. This largely geopolitical circumstance can be seen in Libya and Mauritania, which are buffers for the North African core sector, and in Burma, which is a buffer for the mainland Southeast Asian core sector.

Aberrations in the Periphery

The fluid nature of the periphery occasionally makes it necessary to qualify its delineation. In this section we shall identify two groupings of peripheral states in West Europe and we shall also discuss the problem of borderline peripheral states. Both the large size and certain dichotomous features of the West European periphery suggest that it can be divided into Northern and Southern groupings (see Table 1). The Northern peripheral states are more industrialized, more developed economically, and more democratically governed than the South; as a consequence, most of these states have a higher core potential. They are also distinguished from the South because they are more Protestant and linguistically more Nordic, Anglo-Saxon, and Germanic. This distinction does not, however, affect the method of core-periphery analysis already presented, because it is offset by the importance of intrasector organizational and economic cohesion.

A few of the states which we have described as peripheral are, by virtue of their activities, divided between the peripheries of two subordinate systems. In terms of our four pattern variables this generally appears to occur when certain states (notably Turkey, Finland, Afghanistan, and Burma) can be identified with one subordinate system in terms of cohesion and communications while they interact with another in terms of power and the structure of relations. In addition, the Anglophonic area of the Caribbean appears to lie astride both the North American and Latin American subordinate systems, as elements of the four pattern variables and geography pull these micro-states in both directions in this period of transition from colony to independence.[16] Some degree of verification of the

marginal character of borderline states is provided by the fact that our consideration of them reveals that they are always located in a periphery, and never in a core. Thus, although borderline peripheral states are difficult to locate within a specific subordinate system, it is possible to examine their position by utilizing this comparative regional approach.

Relations Between the Sectors

As the definition of the peripheral sector indicated, the periphery is in part defined by its relationship to the core. In relations between the core and the periphery, alienation is a central factor, as was cohesion in our discussion of relations within a sector.

The core, as the center of political gravity in the subordinate system, relates individually to isolated states or to small groups of states in the periphery. Their alienation may arise for a variety of reasons. Geography is frequently a complement to other factors, but it is not ordinarily the only element leading to alienation from the core, and in fact may not be an element at all, as the case of Israel shows. In West Europe, geography has contributed to Great Britain's alienation from the core, but political developments have also been crucial. Were Britain to be admitted to the Common Market, she would thereby become a member of the core, since organizational cohesion is the most important element in determining the West European core. In the Middle East, on the other hand, social cohesion is extremely important in delineating the periphery; therefore, the three non-Arab states, Iran, Turkey and Israel, form the periphery.

The degree of alienation between the two sectors can perhaps be seen in the distinction between states with, and states without, the potentiality of becoming part of the core (for example, Taiwan and Great Britain versus Jamaica and Israel). A high degree of political and

---

[16]Further examples of states which may be placed in more than one subordinate system may readily occur to our readers (for example, Mongolia, Yugoslavia,

Mauritania). At this stage in our study, an examination of conditions in terms of the four pattern variables yielded only the borderline peripheral states which are listed in Table 1, although the addition of others is possible as further research continues.

organizational cohesion in the core tends to breed peripheral states which are potential members of the core sector, while a high degree of social cohesion in the core tends to preclude peripheral states from having such potentialities (see Table 1).

There is frequently disaffection between the core and the periphery. Among the fifteen subordinate systems of the world, some form of tension between the two sectors is especially severe in the Middle East, East Europe, Latin America, East Asia, and South Asia. Only in Southeast Asia and North Africa does tension within the core exceed the tension between the sectors. As for tension within the periphery, this hardly exists, because of the low level of interaction in the periphery. The major exceptions are Greece and Turkey (when Turkey is viewed as a member of the West European periphery); Albania and Yugoslavia in East Europe, the Koreas in East Asia, and Ethiopia and the Somali Republic in East Africa. States which are potentially part of the core and those which are not seem to be equally likely to find themselves in antagonistic relationships with their core. In some cases the differences which contribute to the difficulty of becoming part of the core create an antagonistic relationship with some or all of the core states (for example, Israel, Pakistan, Mauritania), although frequently the potentiality of joining the core itself seems to create alienation and conflict (for example, Taiwan, Albania, and Cuba).

IV. THE INTRUSIVE SYSTEM

An instrusive system consists of the politically significant participation of external powers in the international relations of the subordinate system. While the core and peripheral sectors both involve the states located within the region, an analysis of almost every region reveals that these states are not the only ones which play a role in the activities of the subordinate system. As one would expect in an international system with a hierarchy consisting of seven types of nations, external countries involve themselves in the international politics of subordinate systems other than their own. This pattern is only absent in the North American core and in the Soviet Union,

where the level of power is extremely high. Additionally, in the core of North America, the level of cooperation between the two members, the United States and Canada, is extremely high.[17]

There are two types of externally based regional participation: politically significant involvement and politically insignificant involvement. Politically insignificant involvement comprises material aid, trade, economic investment, and cultural and educational efforts which do not usually produce participation in the balance of power of the region. Middle powers, and to some degree secondary powers, are most likely to undertake this type of involvement. Spanish involvement in the Middle East and Canadian aid to India are examples. Much of Japanese and West German aid (except West Germany's activity in East European politics and its Hallstein Doctrine) has not been politically motivated or accompanied by a desire to participate in local international relations. These conditions may change, however.

Politically significant involvement, on the other hand, produces participation in the balance of power of the subordinate system and may affect the dominant system's balance as well. This participation is expressed by the possession of a colony; economic or military aid producing an alteration in the balance of power in the region; formal alliance, troop commitment, or any agreement which causes the external power to act in ways which resemble the types of actions that would ordinarily be taken by a country indigenous to the region. This type of involvement is also determined by reference to the objectives, power, motivation, location, and international position of the intruding nation. Since only politically significant members can be defined as being members of the intrusive system, we will primarily be concerned here with these types of external powers. Even politically significant involvement by one state, once identified as such, has to be judged further in relation to other intrusive powers. Thus, for example,

---

[17]It might be suggested that French and British involvement in Canada is in form similar to intrusive action in other subordinate systems. The authors rejected this interpretation, however, because of both the indigenous power of Canada and its close relationship with the U.S.

Australia and Portugal meet the minimum requirements for politically significant involvement in Southeast Asia, but their participation is nowhere near as significant as that of the United States, China, or the Soviet Union.

We can isolate nine characteristic ways in which external powers participate in the politics of a given region. These are: multilateral arrangements; bilateral arrangements; trade and economic investment; possession of a colony; military intervention; subversion; use of the United Nations; cultural and educational activities; and propaganda. All of these are employed in one situation or another by politically significant external powers, while a few—particularly the economic and cultural avenues—are used occasionally by those which are politically insignificant.

These characteristic ways of participation in the intrusive system have both positive and negative effects upon the four pattern variables of the subordinate system: cohesion, communications, power, and the structure of relations.

Cohesion

The social, economic, political, and organizational aspects of the cohesion of a subordinate system are affected in a number of ways by the participation of an external power. Social cohesion can be enhanced by the educational efforts of an external power, if these efforts reinforce the pre-existing educational and linguistic patterns within the system. An example of this type of activity is the continued educational efforts of the French in their former colonies in North Africa and sub-Saharan Africa. Another way an intrusive power may affect social cohesion is to assist in the transfer of populations (for example, the Russians, in moving the German and Polish populations westward after World War II). In general, however, external powers are less able to affect social cohesion as such. Economic cohesion can be increased if economic assistance programs have as their aim the enhancement of economic complementarity through the encouragement of industrialization, improved methods of agriculture, or economic integration. Examples of external attempts to influence economic cohesion

include American efforts in Latin America and West Europe, Russian efforts in East Europe, and British efforts in East Africa. In each case the purpose of external pressure and effort has been at least in part the encouragement of a division of labor within the region. The effect of external participation upon political cohesion may be seen when the support of a given power serves to perpetuate a conservative, radical, or moderate regime in power, or to prevent a particular type of regime from coming to power, thereby reinforcing or reducing cleavages within the system. In addition, there are instances where the concern of an external power with regional security arrangements or economic arrangements has either contributed to or hindered the organizational cohesion of a subordinate system. Intrusive powers have been able to act whether or not they have actually been members of these international organizations (for example, NATO, CENTO, COMECON).

Communications

External powers influence communications within subordinate systems in a variety of ways. Economic assistance programs have aided in mail delivery and telephone and telegraph facilities. In a variety of circumstances they have also led to improvements in transportation systems and have expedited the introduction of radio and television. The activities of an external power in a region can also encourage interchange of elite groups. Diplomatic visits and education within the region have been promoted by intrusive powers. Moreover, students and diplomats have found themselves in contact with members of other elite groups of their own region, on the territory of an intrusive power, at its universities, and at conferences sponsored by it.

Level of Power

It is upon the pattern variable of level of power that external powers have perhaps their greatest effect. External powers can promote the material power of members of subordinate systems by providing economic aid, food, technical assistance, favorable trade terms, birth control assistance, teachers, and administrative advice. Of more direct effect on the balance of power of a subordinate system is a change in military power. In ascending order of importance, the types of this kind of aid external powers can give members of the subordinate system are: economic aid which frees funds for arms purchases; grants or sales of arms and the training necessary for the use of these arms; transfer of the technology, know-how, and material necessary to permit indigenous manufacture of weaponry; and finally, the commitment of troops.

Of the three factors of power, the motivational factor is here the most significant. Through their participation in the region, external powers may affect the political, social, and ideological direction which particular nations in the subordinate system follow. Exterior powers will decide whether to support existing governments or whether to support opposition or rebellious groups, and they may either moderate or encourage the desire of indigenous countries for increased influence of their own. External powers may then play an essential role in determining which elite comes to power in a large number of states of the region and which kinds of political institutions will prevail. In extreme cases, they may even affect the number of states which exist in the subordinate system.

Structure of Relations

As this analysis of the risks attendant upon the involvement of intrusive powers suggests, external powers affect and indeed at times determine the structure of relations within a subordinate system. The high degree of cooperation in both East Europe and Latin America is affected by the primacy of the Soviet Union and the United States, respectively, in these intrusive systems. It is interesting to note that when either the United States or the Soviet Union loses power in either of these regions, regional conflict tends to be aggravated. On the other hand, the competition of intrusive powers exacerbates conflict in the Middle East, Southeast Asia, East Asia, North Africa, and West Africa. In the Middle East and Southeast Asia particularly, sustained crisis and direct military conflict have become prevalent as

the conflicts of the dominant and subordinate systems have fused.

The type of military aid and involvement of intrusive powers affects the means of relations. Consultation and amelioration are facilitated by one or more of the intrusive powers in West Europe, Latin America, East Europe, North Africa, and South Asia. In Southeast Asia and the Middle East, on the other hand, massive military aid has raised the level of conflict and made it far more dangerous. In addition, China has contributed to the turmoil in Southeast Asia through its conceptual and practical assistance in guerrilla warfare. The great influence of the intrusive powers upon the means of relations in Southeast Asia is attested to by the fact that regional wars are frequently accompanied by peace conferences attended by several great powers.

Intrusive powers usually have less influence on the causes of relations than on the other elements of the structure of relations. They may not be responsible for local religious and racial rivalries, but as we have already suggested they are capable of fanning the flames of contention by introducing ideological rivalries, by imposing their own political competitions on the area, and by encouraging local adventurism. The division of Korea and of Vietnam may be cited as examples of external powers influencing local conflict. In like manner, although to a lesser extent, they can organize local blocs and alliances to support their policies (for example, NATO, Warsaw Pact) and thereby enforce cooperation among local parties. In general, the experience of intrusive powers has been that it is easier to impose conflict than cooperation upon the members of a subordinate system.

External powers can thus serve to intensify or reduce the level of conflict of subordinate systems. Their presence may encourage division or integration among the nation-states of these areas. Intrusive powers may promote regional associations as a means of extending their control or of aiding the economic development of the indigenous states. On the other hand, their presence may limit regional cohesiveness and produce fissiparous tendencies. Whatever their effect, the external powers must be viewed as an integral part of the international politics of almost every region without which the form of each subordinate system would be considerably dissimilar.

V. RELATIONS BETWEEN SUBORDINATE SYSTEMS

The final subject to be considered here is the relationship between subordinate systems. We can distinguish two fundamental types of such relationships, that oriented toward cohesion and that oriented toward power. Relations which are oriented toward cohesion are based primarily (although not solely) on the effect of the first two pattern variables: cohesion and communications. They tend to occur among subordinate systems which are geographically proximate, have similar political and social backgrounds, and have a high degree of interaction. Examples of such relations between systems are the Middle East and North Africa, and Central Africa and West Africa. Power oriented relations are influenced primarily by the pattern variables of level of power and the structure of relations, and are characterized by the presence of intrusive systems. The most powerful subordinate systems are the most highly interactive. In general, relations oriented toward cohesion exist between regions which are similar in power, and power-oriented relations exist between subordinate systems unequal in power. Of course, subordinate systems do not always relate to each other as a whole; in particular cases, one sector or even one country may be more important than others in determining the pattern of relations with another region. In individual cases, then, we must investigate the countries or group of countries which relate to another system, as well as the role of the periphery and the core in these relations.

Let us select a single subordinate system by way of illustration. In the Middle East, relations with North America, the Soviet Union, West Europe, East Europe, and, to a minor degree, East Asia are power-oriented. They are determined largely by the level of power and the spectrum of relations with geographic proximity also playing an important role in some cases. On the other hand, the factors of cohesion and communications are particularly—although not solely—significant in the cohesive relations of most Middle Eastern states with North Africa and, to a much lesser degree, with West, East, and Central Africa. Factors of cohesion and geographic proximity are most important in the region's cohesive relations with South Asia and, to a lesser extent, in its cohe-sive relations with Southeast Asia, where the Islamic solidarity between most of the Middle East and Malaysia and Indonesia is the most significant influence. Israel, unlike the other states in the Middle East, conducts power-oriented relations with many countries in sub-Saharan Africa, Southeast Asia, and parts of Latin America.

Besides identifying the factors which contribute to relations between two or more systems, it is necessary to form some estimate of the intensity of these relations between subordinate systems. In this regard, one of the most significant indices is the degree of shared participation in international organizations, which may operate either toward cohesion or power. For example, OECD and NATO represent the cohesive interconnectedness of West Europe and North America, but they also are significantly power-oriented. The Arab League is an indicator of the cohesive ties between the Middle East and North Africa, and the OAU links the various regions of Africa in a broader manner. To a lesser extent, power-oriented organizations encourage more cohesive relations between subordinate systems: the Colombo Plan has encouraged greater cohesive contacts between South and Southeast Asia; OCAM links Francophonic Africa; the British Commonwealth, in a much broader way, has served to increase incipient cohesive links between a variety of subordinate systems. In this way, international organizations like OECD, NATO, the OAU, OCAM, the Arab League, and the British Commonwealth can be viewed as supraregional in character; that is to say, they tend to function as aggregators of regions. By providing forums for greater interchange they enable particular subordinate systems to intensify their interactions toward either cohesion or power.

Thus, relations between subordinate systems, while largely unstructured and uneven, can have a significant effect upon the international politics of particular areas of the world. The relationships between diverse subordinate systems, between individual countries in different regions, and between cores or peripheries of different regions, can affect local balances, local intrusive systems, and the dominant system. Consequently, in any complete analysis of the international system it is insufficient to consider each subordinate system in isolation. Its relationship to other systems must also be explored.

VI. CONCLUSION

We have been engaged in the exploratory venture of attempting to characterize the nature of the international relations of a region. As our point of departure, we have endeavored to treat the region as a unit of analysis unto itself, a unit which possesses its own internal dynamic processes. We have attempted to do this by means of an inductively arrived at classificatory system which can be used to specify how the subordinate system can be identified and what its component elements can be said to be: core sector, peripheral sector, and intrusive system. Our introduction of the four pattern variables—level of cohesion, nature of communications, level of power, and the structure of relations—was intended to establish that these matrical elements are of intrinsic importance to the delineation and understanding of the core and peripheral sectors and the intrusive system.

As part of the four pattern variables, we included a seven step ranking system to estimate the level of power of each member state of the international system, as well as a spectrum of international relations which encompasses conditions of cooperation and antagonism. We attempted to show, by means of these categories, that both antagonistic and cooperative relationships contribute to the delineation of a subordinate system and its sectors. Both antagonistic and cooperative relationships exist within the core and the peripheral sector, and between the core and peripheral sectors, and these assist us in identifying a particular subordinate system.

We cannot fully understand the inner dynamics of a subordinate system, however, until the effects of politically significant participation by external powers in what we have called the "intrusive" system have been added. Only a consideration of the antagonism and cooperation inculcated within the subordinate system by external powers can provide a complete panorama of the full network of relations at work within any particular subordinate system. As we have seen, the support or withdrawal of support of an external power can radically alter the internal balance of a subordinate system.

Thus, our attempt here has been to provide a schema for the comparison of the international relations of regions. We have sought to produce a basis for analyzing units of international relations of diverse social and political backgrounds. Any such effort runs the risk of ignoring crucial factors or magnifying minor elements. We have entertained such a risk, being convinced of the significance of beginning to categorize and illustrate the patterns and processes at work in the intermediate arena of the international system—the subordinate system. For in this era of the collapse of European influence in international affairs and of the decolonization of formerly dependent peoples, the region has become one of the crucial units of international politics.

Discussion and Questions

1. ➤ Do you agree with the definition of region provided by Cantori and Spiegel? ➤ How does it compare in concept and application with Russett's effort to delineate regional boundaries by the confluence of behavioral indicators of interrelatedness? ➤ Do you agree with the exclusion of associations of states such as "the Communist International System" or "the British Commonwealth" from the scope of regional studies? ➤ How about the exclusion of multinational continentwide states?

2. ➤ Do you find the central concepts of "core," "periphery," and "intrusive system" useful for purposes of cross-regional comparison? ➤ Would you add any other concepts? ➤ Are these concepts susceptible of rigorous application? ➤ Do you find the table of classification persuasive? ➤ How would you argue against the classification given a particular country in a subordinate system? ➤ Are the "pattern variables" well-defined and appropriately selected?

3. ➤ Do you think that Cantori and Spiegel give excessive emphasis to issues of conflict within the world system? ➤ To what extent is their approach useful to assess prospects for first-order and second-order integration potential at the regional level?

16

The Middle East as a Subordinate International System

LEONARD BINDER

I

Recent developments in the study of international politics reflect two major emphases. One comprises a variety of attempts at systematization and stresses the "frame of reference" approach;[1] the other seeks specific knowledge of national policies in greater detail and stresses the "area studies" approach.[2] Theoretically, the first explains international politics in terms of broad generalizations applicable to all international actors insofar as they conform to an ideal model or depart therefrom in a calculable manner. The second seeks to understand international politics in terms of the relationship of foreign policy to the total social and historical context from which it emerges.[3] This article is an attempt to find a middle ground between these two emphases.

The variety of attempts at systematization are in the main derivations from or modifications of balance-of-power theories, but contemporary interest has focused primarily upon the notion of power rather than balance.[4] There is another

Editor's Note: This article was written prior to the formation in February 1958 of the United Arab Republic and the Arab Federation. The author has appended a brief discussion of these developments in the light of his analysis of the Middle Eastern international system.

[1] For a discussion of some of the issues involved, see Fred A. Sondermann, "The Study of International Relations," *World Politics*, x, No. I (October 1957), p. 102; and Kenneth W. Thompson, "Toward a New Theory of International Relations," *American Political Science Review*, XLIX, No. 3 (September 1955), pp. 733–46.

[2] Despite Sondermann's views, it seems to me that a strong rationale for this approach is presented in Ernst B. Haas and Allen S. Whiting, *The Dynamics of International Relations*, New York, 1956.

[3] To be distinguished from Sondermann's "freight car" category.

[4] Especially Hans J. Morgenthau, *Politics Among Nations*, New York, 1948.

From *World Politics*, vol. 10, no. 3 (Copyright © 1958 by Princeton University Press), pp. 408–429. Reprinted by permission of Princeton University Press.

tendency to substitute patterns of interrelationship of varying degrees of intricacy for the notion of balance.[5] Implied in this theoretical approach is the hypothesis that such patterns of interrelationship (sometimes called "system") are a function of the distribution of power among states (sometimes called "structure").[6] While system/structure theories are an improvement upon the crude notion of multilateral power maximization through a restricted number of diplomatic-military gambits, they lack the refinements necessary for dealing with "aberrant" action unrelated to power. One of the reasons for this lack of refinement is overemphasis upon US-USSR relations, an over-emphasis usually summed up in the loose term "bipolarity."

An underlying assumption of most such approaches is that international politics is total and global. This assumption is based upon the possible character of modern warfare, and is therefore potential rather than actual. Insofar as the security considerations of the United States and the USSR have no territorial limit, international politics is global and total for these states. But the great-power view of world politics is not necessarily reciprocated by the lesser powers. While neither the great-power nor the smaller-power view tells the whole story, the view of the smaller powers is sustained by the development of a situation of mutual deterrence. Insofar as a situation of mutual deterrence obstructs great-power intervention, the smaller powers are free to act. Hence international politics is not global or necessarily total for the lesser powers.

The consequence of the non-global character of international politics for system/structure theories is clear. Any system or pattern of scientific rules which adequately describes US-USSR relations must fail to explain the politics of the uncommitted states. All that such theories may do for politics that are not oriented to the cold war is to define the conditions under which they exist. Of course, this is only a technical limitation, for if we understand power in its broadest sense and if we make no artificial distinction between domestic and international politics when considering system, the same general principles will be applicable to the uncommitted states. But it must be stressed that the identity of the principle from which systems are derived does not require that all systems so derived be identical. Thus it is the purpose of this article to establish a link between system/structure theory and the area studies approach by positing that we are confronted not with a single global international system, but with several in a variety of relationships.

Thus far our problem has been approached from the side of system/structure theory; but there are difficulties on the side of area studies as well. The major problem is the possible conflict between the theoretical universality of the social science disciplines and the delimitation of a group of countries for special study. Do area studies comprise a merely convenient or practical method, but entail a nevertheless arbitrary subdivision of the subject matter of the social sciences? One of the purposes of this article is to suggest that area studies may be justified in terms of a discipline; or, rather, to assert that it is both possible and necessary to justify area studies and to delimit areas in terms of the discipline by means of which an inquiry is to be pursued. Obviously, this means that the "Middle East," for example, may not signify the same thing to a political scientist and an anthropologist; but that is less harmful than area dilettantism. Furthermore, the burden of proof that an area exists rests with the area specialist, and must be referred to substantive problems which cannot be solved without the concept of area.

Just how many international systems exist, and the precise nature of their diverse relationships, are problems for area specialists and political scientists to work out together. In what follows, it will be assumed that there exists a system of US-USSR relations characterized by bipolarity in the sense that there are only two actors of importance involved. If this assumption is granted, it will be readily agreed that this bipolar system is the dominant one in the world today, and that the relationship of other systems to it is that of subordination—in the sense that changes in the major system will have a greater effect on a minor system than the reverse. The Middle East alone

---

[5]Especially and most recently, Morton A. Kaplan, *System and Process in International Relations*, New York, 1957.

[6]See William Reitzel, Morton A. Kaplan, and Constance G. Coblenz, *United States Foreign Policy, 1945-1955*, Washington, D.C., 1956, especially Ch. XVI.

will be used as an example of a subordinate system because of the writer's interests and limitations.

The substantive problem which concerns us here is the inapplicability of the theory of bipolarity to Middle Eastern international politics. The term "bipolarity" has been defined above as characterizing an international system in which there are only two actors. To this definition must be added the qualification that the persistence of the system is due to the roughly equal power of both actors.[7] In what sense may bipolarity characterize a universal system?—i.e., in what sense can bipolarity explain the international politics of the Middle East? Two possible meanings of bipolarity present themselves, the first emphasizing structure and the second emphasizing system: (1) where the power of the United States and the USSR is in each case very much greater than the power of all other states, and where we are unable to ascertain whether or by how much the power of one exceeds the other, and where our estimates of power in each case may err in either direction by the same amount, and where the difference between actual and estimated power is greater than the sum of all uncommitted power;[8] (2) where the dominant factors of international relations are the very great power of the United States and the USSR and their rivalry, which leads each to attempt to counter every action of the other regardless of its locus or circumstances, and where the inferiority in power or the disunity of the uncommitted states renders them unable to resist effectively this pattern of great-power action.[9]

The systematic consequence of the first conception of bipolarity is the ability of the great powers to disregard the uncommitted states; and suggests that any attempt of one of the great powers to secure a foothold in an uncommitted state is a manifestation of a gratuitous imperialism. The structural consequence of the second conception is that the approximate equality of the power of the United States and the USSR is precarious, and so the uncommitted states may not be ignored.[10] Neither conception is fully explanatory of recent great-power policies in the Middle East, and if the second seems more accurate at present, it does not explain the success or failure of particular great-power actions.

From the point of view of the uncommitted states, neither of these conceptions represents a desideratum: their goal is to break bipolarity, or to insulate their own affairs against its effects, or to make use of it to gain their own ends.[11] This final alternative suggests the temporary reversal of the subordinate relationship of the Middle Eastern system, but our preferred explanation is that bipolarity characterizes only US-USSR relations and not their relations with third powers.

II

While historically minded persons will find no difficulty in tracing the evolution of Russian interests and aspirations in the general area of the straits and the Persian Gulf, they will be unable to explain the comparative inactivity of the Soviet Union in the Middle East from, say, the end of 1948 until mid-1955.[12] As evidence of American interest in the Middle East, the historian must be satisfied with the activities of a few devoted missionaries until the middle of World War II.[13] From 1945 on, the United States took an increasingly keen interest in the area. Since 1950 the United States has concentrated on organizing the defense of the Middle East, while renewed Soviet activity seems to have developed only after the initial and limited American success in bringing the Baghdad Pact into existence.

Soviet action in the Middle East to the end of 1948 was apparently aimed at deriving the maximum of territorial gain and political influence during the disorganized circumstances following the war. Subsequent American efforts to organize the defense of the area were rationalized by reference to aggressive Soviet behavior during the

---

[7]See Kaplan, *op. cit.*, p. 40 (the fourth "condition").

[8]This is similar to Kaplan's "tight bipolar system," *ibid.*, pp. 43f.

[9]Similar to, but not quite the same as, Kaplan's "loose bipolar system, *ibid.*, p. 36.

[10]*Ibid.*, p. 40 (the fifth "condition").

[11]The final alternative contradicts Kaplan's fifth condition cited above, as well as his rules 7, 9, and 10, *ibid.*, pp. 38–39. This difference is an additional reason for the present writer's preference for the concept of subordinate systems to that of "loose" bipolarity.

[12]Walter Z. Laqueur, *Communism and Nationalism in the Middle East,* New York, 1956, pp. 260f.

[13]E. A. Speiser, *The United States and the Near East,* rev. ed., Cambridge, Mass., 1950.

preceding period, but such efforts could also be related to the goal of sustaining British influence in the Middle East to the maximum possible degree, or to the principle of collective self-defense outside of the United Nations. Against a background of Soviet inaction and wide acceptance of the notion of bipolarity, American rationalizations have been unconvincing. We cannot know the reason for Soviet inaction until 1955, though several possibilities present themselves. The Soviets, no less than we, were concerned elsewhere, in Europe and in the Far East. The Soviets may have considered the Middle East of little importance. They may have judged the Middle East quite unready for the nationalistic-*cum*-Communist ideological offensive which worked so well elsewhere in Asia. Or they may simply have preferred to rely on the anti-imperialistic attitude of Middle Eastern leaders as sufficient to preclude the success of Western efforts.

Of more importance than the reason for Soviet inaction in the Middle East until mid-1955 is the circumstance under which Soviet activity was resumed with great intensity. The limited success achieved by the United States in the signing of the Baghdad Pact has already been mentioned. Aside from a series of dire warnings, the initial Soviet reaction was nil.[14] What elicited a far stronger reaction was the development of an important breach in Arab unity over the Pact. Thus, the Soviet Union was encouraged to act in the Middle East not primarily as a consequence of an American success, but as the result of the provision of favorable intra-area circumstances.[15] These circumstances—i.e., the Egyptian-Iraqi dispute—were the indirect result of wholly indigenous conditions characterizing the Middle Eastern international system.

More recent action by the United States in Jordan and with regard to Syria has tended to fall into the same pattern.[16] This tendency has not

been complete, however, as exemplified by the Eisenhower Doctrine. The Doctrine was a reaction to a Soviet success, but its implementation was not at all suited to the circumstances provided by the indigenous system of Middle Eastern relations. The Doctrine was directed against a hypothetical act of Soviet aggression, so that adherence to its goals by some Middle Eastern states may be likened to an act of pure devotion. For those who saw no threat of overt Soviet aggression, and who accepted the general idea of bipolarity, the Doctrine was interpreted as an act of imperialism.

If overt Soviet aggression was considered unlikely in the Middle East, intra-area aggression and subversion had become more likely, if only because the Suez invasion nullified the Tri-partite Declaration of 1950, destroyed the Anglo-Egyptian Treaty of 1954,[17] and gravely weakened the Anglo-Iraqi arrangement under the Baghdad Pact. Unilateral American support for the Tri-partite Declaration was both unconvincing and inadequate.[18] Developments in Jordan, however, presented the United States with its first opportunity for limited but effective action aimed not at "constitutional" change of the Middle Eastern structure, but at its preservation. Support of King Husain of Jordan by all manner of unconventional means, without eliciting any formal declaration from his government and without obtruding our disproportionately great power in the area, was at least temporarily successful.

This successful example of playing the Middle Eastern game by its own rules was followed more recently by a perhaps typical example of American exaggeration. The temporary stabilization of the Hashimite Jordan regime was accompanied by some revulsion of Saudi feeling against too-close association with Egypt. After a long cold war

---

[14]E.g., *Pravda* of March 8, 1955, cited in Committee on Foreign Relations, U.S. Senate, *Events in the Middle East,* Washington, D.C., 1957, p. 9.

[15]See Guy Wint and Peter Calvocoressi, *Middle East Crisis,* Penguin Special, 1957, pp. 52–53.

[16]Re Jordan: Department of State, *US Policy in the Middle East,* September 1956–June 1957 (Documents), p. 69, "News Conference of Secretary of State Dulles, April 23, 1957." See also note 63, *ibid.* On April 30, 1957, six US naval vessels of an amphibious force visited

Beirut: "Developments of the Quarter," *Middle East Journal,* XI, No. 3 (Summer 1957), p. 286. Re Syria: see *New York Times,* August 17, 1957, *et seq.,* especially August 21 dispatch by D. A. Schmidt, ". . . the US by itself cannot do anything. . . . It is up to the governments of the Middle East . . ." (p. 1 in nearly all cases)

[17]The British government still insists that the treaty is valid.

[18]The latest reaffirmation of the Tri-partite Declaration stressed its applicability to the Israeli-Arab dispute only; Department of State, *op. cit.,* p. 65, "News Conference Statement by President Eisenhower, April 17, 1957."

of their own, the Hashimite and Saudi houses began to discover a common interest in the institution of kingship and the aristocratic orientation of their regimes. When the extent of the Syrian commitment to the Soviet Union became better known (and perhaps increased as a result of frustrations in Jordan), the United States attempted a vigorous counteraction. The idea was ineptly phrased as a "quarantine" of Syria by neighboring states, but the slogan was never defined.[19] In spite of the wide popularity of the notion of Arab unity, publicity was given to a policy of dividing the Arab world while an American representative was canvassing support in the area. In view of subsequent events, especially the Syrian rejection of King Saud's offer to mediate the Syro-Turkish dispute, it would seem that the "quarantine" policy was out of keeping not with the inclination of Middle Eastern governmental relationships, but with their capabilities.

It is risky to generalize from so few examples, but certain suggestions present themselves for further study. From these examples it seems that initiative must be left to Middle Eastern states themselves. It would also seem that great-power involvement within the Middle Eastern system must be as unobtrusive as possible if it is to be successful. And, as might be expected in view of the low level of power in the area, action to maintain the status quo will be more successful than revisionism.

Domestic politics in the Middle East, as elsewhere, are of great importance in determining the nature of its system. Here, however, the nature of domestic political issues is distinctive, and their bearing on international developments unique. It is fairly well known that the foreign policies of various Middle Eastern countries are designed to have a maximum of impact upon the domestic affairs of target countries within the system. Political and constitutional instability, coupled with the attraction of Islam and Arabism as political symbols, make the direct interventionist appeal a rewarding circumvention of the frequently inadequate or inefficient diplomatic process. However, the degree to which non-area states may engage in these tactics is strictly limited by the anti-imperialist bias of Middle Eastern political leadership. Furthermore, what may be done in the name of Islam or Arabism may not be done in the name of Western security or even Middle Eastern security. If the withdrawal of aid for the Aswan High Dam project was directed at weakening the Nasir regime domestically,[20] the move clearly backfired, and demonstrated the limitations upon non-area states attempting to play by Middle Eastern rules.

It would appear that the existence of a bipolar system, or the counterbalancing of the United States and the Soviet Union, cannot explain all post-World War II developments in the Middle East. The fact is that the most vigorous of American efforts were pressed at the very time of the most complete Soviet inaction. The failure of American policy was not due to Soviet counteraction, but to indigenous circumstances militating against the acceptance of American overtures at their face value. These same circumstances explain why King Saud could accept American aid, could attempt to construct an anti-Egyptian Arab alignment, could welcome—if not accept—the Eisenhower Doctrine; and yet support Syria against the United States and Turkey at the United Nations. These same circumstances explain why Israel may act against structural change in the Middle East, and Turkey may not. And, on the brighter side, they explain why Communist arms sales to Egypt and Syria probably will not lead to the incorporation of these states in the Soviet bloc.

It is erroneous to look upon the Middle East as being in the "middle" between the United States and the Soviet Union. It is clear that the great-power relationship has an important bearing on Middle Eastern affairs, but the latter may not be understood wholly or even primarily in terms of the major international system. If power were to be likened to rays of light, we might say that extra-area power is "refracted" when projected into the Middle Eastern element. If we are ever successful in quantifying power for purposes of international political analysis, we shall have to give that power separate coefficients in each system. The concept of subordinate systems complicates the problem of reducing international system to a set of rules. Progress toward the latter

---

[19] *New York Times*, August 23, 1957, p. 1, dispatch from Washington by D. A. Schmidt, in which the term "isolation of Syria" is used. "Quarantine" was the revised version of this slogan.

[20] Wint and Calvocoressi, *op. cit.*, p. 69.

goal, if it is at all attainable, must first depend upon identifying the unique characteristics of each system.

III

A preliminary and perennial problem is that of defining the area of the Middle East. Official definitions such as that of a foreign ministry or a United Nations body are arbitrary and meaningless in terms of a disciplinary approach. Possible criteria for delimitation of the area in terms of the study of international affairs might be the existence of regional organizations or defense pacts, but this is to neglect the close interrelationship of domestic and international politics, to take no account of power, and to fail to reflect conflicting intra-area policies. Elsewhere the existence of a religious opposition to nationalism has been cited by the present writer as a criterion for delimiting the Middle East in terms of the study of comparative government, and this characteristic was supplemented by reference to the shorter colonial experience of Middle Eastern states.[21] On this basis the Middle East proper stretches from Libya to Iran, with fringe areas including Afghanistan, Pakistan, and the Maghrib, and a core area including the Arab states and Israel. This definition may be allowed to stand for present purposes, with some refinement to be added in terms of the applicability throughout this area of the characteristics to be discussed.

With the exception of Iran, all parts of the Middle East proper—the Arab states, Israel, and modern Turkey—were once part of the Ottoman Empire. They share disparate elements of the formerly common Ottoman legal system, and vestiges of the old millet system. Wherever a landed aristocracy exists, it can usually trace its roots back to Ottoman times. All of these states have a common administrative tradition from which they have only partially departed. Except for Israel and, to a lesser extent, Lebanon, all are susceptible to a common Pan-Islamic ideal. Because of the location of Mecca and Medina within Saudi Arabia, that state may perhaps most advantageously manipulate the symbols of Islam. Pan-Arabism

ties all these states, except for Turkey and Israel. Because of the middle-class appeal of Pan-Arabism, the monarchical states are at a disadvantage in using the symbols of Arab nationalism in their foreign policies. Until the recent imposition of political boundaries upon the area, communication was comparatively unobstructed for those who desired or were compelled to travel or maintain commercial contacts throughout the empire. Despite administrative divisions and varying degrees of autonomy in outlying or inaccessible districts, the clergy of each faith comprised a single cohesive group.

The political boundaries which have been established in the area have little historical significance and frequently less ethnical validity. Moreover, these boundaries are often associated with imperialist intervention, and consequently lack legitimacy. The existence of such boundaries over a relatively short period of time has tended to fix them in a legal and political sense for the present, but they must be recognized as inherently unstable. If they are to be retained for any purposeful reason, such policy will require positive action.

A phenomenon which may be directly related to the common political-territorial heritage of all these states is that nearly all are in some degree revisionist. Those that are not—Libya, the Sudan, and Lebanon—are relatively unimportant or inactive; while Iran, like Turkey the residuum of a once great empire, is at least potentially revisionist. Nearly universal revisionism has resulted from the usual incongruity of nation and territorial state, from the persistent conception of certain parts of the area—the Gezira, the south Syrian Desert, Palestine, "geographical" Syria—as territorial units, and from the fact that none of the Middle Eastern states was a "winner" in the partition of the Ottoman Empire. Under these circumstances, diplomatic relations are more than usually tense and suspicious. Alliance is impossible except where states have no common border (Egypt and Syria) or an unimportant one (Iraq and Jordan, Egypt and Saudi Arabia). The Turco-Iraqi alliance is therefore an exception to be explained in terms of the provision of a wider framework involving the major system, and in terms of the peculiar domestic political position in Iraq. The only other basis for alliance is a wide one, involving mutual self-denial through acceptance of the status quo. The Arab League Pact was diverted to this purpose by Egyptian policy,

---

[21]"Prolegomena to the Comparative Study of Middle East Governments," *American Political Science Review,* LI, No. 3 (September 1957), pp. 651–52.

and thereby earned general Arab support and even the capacity to recruit non-charter members. The negative character of the alliance was demonstrated in the lack of Arab concert during the Palestine war.

In view of this nearly universal revisionism, alliances with non-area powers are extremely suspect and highly unstable, because area interests generally receive a higher priority than non-area interests. It would seem that any attempt by an extra-area state to establish close relations with two or more Middle Eastern states which have themselves been unable or unwilling to establish a bilateral alliance will be doomed to failure. Such seems to have been the fate of the proposed Middle East Defense Organization. Insofar as Iraq was concerned, the Baghdad Pact was more important as a revision of Anglo-Iraqi relations than as establishing close Turkish-Iraqi relations. Obviously, Turkey will play but a minor role in determining Baghdad Pact policy, and it remains to be seen what kind of intra-area co-operation will result from the recent change in emphasis from military to political defense.

Another consequence of the former political unity of the area is the ease with which domestic politics may affect affairs in neighboring countries. Recently even Iran has grown closer to former Ottoman territories in this regard. The policies of Musaddiq undoubtedly affected the Egyptian position on the Suez Canal, while the fate of Faruq had its implications for the Shah of Iran. Turkish nationalist policies have had a tremendous impact throughout the Middle East, and not least in Iran. The fate of Islam in Turkey will elicit responses in all Muslim countries, as did the suppression of the Muslim Brethren in Egypt. Among the Arab states, it is well understood that an Egyptian editorial will threaten the stability of the Jordanian government, while a Syrian military coup will encourage Iraqi politicians or terrify Lebanese leaders. In the confrontation of Israel and the Arab states this characteristic is less well defined, but domestic power shifts that portend alterations in the Middle Eastern international structure have an immediate effect on Israeli policy, as the treatment of Jews throughout the area affects domestic Israeli affairs.

With only partial exceptions, the power structure of the area must be reckoned in terms of population and foreign aid. Generally speaking, the entire area is characterized by profound weakness, governmental instability, and administrative inefficiency. The general lack of resources, low level of economic development, and low level of education are the fundamental causes of this weakness. Turkey, which is best endowed in regard to nearly all of these factors, has about the largest population in the area and has received the largest amounts of foreign military and economic aid.[22] Turkey is the strongest Middle Eastern power. Egypt, because of the size of its population (about equal to that of Turkey), would be of comparable power were it better endowed with mineral resources, were its population better educated and in better health, and were it the recipient of larger amounts of foreign aid and technical assistance. Israel has a small population, but has the best-educated population, a fairly efficient administration, and a relatively stable government. Israel has the highest standard of living in the area and has been the recipient of the largest per capita amounts of foreign aid. Israeli industry and technology are relatively advanced for this area as well. Israel probably stands next to Turkey in power. The population of Iran is the third largest in the Middle East (excluding Pakistan) but this population is spread over the largest land area and is characterized by much disunity. The Iranian situation is much the same as that of Egypt, except that it has a smaller population and has received larger amounts of foreign aid. Iraq, with a somewhat larger population than Syria, and having always enjoyed greater military and technical assistance, is the more powerful. More recently the expansion of Iraq's petroleum production has provided an adequate financial basis for economic development, so that Iraq may grow rapidly in power. Jordan has a small population, but, until recently, its power could be measured in terms of the British-trained, led, equipped, and subsidized Arab Legion. The efficiency of this organization has probably fallen since its last test in 1948, so that it may be considered a sufficient achievement if the Legion can keep order in Jordan and sustain King Husain.

If it is granted that foreign aid and population are the key elements in the Middle Eastern power structure, then it follows that the scope of foreign intervention in the area is wide. Given the general

---

[22]"United States Aid to the Middle East, 1945–1957," *Middle Eastern Affairs*, VIII, No. 11 (November 1957), pp. 385f.

weakness of the area, relatively large amounts of both material and technical aid can develop a temporary superiority of power even in such a state as Jordan. If such power could be turned to the purposes of an extra-area state, it might disrupt the entire Middle Eastern system. On the other hand, no Middle Eastern government need become the instrument of an extra-area state because extra-area power may not be transmitted at full strength from the dominant bipolar system, nor can it become such an instrument because of the orientation of domestic Middle Eastern politics. In other words, it is possible for an extra-area state to help a Middle Eastern state achieve its own ends, but unlikely that an extra-area state can compel a Middle Eastern state to serve extra-area interests. Moreover, even in helping Middle Eastern states to achieve their own goals when these coincide with extra-area goals, the scope of foreign intervention is limited by the greater ease in maintaining the status quo than in changing it.

If the Suez invasion illustrates anything besides poor military execution and even worse political direction of the military, it illustrates the limited ability of extra-area states to commit power to the Middle East and the limited period during which such a commitment may be maintained. The time limit may be important, for it determines that, in the long run, the crucial power factor will be population (and possibly petroleum) rather than foreign aid. But this eventuality would require the complete insulation of the Middle Eastern system from all external influence—and such a situation is hardly conceivable at present. A more immediate consequence of the wide, if nevertheless limited, scope of external influence is the near-equality of the role of each Middle Eastern state within the subordinate system, limited only by domestic political circumstances. These factors add up to an inherent instability of system, suggesting further that, should external vigilance be relaxed or a domestic (and therefore inaccessible) upheaval take place, violent changes will occur throughout the area. It is more than likely that extra-area states will be unable to control or direct these changes because of the negative character of their influence and because in some cases there may be no widely accepted political authority through whom such influence may be channelled. For the present these questions are academic, because the tendency in recent years

has been for foreign influence (of both the United States and the USSR) to gain strength and further to support the status quo.

National security may be the irreducible minimum goal of any foreign policy, but the nature of the security problem in the Middle East is only vaguely related to the security problem in the major international system. Certainly, the concept of security in a nuclear war is so far beyond the scope of Middle Eastern governments as to be nearly meaningless. Even among the members of the Baghdad Pact, only Turkey seems to have given the problem some thought. In a more concrete if less humane approach to "nuclear security," we may say that the nature of the security problem in the Middle East differs from that in the major international system because of the relatively low public capital investment in these countries and the small portion of the population resident in urban centers. Middle Eastern countries do not make good targets for nuclear missiles.

To be meaningful for purposes of analyzing the international relations of the Middle East, the dominant security consideration must be related to actual foreign policies and hence to "local" problems. The Middle Eastern security consideration must be predicated upon the continuance of the present system. That is to say, national security in the Middle East means the security of existing individual states, and not the security of the free world or of Islam or of Arabdom.

There are some who argue for an Arab national interest in terms of an Arab nationalist ideology.[23] This argument suggests either that the interest of the Arab peoples is opposed to that of their governments in most cases or that an ideal is in some manner an interest, and that an interest may exist quite apart from benefiting any specific group of individuals. However that may be, the notion of an Arab national interest, insofar as it insists upon the political unity of the Arab states and possible territorial expansion at the expense of Israel, Turkey, and Iran, is a threat to rather than a substitute for the security interest of all existing states in the Middle East.

By relating the security consideration to existing states and by distinguishing it from at least one constitutionally transcendent ideology, it is

---

[23]H. Z. Nuseibeh, *The Ideas of Arab Nationalism*, Ithaca, N.Y., 1956, pp. 84f.

a simple matter further to relate that consideration to the interest of a ruling elite. While the popular support for existing governments varies from state to state, it is clear that those governments, politicians, administrators, military officers, and allied groups have the greatest stake in continued independence. If this point of view is pressed far enough, we may find in some cases that the threat to the security of the state is as much internal as it is external. This seems to be the case in Iran and most of the Arab states.

The domestic political process in these states has an important bearing on the manner in which this kind of security is pursued.[24] The dominant characteristics of this process are the stringent limits upon access to or participation in decision-making and the erratic uncontrolled progress of social mobilization. The latter characteristic results in short-lived and disoriented political or interest organization and correlative erraticism in political action, frequently punctuated by disjointed acts of violence.[25] Lacking popular support in most cases, and often lacking reliable information, Middle Eastern governments are at a loss to provide against sudden upheavals. One of the greatest weaknesses of these governments in the last analysis is the lack of means to satisfy increasing demands for jobs and higher standards of living, or demands by the military for better equipment and a larger establishment, or both of these at the same time. Problems such as these induce Middle Eastern governments to accept foreign aid, not primarily as a means of strengthening or developing their country, or as a means of guaranteeing their security against extra-area aggression, but as a means of staying in power.

IV

Within the Arab core of the Middle East the preceding generalizations apply with the greatest relevance. The overlapping of domestic and foreign politics, the relative equality of all international actors, and the paradoxical inadequacy of the diplomatic process are all enhanced by the common ideal of pan-Arabism. While certain recent developments permit us to talk of groupings of Arab states—the Three Kings group and the Cairo-Damascus entente—subsequent events have demonstrated that such groupings have not basically altered the Middle Eastern system.

It is among the Arab states that the equality of role of each participant is most out of keeping with the facts of international power. How else can we explain the rivalry of Egypt with its 23,000,000 people and Iraq with only 5,000,000? How else can we explain the threat that King Abdallah posed for Syria? The posture of individual Arab states may change: Jordan from Abdallah's aggressiveness to Husain's defensiveness, Iraq from pressing for unity with Syria to acting against Syrian attempts to subvert its government, Saudi Arabia from close association with Egypt to a cool, correct relationship and from financial support of Syria to financial support of Jordan; but all remain as though fixed in place because of domestic political circumstances, because of extra-area influence, and because Israel exists in their midst. Intra-Arab rivalries have, therefore, an air of unreality about them, and many an ingenious diplomatic program has been cast on the trash heap.[26]

There is another sense in which four of the Arab states are equal. Egypt, Syria, Iraq, and Saudi Arabia can each make an impressive claim to be the political nucleus about which the future inclusive Arab nation-state will form. Egypt's claims are based upon its larger population, more important contemporary cultural achievements, and its recent international successes. Syria can assert its conception and early nurturing of the Arab movement, its provision of a throne for King Faisal ibn Husain, and its historical position as the locus of the "Arab" caliphate. Iraq's claims

---

[24]See Danwart A. Rustow, *Politics and Westernization in the Near East*, Princeton, N.J., Center of International Studies, 1956.

[25]See George McT. Kahin, Guy J. Pauker, and Lucian W. Pye, "Comparative Politics of Non-Western Countries," *American Political Science Review*, XLIX, No. 4 (December 1955), pp. 1024–27.

[26]E.g., Egyptian-Syrian-Saudi Joint Command announced March 6, 1955; Five-Year Egyptian-Saudi Defense Treaty announced October 27, 1955; Jordan-Saudi-Syrian-Egyptian "Unified Frontier" plan announced March 23, 1956; Egyptian-Saudi Yemeni Five-Year Defense Pact announced April 21, 1956; Lebanese-Jordanian co-ordinated Defense Pact announced May 21, 1956; similar Jordanian-Syrian arrangement of May 31, 1956; and the Egyptian-Saudi-Syrian agreement of January 19, 1957, to subsidize Jordan.

stem from its early achievement of independence, its superior power in the Fertile Crescent, its initiation of political pan-Arabism after World War I, and its not inglorious history as the center of the Abbasid caliphate. Saudi Arabia is, however, the original Arab homeland, the seat of the "Rightly Guided" caliphate, and the center of the Islamic religion. Neither Lebanon, nor Jordan, nor Libya, nor the Sudan can make similar claims, but all are quite content with the coexistence of these rival aspirations.

Despite the rough equality of role among the Arab states, the pattern of their interaction is marked both by variations in intensity and by incomplete multilateralism. The greatest intensity exists in the relations of the Fertile Crescent countries. Egypt has become a full participant in this intense pattern as a result of the conflict with Israel and Israel's logical choice of Egypt rather than Jordan as the country to defeat, as a result of the disagreement with Jordan over the future of the Arab portions of Palestine, and as a result of recent Egyptian diplomatic successes in Syria. The source of the greater intensity of Fertile Crescent relations is the more extreme applicability of the earlier generalizations on boundaries, revisionism, domestic politics, and pan-Arabism. These same factors determine that the intensity of relationship is almost completely multilateral in character. Libya and the Sudan participate in this system only through their relations with Egypt, and these relations are for the most part bilateral. Saudi Arabian policy among the Arab states has been marked by both astute caution and a curiously anachronistic element. Saudi caution is based upon the inability of the Saudi government to project its power beyond its own borders, and upon the extreme vulnerability of the existing social and political structure of that country to the influences of middle-class Arab leadership in the more "modern" states. The anachronistic element enters in the tendency of the king to utilize internationally the quasi-diplomatic methods which have served the House of Saud so well domestically. The domestic success of these methods is due to the combination of dignity, honesty, and power maintained by the king; but their lack of international success is due to the absence of international power. Saudi Arabia is, of course, vitally interested in the Fertile Crescent, and for a time its foreign policy was dominated by the dynastic feud between the houses of Hashim and Saud. But the intensity of Saudi action internationally has been notably less than that of the others (except for Libya, the Sudan, and the Yemen), first because the Hashimite states were dominated by the common British ally, later because Egypt was better able to accomplish Saudi purposes in maintaining the division of the Fertile Crescent, and more recently because of the recognition of common interests with the Hashimite states. Recent developments in Syria, perhaps coupled with some pressure from the United States, have prodded King Saud to attempt too much. His failure to mediate in the Syro-Turkish dispute will probably result in the more usual lower level of international activity. The preceding analysis suggests that Egypt is the hub of Arab relations, and the essential element in the success or failure of extra-area policy. It further suggests, in contradiction of the news reports which have followed King Saud's visit to the United States, that a successful Middle Eastern policy may not be built on that king's prestige.

Turkey, Iran, and Israel stand in a special relationship to the Arab "core" of the Middle East. Turkey retains the aspect of a former imperialist overlord, an aspect which is enhanced by Turkey's insistence upon its European status. Prevalent anti-Western attitudes involving the use of the slogans of neutralism and anti-imperialism may be applied against Turkey with little shifting of ideological gears. Turkish membership in NATO and the official secularism of the state are further distinguishing characteristics. The total effect of these special features has been to hamstring the operation of dominant Turkish power in Middle Eastern affairs.

During the postwar period, the Turkish government has made several overtures to the Arab states with a view to engaging them in closer relations. For a long while the United States hoped to use Turkey as the cohesive element in organizing the area for defense. Except for Iraq, which has always been somewhat more favorably inclined toward Turkey, the response of the Arab states has been negative. And well it might be, too; for a continuing Middle Eastern problem is how to prevent renewed Turkish domination of or intervention in Arab affairs. The global problem of security against the Soviet Union runs a poor second to this local structural problem.

The systematic tendency of the Arab states has been to exclude Turkish influence, and this was matched earlier by Turkish aloofness from Arab problems, Turkish recognition of Israel, and the relation of Turkish security to that of Western Europe. The change in Turkish policy was due to American predilection, and was based upon calculations related to the global conflict in the major system and not the peculiar characteristics of the subordinate Middle Eastern system. Obviously, this policy failed, and for good reason, but it established the special role of Turkey in the Middle East. That special role is one of bridging the gap between the major and the subordinate systems, for the position of Turkey has a good deal of ambiguity. The imperialist epithet may be applicable to Turkey in a historical sense, but not in terms of the immediate post-World War I policies of nationalist Turkey. Turkey, too, can be seen as a new nation-state pointing the way to a successful political renaissance for other new non-European states. It is the latter aspect of Turkish history that would have to be stressed for Turkey to play a more effective role in Middle Eastern affairs.

Iran also has a special relationship to the Arab states, and it, too, tends to bridge the gap between the major and the minor systems. There is no tendency for Iranian policies to be construed as imperialist; usually Iran has been the most abject of those suffering imperialist intervention. The particularly unfortunate position of Iran was that of being coveted by both Britain and Russia while being allied to neither. But for rather special circumstances the fate of Iran might have been that of nineteenth-century Poland. To escape from this position Iran has recently sought to emulate the part of Turkey in alliance with the West, a possibility opened to Iran only by the decline of British power in the Middle East.

Iran is separated from the Arab states by the divergence of its sectarian Islam and by the historical effect of a four-century-old political boundary. Despite the vagueness or shifting character of this boundary, it has had a persistence which has served to prevent the complete cultural and political assimilation of Iran and Iraq. On the other hand, the existence of important Shi'i holy places in Iraq exemplifies the usual Middle Eastern overflow of domestic into international politics. The competitive Iranian oil industry rivals that of neighboring Arab states, but it is not a truly divisive factor. While Iran may benefit from the disruption of oil production in the Arab states, as those states benefited from the interruption of Iranian oil production, such competition implies a close interrelationship rather than a disinterested lack of relationship.

Despite its adherence to the Baghdad Pact, Iran has a close relationship to the Arab states in many ways. The sense of unfulfilled nationalism in Iran is familiar and makes Iran a respected member of the new-nation international. While Iran, or the Shah, has preferred an alliance with the West to the equal pressure of both East and West, it is clear that the highest good for Iranians is the absence of all pressure. In this sense Iran joins with most neutral states in desiring to break bipolarity. The pressure of the Soviet Union is so great, however, and the domestic position of the Shah would be so weak in the absence of external aid, that it is unfeasible for Iran to act upon this favored policy.

Because of its non-Arab character, Iran cannot interfere in inter-Arab relations; but because of its history as a victim of imperialist exploitation, Iran more than Turkey dignifies the Baghdad Pact with a sincerity which has some appeal in the Middle East. Under Musaddiq some effort was made to win Arab support against the British, and it seemed as though a close relationship might develop between Egypt and Iran. Nothing came of these beginnings because of the extreme disparity in the kinds of problems faced by each country, and because neither had the power to help the other. Furthermore, Iran's typical response to pressure is to confound the outsider by a demonstration of weakness and anarchy rather than strength and defiance. A strategy of this kind does not encourage alliance nor does it produce international leadership.

Should Iranian power increase, and should the pressure from the north abate, it may be expected that Iran will return to more aggressive policies abandoned over a century ago. A truly strong and stable Iran might willingly attempt to involve itself in the diplomatic maneuvering among the Arab states, and might be better able to lend support to the government of Iraq should that state become isolated from other Arab states.

Israel, like Turkey and Iran, is another link connecting the Middle Eastern and the major global system, but it is the weakest systematic link of the three. Its function in this regard is largely negative. Since the Arab states cannot themselves cope with what they consider to be a disruptive element in their region, the role of the great powers in confirming the partition of Palestine has had a continuing impact on the Middle East. The existence of Israel, not yet accepted by the Arab states, lends constant validity to the dependence of the Middle Eastern structure upon the major bipolar structure. This situation tends to foster the notion that the Palestine question may be solved to the satisfaction of the Arab states only if the influence of the great powers is entirely withdrawn. Since the Soviet Union did in fact withdraw from the Middle East after 1948, emphasis was placed upon the withdrawal of the Western powers. Lately the Soviet Union has been invited into the area to counterbalance American influence—an example of members of the subordinate system attempting to exploit the possibilities of the major bipolar system.

Within the Middle Eastern system itself the place of Israel is important; but again it functions in a largely negative manner. Israel has functioned as a stabilizing influence in inter-Arab affairs by preventing important structural shifts and diverting the energies of the Arab nations from their own disagreements or internal difficulties. If, in time, peaceable political unity ever comes to the Fertile Crescent, its success would seem to depend upon Israel continuing to moderate the application of Egyptian pressures on Syria and Jordan. The demise of the Kingdom of Jordan will probably be delayed more by the presence of Israel than by external financial aid and military support.

The state of Israel was established at least as much by military action as by resolution of the General Assembly, and this fact has tended to focus attention in and around Israel on the question of armaments. The continued state of quasibelligerency has perpetuated this tendency, not only because of recurrent border incidents, but also because of the diplomatic boycott of Israel. The diplomatic boycott has compelled Israel, in seeking to exert its structural weight in the area, to participate in the Middle Eastern system by the measured use of force. The tendency to stress armaments diverts scarce resources from economic development, and thus has a deleterious effect on all concerned which external intervention has been unable to prevent.

V

The preceding discussion of the special characteristics of the Middle Eastern international system, though far from providing a manageable group of systematic rules, should serve to illustrate its distinctive nature. If bipolarity is a useful term in describing certain contemporary aspects of international politics, it is clear that it is inadequate to describe either relations within the Middle East or between the major bipolar system itself and this subordinate system.

It is much more difficult to derive policy suggestions from this kind of preliminary analysis, but one point does stand out. It seems clear that policies based upon the assumption of global bipolarity will be unsuccessful in the Middle East. It may be further suggested that policies derived from the assumption or reality of a situation of "mutual deterrence" in the major system will effect no progress toward the solution of disputed problems in the minor system. If the mutually deterrent system is to work in the subordinate area, each of the great powers must indicate its willingness to fight over the most minor issue, while the indigenous states must act in so responsible a manner as not to change mutual deterrence into mutual destruction. Since Middle Eastern states are neither responsible nor keenly aware of the relationship between the major and minor systems, it does not seem likely that they will act to sustain the situation of mutual deterrence. It is far more likely that the Middle Eastern states will feel compelled to act in terms of their own complex system so as to preserve their individual positions within the Middle Eastern structure; and that they may feel that mutual deterrence is a condition which exists independently of their action, i.e., that the United States and the Soviet Union will, in the last analysis, not react to the moves of third parties in the Middle East if such action would entail a global nuclear war. In this sense Middle Eastern states, and the Arab states in particular, may believe that there is more room for maneuver along the brink than actually exists.

An attempt has been made in this article to describe the major patterns of interaction of Middle Eastern states without imposing a rigid set of rules upon such action. The most important conclusion arrived at is that Middle Eastern patterns are relatively independent of the "rules" regulating the dominant bipolar system. The rapid development of events compels us to add that this analysis is dynamic only in the sense that emphasis upon the relative independence of intra-area action permits alteration of the system itself, but static in the sense that it describes only existing patterns and the existing distribution of power.

Three new constitutional arrangements have arisen among the Arab states to complicate the symmetry of complete multilateralism and formal structural equality. These are the United Arab Republic, comprised of Egypt and Syria; the United Arab States, including both of these countries and the Yemen in a kind of league rather than a federation; and the Arab Federation of Iraq and Jordan. Despite the continued obscurity surrounding the personal and factional motivations of Syrian leaders, it is apparent that the Syro-Egyptian union may result in far-reaching structural changes in Middle Eastern international relations. The remaining combinations, and probably any that may follow in the near future, merely continue preceding patterns with formal changes calculated to sustain the challenge of a practical move toward Arab political unity.

The basic question to be answered at this point is whether the structural change brought about by the Syro-Egyptian union is of such magnitude as to require the use of the past tense in the preceding analysis. There seems to be little question but what the union itself and the disappointment or surprise which it has occasioned in both Moscow and Washington may be easily explained within the framework of that analysis. But is that analysis *still* valid?

The immediate effect of the Syro-Egyptian union has been to limit the alternatives heretofore available to Middle Eastern leaders. In the first place, there is no longer any possibility (given the success of the union) that Syria will act otherwise than in concert with Egypt. It also seems highly unlikely that any form of Arab political integration short of complete union will receive general approval. Syrian initiative in bringing about the union has been paralleled by President Nasir's decision to play all his cards at once. As a consequence, King Saud has been prevented from pursuing an ambiguous policy of mediating between the union and the federation. While it seems inevitable that the rivalry between Egypt and Iraq will be the dominant aspect of Arab relations, Lebanon, Saudi Arabia, the Sudan, and perhaps even Jordan are determined to alter their policies only to the minimum extent deemed necessary. A definite answer to our question must await future events, but for the time being it is possible to come to the limited conclusion that the Middle Eastern system described above has not been greatly altered by recent constitutional changes.

It would, however, be incorrect to assume that this system is fixed and unchangeable. In the first place, the system is of relatively recent vintage, having prevailed only for the last decade or so. In the second place, as we have seen, it contains within itself the seeds of its own destruction. To the extent that Egyptian policy is successful among the Arab states, President Nasir may more directly challenge the great powers on their own ground. Since the policies of the non Arab states of the Middle East are already more closely dependent upon great-power preferences, such a development would mean the end of the Middle Eastern system as presently constituted—and further dilution of the bipolar character of the dominant system.

Discussion and Questions

1. ➤ How does Binder's analysis relate to Young's presentation? ➤ Is Binder sensitive to the linkages between the global system and the subsystem? ➤ Is a subordinate international system also a bloc in the sense meant by Roger Masters? Does the development of an equilibrium within a subsystem necessarily promote world order? ➤ Under what circumstances does the insulation of subsystems from the dominant global system promote world order? ➤ What kinds of relations between subsystems would create the most favorable conditions for second-stage integration?

2. Binder states that foreign aid and population are the key elements of the Middle Eastern power structure. ➤ Is this approach valid? ➤ What about such factors as mobilization of pan-Arab ideology, oil wealth, respect for leaders, and so forth? Binder identifies Turkey as the most powerful state within the subordinate system. ➤ What does this mean, considering Turkey does not generally participate very actively in Arab affairs? ➤ Should we think in terms of *actual* and *potential* power within a system? ➤ Should a nation that does not exercise its power be considered a part of the subsystem?

3. Binder emphasises that pan-Arabism creates a bond among Arab states. ➤ Is this a strong unifying bond or a disruptive issue? Consider the conflict between Ba'thism and other types of pan-Arab ideology. Also consider the conflict between the Palestinian liberation forces and the Hashemite Dynasty of King Hussein in Jordan. (Consult Phillip K. Hitti, *The Arab Ba'th Socialist Party* [Syracuse University Press, Syracuse, 1966]. Also Malcolm H. Kerr, *The Arab Cold War, 1958–1967* [Oxford Press, New York, 1967]. For a more general discussion, see Sylvia G. Haim, Ed., *Arab Nationalism, An Anthology* [University of California Press, Berkeley, 1962].)

4. The Binder article was written in 1958 in the context of the demise of the CENTO organiza-

tion. The author thus places strong emphasis on the extent to which the great powers are limited in their capacity to influence Middle Eastern politics. ➤ Has the limitation on great-power influence been lessened since 1958? Note the development of Soviet influence in Egypt, Syria, and Iraq, especially since the June War of 1967. ➤ How has Soviet power affected Middle Eastern regional politics? ➤ Are there prospects for a counter-balancing development of direct American influence? ➤ What strategies have Middle Eastern states pursued to maintain their independence and achieve their external goals?

5. The phenomenon of Arab socialism is ignored in the Binder article. ➤ How significant a linkage is this between Arab states? Saudi Arabia and Kuwait are, of course, very traditional, almost feudalistic, Arab states, and are in ideological conflict with socialist states, as in the Yemen War. ➤ What is the connection between Arab socialism and Arab traditionalism and pan-Arabism? ➤ How does the conflict between socialism and traditionalism affect prospects for the development of regional order within the Arab League?

6. ➤ How do Israel, Iran, and Turkey relate their participation in the global system with their role in the subordinate system? ➤ How much influence does the subordinate system wield directly in international politics? (See Muhammed Afifi, *The Arabs and the United Nations* [Longmans, London, 1964]. Consult also Charles Cremeans, *The Arabs and the World: Nasser's Arab Nationalist Policy* [Praeger, New York, 1963].)

7. ➤ What is the likely structural effect of the Arab-Israeli War of 1967 on the Middle Eastern system as outlined by Binder? ➤ Aside from the increase in Soviet influence, which states gained and lost power as a result of the conflict? ➤ How has Israel's role within the system changed? ➤ Has the subsystem grown more or less stable as a result of the war?

International Relations and Asian Studies: The Subordinate State System of Southern Asia

MICHAEL BRECHER

I. INTRODUCTION

Asian studies have long since ventured beyond the traditional limits of Orientalia to embrace history and the social sciences; they have not as yet, however, applied the insights of international relations to an area framework. Similarly, international relations specialists have all but ignored the relevance of their discipline to Asia.[1] The purpose of this article is to help bridge the serious gap between these two fields.

Until a few years ago the sole level of analysis in international relations was the nation-state. Almost all texts adopted this approach,[2] and many included surveys of the foreign policy of selected states.[3] One reason was the relative abundance of data on the state actors. Another was the

Note: I am grateful to Dr. Howard Wriggins for inviting me to prepare this paper, which was presented, in a slightly different form, to the Fourteenth Annual Meeting of the Association for Asian Studies in Boston on April 3, 1962. An earlier draft also benefited from the comments of Professor Michael Oliver, Dr. Blema Steinberg, and Mr. Paul Noble of McGill University.

[1] Whether or not international relations is an autonomous discipline, an emerging discipline, or simply a branch of political science is still subject to sharp controversy. See C. A. W. Manning, *The University Teaching of Social Sciences: International Relations* (Paris 1954); P. D. Marchant, "Theory and Practice in the Study of International Relations," *International Relations*, 1 (April 1955), 95–102; Charles A. McClelland, "Systems and History in International Relations: Some Perspectives for Empirical Research Theory," *General Systems: Yearbook of the Society for General Systems Research*, III (1958), 221–47 [these two articles are reprinted in whole or in part in James N. Rosenau, ed., *International Politics and Foreign Policy* (New York 1961), 18–23 and 24–35, respectively]; and Morton A. Kaplan, "Is International Relations a Discipline?" *Journal of Politics*, XXIII (August 1961), 462–76.

[2] A notable partial exception is Hans J. Morgenthau, *Politics Among Nations: The Struggle for Power and Peace* (3rd edn., New York 1960).

[3] See for example, Frederick L. Schuman, *International Politics: The Western State System and the World Community* (6th edn., New York 1958).

From *World Politics*, vol. 15, no. 2 (Copyright © 1963 by Princeton University Press), pp. 213–235. Reprinted by permission of Princeton University Press.

lack of effective supra-state authority to ensure orderly relations among them, thereby accentuating their individual roles.

The unit or actor focus is not without great merit. It can provide studies in depth of state behavior that are essential to a comparative analysis of foreign policy.[4] It encourages the gathering of data useful for the study of decision-making, motives, and elite images of the external world. And it permits an inquiry into the content of "national interest."[5] This focus, micro-analysis, will probably continue to be the most widely used because "as things stand today—and are likely to remain for an indefinite period—there can be no serious doubt about the paramount position of the nation-state or about the superiority of its influence and power"[6] Yet new macro-perspectives have emerged.

Some of the ablest minds in international relations have set out on "the long road to theory," as part of the general search for a science of politics.[7] Their most suggestive innovation, creating

a new level of analysis, is the concept of an "international system." As so often in the past, the more rigorous models of economic theory have provided both a challenge and an assumed analogy. Since an international economic system exists apart from the national economic systems within it, there must also be an international political system related to, but distinct from, the political systems of nation-states; such is a rationale of the new approach.[8]

The body of literature is already impressive and the range of method striking. At one extreme is the pure theory of Morton Kaplan, who postulates six types of system: "balance of power," loose bipolar, tight bipolar, universal, hierarchical, and unit veto; only the first two have historical counterparts and "essential rules," but all are logically plausible.[9] At the other extreme is the inductive method of Stanley Hoffmann, based on "systematic historical research" or a comparative historical sociology.[10] Others concentrate on the contemporary international system, the most stimulating model being that of John Herz in *International Politics in the Atomic Age*.[11]

The basic features of this contemporary system, as viewed by Herz and others, may be noted briefly. *First* is its universality, its geographic expansion to global terms with the coming of independence to Asia and Africa; the state membership has more than doubled in fifteen years. *Second* is the continued absence of law and order within the system and a fragmentation of power; this is in sharp contrast with the authority pattern in the state units of the system, where a monopoly of the means of violence usually obtains. *Third* is a unique pyramid of power, which takes the form of bipolarity, with two superpowers acting

---

[4]A preliminary effort in this direction, not entirely satisfactory, is Roy C. Macridis, ed., *Foreign Policy in World Politics* (2nd edn., Englewood Cliffs, N.J., 1962).

[5]This has long been concealed by the exponents of metaphysical realism. See Hans J. Morgenthau, *In Defense of the National Interest* (New York 1951).

[6]Arnold Wolfers, "The Actors in International Politics," in William T. R. Fox, ed., *Theoretical Aspects of International Relations* (Notre Dame 1959), 101. For dissenting views on this point, see Edward Hallett Carr, *Nationalism and After* (London 1945), esp. 53ff.; and John H. Herz, *International Politics in the Atomic Age* (New York 1959), Part 1, esp. 96ff.

[7]The rapidly growing interest in theory and method is well reflected in five recent collections of papers and one volume: Fox, ed.; Stanley Hoffmann, ed., *Contemporary Theory in Internatonal Relations* (Englewood Cliffs, N.J., 1960); *The Place of Theory in the Conduct and Study of International Relations*, special issue of *Journal of Conflict Resolution*, IV (September 1960); Rosenau, ed.; Klaus Knorr and Sidney Verba, eds., *The International System: Theoretical Essays*, Special issue of *World Politics*, XIV (October 1961); and Quincy Wright, *The Study of International Relations* (New York 1955).

Among the notable illustrations of model-building in international relations are Morton A. Kaplan, *System and Process in International Politics* (New York 1957); and George Liska, *International Equilibrium* (Cambridge, Mass., 1957). For a critique of "scientism" in American political science, see Bernard Crick, *The American Science of Politics; Its Origins and Conditions* (London 1959).

[8]See Fred A. Sondermann, "The Linkage Between Foreign Policy and International Politics," in Rosenau, ed., 10. A notable earlier example of the use of economics concepts for the analysis of international politics is the "developmental" and "equilibrium" concepts in Harold D. Lasswell, *World Politics and Personal Insecurity* (New York 1935), ch. 1.

[9]Kaplan, *System and Process*, ch. 2. See also his "Problems of Theory Building and Theory confirmation in International Politics," in Knorr and Verba, eds., 6–24.

[10]Stanley Hoffmann, "International Relations: The Long Road to Theory," *World Politics*, XI (April 1959), esp. 366ff.

[11]New York 1959.

as centers of decision, military organization, economic coordination, and diplomatic cooperation involving a large segment of the system—though not all its members. *Fourth* is the presence of new types of actors; states still predominate in number and influence, but there are also bloc actors, a universal actor (the United Nations), and various regional actor organizations. *Fifth* is the decline of Europe, a shift in the power center from the continental core of the Western state system to the periphery (Soviet Union) and beyond the seas (United States); this was due partly to the end of empire, partly to the division of Europe by power and ideology into two blocs, and partly to a technological revolution, the *sixth* and most vital feature of the contemporary system.

Massive technological change, especially the development of nuclear weapons and missiles, has tended to undermine (Herz says, has ended) the physical defensibility or impermeability of states, the material basis of the preceding system. Even if exaggerated as far as the superpowers are concerned, the "decline of the territorial state" and the technology responsible for it have had a tremendous impact on the system. They have created both the possibility and the necessity for the creation of blocs, in order to provide greater security for related units; they have produced the new type of actor, the superpower, which raises the level of fear for all other units and thereby induces bloc formation; and they have destroyed the classical balance of power. The very presence of superpowers eliminates the role of balancer—in global terms—and the traditional balancing process. What exists today is a balance of terror, which performs only the negative function of the classical balance—namely, to deny preponderance of power to states seeking to change the *status quo* by violence—not the positive function of facilitating preponderance on the side of the *status quo*.[12]

A *seventh* characteristic of the contemporary system is the rise of ideology to prominence, another component of the multiple revolution still in progress. In the Europe-centered nineteenth-century system, interstate conflict was for limited power, prestige, and profits, with exceptions—notably, Napoleonic France. The coming of Fascism, Nazism and communism, however, sundered the value consensus of the international system. The last, especially, helped to accentuate intra-bloc rigidity and inter-bloc rivalry—in short, underpinned the fragmentation of the system into blocs. Ideology and power became intertwined, each strengthening the intensity of the other; the result was to aggravate the tendency of actors to seek unlimited power, now possible because of the technological revolution.

This, in turn, points up *another* critical feature —the total character of the political process in the contemporary system, in every sense. The goals have become total, whether defined in terms of Morgenthau's "nationalistic universalism" or "liberation" or world communism; the instruments have become total, with weapons of unparalleled destructive capacity; and the consequences have become total, for people everywhere on the planet.[13] The globalization of politics, referred to earlier, has also marked the disappearance of the colonial frontier, at least in the traditional meaning of that term.[14] *Finally*, there is an ever-widening gap between the rate of progress in means of destruction and the rate of progress towards international order, incomparably greater than at any other time in history.

Much of the literature on international relations in the past decade or more reveals an almost pathological concern with Soviet-American relations, most of it policy-oriented and transitory. Even among the few, like Herz, who have constructed a sophisticated model, there is evident a preoccupation with the dominant system of inter-state politics, i.e., the bipolar bloc system. This is natural and appropriate, for as William Fox observed many years ago, ". . . we will never reach [a well-ordered world] by ignoring the differences between the elephants and the squirrels of international politics."[15] Apart from assisting a

---

[12]Ernst B. Haas, "The Balance of Power: Prescription, Concept or Propaganda?" *World Politics*, v (July 1953), 442–77.

[13]Morgenthau, *Politics Among Nations*, ch. 22.
[14]For a stimulating general analysis of the Western colonial epoch in Asia and Africa, see Rupert Emerson, *From Empire to Nation: The Rise to Self-assertion of Asian and African Peoples* (Cambridge, Mass., 1960), esp. Part 1.
[15]W. T. R. Fox, *The Super-Powers—The United States, Britain and the Soviet Union: Their Responsibility for Peace* (New York 1944), 3.

rational process of framing policy, the primary stress on the Dominant (bipolar bloc) System provides data to test and refine models of international systems—notably, Kaplan's loose and tight bipolar types.

By the same token, it is dangerous to assume that the elephants are the only members of the system or to ignore the squirrels by virtue of a specious claim that the elephants determine all or most of their actions. Yet this is often done. The focus on the superpowers rests on the premise, rarely stated, that the Dominant System is synonymous with the International System. This assumption is then elevated to the status of truth and is invoked to justify the exclusion or neglect of all other inter-state patterns. For certain features of contemporary international politics the assumption is valid. But there is an array of inter-state problems, conflicts, and relationships among actors outside the blocs that have nothing or little to do with the bloc system, in the Americas, Africa, Asia, and even in Europe; and these are ignored, or distorted, by a model that identifies the bipolar bloc system with the totality of inter-state politics. More important, this assumption obscures another vital pattern of relations—the *Subordinate State System.*

The existence of this pattern would seem to be obvious. A few writers pay lip service to it.[16] Kaplan's type-models and Hoffmann's historical systems can theoretically be applied with this focus. Yet thus far there have been few efforts to explore a specific subordinate system of inter-state politics.[17] This gap in both international relations and Asian studies suggests a need to apply the combined skills of a discipline and area knowledge.[18]

The foregoing dicussion gives rise to the following propositions: (*a*) There are two broad levels of analysis, the unit (nation-state) level and the systems level; the latter, however, reveals three distinct foci of attention—in ascending order,

Subordinate Systems, the Dominant System, and the World or Global Political System; in theory, the Dominant System may be geographically and organizationally coterminous with the Global System, but this threefold classification is valid for the contemporary world.[19] (*b*) There are at least five definable subordinate systems at present —Middle Eastern, American, Southern Asian, West European, and West African. (*c*) The World System is not merely the sum of relations within the Dominant (bipolar bloc) System and in all subordinate systems; rather, there is a need to link a model of the Dominant System with those of the subordinate systems in order to devise a comprehensive model of the World System. This task has not even been started.

The focus of this article is the Subordinate State System of Southern Asia. Some of its features will be sketched and, where appropriate, comparisons with other systems will be drawn. The strokes will be sweeping, as befits a preliminary inquiry. The operative terms are "structure" and "texture." "Structure" will be used here to denote the basic features of the pattern of relations among and between the units of the system.[20] "Texture" connotes the broad characteristics of the environment—material, political, ideological— in which those relationships function.

What is the rationale for exploring the Southern Asian System or any Subordinate System? In the broadest sense, it will enrich both area study and international relations. The concept of system gives the one-country Asian specialist a region-wide perspective that can deepen his insight into the foreign relations of his particular state. Moreover, this approach can contribute a common analytical framework and hence comparable data to all students of Asia with an international relations interest, and thereby enrich the study of inter-state relations in the region as a whole; the area has too long been characterized by isolated, one-country, compartmentalized study. Stated in different terms, this focus will permit a study of the *interaction* among states in Southern Asia rather than *action* alone, i.e., the foreign policy of one state. To the international relations specialist,

[16]See, for example, Rosenau, ed., 77–78.

[17]Leonard Binder, "The Middle East as a Subordinate International System," *World Politics*, x (April 1958), 408–29; Goerge Modelski, "International Relations and Area Studies: The Case of South-East Asia," *International Relations*, II (April 1961), 143–55; and Thomas Hodgkin, "The New West Africa State System," *University of Toronto Quarterly*, xxxi (October 1961), 74–82.

[18]A thoughtful policy-oriented paper is Guy J. Pauker, "Southeast Asia as a Problem Area in the Next Decade," *World Politics*, xi (April 1959), 325–45.

[19]For a discussion of levels of analysis, see David J. Singer, "The Level-of-Analysis Problem in International Relations," in Knorr and Verba, eds., 77–92.

[20]Used in this way, "structure" is very similar to Herz's "system." (Herz, 7.)

the application of systems concepts to a region will increase greatly the data for case studies of state systems. There have been relatively few Dominant Systems in history; the Subordinate System focus will permit tentative hypotheses about unit behavior in comparable milieux. It will, therefore, be a step towards an empirically oriented theory of comparative systems.

Various specific reasons strengthen the case for this approach. *First,* a system sets limits to the foreign policy choices of all actors within it—i.e., it creates external givens that impinge on both the content (goals) and the conduct (techniques) of all actors' foreign policy. Some writers attach great importance to the notion of "system determinism"—i.e., that policy is determined by the character and distribution of power within the system of which it is a member.[21] Although this may be exaggerated, it points up the vital fact that a state's foreign policy is the product of external, as well as internal, conditions. A *second* factor is that states operate at different levels and usually have various associations. Aside from being part of the Global System, they may be members of the Dominant System and one or more subordinate systems. Different actions and decisions derive from different associations; it is useful to separate and correlate policy acts with specific membership roles. Thus, for example, Pakistan belongs to two subordinate systems (Southern Asian and, marginally at least, Middle Eastern), the Dominant (bipolar bloc) System, and the Global System. Its policy on Kashmir, Israel, Germany, and nuclear tests may be viewed in terms of these four associations respectively.

A *third* justification, noted earlier, is that an exclusive Dominant System focus distorts all inter-state relations except those within the bipolar bloc system—and most exist outside that framework. The constant intrusion of that focus leads to errors of judgment and, frequently, of policy as well. *Finally,* the study of subordinate systems would help to resolve a sterile debate on the merits of deductive and inductive approaches to a more rigorous discipline of international relations.[22] Both methods have a legitimate place in this quest. An application of existing models will test their validity and lead to refined theory. The accumulation of data about subordinate inter-state politics will facilitate inductive hypotheses to be tested frequently in the light of steadily increasing data. In the cross-fertilization of international relations and Asian studies, both will benefit.

II. DEFINITION OF THE SOUTHERN ASIAN SYSTEM

Any concept must be defined precisely if it is to serve a useful analytical purpose. Yet, as James Rosenau observed, since all bilateral interaction may be viewed in a systems framework, the one hundred contemporary states can theoretically form almost five thousand dyadic systems.[23] The concept of Subordinate State System is more rigorous and requires six conditions: (1) its scope is delimited, with primary stress on a geographic region: (2) there are at least three actors; (3) taken together, they are objectively recognized by other actors as constituting a distinctive community, region, or segment of the Global System; (4) the members identify themselves as such; (5) the units of power are relatively inferior to units in the Dominant System, using a sliding scale of power in both; and (6) changes in the Dominant System have greater effect on the Subordinate System than the reverse. In the present Global System, as we have said, there are five subordinate systems—Middle Eastern, American, Southern Asian, West European, and West African; others may emerge.

Using conventional geographic terminology, Southern Asia extends from Pakistan to Indonesia; the state members are Pakistan, India, Nepal, Ceylon, Burma, Thailand, Cambodia, Laos, North Viet Nam, South Viet Nam, Malaya, the Philippines, and Indonesia. China is not formally within the region and is usually excluded from the designation "South and Southeast Asia" or the more recent category, "Southern Asia." However, the Subordinate System is a political as well as a geographic concept; the region is a necessary but not a sufficient basis for definition.

China is a vital peripheral state, analogous to Russia in the eighteenth-century European system, Macedon in the Greek city-state system, and

---

[21]See, for example, Herz, 115; and Sondermann, in Rosenau, ed., 13.

[22]For extreme formulations, see Singer, 92, and Hoffmann, "International Relations," 356–58, respectively.

[23]Rosenau, ed., 77.

Ch'in in the Chou system of China before the seventh century B.C. Moreover, the subsequent roles of Macedon and Ch'in are not wholly irrelevant to China and the present Southern Asian System.[24]

There are other persuasive reasons for China's inclusion in this system. The presence of 12 million Chinese in the states of Southeast Asia gives China great influence within that region, comparable to that of the scattered German communities in Eastern Europe in the past half-century; more pointed is the analogy of the Chinese in Singapore-Malaya and the Germans in Sudetenland. Closely related is the unstabilizing effect of China's minorities on the internal politics of various states; this accentuates her influence in the system. Another reason derives from Chinese territorial contiguity with many states of the region; this permits continuous Chinese interaction with these weaker units, a vital test of membership in any international political system. This pattern assumes special significance in the light of China's historic hegemony in Southeast Asia and its goal of renewed domination of that area.[25] Thus this article treats China as a member of the Southern Asian System.[26] She is, of course, a member of other systems, too.

China's inclusion suggests a system comprising three overlapping fields—South Asia, Southeast Asia, and China.[27] Only two actors, India and China, have a high intensity relationship to and influence on most actors in all three fields, both through bilateral links.

This section of a date for the *Origin* of the system is somewhat arbitrary. The year 1949 would

---

[24]A brief description of inter-state politics in antiquity is to be found in Schuman, ch. 1.

[25]See Victor Purcell, *The Chinese in Southeast Asia* (London 1951).

[26]For a different view, excluding Great Powers from subordinate systems—in this case, India and China—see Modelski, 148-50.

[27]Neither Japan nor either of the Koreas is included in the Southern Asian Subordinate System. Unlike China, they do not meet conditions (3) or (4) as noted earlier—i.e., they are not (usually) treated as part of that system by outside actors and do not so identify themselves. They do, of course, have relations with some states in Southern Asia and, in theory, could become full members of the system. Apart from periods of disunity, by contrast, China had regarded itself as part of the Southern Asia System and has, throughout history, played a major role therein.

seem to be valid, for it marks the rounding out of the system—with the coming of independence to Indonesia and the emergence of a united mainland China, following on the transfer of power to the Philippines, Ceylon, Pakistan, India, and Burma. The remaining two phases, the creation of four weak units in Indo-China in 1954 and the end of British rule in Malaya in 1957, were marginal to the system. Prior to the end of World War II, the entire area, except Thailand and a weakened China, was totally dependent on European actors; Southern Asia was a geographic, economic, and political appendage of the Dominant (European) System. The countries of the region were objects, not subjects, of politics; they lacked autonomy of power and freedom of decision-making in external affairs.

Having delineated the State System of Southern Asia in space and time, we may now turn to its salient structural and textural characteristics.

III. STRUCTURAL FEATURES

A key structural feature of any system is the *Configuration (Distribution and Level) of Power*. The general level in Southern Asia is low, in both absolute and relative terms. No member of the system appears to be capable of producing nuclear weapons or missiles; the armed forces of all states, except China, are small in number and severely limited as to skills and weapons. All units are characterized by an arrested economy, a low standard of living, a stagnant agriculture, a shortage of capital and skills, little heavy industry, and (most states) a disturbing rate of population growth.[28] Only India and China are potential "Great Powers"; Pakistan, Indonesia, and the Philippines are "Middle Powers"; all the rest are squirrels.

In systems of advanced technology—for example, where two actors possess thousands of H-bombs and adequate delivery systems—the power margin is inconsequential. In Southern Asia the differences *tend* to be accentuated by

---

[28]Strictly speaking, the level of technology and economy is an environmental or textural feature. However, the level of power is a direct function of technological and economic characteristics in the area covered by this system. In short, this is an overlapping feature, falling into both Structure and Texture categories.

the low general level. Yet this tendency is offset by other factors. Vast geographic distances, along with an underdeveloped economy, confine the effectiveness of India's and China's power to their respective fields; India's superior military strength may be effective vis-à-vis Nepal, Pakistan, and Ceylon, but it diminishes rapidly and steadily farther east. For China's influence, the barriers of distance and technology are especially noticeable in the offshore island areas of Southeast Asia; there, the lack of naval and air power is crucial. For all other actors in the system, their low level of power and technology restricts the exercise of influence, at best, to neighboring states.

This general weakness also invites intervention by superpowers and blocs to fill the power vacuum, a penetration that is resented and feared by many states in the Subordinate System.[29] Indeed, it is the low level of power in Southern Asia that gives China, an extra-area actor, virtual *carte blanche* access to the system, as well as *de facto* membership in it. Moreover, the presence of a relatively powerful peripheral state, China, further diminishes the application of India's power, not only in Southeast Asia but also with respect to immediate neighbors, such as Nepal and Pakistan. There is, then, diffusion of power in Southern Asia, with neither of two potential Great Powers able to dominate the system because of technological underdevelopment.

How does this power configuration compare with other systems? The pattern in Southern Asia is much more pyramidal than in *nineteenth-century Europe*, where there were five relatively equal Great Powers—England, France, Prussia (Germany), Austria, and Russia. Another striking difference was the absence of a major peripheral state upsetting all power calculations within the system proper; Russia had by then become a formal member, and the United States, the only possible analogy to China vis-à-vis Southern Asia today, remained a passive onlooker until the last years of the European system's century of peace. Like China in Southern Asia, when the United States became an active participant in 1917, it, too, acquired *de facto* membership in the system.

The distribution of power also differed in the state system of *ancient China*. Among the multiplicity of states were seven major units—notably, leagues of states under the leadership of Ch'u, Chin, Ch'in, and Wu. Gradually, over the course of centuries, a bipolar pattern emerged, with Chin and Ch'u as the superpowers—until the peripheral state, Ch'in, established its hegemony.[30] A similar pattern is observable in *ancient Greece*, with most city-states ultimately being linked to Athens or Sparta—and Macedon destroying the system. Southern Asia today does not reveal a bipolar pattern. Moreover, neither China nor Greece was a subordinate system; both were autonomous during most of their existence.

The hierarchy of power in Southern Asia is superficially akin to the *contemporary Dominant System*, with its two superpowers, its four "Middle Powers"—England, France, Germany, and China—and the host of squirrels. There are, however, striking differences. The general level of power in the Dominant System is infinitely higher. And the power margin of the superpowers in the Dominant System is greater both quantitatively and qualitatively. This, in turn, has two vital consequences: it makes each a hegemonial state within each bloc, to a much greater degree than India in South Asia; and it enables both to exert a life-and-death influence on all actors in the Dominant System, which neither India's nor China's power margin permits in the Subordinate System. The substantive differences, then, are very great indeed.

The level of power in Southern Asia is comparable to that of the *Middle East System*, but the distribution is markedly different. There is no Great Power in the Middle East, real or potential. Most units in the Arab core are of the same order of power; Egypt and Iraq are the strongest, but neither has the power status of India or China in Southern Asia. In fact, two of the peripheral states, Turkey and Israel, are at present stronger than any single Arab actor—though the

---

[29]An extreme illustration of resentment was Krishna Menon's comment on SEATO: ". . . this is not a regional organization. . . . It is a modern version of a protectorate. . . . " (*Daily Indiagram* [Ottawa], August 30, 1954.)

[30]On this and other aspects of inter-state politics in that autonomous system, see Richard L. Walker, *The Multi-State System of Ancient China* (Hamden, Conn., 1953).

margin is not decisive. The distribution of power in the *American System* reveals still another pattern, that of a superpower whose superior technology and military and economic strength give it hegemonial status. Not even the Soviet Union can claim such unqualified domination within its bloc in the Dominant System.

Another structural feature concerns *organizational integration* (as distinct from social integration). Southern Asia is acutely underdeveloped in this respect. There is no system-wide political institution, judicial body, or security machinery. And neither of the two economic organizations embracing almost all units plays a vital role. Indeed, the process of integration has barely begun.

The *political* sphere is characterized by infrequent conferences among the actors of the system. Noteworthy events were the Asian Relations Conference in 1947, the Delhi Conference on Indonesia in 1949, and the Bandung Conference of 1955. No permanent machinery for regional cooperation emerged, despite serious efforts at the first and third of these conclaves. One reason was the rivalry of India and China, neither willing to concede Asian leadership to the other. A second was fear among the smaller states that one or both giants would dominate the system. As for the Colombo Powers, formed in 1954, or the Asian Group within the Afro-Asian bloc at the United Nations, they lack organic unity or even a common attitude to the Dominant System and its conflicts. Yet Bandung was a turning point in the evolution of the Southern Asian System, for it symbolized rejection of the Western view that everything was secondary to the Cold War. By asserting the primacy of anti-colonialism, the Conference proclaimed the regional autonomy of this Subordinate System and its noninvolvement, where possible, in the bipolar struggle for power.[31]

The lack of integration in the *security* field is even more striking. The only formal organization, SEATO, includes but three units of the system—Pakistan, Thailand, and the Philippines—and is dominated by extra-area Powers; it is also opposed by various states within Southern Asia. Nor are the members' obligations impressive—"to meet the common danger in accordance with [their] constitutional process" in case of aggression, and to consult immediately on appropriate measures in case of subversion (Article 4); and even this is aimed at only one kind of danger, the threat from Communist China. Finally, the organizational links are minimal and the military power of the Southern Asian members grossly inadequate; it is extra-area power, that of the United States, which gives SEATO meaning.[32]

The efforts to forge *economic* unity are more impressive and more successful. The U.N. Economic Commission for Asia and the Far East (ECAFE) has functioned since 1947, and the Colombo Plan since 1950. Both include most states in Southern Asia, as well as extra-area units. Both were designed to assist the process of economic development, but both are advisory in character. ECAFE possesses a permanent secretariat that conducts valuable research and recommends policies to members, who meet annually in formal conference and more frequently in sundry committees; the Commission proposes, but the states dispose. As for the Colombo Plan, really a collection of individual state plans, the organizational links are even less developed. A Consultative Committee meets annually to hear reports and to facilitate an exchange of views. The Bureau in Colombo acts as a clearing house for information, technical assistance, and the like. Both institutions have achieved much in promoting international cooperation and in creating a climate of opinion conducive to the granting of aid by wealthier actors outside the area.[33]

[31]For accounts of Bandung, see George McTurnan Kahin, *The Asian-African Conference* (Ithaca 1956); and A. Appadorai, *The Bandung Conference* (New Delhi 1955). On the steps taken in the direction of political integration, see Russell H. Fifield, *The Diplomacy of Southeast Asia, 1945-1958* (New York 1958), ch. 10; Guy Wint, "South Asia: Unity and Disunity," *International Conciliation,* No. 500 (November 1954), 162-73; and William Henderson, "The Development of Regionalism in Southeast Asia," *International Organization,* IX (November 1955), 463-76.

[32]See Ralph Braibanti, "The Southeast Asia Collective Defense Treaty," *Pacific Affairs,* XXX (December 1957), 321-41; and Royal Institute of International Affairs, *Collective Defense in South East Asia: The Manila Treaty and Its Implications* (London 1956).

[33]For the work of ECAFE and the Colombo Plan, see, respectively, United Nations: *Economic Survey of Asia and the Far East for* . . . (annual since 1947, New York); and Colombo Plan: Consultative Committee, *Annual Report,* Colombo Plan for Cooperative Eco-

The level of organizational integration in Southern Asia is much lower than in other systems. Although not highly institutionalized, the Concert of Europe performed security and political functions from 1815 to 1848, and in a modified form throughout the nineteenth century. The Permanent Court of Arbitration provided quasi-judicial services towards the close of the *European System*, and a series of technical interstate organizations emerged to serve member needs.[34] Each bloc in the *current Dominant System* has a high degree of integration. Thus, in the U.S.-led bloc there is a sophisticated security institution (NATO), a judicial body (European Court), a host of economic organizations (OECD, Schuman Plan, Common Market, etc.), and a legislative-executive organ (Council of Europe).[35] The Soviet bloc also possesses a security machine (Warsaw Pact), an economic organization (council for Economic Mutual Assistance), specialized organs (Danube Commission and the Institute for Nuclear Research), and a multitude of bilateral agreements covering a wide range of inter-state cooperation. Underpinning these institutional aspects is the Communist Party; frequent meetings of Politburo (Presidium) members and gatherings at Congresses enhance the integration process.[36]

An extreme contrast to Southern Asia in this respect is the *American System*. Indeed, the Organization of American States (OAS) provides the most comprehensive, formal machinery in the history of state systems. There is a legislative organ (Inter-American Conference), a permanent executive body (the Council), a secretariat (Pan American Union), a multifaceted security machinery (Foreign Ministers' meetings, Inter-

American Peace Committee, Defense Board and Advisory Defense Committee), specialized organs (Economic and Social Council, Cultural Council and Council of Jurists) and specialized agencies (Commission of Women, Statistical Institute, Sanitary Bureau, etc.), and, finally, an abundance of conferences and congresses on functional matters. The structure is impressive on paper, but its effectiveness as an instrument of cooperation among the twenty-one republics is often wanting.[37] Similar duality obtains in the *Middle East System*. The counterpart of the OAS is the Arab League, which has an organ of consultation (Majlis or Council), seven permanent committees to deal with political, economic, social, cultural, and health matters, a secretariat, a security machine (Joint Defense Council, Military Organization, Chiefs of Staff Committee, etc.), and a growing number of specialized agencies. The League is even less effective than the OAS in security and other spheres, but it has the organizational foundations that are still lacking in Southern Asia.[38]

The degree of integration is closely related to a third structural feature—*Character and Frequency of Interaction* among the members. Of all the states in the system, only India has active relations with almost all other units. Apart from formal diplomatic ties, other actors have limited inter-state relations—for example, Pakistan with India and, through SEATO, with Thailand and the Philippines; Ceylon with India; Burma with India and China; the Philippines with her SEATO partners; Malaya with Indonesia; Thailand with Burma and Cambodia, etc. Interaction among the members is, then, incomplete or spatially discontinuous within the system. Moreover, it is almost entirely bilateral in

nomic Development in South and Southeast Asia (London, Wellington, Singapore, *et al.*). See also P. S. Lokanathan, "ECAFE—The Economic Parliament of Asia," in *Indian Year Book of International Affairs, 1953*, II (Madras 1953), 3–26.

[34]See Gerard J. Mangone, *A Short History of International Organization* (New York 1954), chs. 2 and 3.

[35]See Ernst B. Haas, *The Uniting of Europe: Political, Social, and Economic Forces, 1950–1957* (London 1958) and *Consensus Formation in the council of Europe* (London 1960).

[36]See Zbigniew Brzezinski, "The Organization of the Communist Camp," *World Politics*, XIII (January 1961), 175–209; and George Modelski, *The Communist International System* (Center of International Studies, Princeton University, 1960).

[37]See Manuel S. Canyes, ed., *The Organization of American States and the United Nations* (4th edn., Washington 1958); C. G. Fenwick, "The Inter-American Regional System: 50 Years of Progress," *American Journal of International Law*, L (January 1956), 18–31; Martin B. Travis, Jr., "The Organization of American States: A Guide to the Future," *Western Political Quarterly*, X (September 1957), 491–511; and Arthur P. Whitaker, *The Western Hemisphere Idea: Its Rise and Decline* (Ithaca 1954).

[38]See T. R. Little, "The Arab League: A Reassessment," *Middle East Journal*, X (Spring 1956), 138–50; and Paul Seabury, "The League of Arab States: Debacle of a Regional Arrangement," *International Organization*, III (November 1949), 633–42.

form, the only examples of multilateralism being ECAFE and the Colombo Plan, SEATO, and the United Nations, which do not bind the actors. Most inter-state relations are of low intensity, though there are variations, the extremes being near-continuous tension between India and Pakistan and rarely disturbed tranquillity between India and Indonesia. Mainland China has resumed active relations with many states in Southern Asia since Bandung, but these remain less stable than those of India.[39]

In this sphere, too, Southern Asia is less developed than other systems. In the *Middle East*, for example, relations among the core Arab members are spatially continuous and complete, intense and acutely multilateral. The half-dozen actors are in constant contact, at every level, and use every form of interaction—diplomatic, political, social, economic, cultural, personal; the process of interaction even includes close links between domestic politics in any one state and the internal and external affairs of all others. At the same time, there are no relations with one peripheral unit, Israel, and limited ties with two others, Turkey and Iran.[40]

The pattern differs somewhat in *America*. All actors have continuous bilateral ties with the hegemonial power. Multilateral lines in the system as a whole are channeled through the OAS. And contact among the twenty Latin units varies in intensity. It is at a high level in Central America, which resembles the Arab core in this respect, fairly high in the deep south of the hemisphere, and declines sharply among the others.

Apart from these three basic structural features, which apply to all systems of inter-state politics, there is the question of the *linkage between the Subordinate and Dominant Systems* of the time. An inquiry into the nature and extent of penetration (or interpenetration) of the two systems will shed light on the degree of autonomy of the Subordinate System and its units. It will also represent a first step towards achieving the goal noted earlier—an all-inclusive model of the World Political System.

All states in Southern Asia are members of the Global System, and almost all belong to the universal international organization, the United Nations. Some also participate in the Dominant System—Pakistan, Thailand, the Philippines (and South Viet Nam) via SEATO; China and North Viet Nam via the Soviet bloc. Others are relatively free actors—India, Indonesia, Burma, Ceylon, and Malaya.[41] All, of course, are also units of a subordinate system.

Perhaps the most important feature of the Southern Asian Subordinate System is the constant penetration by the Dominant System. The Western bloc penetrates through a security instrument (SEATO), an economic organization (Colombo Plan), a multipurpose association (Commonwealth), bilateral aid, and propaganda. The Soviet bloc penetrates through a security instrument (Communist military bloc), bilateral aid from Moscow and Peking, subversion (Chinese minority), a political organization (Communist Party), and propaganda. Both blocs court the uncommitted states in Southern Asia—notably, India and Indonesia. Both blocs also intrude in the problems of the area—directly in Laos and Viet Nam, indirectly in Kashmir and West New Guinea (West Irian).[42] This intervention is facilitated by three conditions: the dire need of Southern Asian states for economic aid, which can be provided only by extra-area Powers; ideological disunity and the lack of integration; and the political instability of most units within the system.

Among all members of the Subordinate System, only India reciprocates actively. Indeed, it penetrates the Dominant System effectively and continuously, through a conscious mediatory role at the United Nations and elsewhere, in regard to the Middle East, the Congo, Laos, disarmament, and Berlin. For all states but India and China, the Subordinate System is the primary, if not exclusive, framework for foreign policy. Even those units that are militarily linked to a bloc are motivated essentially by regional considerations—Pakistan fears India and desires aid in the struggle

---

[39]On China's role in international politics, see H. Arthur Steiner, "Communist China in the World Community," *International Conciliation*, No. 533 (May 1961); and Howard L. Boorman, "Peking in World Politics," *Pacific Affairs*, xxxiv (Fall 1961), 227–41.

[40]Binder, 423–26.

[41]Nepal, Cambodia, and Laos are too exposed to be termed "free actors." At the same time, they do not participate formally in bloc military alliances.

[42]As reflected in various Anglo-American-sponsored resolutions on Kashmir in the Security Council and the Soviet vetoes, and the U.S. (Bunker) mediation between the Netherlands and Indonesia.

for Kashmir; Thailand and the Philippines fear Chinese expansion.

India's policy towards some issues reflects a local ("national interest") or subordinate system outlook—for example, Goa, Kashmir, and the treatment of Indians in Ceylon, Burma, or Malaya. On other vital questions, however, there is a primary stress on implications for the Global System or the Dominant System—Tibet in 1950, Laos since 1954, South Viet Nam today.

China's motivations are more difficult to unravel. In some cases, her role in the Dominant (bipolar bloc) System is primary, as with her aid to Castro and the F.L.N. in Algeria, and her attitude in the Congo and in Hungary in 1956. In others, her membership in the Subordinate System is decisive—for example, the border disputes and settlements with Burma and Nepal, her performance at Bandung, and the placatory offer to Asian states on the double nationality problem. But in another category the lines are blurrred, with both systems appearing to fuse; the outstanding examples are Formosa and the border conflict with India. China's aim of hegemony in Southern Asia is clearly involved, but so is the larger struggle in the Dominant System— between the blocs in the Formosa case, within the Communist bloc in the Indian border case. For the two giants of Southern Asia, then, inter-penetration is frequent and vital.

The *Middle East Subordinate System* is similar to the Southern Asia in this respect, but not altogether. The blocs penetrate through security or military ties (CENTO and Soviet aims aid to Egypt), economic assistance, and propaganda. They also intervene in regional problems—the Arab-Israel conflict continuously, Jordan and Lebanon in 1958, Kuwait in 1961, etc. The basic difference is the absence of a reverse penetration, except by Egypt on a rare occasion, as a prominent Afro-Asian neutralist. The *American System* was strikingly different until 1959. Apart from limited diplomatic contacts and the presence of some weak Communist parties, effective Soviet bloc penetration was prevented by United States hegemony; this is simply another way of saying that Southern Asia was a power vacuum, open to extra-area pressure, and that America was not. This has changed somewhat with the rise of Castro, facilitating Soviet bloc entry into the American Subordinate System on an unparalleled scale. Like the Middle East, and unlike Southern Asia, reverse penetration is nonexistent, except at the United Nations, for no Latin American state is powerful enough or sufficiently uncommitted to play India's role.

IV. TEXTURAL FEATURES

Various textural features of Southern Asia merit attention, however brief. One is the *low intensity of communications and transport* within the system. Another is the complex of *common and conflicting ideologies and values*. A third is the *diversity of political systems*. And a fourth is *internal instability within the member-units*. Contrasts and similarities with other systems are striking.

Distances are vast in Southern Asia, topographic barriers are great, means of transport are limited, and extreme poverty restricts travel to a few. Inter-state radio contact is minimal, except for India-Pakistan, India-Ceylon, India-Burma, and bilateral links in parts of Southeast Asia. Press communications are also minimal, though some leading Indian, Pakistani, and Ceylonese newspapers may be available in the other countries. Television is practically nonexistent. And the language barrier is formidable, not only within the system, but often within individual states as well—for example, fourteen languages in India, two or more in Pakistan and Ceylon, and no less diversity in other lands. Indeed, inter-state communication is confined to the elite—at the United Nations, diplomatic conclaves, regional conferences, and the like. The communications network of each unit is virtually closed to the others, hardly an inducement to integration and cooperation.

The *Middle East System* lies at the other extreme of communications interaction. Distances are much less, states are territorially contiguous, and topography, though a barrier, is not insurmountable. The great contrast, however, is the common language of the Arab core, which eases communication via press, radio, visiting leaders, and the spoken and written word generally. Face-to-face contact is much greater. Arabic is also widely understood in the peripheral states —Israel, Turkey, and Iran. There is, in short, an open communications system, which strengthens the interaction process. The *American System* is similarly endowed with an integrated communications network. A common language is an asset, though the hegemonial power and Brazil stand apart. A developed air transport service assists the process. And radio, press, and TV knit the actors together in an information sense.

All states in Southern Asia share the goals of economic development, social progress, and a viable political order; this permits widespread cooperation in such associations as ECAFE and/or the Colombo Plan. Most have a common experience of foreign, white, rule, inducing a common reaction to many international issues involving the ills of colonialism and racialism. They are also deeply attached to nationalism and fear renewed domination. In all these important intangibles they are psychologically knit together in a community, fulfilling the fourth condition of a Subordinate System; this is also a temporary substitute for organizational integration.

Beyond these, however, is a wide gulf in regard to values. There is a clash between the secular and religious orientation to public policy, as illustrated in Indian and Pakistani constitution-making.[43] A variant is the conflict between modernist and traditionalist approaches to the achievement of common goals. Some follow the liberal path in politics and economics, others the Communist way, and still others various types of a "middle way." There are sharp cleavages within the system on the proper attitude to the bloc struggle within the Dominant System. Unlike Western Europe or America, there are several distinct civilizations—Buddhist, Muslim, and Hindu. Their economies are competitive. Enormous distance is a barrier to close contact. Racial, linguistic, and cultural differences are numerous and deep. Historic antagonisms persist, especially fear and resentment by the weaker peoples and states in Southern Asia. And, as in Africa, there are zones of English, French, and Dutch influence, with different traditions of education, law, and administration. No wonder, then, that the initiative for inter-state organizations in Southern Asia has usually come from outside the system, as with SEATO, ECAFE, and the Colombo Plan.[44] Yet their existence testifies to the presence of the third condition

of a Subordinate System—objective treatment by outside actors as a distinct system or community.

In *nineteenth-century Europe*, too, there were differing values and ideologies—liberalism versus conservatism, revolution versus legitimacy, democracy versus absolutism. It is true that Christian civilization provided a unifying thread and common standards of behavior—until 1917. And yet the great gulf in values between the blocs today does not detract from their membership in a system—indeed, the *Dominant System*. Nor does ideological diversity, *per se*, deny the existence of a Southern Asian System. The *Middle East* Arab core is far more united in values and ideology; it has a common religion, for the most part, a common way of life, thought, and action, and the common experience, problems, and aspirations of Southern Asian states. Yet there is a basic clash in values with other members of the system. Apart from the United States, the *American System* is immeasurably more homogeneous in terms of cultural and ideological foundations—a common history, religion, way of life, and basic values.

There are three general types of political system in Southern Asia. Democracy, based on the Anglo-American models, may be found with deviations in India, the Philippines, Malaya, and Ceylon. The Soviet or Communist model is evident in China and North Viet Nam. All other states reveal some form of authoritarianism. It may be mild, as in Pakistan since 1958, or severe, as in South Viet Nam since 1955. It may be military rule, as in Thailand and Burma, or civilian dictatorship, as in South Viet Nam, or an uneasy blend of civil-military control, as in Indonesia, or absolute monarchy, as in Nepal. In all of these cases the essential components of democracy are absent, in whole or in part. In some, the disregard for civil liberties is as great as in Communist lands, and the instruments of control are no less oppressive. In most, the army has become a major political force, either exercising power directly or standing in the wings ready to seize control from a faltering civil authority and acting as guardian of the political order. But in none of these states is authoritarianism total; this is one vital distinction between Communist governments and those of the middle zone. Another is the commitment in principle to democracy, though this has lessened in recent years. For the present, however, they remain

---

[43]See, for example, Leonard Binder, *Religion and Politics in Pakistan* (Berkeley and Los Angeles, 1961).

[44]Exceptions are the quiescent Asian Relations Organization and the Association of Southeast Asian States.

almost as far removed from democracy as is communism; and many are less welfare-oriented than either of the polar models. All three types of political system in Southern Asia are "Western" in the sense that they are legacies of the Western epoch in Asian history. Democracy is the direct intrusion of colonial rulers. Communism is the product of Western ideas and the example of a non-Asian state. And even the non-Communist authoritarians use Western-derived techniques and political forms to maintain power.

Diversity in political forms and substance is not unique to Southern Asia. Nor is it a necessary source of conflict within the system. *Nineteenth-century Europe* had constitutional democracy (England) coexisting with autocracy, constitutional and others (Prussia, Austria, Russia, etc.). In the *Middle East* today there is democracy (Israel and, with qualifications, Lebanon) and non-Communist authoritarianism of different forms—military (Egypt, Iraq, Turkey, and Yemen), absolute monarchy (Saudi Arabia), and constitutional autocracy (Iran and Jordan). As for *America*, all three types are represented— democratic (U.S., Uruguay and, occasionally, others), Communist (Cuba), and authoritarian (the majority, most of the time).

The dominant feature of internal politics in Southern Asia is instability. The record is emphatic on this theme.[45] Pakistan and Indonesia are the most persuasive illustrations. In the first eleven years of statehood, Pakistan had four heads of state and eight cabinets; there were seven Chief Ministers of Sind from 1947 to 1955. Constitutional government broke down in the provinces three times—in the Punjab (1948–1951), in Sind (1951–1953), and in East Bengal (1954– 1955). No national election was ever held. A grave constitutional crisis occurred in 1954. Politics was controlled by a club of 150 opportunistic men engaged in a dismal game of political chairs. The rot was swept aside in 1958 by Mohammed Ayub Khan. The military remained in power until 1962, and Field Marshal Ayub continues to rule as President under the new constitution.[46]

The crisis of instability was as severe in Indonesia. Violence has been endemic since the Japanese departed in 1945. Banditry has never been stamped out. Nor has guerrilla war. The main area of disorder has been the outer islands, scene of four major insurrections in the 1950's. In the political arena, too, fragmentation has been the keynote. None of the three major parties—the Nationalists, Masjumi, and the Communists—was strong enough to establish a firm majority, leading to coalition government, often the bane of political order. Only Sukarno, President since independence, created the image of continuity. With the coming of "Guided Democracy" in 1958, the search for a viable polity took a new path.[47]

The pattern of instability in the *Middle East System* is similar—if anything, more acute. There, it has led to sharp change in foreign policy, as with Nasser in Egypt and Kassem in Iraq since 1958. In the *American System*, only when the entire political order is transformed, as in Cuba, does instability lead to a new path in external affairs. Thus far, the ubiquitous flux of Southern Asian politics has not seriously undermined the continuity of foreign policy—in Burma, Pakistan, or Indonesia, for example. However, this is a potential effect on the actors. Moreover, political change within the states makes a prediction of probable actor behavior more difficult. It also accentuates the image of power weakness in the system as a whole.

V. CONCLUSION

The foregoing analysis suggests certain observations. The state system of Southern Asia consists of fourteen units, most of which are weak and under grave internal stress. Each jealously guards its newly won status and asserts the primacy

[45] The record and the causes are examined in Michael Brecher, "Political Instability in the New States of Asia," in David E. Apter and Harry Eckstein, eds., *Comparative Politics: A Reader* (forthcoming).

[46] For acute analyses of Pakistan's politics, see Keith Callard, *Pakistan: A Political Study* (London 1957) and *Political Forces in Pakistan, 1947–1959* (New York

1959); Mushtaq Ahmad, *Government and Politics in Pakistan* (Karachi 1959); and Khalid bin Sayeed, "Collapse of Parliamentary Democracy in Pakistan," *Middle East Journal*, XIII (Autumn 1959), 389–406.

[47] See George McTurnan Kahin, ed., *Major Governments of Asia* (Ithaca 1958), chs. 21–23; Guy J. Pauker, "U.S. Foreign Policy in South-East Asia," in *United States Foreign Policy: Asia* (Conlon Report, Washington 1959), esp. 56–62; and John D. Legge, *Problems of Regional Autonomy in Contemporary Indonesia* (Ithaca 1957).

of national interests over group interests that could induce organizational integration. The process is rudimentary and is likely to remain so in the foreseeable future. Indeed, Southern Asia is clearly the most underdeveloped of all contemporary Subordinate State Systems.

The vast majority of states lack sufficient power to ensure their independence. Apart from India and China, it is certain that no actor will have the surplus power to play a major role outside the system in the coming decades. The region of Southern Asia is a power vacuum buffeted by both blocs in the Dominant System. The presence of American and Soviet-Chinese power, real and potential, creates a precarious equilibrium and a dangerously rigid link between Dominant and Subordinate Systems.

Viewed in these terms, Southern Asia bears a striking resemblance to the Balkans before 1914. It lies between two centers of power and ideology. Its units are very weak compared with extra-area powers, three of which have actively intervened—like Germany and Russia in the Balkans; indeed, one of them is a member of the system. And conflicts within Southern Asia—for example, in Laos and Viet Nam—attract intervention by the superpowers.

The real danger in such an unstable system of power is that one or more of the units will disintegrate or even come under the control of outside states. If this were to occur in a unit like India or Indonesia, the consequences would be far-reaching. The whole system would be unsettled, and pressure from without would increase for all Southern Asian states. The line dividing Dominant from Subordinate System would disappear, and bloc rigidity would be further accentuated. In case of Indian disintegration, probably nothing could prevent the rapid assertion of Sino-Soviet domination over the whole system. In brief, the domestic stability of most units in Southern Asia is necessary for the maintenance of a system at all. And the maintenance of an autonomous system in Southern Asia is conducive to stability in the World Political System.

One final observation is in order. Space limitations have not permitted discussion of the next two logical stages of the analysis. The first is a demonstration of how the Subordinate System of Southern Asia *qua* system helps to shape the broad outlines and specific acts of the foreign policy of member-states. The other is a projection of the likely evolution of the system as a whole. This article has attempted only to provide an analytical framework within which these tasks can be performed fruitfully. It is now up to those with special knowledge of individual states in Southern Asia to link the system and the foreign policy of a particular unit. Only then can the broader task of charting the future of the system be undertaken.

Discussion and Questions

1. Brecher's analysis of the Southeast Asian subordinate system is based upon China's prenuclear status. The development of a Chinese nuclear capability together with a rudimentary delivery system has vastly changed the basis of Southeast Asian politics. Consider carefully how these relationships have been altered and how these changes affect the stability of the region and its autonomy from Soviet-American influence. (Consult Morton Halperin, *China and the Bomb* [Praeger, New York, 1965].)

2. Brecher's article was written before the upsurge in Southeast Asian organization activity in ASA, MAPHILINDO, and the Asian and Pacific Council. ➤ How significant are these institutions for the development of regional

order? Consider their significance in relation to the probable outcome of the Indochina War. (See "Regionalism and Instability in Southeast Asia," *Orbis*, vol. 10, no. 2 [Summer 1966], pp. 438–457. For a general review of Southeast Asian institutional efforts, see Lalita Singh, *The Politics of Economic Cooperation in Asia: A Study of Asian International Organizations* [University of Missouri Press, Columbia, 1966].)

3. The military failure of the United States in Vietnam will have a profound effect upon the Southeast Asian system as a demonstration of the inability of even a great power to control the outcome of an internal conflict in a small undeveloped Asian country. Whatever the political outcome of the war, the U.S. military failure will have an enduring impact. ➤ How will the evidence of great-power failure affect the subordinate system? ➤ Will the system become less hegemonial? or is U.S. influence likely to be replaced by Chinese, Japanese, or Soviet hegemony? ➤ Is it feasible to exclude hegemonial conceptions from Southeast Asian patterns of order?

4. Prior to World War II, Japan was the dominant factor in Southeast Asian politics. Japan has already reestablished a strong economic influence in the region, and there are various signs of a renewed Japanese interest in playing a leadership role within the region. ➤ How will Japanese participation affect the structure of power within the system? ➤ Can Japan project its influence without reviving old fears of Japanese domination?

5. The fundamental causes of weakness and permeability of the smaller Southeast Asian states are the lack of economic development; the instability of political regimes; and the divisions and conflicts between tribes, sects, and religions within states. Fundamentally, the creation of an organizationally developed, autonomous region able to handle its own security affairs and to take a constituent role in a regional pattern of world order, depends upon progress toward solution of these problems and the development of more highly integrated and viable nation-states. (To carry on further inquiry on these matters, consult such sources as Maynard Dow, *Nation-building in Southeast Asia* [Pruett Press, Boulder, Colorado, 1966]; George McT. Kahin, *Governments and Politics of Southeast Asia* [Cornell University Press, Ithaca, 1964]; Tillman Durdin, *Southeast Asia* [Atheneum, New York, 1966]; Bernard K. Gordon, *The Dimensions of Conflict in Southeast Asia* [Prentice-Hall, Englewood Cliffs, N.J., 1966]. A useful but highly ideological study of revolution in South Vietnam is by Dennis Duncanson, *Government and Revolution in Vietnam* [Oxford Press, London, 1968]; a more balanced presentation is John T. McAlister's *Viet Nam: The Origins of Revolution* [Knopf, New York, 1969].)

18

Africa as a Subordinate State System in International Relations

WILLIAM ZARTMAN

Interpretations of patterns and trends in postwar international relations have frequently noted the outmoded position of the nation-state, the shrinking nature of the world, the extension of a single international relations system to global limits, and the rising importance of superpowers and regional organizations. It was then often concluded that the coming unit of international politics was likely to be not the territorial state, as in the past, but new regional groupings of states, where the component members would collectively acquire greater power by individually giving up some of their sovereignty to a bloc or group.[1]

If events in Europe, the North Atlantic, and the Soviet bloc have tended to give temporary supporting evidence to this view, the actions of the rest of the world have scarcely followed suit.[2] Logical as this preview of world politics may be, it seems to have been disavowed by actual happenings. Yet the divorce between analysis and reality is not total. Many characterizations of the bloc-actor concept appear simply to have gone too far in the right direction. Instead of a global system of interacting regional blocs there has

---

[1] See the discussions in Roger D. Masters, "A Multi-Bloc Model of the International System," *American Political Science Review*, December 1961 (Vol. 10, No. 4), pp. 780–789; Stanley Hoffmann, *Organisations Internationales et Pouvoirs Politiques des Etats* (Paris: Colin, 1954), especially pp. 416–417; John Herz, *International Relations in the Atomic Age* (New York: Columbia University Press, 1959), pp. 96–108; John Herz, "The Rise and Demise of the Territorial State," in James N. Rosenau (ed.), *International Politics and Foreign Policy* (New York: Free Press, 1961), pp. 80–86; and Kurt London, *The Making of Foreign Policy: East and West* (New York: J. B. Lippincott, 1965). For commentary see Arnold Wolfers, *Discord and Collaboration: Essays on International Politics* (Baltimore, Md: Johns Hopkins Press, 1962), especially pp. 19–24.

[2] Latin America, or the western hemisphere, is a borderline case that deserves examination as a subsystem.

From *International Organization*, vol. 21, no. 3, Summer 1967, pp. 545–564. Copyright 1967, World Peace Foundation, Boston, Mass. Reprinted by special permission.

appeared . . . a dominant system of bipolar configurations, covering a number of autonomous, subordinate state systems, each limited to a geographic identification area and reflected in a regional organization. A pioneer analysis has already been made of the surbordinate system in the Middle East, and attempts have been made to apply the same concept to southern Asia.[3] This study deals with the subordinate state system of Africa.

As frequently occurs in social sciences there is some confusion about the basic concept: Is the subordinate system—indeed, any international relations system—a fact, a goal, or a tool of analysis? Is it to be discovered, created, or invented? Does it have objective existence independent of volition, is it a quality to be attained, or is it a way of ordering and interpreting observable qualities and quantities?[4] Although different, these three aspects of the concept are not necessarily mutually incompatible. A "team" can be at the same time an existing situation of relationships between co-workers, a goal of a group leader, and a yardstick for evaluating relations. Like a team, a subordinate system may be both a conscious creation of some statesmen and the unintended result of other statesmen's actions for

other purposes. As in the case of a team—or of a state, a government, or many other subjects of political science—it is easier to identify a system than to ascertain when it was born or when it disappeared. The purpose of this study will be to describe and analyze the subordinate state system of Africa as a fact in contemporary world politics, showing the actions that have expressly or involuntarily tended to perpetuate it.

I

To do this it will first be necessary to establish the *components* of a subordinate state system and ascertain their relevance to African relations.[5] The first component is a *geographic region* that serves both as a territorial base and as an identification area. The use of "Africa" and "African" as a reference symbol by outsiders and an identity symbol by Africans makes the geographic region appear obvious.[6] Even if there has been some rational antagonism between Africans north and south of the Sahara, negritude has never been adopted as a basis for identification in international relations; by the same token the ethnic distinctness of the Malagasy population has not prevented it from being part of the African system.

Nevertheless, the limits of geographic region are less obvious than the insularity of the continent might imply. On the one hand, the close relations between independent African party-governments and nationalist movements in still dependent territories suggest a continental area of interaction. On the other hand, the fact that African leaders aspire to the extension of the system to the entire continent by the liberation of Africans from white rule indicates that the subordinate international system has not yet

---

[3]Leonard Binder, *The Ideological Revolution in the Middle East* (New York: John Wiley & Sons, 1964), pp. 254-278; Michael Brecher, *The New States of Asia* (New York: Oxford University Press, 1963); and George Modelski, "International Relations and Area Studies: The Case of South-East Asia," *International Relations* (London), April 1961 (Vol. 2, No. 2), pp. 143-155. See also Thomas Hodgkin, "The New West Africa State System," *University of Toronto Quarterly*, October 1961 (Vol. 31, No. 1), pp. 74-82; and Stanley Hoffmann, "Discord in Community: The North Atlantic Area as a Partial International System," *International Organization*, Summer 1963 (Vol. 17, No. 3), pp. 521-549.

[4]More specifically, what is to prevent an analyst from describing a subregion as a system, as in Hodgkin, *University of Toronto Quarterly*, Vol. 31, No. 1, pp. 74-82 (although Hodgkin was writing before the continentality of the system was totally apparent)? Essentially nothing, except the ineffectiveness of the argument, suggesting that a subordinate system may be more a tool of analysis than a reality. However, it seems difficult to avoid key elements of autonomy and limits of the system; yet these are underemphasized in Brecher. In fact, subregions such as West or North or East Africa are relatively autonomous on some levels of relations and will be referred to here as subregional constellations (see below). Their integral membership in the African subordinate system, however, seems undeniable.

[5]The phrase "regional system" may be less likely to raise political connotations to people sensitive of a colonial past, but "subordinate system" is retained here because of its established use; see Binder, and Brecher. Binder calls his system an "international system" and Brecher a "state system"; both terms are adequate.

[6]See the excellent discussion by Ali A. Mazrui, "On the Concept of 'We Are All Africans,'" *American Political Science Review*, March 1963 (Vol. 57, No. 1), pp. 88-97, reprinted in Ali A. Mazrui, *Towards a Pax Africana: A Study of Ideology and Ambition* (Chicago: University of Chicago Press, 1967), pp. 42-58.

attained its maximum geographic limits. The way out of these conflicting criteria is to identify the inner limits of the system as containing the independent, anticolonialist states of Africa. The remaining, white-ruled territories then form a fringe area, in a position similar to that of Israel in the Middle Eastern system. The antagonistic relations between the system and the fringe area are one of the elements that help keep the system together.[7]

The very term "Mother Africa" suggests that the identification area is highly sentimentalized, reinforcing the outer limits of the region. This view is clearest in the Pan-African school of African nationalism that considers itself and its national parties as merely territorial representatives of a continental movement and regards state independence as incomplete, if not insecure, until all the continent has been liberated. Thus, sentimentalization of the area serves as the basis for political action to bring "colonialist" territories within the system. Even "moderates" and "state nationalists" think of themselves as Africans although they may differ over the policy consequences to be drawn from this identity. In both cases the "macronationalistic" or continental identification supports and holds in place—as well as rivals—the "micronationalistic" or state-nation identification in the same way as a man (and his wife and children) distinguishes himself from brothers and cousins without destroying the sense of family or clan.[8]

To the African this continental self-consciousness is first of all negative, the rejection of European control and European-defined identification. Thereafter it becomes positive, both the assertion of and the search for distinguishing characteristics. Shared experiences—such as the colonial struggle, denigration by colonialists, confrontation with modernization, similarity of aspirations—form the basis of a sentimentalized continental identity.

The inner limits of the system coincide with an organizational definition of the area. The Organization of African Unity (OAU), which will receive more attention below, is open to "each independent sovereign African State," members pledging themselves "to observe scrupulously the principles . . . of the present Charter."[9] An *international organization* may be considered a second component of a subordinate system, although not as necessary to its existence as the other components—any more than an organization is necessary to the existence of a world system of international relations. The African organization serves a double purpose. In its inward focus it serves as a framework for relations between its members, replacing their former patterns of relations with a forum for problem solving and an arena for competition. In its outward focus it becomes an alliance avowedly directed against the colonialist governments of the nonliberated territories with the purpose of defending and extending the system.

The third characteristic is intrarelatedness or *autonomy*, a condition wherein a change at one point in the system affects other points and where intrasystem actions and responses predominate over external influences. Despite the continuing influence of France and, to a lesser extent, the United Kingdom and the effects of the Cold War on African foreign policies, relations between African states are primarily governed by intra-African stimuli; in fact, the independence movement has the primary purpose of making this so, and African solidarity and support behind the struggle for independence in various countries have had the dual effect of breaking ties with the metropole and strengthening relations between African states. The formation of African groups and alliances has been the result of African events—the African independence movement, the Congo breakdown, internal government changes. After major internal events—Algeria's 1965 coup, Ghana's 1966 coup, Morocco's Ben Barka affair, Nigeria's military takeovers—diplomatic missions have been sent to other African states to explain

---

[7]Dependent territories such as the Spanish Sahara and Portuguese Guinea play an important buffer role in intra-African relations, an indication that fringe areas—particularly those outside of the southern redoubt—may have some of the characteristics of membership in the system.

[8]On the two types of nationalisms see Doudou Thiam, *The Foreign Policy of African States* (New York: Frederick A. Praeger, 1965); on the state-nation see I. William Zartman, "Characteristics of Developing Foreign Policies," in William H. Lewis (ed.), *French-Speaking Africa: The Search for Identity* (New York: Walker and Co., 1965), pp. 179–193.

---

[9]Articles IV and VI of the Charter of the Organization of African Unity. The text of the Charter can be found in Mazrui, *Towards a Pax Africana*, Appendix I, pp. 219–229.

the official position. Moroccan and Somali irredentism, Tanganyikan appeals for an African force to replace the British after the 1964 mutinies, the OAU provision for solution of African problems by African states, and African conferences on the Togolese assassination, the Algerian-Moroccan and Somali-Ethiopian wars, the Congo rebellions,[10] and the Rhodesian problem have all been evidences of autonomy or intrarelatedness.

Obviously, the subordinate system is autonomous but not independent; that is, it is not free of influences and relations involving outside areas. One problem in this context arises from overlapping systems. Both the African and Mideastern subordinate systems include the Sudan, the Maghreb, and the United Arab Republic (Egypt). The oft-discussed question, "Is Northern Africa Arab or African?," is not answerable in yes-or-no terms; all of Arab Africa is in both areas. The Maghreb has used its membership in the African system to counterbalance Egyptian dominance in the Arab system and to give itself the greater independence that comes from choice. Egypt has used its membership in both systems to give it greater influence in foreign relations; Nasser's "three circles"—the Arab, African, and Muslim "worlds"—all include African states.[11] The recognition of overlapping systems in interpreting foreign policy alternatives and possibilities for states with dual membership is both a more helpful and more realistic way of looking at foreign policies than is the attempt to force such states exclusively into one area or the other.

In sum, an autonomous, subordinate, African system with certain identifiable characteristics does seem to exist and to be capable of performing limited functions under certain conditions. These functions fall into two broad categories: problem solving and self-maintenance. Where the capabilities of the system are overburdened and the system can no longer perform its functions, the door is opened to external influences. The most readily available are France and

Britain, former metropoles, and the Union of Soviet Socialist Republics and the United States, cold-war protagonists. Africa's lack of sufficient resources to achieve its own economic development causes it to turn to outside sources of aid, for example, opening the system to foreign penetration and threatening its autonomy. Its low capability of controlling the use of violence has led to similar outside appeals. Thus, Tanganyika called on Britain to control its mutinous army, the Democratic Republic of the Congo called on the UN and on mercenaries to turn chaos and rebellion into order, the OAU called on Britain to intervene militarily in Rhodesia, and Gabon (and allegedly some other states) appears to have called on France to put down internal revolt.

The system can handle its functions only when problem solving and autonomy are the subject of consensus and are higher values than political advantage, ideological commitment, or a *particular* outcome of a dispute. When the latter predominate (when consensus is absent) and Africa is split, African states scramble for outside allies and the system fails. Thus, the autonomous African system which replaced the Eurafrican colonial system is no more perfect than it is totally independent of outside influence; when burdens exceed capabilities, postcolonial or cold-war influences enter, often by African invitation. Many of Africa's foreign policy troubles are found in the dilemma posed by the two functions. The desire to solve problems, which often exceeds system capabilities and requires outside help, clashes with the desire to maintain the autonomy of the system.[12]

II

The description of the system's internal operations begins with the *configuration of power*. Power is a relative situational consideration and may be defined as the capability of achieving a

[10]On the Congo conflict as an "attempt to keep the Cold War out of Africa" see Robert C. Good, "The Congo Crisis: A Study of Postcolonial Politics," in Laurence W. Martin (ed.), *Neutralism and Nonalignment: The New States in World Affairs* (New York: Frederick A. Praeger, 1962), pp. 34–63.

[11]Gamal Abdel Nasser, *The Philosophy of the Revolution* (Cairo: Government Printing Office, 1958), pp. 66–67.

[12]The conflict between these two functions also has important ideological ramifications in internal politics. See Herbert Feith, *The Decline of Constitutional Democracy in Indonesia* (Ithaca, N.Y.: Cornell, University Press, 1962), on problem solvers and solidarity makers; see also I. William Zartman, "Ideology and National Interest," in Vernon McKay (ed.), *African Diplomacy: Studies in the Determinants of Foreign Policy* (New York: Frederick A. Praeger, 1966).

goal. The items to be considered under the con-figuration of power include its level, distribution, basis, and use. The *level* of power in Africa is low, both within the system and toward outside states. This means simply that African states have little capability of influencing the decisions of other African and non-African states. The reasons for this situation are found in the other components of power configuration. The second component is the *distribution of power*, which is highly diffused within the system rather than being hierarchically structured. This characteris-tic is highly important to the nature of the sys-tem, for it means that there is little chance for a polar pattern of relations, with power concen-trated in one or two states, and that even within camps, groups, or alliances, relations will be between relative equals rather than centered about single states. The distribution of power brings the legal fiction of states' equality—so important in the world view of the new nations— closer to reality in Africa than in many other areas of the world.

There are, however, a number of present and future qualifications to this general description of African power. Although the distribution is rela-tively egalitarian on a continental level, there are important differences within certain regions. Among its Conseil de l'Entente partners Ivory Coast has a dominant position. Algeria, Egypt, and Ghana have enough power to be seen as a threat by some other African states, giving rise among the latter to policies designed to reduce the three states' influence. Other states appear to be destined for a more powerful position in the future because of their size or development potential, and in some cases they are already cashing in on this potential with increased in-fluence in the present. Such states include Ni-geria, Kenya, the Congo, and, again, Algeria. Finally, there are states whose poverty in re-sources, smallness of population and territory, and/or general underdevelopment are character-istics of long-term weakness. Libya, Mauritania, Togo, Niger, the Central African Republic, Chad, Rwanda, Burundi, and Somalia may be in this category although situational peculiarities may from time to time suddenly give them a position of importance.

The *basis* of power is found in the classical elements of national power although an examina-tion of the African system may suggest that there are some new elements to be considered. Size alone is no direct index to power; in Africa it is especially illusory since many of the largest states include large areas of desert and jungle, and even in those which do not the effectiveness of territory as a power base is reduced by the inadequacy of transportation and communication systems. Population is a relevant element of national power; but a closer examination of the reasons for its importance—a source of military strength, a consuming market, productive and exportable skills—suggests that raw figures must be tempered by considerations of illiteracy, het-erogeneity, underemployment, ruralism, poor in-tegration, and apathy. Again, the only valid generalization that can be made is that states with the smallest territories and populations tend to be the weakest.

Military size, preparedness, and armaments also form one of the important elements of na-tional power, and armies in Africa range from fewer than 1,000 men (Burundi, the Central African Republic, Gabon, Malawi, Chad, and Gambia) to 100,000 or more (Egypt). Yet there are important inhibitions to the use of African armies, including their inadequacy for the local terrain, their primary utilization for internal security, the general disapproval of military means as contrary to African unity, and the danger of inviting cold-war intervention. On their own, African armies are unable to face each other in decisive combat for a long time. More important to the military power of African states is the whole range of paramilitary means avail-able, ranging from the more or less uncontrolled marauding bands that are a fact of African fron-tiers (Shiftas, Somalis, Reqeibat, Tuareg) to the actual training and arming of insurgent move-ments inside another country (from Egypt to Eritreans and Libyans, from Algeria to Moroc-cans, from Algeria and the Sudan to Congolese, from Mali to Senegalese, from Guinea to Camer-ounians, from Ghana to Nigerois).

Diverse economic elements form a variable basis for power in Africa. Energy and mineral resources—oil, gas, aluminum and iron ore, and electricity—all provide some African states with a means of influence over others, particularly in the supply of needed energy or the location of industries. Agriculture is less significant since there is not a great deal of intra-African trade and even less interdependence on food supplies.

Economic development is a matter of growing importance, and differences in development are bound to increase in the future. At present the difference in development (as measured, for example, by the continental range of per capita incomes from $40 in Chad, the Congo [Brazzaville], Niger, Rwanda, Somalia, Upper Volta, and the Central African Republic to about $200 in Algeria, Gabon, Ghana, and Ivory Coast) is not enough by itself to give one state a decisive advantage over another, largely because development has not concentrated on items of leverage over other states and because African states have not had the occasion to bring their development to use in foreign policy.

A final element of national power—geographical position—has had more importance. Coastal states which control inland neighbors' access to the sea and states which lie astride river, rail, or pipeline routes enjoy a certain amount of influence. States whose geographical position favors a buffer policy, such as Libya, Mauritania, Togo, and occasionally Dahomey, are also able to "borrow power" from their stronger neighbors. It should be noted, at the end of this listing of power elements, that the relation between the basis of power and the actual power a state possesses in a particular situation is neither direct nor constant nor as simple as standard enumerations of the elements of national power might imply.

With some of the more tangible elements of national power in Africa suffering from underdevelopment power within the system appears to rest on more elusive bases. One is each state's vote in international organizations: the United Nations, the Organization for African Unity, and subregional groups and alliances. Here, at least, individual members possess an item in demand by other states and can bargain over its use within limits imposed by their own interests, policies, and ideologies. It is the latter element, ideology, which also acts as a basis for power as states attempt to become centers of authority for others which are susceptible to appeals to "correct," or "truly African," or "revolutionary" action.[13] If a state can monopolize popular symbols without destroying their universality, it can create rules of conduct for fellow believers. African states have often been very effective both inside and outside the system in "decreeing the unthinkable" in matters of neocolonialism, foreign bases, and external alliances, thus exercising power over other states' policies. A related element of power, intangible but important, is the prestige of African leaders which has given Kwame Nkrumah, Gamal Abdel Nasser, Modibo Keita, Félix Houphouët-Boigny, Haile Selassie, and others a sympathetic audience among their peers. Finally, Africa also has its share of persuasive diplomats who can appeal to principles, reason, and interest in order to influence others.

On the basis of these elements what is the *use* of power within the African system? Power can be exercised in many ways, involving the use of real or implied gratifications or deprivations. In Africa the means—other than psychological—for gratifying or depriving other states are slim. Except for a restricted list of items—ideological approval, a few ores, ports, and transportation lines, and limited skills, monies, and trade items—African states have few items that other African states want or need. The same is true in regard to their weight in the dominant cold-war system where their political neutrality and their openness to foreign economic interests are about all they can offer.

The situation is somewhat different in regard to the territories between the inner and outer limits of the system.[14] Here independent African states have financial resources, bases, arms supplies, and military or paramilitary forces to exert their power, as well as port and airfield rights, votes in international organizations, and diplomatic means of persuasion. All of these items are in short supply but are available. Portugal, Rhodesia, and the Republic of South Africa, on the other side, have larger military and economic resources but smaller voices on the world stage; they also have trade items which African states want or need. The simple balance sheet indicates why independent Africa has concentrated on nonmilitary sources of power. The inherent difficulty

---

[13]See Zartman in McKay; and Joseph S. Nye, Jr., *Pan-Africanism and East African Integration* (Cambridge, Mass.: Harvard University Press, 1965).

[14]See Waldemar Neilsen, *African Battleline* (New York: Harper & Row, 1965); Amelia C. Leiss (ed.), *Apartheid and United Nations Collective Measures: An Analysis* (New York: Carnegie Endowment for International Peace, 1965); and Ronald Segal (ed.), *Sanctions Against South Africa* (Baltimore, Md.: Penguin Books. 1965).

in this situation is also evident: Africa's greatest strength is in those elements that are slowest in producing results.

The characteristic, egalitarian weakness in the different components of the African subordinate system's power configuration has had an important effect on the dominant world view within the system. Globally revisionist, African attitudes frequently reject power as a basis for international relations, both in its past manifestation—the colonial system—and in the present—the Cold War. The African world view regards recent history as a struggle between power and justice, with Africa on the losing side of justice both under colonialism and within the present great-power confrontation.[15] Since Africa is deficient in the current coin of world politics, it rejects relations on a power basis (often including parts of current international law, which appears only to consecrate *de facto* power dominance). Since nationalist movements generally benefited from colonial withdrawal by the powerful European states with relatively little direct pressure (deprivation) or reward (gratification) and without resorting to the ultimate use of power, force, the possibility of creating a new world order without power and based on justice seems real to them. This aspiration also appears to be necessary since to the African neutralists the cold-war protagonists seem irresponsible and dangerous in their handling of overwhelming power, threatening to destroy the world for conflicting goals that are not worth the cost. In sum, in a world where Africa does not have the power to protect itself and promote its own goals, it proposes a new system of international relations that emphasizes its rights and deemphasizes the classical means to attain them. The inherent contradiction, sharpened by the fact that the faster developing states in Africa do in fact seek to increase their power and use it in classical ways, is typical of an idealistic view of international relations.

[15]Some examples to substantiate this gross generalization, "the African world view," are found in Thiam; Sékou Touré, *The International Policy and Diplomatic Action of the Democratic Party of Guinea* (Conakry: P.D.G., n.d. [1962]); Kwame Nkrumah, *Consciencism* (New York: Frederick A. Praeger, 1963); Mamadou Dia, *The African Nations and World Solidarity* (New York: Frederick A. Praeger, 1961).

III

The second element in the description of a subordinate system concerns the *nature of relations*, including quantity, quality, intensity, and patterns. The first three components are related but are extremely difficult to analyze, particularly on the political level. Some indication can be made by studying commercial relations between African states.[16] Two significant characteristics are visible: the existence of distinct subregional trading

[16]Postal and telecommunications would also tell something of intra-African relations, were the raw data available. See Karl Deutsch, *Nationalism and Social Communication* (New York: John Wiley & Sons, 1953). The few independent African countries for which statistics are reported (five plus South Africa) provide a basis only for observations, not conclusions. Generally, correspondence within Africa is numerically inferior to correspondence with the former metropole and is largely shaped by linguistic lines. Specifically, Senegal has frequent exchanges with the Entente and only secondarily with its four neighbors; Togo shows frequent exchanges with the Entente and Senegal and only secondarily with Ghana and Nigeria; Egypt corresponds first with Northeast Africa and second with Northwest Africa (Maghreb), far more than with Black Africa but far less than with the Middle East; Morocco corresponds with the Maghreb, Egypt, Mali, Senegal, and the Entente, in that order, while Nigeria shows an equally broad scattering, with its coastal neighbors, Sierra Leone, South Africa, Liberia, and the Democratic Republic of the Congo high. Further information would be instructive, for mail exchange in the countries noted does tend to confirm some political patterns. (Data taken from *Statistiques des Expéditions dans le Service Postal International*, 1961 [Berne: Universal Postal Union, 1963].) A chart of commercial relations on which the following conclusions are based was made from data given in the *Yearbook of International Trade Statistics 1963* (New York: United Nations, 1965). The expression "East-Horn" is used because the region is composed of two subgroups: East (three East African Common Services Organization [EASCO] states plus three ex-Belgian states) and Northeast (Egypt, the Sudan, Ethiopia, and Somalia) Africa. Northern Africa comprises the five Mediterranean states; Central Africa refers to the five ex-French equatorial states plus the Democratic Republic of the Congo and Nigeria. Separate data are not available for the states of the former Central African Federation; the Republic of South Africa and colonial territories are not included in the conclusions. For analytical use of transaction flows in intra-African relations see William J. Foltz, *From French West Africa to the Mali Federation* (New Haven, Conn: Yale University Press, 1965); and L. P. Green and T. J. D. Fair, *Development in Africa* (Johannesburg: Witwatersrand University Press, 1962).

groups (West, Central, East-Horn, and Northern Africa) and the existence of certain "hinge" states which are members of two groups (Senegal and Nigeria trading with both West and Central Africa, the Democratic Republic of the Congo in both East-Horn and Central Africa, Egypt in both East-Horn and Northern Africa, and Morocco-Algeria-Tunisia in Northern Africa but trading with the Central and Western subregions). These same characteristics also appear in political relations.

When applied directly to political matters, *quantity, quality,* and *intensity* are valuable concepts but difficult to reduce to any summary appreciation. Quantity refers to the number of contacts, including visits by delegations and meetings at international conferences; quality refers to a range of feelings from amity to enmity; and intensity refers to the emotional level of these feelings. However, since bilateral relations tend to change rapidly in Africa, a new political "weather map" for the continent would be necessary every six months. Although quality and intensity could easily be estimated, a sounder way of measuring these components would be through a quantitative analysis of each country's newspaper or leaders' speeches.[17] Such a task is beyond the scope of this article, but a qualitative evaluation of relations shows several characteristics.

One is the presence of subregional constellations within the continental pattern, in the Maghreb, West Africa, and East Africa, with less of a subregional pattern in Central and Equatorial Africa. Another characteristic is the creation of "bridges" between regions, for example, by conflict between Morocco and Mauritania, attraction between Mali and Algeria, friendship between Nigeria and the Congo, influence of Ghana in East Africa, and varied reactions to Egyptian policy. The first and second Congolese crises have had the visible effect of creating a continental pattern of interactions; the problems of the Portuguese territories and, to a growing extent, the Rhodesian affair work in a similar direction. A

third characteristic is the kaleidoscopic nature of African relations where a slight turn of events brings dramatic new patterns; until firmer patterns of friendship and rivalry are established, yesterday's friends can become today's enemies—as relations between Rabat, Algiers, Tunis, and Cairo, between Dakar and Bamako, between Brazzaville and Leopoldville, or between Conakry and Accra have shown—and then become tomorrow's friends—in many of the same cases. A last characteristic is that while enemies usually have different close friends (with some notable exceptions), the converse is not necessarily true: Close friends usually do have different enemies. In addition, few friendships and enmities are of such serious nature that they involve the entire continent. Thus, African disputes have never separated all states in the system into two opposing camps; there have always been some uninvolved or unaligned states to serve a mediatory function. This characteristic corroborates some aspects noted in the configuration of power.

The final component in the nature of relations refers to multilateral *patterns.*[18] In a sense Africa's search for a definition of unity, which has been the dominant theme of intra-African relations, has been an attempt to find satisfying patterns of relations as states balance the demands that unity places on their policy against those imposed by other ideological imperatives. Since the period leading to the formation of the OAU—and only to a lesser extent the subsequent period, still not ended—was a time of search, patterns could be discarded one after another until some satisfying definition of unity was found. What is even more significant is that the new African states apparently stumbled on some of the classical patterns of international relations, suggesting that theoretical concepts used in the West do have relevance in other areas.

The simplest pattern of relations is a multilateral extension of bad-neighbor relations. Although it is usual, if not normal, that a state has more difficulties with its neighbors than with

---

[17]See Ithiel de Sola Pool, *Symbols of Internationalism* (Stanford, Calif.: Stanford University Press, 1951); Kenneth Boulding, "National Images and International Systems," in Rosenau, pp. 391-398. On the need for such "maps" see Charles A. McClelland, *Theory and the International System* (New York: Macmillan, 1966), p. 106.

[18]"Pattern" is used here where most analyses have used "system." The change in term seems necessary; a pattern is only one element in the operation of a system, and a system can continue to exist in transition between two patterns of relations. Masters (*American Political Science Review,* Vol. 10, No. 4, pp. 780-789) uses the term "structures."

other states, such a situation only becomes a pattern when the state takes the next logical step and forms an alliance with its neighbor's neighbor because they both have the same enemy (the state in the middle). The result may be called a *checkerboard* pattern or a Kautilyan pattern after the Indian statesman who so well described it.[19] It has frequently appeared in Africa. The interlocked alliances of Guinea, Ghana, and Mali (Union of African States [UAS]) and of Ivory Coast, Upper Volta, Niger, and Dahomey (Conseil de l'Entente) are one example of this pattern. In the horn of Africa a similar pattern began when two objects of Somali irredentism, Kenya and Ethiopia, signed a mutual defense pact in late 1963, but the pattern did not extend as far as in North and West Africa; that is, Somalia did not then ally with Uganda or the Sudan although it did tighten relations with Egypt. Why did the pattern stop in East Africa instead of spreading as it did in North and West Africa? The simplest answer is that the Somalia conflict has had no interest for the second ring of states around Somalia; whereas relations within West Africa were so intertwined that, once begun, a pattern spread to other states in the subregion, Somalia's subregion included few members and Somalia could not find other states to share its goals or its enemies.[20]

The primitive checkerboard of West Africa soon turned into a more sophisticated pattern of relations, the *balance of power*, and in the process turned the pattern from a subregional to a continental complex of relations. The balance of power is a mobile pattern of alliances whereby any state or group of states is prevented from achieving hegemony; it can be ended by failure (one side achieving dominance), breakdown (both alliances falling apart), or resolution (alliance members forgetting the conflict or the hegemony issue and moving on to another pattern). The African balance-of-power pattern grew out of the Western African checkerboard.[21] The first step was the formation of the Brazzaville Group of moderate states (including the Entente) in 1960 for the purpose of (1) checking the Moroccan campaign for hegemony over Mauritania, (2) checking the radical states' efforts in the Congo, and (3) seeking an agreeable definition of African unity. The counter-alliance was the Casablanca group (including the UAS), formed in 1961 to promote its activist members' policies in the same three areas. Both alliances then sought to expand, but only the Brazzaville Group was successful; it gained new members and formed the Monrovia-Lagos Group. However, by this time (1962) the first two issues had died away, another issue which had kept the alliances apart—recognition of the Algerian Provisional Government (a member of the Casablanca Group)—was obviated by Algerian independence, and the African unity issue was the only problem left. In this situation the balance of power was no longer relevant, and it disappeared in the process described above as resolution as African states sought another pattern of relations centered about the remaining issue of unity. Because the expanded moderate alliance in the last stage was stronger than the radical counter-alliance, however, its ideas on the new pattern would be expected to predominate, as in fact happened at Addis Ababa with the founding of the OAU.

A third pattern of relations came into effect in 1963 with the formation of the OAU, which at the same time serves as the organizational framework for the system. The new pattern of relations bears many similarities to the *concert* as practiced in other parts of the world.[22] In a concert pattern states meet regularly to handle common prob-

---

[19]Kautilya, *Arthasastra*, trans. R. Shamasastry (Mysore: Mysore Printing and Publishing House, 1960), especially pp. 289–293; and George Modelski, "Kautilya: Foreign Policy and International System in the Ancient Hindu World," in *American Political Science Review*, September 1964 (Vol. 58, No. 3), pp. 549–560.

[20]It is remarkable that a checkerboard pattern did not appear in North Africa, i.e., that Morocco and Tunisia never united against the Algerian revolution and sporadic interference. To the contrary, the period between 1958 and 1962 was filled with alternate Tunisian and Moroccan attempts to win the National Liberation Front (FLN) to *their* side, to the exclusion of the other neighbor. The only checkerboard that has appeared was the Algerian-Egyptian "entente" under Ahmed Ben Bella, with Morocco, Tunisia, and Libya in various positions of enmity but never allied in a counterentente.

[21]For a more detailed analysis of these events see the author's *International Relations in the New Africa* (Englewood Cliffs, N.J.: Prentice-Hall, 1966).

[22]The concert system (pattern) is described in Richard Rosecrance, *Action and Reaction in World Politics* (Boston: Little, Brown, 1963), pp. 156–159.

lems on the basis of some common ideals (including agreement that problems should be handled by members of the system); the formation of firm alliances is excluded although differences of opinion are not. The OAU has served such a purpose, sometimes inconclusively but with enough prestige derived from its nature as the embodiment of the African unity mystique to be effective in its role. The principal organ of the OAU, the Assembly of Heads of State and Government, was busy enough setting up institutions during its first two sessions (Addis Ababa in May 1963, Cairo in July 1964) to keep this prestige. Council of Ministers' meetings precede and prepare the work of the annual summit although the Council's other meetings have been less successful in dealing with concrete problems, such as support of nationalist movements in dependent territories, solution of disputes between members, or resolution of the Congo problem. The Commission of Mediation, Conciliation, and Arbitration has never functioned, and the Defense Commission and the Liberation Coordination Committee have been ineffectual. The Secretariat, under Diallo Telli, has been caught between the need for vigorous efforts to keep the Organization going and criticisms coming from member states jealous of their sovereignty; it has, however, been prevented from becoming a supranational power center in its own right, thus keeping the pattern of relations on a concert level.

During 1965 some of these specific weaknesses caused member states to complain of the ineffectiveness of the Organization and to search about for new patterns of relations. In general, the radical members, seeking to strengthen the Organization and use it to impose their concept of orthodoxy on the policies of member states, tried to organize relations on a hierarchical pattern. Many of the moderate states reacted to this pressure by reinforcing the only remnant of the balance-of-power pattern that had continued to exist, the Brazzaville Group, reconstituted and enlarged as the Afro-Malagasy Common Organization (OCAM). At one point, in March 1965, it appeared as if the radicals would take up the challenge and return to a balance-of-power pattern, but preliminary meetings at Bamako and Conakry did not result in the formation of a new counteralliance. At the same time the radicals for a second time failed in their attempt to change

the Congolese government and the concert pattern was preserved. Boycotts and walkouts during the OAU Council of Ministers and third Assembly of Heads of State meetings in the latter months of 1965, followed by bitter fights over the size and use of the budget and ineffectiveness of liberation policies at the Councils of Ministers and fourth Assembly in 1966 have all contributed to increased disenchantment with the Organization. Nothing, however, indicated a return to a balance of power since the OCAM group remains quiescent and no counteralliance appears to be forming. A continuation of the present concert-like pattern, despite its troubled record, seems best to fit other characteristics of the system, particularly the configuration of power.

IV

The third element in the description of the African subordinate system may be called the *normative characteristics* of the system. These "rules" are *de facto* guidelines of policy, established by consensus through the development of the subordinate system and resulting from its power configuration. Like any laws, they are not universally accepted and have been broken in the past. Each time that they are used as a basis of a state's policy decision, their effectiveness is reinforced; conversely, if they are broken too frequently or in particularly important cases, such action creates pressure for normative readjustment. Thus, the conflict between the radical, intervention school and the moderate, sovereignty school in the second Congo case was a basic conflict over rules to govern relations in the system as well as a conflict between camps and ideologies. Consensus on normative behavior is particularly important to the existence of a true concert pattern of relations.[23]

Rule One is that intrasystem solutions are to be preferred over extrasystem solutions to African problems whenever possible. The effect of this rule is to maintain the autonomy of the system.

---

[23]On norm making at Addis Ababa see T. O. Elias, "The Charter of the Organization of African Unity," *American Journal of International Law*, April 1965 (Vol. 59, No. 2), pp. 243–264.

Examples have already been given in the discussion of autonomy; others include the whole African independence movement which seeks to put problems of government into the hands of national elites, the Ghanaian (1960) and Congolese (1964) appeals for African troops in the Congo, the Zambian negotiations (1965–1966) to circumvent the Mozambique outlet to the sea, the Moroccan-Algerian rejection (1963) of the Arab League good offices in their border dispute, to name a few. A less tangible but more striking example is the frequently successful attempt of African states to change the rules governing postcolonial bases, neocolonialism, colonial return, nuclear armament, and indeed general foreign intervention, putting them outside the realm of "thinkable" actions of foreign states in Africa.

It is worth pausing a moment to notice the relation between this attempt to change external rules and the characteristics of the system already noted. In a world context Africa's security problems are largely out of its hands; the absence of effective modern armies, atomic weapons, and industrial power (including a self-sufficient armaments industry) all put Africa at the mercy of the outside, should power be reduced to its raw terms of force. Even if the chances of military intervention are in fact slight, such a situation of basic insecurity is difficult for any state to live with, and especially so for a new one that is sensitive about its sovereignty and independence. Thus, it becomes imperative for African states to minimize the chances of military intervention—one of the basic functions of a neutralist policy—and to create psychological barriers (in the absence of military barriers) to intervention. Restated, this means that African leaders are deeply aware of the existence of a power vacuum;[24] since they are aware that it is caused by their inability to fill it, they attempt to strengthen the walls that contain it. If African states can make intervention "unthinkable" and can also make it unwarranted by handling their own problems, insecurity is reduced.

Rule Two establishes a hierarchy among the three primary goals of African states: independence, development, and unity, in that order. The fate of the North African Tangier Conference (1958), of the Mali Federation (1960), of plans to consolidate the East African Common Services Organization (1963) and former French Equatorial Africa (1959) as federal or confederal units, and more broadly of the "Africa Must Unite" school all show the priority of independence over unity. Decidedly, despite the contrary pressure of Pan-Africanism, the state as the African political unit seems here to stay. By the same token, examples such as the West Africans' problems in locating a common steel mill, the North Africans' emphasis on an economic approach to Maghreb unity, and the East Africans' attachment to a common market, among others, show that national development is preferred to regional development but that if regional "unity" is to take place, it will probably do so first on economic grounds. This hierarchy simply brings out the continuing reasons why political unity is so difficult to accomplish, despite its mystique in Africa, and shows that under the present rules unification is not a foreign policy alternative among African states. The only exception is the case of Zanzibar, which falls only slightly short of joining the other cases of unification (Morocco, Ethiopia, Somalia, Cameroun, and Ghana), all of which took place before or with independence.

Rule Three states that wars of conquest are not policy alternatives. This rule derives from military weaknesses of African states, from their fear of foreign intervention, and from the inhibitory effect of such values as legitimacy (independence) and unity. Morocco's restraint in the Moroccan-Algerian war and in its irredentist campaign against Mauritania, Ghanaian restraint against Togo, Somali reluctance to engage its army in its irredentist campaign, and the Egyptian withdrawal in the 1958 border dispute with the Sudan are all cases in point. This rule has even been codified in the OAU Charter provisions against use of force and against intervention in internal affairs.[25]

---

[24]See the discussion in Cecil V. Crabb, Jr., *The Elephants and the Grass: A Study of Nonalignment* (New York: Frederick A. Praeger, 1965), especially pp. 96–99. On neutralism see also Francis Low-Beer, "The Concept of Neutralism," *American Political Science Review,* June 1964 (Vol. 58, No. 2), pp. 383–391; and Martin (ed.).

---

[25]See Article III of the OAU Charter and, more specifically, the resolutions of the first Assembly of Heads of State, Cairo, July 1964, reprinted in Colin Legum, *Pan-Africanism* (2nd ed.; New York: Frederick A. Praeger, 1965), pp. 303–304.

The combined effects of Rules Two and Three are important.[26] With unification and military conquest ruled out as policy alternatives the strongest form of good and bad relations becomes economic cooperation and political warfare, respectively. The OAU nonintervention clause and political actions such as the OCAM stand on the Congo and against Ghanaian subversion in neighboring countries are attempts to further reduce policy alternatives by removing the possibility of political warfare, but without complete success. Lesser forms of intervention, such as propaganda, conspiracy, subversion, terrorism, and guerrilla warfare,[27] still are used. Lessons of experience, such as the Sudan's decision to stop arms supplies to the Congolese rebels when it found out that the arms were actually going to the Sudanese rebels, may help to accomplish what appeals to virtue have failed to attain. Another attempt to enforce the antisubversive extension of Rule Three through the use of one available element of power was OCAM's threat not to attend the third OAU summit at Accra, and thus weaken Ghana's prestige, if subversion did not stop. This attempt was successful in suspending political warfare in early 1965 and in weakening Nkrumah's regime internationally.

Rule Four is that all available means will be used to extend the boundaries of the inner system to its outer limits. This is a restatement of the emphasis on independence for the entire continent, but Rule Two also indicates the limitations on the means. For power will be applied only to the extent that it does not jeopardize the independence of the existing states, either by sapping their resources or by opening them to serious retaliation. This rule was already in formation during the Algerian war, when it created dilemmas for Tunisia and Morocco in their support of the Algerian nationalists, and it has severely limited support for nationalist movements "south of the battle line," including intervention in Rhodesia. In fact, it was not just Moïse Tshombe's political views that limited Congolese

support for Angolan nationalism but a realistic evaluation—visible in Zambia and Malawi as well —of an exposed position (indeed, the latter fact may be viewed as instrumental in producing the former). So long as the interests of the states north of the battle line are not brought seriously into question by the Southern African regimes, Rule Two—independence over unity, state over revolution—will undermine the active solidarity behind liberation.

V

The enumeration of characteristics of the African system enables a tentative concluding analysis of possible future changes and their effect on intra-African relations. The most likely change in a component of the system, capable of causing its breakdown, is the destruction of its seemingly fragile autonomy. If African events become of direct and primary interest to outside—particularly cold-war—states to the point where outside stimuli outweigh African sources in triggering African responses, the very existence of the system is in danger. This would take place, as seen, if African states gave up their neutralism to take active part in an outside conflict or if an African conflict was beyond the continent's ability to contain and drew in major participation of outside powers. While the former is unlikely, the entire southern African conflict is a possible case of the latter and could mean an even more serious dislocation of the African system than the first Congo crisis which arose during its early formative years. Direct involvement by cold-war protagonists in a prolonged Rhodesian war, a South West African invasion, a South African revolution, or a guerrilla campaign in Portuguese territories would take the control of African relations out of African hands. Yet foreign involvement may, from the African's point of view, be the only way to accomplish a desirable policy objective. The dilemma is evident: Is liberation worth the price of the loss of autonomy and nonalignment? The answer to the same question concerning development has been negative, the Africans rejecting increased aid when it involves political strings and alignment. In both cases, however, the dilemma has been tempered by the disinclination of outside powers to threaten autonomy, either through active participation in the liberation

---

[26]In other language, what is in formation is an integrated security community which rejects attempts at amalgamation. See Karl W. Deutsch and others, *Political Community and the North Atlantic Area* (Princeton, N.J.: Princeton University Press, 1957), pp. 5–6.

[27]See Zartman, *International Relations in the New Africa*, p. 88.

campaign or through major increases of aid to aligned states.

Another source of change in the system concerns the level and distribution of power. At the present time power is so highly diffused that increases or decreases forseeable in the short run are unlikely to affect the nature of intra-African relations. Nor is the advent of new states, through either the further breakup of present units (e.g., Nigeria) or the independence of present territories (e.g., Portuguese Guinea or Rhodesia), likely to alter the configuration of power in the continent, particularly since any new states can be expected to have their power reduced by problems of domestic consolidation after independence. The formation of new states through the integration of present units into a larger regional complex would certainly change the power configuration although such an event seems unlikely to take place, as has been seen.

A very few countries, however, could increase their power significantly enough to alter at least regional and perhaps eventually continental relations. The most notable example is Algeria, which already has a sizable army and a substantial economic infrastructure; politically, it has a strong attachment to African liberation and revolution, derived from its own experiences. If domestic political stability can be added, Algeria will have united basic conditions for a role of increased activity in African relations. The result could be predominance in the region (Maghreb), leadership of a radical policy in the continent, and/or catalyzation of alliances and counteralliances. It is difficult to see any states south of the Sahara and north of the battle line capable of a similar short-run power increase, Ghana being the only state with the beginnings of a heavy industrial base but handicapped by unstable politics, a small population, and an unclear foreign policy direction.

One possible change in the nature of relations would be the reinforcement of the present regional constellations to the point where several autonomous systems of interaction would come into being. This would depend on African states turning their attention to conflict and cooperation with their neighbors, losing their interest in African events in other parts of the continent and in the OAU, and following the lead of the regional committees of the Economic Commission for Africa (ECA) in focusing on regional eco-

nomics; it would also suppose a decrease in the importance of the "hinge states," a disenchantment with the liberation struggle, and a disappearance of "bridging" issues. There is no reason to infer that such a change would necessarily bring about either harmony or conflict although, whatever the quality of relations, the increased quantity in a regional context would probably also involve increased intensity as other focuses of relations fell in importance.

Another likely change in the nature of relations would be a return to a balance-of-power pattern of ideological alliances and counteralliances. OCAM has concentrated on economic and cultural harmonization and has not reassumed the politically active role it played as the Afro-Malagasy Union (UAM). Meetings of the radical states—Algeria, Egypt, Mali, Guinea, the Congo (Brazzaville), and Tanzania—were to have been held in Cairo in February 1967 and in Algiers in May but were postponed. It is this group, however, which has the greatest potential for introducing a new alliance pattern since it is minority, activist, and generally dissatisfied with the content of African policies, including those in the OAU. The likelihood of such a turn of events would be enhanced by the development of new African issues of the magnitude of the Algerian or Congolese issues in 1960-1961; again Rhodesia affords the most explosive possibility although Djibouti or Spanish Sahara would be more divisive in their effects. Prolonged internal unrest in an African state involving outside assistance could also act as a catalyst for the formation of rival alliances although the events of Nigeria and Ghana show that, to the present, African states have been unwilling or unable, respectively, to intervene directly in internal unrest, and the second Congo crisis shows that, to the present, even when undertaken such intervention is ineffective.

In this light the attempts to establish norms ruling out guerrilla warfare for purposes of intervention in internal affairs have been more effective than might initially be suspected. Indeed, even terrorism, subversion, and conspiracy, while not eliminated, have been relatively ineffective as policy alternatives, and their ineffectiveness reinforces the norm. However, next to Rule One, discussed above, Rule Three is the most likely of the four present normative characteristics to undergo change. Two types of wars of conquest are possible: the border war that culminates a period of bad blood and the Goa-type incident, often involving competing African armies. There are numerous occasions for the former, particularly where nomadic forays along a permeable frontier are followed by a military riposte; they are likely to be as inconclusive in terms of territorial conquest as they have been in the recent African past.[28] The Goa-type incident has greater potential for disturbance, particularly in colonies claimed by two African states, such as Djibouti (Ethiopia and Somalia) and Spanish Sahara (Morocco and Mauritania supported by Algeria) although the colonial power in both cases presently is in a stronger position than Portugal was in Goa. The foreseeable limits of military strength in the near future suggest that Rule One would be broken along with Rule Three, for prolonged military measures cannot be sustained by African armies without concurrent outside help.

The preceding review is an attempt to indicate areas where the nature of the current system could change. If such changes now appear unlikely, this is only to say that certain presently identifiable characteristics of intra-African relations exist, not that they are immutable. Nor is it to predict that such changes are imminent, a task beyond the capabilities of political science. If it has been able to indicate areas where changes might take place and to isolate characteristics

useful for analyzing present relations and future changes, it will have been useful.

It will also be of value if it can be used to indicate further areas where research is necessary and relevant to a coordinated study of international relations. The need for detailed research in quantity, quality, and intensity of relations has already been cited, together with some suggestions on methodology. More conceptual and empirical work is required on the types and tactics of international organization, including the dynamics of alliance formation and the behavior of states in a concert organization such as the OAU. Africa is also a particularly apt area to study two other major problems in dealing with international relations: the choice and use of policy alternatives when power is consistently low, and the formation and enforcement of norms. Finally, the concept of the subordinate state system suggests further investigation of the question of systems overlap, partially analyzed above. How do states use dual membership? What types of relations are handled in which system and at what level? When and for what types of problems does a state have recourse to a universal organization (UN), a continental organization (OAU), a regional organization (e.g., Entente), and/or its own individual resources?

Discussion and Questions

1. Zartman stresses the importance of subregional clusters and institutional integration in Africa. Indeed, subregional activity seems to have preempted much of the interest and energy that might otherwise have been devoted to regional

ordering activity within the OAU and other all-African institutions. ➤ What factors account for this tendency? ➤ What is the significance of the subregional phenomenon for the creation of an African regional unit in world order? ➤ Can these subregions serve as constituent units of regional order within Africa? (See Arthur Hazlewood, Ed., *African Integration and Disintegration* [Oxford University Press, London, 1968]. Also Immanuel Wallerstein, *Africa: The Politics of Independence* [Vintage, New York, 1961].)

[28]See Zartman, *International Relations in the New Africa*, pp. 87–119, 165–166; and Ravi L. Kapil, "On the Conflict Potential of Inherited Boundaries in Africa," *World Politics*, July 1966 (Vol. 18, No. 4), pp. 656–673.

2. ➤ What is the first-stage integration potential of Africa as compared to Asia? ➤ Enumerate favorable and unfavorable factors. (see Ali Mazrui, *Towards a Pax Africana: A Study of Ideology and Ambition* [Weidenfeld and Nicolson, London, 1967].) ➤ Is the Arab Middle Eastern opposition to Africa and the African opposition to Southern Africa a positive ordering factor? ➤ For what purposes of analysis is it desirable to include regional enemies within the boundaries of a subordinate international system? Note that Zartman excludes white-governed South Africa, whereas Binder includes Israel. ➤ Which decision is to be preferred or are both acceptable interpretations of sybsystemic variations?

19

The Concept "Subordinate International System": A Critique

KAY BOALS

As a discipline in a preparadigmatic phase of development,[1] political science offers a wide range of approaches, theoretical frameworks, and methodologies. Although in comparative political studies a relatively large number of approaches compete with one another,[2] in the field of international politics the alternatives have tended to remain limited to the choice between systems and unit-actor analysis. In practical terms, a choice is usually made between the global or dominant international system and the nation-state as actor as the level on which to undertake analysis.[3] The latter has often involved a phenomenological perspective and methodology much different from the perspective and methodology of systems theory.[4]

Since each approach has distinct advantages,[5] it is not surprising that attempts have been made to find a "middle ground" between them that would combine their advantages and minimize their disadvantages. One of the most suggestive, though little developed, efforts is the concept "subordinate international system" first outlined

[1]A concept from the philosophy of science developed by Thomas S. Kuhn, *The structure of Scientific Revolutions* (Chicago: University of Chicago Press, 1962).

[2]For example, the group approach, structural-functional analysis, and the elite and political culture approaches, as well as systems analysis.

[3]J. David Singer, "The Level-of-Analysis Problem," in Klaus Knorr and Sidney Verba, Eds., *The International System: Theoretical Essays* (Princeton, N.J.: Princeton University Press, 1961, pp. 77–92.

[4]In the sense that systems theorists are usually not interested in detailed causal explanation of how and why particular decisions are made. Further, the phenominological approach rests on a number of assumptions set forth by Singer (*ibid.*), which the systems theorist is likely to reject.

[5]Singer suggests that focus at the actor level-of-analysis permits greater explanatory depth and intensity as well as more comprehensive, richer empirical description; on the other hand, focus at the systemic level allows for greater comprehensiveness, and elegance.

Reprinted by permission of the author.

by Leonard Binder in 1958 as an approach to study of the Middle East[6] and thereafter applied by others to different regions.[7]

I propose on the basis of this existing literature to undertake a critique of the concept, including a revision intended to increase its conceptual clarity. I shall be attempting to discover what the concept "subordinate international system" adds to the concept "system" as used in the discipline of political science and to evaluate that contribution, as well as to suggest an alternative concept that appears promising.

THE CONCEPT "SYSTEM"

Despite—or perhaps because of—the frequent use of the concept "system" in political science, there exists great confusion concerning its definition and conceptual implications. For some theorists "system" implies a highly autonomous structure; for others, a structure that changes only because of the impact of external forces. Although some have used the concept to refer to a structure all of whose parts are necessary for the persistence of that structure,[8] others have embodied in the concept notions of functional unity, interdependence of the system's parts, or tendencies to self-maintenance or homeostasis.[9]

Confusion is further compounded by technological differences. For example, though some writers use the term "structure" to refer to the "orderly patterning of the elements of the system,"[10] others use the terms "structure" and "system" as synonyms, as was done in the paragraph above.[11] Thus, for some theorists the concept "system" apparently includes only "a network of relations between interacting actors,"[12] for others it includes those actors (or elements) as well. Clearly, any network must exist between or among elements, but, for purposes of conceptual clarity, it is important to know whether such elements are part of the analytic notion of system.

In addition, much conceptual muddiness has arisen from the failure to distinguish clearly whether the concept "system" refers to "a fact, a goal, or a tool of analysis."[13] Although the three may not be mutually exclusive,[14] failure to distinguish among them analytically has led to numerous instances of reification, misleading terminology,[15] and confusion between "system" as an analytic concept and as an empirical referent.

In view of these confusions one is tempted to agree with the viewpoint that "far from being a heuristic tool, the system concept, even in its narrow sense, is in danger of becoming a substantive bone of academic contention and interpretation."[16] According to this view, "as things

---

[6]Selection 16: Leonard Binder, "The Middle East as a Subordinate International System." [*World Politics*, 10 (April 1958), pp. 408-29.]

[7]Selection 17: Michael Brecher, "International Relations and Asian Studies: The Subordinate State System of Southern Asia." [*World Politics*, 15 (January 1963), pp. 213-35]; Selection 18: William Zartman, "Africa as a Subordinate State System in International Relations." [Mimeographed, 1964]; George Modelski "International Relations and Area Studies: The Case of Southeast Asia," *International Relations*, vol. II no. 2 (April 1961), pp. 143-155; Thomas Hodgkin, "The New West Africa State System", *University of Toronto Quarterly*, 31 (October 1961), pp. 74-82.

[8]For example, Carl J. Friedrich, who defines "system" as follows: "When several parts that are distinct and different from each other compose a whole, bearing a defined functional relation to each other which establishes a mutual dependence of these parts upon each other so that the destruction of one entails the destruction of the whole, then such a constellation shall be called a system." Cited by Peter Nettl, "The Concept of System in Political Science," *Political Studies*, 14 (October 1966), p. 307.

[9]This list of the various theoretical implications of the concept "system" was suggested by Harry Eckstein. The functionalist concept of system has been presented by numerous theorists, including Parsons, Levy, and Merton.

[10]Herbert Wiseman, *Political Systems*, (London: Routledge & Kegan Paul, 1966), p. 2.

[11]It was so used there strictly for convenience rather than to prejudice the argument.

[12]Wiseman, p. 2.

[13]Zartman, *op. cit.*

[14]*Ibid.* It would seem, however, that there is some mutual exclusivity between "system" as a fact having "objective existence independent of volition" and as "a quality to be attained," at least if one is speaking of objective existence at the same point in time at which the system is still to be attained.

[15]A notable offender on this score is Kaplan, who, despite his logical definitional rigor, allows himself to employ anthropomorphic terminology in describing system reactions.

[16]Nettl, p. 314.

stand now, the concept of systems as such wields no automatic focus of meaning, no immediate signaling of any particular form of analysis or analogy. . . ."[17]

It is possible, however, to see the various definitions of "system" as variations on a common theme, all of which have "a common core of meaning," defined as "a set of elements or components or units which are observed to exist or to function in accordance with a discernible pattern.[18] More simply, a system has been defined as "any pattern of elements and linkages persisting over time."[19] Such definitions do not eliminate all confusions connected with the concept "system," but they do permit us to view concepts of system that incorporate notions of autonomy, homeostasis or functional interdependence as simply elaborations or special cases of a more general concept.[20]

Further, these more general definitions, while minimalist in their implications, avoid using the term "system" in a nonconceptual sense to refer to "merely a (related) set of variables and nothing more."[21] Although it is certainly true that "any set of specified variables may be considered a system,"[22] that is only to say that such a set may be examined as if it were a system, that is, to see whether in fact a pattern or order can be discerned. It does not mean that any such set in fact fulfills the minimal specifications of the concept "system."[23]

The second confusion, that arising from divergent uses of the terms "system" and "structure", might be resolved on a purely linguistic level, if not by general agreement on usage, at least by definitional clarity on the part of theorists using these terms. On another level, however, the equation of both "system" and "structure" with "patterns of interrelationship"[24] or "a pattern of relations"[25] rather than with both elements and linkages appears undesirable. By excluding from the analytic notion of system those elements (actors) among whom patterns of interrelationship are discerned, such an equation makes extremely difficult discussion of system change, stability or transformation with even a modicum of conceptual elegance and obviates questions of system autonomy, interdependence, and functional unity.[26]

Consequently, it seems advisable to include within the concept "system" both elements (actors) and linkages (patterns of interaction), thereby distinguishing more meaningfully between a system and its environment. The term "structure" could then be used to refer to the discernible ordered pattern of relationships among elements of the system, a usage which is in fact general.

Perhaps the most frequent and dangerous confusion is that between system as fact and system as tool of analysis, that is, between concrete and abstract systems. Although there is, of

---

[17]Nettl, p. 324.

[18]Harold and Margaret Sprout. *The Foundations of International Politics* (Princeton, N.J.: Van Nostrand, 1962), p. 66.

[19]Manfred Halpern, "Toward a Theory of Modernization: Notes for Work in Progress" (mimeographed).

[20]As theorists like Eckstein and Halpern have argued, they have the added advantage of not building into one's concepts and definitions attributes that are better left as part of the empirical investigation to be undertaken.

[21]Nettl, p. 307. Nettl distinguishes between a concept, which is "essentially a system of thought" (p. 300) derived from both statements about reality and hypotheses, and a simple word or term used without conceptual significance. Thus, for example, the concept "system" is intimately bound up with "notions of stability, continuity, and structure," (p. 311), whereas a nonconceptual use of the term "system" lacks such focus.

[22]Morton Kaplan, *System and Process in International Politics*, New York: Wiley, 1957, p. 4.

[23]Thus, Kaplan's reasoning that his own definition of system is technically faulty because any variables may be considered a system appears invalid. Kaplan's definition of a "system of action" is as follows: "A set of variables so related, in contradiction to its environment, that describable behavioral regularities characterize the internal relationships of the variables to each other and the external relationships of the set of individual variables to combinations of external variables" (p. 4).

[24]Binder, *op. cit.*

[25]Brecher, *op. cit.*

[26]Since the elements or units among which interaction takes place are themselves part of the system's environment, interdependence and functional unity—both of which are assumptions concerning the elements—become irrelevant. Similarly, system autonomy is presumably not in question since the patterns of relation can hardly be in any meaningful sense autonomous of the interacting elements.

course, no escape from abstraction, whether in scientific endeavor or other perceptual activities, and thus the question is more properly posed in terms of levels of abstraction, nonetheless the terms "concrete" and "abstract" are helpful in discussing the problem at hand. Many writers who employ the concept "system" imply that the "system" they are discussing is somehow "out there" somewhere in the empirical reality under investigation rather than being simply their own framework of analysis. Thus, for example, Zartman proposes to "describe and analyse the subordinate state system of Africa *as a fact* in contemporary world politics."[27]

It has been suggested that there are academic and linguistic reasons for confusing facts and concepts, among them, the necessary inclusion within concepts of the presumption of certain facts and the constraints on thinking inevitably arising from use of a particular concept, such that certain kinds of facts "leap forward teleologically at the summons of the system concept.[28] Also, confusion is perpetuated by the dual use of the term "system" in both concrete and abstract senses. Misleading shifts from one sense to the other can easily occur.

Consequently, I shall use the term "system" to refer only to those elements and linkages that have been abstracted as a system and shall use the term "systemic empirical referent" to denote that portion of empirical reality from which they have been abstracted. For example, the phrase, "Middle Eastern subordinate international system" would connote only a particular pattern of elements and linkages chosen for abstraction as a system; its systemic empirical referent would be the totality of events and actions both within the region conventionally abstracted as "the Middle East" and all those in other regions in which Middle Easterners participated.

Essentially, then, to say that a set of elements (variables) is a system is to say that certain ele-ments abstracted from the flux of concrete reality are perceived to be related in describable and regular ways to one another and, as a whole, to their environment.[29] This formulation, while cumbersome, offers the advantage of clarifying the relationship of the analytical construct "system" to the empirical reality to which it is applied for purposes of description, explanation or prediction.

In summary, it is my view that despite the disagreements and confusion surrounding use of the concept "system" in the social sciences, it is possible to arrive at an unambiguous and useful delineation of the concept by (1) defining the concept by its common core of meaning as used by different theorists; (2) using "system" to refer to both elements and linkages and "structure" to refer to the discerned orderly patterning of those elements; and (3) using "system" to refer to elements and relationships abstracted from reality rather than to the empirical reality from which they have been abstracted.

It is on this basis that the concept "subordinate international system" will be examined.

THE CONCEPT "SUBORDINATE INTERNATIONAL SYSTEM": AN INTRODUCTION

Before considering in detail the conceptual impli-cations of the concept "subordinate international system,"[30] it is perhaps relevant to discuss briefly the reasons for which the concept was originally put forward. One of these was to link area studies and international relations; the second was to call into question what was seen as an overemphasis on bipolarity in international-relations theory.

Binder, who first developed the concept, sought a "middle ground" between "frame of reference" theories, that is, broad generalizations based on an ideal model, and area-studies approaches that

---

[27]Zartman, *op. cit.*

[28]Nettl, *op. cit.* According to Nettl, concepts are formed both from statements about reality and from hypotheses or assumptions. Thus, certain presumed facts become intrinsic to the concept and quasi-insepar-able from it. At the same time, "sensitizing" concepts direct the investigator's attention to certain aspects of reality rather than others, that is, they shape percep-tions.

[29]Cf. Kaplan's definition of "system of action", above, note 23.

[30]The term "subordinate international system" will be used throughout to refer to the concept discussed by Binder, Brecher, and Zartman, although the latter two use the term "subordinate state system." Both refer to Binder's earlier article and are obviously using the concept he developed; therefore, use of a single term appears justified.

stress the relation of foreign policy to socio-historical context.[31] Brecher also sought to bridge the gap between international relations and area studies.[32] Yet it appears that the two meant rather different things despite similar formulations.

To clarify this point it will be necessary to distinguish between two questions that seem intertwined in Singer's discussion of what he calls the level-of-analysis problem. I would suggest a distinction between level-of-analysis, that is, unit-actor versus the system under consideration as a whole, and level-of-abstraction, that is, the "distance" from the richness and detail of concrete experience.

Although it is generally true that the two tend to vary together—a high level-of-analysis (for example, the total international system) being associated with a high level-of-abstraction (for example, Kaplan's pure models), and a low level-of-analysis (for example, a national actor) with a low level-of-abstraction (for example, detailed decision-making studies, phenomenological methodology, noncomparative configurative studies)—it is by no means necessary that they do so. For example, Hoffmann's inductive historical sociology combines high level-of-analysis with low level-of-abstraction; likewise, some of the propositions given by Singer[33] combine low level-of-analysis with high level-of-abstraction.

What does it mean, then, to seek a bridge or middle ground between area studies and international relations? Limitation to a partial rather than the total international system does not in itself predetermine the question of level-of-analysis, since it would remain possible to approach it from either the unit-actor level or the system level. On the other hand, focus on any system *qua* system would seem to imply a tendency toward a high level-of-analysis. From the perspective of the total international system, however, focus on a partial international system at the systemic level-of-analysis might be said to constitute a middle level-of-analysis, especially if the interactions of that partial system with other partial systems are analyzed.

The level-of-abstraction would also seem to be "middle," that is, focusing on the determinants of action common to a group of states with certain shared socio-historical characteristics rather than either on one particular state in its uniqueness or on more general factors shaping the behavior of all states in the international system. This interpretation would seem applicable at least to Binder's aims.

Brecher, however, speaks also of using the concept to explore "unit behavior in comparable milieux" by which he appears to mean seeking propositions at a high level-of-abstraction to describe and explain unit-actor behavior (low level-of-analysis) in all subordinate international systems.[34] Thus, while Binder's "middle ground" appears to involve middle levels of both analysis and abstraction, Brecher's "bridge" is primarily a technique for cross-fertilization of inductive and deductive approaches to the study of international relations,[35] and does not necessarily imply any particular level of either analysis or abstraction.

In connection with the second reason for developing the concept "subordinate international system," that is, as a reaction to overemphasis on bipolarity, Binder and Brecher again begin with similar formulations. Binder begins with the premise that the theory of bipolarity is inapplicable to Middle East international politics, since "rules for US-USSR relations can only define the conditions under which politics of the uncommitted exist, not explain them."[36] For Brecher there exists an array of relationships among nonbloc actors having very little to do with the bipolar bloc system.[37] Zartman as well notes the existence of a "dominant system of bipolar configurations" that cover a number of subordinate systems.[38] Thus, all three posit a dominant bipolar system, separate subordinate systems, and a world system made up of the interactions within and between all of them.[39] All share this common basic insight; however, they differ significantly in its application and elaboration.

[31]Binder, *op. cit.*
[32]Brecher, *op. cit.*
[33]See the citation in note 3, above.

[34]Brecher, *op. cit.*
[35]*Ibid.*
[36]Binder, *op. cit.*
[37]Brecher, *op. cit.*
[38]Zartman, *op. cit.*
[39]Brecher's formulation is clearest on this point (p. 217); it remains implicit in Binder's treatment.

One of the major differences appears to be the basic question to which each directs his use of the concept. Binder, for example, seems to be asking how much, in what ways, and why do patterns of interaction among states in the Middle East restrict the goals and methods of super powers acting within the region. Brecher, on the other hand, is apparently basically concerned with the question of how the subordinate system shapes the general and specific foreign policy of its members. Thus, while Binder examines the system from the perspective of an external super power seeking to act within the region in which that system exists, Brecher does so from the viewpoint of states within the system whether they act outside or within the region.

In essence, of course, both are asking what effect the system has on the behavior of its units, but the difference in perspective is relevant to the kinds of more specific questions one may ask about the system's functioning. For example, from the perspective he has chosen, Brecher need not be concerned at all with the question of system autonomy;[40] by contrast, Binder is necessarily brought to deal with it. Likewise, for the question Binder has posed, he need only be concerned with those aspects of the system's influence on its members that concern their response to the actions of super powers; Brecher's question, on the other hand, leads more naturally to concern with the system's influence on intra-area responses as well. Presumably, therefore, the perspective chosen—whether that of an actor within the system, an actor outside it, or an observer from the systemic level[41]—will have significance for the concept's development.

If, however, Kaplan is correct in stating that systems analysis in general is concerned with describing the characteristic behavior of actors within a given system, then it would appear that Brecher's question about how the system affects its members is central, since it is only after having answered that question that one can proceed to deal with Binder's query about extra-area powers. The major focus of discussion in using the con-

cept "subordinate international system," in other words, is likely to be the internal workings of that system as it affects and is affected by the actions of its units. This idea is of some importance to the discussion that follows, since the concept's power to provide insights concerning intrasystemic relations in certain types of partial international systems will therefore be significant in evaluating its clarity and usefulness.

THE CONCEPT "SUBORDINATE INTERNATIONAL SYSTEM": CLARIFICATION AND REVISION

It is worth considering the concept "subordinate international system" from the perspective of its conceptual clarity before going on to discuss its applications and usefulness. It is certainly true that a major criterion of a good concept is its usefulness in providing insights that help to answer the theorist's questions about reality; in addition, a concept may also validly be examined for elegance, simplicity, and clarity.

Each of the three theorists has components or conditions for the existence of a subordinate system. For Zartmann they are (1) a geographic area, (2) an international organization, and (3) autonomy. For Brecher they are (1) a geographic area, (2) at least three actors who (3) form a distinctive segment or community in their own and others' eyes and (4) are relatively inferior to the units in the dominant system; and (5) the fact that changes in the dominant system have a greater effect on the subordinate system than the reverse. Although Binder does not explicitly set forth conditions, by inference they include (1) geographic area, (2) the greater effect of changes in the dominant system, and (3) the "refraction" of power from the dominant system when applied within the subordinate system.

We suggest that it is possible to eliminate most of these components while retaining the essence of the concept. The first candidate for elimination is the existence of an international organization coterminous with the "inner limits"[42] of the

---

[40]And, indeed, his discussion of penetration of the Asian subordinate system by the great powers indicates lack of interest in this aspect of the subordinate systems.

[41]This is the perspective taken by Zartman, who appears to be asking a question similar to that asked by Brecher.

[42]Zartman's formulation, which stresses geographical area, contains the idea of inner and outer limits of a subordinate system, with the inner limits comprising independent, anticolonialist African states and the outer limits extending to the whole continent, including still-dependent and white-ruled "fringe areas" (*op. cit.*).

system. If this criterion were applied, there would as yet be no subordinate system in Asia, that of Africa would date only from the creation of the Organization of African Unity in 1962, and that of the Middle East only from 1945 at best. Brecher, however, applied the concept to Asia; further, the reasons adduced by Binder for the existence of a Middle Eastern subordinate system date back at least to 1919. Thus, it would appear desirable to eliminate an international organization as a condition rather than keeping it, as does Zartmann, as a component "less necessary" than the others.

Secondly, Brecher's condition that units in the subordinate system be relatively inferior (in power?) to those in the dominant system appears somewhat redundant, since presumably if that were not the case the subordinate system would become dominant. Likewise, it is not clear why at least three actors are needed to constitute a subordinate system. Since dyadic systems are clearly possible,[43] what of India and Pakistan? Or the United Kingdom and Ireland?

Fourthly, it would not be in principle impossible to think of circumstances under which changes in a subordinate system would have potentially transforming effects on the dominant system. If, for example, the "new" states attained sufficient internal stability and external capabilities to function as full-fledged independent members of the international community, the whole climate of the dominant system in which at present conflict has been largely diverted to intervention (directly or by proxy) in the third world might be radically altered.[44] To take a less extreme case, the present crisis in the Middle East offers one instance of the potential of events within a subordinate system[45] to affect the dominant system. Thus, although it is clear that drastic changes in the present bipolar dominant

system would affect subordinate systems, the condition for subordinate systems as stated by Binder and Brecher is far from clear and might better be dropped.

The basic insights contained in the concept "subordinate international system" appear to be best expressed in Brecher's third and Binder's last conditions, that is, that the system's members form, in the general view, a distinctive segment of the world community and that power is somehow refracted and deflected coming from the dominant to a subordinate system.

If that is the case, then the component of geographic area can also be called into question, since its function is presumed to be the provision of a "territorial base" and an "identification area" for the system's members. Why could these functions not be performed by nongeographic factors? In the modern world, with the development of worldwide communications, the spread of certain languages, and the strength of ideological affiliations of various kinds, it would not be inconceivable to satisfy the two conditions stated in the preceding paragraph for states not geographically contiguous. To take actual cases, Egypt is in fact separated from the Arab East by Israel, and the concept of an Atlantic Community does not seem to depend primarily on territorial identifications.

One major advantage of eliminating the component of geographic area would be to include for comparative study of subordinate systems such cases as the British Commonwealth and the Afro-Asia group. It might well be found after investigation that geographic area is in fact an important factor in the character and cohesion of subordinate systems, but there seems to be no valid justification for foreclosing the question definitively.

Finally, there is the component "autonomy," which Zartman uses to signify "a condition wherein relations within the area are composed of intra-area actions and responses" or where, in Africa for example, "relations among African states are primarily governed by intra-African stimuli."[46] Zartman distinguishes autonomy from independence by maintaining that the former does not imply freedom from influences from

---

[43]Brecher agrees with Rosenau on this point, but still requires at least three actors.

[44]This view of the nature of relations and conflict in the dominant system in the contemporary world has been advanced by Richard A. Falk and Manfred Halpern, among others.

[45]If, that is, Israel and the Arab States are considered part of one subordinate system. As we shall argue below, however, on the basis of components retained as part of the concept "subordinate international system," this does not in fact appear to be the case, although Binder considered the Middle East as a whole as such a system. Other examples can be found, including the

---

India-China conflict or the Indonesian-Malaysia dispute, though neither of these in fact affected the dominant system extensively.

[46]Zartman, *op. cit.*

outside powers; yet it is obviously difficult in practice to determine what degree of influence is compatible with autonomy even in that restricted sense. It seems, in any case, to imply a higher degree of freedom from extra-area influence than does Binder's "refraction" of dominant system power, although the two notions deal with the same phenomenon.

Since system autonomy has come to carry connotations of independence from the environment greater than that which Zartman appears to find necessary for the existence of a subordinate system, it would seem preferable to retain Binder's more general idea while leaving the question of the degree and kind of autonomy within a particular subordinate international system for empirical research. A further reason for doing so is that Zartman's definition of autonomy is limited to intrasystemic relations, but Binder's idea encompasses intersystemic relations as well.

Having eliminated six of the components originally listed, we are left then with a concept "subordinate international system" that distinguishes certain partial international systems[47] from others on the basis of two criteria: (1) whether or not the system is composed of members who feel themselves to be and are considered by others to be a distinctive segment or community; and (2) whether or not there is a "refraction" of dominant system power by the subordinate system.

The two appear intimately linked together when it is seen that the implicit hypothesis underlying the notion of refraction is that the members of a subordinate international system, linked by a feeling of community or distinctiveness, will react to both intra- and inter-systemic stimuli primarily in terms of their position within that subordinate system, that is, with a view to the effects of their response on their interests and position within that system.

In this form the concept appears of use in making both policy-makers and theorists aware of factors that may be of great significance in explaining and predicting international behavior. When we attempt to relate the concept of subordinate international system in this form to the concept "system" discussed in the first section, however, certain problems arise.

First of all, Binder's definition of "system" as "patterns of interrelationship" and Brecher's as a "pattern of relations" have already been criticized for restricting the notion of system to linkages rather than to both elements and linkages. This definition leads to much confusion, since both writers quickly make an implicit identification of "system" with "area," that is, with what we have called the "systemic empirical referent." Likewise, the units of the system become identified with the units formed by the geographic boundaries of existing political entities.[48] Consequently, it is very difficult to determine in any given statement whether the abstracted system or its empirical referent is meant.

Also, as a result of the blurring of the crucial distinction between systemic empirical referents and systems, the authors fail to deal directly with the question of exactly what features of concrete reality have been abstracted as the elements and linkages of the subordinate international system. In addition to loss of conceptual clarity, this failure results, as we shall argue below, in a less than optimal utilization of the concept on the Middle East, the area to which it was first applied.

Implicitly, in any case, the authors appear to conceive of the actual actors as the incumbent governments of the states included within the area that comprises the empirical referent of the subordinate international system and to conceive of the linkages as the totality of intergovernmental interactions. Our definition of system, however, includes the idea of a pattern of such elements and linkages over time. What this pattern is within any particular subordinate system is never really dealt with by any of the authors, a deficiency that perhaps derives from their lack of a clear definition of "system."

---

[47]A partial international system is one that does not include the totality of international actors.

[48]Nettl suggests that identification of "system" with an area is usual in the functionalist concept of system, for which "system" is defined only as the structural complement of function. Whereas in functionalism there is a conception of a concrete system with abstract functional subsystems, in the literature on subordinate international systems there may be an inversion such that the subsystems (units) are conceived of concretely and the subordinate international system is viewed as an abstract (supra) system. In fact, however, even the subordinate system itself is often identified with a concrete geographical area.

In addition, at least one of the authors identifies "structure" with the configuration (distribution and level) of power within the system[49] rather than with the network of interactions, as is usually done by systems theorists. Thus, the attempt to relate the concept "subordinate international system" to the basic concept "system" encounters much terminological difficulty, even using the minimalist definition of "system" we earlier adopted;[50] this difficulty is in addition to that which arises from confusion between the concrete and the abstract.

A further result of such confusion is the difficulty of discussing clearly notions of system stability and system transformation, since it becomes difficult to tell whether stability refers to the continued existence of the concrete system or its units, of particular patterns of interaction, or of types of interaction patterns.[51] Likewise, unless the distinction between the abstracted system and its empirical referent is clearly made, confusion arises as to what constitutes system transformation. If, on the other hand, the distinction is made, then only those changes in the system's empirical referent or in inter-systemic linkages that have transforming consequences for the abstracted patterns of interaction of the subordinate international system will be relevant. For example, the revolution in Egypt in 1952 has had transforming consequences for Egypt's domestic political system, but would not be considered a factor of system-transformation in the subordinate inter-Arab system unless it could be shown that it in fact had transforming consequences for that system's pattern of interaction.

In summary, then, although the concept "subordinate international system" can be clarified and revised on a conceptual level, its usefulness as a contribution to systems theory is limited by its users' failure to distinguish clearly between the abstracted system and its empirical referent. Although the basic insights that led to the development of the concept appear fruitful, the concept itself requires further elaboration and clarification.

Up to the present, its use has resulted primarily in a descriptive characterization of particular subordinate international systems along dimensions such as the configuration of power, the nature of relations within the system (frequency, intensity, and multilateralism), and linkages to the dominant system in terms of extra-area penetration into the subordinate system.[52] The purpose of such characterization on a descriptive level has been to "produce hypotheses" to explain state behavior and "to serve a limited predictive function" as long as the system as described continues in being.[53] What Zartman and Brecher have done is to provide an "analytic framework"[54] to be applied to the study of certain partial international systems. Binder, on the other hand, though less systematic in his formulations, provides in addition a series of explanations for why

---

[49]Binder equates "structure" with "the distribution of power among states" (*op. cit.*). Both Brecher and Zartman include configuration of power in their discussion of the system, Brecher as one of the "structural" features, and Zartman as part of the system's "internal workings."

[50]The more restricted and elaborate concepts of system are even less related. As mentioned in note 48, subordinate-international-systems theorists differ from functionalists in conceiving of the sybsystems (units) as concrete rather than abstract; in any case, functional analysis appears unsuited to international politics in the absence of structural differentiation along functional lines. Further, whereas in functional analysis there is an assumed hierarchy between system and subsystem such that the latter exists for and contributes to the former, in international politics the reverse would appear to hold true. Although Nettl's description of "system as analogy" appears related to our writers' concern with boundaries and system autonomy, the use of "environment" by such systems theories is unhelpful to those concerned with relations between dominant and subordinate systems and does not allow for inputs from inside the system.

[51]Under this heading Zartman, who is the most comprehensive of the three on this point, discusses the level, distribution, basis, and use of power. Making configuration of power a central feature of subordinate systems analysis while leaving power unsatisfactorily defined raises many questions, especially since the authors are attempting to demonstrate that global configuration of power (however defined) is clearly inadequate in itself to explain state behavior in many circumstances.

[52]Additionally, Zartman discusses what he calls the "normative characteristics or rules" of the system, for example, a rule establishing a rank ordering among the primary goals of independence, development, and unity, in that order (*op. cit.*).

[53]Zartman (*op. cit.*) adds that the analysis cannot predict system change, although it can sensitize to changes which may be important.

[54]Brecher, *op. cit.*

the Middle Eastern subordinate international system functions as it does.

Consequently, in order to evaluate the usefulness of the concept "subordinate international system" when applied to concrete reality, we shall examine Binder's thesis about the Middle East in some detail.

The Concept "Subordinate International System": Application

Binder delimits the Middle East subordinate international system as a geographic area from Libya to Iran, with a fringe area formed by Afghanistan, Pakistan, and the Maghrib, and a "core" of the Arab States and Israel. In so doing he considers not only geography, but also certain factors common to the history of the states in this area, including religious opposition to nationalism, relatively short colonial periods, the Ottoman Empire, pan-Islamic ideals, and pan-Arabism.[55]

In terms of the components we have retained for the concept "subordinate international system," however, since it would be difficult to assert that people in all the states in the area are considered and consider themselves as a distinctive segment or community, the concept would seem more applicable to Binder's "core" alone, excluding Israel. At least seven states would then be included: Iraq, Egypt, Jordan, Syria, Saudi Arabia, Yemen, and Lebanon.[56]

Such modification of Binder's delimitation appears justified by the fact that most of the hypotheses he suggests in fact deal with the Arab

states alone. Moreover, unless we retain the criterion proposed by Brecher it becomes almost impossible to distinguish subordinate international systems conceptually from other partial systems. For example, there are presumably conflict situations between states outside the dominant system that are not part of the same subordinate system in which Binder's phenomenon of dominant system power "refraction" would occur.[57] Furthermore, retention of the criterion of delimitation in terms of distinctive segments or communities would help in answering such questions as whether West Africa should be considered as a subordinate international system in itself or rather as part of a larger African system.[58]

The main portion of Binder's article is devoted to the presentation of a series of explanatory statements and hypotheses about the inter-Arab subordinate international system, some of the most interesting of which are unfortunately made unintelligible by the use of terms such as "these factors" without a clear referent.[59] His aim is to show the limitations of great-power action in the area, and he succeeds in providing a set of reasons for those limitations. In the form in which they are presented, however, those reasons are not causally interconnected.

It is quite possible, nonetheless, on the basis of the material that Binder provides, to find a

---

[55]Binder, *op. cit.*

[56]More questionably, one might include Morocco, Algeria, Tunisia, Libya, and Kuwait, since all participate in the Arab League. But their contacts with the Arab world, although close, are of a rather different order from relations among the others. Libya and the Sudan are connected to the system primarily through bilateral relations with Egypt; Kuwait is a newcomer in a rather special position vis-à-vis the rest of the Arab world due to her continued closeness to Britain and her great wealth. Yemen's inclusion too is somewhat doubtful. Perhaps the idea of fringe areas would be appropriate, since the basic tendencies discussed below operate in these states as well, but in somewhat attenuated form. Not to include them in some fashion would call into question the criterion of distinctiveness as a community.

[57]As, for example, a hypothetical conflict between Ethiopia and Saudi Arabia or the actual conflict over Cyprus between Greece and Turkey. Indeed, there is evidence that the "refraction" phenomenon is generalized as bipolarity becomes loosened, and, in addition, that even "the range of mixed types between the poles of bipolarity and multipolarity" is not "sufficient for the analysis of ongoing shifts." (Oran R. Young, "Multiple Power Balances and Political Discontinuities," mimeographed). Young's article proposes a "discontinuities model" for the study of international relations to take into account factors usually neglected by analysts, including the (subordinate) system in which action takes place.

[58]Thomas Hodgkin did so in "The New West Africa State System," *University of Toronto Quarterly*, vol. XXXI, (October 1961) pp. 74–82, but Zartman took issue with this delimitation (*op. cit.*).

[59]As, for example, the following (p. 419): "These factors add up to an inherent instability of system, suggesting further that, should external vigilance be relaxed or a domestic (and therefore inaccessible upheaval take place, violent changes will occur throughout the area." It is not at all clear from what goes before what "these factors" are.

central explanatory factor: the illegitimacy of existing political boundaries, itself a result of former political unity, common language and culture, and aspirations for renewed unity. As a consequence of this illegitimacy, existing boundaries are inherently unstable and revisionism is universal;[60] inter-Arab politics have substantial impact on domestic politics within the individual states[61] and vice versa;[62] direct appeals are made by the government of one state to the people of another;[63] and interactions with extra-area powers are shaped and limited by their effects on an area government's position vis-à-vis other area governments and its own and their people.[64]

Thus, the illegitimacy of existing political boundaries and aspirations for unity are factors that allow other systemic phenomena to be meaningfully linked, including the phenomenon of power refraction crucial to the concept "subordinate international system."[65] Consequently, it would seem that any concept designed to throw light on inter-Arab relations should stress the unstable, illegitimate boundaries of the Arab East.

We would propose, therefore, the concept "potential national system"[66] as a concept more useful than "subordinate international system" in sensitizing the analyst to the fundamental forces and currents operating in the contemporary Arab world.[67] The phrase "international

system" when applied to the Arab world is misleading in its connotations, since it implies the notion of nation-states as unitary entities interacting with other such entities. Although it is true that such intergovernmental interactions take place in the Arab world, to focus upon them is to ignore much that is significant for understanding even those interactions themselves.

Using "potential national system" as a concept shifts attention not only to the intimate interrelatedness of domestic and inter-Arab politics, but also to the existence of transnational parties and political movements,[68] pan-Arab ideologies and sentiments as myth and ideal, and to counterelites as well as incumbent elites as actors within the system. Thus, the concept directs attention to factors usually ignored in the study of international politics. Analysts of international politics tend all too often to assume that incumbent governments are the only relevant actors in the system—or, worse, to talk simply in terms of states as the only actors. This assumption may once have made sense. In the comtemporary world, however, it is often as important for analyzing international politics to focus on opposition movements and parties as it is to focus on incumbents; as crucial to be aware of transnational or subnational politicized groups as it is to analyze those groups whose scope corresponds to state boundaries; and as important to pay attention to underlying changes in class structure and popular opinion as it is to keep up with governmental policymaking. This is particularly the case in the Arab world.

The very fact of existing political boundaries, however unstable, guarantees that the "international" aspect of inter-Arab politics will receive sufficient emphasis. What appears necessary, then, is a concept that calls attention to aspects of systemic interactions that might otherwise be neglected. Perhaps the concept "potential national system" might serve this function. The

---

[60]Binder, p. 416.

[61]The most striking example is provided by Jordan, where Cabinet changes frequently result from political events in other parts of the Arab world.

[62]The domestic situation in Yemen provides the most striking example; another is domestic politics in Syria.

[63]Nasser's government was especially adept at this technique, using such methods as radio broadcasts over the Voice of the Arabs, and newspapers that reach a wide audience in the Arab world outside Egypt.

[64]These interactions include defense pacts and alliances notably, and may even affect foreign aid.

[65]See below.

[66]This idea was developed in conversations with Ian Garth Stevenson in March 1967.

[67]Nettl contrasts sensitizing concepts, which involve inferred or suggested references without definition of a relationship, with empirically determinate concrete and with systemic concepts (p. 308), and says they are a way of ordering propositions or facts (p. 309). Given the conceptual difficulties discussed above with the subordinate international system concept, it seems clear that the real function that has been served by that concept has been to sensitize analysts to important

factors that need to be considered. It has not, however, been sufficiently clarified or developed to go beyond this sensitizing function. The alternative concept of a potential national system being proposed here also remains only a sensitizing concept at this point but is being proposed as one that may prove fruitful.

[68]For example, the Muslim Brotherhood, the Ba'ath Party, and various Nasserite groups in almost all Arab countries.

terminology is somewhat awkward, since I do not mean in any way to suggest that Arab unity is imminent or even probable. Indeed, with the passing of time chances for unity may well decrease as social and economic life becomes structured by existing boundaries. Yet even as myth, ideal, and aspiration, the idea of Arab unity has, as we have seen, important consequences for the inter-Arab system.

Since we have seen that the instability of political frontiers is crucial in explaining the "refraction" of dominant system power in the Arab world, leading to the idea of "subordinate international system," it may well be that the same factor, albeit for different reasons, operates in the subordinate system of Africa in somewhat the same way. In Africa, as in the Arab world, existing frontiers are illegitimate because of the belief that unity ought to exist. This situation is in contrast to the Asian subordinate international system. Perhaps the relative penetrability and lack of integration of the Asian subordinate system as opposed to the African and Arab subordinate systems can be at least partially explained by the hypothesis that the first is not a "potential national system," but that each of the latter two is a "potential national system" in some sense.

If the latter concept seems worth exploring and developing, it then becomes necessary, if only to avoid the criticisms we have made of subordinate-international-system theorists, to link the concept to the more basic concept of "system," defined as a pattern of elements and linkages. The systemic empirical referent would remain the same as for the subordinate system concept, that is, the totality of actions performed by the individuals who are members of the collectivities under investigation. In the abstracted system, however, the actors would have to include not only incumbent governments, but also whatever opposition movements or other groups and individuals appeared relevant to the particular potential national system under study. For the inter-Arab system, for example, actors would include transnational political movements, domestic opposition groups, and the politicized portion of the general populace. As is evident, it becomes much more difficult to specify clearly what kind of units and what particular units should be abstracted as actors.

In addition, the potential-national-system concept complicates the specification of linkages and makes less relevant as well as harder to delineate such factors as configuration of power, which have been taken as central features of subordinate international systems. On the other hand, it may usefully shift attention to qualitative differences among kinds of linkages, whether of cooperation or conflict. rather than merely talking about linkages in terms of intensity, frequency, and multilateralism.

CONCLUSION

This article has been primarily an exercise in the careful delimitation and specification of concepts, in particular the "subordinate international system" concept as developed and applied by a number of scholars. I would like, however, to close on a rather different note, namely, with the suggestion that precision and conceptual clarity are not the only—and perhaps not even the most important—criteria by which concepts should be evaluated. As others have argued,[69] one important function of concepts is that they sensitize researchers to particular aspects of empirical reality that are singled out as being of especial importance for the problem under investigation. To the extent that such a sensitizing function is primary, then, competing concepts need to be evaluated in terms of their range of associations and suggestive richness, as well as in terms of their precision and clarity. That is not to say, of course, that careful delimitation and specification of concepts is not a useful and even an indispensable exercise. It is, however, to suggest that an exclusive focus on those evaluative criteria is both inappropriate and likely to be unproductive. Thus, the fundamental problem with the "subordinate international system" concept is not that it is imprecise and unparsimonious, although those difficulties exist; rather, the fundamental problem is that it does not help to reorient our thinking to crucial but heretofore neglected aspects of the political process within regional subsystems.

---

[69]For example, Peter Nettl, "The Concept of System in Political Science," *Political Studies* 14 (October 1966).

Discussion and Questions

1. ➤ Is it misleading to describe a multinational relationship as a "potential national system"? ➤ Would it be preferable to refer to it as a "partial supranational system"? or as a "potential regional polity"?

2. ➤ Define the terms "system" as used by Binder, Brecher, and Zartman. Does it refer to the *states* involved, the pattern of relationships between those states, or both? Is the system they talk about an actual, concrete entity or an intellectual construct abstracted from political reality?

3. How do the criteria by which Binder, Brecher, and Zartman define a subordinate system differ? Do the differences in their definitions affect the usefulness of systems analysis in conceiving subsystemic units of world order? For example, Zartman includes membership in an international organization as a criterion, whereas Binder and Brecher ignore this factor. How do the criteria used by these three authors compare with Russett's behavioral analysis of international subsystems? with Northrop's analysis of cultural subsystems?

4. ➤ Compare the idea of "subordinate international system" with that of a "potential national system"; to what extent are these units subject to historical transformation?

5. Binder, Brecher and Zartman maintain that their subordinate systems are "autonomous." ➤ What is meant here by autonomy? ➤ To what extent is any nation within a subordinate system free of great-power influence even when dealing with intrasystemic issues and states? For example, Binder states that the primary determinants of power in the Middle Eastern system are population and foreign aid. The U.S. and the Soviet Union, as the principal dispensers of aid, thus affect Middle Eastern power relationships even if the two great powers do not actively intervene in the subsystem. In another instance, African nations may not be able to resolve intrasystemic conflicts because they lack the arms that only the United States and the Soviet Union (or their allies) can provide. Consider also the effect of the U.S. Sixth and Seventh Fleets in the Mediterranean Sea and Pacific Ocean on politics in these subordinate systems—even if these naval forces do not engage in overt military action. ➤ Considering these factors, to what extent is the concept of a subordinate system helpful in approaching the study of international politics? If you feel it is helpful, think carefully about the extent of latitude nations within these systems possess.

Regional Organizations and Subordinate Systems

LYNN H. MILLER

. . . What follows, first of all, is an attempt to indicate the potential relevance of regional organizations to the systemic study of the international relations of regions.[1] An effort is made to bring together here the two worlds of description and analysis based on formal-legal structures, on the one hand, and the more sociologically-oriented approach of the systems theorist, on the other. Second, this article is a partial attempt to consider the factors involved in intersubordinate system relations to the extent that they relate to the activities of regional international organizations. As Cantori and Spiegel have noted, "one of the most significant indices [of intersubordinate system relationships] is the degree of shared participation in international organizations, which may operate either toward cohesion or toward power."[2] This is to say we may expect the participation of states in intergovernmental organizations to constitute one of the chief vehicles for the conduct of intersubordinate system relations, or for discovering the linkages which exist between subordinate systems.

A number of university level texts on international relations devote a section, usually brief, to a description of the more important regional organizations of the post-World War II period. While such descriptions often supply useful information to the student as to the contexts in which many important international decisions are made, no view of these structures alone permits an assessment of the vast complexities of the political and social process in which legal struc-

From Louis J. Cantori and Steven L. Spiegel, *The International Politics of Regions: A Comparative Approach*, © 1970, pp. 357–378. Reprinted by permission of Prentice-Hall, Inc., Englewood Cliffs, N.J.

[1]Cantori and Spiegel have noted [*International Politics of Regions*, Chap. 1, footnote 3] their own deliberate avoidance of the technical vocabulary of systems theory as used by a number of contemporary political scientists. They also note, however, "the suggestiveness of what we have to say for systems theory in political science." The present essay, too, is meant to be primarily suggestive for systemic analysis of regional organizations, for reasons indicated above.

[2]See above, Chap. 1, p. 38.

tures are set. To take an extreme case, a man stranded on a desert isle in 1950, with only a copy of the Charter of the North Atlantic Treaty organization in his pocket, would have no way of predicting, no matter how carefully he read that document, such things as the NATO debates on nuclear strategy that have been a continuing feature of the organization or the disaffection of General de Gaulle from the alliance structure. The analysis and praise of the League of Nations Covenant that was so common during the 1920's and 1930's had little bearing upon the problems which beset and ultimately destroyed the League.

In contrast, the more complex, sociologically oriented approaches to the study of international political phenomena, of which the subordinate systems emphasis of the present volume is one example, have attracted the attention and interest of social scientists in recent decades because of their greater sophistication and methodological rigor. Their intelligent use may permit the gradual accumulation of a scientifically verifiable body of knowledge about social and political life out of which eventually might come greater understanding of these phenomena. Different approaches obviously have differing utilities, and must be selected with a view to the kinds of information needed in the problem area to be explored. The very complexity of a systemic approach, with its multiple variables and nearly limitless applicability to any congeries of social processes, may make it appear ill-suited to the interests of legal scholars and others concerned with international institutions. However, there are several reasons for dual attention to formal-legal structures and to trans-national systems and processes. When the subordinate international system is the object of attention, there are reasons also for focussing upon regional international organizations.

Before indicating what those reasons are, it would be useful to consider some of the confusions to be avoided over the term "regional organization."

I. THE CLASSIFICATION OF REGIONAL ORGANIZATIONS

Although international organization is by no means an exclusively contemporary invention,

this phenomenon is probably more important today than ever before. Certainly, it is a more complex process today than at any time previously in the nation-state period, if for no other reason than that different kinds of international organizations have multiplied on a vastly greater scale in the last several decades. Since different organizations have very different purposes and memberships, certain basic distinctions must be made before any kind of comparison or generic treatment can be meaningful.

First, it is obvious that a fundamental distinction can be made between the universalistic international organization, the United Nations, and all of the "regional" international organizations.[3] In this connection, the regional organizational category is broad enough to include all limited-member associations, whether or not they are genuinely regional in the sense of comprising states that are geographically proximate. Thus, the Commonwealth, whose members are now scattered throughout the world, can be considered to be as much a regional organization as the Nordic Council, whose membership is limited to the countries within the geographically compact Scandinavian area. What all of these associations have in common is what distinguishes them from the United Nations—an absence of intention to become universalistic or nearly universalistic in scope. Although the reasons for the limited membership of these associations may vary widely, in general it is safe to assume that these reasons are historical in nature, the product of perceived political, cultural, economic, or military ties.[4]

---

[3] It may not be too far-fetched to suggest an analogy between the concepts of dominant and subordinate international systems, on the one hand, and the United Nations and regional organizations, on the other. In both instances, study of the politics of the dominant system or universalistic organization alone tends to ignore, and sometimes distort, the politics of various subordinate systems (regional organizations).

[4] Thus, the Commonwealth is the product of the mutual experience of its members within the British imperial system; Benelux is almost purely the result of economic imperative for three small and highly developed European states confronted with the great economic competition of larger units in the mid-twentieth century; the Arab League reflects, at least to a limited extent, the common culture of its members; NATO is clearly the product of a commonly perceived security threat to the states of the North Atlantic area.

Yet, even the distinction between the one universalistic organization and the limited-member associations is not as clear-cut as might be supposed, particularly in specific types of international activity. The United Nations system is itself a complex network, and some of its more important work in the area of economic development is carried out in the framework of regional Economic Commissions—for Europe, Latin America, Africa, and Asia and the Far East.[5] Participation in these Commissions is not limited to individuals representing countries within the area, although their purpose is to provide forums that are as efficient as possible for considering the economic problems—often very different from one region to another—of UN member states. The activities of certain UN Economic Commissions clearly may be relevant for certain types of investigation focussing upon subordinate systems, particularly those involving economic interrelationships. It may be found in some instances that they provide (a) an instrument for increasing the stability or cohesion of the subordinate system (or systems), (b) an avenue for permitting the economic intrusion of the dominant system, or some members of the dominant system, into the area, or (c) a formalized link between the subordinate system and most of the rest of the world system as it is manifested in the United Nations Organization.[6]

The picture is further confused by the existence of numerous UN specialized agencies, whose memberships are not identical with, but approximate, that of the United Nations itself. These agencies all have specific "functional" concerns,[7]

in the sense that each is designed to grapple with particular issues—from international postal problems, to health issues, to scientific and artistic projects—which are the common concerns of many states in an age of growing interdependence at many levels. While none of the specialized agencies is a regional organization in the sense that it has a deliberately limited membership, very often some of its activities, like those of ECOSOC's regional economic commissions, have a distinctive impact upon a particular region or subordinate system. Examples might be the World Health Organization's campaign to eradicate the tsetse fly in tropical Africa, UNESCO's drive to save the ancient temples of Luxor from inundation by the Nile above Aswan in Egypt, or various of the technical assistance projects under the direction of the United Nations Development Programme.[8]

Other illustrations of ways in which activities originating in the United Nations system may bear upon the cohesion of subordinate systems no doubt could be found. Perhaps enough has been said, however, to indicate the reason for this brief excursion into some aspects of the UN organization, that is, various processes at work even within the universalistic international organization may relate directly and yet discretely to particular subordinate international systems. As such, they constitute part of the fabric of systemic, although not of regional organizational, analysis. Now we need to turn to the even greater challenge posed to rigorous analysis by the very diverse kinds of limited-member associations which go under the name of regional organizations.

Although many writers have objected to the ambiguous use of the term "regional organiza-

---

[5]As is typical in United Nations parlance, these Economic Commissions commonly are referred to by their alphabetic acronyms: ECE, ECLA, ECA, and ECAFE. All are technically under the jurisdiction of one of the principal organs of the United Nations, the Economic and Social Council, or ECOSOC.

[6]There may even be the possibility that the work of such regional commissions may aid in the creation of new regional systems where they have not previously existed. For example, a recent study on the ECE specifically describes it as fundamental to an emerging European system. See Jean Siotis, "ECE in the Emerging European System," *International Conciliation*, No. 561 (January, 1967).

[7]Here the term "functional" is used in the sense employed by David Mitrany and others, to describe inter-

national cooperative efforts, particularly on economic and social questions, intended to provide a basis for the ultimate solution of the most divisive political conflicts. For the classic elaboration of the functionalist thesis, see especially Mitrany's *The Progress of International Government* (New Haven: Yale University Press, 1933) and his *A Working Peace System* (London: Royal Institute of International Affairs, 1946).

[8]The UNDP is not a specialized agency of the United Nations, but is under the authority of the General Assembly and ECOSOC. Yet it is functionally oriented and its work is in many respects analogous to that of the specialized agencies.

tion," and some have attempted to make the concept more precise, most statesmen and many observers continue to use the term so loosely as to prevent general agreement upon its precise meaning.[9] As a result, according to one writer on the subject, "ambiguity of definition has forced regional arrangements to bear a double burden they were never meant to assume. On the one hand, the very looseness of the term has made regional arrangements seem to be little more than a series of treaty structures creating bilaterally assumed obligations within a context limited as to area or as to function. There came in popular parlance at least, to be a difference of degree, but not of kind, between the treaties and agreements similar to those traditionally signed among states and *organizations* created by a collectivity of states for security, economic, or other purposes."[10] Some have insisted, in the attempt to narrow somewhat the vast category of limited-member associations, that at a minimum a "regional" organization must be associated in some way with a particular geographic region of the world.[11] Others have applied the term to so dispersed an association as the Commonwealth, asserting that "regional" simply connotes a community of interest.[12]

This last dispute is perhaps largely irrelevant to a concern with subordinate international systems which, by definition, are composed of states that are geographically proximate. Such concepts as core, periphery, and intrusive system are largely meaningless when applied to the Commonwealth.

However, this does not mean that the Commonwealth or any other international association whose members are widely dispersed cannot be analyzed systemically; rather, to the extent that the analytic framework of the subordinate system applies to them at all, they probably must be considered as aggregators of such systems. For example, meetings of Commonwealth prime ministers no doubt constitute unusual opportunities for communication between the leaders of different subordinate systems.

Undoubtedly there are more useful ways to narrow the category of limited-member international organizations than simply by throwing out all those in which geographical proximity of the members is not a factor. A classificatory scheme is needed, based upon the isolation of a pattern variable crucial in all regional organizations. No single such variable—and hence, no single classificatory scheme—is preferable *a priori* to every other such variable. What follows is, therefore, but one possible approach which permits a classification of types of regional organizations.[13]

Three broad types of regional organization can be distinguished on the basis of the single variable of the *security orientation* of component states as expressed through the organizational structure. We begin by assuming that, within the spectrum of international relations, regional organizations are most likely to come into being among states whose relations already have been marked by at least a modicum of cooperation. It is virtually a contradiction in terms to suggest that limited-member organizations are likely to be produced among states whose relations with each other typically are those of sustained crisis or direct military conflict. But if we are safe in assuming that regional organizations will only arise among states that interrelate on the cooperative side of the spectrum of relations, we still must acknowledge that there are obvious gradations in cooperation among the members of various regional groupings. The security orientation of the grouping gives some

---

[9]A sampling of the writers who have attempted definitions might include Norman J. Padelford, "Regional Organization and the United Nations," *International Organization*, VIII, 2 (May, 1954), 203–16; Amry Vandenbosch and Willard N. Hogan, *Toward World Order* (New York: McGraw-Hill Book Company, 1963); Ann [V. Thomas] and A. J. Thomas, Jr., *Non-Intervention: the Law and Its Import in the Americas* (Dallas: S. M. U. Press, 1956); J. Lloyd Mecham, *The United States and Inter-American Security, 1889–1960* (Austin: University of Texas Press, 1961); Peter Calvocoressi, *World Order and New States* (New York: Frederick A. Praeger, Inc., 1962); Edgar S. Furniss, Jr., "A Re-examination of Regional Arrangements," *Journal of International Affairs*, IX, 2 (May, 1955), 78–89.

[10]Furniss, "A Re-examination of Regional Arrangements," p. 81.

[11]Vandenbosch and Hogan, pp. 265–66.

[12]Thomas and Thomas, pp. 177–78.

---

[13]Note that Cantori and Spiegel, for example, demarcate the subdivisions of subordinate systems on the basic of four pattern variables: (1) nature and level of cohesion, (2) nature of communication, (3) level of power, and (4) structure of relations.

indication both of the degree and kind of cooperation perceived by the member states.

"Security orientation" is a broader and more inclusive term than "security capability"; the latter implies the existence of a distinctive military concern (for example, nation-states and traditional military alliances possess some sort of security capability), while the former does not *necessarily* do so. In the broadest sense, all contemporary international organizations are maintained, at least in part, because of a desire of participating states to enhance security through organization. Unless some measure of insecurity were perceived by national actors, there would be little reason for them to organize. Obviously, this insecurity is not always perceived simply in terms of a military threat from outside. It may also relate, for example, to economic instability or to political tension, which is scarcely peace-threatening but, nonetheless, regarded as unfortunate and unnecessary. The organizational response, then, to whatever the source of insecurity that is perceived by organizing state actors constitutes that organization's security orientation.

On this basis, several hypothetical orientations are possible. *First,* the organization's structure and practice may be designed to aid in settling disputes among its own members either through the diplomatic process or through more elaborate peacekeeping machinery. *Second,* the organization may be designed to present a common military and, perhaps, diplomatic front against an outside actor or actors. *Third,* both of the above issues may be regarded as irrelevant to the purposes of the organization (perhaps because other organizations with similar memberships respond to them). Hence, the rationale of this third type of organization is to be found in perceptions of what might be called "functional insecurity," that is, in the mutual desire to improve economic relations to deal with other technical problems resulting from proximity and growing interdependence. The functional organization's relationships with other groupings and processes concerned with security capabilities explains its lack of concern with military policy. All existing regional organizations can be classified on the basis of these three kinds of orientation: (1) Cooperative, (2) Alliance, and (3) Functional.

Cooperative. This group includes organizations that combine, to a greater or lesser extent, both the first and second security orientations described above. These are associations which have arisen as the expression of some sort of regional solidarity in the face of the politics of the outside world, and which also possess the machinery, at least in embryo, to control the use of force within their own region. In the most fully developed of these groups, the Organization of American States, the machinery involved permits both (*a*) the development of a common policy in the face of intervention from outside the organization and (*b*) the settlement of disputes among member states. For the other two groupings which fall into this regional type (the Organization of African Unity and the Arab League), the provisions for settlement of inter-member disputes are less fully developed than are those for creating common policies. Characteristic of this type, however, is the fact that they are not alliances in the traditional sense, but are "ostensibly more permanent groups whose professed first aim is to keep the peace within a given area."[14] Their *raison d'etre* springs from territorial unity, which itself may contribute to an ethnic or ideological common ground. Yet, cooperation obviously has not advanced among the members to the point of their pluralistic integration,[15] or there would be no need for organizational machinery designed to facilitate the settlement of disputes in which force is used or threatened.

Alliance. A second group of associations sometimes labelled regional organizations is composed of states bound together by multilateral defense treaties. This category includes many of the alliances of the postwar world, such as NATO, the Warsaw Pact, ANZUS, SEATO, and CENTO. The only treaty arrangements including a common defense pledge that do not fall within

---

[14]Calvocoressi, p. 59.
[15]The term is employed here as defined by Karl W. Deutsch and his associates in *Political Community and the North Atlantic Area* (Princeton: Princeton University Press, 1957), pp. 5-6. A pluralistic security-community is one composed of two or more "sovereign" states, formally independent, whose interrelations are marked by "dependable expectations of 'peaceful change' among its population."

this category, in fact, are those which are bilateral and not multilateral. (These lack the so-called permanent institutions of the multilateral arrangements, such as secretariats, councils, and the like, and generally make no provisions at all for a coordination of military policy prior to outright military involvement with a third power.) As to the multilateral arrangements, it is evident that it is only the second kind of security orientation that is meant to be entailed here.[16] These are "outer-directed" associations which have come into being as the result of a felt threat from a common external enemy, and they do not possess the structures, unless, perhaps, incidentally, to regulate the use of force within the group.

Functional. The third group includes organs of economic and political consultation and action which make no attempt to provide military collaboration. Far more of the extant regional groupings in the world today—groupings which differ from each other in important respects—belong to this type than to the other two. Such organizations as the European Coal and Steel Community, the Common Market, the Nordic Council, have in common their "inner-directed-ness" as transnational ventures. They either (a) have come into being only after there is reasonable assurance that the participants will be able to resolve their own disputes without resorting to the use of force, or else they (b) are organs of economic or technical cooperation which presumably would fail to function in the unlikely event of overt armed violence among the member states.[17] This type of organization is not con-

cerned with presenting a united military policy to external actors. For these organizations, inter-member security and organizational security *vis-à-vis* external actors is irrelevant to the purposes of the organization. They may be closely associated with other regional associations which direct themselves toward security capability so that they may seem to possess it themselves, but in fact their concerns are not with the regulation of force.[18]

Some such classificatory scheme as this provides the basis for more precise analysis of the regional organizational phenomenon than is possible if the very different kinds of organizations are lumped together for study and generalization.[19] Once such distinctions are made, it is possible to examine particular regional organizations

---

[16]*Supra*, p. 8.

[17]Organizations which might fall into the category of sub-type (a) above would include, in particular, the European Communities, wherein pluralistic integration already has proceeded some distance and the potentiality even exists that with increased integration the grouping will function, for all practical purposes, as a single actor in international affairs. In that event, such a development obviously would transcend the stage of organization, as that term is commonly used, and the analytic framework would have to be altered accordingly.

Sub-type (b) organizations of functional cooperation would include such groupings as the European Free Trade Association, the OECD, and other limited-member associations designed to promote mutual welfare and economic or technical assistance.

[18]For example, the Organization for Economic Cooperation and Development, like its predecessor, the Organization for European Economic Cooperation, "may appropriately be regarded as the framework for North Atlantic Community economic activities" in view of the fact that all NATO members are also members of the OECD. [Ruth D. Lawson, *International Regional Organizations, Constitutional Foundations* (New York: Frederick A. Praeger, Inc., 1962), p. 11.] Yet, the two organizations 'are constitutionally and functionally distinct, and OECD, as such, lacks the critical variable of the force-controlling potential.

[19]The only major international association, sometimes called a regional organization, which is difficult to classify on the basis of the above scheme, is the Commonwealth. It combines some of the characteristics of both the Functional and Cooperative organizations: it does not possess the force-regulating machinery of Cooperative organizations in any formal sense yet, unlike the Functional groups, Commonwealth members do concern themselves with the resolution of disputes among the members, and there is consultation on foreign policy to the extent that there is some unity on certain issues *vis-à-vis* external actors. Moreover, another of the characteristics of Cooperative organizations is lacking in the Commonwealth in the absence of territorial unity.

As the imperial experience which once bound Commonwealth members together continues to recede into the past, we probably may expect lesser, rather than greater, cohesion on political issues within the grouping. The day may soon come, if it has not already arrived, when the Commonwealth will cease to be a meaningful grouping with any discernible impact upon international affairs. Already, most of its states are members of various other regional associations, some of which appear to command their greater allegiance and attention than do the affairs and ties of the Commonwealth.

systemically, in terms of inputs, transformation processes, and outputs. Now, however, we need to consider some of the utilites of systemic analysis for the student of regional international organizations. While these are considerations which draw us away from the specific issue of subordinate international systems to some extent, they are meant to suggest an additional, rigorous approach to the study of regional organizations.[20]

II. SYSTEMS ANALYSIS AND REGIONAL ORGANIZATIONS

First, to state what should be perfectly evident, "systems" and "organizations" are by no means mutually exclusive terms. An organized unit is as much a system as is an integrated community, a biological organism, or world society. That is, all of these phenomena may be conceived of and studied as systems, even though their stability in systemic terms obviously will vary depending upon the amount and kind of cohesion that exists among component structures and functions. The real point is that the term "system" is instrumentally neutral as used in the social sciences: it neither assumes an inevitable growth in cohesion and stability on the part of the processes studied nor does it prescribe for such growth. Thus, within the international arena, it is possible to conceive, in systemic terms, of action taking place entirely within a bloc, at one extreme, and that involving direct military conflict, at the other.[21] In contrast, an organization is a more specific concept, entailing some form of legal structure binding several actors. When the organization in question is a regional international one, as noted earlier, it is most likely that it will be found to exist only at the most cooperative end of the spectrum of relations, that is, among states that interact either in terms of a bloc or an alliance framework.[22] It becomes difficult, if not impossible, to conceive of organizations other than as instruments *for* something. As the conscious creations of individual men, organizations presumably are brought into being to produce certain results. Significantly, however, any very precise analysis of the organization's progress in achieving specified goals or even in self-maintenance must depend upon techniques other than mere exegesis of its formal-legal structure. It is systemic analysis which is preeminently suited for such a purpose, for while it is instrumentally neutral as an analytic technique, such analysis is specifically designed to permit examination of cohesive and disruptive aspects of social processes conceived as an interrelated unit. Any analyst of particular international organizations, then, would do well to follow the path of systemic analysis since, in general, such an approach is well suited to revealing the political and social development of such organizations.

A second point is to some extent the other side of the same coin. If systemic analysis is useful to the student of regional international organizations, so are many of these organizations potentially important in themselves as objects of systemic analysis. To focus upon regional organizations is to direct attention to certain international developments that are of undoubted importance in the contemporary period. While regional international organizations vary greatly in their viability and importance, the organizational phenomenon is one to be reckoned with in the international arena of today. It is increasingly evident that the traditional Hobbesian model of the international system—as a state of nature in which total anarchy prevails—is no longer fruitful as an explanatory concept for many of the actions that we witness today within the international arena. Much state conduct, not to mention many of the activities of various international agencies and institutions, is difficult to reconcile with the state of nature concept, in which all actors are "sovereign" nation-states and no political authority exists outside those nation-states. On the other hand, to view the international system in terms of the model of an integrated community is not very helpful. Transnational, integrated communities

---

[20]See note 1, above.

[21]See above, Chap. 1, Table 1–2.

[22]*Ibid*. Obviously, on the other hand, a universal international organization such as the United Nations

can and does encompass states, some of whose interrelationships are manifested from time to time in terms of the least cooperative categories of the spectrum of relations, those of sustained crisis and direct military confrontation.

may indeed exist in the world today, but they quite clearly do not encompass all the world's people.[23]

More specifically, the concept of "organization" may permit practical analysis of a phenomenon which constitutes a sort of half-way house between the state of nature (that is, the absolute sovereignty of component states within the world arena) and the thoroughly integrated world community. It is no longer sufficient to attempt explanations of all international political behavior in terms which view all transnational associations as transitory aberrations from the state of nature, characterized by the war of all against all. Neither is it realistic to view all such transnational undertakings as inevitable first steps down the path to worldwide (or even regional) integration. To discuss regional organization solely from a traditionalist or state oriented point of view, as it relates to the conduct of multilateral diplomacy, to alliance policy, and so forth, is to assume as given what is open to question: that nation-states are to continue indefinitely as the only significant actors in international politics.[24] On the other hand, to ignore inter-member conflict within regional groupings, through analysis concerned only with organizations as integrated actors in the world community, is to assume the existence of a regional community where there may be none. Analysis which accounts for both viewpoints probably must answer ambiguously the question as to which units currently constitute the significant international actors. In some circumstances, state actors remain crucial; in others, it is the regional organizations that act as a unit; in still others, the universal international organization may play a dominant role.

A third general reason for the systemic analysis of regional organizations lies in the increased importance that constitutional analysis can achieve in such a context. Each organization is built upon a constitutional framework, a treaty structure which creates the organization and sets forth its basic goals and operative procedures. It is true that formal-legal analysis of the basic enabling documents of international organizations, when divorced from considerations of political practice, may in fact lead to distortions of political reality rather than accurate perceptions of it. But if the organization in question is examined as a system— which is to say, as an entity of interdependent parts which is developing and evolving or stagnating and disintegrating—it becomes useful to consider its formal constitutional structure as a model to compare to its systemic processes. If this is done, one may expect to learn two kinds of things, both crucial to meaningful political analysis. First, the direction of the organism's growth and evolution from its constitutional "birth" can be plotted with some accuracy (and if, in fact, it is not growing, but dormant, that too, should be ascertainable). Secondly, tools are provided for determining the relative importance to the particular body politic of practice that conforms to the formalistic demands of the constitutional documents.

The latter is a point that can be of great importance in assessing the relative deference given in differing political groups to authoritative norms and rules. Such analysis may be able to account for at least three kinds of phenomena, all of which must be increasingly explored and understood by social scientists interested in the process of community building at transnational levels. First, such an approach can explore and, perhaps, define differences in personalistic versus legalistic considerations on the part of various groups in their creation and development of authority structures. For example, it may be that the nations of the West, with their traditions of domestic constitutionalism and development of positive international legal standards, would be rather inclined to emphasize formalistic criteria in their international organizational relationships. In contrast, perhaps, the personalism of the Middle Eastern political culture suggests that examination of the organic law of, say, the Arab League cannot permit very confident generalizations about Arab League practice in most areas. Yet this kind of cultural approach to the issue is not the only one involved.

In the second place, an awareness of the relative importance of practice that is "law-abiding" in different regional organizations can permit

[23]See Deutsch's formulations of "integration," *Political Community and the North Atlantic Area*, pp. 1-10.

[24]See Stanley Hoffmann's critique of Hans Morgenthau on this point, in his *Contemporary Theory in International Relations* (Englewood Cliffs, N.J.: Prentice-Hall, Inc., 1960), p. 36.

realistic treatment of the kinds of political relationships that do exist among the states within the organizations. If a particular relationship is clearly one of the overt domination and political control of quasi-sovereign entities by an imperial power, a constitutional organizational document which treats these units as equals is not likely to reveal much of importance about the structures and functions of the grouping. Systems analysis is needed for that. For instance, it has been customary in the West to dismiss the Warsaw Pact as a scrap of paper without genuine relevance to the political realities of the Soviet bloc. Only recently, with the clear loosening of the satellite status of the East European states, has it been suggested in the West that the Warsaw Pact may be evolving into a genuine political coalition somewhat more like NATO than it has been previously.[25] As this development continues, formal-legal analysis of the pact may become more meaningful because more closely related to operative political restraints within the area.

This example leads to the third relevant factor in this regard. The more complex the legal-political "mix" of relationships among member states, the more important formalistic provisions are likely to be as a basis for analyzing political practice. The study of U.S. constitutional law is an important approach to analysis of the American political process at least in part because the complexities of American federalism and separation of powers have forced more important political conflicts in this country into constitutional channels. Similarly, in the Organization of American States, international law has been relied upon strongly as a means of harmonizing the potentially very unharmonious relationships of the American states. The *de jure* equality and *de facto* inequality of the members combine to make the political-legal status of the members complex in relation to each other, and to encourage reliance upon formalistic approaches to issues—a reliance that is also compatible with the political cultures of these nations.

Undoubtedly, other reasons could be adduced for combining an interest in regional international organizations with systems analysis. Perhaps the point has been made clearly enough, however, that attention now may be directed toward a few generalizations about regional organizations and the subordinate systems of this study.

III. REGIONAL ORGANIZATIONS AND SUBORDINATE SYSTEMS

In this connection it may be useful to reexamine the world's subordinate systems as these are defined by Cantori and Spiegel, in terms of membership by states listed in various regional international organizations.[26] What follows is only a brief overview, intended to indicate some of the kinds of issues which exhaustive treatment of particular organizations and subordinate systems may need to consider. There are, however, at least four kinds of gains which may be derived from such an overview of membership in regional organizations on the part of states which participate in subordinate systems. First, it may permit a more useful classification of regional organizations for purposes of their consideration in systemic analysis. Here, such factors as the relationship between organizational membership and membership in the subordinate system's core, periphery, or intrusive system sectors may reveal certain patterns useful for differentiating types of organizations. Secondly, such an overview may provide the basis for assessing the viability of regional organizations by examining their congruence or noncongruence with the parameters of subordinate systems. Thirdly, and conversely, it may permit an assessment of the viability of the subordinate system in relation to its congruence with particular regional organizations. Fourthly, and most importantly, it provides a graphic point of departure for a consideration of the role of regional organizations in intersubordinate system relations.

---

[25]See especially Thomas W. Wolfe, *Soviet Strategy at the Crossroads* (Cambridge: Harvard University Press, 1964). Chap. 17 treats the development of cooperation on military policy within the Warsaw Pact area.

---

[26]See Cantori and Spiegel, Table 1-1, "Subordinate Systems of the World and Their Subdivisions," Chap. 1.

Table 1
Subordinate Systems and Regional Organizational
Membership (Notes follow table.)

Cooperative

Arab League: AL	*Organization of American States: OAS*
Joint African and Malagasy Organization: OCAM[27]	*Organization of African Unity: OAU*

Alliance

Central Treaty Organization: CENTO	*Western European Union: WEU*
North Atlantic Treaty Organization: NATO	*Southeast Asia Treaty Organization: SEATO*
Warsaw Pact: WP	

Functional

A[28]

East African Community: EAC	*European Coal and Steel Community: ECSC*
European Economic Community (Common Market): EEC	*European Atomic Energy Commission: Euratom*

B[29]

Association of Southeast Asian Nations: ASEAN	*Guinea-Ghana-Mali Union: UAS (Union of African States)*
Belgium, Netherlands, Luxemburg Union: BENELUX	*Latin American Free Trade Association: LAFTA*
Conseil de l'Entente: CE	*Central American Common Market: CACM*
Council for Mutual Economic Assistance: COMECON	*Organization for Economic Cooperation and Development: OECD*
European Free Trade Association: EFTA	*Nordic Council: NC*

---

* = *Peripheral states with core potential*

(Angola) = *Colony*

—Afghanistan— = *States which could possibly be members of a second periphery*

---

[27]OCAM ("Organisation commune africaine et malgache"), which was founded by thirteen French-speaking states in February, 1965, is intended to operate within the framework of the OAU and to reinforce cooperation among the African states and Madagascar. Its aim is to accelerate the development of these states in the political, economic, social, technical, and cultural spheres.

[28]This is the Functional sub-type wherein the organizations might be described as community-oriented, that is, as intended to eliminate the traditional barriers of state sovereignty in specified, functional areas. For this purpose, supranational authority is the ultimate goal.

[29]This is the Functional sub-type whose organizations are intended to improve functional conditions in such areas as trade and economic development, but without providing a supranational administrative authority in the process.

Table 1 (*continued*)

Region	Core	Periphery	Intrusive System
Western Europe	France EEC, ECSC, Euratom, NATO OECD, WEU W. Germany EEC, ECSC, Euratom, NATO, OECD, WEU Italy EEC, ECSC, Euratom, NATO, OECD, WEU Belgium EEC, ECSC, Euratom, NATO, OECD, WEU, BENELUX Netherlands EEC, ECSC, Euratom, NATO, OECD, WEU, BENELUX Luxemburg EEC, ECSC, Euratom, NATO OECD, WEU, BENELUX	*U. Kingdom EFTA, NATO, OECD, WEU *Ireland OECD *Switzerland EFTA, OECD *Austria EFTA, OECD Greece NATO, OECD Iceland NATO, OECD, NC —Turkey— NATO, OECD Cyprus *Spain OECD *Portugal EFTA, NATO, OECD *Denmark EFTA, NATO, OECD, NC *Sweden OECD, NC *Norway EFTA, NATO, OECD, NC Malta —Finland— NC, EFTA (Assoc. status)	U.S. NATO, OECD U.S.S.R. Canada[30] NATO, OECD
Eastern Europe	Poland COMECON, WP Czechoslovakia COMECON, WP Hungary COMECON, WP	*Albania[31] *Yugoslavia Finland EFTA E. Germany COMECON, WP	U.S. France W. Germany U.S.S.R. COMECON, WP P.R. China

[30]Canada is not included in the Cantori-Spiegel Table 1-1, but I have done so here, under the heading of "intrusive system" because of Canada's participation in two West European-oriented organizations.

[31]Albania orginally was a member of both COMECON and the Warsaw Pact, but has not participated in either for several years.

(continued)

	Rumania COMECON, WP Bulgaria COMECON, WP		
North America	U.S. NATO, OAS, OECD SEATO, (CENTO)[32] Canada NATO, OECD	—Trinidad and Tobago— OAS —Jamaica— —Barbados— OAS —(West Indies Associated States)—	
Latin America	Argentina LAFTA, OAS Bolivia LAFTA, OAS Brazil LAFTA, OAS Chile LAFTA, OAS Colombia LAFTA, OAS Costa Rica OAS, CACM Dominican Republic OAS Ecuador LAFTA, OAS El Salvador OAS, CACM Guatemala OAS, CACM Honduras OAS, CACM (British Honduras) Mexico LAFTA, OAS Nicaragua OAS, CACM	*Cuba[33] Trinidad and Tobago OAS Jamaica Barbados OAS Guyana Haiti OAS (Surinam) (West Indies Associated States)	U.S. OAS U.S.S.R. U. Kingdom Netherlands France P. R. China

[32]The United States is not a treaty member of CENTO but is "associated" with it, and has participated fully in its activities.
[33]Cuba remains officially a member of the OAS, but the Castro government has been prevented by vote of the members to participate in any of the organization's activities.

Table 1 (*continued*)

Region	Core	Periphery	Intrusive System
	Panama		
	OAS		
	Paraguay		
	LAFTA, OAS		
	Peru		
	LAFTA, OAS		
	Uruguay		
	LAFTA, OAS		
	Venezuela		
	LAFTA, OAS		
East Asia	Peoples Republic of China	*Taiwan North Korea South Korea *Mongolia Japan (Hong Kong) (Macao)	U.S. Portugal U. Kingdom U.S.S.R.
Southwest Pacific	Australia SEATO New Zealand	(Islands of South Pacific) Western Samoa	U.S. SEATO France[34] U. Kingdom SEATO U.S.S.R. Japan
Southeast Asia	I. Maritime Indonesia ASEAN Malaysia ASEAN Philippines SEATO, ASEAN II. Mainland Laos North Vietnam South Vietnam Cambodia Thailand SEATO, ASEAN	Singapore ASEAN (Territory of New Guinea) (Territory of Portuguese Timor) Burma	P. R. China Japan Portugal Australia SEATO U.S. SEATO France[34] U. Kingdom SEATO U.S.S.R.

[34]France is an original member of SEATO, but has refused to participate in its activities for several years.

(continued)

Region	Core	Periphery	Intrusive System
South Asia	India	*Ceylon	U.S.
		*Nepal	SEATO
		*Bhutan	U.S.S.R.
		*Sikkim	U. Kingdom
		Afghanistan	SEATO, CENTO
		Maldive Islands	P. R. China
		Pakistan	
		SEATO, CENTO	
		—Burma—	
Middle East	U.A.R.	Israel	U.S.
	AL	Turkey	(CENTO)[32]
	Yemen	CENTO	U.S.S.R.
	AL	Iran	France
	S. Arabia	CENTO	U. Kingdom
	AL	—Afghanistan—	CENTO
	Kuwait		W. Germany
	AL		P. R. China
	Iraq		
	AL		
	Lebanon		
	AL		
	Sudan		
	AL		
	Jordan		
	AL		
	Syria		
	AL		
	S. Yemen		
	AL		
North Africa	Morocco	Mauritania[35]	France
	AL, OAU	OAU	U.S.S.R.
	Tunisia	Libya	U.S.
	AL, OAU	AL, OAU	P. R. China
	Algeria		Spain
	AL, OAU	(Span. Sahara)	Portugal
		U.A.R.[36]	
		AL, OAU	
		Sudan[37]	
		OAU	

[35]Mauritania was an original member of OCAM, but subsequently withdrew on grounds that its purposes would undermine those of the OAU.

[36]The UAR is not included by Cantori and Spiegel as a part of the North Africa subordinate system. I have included it here, however, because of its membership in the Arab League and the OAU.

[37]The Sudan is not included by Cantori and Spiegel in the North Africa subordinate system. I have included it as a peripheral state because of its membership in the OAU.

Table 1 (*continued*)

Region	Core	Periphery	Intrusive System
West Africa	Ivory Coast	Nigeria	U.S.
	OCAM, OAU, CE	OAU	U.S.S.R.
	Dahomey	Liberia	France
	OCAM, OAU, CE	OAU	U. Kingdom
	Guinea	Sierra Leone	
	UAS, OAU	OAU	
	Senegal	Gambia	
	OCAM, OAU	OAU	
	Upper Volta	Ghana	
	OCAM, OAU, CE	UAS, OAU	
	Mali	(Port. Guinea)	
	UAS, OAU		
	Niger		
	OCAM, OAU, CE		
	Togo		
	OCAM, OAU		
Southern Africa	South Africa	Malawi	U.S.
	Rhodesia	OAU	U.S.S.R.
	(Angola)	Malagasy Rep.	France
	(Mozambique)	OCAM, OAU	U. Kingdom
	(South-West Africa)	Lesotho	
		OAU	
		Botswana	
		OAU	
		Zambia	
		OAU	
		Swaziland	
		OAU	
		Mauritius	
Central Africa	Congo (Kinshasa)	Cent. Afric. Rep.	U.S.
	OCAM, OAU	OCAM, OAU	Belgium
	Rwanda	Chad	P. R. China
	OAU	OCAM, OAU	U.S.S.R.
	Burundi	Cameroon	France
	OAU	OCAM, OAU	Spain
		Gabon	
		OCAM, OAU	
		Congo (Brazza.)	
		OCAM, OAU	
		Equatorial Guinea	
		OAU	

(continued)

Region	Core	Periphery	Intrusive System
East Africa	Uganda	Ethiopia	U.S.
	EAC, OAU	OAU	U.S.S.R.
	Kenya	Somalia	France
	EAC, OAU	OAU	P. R. China
	Tanzania	(French Somali.)	U. Kingdom
	EAC, OAU		

Some twenty-two regional international organizations are included in the following table. This is not an exhaustive listing, but is meant to include important samplings of Cooperative, Alliance, and Functional types.

As previously indicated, this table permits a useful focus at several different levels. The first involves types of regional organizations and the kinds of distinctions among them that may be meaningful for analysis. In this connection, it is clear that only Functional organizations correlate effectively to the membership of subordinate systems. That is, every Functional organization listed (with the exception of Finland's membership in EFTA) possesses a membership exclusively contained within a particular subordinate international system, if core, periphery, and intrusive states all are included. Furthermore, only the "community-oriented" sub-type of Functional grouping[38] is composed of states all of which also constitute the entirety of the subordinate system's core (in West Europe, the members of the three European Communities). In contrast, both Cooperative and Alliance organizations tend to have memberships drawn from more than one subordinate system. Exceptions are the OAS among Cooperative groupings, and NATO and the Warsaw Pact among Alliance organizations, again if members of the intrusive system are included along with periphery and core members. The Arab League contains members included in two subordinate systems (the Middle East and North Africa); the OAU's members are drawn from the five subordinate systems of the African continent; CENTO states are included in both the Middle East and South Asia; and SEATO's membership is drawn from states ranging across three subordinate systems (Southwest Pacific, Southeast Asia, and South Asia).

In addition, important members of Alliance organizations generally are to be found within the intrusive system rather than either the core or periphery. This is true of the United States in CENTO, NATO and SEATO, of Britain and France in SEATO, of Britain in CENTO, and of the Soviet Union in the Warsaw Pact.

None of this constitutes a true "test" of the utility of classifying regional organizations as Cooperative, Alliance, or Functional. It at least suggests, however, that differences in the security orientations of the three types may relate directly to the position of member states in core, periphery or intrusive systems. With the addition of more regional organizations and associations than have been included here, it may be possible to distinguish other types, or varieties of types, for purposes of greater precision in the analysis of organizations.

Secondly, what of the viability of regional organizations as suggested by their relative congruence with divisions within and between subordinate systems? It is probably not accidental that the most highly integrated regional groupings in the world today are the European communities, all of whose members together constitute the core of a single subordinate system. In contrast, should we expect the least viable regional organizations to be those whose memberships do not correlate closely with particular subordinate systems? So sweeping a conclusion may not be warranted; yet, when the correlation factor is considered in the light of differences in organizational type, some tentative conclusions may be possible.

---

[38]See above, notes 28 and 29.

Among Cooperative organizations, the OAS correlates most closely to a single subordinate system, the Arab League is included in two, and the OAU in five. Yet, Cooperative organizations, by definition, are created in part to deal with the peaceful resolution of inter-member conflicts. This may suggest that such groupings are capable, within limits, of containing members from more than one subordinate system. In other words, perhaps the existence of structures within these organizations for the resolution of disputes among the members reflects the fact that those members are not all situated within the core of a single system, but range into the periphery, the intrusive system, and even other systems. On the other hand, it is clear that the OAS has proceeded further in the direction of developing structures for the resolution of inter-member disputes than has either the Arab League or the OAU. Is this explainable in part because of the greater congruence of its membership with a single system than is the case for the other two organizations? It would be interesting to ascertain, for example, the extent to which conflicts within the Arab League tend to produce opposing alignments between the member states of the Maghreb and those of the area nearer the Red Sea.[39] Is there any likelihood of the OAU breaking up or evolving into several Cooperative and Functional organizations, whose membership would correspond more closely to those of the various African subordinate systems? Some such development may, in fact, be taking place in the creation of such infant groupings as the West African Regional Group, the Union of Central African States, and the Organization of Riparian States of the River Senegal.

In Alliance organizations, which theoretically are not concerned with treating issues of inter-member conflict, is a lack of congruence between subordinate system and organizational membership a more ominous sign of ultimate weakness than is the case where similar conditions exist in Cooperative organizations? The experience of the two Alliance groupings whose members are most widely scattered would seem to indicate this. Neither SEATO nor CENTO has shown marked effectiveness as an instrument of multilateral defense. In both, intrusive system members are the only important military powers involved; moreover, even the weaker, "regional" members of these groupings are not confined in either treaty system, to a single subordinate system. This at least suggests that the interests of the states within the region may be rather different and that, therefore, organizational attempts to achieve a common military policy probably will not proceed very far. NATO is less divided in this respect, which may be another way of suggesting why NATO constituted a rather formidable defense establishment with an elaborate organizational system for a number of years. Yet here, too, the presence of an intrusive power as the most important member clearly has taken its toll (perhaps increasingly in recent years) on organization-wide harmony. As a result, there is a growing tendency to question the long-range viability of NATO as an arrangement for formulating common defense policy, not to mention common foreign policy generally.

Thirdly, to reverse the viewpoint, what does this table suggest as to the viability of particular subordinate systems on the basis of their congruence with regional organizations? Clearly it would be misleading to suggest that the most stable systems are those with the most regional organizations. To do so would be to ignore the likelihood that imperial or quasi-imperial relationships may exist among certain states within a subordinate system, insuring a large measure of systemic stability even in the absence of formal, transnational structures. It also would ignore the possibility that historical factors and the foreign policy orientations of particular states inhibit their joining together in regional organizations, even though they may be members of relatively stable subordinate systems.[40]

---

[39]Tunisia was virtually read out of the Arab League when, several years ago, President Bourguiba called publicly for Arab accommodation with Israel. Both his action and the reaction it provoked within the League may be partially explainable in terms of Tunisia's comparative distance from Israel and relative uninvolvement through the years with the problems of the Israeli presence in the Middle East.

---

[40]"Historical factors" have inhibited wide participation by the divided nations of Vietnam and Korea in international organizations, although this has been less true at the regional level of the two Germanies. The latter is, no doubt, largely due to the eagerness of states in both West and East Europe to integrate the Ger-

With this in mind, it may be meaningful to explore the relationship between a subordinate system's stability and the number (or kind) of transnational organizations it has generated. A system all of whose core states are members of a Cooperative organization (such as West Africa and the OAU) may be somewhat less stable than one whose core states are united in a community-oriented Functional grouping (such as West Europe and the European Communities). A subordinate system, some of whose core members belong to organizations that cross systemic boundaries while their relations with other core members are by no means cohesive, should no doubt prove to be rather unstable as a system (as, for example, Southeast Asia).

Moreover, the view of organizational membership presented here may suggest that certain states that have not previously been so considered ought to be regarded as members of particular subordinate systems. Thus, the membership of Sudan and the U.A.R. in the OAU may qualify both states as participants in the periphery of the North Africa subordinate system. Similarly, Canada's participation in both NATO and OECD may suggest a role within the intrusive system of Western Europe. Addition to the table of other regional groupings might suggest other potential participants.[41]

Finally, the table suggests the various roles regional organizations may play in *intersubordinate system relations*. The issue is obviously one ripe for fuller investigation, and only a few observations will be attempted here. It is clear that Cooperative and Alliance, but not Functional, organizations are most relevant to such relations. As we have noted, community-oriented Functional organizations, in particular, are confined to states within the core area of a single subordinate system. This is not to say that community-oriented Functional groupings may not have a considerable impact upon relations with other subordinate systems—by strengthening the groupings's political or economic potential *vis-à-vis* other such systems, for instance. But it is the Cooperative and Alliance organizations which include states from the core, periphery, and intrusive system of a single area, as well as those from more than one subordinate system in certain cases. These are the types of organizations that can be expected to play important roles as agents of intersubordinate system relations.

Furthermore, the existence of these latter two types of regional organizations relates in interesting ways to the patterns of intersubordinate system relations described as power-oriented and cohesive-oriented.[42] The three Cooperative organizations—the OAS, the OAU, and the Arab League—all are instrumentalities for the conduct of intersubordinate system relations, since all three combine states from more than one system within the organization. Yet it is only the OAS which is the vehicle for the conduct of power-oriented relations in the Latin American system. Relations between the two systems encompassed within the Arab League and the five systems within the OAU are cohesive-oriented. In other words, none of the relations which occur between intrusive, external systems and either the Middle East or the African subordinate systems are channeled through a Cooperative organizational framework. While U.S. intrusion into the Latin American system historically has been characterized by sporadic tension and conflict, it remains, as manifested in the existence of the OAS, a more thoroughly regularized and accepted intrusion than is characteristic in other power-oriented relations throughout the world.

Clearly, however, some power-oriented relations may be marked by a good deal of harmony even in the absence of a Cooperative organization for the states involved. At present, Soviet intrusion into the Middle East appears to fit such a description. Yet it may be precisely because no institutional arrangements have yet been produced to "legitimize" this or some other intrusive relationship, that the Middle Eastern subordinate system remains the seat of such potentially explosive political rivalries. Thus, the quality of Soviet-Arab

---

manies as fully as possible into their own systems as an attempt to prevent future German imperialism.

"Foreign policy factors" certainly have inhibited India, and perhaps also the Peoples' Republic of China, from becoming involved in regional organizations.

[41] For example, Finland is included in the periphery of West Europe by virtue of its participation, with Norway, Sweden, Denmark, and Iceland in the Nordic Council.

[42] See the discussion above by Cantori and Spiegel, Chap. 1, pp. 37–39.

relations generally is perceived (at least by other actors) as more *ad hoc* and temporary than, say, U.S.-Latin American relations. One of the functions of Cooperative organizations, in other words, may be to signal potential intruders that existing power-oriented relationships generally are acceptable to all participant states.

But what of the fact that in several instances power-oriented intersubordinate system relations are marked by the existence of Alliance organizations (CENTO in the Middle East, SEATO in three different systems in Asia, NATO in West Europe, and the Warsaw Pact in East Europe)? Because of the fact that these organizations are of a different type, different kinds of problems for intersubordinate system relations are involved. Since Alliance organizations, by definition, do not possess the machinery for the resolution of inter-member conflict, they are predicated upon the assumption that dependable expectations of peaceful change already exist among the members. Yet, because of the fact that they lack such machinery, Alliance organizations should not be expected to serve as particularly effective instruments for the conduct of intersubordinate system relations. As the postwar experience with NATO and other such groupings has shown, the existence of such Alliances may increase the level of relationships, yet when the conflicts of interest arise that are inevitable between states in different subordinate systems, Alliance machinery *per se* is not always capable of treating them effectively. In contrast to Cooperative organizations, Alliance groupings are more likely to increase the interrelationships that states of one subordinate system may have with those of another without promoting greater cohesiveness in the quality of those relations in the process.

The long-range effect of such a situation may be to undermine the effectiveness of the coalition as a single actor in the world arena even while intersubordinate system relations increase in scope and number. Among current groupings, this is perhaps most clearly true of SEATO, which is progressively less viable as a military alliance, even while it remains one of the principal vehicles of the power-oriented politics of the United States into the various subordinate systems of Asia. To a lesser extent, this phenomenon also appears to be true of all the other Alliance organizations of the postwar period. An increase in the "amount" of relations—whether cohesive- or power-oriented —among States in an Alliance organization may well create new problems with which a Cooperative organization is better equipped to deal. Moreover, an Alliance organization that is created as the instrumentality for the intrusion of the states of one subordinate system into another, such as SEATO or CENTO, may even prompt the strengthened resistance of rival state actors, thereby increasing rather than ameliorating tensions.

These are but a few of the most obvious questions and issues that can be raised, both about subordinate systems and regional organizations, when analysis proceeds along the lines suggested here. It is hoped that serious future attempts will be made to investigate the conditions involved in the development of social systems at transnational levels. While the mere existence of legal structures at regional levels by no means provides a certain catalyst in this development—as contemporary experience amply proves—neither may such structures safely be ignored in a period when many of them clearly are contributing to the transformation of the international political system.

Discussion and Questions

1. ➤ How does Miller define "system"? "regional organizations"? ➤ What are the advantages of systemic analysis of regional organizations?

2. ➤ How do the concepts of core, periphery, and intrusive system relate to each of the three types (Cooperative, Alliance, Functional) of regional organization? (See John D. Mitchell, "Cross-cutting Memberships, Integration, and the International System," *Journal of Conflict Resolution,* vol. 14, no. 1 [March 1970], pp. 49–55.

Mitchell feels that crosscutting memberships are the result, not the cause, of international integration.)

3. ➤ Which regional organizations are most viable, according to the criteria Miller provides? ➤ Is any one type of regional organization more viable than any other type?

4. ➤ What are the various roles that regional organizations may play in relations among subordinate international systems?

PART **VI**

THE FUTURE OF REGIONALISM

Regional experiments are still few and incomplete; hence any assessment of regionalism should be tentative in spirit and provisional in form. It is difficult to anticipate the prospects for regionalism in the remainder of the century. It is too early to pass judgment on the extent to which the growth of regional institutions represents a trend that will increase in the future or to determine whether these institutions will realize adequately the values of security, welfare, dignity, and environmental quality for political units constituting a "region" or in relations among "regions".

Several forces should be kept in mind in evaluating the future course of regionalism. First, certain functional imperatives arising, for example, from environmental deterioration will be augmenting pressures for reliable forms of continuing regional cooperation. Second, to some extent statesmen are already comfortable about according actors other than states a central role in the international political system of the future, and this attitude can be expected to continue its growth: consider President Nixon's emphasis on

the emergent "five-power world," which includes the "regional unit" of Western Europe alongside four state actors.

Over the next decade or so we anticipate a jagged course of regionalist development, marked by uneven growth between the main regions of the world. A third force is that a pro- or contra-regionalist bias of a key government (or even of a key head of state, as in the instance of de Gaulle's influence on European regional prospects) may exert a dramatic impact on short-term tendencies in a particular region. Fourth, the success or failure of global efforts to foster international cooperation is likely to influence regional prospects— the greater the global success at cooperation, the less likely the regional development. To some extent, however, institutional cooperation at different levels is complementary, with distinctive regional problems warranting regional forms of cooperation, and global problems warranting global forms.

In order to promote the goal values mentioned in the General Introduction, world-order changes of systemic magnitude will have to occur. Bold regionalist models of the future provide one significant way of conceiving of such changes.

In Part VI we present two positions offering significantly contrasting views of how the future of regionalism could be developed. The first selection by Leon N. Lindberg and Stuart A. Scheingold, entitled "The Future of the European Community: Equilibrium and Beyond," is an assessment of regional integration efforts in Western Europe. This article represents the incrementalist view of the integration process, showing how integration might proceed in Western Europe in the future and illuminating problems and prospects of engendering a regional movement. Our main interest is whether such incremental regional integration in Europe and, by extrapolation, elsewhere is likely to promote the realization of preferred world-order values.

The second selection can be characterized as a drastic system-change approach to the realization of world-order values. *Preliminary Draft of a World Constitution* was prepared by a group of scholars in Chicago during the period 1946–1948. The Chicago group's comprehensive undertaking makes a serious effort to propose a unified world polity, administered and represented largely by reliance on the authority of regional units, thereby overcoming the destructive tendencies of statism

without risking the totalitarian potentialities of a more centralized world-government. Constitutional strategies of the Chicago group stress authority structures to achieve global order. This approach, both because of its emphasis upon drastic system change and its implicit view that there will be a constitutional convention that will bring a new system into being, has frequently been labeled utopian. And one of the questions that should be faced seriously by students of world-order change, is whether or not such a method for achieving change is indeed utopian or likely to be essential at some point. At any rate, this view of drastic system change can be contrasted with strategies relying upon a revised conception of the goals of statecraft. See, for example, E. H. Carr, *Conditions of Peace* (Macmillan, New York, 1942); Carr, *Twenty Years' Crisis, 1919–1939* (Macmillan, London, 1961), pp. 228–31; Walter Lippmann, *U.S. War Aims* (Little, Brown, Boston, 1944), pp. 80–85. Finally, this comprehensive constitutional concept should be compared with the more restricted concept of limited world government embodied in the Clark-Sohn Plan. In what situations would either of these two concepts be more successful than the other in promoting the five world-order goals set forth in the General Introduction to this volume?

21

The Future of the European Community: Equilibrium and Beyond

LEON N. LINDBERG AND STUART A. SCHEINGOLD

From Leon N. Lindberg and Stuart A. Scheingold, *Europe's Would-be Polity: Patterns of Change in the European Community,* © 1970, pp. 279–310. Reprinted by permission of Prentice-Hall, Inc., Englewood Cliffs, N. J.

1. INTRODUCTION

Broadly speaking, we perceive three possible future outcomes for the European Community: (1) The Community will continue to grow, but at a decreasing rate, eventually approaching an overall equilibrium state. (2) Growth pressures will mount with time and will lead to a series of forward linkages which could eventually transform the Community system's scope and capacities into a federal or quasi-federal pattern. (3) The system will be beset by a cumulation of crises that will lead to general spillback and a reconfirmation of national decision-making patterns.

On the basis of the evidence presently available to us, a straight-line or "surprise-free" projection in terms of the categories of our model and the findings of our case study analyses shows a Community which is clearly tending toward an overall equilibrium or plateau, but which has relatively good short-term growth prospects. Most of this [discussion] will be devoted to filling out this basic scenario and to exploring what some of the implications of such a future might be. We cannot completely neglect the alternatives, however. It is certainly possible to envisage a combination of events that could either reinvigorate the Community's growth processes (e.g., by incorporating new actors or constituencies, by changing actor goals, etc.) or set off a slow or precipitous decline. It is widely speculated on both sides of the Atlantic that now that General de Gaulle has left the scene, successor governments will very likely be more "European" in orientation. Most seem convinced that the log jam over British entry will quickly be broken. Similarly, many argue that when Britain finally joins the Community, she will give it the needed impulse to enable the growth pressures to overcome inertial forces.[1] This may

---

[1] For a recent persuasive presentation of this argument see J. L. Zaring, *Decision for Europe: The Necessity of*

happen, but we are inclined to be skeptical. British entry will certainly be perceived by most actors as a dramatic alteration of the system. . . . The Community's foreign and domestic policy image may well be very different with Britain, and perhaps other EFTA countries as participants. Cost and benefit calculations will certainly change. The euphoria of a newly enfranchised Britain and a more cooperative France may lead temporarily to a spurt of progress in some long stalled areas of activity. But our feeling is that this does not necessarily mean that the longer term growth prospects of the Community will be much improved. What we suspect is that the Community is nearing the end of its initial growth period. During this period the outstanding phenomena were the gradual expansion of its functional scope and the development of a characteristic set of institutional capacities. The dynamic factors were actor goals and goal-oriented behavior in the form of demands and leadership efforts, all operating in a particular sociopolitical environment (i.e., postwar reconstruction and recovery, pluralist polities, technocratic and de-ideologized politics, etc.). But this environment may well be in rapid transformation . . . , and the dynamic factors may soon be exhausted. The next stage(s) in the life of the Community could involve substantially different phenomena and the operation of new factors and environmental conditions. Understanding of this period will hence probably require the construction of new models and new theories.

Unanticipated events such as internal or external crises might confound a straight-line projection. Certainly crises have stimulated growth in the past. Hence, we have included a discussion of some possible variations in the flow of demands and leadership to the system that may arise as a result of different kinds of hypothetical crisis situations. Any of these could produce either forward linkage or spillback. We have no really systematic way of estimating which is the more likely. That will depend on matters of timing, the severity of the crisis, who is in power where, etc. Nor can we assign a probability of occurrence or nonoccurrence to any of

the hypothetical crises. There are many who argue that if the Community stops growing it will *inevitably* founder because partial economic integration will create intolerable pressures that must be answered either by more integration or less. Unfortunately, little empirical research has been accomplished on this point and we remain with little more than conjecture.

In the next two sections we will make projections about future growth pressures and about *system generated* constraints on growth. It is on the basis of these findings that we project a Community moving into a more or less stable equilibrium state. After a digression to consider how crises could alter this projection, we will conclude with some speculations about its economic, social, and political implications. These lead us to urge that future students of the Community adopt new perspectives which will be more appropriate to the kind of polity that seems to be emerging.

Before proceeding we must indicate clearly some of the limitations of this exercise in prognostication. There are, first of all, certain risks in projecting the future on the basis of an analysis that is rooted in the past experience of the Community. In extending it into the future we are asserting that change is most likely to occur in response to X or Y, *all other things being equal*. Some may think this a dubious assumption, as we will see later, but as Lincoln Bloomfield has pointed out, "That all things are never equal is irrelevant, since one can only predict on the basis of orderly assumptions."[2] If events prove us wrong, it should prove possible to pinpoint our errors. Either our facts are incorrect, our assumptions unwarranted, or our model or theory faulty or incomplete. In any case, correction will contribute to a better understanding of the Community enterprise, which is after all our ultimate purpose.

Secondly, in talking about growth pressures and constraints on growth we have not considered all the possible ways in which political actors might develop pro- or anti-integration incentives, but have for the most part focused on the incen-

---

Britain's Engagement (Baltimore: The Johns Hopkins Press, 1969).

[2]Lincoln P. Bloomfield, "Western Europe, 1965–1975: Five Scenarios," Project DOWNGRADE, Bendix Systems Division, Bendix Corporation, April 1, 1965, pp. 2–25, 26.

tives they seem likely to develop via the coalition-formation mechanisms, that is, as a result of the continued operation of the customs union, the incipient economic union, and the Community's institutional system. International events, unforeseen crises, changes in government or in ruling elites, the entry into politics of new groups or actors, could fundamentally change the picture, but our model gives us no way to systematically predict whether any of these things will happen.

Finally, projecting or predicting what political actors will do is always a risky business, even when one bases one's judgments on a careful analysis of their past behaviors present attitudes, and interest perceptions, future aspirations, and the concrete situation in which they are likely to find themselves. Unfortunately, we do not as yet have this kind of information for crucial categories of political actors in the countries of the Community. All we have had to go on is our own scattered and fragmentary impressions based on limited interviewing, our reading of the specialized press,[3] and a few partial studies.[4] Even if we had complete data we still would not be able to predict whether or not actors would or could in fact act "rationally" to further their interests, or whether or not the necessary intranational and international bargains among actors and between sectors or issue areas would or could be struck.

2. PROJECTING GROWTH PRESSURES

We think of our approach to the analysis of integration as a voluntaristic, actor-oriented one, emerging out of neofunctionalist thought, but distinct from it in the extent of its voluntarism. According to our basic model of system change, political actors engage in two kinds of

activities that are crucial to integration. They can develop and articulate demands and they can make available to the system vital skills, imagination, and energy in the form of leadership. Background or environmental factors will, of course, help determine which actors will be in power, what they must respond to, what their alternatives will be or what they perceive them to be. The international system and their domestic political systems are both important sources of constraint on their freedom of action.

The Community system itself has a certain built-in potential for growth that can also move actors along to positions they did not clearly opt for in advance. But we have analyzed this potential in terms of *mechanisms* and the relatively static metaphor was used advisedly. Our analysis tends to show that the Community's potential needs to be *activated;* the mechanisms are not *in themselves* processes or agents of integration or system growth. And it is the flow of demands and the relative availability of leadership that can serve the function of activator. Let us summarize briefly some of our more important findings about demand flow (points 1–5) and leadership (points 6–7) in the growth process.

To the extent that the following conditions are fulfilled, growth is more likely to occur.

1. Political actors with system-wide power or with a substantial constituency (i.e., interest groups) within several member countries come to identify their interests with the creation of a Community decision-making capability, i.e., with an extension of the scope or capacities of the system.

2. Political actors in control of one or more governments perceive progress in a particular area or sector to be a central item on their agenda.

3. Political actors can anticipate redistributive benefits in the area of most concern to them as a result of the change to the Community arena.

4. The goals sought by actors are generally consistent with each other, i.e., the demand pattern is identical or convergent rather than conflictual. Growth will be a function of the *balance* among supporters, opponents, and "conservers," as well as the kinds of actors (dramatic-political, incremental-

---

[3] By far the most important source is *Agence Europe*, a daily newsletter published in Brussels. Also useful are *Common Market, Agenor,* and *European Documentation*, and *Trade Union News*, publications of the European Parliament that attempt to keep track of Europe-related statements and activities of individuals, groups, or political parties in the Six.

[4] Miriam Camps, *European Unification in the Sixties* (New York: McGraw-Hill Book Company, 1966), esp. chap. 6; Jensen and Walter, *The Common Market:* John Newhouse, *Collision in Brussels: The Common Market Crisis of 30 June 1965* (New York: W. W. Norton & Co., Inc.).

economic, systemic, subgroup) that pursue these different kinds of goals.[5] The likelihood that a pro-integrative balance will emerge seems to vary as follows:

a) It will be *high* if:

(1) Systemic actors and subgroup actors with dramatic-political and incremental economic aims favor the measure, even if for different reasons

(2) If there is opposition only from some subgroup actors

b) It will be *moderate* (50/50) if:

(1) Systemic actors with incremental economic aims are opposed, but they are offered side-payments, or subgroup actors are mobilized to support the measure, or systemic actors with dramatic-political goals are in favor

(2) If opposition can be isolated to one or two countries and to one level or type of aim (except systemic dramatic-political)

(3) Only incremental-economic elites are mobilized.

c) It will be *low* if:

(1) Systemic actors with dramatic-political aims oppose the measure

(2) Systemic, dramatic-political actors favor integration but pursue inconsistent goals

(3) Both kinds of actors at both levels oppose

(4) Most kinds of actors in any one country oppose the measures

5. Intra- and intersectoral bargaining remains open enough to yield a rough equivalence of benefits (gains and losses as a result of integration) among the member countries.

6. The top officials of the European Commission (Commissioners and occupants of A1–A3 classifications) perceive their role as an activist-political one that is rooted in the double necessity of gaining the assent of the governments while taking incremental steps to increase Community capability.

7. Top national leaders affirm their support for the goals and procedures of the Community enterprise and demonstrate in bargaining behavior their readiness to take into account the needs and preoccupations of other member countries.

One thing that stands out from this list is that it says little about *basic causes*. What we offer is a set of "if . . . then" statements, relating variations in certain variables (broadly speaking, in demand flow and leadership) to different change patterns. Only rarely—and then only speculatively—have we probed back into the questions of the historical, structural, or economic determinants of the style and content of actor demands or leadership. In other words, we take the variations in demand flow and leadership as *givens*, and then analyze their consequences for change in the Community system.[6]

This may put us in the position to ask the right questions about the future. But how can our findings have any utility for the actual projection or prediction of future variations in demand flow or in leadership? Our answer to such a question is that, while we have not probed into basic causes or determinants, we have explored in some depth an intermediary level of causation via our analyses of mechanisms of coalition formation and how they interact with demands and leadership to produce change. We have seen how functional spill-over, log-rolling and side-payments, socialization, and feedback can operate through the Community system to help induce political actors to perceive an interest in integration and to join growth supporting coalitions.

By means of projections about pro- and anti-integration incentives we can make tentative statements about the probability that future growth pressures will develop, this in turn based upon our estimate of the extent to which condi-

---

[5]For an earlier effort to develop propositions of this sort see Haas, "*The Uniting of Europe* and the Uniting of Latin America," in *Journal of Common Market Studies,* 5 (June 1967), 329.

[6]The most obvious defect of our method is that it assumes that such basic parameters or background conditions as pluralism, technology, de-ideologization, de-politicization, etc., do not change much. Fundamental changes in these "external parameters" (i.e., transformation of the internationsl system or of the domestic political systems of so-called "post-industrial" societies) can be expected to require a substantial revision of our model, if not the development of entirely new analytical approaches.

tions 1–5 above are likely to be fulfilled in any particular issue area, that is, what kinds of actors seem likely to be mobilized? To what extent will they pursue compatible goals? Will they perceive redistributive or at least equivalent benefits as the likely result of an integrative move?

Our projections will assume that there will be no dramatic variations in the future availability of supranational and national leadership. Although we have noted a trend toward a conservative, crisis management leadership on the part of the Commission, there are no clear signs that it is likely to be reduced to complete impotence or inactivity. Indeed, we would expect it to play more or less the same role it has since the 1965–1966 crisis over the French boycott, still politically ambitious, but much more cautious in its strategies. It will probably limit itself to modest policy initiatives that can be clearly justified on the basis of economic necessity, the adaptations or incremental decisions required to make the common market work. We do not expect to provide major new impetus for growth.

We expect much the same to be true of national leadership. In spite of some evidence of a tendency toward a decline in the participation and attentiveness of dramatic-political actors as decision-making is routinized, we anticipate that national leaders will continue to make demands, show support, or seek to facilitate bargaining on a case by case basis when (and if) they develop appropriate system-based incentives to do so. However, we see few signs of reduction in the present level of ambiguity and disagreement among the governments as to the future of the Community per se (e.g., how much should it grow in scope and authority? What policy postures ought it to take? etc.). De Gaulle's departure may facilitate a better political climate within the Community, and thus increase the likelihood that Britain and several other EFTA members will gain entry. It is difficult to see how this will reduce the diversity of views in the Community, however. Social and economic interests, images of the world, domestic policy preferences can be expected to diverge for some time to come. Ambiguity over how politically active the Commission ought to be is likely to persist or even increase. Hence, we do not consider it at all likely that national leaders will make dramatic proposals implying important new tasks or powers for the Community system. If such proposals are made, they seem likely to be rejected.

Strong Growth Pressures

There are a number of interrelated economic policy areas in which we expect substantial growth pressures to arise via the functional and bargaining mechanisms, namely in fiscal, countercyclical, and balance of payments policy.[7] Growth pressures in these areas appear likely to be strong primarily because those who stand to gain from the customs union, as well as the technocrats in charge of the area in each country, perceive a common interest in avoiding competitive distortions that might counteract the effects of having lowered tariff and quota barriers. Governmental decision makers of both types also share an interest in keeping to a minimum the potentially destabilizing effects that participation in a common market or customs union can have on national efforts to maintain full employment, resist inflationary trends, or encourage economic growth.

Divergent fiscal systems (both indirect and direct taxation) can neutralize or even reverse the trade-producing effects of integration by, for example, substituting excise taxes for tariffs and hence restricting the free flow of goods within the Community. Sharply divergent business profits taxes on earnings retained, or profits distributed could cause capital to flee one country for another as capital mobility increases. Much the same would be the case with countercyclical and balance of payments policies. Maintaining full employment, price stability, and economic growth in any one country alone will become increasingly difficult as the customs union is solidified and beginnings are made towards economic union. Unless coordinated approaches are developed, any one country's efforts to stimulate or

---

[7]Actor socialization will probably play a role too. Cabinet ministers and national experts along with Commission staff in these fields have established an extensive and apparently productive series of committees and working groups in which they have over the years regularly exchanged information and considered possible future means of cooperation and coordination.

cool off its economy could be undone if her neighbors pursued contradictory policies.[8] Similarly, maintaining balance of payments equilibrium is complicated by involvement in a customs union, since countries are not free to use some of the standard policy tools such as restricting the inflow of goods, limiting short-term capital movements, and changing exchange rates.[9] In view of recent international monetary crises, the apparent fragility of major currencies, and the serious balance of payments problem experienced by France in 1968, we can expect that dramatic-political actors will also be mobilized to push for some kinds of Community-level activity in these areas. The Commission too would seem to be in a good position to play an active role, because of the close functional linkages between the customs union and the fiscal, countercyclical, and balance of payments fields. It certainly has an incentive to do so if it is to defend what has been achieved in economic integration.

Nevertheless, an increasing number of scholars have recently argued that there is little evidence that national technocratic bureaucrats, political leaders, or the Commission for that matter,[10] are at this point interested in more than a minimal policy coordination as needed to cope with short-term crises.

> The problems within the system that are likely to arise in the next few years can probably be handled by reaching ad hoc agreements among the national authorities. Very probably these arguments will be worked out within the existing committee structure of the Community. . . . But . . . the pattern seems likely to be essentially one of intergovernmental cooperation, not, as had earlier been planned and hoped, the progressive adoption of common policies and the gradual development of an instituional infra-structure capable of sustaining a unified system.[11]

Thus while there is a good chance that there will be a clear increase in the scope of collective decision-making (i.e., shifts in the locus of decision-making), it does not seem at all assured that it will take the form of the development of common policies on the scale of the common agricultural policy.[12]

The first hesitant steps being taken in the area of medium-term planning are a case in point. In anticipation of growing problems of maintaining internal and external balances by means of coordinating short-term stabilization measures, the member countries have turned to a form of nascent economic planning. In a Medium-Term Economic Policy Committee high level national planners and policy makers meet to examine five-year projections of aggregate economic performance and to develop guidelines for private and governmental investments, etc.

> The Medium Term Economic Policy Committee can issue guidelines for noninflationary increases in government spending on the basis of the projections. All of these yardsticks for behavior are meant to prevent the excesses of inflation and deflation in member countries which could upset the economic stability of the Community—and require painful internal adjustments.[13]

Although such a committee could eventually develop into a Community-wide planning apparatus, the immediate prospect is for an intensive intergovernmental communications network which, although it may increasingly influence national policy decisions, will not generate collective policy decisions.

---

[8]See Krause, *European Economic Integration and the United States*, p. 167, n. 25.

[9]*Ibid.*, pp. 168–72.

[10]A working program for the next three years proposed by the Commission to the Council in March 1969 tends to confirm the same conclusion, i.e., that the emphasis is on coordination and harmonization rather than on common policies. See Commission des Communautes Europeennes, "Programme de Travaille des Communautes" Brussels, March 20, 1968.

[11]Miriam Camps, *European Unification in the Sixties*, p. 204. See also Krause, *European Economic Integration and the United States;* Scheinman, "Some Preliminary Notes on Bureaucratic Relationships in the European Community," *International Organization*, 20 (Autumn 1966), and "The European Community in 1969,"*Common Market*, 9 (March 1969), 47–48.

[12]Nor is the prospect bright for increases in institutional capacity. All indications are that the best the Community can hope for is to salvage the supranational structures and decision rules at their present level. Indeed, a gradual erosion of both facets is a distinct possibility.

[13]Krause, *European Economic Integration and the United States*, p. 173.

Another area that seems to hold promise for substantial growth in the relatively near future is that of technological research and development. The spectacular success in Europe of Servan-Schreiber's *The American Challenge* may well be symptomatic because of its themes that Europe is falling farther and farther behind in those areas of technology that are likely to become the main sources of economic growth and profit in the future and that the only alternative to economic submersion is a federal Europe. There has certainly been a deluge of books, pamphlets, position papers, interest group statements, and the like developing a plethora of variants on the same general theme. Indeed, the Community's own Committee on Medium-Term Economic Policy has asserted that without much more extensive cooperation and pooling of markets and resources, the member countries will remain "the main world importers of discoveries and exporters of brains, they will be condemning themselves to a cumulative underdevelopment which will soon render their decline irremediable."[14]

Both incremental-economic and dramatic-political actors seem likely to become increasingly susceptible to proposals to increase cooperation and coordination in scientific research and development in such areas as aircraft, electronics, and atomic energy. The argument that this would inevitably enhance the individual and collective position of the member countries is generally accepted. And the redistributive outcome would be the best imaginable, everybody in the Community standing to gain, and nobody really losing (except possibly the United States by a reduction in its technological superiority over the Europeans).

Serious obstacles, however, remain to be overcome, for example, the absence of common goals and purposes, both scientific and diplomatic-political, and the present unavailability to the Community of Britain's considerable technological capability. Nevertheless, there are clear signs that a beginning is being made. On December 20, 1968, the Council of Ministers in the course of deciding on a limited joint program of research in the nuclear field (provided for in the Euratom Treaty), voted in principle to extend Community cooperation to other fields and a Scientific and Technological Research Policy Committee was set up to work under a tight schedule to report back studying the feasibilities and priorities of cooperation in such fields as data processing, telecommunications, new kinds of transport, oceanography, metallurgy, air and water pollution, and meteorology.

It is generally agreed that the Community's first effort at scientific cooperation, the European Atomic Energy Community, failed dismally. It remains to be seen if the problems that accounted for the failure can now be overcome. On the level of theory it would seem that a strong positive argument can be made. Schienman[15] has attributed Euratom's difficulties to

1. Reduced incentives to engage in cooperation because of the development of alternative supplies of energy,
2. The disparity of national interests and of national capabilities in the nuclear area (France was predominant in nuclear research and the only nuclear military power.),
3. The reassertion of political and economic-commercial nationalism which substituted national priorities for collective ones,
4. A lack of dynamic and resolute leadership on the part of the Euratom Commission,
5. A bargaining context that was limited to one area, and which thence allowed little room for cross-sectional bargaining as a way of adjusting competing interests.

Most of these conditions might well be eliminated or their effects at least muted in the current atmosphere of urgency and in the broader bargaining contexts being proposed. A wide range of political actors is available. Redistributive outcomes seem possible and everybody stands to gain. No single nation will predominate in all areas, and extensive log-rolling and side-payments should be possible as the prime mechanism of coalition building.

[14]Quoted in Robert Gilpin, "European Disunion and the Technology Gap," *The Public Interest*, 10 (Winter 1968), 54.

[15]Lawrence Scheinman, "Euratom: Nuclear Integration in Europe," *International Conciliation*, 563 (May 1967), 27–63.

The situation in agriculture also seems likely to generate growth pressures, as we already suggested in our earlier case study. Mounting problems of surpluses and the resultant skyrocketing budgetary outlays[16] can probably be dealt with effectively only by extending Community policy-making into the areas of production controls and structural and social policy. Germany's interests in limiting the extent of future transfer payments to the French and the Dutch via the agricultural budget, the French concern with inflationary pressures as a result of existing high agricultural prices, the Italian desire for increased subsidies for basic structural reforms, and the accumulated success and skill of the Commission in this area should constitute a favorable set of circumstances for future growth.

In December 1968 Commissioner Mansholt proposed a ten-year plan for a radical reform of agricultural policy (dubbed Agriculture 1980) according to which less emphasis would be placed on market and price policy, the farm acreage in the Community would be decreased and the average size of farms increased, and the drift from the land to the towns and cities accelerated.[17] Under the new Mansholt plan expenditures for market support policy would be decreased and those for structural reform increased substantially (to an average of $2500 million per year) at least over the period 1970–1980. If the plan were adopted Mansholt estimated that total agricultural expenditures could be reduced to under $2000 million a year after 1980. Conversely, under the present policy they could explode to $8500 million a year![18]

Because of the radical nature of the proposals, Mansholt and agriculture immediately became once again a center of attention and controversy throughout 1969. Politicians, political parties, and interest groups have rushed to take positions for and against, and the stage seems set for yet another long series of agricultural debates in the 1970's.

The Community's short-run growth prospects are not at all poor, at least on the one dimension of functional scope. Yet in fiscal policy, counter-cyclical and balance of payments policy, and research and development, political actors seem to be proposing little more than minimal measures designed to better facilitate the execution of existing national policies that will still largely be based on national priorities and purposes. Even the far-reaching Mansholt Plan seems to confirm the same trend, away from Community-level centralized administration and policy-making, and toward programs "conceived in Community-wide terms" with implementation largely decentralized . . . the responsibility of the member states."[19] Political actors seem to be inclined primarily to taking limited, defensive steps designed to lead to compatible national policies, rather than to seek to pool policy-making institutions and processes in search of new, potentially redistributive benefits. Even if such steps toward policy compatibility were taken in a salient area like monetary policy, or even defense, it would probably not transform the qualitative nature of the system although it might well have enormous practical significance.

This trend toward more minimalist goals certainly reflects persisting policy disagreements among political actors, the national preoccupation and inertia of most bureaucracies, interest groups and political parties, and the general decline of pro-integration enthusiasm. But it may also develop as a result of political actors becoming more and more concerned with protecting initial gains and less and less with supporting possibly risky projects for more integration. Let us turn now from system-generated incentives for growth to a more systematic investigation of how constraints on growth can also be generated by the system itself.

3. SYSTEMIC CONSTRAINTS ON GROWTH

One of our basic conclusions about the Community system is that there seems to be a tendency for individual sectors to move towards

---

[16]In 1967 it had been estimated that market support expenditures for the year 1969–70 would be on the order of $1500 million; by 1969 it seemed likely they would in fact reach $2600 million.

[17]Commission of the European Communities, "Memorandum on the Reform of Agriculture in the European Economic Community," Brussels, December 18, 1968.

[18]"Agricultural 80: avec Mansholt et au-dela," AGE-NOR 9 (January-March 1969), p. 64.

[19]"Memorandum on the Reform of Agriculture," p. 36.

equilibrium. That is to say, once the basic coalition is struck and once decision-making begins in earnest, the initial goals of the more important actors are likely to be satisfied. And contrary to standard neofunctional interpretation, we do not believe that initial satisfaction necessarily leads to new demands for broader or more intensive decision-making. This may happen, of course, but a countertendency is at work: the actors' concern with protecting their initial gains. This is not to argue that crises may not, from time to time, undermine the existing equilibrium, or that outputs may not fail to materialize in some sectors. Similarly, movement from spillback or output failure to forward linkage may well develop. Still, within a continued mix of patterns of sectoral outcome, we expect the proportion of equilibrium sectors to grow. This would in turn strengthen the processes in the system that are associated with equilibrium, or routinized kinds of conflict, and these are not, of course, the processes that are associated with growth. On the contrary, equilibrium processes nurture pressures that inhibit growth. Put in the most general terms, individual sectors lose their dynamic quality when they reach equilibrium; in addition the actors in these sectors may work against growth elsewhere in the system.[20]

Ironically, then, the success of integration tends to retard growth. The realization of initial goals renders important groups and actors rather quiescent. Once they have a stake in the system, they are inclined to protect the system from the disruption that often accompanies growth. Such behavior is neither startling nor novel. The conservative instincts which often accompany success are well understood, and their impact on the European Community has been noted before. A study of interest group responses to de Gaulle's 1965–1966 boycott concluded that their basic instinct was to try to keep the customs union and

common agricultural policy intact and functioning, even if that meant accepting a weekening of the Commission's prerogatives, giving up on efforts to increase parliamentary control, and tolerating an implicit right of a French veto over all important future Community decisions.

> The "New Europe" has indeed created its own vested interests! But the irony is that the successes of integration can be, and in my view were, used against the architects of that success . . . groups committed primarily to the infrastructure of integration may not perceive the institutional system and its operational rules as vital to the persistence of that system. . . . Thus the success of integration, which has been the work of the institutional system and its code, has strengthened the hand of the most consistent opponents of that system and weakened that of its supporters![21]

However, the sectoral frame of reference directs our attention to the whole series of mechanisms of coalition formation which offer the possibility of a more detailed understanding of the braking pressures generated by sectors being in equilibrium. Indeed, it is a second irony of the system that the same mechanisms of coalition formation that are often identified with growth can produce pressures that inhibit growth. What this second irony indicates is, of course, that growth opportunities do not necessarily vary directly with the scope and capacities of the system. Our model notation, $dS = f[(S + Su)(dD + dL)] + e_n$ indicates that change (dS) is some function of the other major variables—including, of course, the existing political system (S). If, however, an increase in the scope and capacities of the system is associated with growth only up to a point where the conservative forces take hold, then it is clear that the relationship between the system and support for the system is not linear—but more probably curvilinear. This relationship might be symbolized graphically by Figure 1. In sum, what we envisage is the conservative portion of the system growing larger and perhaps in the long run frustrating demands for growth elsewhere in the system.

---

[20]Our conclusions here are based to a substantial degree on the results of our study of the customs union and the coal sectors. We recognize that equilibrium in other areas may not have the same consequences for demand flow and leadership. Further study should certainly be undertaken to validate or modify our perspective. We are moved to generalize from the one case because of the quantitative significance of the customs union itself and because of the clear trend in areas like agriculture, competition, transport, etc., to create complex systems of rules and procedures quite analogous to what exists in the customs union.

[21]Leon N. Lindberg, "Integration as a Source of Stress on the European Community System" *International Organization*, 20 (1966), 245.

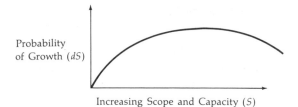

Figure 1

Let us now look more carefully at the manner in which mechanisms of coalition formation generate conservative pressures. Our analysis suggests that virtually all Community decision-making leads to the socialization of the participating actors. It is, in addition, reasonable to believe that the settled patterns of long-term cooperation in sectors in equilibrium might be particularly conducive to effective socialization. At the same time, we know that the routinized decision-making of sectors in equilibrium is not likely to be very appealing to system-level actors and particularly to dramatic-political actors; indeed, the latter may even be less effective in equilibrium situations. Not only the participation but also the attention of dramatic-political actors is likely to fall off as matters become increasingly routinized with, for example, cabinet ministers increasingly delegating Community responsibilities to their subordinates. Routinization then tends to restrict the circle of political actors who regularly interact in the Community setting to what we have called subgroup actors, i.e., interest groups, business firms, technical experts, and lower level officials. While socialization of these actors may occur, the processes whereby perspectives may change, new common goals may be developed, and decision norms may be established are increasingly cut off from more politically salient elites as more and more areas of the Community move into equilibrium. Thus, we would expect the system's future growth possibilities to suffer if system-level actors, both incremental-economic and dramatic-political, were to be less and less actively involved in joint problem-solving.

With respect to supranational leadership, there is at least impressionistic evidence of these same trends in the way in which leadership of the High Authority passed from political personalities like Jean Monnet and perhaps even René

Mayer to lesser-known figures like Piero Malvestiti and Rino Del Bo. The contrast between Monnet, the political activist, and Del Bo, the generally effective administrator, is particularly striking. Whether these tendencies are cause or effect and despite effective socialization, the kind of leadership which seems necessary for effective coalition-building is less likely to be available to the Community—at either the national or the supranational level. Even outside official circles, the most influential politicians and interest group leaders may well turn to other arenas where a satisfactory fundamental consensus has not yet been hammered out. This kind of explanation may well account in part for the difficulty that the Monnet Committee has had in effectively mobilizing its target groups in recent years. That is to say, membership in the Committee and support for the Community continue, but attention, dedication, and inputs of political energy tend to wane.

Another likely concomitant to equilibrium is the increased legitimacy of Community processes and institutions among broader publics, although not necessarily among mass publics as such. After all, equilibrium entails at least minimal satisfaction of the demands of relevant groups, thus implying positive feedback. Moreover, even in the absence of positive feedback, it is reasonable to believe that after joint problem-solving at the Community level has continued for some time, it will increasingly be accepted as normal or legitimate by attentive publics. In using the term legitimacy to cover both the fruits of demand satisfaction and normalization of decision-making patterns, we are perhaps blurring over a distinction which has significant implications for growth. Thus, positive feedback is really an index of the stake that certain groups develop in the continuation of the system. Legitimation stemming from normalization is, in contrast, much more directly akin to the notion of permissive consensus and indicates simply that leadership groups favorable to the Community are likely to have a relatively congenial environment in which to work.

Finally, let us consider briefly the two remaining mechanisms of coalition formation, log-rolling and side payments, and functional spillover. At this point, the analysis becomes particularly speculative, but nonetheless it seems appropriate to indicate at least the general lines of our thinking. We are inclined to think of functional linkages as more or less a constant. Given the complexity of contemporary society, problems are necessarily interdependent and so their solutions tend to impinge on one another, and this is the heart of the neofunctionalist logic. In the long run, of course, if a "total society" is established at the European level, these functional linkages will not be relevant to further extension. However, the Community is far from any such boundaries, and we see nothing peculiar to equilibrium systems which either shrinks or multiplies the available functional linkages. On the other hand, the effect of equilibrium on the two barganing strategies is clearer. As more and more sectors are incorporated into the system and tend towards a state of equilibrium, the opportunities for bargains among sectors (log-rolling) will in all likelihood increase since necessarily more incentives are available with which to bait the bargaining hook. Moreover, incorporation also entails accessibility to supranational leadership and thus provides more groups which can be manipulated by supranational leadership.

The general picture with respect to mechanisms of coalition formation is thus relatively clear. The long-term trend is very likely to result in increases in positive feedback, in the number of actors who are socialized, and in bargaining opportunities. There is no reason to expect the generally abundant possibilities for functional spill-over to decline. But what about the impact of these trends on the system? We would argue that they will tend to stabilize the system and to inhibit its growth.

Specifically, it would seem that the implication of the feedback and socialization process lends some credence to the threshold argument often heard with respect to integration. Most simply, this argument is based on the contention that as the stake of important elites increases the political costs of turning back grow higher. Accordingly, at some point the Community crosses a threshold beyond which it becomes too costly to turn back. No scholar has as yet been able to provide a calculus for determining the threshold point or even for tabulating the costs of giving up, and our analysis does not yield such a calculus either. It does, however, tend to indicate the way in which these vested interests manifest themselves through the mechanisms of feedback and socialization.

The positive feedback adds up to a stake in the continued existence of the system. Even if the leadership of relevant groups allows its attention to wander from the European Community, the leaders would be responsive to any serious threat to their stake in integration. In a sense, socialization is for the actors in question the functional equivalent of a stake in integration although it represents quite a different kind of stake from the concrete benefits implied by feedback. As the experience of the coal sector indicates, this socialization does seem to assure at least minimal cooperation even after the benefits of integration have dwindled. Whereas positive feedback does at least imply a point of no return by the assumption that relevant elites will mobilize in defense of their vested interests, actor socialization is more likely simply to permit the Community to buy time during sustained crisis periods while more permanent solutions are sought. In any case, both mechanisms are likely to be strengthened during equilibrium periods in a manner which will give the Community extra resources for coping with stress.

Directly related, however, to the stabilizing effects of equilibrium processes are a number of growth-inhibiting tendencies. Generally speaking, these growth problems can simply be attributed to the conserving instincts which accompany equilibrium. But beneath the surface lie the demand and leadership effects of equilibrium that we have already indicated. These effects work against growth in normal periods and at the same time reduce the likelihood that it will be possible to capitalize on crises to catalyze a forward linkage or to bring off a transformation of the system.

With respect to normal times, the leadership effects require little elaboration. As we have already argued, the long-run trend of equilibrium is to reduce the availability of the kind of leadership best suited to building growth coalitions: dramatic-political actors will be less concerned with and less inclined to participate in the Community system and supranational leadership positions may increasingly be filled with actors better suited to routine than constitutive bargaining. The demand effects are somewhat more subtle and indirect. What they really do is make rather illusory the idea that equilibrium tendencies increase bargaining opportunities. Thus, as the proportion of equilibrium sectors rises, the total number of demands may not necessarily decrease, even if the demands originating in the equilibrium sectors tend to fall off. This is, of course, because extensive numbers of demands may well be generated in the remaining "dynamic" sectors. It will probably become increasingly difficult, however, to incorporate equilibrium sectors into growth coalitions. In the absence of insistent demands, it is difficult to imagine what the incentives to participation would be. As a matter of fact, given the destabilizing tendencies of growth projects, there is every reason to believe that actors in equilibrium sectors may even work to see that such projects are not undertaken.

When a crisis impinges on the system, the barriers to growth are perhaps lowered. If benefits are reduced or threatened, the demand flow is likely to be reactivated, particularly if the Community has really become the legitimate arena for solving the problems in question. Similarly, the decline in vested interests may well reawaken the gambling instinct. Consequently the scene is set for effective leaders to seize the initiative and promote some sort of growth coalition. Unhappily, there is reason to believe that the less enterprising leadership habits of the equilibrium period may be difficult to reverse. The increased demand flow may be counted upon to reengage dramatic political actors—particularly if the threat to vested interests is significant and widespread. Still, the response may well be rather sluggish since these actors will have to be reintegrated into the system. The problem of supranational leadership is likely to be more serious since Community staffs cannot readily be changed given the combination of fixed terms, national quotas, and civil service guarantees. Moreover, the clashing interests of the crisis period will probably make it difficult to agree on personnel changes.

One limitation of the analysis so far should be noted. Neither national nor supranational leadership can really be identified solely with individual sectors, since the responsibilities of actors often extend to more than one sector. Of course, there are variations, but whereas agriculture and perhaps transport may be narrowly defined, energy and customs union questions may involve several ministries at the national level and perhaps different Commission directorates as well. Moreover, in all problems ultimate responsibility and influence tends to rest with prime ministers, heads of state, the President of the Commission or other key leaders. In other words, the key leadership positions with "transsectoral" responsibility may or may not be filled by different kinds of actors and at the national level they may or may not turn their energies and attention to non-Community problems. Thus, even if we are correct about the tendency towards an increasing number of equilibrium sectors, the total impact may be either greater or less than the sum of its parts.

We do have good reason for believing that success in integration tends to generate conservative pressures, but we know very little about the long-term consequences of such pressures.[22] Will the conservative pressures simply neutralize the forces of growth? Will the clash of conservative tendencies and counterpressures for growth produce a crisis which will lead to further growth? Is it possible that such a clash will destroy the system? Our previous analysis of growth pressures would seem to indicate that the first of these is the most likely, that is, that conserving forces will eventually balance off those pressing for growth, largely because most actors seem likely to be satisfied with relatively low levels of scope and capacity. But crises could cumulate in an unforeseen manner so as to transform actor goals, mobilize new groups, or activate national leadership efforts. Let us identify some of the ways in which this might happen.

---

[22]The broader consequences of a halt in growth will tend to lessen as the system expands. As a matter of fact, some perspective other than growth will certainly become more meaningful as the system fills out in response to the demands of relevant elites. Even if one could, for example, use mechanisms of coalition formation to explain why a particular nation-state was no longer growing, would it really be worth the effort? Growth at the present stage of the Community and, in fact, for the foreseeable future is interesting because the impact of the Community both domestically and internationally will depend on just how many responsibilities it can accumulate. Obviously, beyond some point it begins to matter less if conservative pressures grip the system and, in fact, quesions of growth lose their significance and immediacy.

4. FORWARD LINKAGE-SPILLBACK POSSIBILITIES AS A CONSEQUENCE OF CRISIS

Crises have been important in the history of the Community. Indeed, we have shown that crisis is part and parcel of the integration process. Several have stimulated major surges of growth. After all, it was economic and political crises engendered by World War II that gave birth to the European Coal and Steel Community. And it was the 1955 failure of the proposal for a European Defense Community that triggered the efforts that led to the EEC and Euratom Treaties. Indeed, growth pressures spawned out of crisis might be the only way in which the equilibrium tendencies we have described above will be overcome in the future. Such pressures might arise if the crisis is of sufficient proportions to transform the goals or interest perceptions of actors so as to produce insistent new demands for Community-level decisions; or if it mobilizes new groups or political actors to make demands on the system; or if it endures long enough to force a realignment of leadership at the national and supranational levels; or if it is amenable to solutions that offer the possibility of significant new redistributive benefits.

Crisis may arise in two basic ways. They might originate within the system itself largely as a direct result of the projected slowdown in growth, or they might originate outside the Community as a result of completely exogenous factors. We will not deal extensively with the latter for they are largely outside the scope of this book. Our major concern will be to delineate a number of internal crises which we conceive of as "crises of premature equilibrium." Equilibrium can be considered premature if the system's loss of response capacity were to coincide with the continued input of still powerful demands for action on the part of the system. Persistent frustration of strongly pressed demands could lead to drastic withdrawals of support, both at elite and mass levels, the pursuit of alternative policy strategies (e.g., Atlantic or "Eastern" options), or to a massive campaign to make the Community system more responsive by constructing [a] kind of systems-transforming coalition. . . . Such demands might be generated in a variety of ways:

1. They might be the result of political actors coming to perceive that the level of equilibrium likely to be attained will not produce equivalent benefits.
2. They might be the result of a whole series of output failures in which an increasing number of important groups perceive themselves losing available potential benefits.
3. They might emerge as a result of the mobilization of groups who have hitherto not directly benefited from the Community.
4. They may be spawned by varieties of functional linkages between tasks presently undertaken by the Community system and subsequent tasks that must be assumed but cannot because of the system's loss of vitality.

Equalizing Benefits

One likely consequence of a slowing down of the pace of integration is that political actors will begin to tally up more systematically past gains and losses. While there have always been efforts on the part of national negotiators roughly to equalize the benefits inherent in various integration measures, this goal has not been pursued systematically across the board, and it has still been possible to argue that short-term sacrifices in one area were being made for anticipated future benefits in another. As these future benefits become more problematical, we can expect to hear more and more calls for each nation to receive its "proper return" from the Community. The early signs have already appeared: German Foreign Minister Schroeder's call for "synchronization" after the 1963 crisis over British entry, recent Italian demands that a larger share of the Euratom budget be spent on projects of direct advantage to Italy, growing German opposition to the exploding budgetary outlays required by the common agricultural policy (which burden Germany and benefit France).[23]

Indeed a recent study of all the financial contributions and receipts arising directly or indi-

---

[23]See the article by Walter Grund, German State Secretary in the Ministry of Finance, "Paying for the Common Farm Policy: Why Germany Wants to Change the Rules," in *European Community*, 1 (January 1969), pp. 6–7.

Table 1
Balance of Financial Contributions, Receipts
from Integration 1953–1968 ($ Millions)

Belgium	+92.49
Germany	−946.65
France	+716.07
Italy	+128.20
Luxembourg	+120.24
Netherlands	−110.35

Source: Bernard Heidelberger, "La ventilation des
dépenses communautaires: le juste retour," unpublished
manuscript (September 1968), p. 77.

rectly out of European integration between 1953
and 1968 (e.g., ECSC's levy, readaptation expenditures, loans and research activities; EEC and
Euratom's Social Fund, FEOGA, European
Development Fund, nuclear research, etc.) shows
that at this level there is a striking overall disparity in benefits received.

Of course, integration creates benefits for participants in other ways as well, most notably
through increases in commerce and in overall economic growth. Heidelberger calculates that the
gains from integration in these areas amounted
to approximately $22 billion between 1953 and
1968, almost six times the total of direct or indirect financial outlays. He estimates further that
here it is Germany and the Netherlands who have
been the largest net gainers.[24]

Nevertheless, we might expect that in the
future governments who consider themselves in
a deficit position will more insistently demand
either changes in the existing system designed to
reduce Community activity and the amount of income transfer and hence reduce the economic
advantages of integration for others, or they will
expect to be compensated, perhaps by extending
Community activity into new areas. For example,
Germany may agree to go on paying for the bulk
of the common agricultural policy only in exchange for French concessions on commercial or
monetary policy matters. Thus mounting demands for a "proper return" could have the result
of inducing a spill-back (or a series of them), and
perhaps the risk of a major spill-back could be the
occasion for a future surge of growth.

---

[24]Heidelberger, "La ventilation des dépenses communautaires," pp. 93 ff.

Output Failure

Pressures on the system, either demands for
change or withdrawal of support, can also build
up as a result of the inability of the Community
to take decisive action in a series of policy areas.
Continued deadlock on British entry after de
Gaulle's retirement, ineffectual coping with international monetary problems or with the American technological challenge, inaction on the new
Mansholt Plan or on regional policy measures,
etc., may well force political actors to conclude
that the advantages of integration can no longer
balance off the costs of not having a coherent
policy in certain vital areas. A turn to an Atlantic
area or industrialized nations focus of decision-
making (e.g., on monetary matters) might result,
and this could undermine much of the Com-
minity's present achievements. Nor can we exclude that Germany, frustrated in its efforts to
play a role in a coherent Western European system, will one day be sorely tempted by a Soviet
offer on reunification and the "stabilization" of
Central Europe.

New Groups

Not only have some nations apparently gained
more as a result of integration, but some regions
have gained more than others at their expense
(i.e., center v. periphery problems, northern Italy
v. the South, the Ruhr v. Bavaria and the southeast, the Paris basin v. the southwest, etc.). Similarly, some social groups have been the prime
beneficiaries (employees, businessmen, traders,
some farmers), while others have gained very little
(students, workers) or lost (many small farmers).
[Elsewhere we have] speculated about social
changes that might encourage groups (or regions)
to perceive more sharply their relative deprivation and to demand things such as a more vigorous social welfare policy, regional investment and
programs of income transfer, more meaningful
participation in or control of the decision-making
process, and comprehensive economic planning.
We concluded there that the relatively benign
climate in which the Community was able to
grow during its early years could be transformed
into a politicized, conflictual one, if the response
of the Community and the governments to demands such as these was deficient. The available

evidence would seem to suggest that in the past many groups, most notably workers, have simply deferred judgment on the Community rather than accepting it as truly legitimate and useful. A more stable reservoir of support will thus emerge only if the Community is perceived as relevant and responsive to the needs and aspirations of broader categories of the population.

Functional Linkages

That functional spill-over cannot be viewed in and of itself as a dynamic force making for integration has been a persistent theme in this book. We have not denied that economic functions or tasks were interrelated nor that performing some at a supranational level rather than at a national level would not have wider ramifications for other functions or tasks. But we have observed empirically that there are important discontinuities or lags between tasks or functions that are not clearly explicable in economic or political theorizing about integration. Similarly, there seems to be such a wide range of choice available to makers of economic decisions as to the nature or form of the response, that no automatic projection of either task expansion or retraction of supranational tasks seems possible. Unfortunately, there seems to have been little systematic empirical analysis by economists of the precise ways in which economic sectors and decisions among progressively integrating modern industrialized countries may be intertwined and interdependent. Because this is so, we do not feel justified in excluding the possibility that functional linkages will assert themselves in the future, perhaps after the customs union has been in operation for some years.

One economist, Hans O. Schmitt, has recently argued that such linkages will very likely develop and that the decisive one will be the relationship between the creation of a customs union and the resultant pressures for an integration of capital markets.[25] A customs union cannot operate optimally if capital movements associated with the movement of goods, services, and persons are restricted, or if unequal access to sources of finance can falsify competition between enter-

prises; nor can real allocative efficiency be achieved via trade liberalization alone.[26] Schmitt argues that an integration of capital markets may in turn necessitate a currency unification, which in turn implies "a pooling of sovereignties sufficiently complete to destroy the separate identities of the participating nation states."[27]

> Within national boundaries, money derives its character as a generally accepted means of payment from being a claim not on any individual debtor alone but on the business community collectively. By requiring its collective resources for backing, the establishment of a single currency may in fact be looked upon as the constitutive act whereby such a business community formally comes into existence.[28]

Schmitt finds that there have clearly been persistent pressures for a common European currency as a *sine qua non* of capital market integration, but that this effort has been consistently frustrated because of a reluctance to accept the "hegemony" or leadership of Germany, which seems fated by economic factors to become the financial center of the Community. He speculates that the temptation to withdraw from the Community entirely will be the strongest at the point when creating a common currency seems unavoidable.

> To the extent that Germany promises to dominate the community . . . other countries may conclude that the preservation of separate nation-states offers better opportunities for the exercise of countervailing power (over a resurgent Germany) than any institutional safeguards within a single polity can ensure.[29]

Thus does Schmitt foresee the possible dissolution of the Community as a result of its inability to take a "functionally required" step. Of course, no one can say whether or not the issue will be posed as starkly as he suggests, or whether or not some broader intersectoral bargain on the scale of monetary unification for a European nuclear cooperation in military procurement might not even then be possible. By implication at least,

---

[25]"Capital Markets and the Unification of Europe," *World Politics*, 20 (January 1968), pp. 228–44.

[26]*Ibid.*, pp. 228–29.
[27]*Ibid.*, p. 228.
[28]*Ibid.*, p. 230.
[29]*Ibid.*, p. 244.

the forces Schmitt identifies might also impel the Community forward, particularly if the alternative were seen to be collapse of the customs union itself.

Exogenous Events

The Community may also come under severe pressures as a result of forces that operate largely or completely outside (or independently of) the system or its effects. These may originate in the international system or within individual countries and can range all the way from the holocaust of nuclear war to a domestic social revolution. Some less cataclysmic possibilities might include the following:

1. A reintensification of the Cold War, presaged for many by the Soviet invasion of Czechoslovakia in 1968, could lead to a strengthening of NATO and further divide the Europeans, or it could help bring a Franz Joseph Strauss to power in Germany. Strauss has been increasingly insistent over the years in his calls for a European "political action Community" built around a common nuclear force.[30]
2. A new period of detente or a change in leadership might alter Soviet policy so that the Soviets will come to perceive of a European settlement in terms of Germany's integration into a western European system that would at the same time have looser defense ties with the United States and a freer relationship with Eastern Germany.[31] On the other hand, the Soviet Union might opt for a strategy that would link reunification with a withdrawal from NATO and the Community.
3. There could be a major collapse in the international monetary system such that trade among industrialized nations was seriously disrupted, thus pushing national decision-makers into autarchic economic policies, or toward a monetary integration at the level of the International Monetary Fund or the Group of Ten, or toward the creation of a European reserve currency.

4. The internal politics of member countries could well be trasformed by forces that we can now scarcely describe, much less understand, and in ways whose consequences for integration are unknown. What could be the effects of a new political polarization, of the decline of parties and the emergence of other forms of political organization, of student politicization of the universities?

Challenge and Response

The foregoing catalogue of hypothetical events that could either reinvigorate the Community's growth processes or cause their further deterioration and perhaps even the collapse of the whole enterprise, testifies to the limits of our ability to make exact projections about the Community's future. Doubtless some of these crises are more likely to occur than others and hopefully more research effort by future students of the Community will enable us to eventually make more reliable statements. Doubtless also the ability of the Community and the political decision-makers of its member states to parlay crises and pressures into future growth will vary with time and circumstance. In this regard our analysis of the effects on the Community of the crisis in the coal sector yielded some tentative hypotheses.

1. The longer the time in equilibrium and the higher the level, the more likely is it that the Community will have built up resources, in the form of vested interests and legitimacy, sufficient to resist the effects of most crises.
2. Yet the system's capacity to respond creatively to crisis, i.e., to parlay them into growth, may at the same time be reduced because in equilibrium situations the circle of engaged actors tends to become more and more restricted and the national and supranational leadership available to the system is typically reduced.
3. If a crisis involves primarily issue areas where the existing integrative coalition is based on an identical interest pattern, its effects on political actors are more likely to be symmetrical and hence more readily coped with.
4. On the other hand, since redistributive benefits are less likely to be available in such a situation, the response to a crisis will probably

---

[30]See his *Herausforderung und Antwort* (Stuttgart: Seewald-Verlag, 1968).

[31]See Miriam Camps, *European Unification in the Sixties,* p. 230.

be defensive of what exists rather than involving a search for new benefits from a higher level of integration.

5. A convergent interest pattern will be more vulnerable to crisis and hence, while it involves greater risk, it also may hold out greater potential for parlaying crisis into growth.

6. Whatever the underlying interest pattern, we expect crises to be easier to cope with if their effects are felt by all or by the most important members of the Community. Where only one country is deeply involved, the others seem less likely to be induced to reenter the bargaining lists in order to find common solutions that might be growth inducing.

These hypotheses tend to confirm us in the view that, while it is clear that crises such as those sketched above could in certain combinations transform the Community system in ways that would confound our long-term projection, we are inclined to think that the system does have a substantial capacity to absorb and contain their potentially disruptive effects. This is certainly also the thrust of the threshold argument made earlier in this chapter. It would take a succession of crises in vital sectors and under unfavorable circumstances to do more than nudge the system backward or forward. Although we are inclined to think that this is unlikely we must stress again that we have no systematic way of estimating the likelihood or severity of crises, nor can we confidently predict whether they would be more likely to lead to a decline or to new growth in the system.

In sum, we consider it most likely that crises will be such that the system will be able to cope with them with only marginal alterations in the Community's scope and capacities resulting. Thus, although we cannot with certainty specify the level of scope and capacity at which the system will stop growing, we see that occurring well short of the point where we can talk of federal or pseudo-federal structures. If that is so, then the really interesting question for the future is: "What kind of polity or system will it be?" Before speculating about this hitherto relatively neglected topic, let us summarize the argument we have made up to now about the future:

1. We found that some growth in scope seems quite likely in certain issue-areas, namely monetary and countercyclical policy, balance of payments, research and development, and agriculture.

2. But we also found that individual sectors or issue areas seem to tend toward equilibrium, and that as integration proceeds, more and more sectors are likely to follow suit and the whole system may become both more stable and more resistant to growth. Hence our projection of an overall equilibrium or plateau to be reached some time within the next several years.

3. Even if the French government becomes more European, and even if Great Britain gains entry, our long-term projection is still for an overall equilibrium situation.

4. A substantial measure of uncertainty as to the Community's eventual scope and even to the validity of our basic projection is introduced by the possibility of the occurrence of various sorts of crises. No probability statements are possible as to their effects; they could either induce more growth or cause spill-back or collapse.

5. The long term implications for the system and indeed its ability to survive will in all likelihood vary with its scope (i.e., whether it includes defense, monetary policy, etc.) and its institutional capacities. But that scope and capacity do not seem to us likely to be qualitatively different from what exists today. There will be more or less intensive collective decision-making (more coordination than common policies) in more or fewer issue areas. Many matters will remain to be decided at the national level, and almost all Europe-level decisions will be implemented via national or regional authorities. We see very little prospect of a federal or near-federal European political union.

6. It is an oversimplification to attribute the slow-down in integration that became apparent in the 1960's to the malevolence of one political leader, de Gaulle, or even to a "lack of political will" among political actors more generally. That de Gaulle's influence was primarily negative and disruptive, at least after 1962, cannot be denied. Nor can we deny that political leaders in the countries of the Community are still divided as to long-term goals and as to their conception of what Europe is to become. So they were in the 1950's. Similarly, it is true that nationalism is

more respectable these days and that there is also a growing preoccupation in all Community countries with domestic problems. Perhaps as important as these factors depressing leadership, however, are the two trends we have stressed . . . namely: the conservative dynamics set in motion by the integration process itself, and the possibility that the societal and international parameters that sustained and conditioned the growth of the Community from the 1950's to the mid 1970's are in the process of being transformed.

5.   A NEW KIND OF POLITY?

Even if our basic projection is largely correct one should not conclude that European integration or the European Community will then no longer be of interest or importance. At the projected level of growth the Community will be an unprecedented, but curiously ambiguous "pluralistic" system—in its economic, social, and political aspects alike. Indeed, there seem to be no satisfactory models or concepts in the social science vocabulary to adequately describe it.

The economic area encompassed by the six Community countries seems likely to fall well short of satisfying an economist's criteria of complete economic integration or even of an economic union.[32] Yet the Community has obviously had an enormous economic impact, most clearly at the level of trade, but also on economic policy, on investments, on productivity, etc.[33] One group of scholars has sought to develop a means of estimating "the distance still to be traversed if the EEC countries were to become as integrated in regard to trade as is a nation-state of comparable size."[34] Based upon data on

the average foreign trade turnover for nation states of comparable size and structure (imports plus exports) as a percent of gross national product (GNP), it was found that "EEC-land" was, by the middle 1960's, "less than two-thirds of the way to the level of economic integration normally associated with national states or federations."[35] Although economists are not agreed on the matter, perhaps as a result of not having given it much serious study, there seems to be no strong reason to believe that this kind of partially integrated economy cannot be quite stable. Balassa argues that although economic policy coordination involves a partial abandonment of sovereignty, it need not go as far as the establishment of across the board supranational authority.[36]

Socially, as indicated by our earlier analyses of identitive and systemic support we find a similarly mixed or "pluralistic" picture. There is growing awareness of and support for the decision-making activities of the Community institutions, even if they involve overruling national governments, but there is much less sign of the emergence of a real European "we" feeling. Unfortunately, nobody has carefully studied this seemingly anomalous combination, at least in modern, industrial societies. It is at least conceivable, however, that some sort of relatively stable European social community could be forged out of vertical ties between a number of relatively homogeneous national social communities and a set of European institutions in which all shared membership, rather than out of horizontal ties among the masses or elites of the member countries. This might not be a nation-state in the traditional sense of the term, but then there is in our view no presumptive reason to assimilate the European Community growth process to nation-building per se.

Politically too, the Community system defies ready categorization. It is neither federal nor confederal, intergovernmental or supranational, sovereign or dependent, but it shares some of the characteristics of all. Walter Yondorf, an early student of the European Community, foresaw the

---

[32]For example, see Bela Balassa, *The Theory of Economic Integration*, pp. 3-4.

[33]See Krause, *European Economic Integration and the United States, passim.*

[34]Karl Deutsch, "A Comparison of French and German Elites in the European Political Environment." in Deutsch et al., *France, Germany, and the Western Alliance*, p. 236. The technique involved and the data used are in K. W. Deutsch, Chester Bliss, and Alexander Eckstein, "Population, Sovereignty and Trade," *Eco-*

nomic Development and Cultural Change (July 1962), pp. 353–66.

[35]*Ibid.*, p. 237.

[36]Balassa, *The Theory of Economic Integration*, p. 272.

possible emergence of a new type of political system which he dubbed a "sector integrated supranational system."[37] In such a system responsibility for conflict resolution and other normal governmental functions would be divided among national and "supranational" actors, thus eliminating any "omni-functional supreme decision maker." The organizing principle of a "sector integrated supranational system" would be both territorial (as with the nation state) and functional.

The establishment of a supranational authority signifies that member states have in some respects renounced or limited their right to be the final arbiters of international conflicts. It means that some outside agency now has the right to overrule certain national decisions, or to legislate in areas hitherto exclusively reserved to national control, or to grant relief to and settle disputes among individuals who, in other respects, continue to be subject to national control.

It also means that any third government or national or international agency having business with the supranational community may have to deal with national governments or supranational authorities, or both. If the United States, for instance, wished to supply enriched uranium to a German utility, it would have to negotiate with the German government and the Euratom Commission as well as with the firm directly concerned; and if it wished to obtain a reduction in the external Common Market tariff, it would have to come to an agreement with the appropriate supranational authority (i.e., the Commission acting under Council directives) but it would accomplish little by initiating talks with individual governments.[38]

Yondorf suggested that the authority structure of such a system would resemble a "jagged mountain range" rather than the pyramid suggested by the hierarchical principle expressed in most nation-states. "The peaks would identify the culminating points of national and supranational decision-making systems, and differences in height

and mass would represent differences in competence and power."[39]

If the Community does stop active growth and enters a period of overall equilibrium, either because conservative tendencies counteract pressures for growth, or because pressures for growth lessen in intensity, what are likely to be the survival prospects of the system? Can a partial economic union, with a vertical and segmental social structure and a mixed territorial and functional authority structure maintain itself over time in some sort of steady state?

Most observers have argued that such a "steady state" is both undesirable and impossible to sustain.[40] It is considered undesirable primarily because it is so far short of the finer vision of a united Europe, seen as a vehicle for domestic renovation and reform, and as the means of creating an entity that is capable of playing a positive and self-determining role in international affairs. Indeed, we would argue that the judgment of undesirability has been so overwhelmingly shared that no real effort has been made to study feasibility at all. In other words, . . . [as we have pointed out elsewhere], we have been so preoccupied with the analysis of growth or change that we have by and large failed to countenance seriously the possibility that the system might stop growing, that it might maintain itself at that level, and that such an outcome might even be desirable.

We hasten to say that we are not here taking this latter position, for we have some serious doubts about the survival capacity of such a system. What we are suggesting is that much more attention must be paid to the possibility that a system with the general economic, social, and political characteristics sketched above may well emerge. We must find ways of studying what such a system would be like and how it might function in response to different kinds of internal and external pressures. We cannot assume that because the functional scope and institutional capacities of the European Community system stop growing, that the effects of the activities carried on within that system will also cease to grow. It seems probable that the continued existence of even a European Community in equilib-

---

[37] *Europe of the Six: Dynamics of Integration* (unpublished doctoral dissertation, University of Chicago), Chapter 3, pp. 6–10.

[38] *Ibid.*, p. 108.

[39] *Ibid,.* pp. 111–19.

[40] See, for example, Zaring, *Decision for Europe.*

rium will have now unforeseen (and as yet relatively unstudied) effects throughout the societies that are involved. These effects will not be caught up in the kind of growth model we have employed in this book. They will require that we pose an entirely new set of empirical and theoretical questions.[41] Why exclude the possibility that it is some such symbiotic relationship between nation-states and a European Community that will provide the most adequate, flexible, and responsive combination of resources for coping with the problems of the future? The very fact that we have no serviceable models or concepts should be a stimulus to theoretical creativity. We are in an era of sometimes bewilderingly rapid change, in social and cultural norms, in political behavior, in the structure of the international system, etc. Many of the standard theories or models of social science which had predicted a future of greater centralization, cultural and social homogeneity, secularization, depoliticization have been proven insufficient at best. In such an era we can hardly afford to continue to talk about the European Community solely with a conceptual vocabulary rooted primarily in past forms and experiences.

There are a number of general trends in European societies today that also suggest a future in which authority patterns may well be quite different. Some of these are already well established: changing elite and mass attitudes toward governmental authority, the growth in the size of industry and business and the emergence of the

European or international corporation, the continuing development of ties among governmental technocrats, international bankers, and industry. Others are only beginning to take on any clear form. Among these we would include the anti-bureaucratic ideologies of student movements and the New Left, calls for more participation amidst widespread alienation, the new "regionalisms" in France, Italy, Belgium, and Britain, the experiments in decentralized planning. Perhaps the future will see the development in Europe of something like Yondorf's "sector integrated supranational system" embodying totally new techniques of governance and decision-making which subtly combine international, European, national, and regional and local competences.[42] We would expect the European Community to play an important role in the shaping of such a new polity, not in the least because it may now be giving Europeans invaluable experience in experimenting with problem-solving at different levels of public competence. Thus, if the first period of the Community's existence was one of gradual growth in the scope and capacities of its decision-making system, perhaps the next will see this system and the national systems becoming more and more subtly intertwined with as yet unforeseen consequences at the economic, social, and political levels. Whether such a period would eventually be followed by one in which a European consciousness emerged and a European federal state were established, something on a parallel with the gradual emergence of a German state out of the Zollverein between 1815 and 1867, seems at this point even beyond conjecture.

---

[41] For an example of such questioning from a nation-state centered perspective, see Hoffmann, "Obstinate or Obsolete? The Fate of the Nation-State and the Case of Western Europe," in Nye (ed.), *International Regionalism*, pp. 229–30.

---

[42] For some speculation along these lines see Anthony Sampson in "Europe of Regions?" *The New Europeans* (London: Hodder and Stoughton, 1968), pp. 430–34.

22

Preliminary Draft of a World Constitution

CENTER FOR THE STUDY OF DEMOCRATIC INSTITUTIONS

Contents

Preamble

The people of the earth having agreed
    that the advancement of man
in spiritual excellence and physical welfare
is the common goal of mankind;
    that universal peace is the prerequisite
for the pursuit of that goal;
    that justice in turn is the prerequisite of peace,
and peace and justice stand or fall together;
    that iniquity and war inseparably spring
from the competitive anarchy of the national states;
    that therefore the age of nations must end,
and the era of humanity begin;
the governments of the nations have decided
    to order their separate sovereignties
in one government of justice,
to which they surrender their arms;
    and to establish, as they do establish,
this Constitution
as the covenant and fundamental law
of the Federal Republic of the World.

From *The Constitution for the World,* Center for the Study of Democratic Institutions, Santa Barbara, Calif., 1965, pp. 25–53. Reprinted with permission from the Center for the Study of Democratic Institutions in Santa Barbara, Calif.

Note: This is the verbatim text as written and published in 1947–48 (except for brief omissions indicated by . . .).

*These articles and other parts of the text placed within brackets would disappear from the Constitution after the Founding Convention.

DECLARATION OF DUTIES AND RIGHTS

A.

The universal government of justice as covenanted and pledged in this Constitution is founded on the Rights of Man.

The principles underlying the Rights of Man are and shall be permanently stated in the Duty of everyone everywhere, whether a citizen sharing in the responsibilities and privileges of World Government or a ward and pupil of the World Commonwealth:

to serve with word and deed, and with productive labor according to his ability, the spiritual and physical advancement of the living and of those to come, as the common cause of all generations of men;

to do unto others as he would like others to do unto him;

to abstain from violence,

except for the repulse of violence as commanded or granted under law.

B.

In the context therefore of social duty and service, and in conformity with the unwritten law which philosophies and religions alike called the Law of Nature and which the Republic of the World shall strive to see universally written and enforced by positive law:

it shall be the right of everyone everywhere to claim and maintain for himself and his fellowmen:

release from the bondage of poverty and from the servitude and exploitation of labor, with rewards and security according to merit and needs;

freedom of peaceful assembly and of association, in any creed or party or craft, within the pluralistic unity and purpose of the World Republic;

protection of individuals and groups against subjugation and tyrannical rule, racial or national, doctrinal or cultural, with safeguards for the self-determination of minorities and dissenters;

and any such other freedoms and franchises as are inherent in man's inalienable claims to life, liberty, and the dignity of the human person, and as the legislators and judges of the World Republic shall express and specify.

C.

The four elements of life—earth, water, air, energy—are the common property of the human race. The management and use of such portions thereof as are vested in or assigned to particular ownership, private or corporate or national or regional, of definite or indefinite tenure, of individualist or collectivist economy, shall be subordinated in each and all cases to the interest of the common good.

GRANT OF POWERS

1.

The jurisdiction of the World Government as embodied in its organs of power shall extend to:

a) The control of the observance of the Constitution in all the component communities and territories of the Federal World Republic, which shall be indivisible and one;

b) The furtherance and progressive fulfillment of the Duties and Rights of Man in the spirit of the foregoing Declaration, with their specific enactment in such fields of federal and local relations as described hereinafter (Art. 27 through 33);

c) The maintenance of peace; and to that end the enactment and promulgation of laws which shall be binding upon communities and upon individuals as well,

d) the judgment and settlement of any conflicts among component units, with prohibition of recourse to interstate violence,

e) the supervision of and final decision on any alterations of boundaries between states or unions threof,

f) the supervision of and final decision on the forming of new states or unions thereof,

g) the administration of such territories as may still be immature for self-government, and the declaration in due time of their eligibility therefor,

h) the intervention in intrastate violence and violations of law which affect world peace and justice,

i) the organization and disposal of federal armed forces,

j) the limitation and control of weapons and of the domestic militias in the several component units of the World Republic;

k) The establishment, in addition to the Special Bodies listed hereinafter (Art. 8 and 9), of such other agencies as may be conducive to the development of the earth's resources and to the advancement of physical and intellectual standards, with such advisory or initiating or arbitrating powers as shall be determined by law;

l) The laying and collecting of federal taxes, and the establishment of a plan and a budget for federal expenditures,

m) the administration of the World Bank and the establishment of suitable world fiscal agencies for the issue of money and the creation and control of credit,

n) the regulation of commerce affected with federal interest,

o) the establishment, regulation, and, where necessary or desirable, the operation of means of transportation and communication which are of federal interest;

p) The supervision and approval of laws concerning emigration and immigration and the movements of peoples,

q) the granting of federal passports;

r) The appropriation, under the right of eminent domain, of such private or public property as may be necessary for federal use, reasonable compensation being made therefor;

s) The legislation over and administration of the territory which shall be chosen as Federal District and of such other territories as may be entrusted directly to the Federal Government.

2.

The powers not delegated to the World Government by this Constitution, and not prohibited by it to the several members of the Federal World Republic, shall be reserved to the several states or nations or unions thereof.

THE FEDERAL CONVENTION, THE PRESIDENT, THE LEGISLATURE

3.

The sovereignty of the Federal Republic of the World resides in the people of the world. The primary powers of the World Government shall be vested in:

a) the Federal Convention,

b) the President,

c) the Council and the Special Bodies,

d) the Grand Tribunal, the Supreme Court, and the Tribune of the People,

e) the Chamber of Guardians.

4.

The Federal Convention shall consist of delegates elected directly by the people of all states and nations, one delegate for each million of population or fraction thereof above one-half million, with the proviso that the people of any extant state, . . . ranging between 100,000 and 1,000,000, shall be entitled to elect one delegate, but any such state with a population below 100,000 shall be aggregated for federal electoral purposes to the electoral unit closest to its borders.

The delegates to the Federal Convention shall vote as individuals, not as members of national or otherwise collective representations [except as specified hereinafter, Art. 46, paragraph 2, and Art. 47].

The Convention shall meet in May of every third year, for a session of thirty days.

5.

The Federal Convention shall subdivide into nine Electoral Colleges according to the nine Societies of kindred nations and cultures, or Regions, wherefrom its members derive their powers, such Regions being:

1) the continent of Europe and its islands outside the Russian area, together with the United Kingdom if the latter so decides, and with such overseas English- or French- or Cape Dutch-speaking communities of the British Commonwealth of Nations or the French Union as

decide to associate (this whole area here tentatively denominated *Europa*);

2) the United States of America, with the United Kingdom if the latter so decides, and such kindred communities of British, or Franco-British, or Dutch-British, or Irish civilization and lineage as decide to associate (*Atlantis*);

3) Russia, European and Asiatic, with such East-Baltic or Slavic or South-Danubian nations as associate with Russia (*Eurasia*);

4) the Near and Middle East, with the states of North Africa, and Pakistan if the latter so decides (*Afrasia*);

5) *Africa,* south of the Sahara, with or without the South African Union as the latter may decide;

6) *India*, with Pakistan if the latter so decides;

7) China, Korea, Japan with the associate archipelagoes of the North- and Mid-Pacific (*Asia Major*);

8) Indochina and Indonesia, with Pakistan if the latter so decides, and with such other Mid- and South-Pacific lands and islands as decide to associate (*Austrasia*);

9) the Western Hemisphere south of the United States (*Columbia*).

Each Electoral College shall nominate by secret ballot not more than three candidates, regardless of origin, for the office of President of the World Republic. The Federal Convention in plenary meeting, having selected by secret ballot a panel of three candidates from the lists submitted, shall elect by secret ballot one of the three as President, on a majority of two-thirds.

If three consecutive ballots have been indecisive, the candidate with the smallest vote shall be eliminated and between the two remaining candidates a simple majority vote shall be decisive.

6.

Each Electoral College shall then nominate by secret and proportional ballot twenty-seven candidates, originating from the respective Electoral Area or Region, for the World Council; with the proviso that one-third and not more than one-third of the nominees shall not be members of the Federal Convention; and the nine lists having been presented to the Federal Convention, the Federal Convention in plenary meeting shall select by secret and proportional ballot nine Councilmen from each list, with the same proviso as above.

The Federal Convention shall also elect by secret and proportional ballot, on nominations, prior to the opening of the Convention, by such organizations of world-wide importance and lawfully active in more than three Regions as shall be designated [for the first election by the United Nations Assembly and subsequently] by the Council, eighteen additional members, regardless of origin; and the total membership of the World Council shall be thus ninety-nine.

7.

The primary power to initiate and enact legislation for the Federal Republic of the World shall be vested in the Council.

The tenure of the Council shall be three years.

The Council shall elect its Chairman, for its whole tenure of three years.

Councilors shall be re-eligible.

8.

Within the first three years of World Government the Council and the President shall establish three Special Bodies, namely:

a) a House of Nationalities and States, with representatives from each, for the safeguarding of local institutions and autonomies and the protection of minorities;

b) a Syndical or functional Senate, for the representation of syndicates and unions or occupational associations and any other corporate interests of transnational significance, as well as for mediation or arbitration in non-justiciable issues among such syndicates or unions or other corporate interests;

c) an Institute of Science, Education and Culture;

each of the three bodies with such membership and tenures and consultative or preparatory powers as shall be established by law and with no prejudice to the establishment of other advisory or technical agencies in accordance with the purposes stated herein before (Art. 1, k).

9.

Within its first year the World Government shall establish a Special Body, to be named Planning Agency, of twenty-one members appointed by the President, subject to vetoes by two-thirds of the Council, for tenures of twelve years [except that the terms for the initial membership shall be staggered by lot, with one-third of it, seven members, ceasing from office and being replaced every fourth year].

It shall be the function of the Planning Agency to envisage the income of the Federal Government and to prepare programs and budgets for expenditures, both for current needs and for long-range improvements. These programs and budgets shall be submitted by the President, with his recommendations, to the Council, as provided hereinafter (Art. 13).

Plans for improvement of the world's physical facilities, either public or private, and for the productive exploitation of resources and inventions shall be submitted to the Agency or to such Development Authorities or regional subagencies as it may establish. The Agency shall pass judgment on the social usefulness of such plans.

Members of the Planning Agency shall not be re-eligible nor shall they, during their tenure in the Agency, have membership in any other federal body.

10.

The executive power, together with initiating power in federal legislation, shall be vested in the President. His tenure shall be six years.

The President shall not have membership in the Council.

The President shall not be re-eligible. He shall not be eligible to the Tribunate of the People until nine years have elapsed since the expiration of his term.

No two successive Presidents shall originate from the same Region.

11.

The President shall appoint a Chancellor. The Chancellor, with the approval of the President, shall appoint the Cabinet.

The Chancellor shall act as the President's representative before the Council in the exercise of legislative initiative. The Chancellor and the Cabinet members shall have at any time the privilege of the floor before the Council.

But no Chancellor or Cabinet member shall have a vote or shall hold membership in the Council, nor, if he was a member of the Council at the moment of his executive appointment, shall he be entitled to resume his seat therein when leaving the executive post unless he be re-elected at a subsequent Convention.

No one shall serve as Chancellor for more than six years, nor as Cabinet member for more than twelve, consecutive or not.

No three Cabinet members at any one time and no two successive Chancellors shall originate from the same Region.

The Council shall have power to interrogate the Chancellor and the Cabinet and to adopt resolutions on their policies.

The Chancellor and the Cabinet shall resign when the President so decides or when a vote of no confidence by the absolute majority of fifty or more of the Council is confirmed by a second such vote; but no second vote shall be taken and held valid if less than three months have elapsed from the first.

12.

The sessions of the Council, as well as those of the Grand Tribunal and the Supreme Court, shall be continuous, except for one yearly recess of not more than ten weeks or two such recesses of not more than five weeks each, as the body concerned may decide.

13.

The budget of the World Government, upon recommendation by the Planning Agency, shall be presented every three years by the President to the Council, which shall pass it, or reject it in whole titles by majority vote; the same procedure to apply when at other intervals the President requests additional appropriations or approval of changes.

14.

Any legislation of the Council can be vetoed by the President within thirty days of its passage. But the Council can overrule the veto if its new vote, by a majority of two-thirds, finds support, within sixty days of the President's action, in the majority of the Grand Tribunal [and no such support shall be required during the tenure of the first President].

15.

The President can be impeached on grounds of treason to the Constitution, or usurpation of power, or felony, or insanity, or other disease imparing permanently his mind.

The vote of impeachment shall be final when three-quarters of the Council and three-quarters of the Grand Tribunal concur and the majority of the Supreme Court validates the legality of the proceedings.

If a President is impeached or resigns or dies in the interval between two sessions of the Federal Convention, the Chairman of the Council shall become Acting President until the new Convention elects a new President; and the Council shall elect a new Chairman.

THE GRAND TRIBUNAL
AND THE SUPREME COURT

16.

The supreme judiciary power of the World Republic shall be vested in a Grand Tribunal of sixty Justices, with the President of the World Republic as Chief Justice and Chairman, and the Chairman of the Council as Vice-Chairman ex officio.

The President as Chief Justice shall appoint the Justices of the Grand Tribunal and fill the vacancies, subject to vetoes by the Council on majorities of two-thirds. He shall have power to overrule any such veto if he finds support in a two-thirds majority of the Justices in office [except that no such power shall be vested in the first President].

No one, except the Chairman of the Council, shall hold membership at the same time in the Council and the Tribunal; nor shall a Chancellor or Cabinet member hold membership in the Tribunal or be eligible to it until six years have elapsed from the termination of his executive office.

17.

The tenure of the Chief Justice and Chairman and of the Vice-Chairman of the Grand Tribunal shall be the time of their tenure of office respectively as President of the World Republic and as Chairman of the Council.

The President shall have power to appoint an Alternate, subject to approval by the Grand Tribunal, for the exercise of such of his functions in the judiciary branch and for such a time within his tenure as he may decide.

The tenures of the sixty Justices shall be fifteen years [except that the terms for the initial membership shall be staggered by lot, with one-fifth of it, twelve Justices, ceasing from office and being replaced every third year].

Justices of the Grand Tribunal shall not be re-eligible, except that a Justice appointed as Chancellor or Cabinet member, having resigned his membership in the Tribunal, shall be re-eligible to it for the unfulfilled portion of his tenure when six years have elapsed from the termination of his executive office.

18.

The sixty Justices shall be assigned twelve to each of five Benches:

the First Bench to deal with constitutional issues between the primary organs and powers of the World Government as well as with all issues and cases in which the Tribune of the People shall decide to appear in his capacity of World Attorney and defender of the Rights of Man:

the Second Bench to deal with issues and conflicts between the World Government and any of its component units, whether single states or unions thereof or Regions, as well as with issues and conflicts of component units of the World Republic among themselves;

the Third Bench to deal with issues and conflicts between the World Government and individual citizens or corporations or unions or any other associations of citizens;

the Fourth Bench to deal with issues and conflicts among component units, whether single states or unions of states or Regions, and individual citizens or corporations or unions or any other associations of citizens when such issues and conflicts affect the interpretation or enactment of federal law;

the Fifth Bench to deal with issues and conflicts, when they affect the interpretation and enactment of federal law, either among individual citizens or among corporations, unions, syndicates, or any other collective organizations of citizens and interests.

Each Region shall be represented in each Bench by at least one member and not more than two.

19.

The Supreme Court shall be of seven members: five representing one each Bench, with the Chief Justice as their Chairman and the Chairman of the Council as their Vice-Chairman ex officio; and the active membership of the Benches shall thus remain of eleven each.

No two members of the Supreme Court shall originate from the same Region.

The representatives of the Benches in the Supreme Court shall be elected by secret vote of the Grand Tribunal in plenary session, with each Justice casting a ballot for five candidates, one from each Bench, and with those candidates elected who have obtained the largest vote, except that any presumptive electee shall be held ineligible whose assignment to the Court would duplicate the representation therein of any one Region or Bench.

If the first vote fails to fill all seats, the vote shall be repeated according to the same regulations.

The tenures of the members of the Supreme Court shall be: for the Chairman and Vice-Chairman the same as their tenures of office respectively as President of the World Republic and as Chairman of the Council, and for the other members six years, at the end of which each of the five elected by the Grand Tribunal may be re-elected or shall be restored to the Bench whereof he was the delegate; but no Justice shall sit in the Court beyond his regular term of membership in the Tribunal; and when the latter term expires before the regular six-year term in the Court is completed, or when an elective member of the Court resigns or dies, the Grand Tribunal shall fill the vacancy for the unfulfilled portion of the term by secret partial election in plenary session, with the same proviso as above in regard to the representation of Regions.

Regions which have not been represented in the Supreme Court for two successive six-year terms shall have mandatory precedence in the elections for the third term.

20.

The Supreme Court shall distribute the cases among the five Benches of the Grand Tribunal according to competences as specified hereinbefore [Art. 18].

Cases where competences overlap or are otherwise doubtful shall be referred to such Bench or Benches jointly as the Supreme Court shall decide.

The Supreme Court shall have power to modify the rules of assignment for the five Benches as specified in Art. 18, subject to approval by the majority of the Council and by a two thirds majority of the Grand Tribunal concurrently.

21.

It shall be the office and function of the Supreme Court to review the decisions of the Benches, within three months of their issuance, said decisions to become effective upon registration by the Court, or, when annulled, to be returned for revision each to the Bench which judged the case, or to another, or to others jointly as the Court may decide; annulment to be pronounced in cases of unfair trial or faulty procedure, and also for reasons of substance when final appeal was filed by the losing party, if the Court at its own discretion choose to take cognizance thereof, or by the Tribune of the People, whose demand shall be mandatory.

22.

The Grand Tribunal, with the approval of the Supreme Court, shall establish Lower Federal Courts in such number and places as conditions in the component units of the World Republic shall require, and a Federal Appellate Court in each Region. It shall also determine the rules and competences of such courts, and appoint their officials on the basis of competitive examinations.

23.

The President or his Alternate and the Chairman of the Council shall not sit as judges in cases affecting the solution of conflicts between the President and the Council.

The President or Acting President or Alternate, or a Justice or the Chairman of the Council in his capacity of Justice, shall not sit as a judge in cases involving his appointment or impeachment or demotion or tenure or in any other way affecting his particular interest.

24.

No member of the Council or the Grand Tribunal shall be liable to removal from office until a criminal sentence on charges of felony or grave misdemeanor is final. But he shall be suspended from office, pending last recourse to the Grand Tribunal, when a sentence of guilty, issued by a lower court, has been confirmed by a Federal Appellate Court.

The Supreme Court shall pronounce final judgment on the legality of the proceedings. It shall also pronounce final judgment on the legal validity of elections and appointments to the Council and the Tribunal, and to the offices of President and of Tribune of the People.

25.

The President in his capacity of World Chief Justice shall have power of pardon over sentences passed under federal law.

THE TRIBUNE OF THE PEOPLE AND THE WORLD LAW

26.

The Federal Convention, after electing the Council, shall elect by secret ballot the Tribune of the People as a spokesman for the minorities, this office to be vested in the candidate obtaining the second largest vote among the eligible candidates; ineligible to the office of Tribune being any candidate having also been nominated by any Electoral College for the office of President in the current Convention, or having been a President or Acting President or Alternate or a member of the Grand Tribunal at any time in the nine years preceding said Convention, or originating from the same Region as the President simultaneously in office.

The Tribune of the People shall not have membership in the Council.

The tenure of the Tribune of the People shall be three years. He shall have power to appoint a Deputy, subject to the same ineligibilities as above, with tenure to expire not later than his own.

He shall not be re-eligible, nor shall he be eligible to the office of President or Alternate or Justice of the Grand Tribunal, until nine years have elapsed from the expiration of his present term.

The Tribune, or his appointed Deputy, shall have the privilege of the floor before the Grand Tribunal and under such regulations as shall be established by law, before the Supreme Court; but no vote in either; and he shall not be present when a vote is taken.

27.

It shall be the office and function of the Tribune of the People to defend the natural and civil rights of individuals and groups against violation or neglect by the World Government or any of its component units; to further and demand, as a World Attorney before the World Republic, the observance of the letter and spirit of this constitution; and to promote thereby, in the spirit of its Preamble and Declaration of Duties and Rights, the attainment of the goals set to the progress of mankind by the efforts of the ages.

28.

No law shall be made or held valid in the World Republic or any of its component units:

1) inflicting or condoning discrimination against race or nation or sex or caste or creed or doctrine; or

2) barring through preferential agreements or coalitions of vested interests the access on equal terms of any state or nation to the raw materials and the sources of energy of the earth; or

3) establishing or tolerating slavery, whether overt or covert, or forced labor, except as equitable expiation endured in state or federal controlled institutions and intended for social service and rehabilitation of convicted criminals; or

4) permitting, whether by direction or indirection, arbitrary seizure or search, or unfair trial, or excessive penalty, or application of ex post facto laws; or

5) abridging in any manner whatsoever, except as a punishment inflicted by law for criminal transgression, the citizen's exercise of such responsibilities and privileges of citizenship as are conferred on him by law; or

6) curtailing the freedom of communication and information, of speech, of the press and of expression by whatever means, of peaceful assembly, of travel;

paragraphs 5 and 6 to be subject to suspension according to circumstances, universally or locally, in time of emergency imperiling the maintenance and unity of the World Republic; such state of emergency, world-wide or local, to be proposed by the Chamber of Guardians and proclaimed concurrently by a two-thirds majority of the Council and a two-thirds majority of the Grand Tribunal for a period not in excess of six months, to be renewable on expiration with the same procedure for successive periods of six months or less but in no case beyond the date when the time of emergency is proclaimed closed, on the proposal of the Chamber of Guardians by simple majority votes of the Council and of the Grand Tribunal concurrently or, if the Guardians' proposal is deemed unduly delayed, by three-quarters majority votes of the Council and of the Grand Tribunal concurrently.

29.

Capital punishment shall not be inflicted under federal law.

30.

Old age pensions, unemployment relief, insurance against sickness or accident, just terms of leisure, and protection to maternity and infancy shall be provided according to the varying circumstances of times and places as the local law may direct.

Communities and states unable to provide adequate social security. and relief shall be assisted by the Federal Treasury, whose grants or privileged loans shall be administered under federal supervision.

31.

Every child from the age of six to the age of twelve shall be entitled to instruction and education at public expense, such primary six-year period to be obligatory and further education to be accessible to all without discrimination of age or sex or race or class or creed.

Communities and states unable to fulfill this obligation shall be assisted by the Federal Treasury with the same proviso as in Art. 30.

32.

All property or business whose management and use have acquired the extension and character of a federal public service, or whereon restrictive trade practices have conferred the character and power of a transnational monopoly, shall become the property of the Federal Government upon payment of a just price as determined by law.

33.

Every individual or group or community shall have the right of appeal against unjust application of law, or against the law itself, gaining access through the inferior courts, local or federal, to the superior and the Grand Tribunal, and securing the counsel and support of the Tribune of the People when the Tribune so decides; and, if a law or statute is found evidently in conflict with the guarantees pledged in the foregoing articles or irreparably in contradiction with the basic principles and intents of the World Republic as stated in the Preamble to this Constitution and in its Declaration of Duties and Rights, the Grand Tribunal shall have power to recommend to the Supreme Court that such law or statute be declared, and the Supreme Court shall have power to declare it, null and void.

34.

The Tribune of the People cannot be impeached except on the same grounds and with the same procedure as specified for the President in Art. 15.

If the Tribune of the People is impeached or resigns or dies, his substitute for the unfulfilled portion of his tenure shall be the candidate to the Tribunate who was next in line in the last Federal Convention, with the same provisos in regard to eligibility as in Art. 26, first paragraph.

THE CHAMBER OF GUARDIANS

35.

The control and use of the armed forces of the Federal Republic of the World shall be assigned exclusively to a Chamber of Guardians under the chairmanship of the President, in his capacity of Protector of the Peace. The other Guardians shall be six Councilmen elected by the Council and the Grand Tribunal in Congress assembled, for terms of three years. [But the Grand Tribunal shall not participate in the first election.]

One former President shall also sit in the Chamber of Guardians, the sequence to be determined term for term, or, if he resign or die, for the fractional term, according to seniority in the presidential office; he shall have the privilege of the floor in the deliberations of the Chamber, but no vote in its decisions.

Officers holding professional or active rank in the armed forces of the Federal Republic, or in the domestic militia of any component unit thereof, shall not be eligible as Guardians.

36.

The election of the six elective Guardians shall be by secret and proportional vote, with each Elector casting a ballot of six names or less; but no three Guardians of the seven, including the President and excluding the ex-President, shall originate from the same Region; and any presumptive electee whose election would contravene this norm shall be declared ineligible and replaced by the candidate fulfilling the norm and having obtained the next largest vote.

Regions which have not been represented among the seven Guardians referred to above for two successive three-year terms shall have mandatory precedences in the subsequent elections; but the Guardian or Guardians originating from a nation or Region where sedition against the World Republic is actual or, according to the majority of the Chamber, imminently expected

shall cease from office and be replaced; unless the other Guardians decide unanimously otherwise.

No Guardian can be impeached or in any way suspended or removed from office for any other reason, except on such grounds and with such procedure as specified for the President and the Tribune of the People hereinbefore (Art. 15 and 34), and for the Guardians hereinafter (Art. 38).

If a Guardian resigns or dies or is in any way suspended or removed, his substitute for the unfulfilled portion of the term shall be chosen by partial election, with the same rules and provisos as in the first two paragraphs of this article, each elector casting a ballot of one or more names as the number of vacancies may be.

37.

The Chancellor shall have access to the Chamber of Guardians as Deputy of the President whose vote he shall cast by proxy if the President so decides.

38.

Appropriations for the budget of Peace and Defense, under control of the Chamber of Guardians, as proposed by the Chamber at the beginning of each term for the whole duration thereof, shall be submitted by the President to the Council, in conformity with Art. 13. But if a state of emergency is declared, in the manner and limits as specified hereinbefore (Art. 28, last paragraph), the Chamber shall have power to demand and appropriate such additional funds as the emergency demands, subject to auditing and sanction by the Council when the emergency is closed; whereafter, if sanction is denied, the Guardians responsible shall be liable to impeachment and prosecution for usurpation of power with the same procedure as specified for the President and the Tribune of the People hereinbefore (Art. 15 and 34).

39.

The Chamber shall have power to propose by absolute majority, subject to approval by two-thirds majority votes of the Council and of the Grand Tribunal concurrently, extraordinary powers, world-wide or local, to be conferred on the President beyond those assigned to him by this Constitution, when a state of emergency, as provided in Art. 28, is proclaimed; such powers not to be granted for periods exceeding six months each and to be relinquished before the expiration of any such period as soon as the state of emergency, in conformity with Art. 28, is proclaimed closed.

40.

The Chamber of Guardians shall answer interrogations from the Council on its general and administrative directives, but no vote shall be taken after discussion thereof, except as otherwise provided in Art. 28 and 39; and the decisions of the Chamber in matters technical and strategic shall be final, and withheld from publicity when the Chamber so decides.

41.

The Chamber of Guardians, assisted by a General Staff and an Institute of Technology whose members it shall appoint, shall determine the technological and the numerical levels that shall be set as limits to the domestic militias of the single communities and states or unions thereof.

Armed forces and the manufacture of armaments beyond the levels thus determined shall be reserved to the World Government.

THE FEDERAL CAPITAL AND FEDERAL LANGUAGE AND STANDARDS

42.

Within one year of its foundation the World Republic shall choose a Federal Capital, or a site therefore, with eminent domain over it and an adequate Federal District.

43.

Within three years of its foundation the Federal Government shall designate one language, which shall be standard for the formulation and interpretation of the federal laws; and for analogous purposes, relative to communication, taxation, and finances, it shall establish in its first year a federal unit of currency with a federal system of measures and a federal calendar.

THE AMENDING POWER

44.

Amendments to this Constitution, recommended concurrently by a two-thirds majority of the Council and of the Grand Tribunal, shall be in force when approved by a two-thirds majority of the Federal Convention in the Constitutional Session following the recommendation.

Constitutional Sessions, of thirty days or less, as the discussion may require and the majority may decide, shall be held immediately after the ordinary electoral session in the third Federal Convention and thereafter every ninth year.

[But no amendment altering the electoral units as listed in Art. 5, or the assignment to them of seats in the Council and the other Federal bodies, shall be recommended to the first of such Sessions.]

RATIFICATION AND PRELIMINARY PERIOD

45.

The first Federal Convention shall be the Founding Convention. . . .

The ways and means for the convocation of the Founding Convention, and the regulations for its inaugural and voting procedures, shall be determined by the General Assembly of the United Nations.

46.

The thirty-day electoral session of the Founding Convention shall be preceded by a preliminary session of thirty days or less for the discussion and approval of this Constitution, such preliminary session to be extended for thirty additional days or less as the discussion may require and the majority may decide.

The delegates to the Founding Convention shall vote individually, and not by delegations; except on the assignment to the nine Electoral Colleges or Regions of such optional states or zones as listed hereinbefore (Art. 5); in which matter the vote of the majority, within the delegation from the state or zone concerned, shall be binding upon the minority; and Art. 5 shall be adjusted accordingly.

47.

The founding convention having discussed and approved by individual majority vote this Consti-

tution, ratification by collective majorities within as many delegations of states and nations as represent two-thirds of the population of the earth shall be sufficient for the establishment of the Federal Republic of the World.]

The Committee to Frame
A World Constitution

Robert M. Hutchins
President
G. A. Borgese
Secretary
Mortimer J. Adler
Stringfellow Barr
Albert Guérard

Harold A. Innis
Erich Kahler
Wilber G. Katz
Charles H. McIlwain
Robert Redfield
Rexford Guy Tugwell

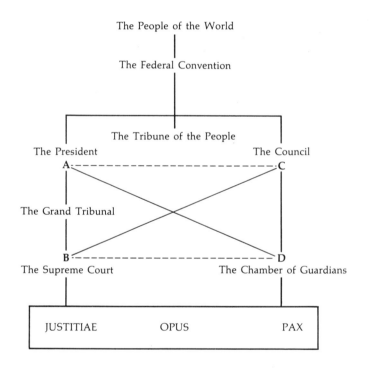

Dotted Line AC symbolizes intervention of Council in tenure of the President's Cabinet and Acting Presidency of the Chairman of the Council during vacancies in the Presidency.

Diagonal AD symbolizes Chairmanship of the President in the Chamber of Guardians.

Diagonal CB symbolizes Council's veto power on appointments to the Judiciary and membership of the Chairman of the Council in the Tribunal and Supreme Court.

Dotted line BD symbolizes intervention of the Judiciary in elections to the Chamber of Guardians.

Discussion and Questions

1. ➤ Do you find Lindberg and Scheingold persuasive with regard to their central argument that the European regional movement is about to enter a period of stable equilibrium? ➤ What are their principal reasons for reaching this conclusion? ➤ What are the principal contingencies that might either lead to increased instability or rapid additional integration in the years ahead and thereby confound their central, but carefully hedged expectation?

2. ➤ Assuming that Lindberg and Scheingold are correct, would the failure of European integration to advance rapidly in the years ahead have a detrimental, neutral, or beneficial impact on the prospects for over-all improvements in the quality of world order? on second-order integration potential? ➤ Does it matter whether integration is proceeding toward a comparable plateau in other regions of the world? ➤ Does it matter whether major steps toward inter-European reconciliation are taken? Whether Soviet-American, Sino-Soviet, and Sino-American relations improve or deteriorate? Japan, as the fastest growing industrial country in the world, may play an important role in shaping the future of regional developments, both by what it does and doesn't do about participating in international society.

3. ➤ Must regional integration move at a faster, more ordered pace than the European incremental process in order to achieve the five goal values posited in the General Introduction to this volume? ➤ Does the pace depend on the region of the world that is trying to become an integrated unit? (That is, could incremental integration be suitable for Europe, whose societies are similar in a great many respects and have drawn closer since World War II, but unsuitable for another region, for instance, Arab countries, among whom great disparities of wealth exist and who have not been drawing closer to operating as a regional unit over the same period? ➤ Is the regional experience of Europe virtually unique because of its security situation and industrial

base, or can we generalize on the basis of the West European experience?

➤ How could the integrative process be speeded up if it were found necessary in order to promote the values? ➤ Could an incrementalist approach be moderated by notions of authority conveyed, for example, through a central guidance mechanism to give a more ordered approach to world-order reform? ➤ Would an incrementalist approach perhaps promote some values and retard others? ➤ How about a more moderated approach through authority structures? ➤ What would it depend on?

4. In projecting the future of the European integration movement, Lindberg and Scheingold eschew the assertion of preferences and do not operate within any framework of values and goals. Their endeavor is scientific in the sense of facilitating understanding by providing that degree of explanation and prediction that can be sustained by available data. ➤ Is this a desirable method of inquiry for the subject matter of international relations? Note that it differs considerably from the value matrix that shapes our study of world order. Our method is a type of social engineering that entails designing models and devising strategies to fulfill certain value requirements.

On page 453 Lindberg and Scheingold write that a stable equilibrium for the European integration movement "might even be desirable." ➤ What does desirable mean, given their nonnormative method of inquiry? ➤ How does it differ from the use of a word like "desirable" in our vocabulary? ➤ Are these two orientations toward this kind of subject matter complementary? ➤ Doesn't the engineer need to know the properties of the existing system as well as possible in order to design alternatives to it? See the General Introduction for some discussion of these issues.

5. In writing about Europe and European unity, Lindberg and Scheingold virtually ignore the split between Eastern and Western Europe.

Indeed, no attention is given to the integration movement in the socialist countries of the East. ➤ Is this limitation of scope a serious weakness in relation to their efforts to forecast the future?

1. ➤ Compare the nine regions of the Chicago Constitution with the seven major cultural units specified by Northrop, pages 259–260, and the seven regions identified by Friedrich, page 177. ➤ What is the ordering function assigned these regional units in the over-all constitutional scheme?

2. For an essay on the Chicago Constitution, see Elizabeth Mann Borgese's "A Constitution for the World" (Center for the Study of Democratic Institutions, Santa Barbara, California, 1965).

3. Regional conceptions are beginning to play a role within the context of present United Nations activities. Measures for structural reform of the principal organs of the United Nations tend to embody *de facto* regional conceptions, especially proposals for enlarging the membership of UN organs to correspond more closely with the distribution of power and values in international society. The activities of regional economic commissions operating within the over-all UN framework have not received much attention. (See W. R. Malinowski, "Centralization and Decentralization in the United Nations Economic and Social Activities," *International Organization*, vol. 16, no. 3 [Summer 1962], pp. 521–41.) The integration potential of these commissions is discussed to some extent following the Gregg selection in Part V.

4. ➤ Is a world-order system based on regional autonomy and regional diversity desirable? ➤ Is it attainable? ➤ Is it preferable to other world-order solutions? ➤ Is it more likely to come about than world government?

Compare the formal authoritative processes of a constitutionally reorganized system of global order with the quest for international equilibrium through the establishment of spheres of influence, blocs, and subsystems as discussed by Masters, Liska, and Yalem. ➤ Can we assess the degree to which such a constitutional scheme would, in fact, serve the four goals set forth in the General Introduction? No doubt the Chicago proposals were motivated by such values, although in a preecological setting.

It should be noted here that the scenario for transition is to be found in articles 45, 46, and 47 of the Constitution. In essence it calls for the General Assembly to be the Founding Convention. It certainly is fair to ask what are the social and political mobilization processes which would have to take place on a global basis to organize the General Assembly for that purpose. Certainly it remains doubtful as to whether the preferred values of the drafters would be the actual values of the power-wielders in the new system, if the present power establishment were to dominate the Founding Convention.

➤ Is there a sufficient number of existing and potential actors in the global community who, if they banded together, might bring about a situation in the General Assembly in which that organ would act as a Founding Convention to achieve a balanced measure of success for the five values? ➤ To what extent could this be done by nonviolent means? ➤ Without a social-political transition outlined, how is this constitution more than a mere statement of ideas in constitutional form? ➤ What effect might this document have, and on whom, in its present state?

5. What circumstances determine whether regionalism is perceived and structured as an *alternative* rather than as a *transition* to a stronger set of central political institutions in international life? ➤ How does regionalism as an *alternative* differ from regionalism as a *transition* in furthering the preferred values?

Regional Politics and World Order/Index